Transport and Logistics

DON BENSON
RALPH BUGG
GEOFFREY WHITEHEAD

WOODHEAD-FAULKNER
NEW YORK LONDON TORONTO SYDNEY TOKYO SINGAPORE

First published 1994 by
Woodhead-Faulkner (Publishers) Limited
Campus 400, Maylands Avenue
Hemel Hempstead
Hertfordshire, HP2 7EZ
A division of
Simon & Schuster International Group

Typeset in 10/12 pt Times by
Photoprint, 9–11 Alexandra Lane, Torquay

Printed and bound in Great Britain by
Redwood Books, Trowbridge, Wiltshire

British Library Cataloguing in Publication Data

A catalogue record for this book is available from the British Library

ISBN 0-85941-907-X

1 2 3 4 5 98 97 96 95 94

Contents

Introduction to the series

In the last fifty years international trade has grown enormously under the influence of international agreements which began in 1944 at the Bretton Woods Conference. These agreements recognised that all nations, whatever their economic organisation, must trade if they are to achieve prosperity. Some degree of international specialisation is inevitable, if only because some countries have raw materials that others do not have, some have climates favourable to particular crops, and some have skills and expertise that others have not yet acquired. The result is that we are now faced with a situation in which every firm must consider an overseas market as a major part of its natural market, while production for the home market must meet serious competition from foreign suppliers. It follows that an understanding of the foundations of overseas trade is of enormous importance to the commercial success of every firm, and there is a great need for trained personnel with this type of background.

In order to ensure an adequate supply of trained, professional personnel in this important field of international trade, there have developed over the years specialised vocational courses by the appropriate bodies which represent the various professions engaged in international trading. The professional bodies concerned include the Institute of Export, the Institute of Freight Forwarders, The British International Freight Association and the Institute of Marketing. These four bodies have agreed and recognised a set of syllabuses for the Advanced Certificate in Overseas Trade, which also forms the basis for Part I of their own qualifying examinations. This has been achieved by offering an optional specialist paper in marketing. Students who successfully complete the Advanced Certificate in Overseas Trade will be permitted to embark upon further advanced courses of study leading to full membership of their respective Institutes.

In addition to these four institutes a fifth institute, the Institute of Logistics, is the focal point for all activities associated with the use of sophisticated computerised systems in all aspects of production, distribution and transport. It is concerned with the more efficient management of supply chains, at every stage of activity where value is added to products. The fourth volume in this series, *Transport and Logistics*, seeks to draw the attention of students and others to this important aspect of both domestic and international trade.

The Chartered Institute of Purchasing and Supply is the largest in its field, and includes this title in its reading for students studying International Purchasing and Supply Chain Management.

The 'Elements of Overseas Trade Series' seeks to cover the four syllabuses in this new Advanced Certificate in Overseas Trade and the Institutes' joint Part I examinations.

Preface

The purpose of this book is to describe the principles of transport and logistics and the practices and procedures followed by the logistical industry. In an increasingly sophisticated world, the authors of textbooks have to keep running faster and faster just to stay where they are, and no industry is advancing as fast as this one.

We have tried to deal with the various activities in as practical a way as possible, mentioning all the problems that can arise. In doing so we are indebted to the many students who have raised difficulties with us over the years. It is impossible to acknowledge their contributions individually, but we hope that those who recognise in the text problems they first raised in the lecture room, or by correspondence after taking employment, will take our use of their material as a token of our appreciation and respect.

Many firms and institutions have kindly provided documents and charts for use in this book and we greatly appreciate their unfailing courtesy and interest in this project. We should particularly like to thank Exel Logistics for helpful advice during the preparation of the book. Every attempt has been made to check the accuracy of the content of the book, but in the last analysis such a book cannot be more than the opinion of its authors of the state of affairs as they see it at the time of going to press. We do urge readers therefore to check with official bodies such as those described in Appendix II for possible developments since publication.

DON BENSON
RALPH BUGG
GEOFFREY WHITEHEAD

Acknowledgements

The courtesy and co-operation of the following firms and organisations in supplying illustrations, publications and general background information are gratefully acknowledged. We hope no one has been overlooked, and apologise in advance if this proves to be the case.

American Bureau of Shipping
Associated British Ports
Australia's Flying Doctor Service
BAA PLC
Baco-liner GmbH
Baltic Air Charter Association
Baltic and International Maritime Council
Boltless Systems Link 51 Ltd
British Aerospace
British Airways PLC
British Association of Removers
British Gas
British International Freight Association
British Ports Federation
British Rail
British Road Federation
British Road Services
British Telecom
Brockhouse-Finspa Handling Ltd
Bureau Veritas
Bus & Coach Council
Carmichael and Sons (Worcester) Ltd
Chamber of Shipping
Channel Tunnel Group Ltd
Chartered Institute of Marketing
Chartered Institute of Purchasing and Supply
Chartered Institute of Transport
Christian Salvesen Distribution Ltd
Civil Aviation Authority
Community Network Services Ltd
Confederation of British Industry
Controller General HMSO
Department of Transport
Dun & Bradstreet International Ltd
East Anglia Forwarding Ltd, Cambridge
Exel Logistics
Felixstowe Dock & Railway Co Ltd
Freight Transport Association
Freightliners Ltd
Gash and Dent Ltd
George Cohen 600 Group Ltd
Gibbon Bros
Goodyear Tyre & Rubber Co (Great Britain) Ltd
Hazchem Signs Ltd
H.M. Customs & Excise
Hoverspeed Ltd
Inland Waterways Association
Institute of Chartered Shipbrokers
Institute of Export
Institute of Freight Forwarders
Institute of Logistics
Institute of Petroleum
Institute of Road Transport Engineers

Institute of Transport Administration
International Air Transport Association
International Chamber of Commerce
International Civil Aviation Organisation
International Transport Intermediaries Club
International Union of Railways
Lancer-Boss Ltd
Lancing-Bagnall Ltd
Lifting Equipment Engineers Association
Lloyd's Register of Shipping
Lufthansa
Lykes Line Agency Inc
Marine Society
Maritime Information Association
Mark Rogers Photography
Matthews Conveyor Co Ltd Canada
MSAS Cargo International Ltd
Norwegian Petroleum Directorate
Overseas Containers Ltd
P & O Containers Ltd
Pallet Handling Ltd, Hildenborough, Kent
Port of London Authority
Port of Tilbury Ltd
Railfreight Distribution
Ready-Mixed Concrete Co Ltd
Richardson Sheffield Ltd
Road Haulage Association
Ryder PLC
St John Ambulance Brigade
Salvage Association
Shell International Petroleum Co Ltd
Simpler Trade Procedures Board (SITPRO)
Society of British Aerospace Companies Ltd
Society of Motor Manufacturers and Traders
Syntegra
Tachodisc Ltd
The Broken Hill Proprietary Co Ltd
Tiphook Rail
TNT Express (UK) Ltd
TNT Materials Handling Ltd
Trade Indemnity PLC
Transport Development Group PLC

1 Transport and the modern world

1.1 Transport in the framework of production

Transport is that part of economic activity which is concerned with increasing human satisfaction by changing the geographic position of goods or people. It may bring raw materials to places where they can be manufactured more easily, or finished goods to places where consumers can make best use of them. Alternatively, it may bring the consumer to places where he or she can enjoy services which are being made available; patients to hospital; the weary to centres of recreation; the young to institutions of education and learning; the bored to places of entertainment.

Many areas of the world, even today, are largely uninhabited and their resources unexploited. We may not experience quite the same thrill that Balboa felt when he climbed a tree on the Isthmus of Panama and saw the Pacific Ocean stretched limitlessly before his eyes, but the television screen daily depicts for us out-of-the-way places where unsophisticated people still lead simple lives ignorant of the wealth that lies in their sun-drenched hills or frozen tundra. Transport can release these resources. It has been said that 'Transport creates the utility of space.' It is a liberating force, setting free natural, manufactured and human resources from situations where they are yielding little satisfaction, and transferring them to places where their full utility can be realised. But equally it may, by giving access, release utilities which have been unable previously to realise their true potential *in situ*. The canals built in Britain in the eighteenth century transformed the districts through which they were cut. The countryside was opened up, populated and developed. Wild heathland became farmland; ores, stone, coal and other natural products could be exploited; villages and towns grew up. It is a process that is taking place even today. It is no accident that the African republics have only now begun to exert an influence on world affairs, for the jet aeroplane has at last liberated their utilities. In a single generation the camel has been replaced by the Boeing

747. The beaches of Kenya have always been beautiful, with coral strands scented with cloves and spices, but until the long-haul jet made them accessible to European tourists, they were of little commercial value.

Transport releases resources from their geographical bondage. It makes available formerly inaccessible utilities. The breakfast cereal made in north London reaches the housewife in Birmingham, Aberdeen or Penzance. The power supply of Kittimat in British Columbia is released when it creates aluminium saucepans for the kitchens of Germany, the United States or Argentina. *We may therefore define transport as a means for increasing human satisfaction by the movement of goods and passengers, so that inaccessible goods may be moved to those points where consumers require them or consumers may be moved to those points where otherwise inaccessible service facilities may be enjoyed.*

Before turning to the study of transport itself, let us first remind ourselves where transport fits into the framework of production.

Production occurs as a result of economic activity of one kind or another. The natural resources and the human resources of the earth are combined for the purpose of creating some marketable product that people want. Usually in this process it is helpful to take advantage of tools, equipment and techniques made available in previous periods. These 'producer goods' or 'capital goods' speed up production and raise output. Economic activity is therefore a combination of three 'factors of production': land, labour and capital. Land, to an economist, means all the non-human natural resources of the earth; 'labour' means all the human resources; and 'capital' means all the accumulated wealth of tools, equipment, techniques of production, etc., inherited from the previous production period. Economic activity aims to satisfy people's wants by creating 'utilities' – the name given by economists to any good or service which yields satisfaction. Food has utility, for it satisfies hunger; clothes have utility, for they keep us warm; dentistry has utility; so have theatrical performances, holidays on the Côte d'Azur and power from atomic reactors. Few of the satisfactions available to people in sophisticated societies are possible without transport, which must either move the goods to where we can enjoy them, or move us to where the goods and services are located. This, then, is where transport fits into the production scene. It moves resources to where they are wanted, from the mines, forests, fields and oceans where they are found. It moves labour into the factories, offices, hospitals, schools, colleges, etc. where they can organise the production of goods and services. Finally, the finished goods are again moved to the countless points where consumers wait to use them or to benefit from the services that are being made available.

1.2 The nature of the modern world

The earth today is commonly described as a 'shrinking' world, one in which transport has reached such a level of performance that very rapid movements of goods and people can be made from one part of the globe to another. Air cargo loaded in Finland or Sweden on Monday arrives in San Francisco by 8 a.m. the next morning. It is possible to leave Seoul on Thursday afternoon, spend a day in Alaska and, with a little help from the international date line, reach London on Friday morning. The distances we have to cover are as great as ever, but the time required to traverse them has shrunk drastically.

The chief features of this shrinking world affecting transport may be listed as follows:

1. A complex pattern of trading nations.
2. A growing population.
3. An increasing affluence of nations.
4. A decline in strategical interferences with transport.
5. A ceaseless quest for economies of scale in transport operations.
6. Increasingly serious environmental problems.

While these are dealt with more fully later, a preliminary glance at the outstanding features is desirable at this point.

1.3 The pattern of trading nations

The modern world still consists of a collection of nation-states, each exerting its own dominion over its territory or territories, and imposing its own legal and administrative controls over its citizens and the economy which provides for them. While peoples' ultimate destiny must be world citizenship, we are not likely to see this attained for many years yet. Instead, we see a tendency for all but the very largest states to associate together in trading groups. These groups at least as far as the free enterprise nations are concerned are not based on the domination of a single powerful member, as in former times. Instead, nations tend to link up with those similar in size and wealth to themselves. Their mutual interests draw them together, and their similar bargaining strengths incline them to arrive at agreements acceptable to all. Since the collapse of a unified Communist bloc in the Soviet Union there are three major world powers, in economic terms. These are the United States, the European Union (EU) and Japan. The United States and the EU are really groups of states, but groups which intend to act together. There is also a residual EFTA (European Free Trade Association) group, most of whose members are anxious to join the EU, and whose prospects for entry are excellent because they are wealthy, sophisticated and at a similar level economically to the present members of the EU. They include Norway, Sweden, Finland, Austria, Iceland and Switzerland (but Switzerland has decided not to apply for membership of the EU).

Despite the confusion in the former Soviet Union since the collapse of communism there is still the potential for industrial and agricultural wealth in these territories once they have made the transition to free market economies, and China is also making rapid progress now that the severity of Communist control has been relaxed. China's progress is export-led, and it remains to be seen whether trade policies will become more restrictive in the last few years of the twentieth century. Any extension of protectionist policies in the United States or Europe would make it more difficult for countries like China and the Commonwealth of Independent States (CIS) (comprised of some states of the former Soviet Union) to achieve growth by exporting. Many smaller free trade areas are also playing their part in helping the world economy grow. The Pacific fringe countries are particularly dynamic, while South and Central America are also making progress. At these less affluent levels the formation of free trade areas, which bring partners of equal strength into co-operative activities, offers good prospects for progress. Other bodies like the Organisation of Petroleum Exporting Countries (OPEC) represent member nations at international conferences on trade and transport matters, and bargain for the best possible terms in international negotiations.

Despite these groupings, the essential feature of the modern world economic scene is the mutual interdependence of all nations. The essence of trade, and the transport associated with it, is that it must be mutually beneficial. Where it is not, the nation that is at a disadvantage will eventually cease to trade. While it is to some extent true that the strong can still extort what they want, and the weak still yield what they must, the general tendency is towards greater egalitarianism. The balance of power is more evenly divided between nations today, and economic power is more susceptible to international opinion than perhaps at any time in history. In transport this has led to a series of international conventions in the last fifty years or so which have regulated most aspects of international carriage. The resulting agreements have done much to ensure fair play between nations and between carriers and customers. They have also done much to eliminate the more wasteful features of free competition.

1.4 The growth of population

One feature of the modern world that affects transport is the enormous increase in population. Tables 1.1 and 1.2 show the same facts in two

Table 1.1 Estimated world population, 1650–2000

Year	Estimated world population (millions)
1650	450
1900	2,000
1960	3,000
1970	3,600
1980	4,000
2000	6,250

Table 1.2 World population trends

Population (thousand millions)	Reached by	Number of years needed to produce an increase of one thousand million inhabitants
1	1830	From the dawn of life, say 100,000 years
2	1930	100
3	1960	30
4	1980	20
5	1990	10
6	2000	10

different ways. In Table 1.1 the growth in world population to the year 2000 is shown, as estimated by the demographers.

A convenient unit for considering the change in population is the gigabirth. A gigabirth is 1,000 million people. The term 'gigabirth nightmare' has been used to describe the incredible growth in world population experienced in the last two decades of this century. In Table 1.2 we have these figures presented in a different way, by showing the speeds with which a gigabirth increase has taken place.

The staggering increase predicted for 1980–2000 (twice as large an increase in twenty years as was produced in the period from the dawn of history to 1830) gives some idea of the transport problems to be faced. Not only will this enormous population need to be fed, clothed and housed, it will increasingly demand to see the world. There have been several occasions in the last twenty-five years when particular problems arose, when the transport systems of the world were barely able to cope. After various crop failures in the Soviet Union and China the movement of grain from the United States and Australia sent freight rates soaring. The shipping capacity was just not available. In 1993, one OECD economist, Michel Andrieu, estimated that in 1990 1,250 million passengers were flown by the world's airlines, and one quarter of the world's manufactured goods also moved by air (22 million tonnes). He estimated that 11,000–12,000 new aircraft costing $850,000 million would be needed in the next twenty years.

There have been some causes for believing that the growth of populations may stabilise, for both good and bad reasons. For example, the Chinese policy of only allowing one child per family held the Chinese population down for a considerable time, though the policy has now been recognised as being too stringent, having produced a whole generation of what are feared will prove to be rather pampered children. Even so, despite this fierce control, in which even eight months pregnant women were aborted, the Chinese officials claiming the right to hold the Olympics in China in the year 2000 used as one argument that China had 1.27 billion people, one fifth of the human race, and that therefore one of the five Olympic rings really represented China. It is unlikely that many nations will follow such a stringent family policy, but several other nations do limit the number of children to two. Less satisfactorily, population is being held down by the spread of AIDS, and by the human misery resulting from wars, civil wars and the genocidal tendencies of religious groups in many countries. That scourge of population, famine, which as Malthus said, 'with one mighty blow levels the population with the food of the world', is often with us. And the greatest increases in population are likely to come in precisely those areas where famines most easily occur. If the population of the developing world is to double by the year 2020, it may well prove impossible to fulfil the demand for shipping in times of emergency. Population growth requires increases in transport – transport of raw materials, vegetables and other crops, meat, milk, cheese and other proteins, of manufactured goods and of the people themselves.

1.5 The increasing affluence of nations

The volume of traffic reflects not only the numbers of people requiring to be fed, clothed and sheltered, but also their affluence. Not only are more nations affluent today than ever before, but the spread of that affluence down into the masses of their populations is greater than at any time in history. Egalitarianism is inevitable in modern societies, for it is easy enough for the dispossessed to disrupt the pleasures of the well-to-do. A rich nation whose wealth is enjoyed by the few generates little trade, and that chiefly in luxury goods. An affluent nation which has an egalitarian structure generates enormous volumes of trade, for there are millions of people demanding broad ranges of goods and services. Home trade, community trade within a free trade area and international trade must grow and generate increased demand for and use of transport facilities of every type.

It is not only the volume of goods transported which increases in an egalitarian society, the people themselves are on the move. Nations pass successively through a bicycle era and a motorcycle era to a private motor car era. A good test of an affluent nation is the extent to which the mass of the people have personal transport. A second guideline is the volume of air passenger traffic, which only becomes possible for the vast mass of the people once they have achieved a certain affluence. The enormous growth of packaged holidays by air has been one of the most significant developments in European transport since 1960, reflecting as it undoubtedly does the increased affluence of the ordinary European.

1.6 The decline of strategical interferences with transport

Transport is vitally affected by geography, particularly the topographical features, mountain chains, plains, valleys and coastlines. These features represent major problems to the various modes of transport. Political and strategic interferences with access are also obviously a great inconvenience, particularly where the natural or shortest route to a given destination lies across territory which may not be traversed for these reasons. The most notable example of such restrictions was the almost total closure of the Soviet Union in the first half-century of Soviet rule. This particularly handicapped the development of rational air routes to the Far East and the Antipodes. The aircraft is the one form of transport which is little affected by geographical topography, but this advantage could not be fully exploited while the trans-Soviet routes were closed.

In the last few years some relaxation of these strategic restrictions has been made, because of the development of satellite observation techniques. When satellites can observe every 90 minutes the developments of even the most inaccessible installations there is little point in preventing air traffic flying along normal corridors. The short air routes across the Soviet Union, first to Malaya and Singapore, later to Vladivostok and Japan, have been opened up, while the Trans-Siberian railway route for containerised traffic has become increasingly important. The latter route does not save much time on the usual shipping routes, but it was, until recently, much cheaper, and it may be again.

1.7 The search for increasing efficiency in transport

At one time the concept of efficiency in production was largely associated with the manufacturing processes. Henry Ford's definition of mass production as 'the focusing upon a manufacturing project of the principles of power, accuracy, economy, system, continuity, speed and repetition' enabled him to achieve enormous economies of scale in the manufacture of motor vehicles. His ideas were quickly copied, not only by rival motor car manufacturers but throughout the whole manufacturing field. By the 1950s firms were forced to look elsewhere for economies which would keep them ahead of their rivals. Naturally, transport and distribution activities came under scrutiny, if only because an increased scale of manufacturing operations inevitably requires longer distribution chains to market the increased output. The result has been the focusing of attention upon the total distribution process, and a continuing search for economies in transport operations. This search for a system offering the 'least total distribution cost' has revolutionised transport since 1960. (For a full description of this concept see page 186.) The most notable changes to achieve economies in physical distribution are the following:

1. An increase in bulk carriage, especially by sea, with the development of specialised bulk carriers for oil, ore, refrigerated gas, wheat, cellulose and other commodities. The enormous increase in the size of vessels has enabled more distant sources of raw material to be exploited, e.g. Brazilian iron ore for Japan. Australia has increased its mineral exploitation out of all recognition, with huge exports of iron ore, manganese, bauxite, coal and phosphates to destinations as far afield as the United Kingdom, the United States and the Middle East, where excess gases from oilfields have led to the development of aluminium smelters.
2. An increase in unit loads, chiefly by containerisation, but also by palletisation, barge carriers, roll-on roll-off systems and by the packaging of timber.
3. An increase in air transport, no longer reserved for valuable lightweight cargo, but extended into a range of other traffics, like the 'Fad today and Fade tomorrow' commodities so appealing to teenagers, and those products where 'total distribution costs' can be minimised by using air freight if it effects savings in other directions such as 'idle plant' costs, warehousing costs and interest on capital tied up in transit.
4. The streamlining of documentation by 'aligned systems', in which a variety of documents is produced from a single master document. This process has now extended into the electronic transmission of aligned documents through electronic data interchange (EDI).
5. Groupage – a process whereby specialist firms assemble the goods of several small shippers into a unit load, for which they assume respons-

ibility for the major part of a transit, dispersing them to their individual destinations on arrival at the foreign port.

6. The growth of the mega-carrier, the large multi-modal carrier, which carries door-to-door on a continental scale using whatever combination of modes is most appropriate to the particular cargo concerned. In assuming the mega-carrier role the carrier also assumes full responsibility for losses or damage suffered, wherever it occurs on the journey. The carrier will meet such claims as are justified (but reserves the right to subrogate the company into the position of the consignee and recover what can be recovered from the person actually at fault, and responsible for the loss). ('Subrogate' is an insurance term, meaning to step into the shoes of another party, and exert all the legal rights that the other party had, by suing the person responsible for the original loss.)

1.8 Transport and the environment

The enormous developments in transport during the last quarter of a century have not been without their social costs, and transport is at present under heavy criticism for the adverse effects it is having on the environment. Much of this criticism is unjust, since transport only reflects people's ordinary aspirations for an increased standard of living. The conservationist who protests loudly about aircraft noise may be found booking a packaged tour with the rest of us. The village resident protesting about juggernaut lorries still buys groceries in the supermarket of the local town where the juggernaut unloaded.

Notwithstanding this inconsistent behaviour of transport's critics, the environmental issue is one that gives most transport personnel cause for concern. No one should plan transport operations without giving at least some thought to ways of minimising the nuisance likely to be caused by any new system that is proposed. The public image of any firm is a matter of concern to its management, and that image is increasingly endangered by transport activities which appear to impact on the environment adversely.

1.9 The study of transport

We have defined transport as a means of increasing human satisfaction by the movement of goods and passengers. The problems of moving goods and passengers are great, and in their solutions to these problems transport engineers and others have shown great ingenuity. The infinite variety of vehicles and units of propulsion means that no comprehensive study of the subject can be short. Transport has its own interesting history, and the pace of development is such that obsolescence overtakes many transport components before their anticipated working life is ended. While this book will do its best to give a world-wide picture, it cannot hope to deal fully with all the branches of transport and of the associated fields which affect and are affected by it. The major headings we shall attempt to cover are as follows:

1. The functions of transport, in particular its part in bridging the gaps between producers and consumers.
2. The physical components of transport; the 'ways' over which vehicles move, the units of carriage and of propulsion, and the terminals where interchanges occur between one transport system and another.
3. The nature of traffic, both goods and passengers. The special characteristics of each type of traffic and the responses made by engineers and others to accommodate the traffic and meet the peculiar nature of each.
4. The modes of transport, road, rail, sea, air and pipeline, and the typical operations of each type.
5. The structure of the industry and its forms of ownership.
6. The associated fields of human activity bearing upon transport, particularly communications, finance, import and export trade, law – in particular international law – industrial relations, the social implications of transport and its effects upon the environment and the biosphere.

1.10 Transport and logistics

As the study of any subject raises the professionalism of those who conduct the activity, new terms are introduced which reflect the wider field of knowledge. Today the term 'logistics' is widely used to describe the processes of physical distribution. Originally a military term used to describe the total problem of moving, feeding and billeting armies on the move, the term is not inappropriate for the modern activity of international physical distribution. We don't need transport only, but all sorts of facilities – ports, airports, container depots, warehouses, helipads, stations, marshalling yards, etc. Even a simple layby can be part of a logistical set-up. If drivers are allowed to drive for an eight-hour day and we can anticipate an average speed of 40 mph (say, 65 km/h), all we need is a layby 160 miles (256 km) down the road and our goods can travel 320 miles (512 km) a day. Two loads, one heading north and the other south, can meet in the layby to change drivers, and each driver will be back home with goods that have travelled 320 miles (512 km) in a day. Logistics is clearly a good term to describe such an efficient use of the humble layby.

In studying transport the use of a lever arch file is recommended, with divisions made from brown paper (old A4 envelopes are quite satisfactory). The chapters of this book are useful titles for the sections. In each section the student should file away the following items:

1. Notes made on the chapter concerned.
2. Notes of lectures attended on the subject.
3. Newspaper and journal articles, etc. relevant to the chapter concerned.
4. Specialist brochures, etc. referring to firms, companies, visits made, etc.
5. Written work done on the subject, including marked essays. However, students should not limit themselves to written work that has been marked, for no lecturer can possibly cope with more than a small amount of marking. You should aim to answer every question in this book, to the best of your ability. Don't worry about who is going to appraise it. You are! That is what happens in real life. When a new regulation comes in you have to read the regulation, decide what it implies for your organisation, write a report for top management about the implication and put it into effect. Don't expect everything you write to be marked by anyone.

Such a collection makes a much more interesting file for revision purposes than just a few notes on the chapters.

1.11 Summary

1. Transport may be defined as a means of increasing human satisfaction by the movement of goods and passengers, so that inaccessible goods may be moved to those points where consumers require them, or consumers may be moved to those points where service facilities such as health care, education, entertainment and recreation may be enjoyed.
2. The features of the modern world are: a complex pattern of trading nations; inhabited by a growing population; increasingly affluent; with rising demand for goods and services of every type.
3. The chief function of transport is to bridge the geographical gaps between goods and services on the one hand, and consumers on the other. Since transport activities take time, it is also necessary to bridge the time gaps involved, so that cargoes do not deteriorate or sustain damage, and are safe from pilfering and large-scale theft.
4. The pattern of trading nations is increasingly one of major and minor trading blocs, each consisting of groups of nations at roughly comparable levels. The major blocs are the United States, the European Union and Japan, but other groups such as the 'Pacific fringe' states and China are making sustained attacks on the traditionally powerful trading nations.
5. A chief feature of transport today is the relentless drive to secure increased efficiency by bulk haulage, the use of unit loads such as containerised and palletised cargo, and higher speeds both in the use of air transport and in improved turn-round times in both sea and air transport.

6. The most serious aspect of transport today is its adverse impact on the environment. This must become a concern of all those interested in transport, so that criticism of this important industry is reduced as much as possible.

1.12 Questions

1. Define transport. Explain how transport works to increase consumer satisfaction in the field of (a) prepared meals; (b) packaged holidays; (c) dentistry.
2. Why is the world said to be 'shrinking'? What transport factors have contributed to the 'shrinking' of the world?
3. What is the link between population increases and the growth of transport?
4. 'Production has become about as efficient as we can possibly get it. If we want to improve efficiency now we shall have to seek it in the physical distribution field.' Explain this statement, made in the 1960s by a 'captain of industry'.
5. 'Transport is good for mankind, but bad for almost every other creature on earth.' What are the environmental effects of transport? What can transport enthusiasts do to reduce the problems referred to in this statement?
6. What is logistics? Refer in your answer to the need to think through fully the likely results of any change in transport and distribution methods.

2 The function of transport

2.1 Transport and economics

Economics has been defined as 'the study of mankind in the everyday business of life'. The everyday business of mankind is concerned with the production of goods and services which satisfy people's wants. There are many solutions to our economic problems, and economies differ according to the pattern of solutions adopted. In the modern world there were until recently three chief types of economy. These were the free enterprise economies, such as the economy of the United States; the centralised economies, such as the economies of the Soviet bloc countries; and mixed economies, of which the economies of the European Union were perhaps the best example. Since the breakdown of the Communist system in the Soviet bloc the strongly centralised economies have lost their 'central' powerbase and are seeking to replace it by a rather haphazard privatisation programme to restore free enterprise. Whatever solutions are found to the problems in providing goods and services to satisfy wants, they are bound to be alike in one respect at least: transport is an essential element in each system.

Only the most primitive economies can operate without transport. The village cobbler of a simple community, having made a pair of shoes, walks with them to his customer's house and a simple cash transaction, or even a barter transaction, takes place. The advanced manufacturing systems of the modern world require more sophisticated arrangements. In economic terms the 'scale' of operations is greater. Large-scale production of footwear requires supplies of skins, hides and synthetic materials to be transported into the production unit. Design staff, production workers, marketing and distribution teams and management have to be attracted to the area and moved in. The finished product has to be packaged, transported to regional depots, warehoused, displayed, sold and finally distributed to the localities where consumers are waiting for supplies.

It used to be thought that the productive person was the factory hand at the workbench, or the labourer in the fields. In today's mass production era this view is out of date. A 'good' has not been fully produced until it has reached the final consumer who will enjoy it. Equally, it cannot even start to be produced until the raw materials, components, etc. reach the factory production-line. Therefore, the transport worker who brings these items to the production-line, or who takes the good from the point of production to the point of consumption, is fulfilling a useful and productive service. Similarly, a service made available at any given point is not productive until someone is present to take advantage of it. The airline pilot who transports holidaymakers to the Costa Brava is productive because he enables passengers to achieve the satisfactions experienced on vacations.

Transport is therefore an element of economics, and the demand for transport derives from the economic needs of mankind.

2.2 The demand for transport

To some extent all economies are free enterprise economies, for it is in the nature of people to find personal solutions to the problems of demand and supply. When we feel a need for some particular good or service, we seek out someone who can supply it, and offer an inducement. Economists have therefore divided elementary economic studies into the studies of demand and supply. When a person wants something sufficiently to be prepared to pay for it – that is to say, will offer an inducement to any supplier prepared to supply it – he or she is said to 'demand' the good. Payment is most often arranged in 'cash': some officially sponsored form of 'legal tender' such as pounds or dollars. The demand for a good or service is therefore that quantity of the good or service which people are prepared to pay for at a certain price.

Many goods are demanded 'directly', that is to say, they are wanted for the satisfaction they yield. The demand for fish and chips arises directly from the hunger of consumers for that particular combination of foods. The demand for houses arises directly from the need for shelter.

There is another kind of demand which is indirect rather than direct. Here the object is not demanded for itself alone, but only as a means to provide other desirable goods and services. The demand for sewing machines is great and continuing, but no one actually 'wants' sewing machines. You cannot eat them, drink them or wear them. We want them because they are producer goods; they help us produce clothing and furnishings which are directly beneficial in our everyday life, bringing warmth, comfort and privacy. The demand for sewing machines is a 'derived demand', derived from our need for clothing, curtains, etc.

The demand for transport is this type of demand, an indirect demand. It stems from our need for goods and services of every type. We demand the transport of Japanese video recorders because we demand the entertainment they provide. Our demand for a taxi to the dentist derives from the demand for the dentist's services. Transport facilities are 'producer goods', i.e. capital goods; goods which have a part to play in the production process. Their particular function is to bridge the geographical gaps between producers and consumers.

2.3 Bridging the producer–consumer gaps

Economists recognise two producer–consumer gaps, the 'time gap' and the 'geographical gap'. The time gap arises because goods produced today may not be required until tomorrow, or next month, or next year. This gap is bridged by the warehousing process, with its techniques for preserving goods against deterioration.

The geographical gap arises because producers and consumers are rarely in the same place. Zambian copper is demanded all over the world, but chiefly in Western Europe, the United States and in Japan. Ghana's cocoa finds its readiest markets in London and in the United States; Volvo cars are sold in Sweden, but also throughout Europe and, indeed, the world. The Spanish hotel industry offers entertainment and recreation to all visitors prepared to pay its very reasonable charges, but the 'consumers' of these services live in Britain, France, Germany, Scandinavia and North America. *It is the function of transport to bridge the geographical gap between producers and consumers, so that goods and services may be exchanged to their mutual benefit.*

Strangely, transport itself is a major factor in producing larger and larger gaps between producers and consumers. It seems paradoxical that a device designed to overcome the gaps between producers and consumers should frequently result in their enlargement, but since time immemorial this has been the case. The explanation is to be found in another economic concept: 'economies of scale'. Generally speaking, it is true to say that larger production units are more efficient than smaller production units. This is because the larger organisation can usually make use of more productive equipment, specialised tools and machinery of every sort. Before the Second World War the 10 million tons of iron ore entering world trade did not travel further than from North Africa to Western Europe. In the early 1980s the world tonnage in iron ore was in excess of 300 million tons and the furthest route was Labrador to Japan, but much of it travelled to destinations half a world away, thanks to the development of oil bulk ore carriers (OBOs) and other bulk carriers. Similarly, the motor industries of most countries started as local factories serving markets in their own countries, often with five or six competing firms producing models in quite small plants. Even Henry Ford started in his mother's kitchen. The economies of large scale led to the growth of larger plants and eventually to the amalgamation of many of the producers to give a few large plants. The market became a world-wide market and part of the expansion was a search for economic transport of finished vehicles which led to the development of car transporters. Today, special car-carrying vessels serve the Japanese and Korean car industries. Bridging the producer–consumer geographical gaps is the major function of transport.

The second producer–consumer gap is the time gap between production and consumption. The time gap is not bridged by transport quite as directly as the geographical gap, which is obviously bridged by our motor vehicles, railway trains, ships, aircraft and pipelines. Many goods coming off production-lines are simply warehoused until required. They may need to be treated with preservatives of various sorts. Additives are added to foods, beverages, etc.; engines are inhibited to prevent rust; fabrics are treated, etc. Goods may need to be refrigerated or even irradiated, and these activities have nothing to do with transport. On the other hand, while goods are on the move they often need these processes to be continued while in transit. We have refrigerated vehicles and vessels, and others which are fully insulated so that goods brought down to very low temperatures before loading are still below freezing point at the end of their transit.

Another aspect of the time gap is the need for vigilance to avoid both casual pilfering and organised theft. This is particularly easy in road haulage, where both cargoes and vehicles are at serious risk. It is also easily effected in air transits, particularly at terminals, or in movements between terminals. The activities of drivers are always to some extent suspect, and sophisticated devices which can track vehicles and say exactly where they are at any moment are now available to trace vehicles diverted from their correct route.

2.4 The concept of 'safe arrival'

Transport provides the means of bridging the geographical gaps between producers and consumers, but its function will not have been carried out properly unless the goods or passengers arrive safely at their destination. Transport is peculiarly susceptible to interference from outside agencies, for by its very nature it requires carriers to go 'over the hills and far away'. Who can say what fate lies in store for those who travel, or what dark deeds may be done by those entrusted with other people's goods. As we shall see later, English law from time immemorial has regarded the carrier as being in a special category of bailee. He has, from early times, been regarded as a 'common carrier' and the peculiar characteristic of the common carrier is that he is liable for every loss that occurs, whether it was his fault or not. He has always been required to put safe arrival before speed – delay is no justification for excessive speed which causes injury to passengers or damage to goods. It is true that later a few exceptions were permitted to this harsh rule of absolute liability: not even a common carrier can be blamed if he is struck by lightning, or if the Queen's enemies fall upon him, but if he is robbed by anyone else he will be held liable. The concept of safe arrival as an essential element in the carriage of goods and passengers has therefore been recognised from very early times.

The concept of 'safe arrival' holds that no transit is complete until the goods have arrived safely at their destination and a 'clean' signature has been obtained acknowledging the delivery. A 'clean' signature is one that certifies that goods have arrived in good order and condition. A more cautious signature might bear the words: 'Received in apparent good order and condition.' A delivery note claused with any other wording would not be deemed a 'clean' signature.

2.5 Transport – an economic catalyst

Transport is demanded to bridge the consumer–producer gaps, and is supplied by those willing, or empowered, to provide facilities. In free enterprise economies transport tends to be provided by enterprising individuals who see prospects of profitability for themselves, yet it confers great benefits on others in the process. When the Duke of Bridgewater built the Worsley–Manchester canal parliament required him to sell his coal in the streets of Manchester at a maximum price of 4d per cwt for 40 years (approx 2p per 51 kg). This was about half the price of coal in Manchester before the canal was dug. Not only did the duke make excellent profits from his canal, but he was able to sell coal at a lower price than 4d per cwt to the general satisfaction of the community. In controlled economies there is some central, nationalised body to provide transport. State railways are extremely common throughout the world, state airlines are to be found in many countries, and even road haulage – an extremely difficult form of transport to nationalise – is operated by nationalised corporations in many countries.

A catalyst – as those who studied chemistry will remember – is a component which enables some other process to be carried on more quickly and efficiently. Transport in many ways acts as a catalyst, raising the level of activity in an economy. It has already been said that it releases utilities trapped in underdeveloped areas of a country, or of the world. It enables the scale of industry to be increased, bridging the producer–consumer gaps on both sides of the production process. Thus the crude oil of the primary producing nations of the Middle East, Indonesia, Nigeria and South America reaches the refineries of the advanced nations, and the sophisticated petrochemicals produced by those refineries make an enormous range of fuels, solvents, plastics, drugs and paints available to customers throughout the world. The commercial activities of business people depend enormously on the contacts they are able to make with one another. While these contacts are promoted and assisted by increasingly sophisticated communications networks, travel for business reasons is still essential. Problems are most easily solved when business people meet face to face, and assess the difficulties at first hand. The expert flies in to extinguish the blazing oil gusher; mini-submarines are rushed to effect spectacular seabed rescues; at more routine levels marketing personnel catch their Inter-City express trains to inaugurate a sales drive, while the goods to be featured in the campaign are containerised to catch the Freightliner next morning.

The catalytic effects of transport on an economy are not confined to business activities, for economic welfare is not achieved by bread alone. We need transport to attain levels of domestic satisfaction not possible in former times. We live in pleasant suburbs and commute to work in busy cities. At least one London businessman lives near Edinburgh and commutes by air daily. We visit our parents more regularly; choose schools for our children at a distance from our homes; travel in to area technical colleges for our education; arrange appointments with consultants at specialist hospitals; fly around the world to the university of our choice; visit theatres, exhibitions, eisteddfods and festivals, and generally enrich our lives by travel.

For the transport operator these catalytic effects of transport on the economy are a challenge and an opportunity. Densely populated urban areas generate traffic: commercial traffic, business passenger traffic, domestic convenience traffic, recreational traffic, vocational traffic and vacational traffic. To the extent that these traffics are catered for by the customers themselves, using personalised transport, the professional operator is prevented from playing a full part. To the extent that he or she can provide more efficient, more economic transport services than the customer with an 'own-account' fleet of vehicles or personal transport, the operator is able to contain personal transport, perhaps with environmental advantages to society in general. We must briefly consider the provision of transport.

2.6 The provision of transport

Transport is only provided if it meets some need, which is brought to the attention of those willing, or empowered, to provide facilities. The demand for a service usually precedes supply. The facilities made available at any time may be regarded as the response of transport engineers and entrepreneurs to the needs of society at that particular time, in view of the technology currently available. These responses have called forth enormous ingenuity from transport engineers, and the variety of prime movers, units of carriage, ways and types of terminal is truly astonishing. Stand on any overpass above a motorway and consider the traffic passing below, if you wish to review the ingenuity of transport engineers. Besides a wide variety of cars and light vans, each with its own specialist features, the enormous range of heavy vehicles is a tribute to their designers' skill. Specialised tankers for fuel oils, chemicals and powders are a main feature of our modern traffic. Articulated vehicles consisting of a motive unit, or tractor, and semi-trailers of enormous variety are a second feature. Ready-mixed cement and similar traffics are a third type of specialised vehicle. The wide range of vehicles fitted with their own lifting devices is a fourth tribute to the ingenuity of the industry. In fact, the development of containerisation was itself dependent on the development of heavier haulage lorries, and would not have been possible a decade earlier, before the heavy articulated vehicle was developed. Subsequently the use of a greater number of axles to spread the load made possible first the 32 tonne, then the 38 tonne and eventually vehicles of 44 tonnes capacity, and greater.

Compared with the traffic of, say, the 1940s, there has been a great leap forward. The increased efficiency, economy, adaptability and capacity of road traffic is matched by other transport systems; the railways, the airlines, shipping and even pipelines display an endless variety and a restless activity. This activity has not only responded to the needs of mankind, it has generated much of the affluence it serves. While some conservationists put their heads in their hands, and their hands over their ears, the transport engineers and operators are seeking new systems which will control the social costs without killing the goose that lays the golden eggs. As he fits a television set to give the driver a view of his reversing vehicle the transport engineer ponders how to make the transport being provided a safe, reliable servant of the community.

Free enterprise firms will only provide transport if they can do so profitably, for profit is the reward for enterprise. Every investment made by a sole operator, a partnership or limited company must in the end yield a return on the capital invested. If it does not, the investment will not be renewed when the existing asset depreciates or becomes obsolete. If left to the free play of the market, transport undertakings would nearly always yield a profit. In times gone by the monopolistic nature of transport made transport undertakings exceedingly profitable. This monopolistic nature may not be apparent to every reader. Clearly, it would be pointless to run two separate railway lines from A to B, with a few trains a day on each line. The capital costs of railways are so enormous that even in the days before taxation, when a man's profit was available for his own use entirely, no one could be found to finance such investments unless reasonable guarantees of a monopoly were given by the state. In Great Britain a running battle between the railways and successive governments lasted for most of the nineteenth century, from 1825 until 1888. The railway monopolists sought to preserve their power and the profits which represented the return on capital invested. The government sought to reduce profit margins to a 'reasonable' level. After 1888, when reasonably firm control of fares and charges was established, the railways began to decline. Investment was less attractive, and, despite the extension of amalgamations to the point where there were only four main companies, with all the economies of scale thus achieved, the railways in the face of competition from new forms of transport ran down steadily into an antiquated and outdated transport service, which only nationalisation could restore.

A nationalised industry provides transport facilities with different reference points from those of the private operator. Often there is a recognition that the services provided cannot be provided profitably. The service itself is the vital thing. Society needs an adequate service, and the industry must provide it. Criteria of efficiency will be laid down, which attempt to predict the nation's needs and the degree of 'loss' that can be suffered. Political decisions replace the test of profitability which is applied by private enterprise, and within the criteria laid down by the legislature the operators provide the services required. The transport facilities are effectively subsidised to the benefit of firms and private citizens who pay through taxation for the balance of the cost. Where services become too elaborate, or overmanning reaches ridiculous levels, or the nationalised system loses freight and passengers to non-nationalised firms, or to the use of personal transport, the nationalised industry may be hit by a vicious spiral of decreasing revenues, and the burden on the taxpayer may become excessive. This leads to calls for privatisation and the return of publicly owned facilities to private hands.

In a mixed economy, where some facilities are provided by private enterprise and some by corporations run as public enterprises, the pattern of transport facilities will be complex. From time to time attempts will be made to improve the arrangements being made, so that the public are better served. Calls for co-ordination of services will be heard, so that trains meet buses and feeder services meet ships or aircraft. Integration of services under a single unified control may be proposed so that these arrangements can be more perfectly made. The transport student, and the reader of this book, must consider all these proposals if he or she is to understand the policies that have been tried, or are being tried, in the transport field.

2.7 Summary

1. Economics has been defined as 'the study of mankind' in the everyday business of life. Transport is part of that everyday business.
2. Transport is an essential element in the production process, for a good or service has not been fully produced until it is available in finished form to the consumer. This means the good must reach the consumer, or the consumer must reach the place where the service (medical care, education, entertainment or recreation) is available.
3. The demand for transport is a derived demand – derived from our desire to obtain the goods we need and to enjoy the services that are available.
4. The chief function of transport is to bridge producer–consumer gaps. There are two such gaps, the geographical gap (which is obviously bridged by transport) and the time gap which is bridged in many ways, but as far as transport is concerned involves the use of refrigerated vehicles and vessels, and a proper attention to security to prevent various types of theft.
5. The concept of 'safe arrival' is an important one for all concerned with transport. It holds that no movement is complete until the goods arrive at their destination and a 'clean' signature has been obtained on the delivery note.
6. Transport is often regarded as a catalyst to economic activity. It speeds up the economy by bringing in raw materials and components easily and cheaply, making possible the use of large-scale methods of production and clearing the production-lines by removing finished products to warehouses, depots and marketing outlets. It also makes movements of consumers of goods and services easy, bringing them to the points where they can experience the pleasures of a consumer society.
7. Transport facilities may be regarded as the response of transport engineers and entrepreneurs to the transport needs of society at that particular time, in line with the technology currently available.
8. Transport facilities are often monopolistic in nature. Efforts to limit exploitation of the monopoly often reduce the return on capital below that level which will induce the operators to continue. Services become run down and nationalisation follows. Nationalised facilities judge their affairs differently from private enterprises, and the resulting range of services requires subsidisation by the government. This leads to calls for privatisation.

2.8 Questions

1. What part does transport play in economics? Refer in your answer to (a) the production of aluminium goods in Bahrain (an island which has none of the raw materials for aluminium), and (b) the Australian iron ore industry, where whole mountain ranges have good quality iron ore.

2. 'Transport is a derived demand.' Explain.
3. Refer to the producer–consumer gaps in the following situations:
   (a) Aku-aku, a member of a primitive South Sea Island tribe, makes fish hooks for relatives and friends.
   (b) Ali, a farmer in the Nile delta, grows market produce for a Cairo vegetable and fruit wholesaler.
   (c) Man Lee, a Singapore manufacturer, makes electronic calculators for the American and European markets.

   In each case assess the role of transport in bridging the gap.
4. (a) 'Only a nationalised railway can solve the problems inherent in a distribution network whose monopoly position has been eroded by competition from road haulage.'
   (b) 'British Rail is totally inefficient and should be privatised.'

   Assess these two views of the UK railway system.
5. 'Private enterprise will only provide transport services if they are profitable, but there is no reason why "social services" should not be financed by official funds.' Comment on this statement.

3 The physical components of transport: preliminary considerations

3.1 Introduction

At first sight there appears to be little in common between an elephant and a jumbo jet, except that the largest of the land mammals has given its name to the largest type of aircraft. They are, of course, both forms of transport. Though widely different in their nature, when we compare them in their transport roles we can find many points of similarity. In fact, if we take any mode of transport and compare it with the others, we find a number of factors common to all. In any attempt to study the various forms of transport we need to examine these common factors to discover the extent to which they affect each particular mode. Having studied the similarities, we can then look at the differences. In this way we can acquire an understanding of the problems which are common to all modes of transport and learn the needs and difficulties of particular modes. We can then assess a particular mode of transport and its suitability for the specific tasks we wish to perform.

In the next few chapters we will be concerned principally with the physical components of transport (sometimes called the elements of transport), but before studying them we need to examine a requirement that is vital to successful transport operation: the need to keep transport moving.

3.2 The need to keep all forms of transport moving

Any form of transport earns revenue only when it is doing the job for which it was designed, viz. carrying people or goods. At all other times it is generating costs.

The need to keep transport moving is so important that it could be called the first principle of successful transport operation. The professional operator who loses sight of this principle could be heading for financial failure. Consider the cases of two small road haulage operators.

> Smith has a lorry engaged on contract work which keeps his vehicle and driver fully occupied for eight hours a day, five days a week. Routine inspection is given to the vehicle at the end of each day and periodic maintenance is carried out at weekends.
>
> Brown has a similar lorry, but has been fortunate in securing a contract under which the vehicle, with two drivers, is used for two shifts each of eight hours a day for five days a week. Inspection and maintenance schedules are similar to those adopted by Smith.
>
> At the end of any given period, Brown's lorry will have carried twice as many tonne/km as Smith's. But what of the costs? Brown's labour, petrol and oil will be double those of Smith; maintenance will be somewhat higher, but the capital cost of his vehicle, premises, tax and insurance will be the same. Brown's total costs per tonne/km will be lower than Smith's, because he has achieved a higher utilisation.

If we take an entirely different mode of transport – shipping – we find ship operators are particularly conscious of the need to obtain maximum utilisation of their vessels. During the anticipated life of their vessels, they must recover the very high capital costs involved and extra funds to replace these assets, which will have risen in price. They must earn the interest incurred on that capital, their operating costs and sufficient profit to make the whole operation worthwhile. This money can only be earned by the carriage of passengers or freight. Every additional journey they can make is an extra opportunity to earn revenue. They are concerned, therefore, to see that as little time as possible is spent in port. Not only does a short turn-round time increase the time available for additional voyages, it reduces the very heavy costs incurred while a vessel is in port. Similar illustrations can be found in all modes of transport, and the higher the cost of the transport facility, the more important it becomes to ensure that the maximum possible utilisation is obtained.

Continuous operation such as is achieved in some industries is rarely attained in the transport industry. Pipelines are perhaps an exception to this rule since they are usually concerned with a single product with a huge demand. Despite peaks and troughs in the demand for transport, operators should be striving to achieve maximum performance within the constraints imposed upon them. These constraints may result from the availability of traffic, national and international legislation, and the physical components of the particular mode of transport.

3.3 The components of a transport system

Every mode of transport uses four major components, or essential elements of transport. These are the *way*, the *terminal*, the *unit of carriage* and the *unit of propulsion*. The 'way' is the route along which the traffic moves. Natural ways are cheap or even free, and have no maintenance costs unless we try to improve them artificially. The sea, the air, the rivers, and footpaths and bridleways are all natural ways. Being natural they are subject to the whims of nature, and this often requires that they be improved artificially. Rivers are subject to controls to prevent flooding in rainy periods and insufficient flow in dry periods. They are dredged to maintain a channel, and locks are built to improve navigation in the upper reaches. Bridleways are made up and turned into roads. Highways and motorways, canals, railways, tramways, tunnels and monorails are similarly constructed. Clearly these are not 'free' like the sea or the atmosphere, but for historical reasons some of the costs may be borne socially rather than privately. If the costs are borne by the ratepayer and taxpayer, we may have what is an apparently free way because no actual charge is made to the user. If the way is privately built, the owner usually has sole use of it. The owner can then charge for its use by other persons to recoup the capital expense.

The terminal is the interface where one transport network ends and another begins. Nearly every journey involves junctions where we can transfer from one form of transport to another. A port is usually regarded as a terminal for ships, but in fact it is also a terminal for trains, roads, pipelines and aircraft. In planning efficient transport systems, commercial firms and transport authorities must view the interchange of facilities as being part of a unified whole. Congestion in terminals in the past has spelt the death of a transport system, as it did when the congestion on the canals led to the growth of railways.

The unit of carriage is that part of the transport system where passengers or goods are accommodated. The efficiency of the mode of transport depends to some extent on the flexibility and adaptability of the unit of carriage used. Road vehicles are more adaptable than railway rolling stock, because they are less rigidly bound to the way they can overtake preceding vehicles and switch to alternative routes with much greater ease than can their railway counterparts. Aircraft and ships are even less tightly bound by the way on which they travel.

The propulsion unit drives the vehicle or craft in use. Every vehicle must be driven, and the choice of a propulsion unit depends on the strength of the vehicle, the speed required, the available fuel and other factors. Today the steam engine, the first great mover, has been largely replaced by the petrol engine, the jet engine, the diesel engine and the electric motor.

In any particular mode we may find two or even three of these components combined. For example, the pipeline is at the same time a way and a unit of carriage, while the pump house, which is the unit of propulsion, is itself an integral part of the way, the product in transit passing through the pump. Similarly, the family car is both a unit of carriage and a unit of propulsion, travelling over a roadway but not using any particular terminal except the family garage.

These four components require detailed study, so that the variations between the components in different modes of transport can be compared. To assist this study each component has been given a separate chapter.

3.4 Summary

1. The essentials of transport are the way, the terminal, the unit of carriage and the unit of propulsion. The different modes of transport each require these four essential elements, and in weighing up the merits of the various modes we are really comparing the efficiency of these elements of transport.
2. The chief modes of transport are road, rail, sea, inland waterway, air and pipeline.
3. The first requirement of any transport system is to keep the goods or passengers moving. The ideal arrangement is continuous operation, but it can rarely be achieved because of constraints imposed by the availability of traffic, national and international legislation and the physical components of any transport system which are liable to break down and delay.

3.5 Questions

1. What are the essential elements of transport in the following transport systems?
   (a) The family motor car.
   (b) Articulated lorries.
   (c) Cross-channel ferries.
2. Compare and contrast a space launch from Cape Kennedy and a pipeline carrying North Sea gas from the point of view of the elements of transport.
3. Apart from recreational purposes, the UK canal network is largely disused. What are the defects in its elementary transport facilities which have rendered it obsolete?

4 The physical components of transport: the way

4.1 Definition

The 'way' is defined as the medium on or through which the transport unit travels in performing its function.

There are three classifications of ways:

4.1.1 Natural ways

The air and the open sea are the examples which spring most readily to mind in the first category, but they are not the only ones. Navigable rivers were the main highways of many countries for centuries before the development of road transport and the advent of the railways, and many continue to fulfil that role today. Large areas of inland water are almost always utilised as commercial highways, e.g. Lake Geneva and the Great Lakes of North America. The importance of these inland lakes and waterways to the development of civilisation can be seen at a glance from maps showing the location of towns and cities two to three centuries ago. The only inland communities of any size had developed on the shores or along the banks of inland lakes and waterways, because these were the only places with supply routes capable of maintaining concentrations of population. Nowadays it is difficult to conceive that in the eighteenth century Welshpool was the head of navigation on the River Severn in England, with gangs of men and horses dragging vessels over shallow areas. Similarly, we see in films of former times the French-Canadian traders carrying their canoes and all their possessions from one navigable stretch of a river to another, with names like Portage La Prairie as the only enduring reminder of this activity.

Throughout the world there are vast tracts of land over which suitably designed vehicles can operate with comparative ease. Deserts and prairie lands are good examples of this type of terrain, where for centuries the unimproved surface of the land has provided the natural ways used by the scattered population. The exploitation of the natural resources of those areas, bringing increased populations and the establishment of towns and cities, has resulted in the provision of artificial ways, better able to serve the needs of the areas. In some parts of the world large areas of swamp and marshlands have lain relatively undeveloped until the past few decades. The development of specialised vehicles such as marsh buggies and more recently hover-vehicles is enabling these areas to develop economically, in a world where land of any sort is a scarce commodity. In the past, the cost of creating artificial ways has been so disproportionate to the economic benefits obtainable that it has been necessary to develop vehicles suited to the natural way rather than provide artificial ways suitable for existing vehicles. Examples are the 'snowcats' used in Arctic tundra conditions, with wide caterpillars which spread the weight of the vehicle over the snow surface. As the demand for land grows, the less difficult areas are being drained and artificial ways created to aid the exploitation of the land.

As the level of economic activity increases, so does the demand for efficient transport. This means, so far as the user is concerned, low-cost, speedy and reliable transport. In the examples given above, natural ways soon become inadequate to meet the demand for efficient transport, and it becomes necessary either to improve the existing natural ways or to provide entirely artificial ways.

4.1.2 Natural ways artificially improved

People soon learned that however useful natural waterways and lakes were, their usefulness could usually be increased by artificial improvements. At first such improvements consisted of such things as removing loose rocks and obstructions, strengthening banks where collapses impeded navigation, and such dredging as could be accomplished with manual labour and crude dredging devices. Then as engineering ability increased, the scale of possible improvements was enormously extended. Where solid rock had formerly frustrated attempts to increase the depth of water, now this could be blasted away to achieve the desired result. Permanent artificial banks could be created, containing the river within fixed limits, so increasing the depth and flow of water, and utilising its 'self-scouring' power. Finally, difficult bends could be removed and where necessary massive engineering projects could be mounted for the purpose even of diverting the river from its natural course.

A good example of this is Glasgow, which commenced its history as a monastic settlement at a fording point above rapids on the Clyde, which protected the settlement from Viking raiders. Subsequently, as its trans-river commerce increased and its merchants developed overseas interests in Canada, it developed Port Glasgow, below the rapids, which in turn were subsequently blasted away to make Glasgow itself a major port.

What medieval people called roads, we would call tracks, i.e. unimproved natural ways across land which offered fairly easy passage. As the need for more efficient land transport grew with the growth of economic activity, it became necessary to improve these natural ways. Considerable improvement could be secured simply by removing obstructions such as rocks and fallen trees, by filling in holes and by draining marshy sections. Further improvement could be achieved by pounding broken rock into the surface, and by digging ditches on either side to assist drainage. This was the pattern of road improvement, other than in towns and cities, in the developed countries, until recent times, and remains the principal form of road improvement in many parts of the world today. It is difficult to conceive that in the United Kingdom the all-weather tarmacadam roads of non-urban areas only date from the first two or three decades of the twentieth century. Today the weight, volume and speed of modern road transport demand roads of a much higher standard, and these can only be created artificially.

4.1.3 Artificial ways

Modern roads are often relegated to a minor position in discussions of artificial ways, because roads have been with us for so long that there is a tendency to think of the majority of them as being natural ways, artificially improved. The opposite is the case, the majority of roads being the conscious creations of engineers and planners. Road transport has reached its position as the most important form of inland transport in many countries because of the universality of its 'ways', i.e. there are few places that are inaccessible by road.

The distinction between natural ways, costing nothing to provide and maintain, and artificially improved ways which may require enormous capital expenditure in their construction and continuous expenditure on maintenance, is significant. Because the former cost nothing to provide and maintain, they can be made free to all – there is no economic justification for restricting their use, although it may be politically desirable or expedient to do so. With artificial or artificially improved ways, the question of 'free' use does not arise. Whether the costs of providing and maintaining the way are borne by the transport undertaking, as in the case of railways and canals, or by the community as a whole, as is the case with most roads, those costs must eventually be recouped. Broadly speaking, railway and canal undertakings recover their costs directly from the users by means of tolls and charges. Where the level of income is insufficient to meet the costs, government subsidies, financed from taxes, may be considered necessary. Roads, on the other hand, excepting certain toll-ways, are financed partly from specific taxes on road users and partly from general taxes on the whole community. However, it does not mean specific taxes are necessarily spent on the roads. In fact, road-related taxes on the personal motor car, petrol tax and VAT on cars are a lucrative source of revenue to supplement general taxation. Personal transport has become the new 'poor man's luxury', and taxes on the 'luxuries' of the poor, such as beer and tobacco, have always been a major source of general revenue. In fact, it is reckoned that vehicle excise duty, petrol tax and VAT on cars far exceeds the total spent on roads in any year, so that the motorist is benefiting the community, rather than being subsidised by the community.

The amount which the community as a whole contributes towards the provision and upkeep of the way must be carefully balanced against the benefit which the community gains from the mode of transport using that way. If the benefit derived from providing ways for one mode of transport is less than that derived from another, then more of the community's resources should be directed towards that mode which proves most beneficial. Unless this is done, adherents of one mode of transport will claim that the elected representatives of the community (e.g. the government) are unfairly favouring one mode of transport to the detriment of others and of the community. Determining the rights and wrongs of such claims is no simple matter, even trying to quantify benefit is a most complex process. In this context 'benefit' is used to denote a concept far wider than simply monetary return against capital outlay, and may even go so far as to embrace the quality of life itself.

4.2 The ownership of ways

We have seen that the provision of ways, other than natural ways, is a costly business, and the money expended must be recovered by some means or another – the user does not get the way for nothing. Some ways may be provided by an individual or an undertaking solely for his or its personal use. Roads or railways, wholly within the boundaries of an industrial estate, are examples of such *private ways* which have been provided solely for the benefit of the undertaking. Members of the public in their dealings with the undertaking may make use of those ways, but they do not have the freedom to use them for purposes of their own (except with the express or implied permission of the owners). The cost of such ways must be borne by the individual or undertaking for whose benefit they were constructed, without the benefit of contributions from other sections of the community.

Other ways, to which the public have access, *for their own private purposes* can be called *public ways*. These may be *publicly owned* ways or *privately owned* ways.

4.2.1 Publicly owned public ways

In this category we find most roads. These are financed from money received from rates and taxes, and their provision is regarded as a service essential to the community. For this reason, some users – e.g. pedestrians and cyclists – make no contribution towards their provision and upkeep, other than through general rates and taxes. Other users, who are considered to obtain a greater benefit from the roads and who, by their heavier use of the roads, create higher maintenance costs, pay an additional charge by way of special taxes, e.g. vehicle taxation coupled with fuel tax.

4.2.2 Privately owned public ways

Some artificial or artificially improved natural ways are provided by private undertakings, for public use. In many cases the provision of the way is intended primarily to benefit the undertaking by providing easier access and more efficient transport, and, by allowing the public to use it, it becomes more attractive financially. This may be because:

1. the financial burden of providing and maintaining the way would be too great for the undertaking to bear; or
2. payment for the use of the way by other members of the public is a source of additional profit.

Many of Britain's early canals, like the Bridgewater Canal completed in 1767, which was constructed to carry coal from the Duke of Bridgewater's estate at Worsley to Manchester and Liverpool, were built primarily to benefit specific undertakings. But because canals were regarded as common highways, they were open for use to all who were prepared to pay the tolls and obey the by-laws of the canal companies. The recovery of capital and maintenance costs, plus a percentage profit, can be achieved by the providers of these privately owned public ways, by two methods:

1. The payment of charges based upon the degree of use, e.g. a charge per tonne or per passenger carried.
2. The payment of tolls, i.e. a charge based on the carrying unit, irrespective of the degree of use; e.g. a per vehicle charge, based on the carrying capacity of the vehicle, not on the load carried.

Where the undertaking providing the way is also the carrier, then the first method is likely to be adopted. Where, as is often the case, the provider of the way does not engage in the actual transport of passengers and goods, then the second method is more likely to be used. If, however, the provider of the way acts as a carrier, alongside other carriers, then a combination of the two methods will probably be adopted.

4.3 The control of ways

Some ways, particularly non-congested ways, are not strictly controlled except by a framework of rules or laws laid down for the mutual benefit of all travellers. They are 'sight' ways, where travellers move so long as they can see their way to be clear. Other ways are rigorously controlled, sometimes with automatic signalling which excludes another unit of carriage from any section of the way that is already in use. Such are the train signals on the London underground railway. Other ways have radar-assisted control points like the air traffic control of modern airports and the estuarial control in busy rivers. These systems and devices are expensive to operate and must be considered when comparing ways.

Where for some reason control breaks down, severe interruptions to traffic may occur. This is particularly so where the system is inflexible, as with rapid transit systems. A single breakdown may hold up all the passenger units behind. A flexible way, by contrast, allows units of carriage to bypass stoppages. This flexibility is an important aspect of ways.

4.4 The characteristics of different ways

4.4.1 Roadways

Roadways are usually public ways. Until the end of the eighteenth century most roads were improved natural ways of ancient origin. The tracks made by our ancestors became pathways, footways, bridleways and eventually highways, deliberately raised above the level of the surrounding countryside to give an advantage against footpads and other outlaws. Some were based on Roman roads laid down during the Roman occupation from AD 43 to AD 410. Others were laid down during the great roadbuilding period from 1760 to 1836, when road transport was greatly improved in Britain. Because of this ancient origin roads have tended to be 'free' – that is, no charges are made to road users for the use of ordinary roads. Certain road tunnels, bridges and in some countries motorways are financed by tolls, and the imposition of charges for the use of congested city centres is continually under discussion, but the freedom of ordinary roads is a chief characteristic of the present day.

A second characteristic is the universality of the road network, which makes all places accessible and forms the link between all other modes of transport. Other specialised ways come to an end at some terminal, and the road is used to link that terminal with the next stage of the transit, or the final destination of the passengers or goods. Of course, there are some places which are not accessible by road, and the helicopter, aeroplane or hovercraft may take over, but these are relatively rare destinations for goods and passengers. The universality of the road network is the great advantage of this type of way – it gives door-to-door service for the vast majority of business firms and private citizens in advanced nations. This door-to-door service is also under the personal control of managements using 'own-account' vehicles. They are able to control the utilisation of their vehicles and the movements of their goods, and with electronic aids like the cab radio can maintain complete control of a vehicle throughout the working day.

Road 'ways' are flexible. By this we mean that each vehicle operates independently of other vehicles. The breakdown of one does not affect the others, which quickly drive round the stoppage or are diverted into alternative routes. Computerised route planning can be employed to select optimum routes for particular vehicles; obstructions, floods or subsidences can be bypassed. It is also flexible in that the way may be used by many types of vehicles. The transport engineer designs vehicles and units of carriage to suit a great variety of traffics. Many of these vehicles are specific to particular products, like milk, cement, petroleum products, etc., but if the demand is constant and continuing, this is no disadvantage.

The road is durable and even permanent, provided reasonable maintenance is carried out. It is of solid construction, usually in concrete, but often of tar macadam, featuring a camber to assist the run-off of water. It is usually controlled and repaired by local authorities charged with the duty of caring for the roadway, but the payment for repairs, lighting, etc., may not be a local matter, but financed from national funds.

Lastly, congestion is a characteristic of the roadway today. With many users, each pursuing his own route and not subject to control, a conflict arises between the demand for road space and its provision, particularly at peak hours. It is impossible to provide enough 'way' at peak periods, and devices such as one-way systems, parking restrictions, clearways, flyovers, traffic lights and roundabouts are introduced as means of increasing the volume of traffic a particular road can support.

Roads do not have any system of traffic control apart from ordinary police activities to detect the bad driver who is breaking the rules. Each driver is legally responsible for the movements his vehicle makes and operates within a framework of laws much of which is embodied in a highway code. A highway code usually includes many recommendations which, though not having the force of law, will tend to enhance or prejudice a case coming before a court of law according to whether or not they have been observed. Traffic lights exercise some degree of control at busy points, and many city centres have closed-circuit television cameras, which allow the traffic authority to survey and monitor the flow of traffic by operating the traffic lights according to the density of the traffic. Infra-red cameras for both night and day use are now being fitted to traffic lights to curb motorists jumping the lights. Photographs of cars breaking the rule have been used as evidence for prosecutions.

In many dormitory areas there is an increasing use of 'sleeping policemen' (traffic calmers) and one-lane width restrictions to reduce traffic speed. The lack of garages in older dormitory areas, built before the age of the car, means that roadside parking, often on both sides of the street, reduces the flow to single-line traffic. Large parking areas are now becoming a necessity at other termini, e.g. railway stations, or public service places, e.g. hospitals, crematoria, colleges, etc.

A final point to make about roads is that major reorientations of traffic can occur when a new facility is built, which alters traffic patterns out of all relation to those used – perhaps we should say endured – for centuries. Consider bridges like the Severn Bridge and the Humber Bridge, and tunnels like the Dartford Tunnel, which in a quarter of a century was dug, duplicated and then supplemented by a bridge to give four lanes in one direction by tunnel and four lines in the other direction by bridge. They have transformed traffic patterns in their areas.

Perhaps the biggest transformation will come when Eurotunnel opens in spring 1994. This is dealt with more fully below (p.36), since it is a railway tunnel, but just to consider road transport using the tunnel is worthwhile. The way is a railway, but the tunnels are large enough to permit special vehicles to shuttle to and fro across the Channel carrying heavy goods vehicles (HGVs).

Le Shuttle is the name Eurotunnel has given to its own cross-Channel transportation service. This operates on a loop between the Folkestone and Calais terminals and will provide a dedicated freight service for the transport of HGVs and their drivers. A separate service will be run for cars and coaches. The railway is thus a roadway service.

A major aspect of Le Shuttle's transportation system is its simplicity. The Channel Tunnel is at the core of a transportation 'corridor', which runs between freight facilities and truckstops at Ashford in Kent and Marck, close to Calais.

At the truckstops on each side of the Channel, there are facilities for the driver, the lorry and the cargo. These include petrol, repair and washing facilities, restaurants, showers, communication centres and shops – in effect, everything the driver may need. There are similar facilities in the freight areas of both terminals.

Getting to and from the terminals is easy. The M20 and A16 motorways are directly connected to the Folkestone and Calais terminals, respectively. From the moment it leaves the motorway, freight traffic is segregated from tourist traffic and HGVs follow their own freight lanes to the toll booths. At the toll booth, transactions can be made using Le Shuttle's rapid service card, by fuel card, credit card, cash or cheque.

Having passed through both UK and French passport controls, the driver heads to an allocation area ready for loading. Loading and unloading is a straightforward, five-step process.

1. The lorry is driven down one of two loading bridges and onto the platform. The first loading bridge allows fourteen HGVs to be driven into the back section of the shuttle, while the second gives a further fourteen drivers access from the middle of the shuttle to the front section. A complete shuttle carries up to twenty-eight vehicles.
2. Using the spacious shuttle loading platform, which allows sufficient room for manoeuvrability, the driver progresses into the carriers.
3. The driver proceeds through to the furthest available carrier, parks, switches off the engine and puts the tachograph to rest. Plug-in points are available in each carrier wagon for drivers who need to maintain the coolchain during the journey.
4. The driver is then transferred to the Club Car at the front of the shuttle to relax during the 35-minute journey and enjoy a first class service. The driver will spend a little over 45 minutes away from the vehicle, thereby qualifying for the mid-shift break.
5. On arrival at the terminal, the driver rejoins the vehicle, drives out of the shuttle, up the loading ramp and straight onto the exit road. With all the control formalities completed on entering the system, the driver is on the way to his/her destination.

4.4.2 Railways

Railways consist of two parallel metal strips which give a smooth, hard surface. Today, rails are made of steel, but in the early days they were made of wood, and later of iron. The surface thus provided offers little resistance to rolling, especially on level ground, and very heavy weights can be moved with relatively small motive power. Railways present major engineering problems during their construction, for it is essential that gradients are kept to a minimum and the problems of overcoming terrain are severe. Bridges, viaducts and tunnels are needed to overcome land barriers and the consequent costs of construction are great. Other solutions to the problems of severe gradients are: (1) *racked railways*, which have steel cogs (the rack) laid between the lines, and pinions on the engines, which engage in the cogs of this rack; and (2) *cable ways*, which engage with the unit of carriage between the rails and haul it up very steep sections of track. Besides the actual way, stations, signalling and other apparatus must be provided and maintained, so that the capital cost is high.

Most railways began as private ventures and the track, when built, constituted a private way for the sole use of the proprietor. In Britain, Parliament introduced into early Railway Acts requirements that the line should be available to other users who had the right to run trains on it. For safety reasons this practice was discontinued, and the operations were performed by the railway company concerned. For a variety of reasons railways are now usually operated as a nationalised industry in many countries. In any case rail movements are outside the control of the owner of goods being moved, who is forced to rely on the efficiency of the railway organisation to ensure that his goods proceed with proper dispatch. This loss of control over one's own goods is a major disadvantage of rail transport. It is offset in continental countries by the increased speed which is possible on long-haul journeys. Over 200 miles (320 km) the advantages of rail transport – high speed and low labour cost – exceed the disadvantages of terminal delays experienced when the terminal is outside the personal control of the consignor. Below 200 miles the advantages can only be achieved if terminals are very efficiently handled, as with the Freightliner system. Medium- and long-distance transport of heavy density is therefore best catered for by railways, with their ability to move large numbers of people and large quantities of goods very easily. For this reason concentration of rail transport on a small number of main lines with heavy through traffic makes good sense.

As far as the United Kingdom is concerned, a major change in the use of the UK rail network is about to happen at the time of writing (1993). The Channel Tunnel is nearing completion and, if properly used by the freight industry, should transform the economics of rail freighting. The essential weakness of the UK rail system as far as freight is concerned is that no two major destinations are much more than 200 miles (320 km) apart, which is about the minimum for a really economic railway transit. Now that Eurotunnel is about to open, the vast majority of long-distance haulage to continental destinations can go by rail. The 'way' is open from Glasgow, Liverpool and Bristol to the Russian border, Constantinople and the Mediterranean. There will be four main services through the tunnel. They are:

1. cars and coaches in passenger shuttles;
2. HGVs in freight shuttles;
3. through passenger trains; and
4. through freight trains.

As explained earlier, a shuttle is a very large train capable of carrying coaches, HGVs, cars and passengers. It is operated by Eurotunnel and travels through the tunnel from the United Kingdom to France. However, the great hope, from the railway viewpoint, is the prospect of getting all those HGVs and their cargoes off the roads – not onto a shuttle but onto a through freight train to be handled by rail all the way to destination (or as near as the railway goes to destination). There are some final difficulties to be sorted out – chiefly, how much should the railways pay Eurotunnel for the right to run a train over the short link between the United Kingdom and France? Another difficulty is that the British Rail side of the high speed link is not yet complete, and until the end of the century the trains will need to use the ordinary BR track (though admittedly this has been upgraded). However, these are trivial matters compared with the real advantage to UK business of switching to rail freight for its major European trading activities.

Eurotunnel has signed a contract with British Rail and the French rail network, SNCF, which will enable the railways to use up to 50 per cent of the tunnel's capacity to run their own services – high speed passenger trains, and freight and intermodal trains carrying swap bodies or containers.

Whether the Eurotunnel will succeed in developing through rail freight depends very much on how its tariff can compete with the ferries. It must be remembered that the road/ferry operations have a much greater flexibility and now an increased capacity since the 44 tonne overall limit has been adopted. It does depend to some extent on how far the goods are to travel beyond the Channel. If the journey is relatively short, the flexibility of the road vehicle will still perhaps give it the advantage. The further the goods have to travel the more the balance will swing in favour of rail freight.

Very high concentrations of commuter traffic over relatively short distances can best be handled by rail, from an operational viewpoint, because of the greater carrying capacity of trains. Unfortunately, this may be inefficient economically because of the under-utilisation of staff and facilities during off-peak hours.

Railways are inflexible in that any interruption along the specialised way holds up all traffic behind. With a dense network of lines it may be possible to re-route trains around an obstruction, but any major accident on a trunk line is going to cause delay to both goods and passengers. Railways today do not provide door-to-door service except to the very largest industrial firms. Private sidings built in earlier times are less useful today since industry has relocated itself in other areas, and only major firms in the motor vehicle, petrochemical and similar industries find it economic today to install private sidings.

Another feature of railway systems today is the reduction of depots and stations. The 'slow train' is generally uneconomic, and in the interests of economic operation the convenience to customers and passengers of the local depot has been sacrificed. By concentrating reception and delivery of goods at a few larger depots the railways achieve economies of large-scale operations and greater total utilisation of the way.

4.4.3 Waterways

Waterways are usually improved natural ways or artificial ways. They have the advantage that a floating unit of carriage is weightless and can be moved by a small motive power unit. This makes for economical transport, but speeds are very slow – even as low as 2 mph. Higher speeds increase the wash to such an extent that the banks are eroded, as those who have visited Venice will appreciate. While the water itself needs no repairing, the way may include artificial banks, locks and other devices which require to be preserved, maintained and possibly manned. In busy waterways radar controls, river police and pilots may be necessary. Barges may be as large as 3,000 tonnes on major river and canal networks, carrying bulk ores, coal, iron and steel products, chemicals, timber and wheat. These traffics are generally non-urgent, so that slow speed is no disadvantage. In recent years the development of 'Lash' ships (lighters aboard ships) makes a very effective use of inland waterway networks (see page 132). A feature of water traffic today is the environmental advantages to be achieved by the use of waterways. Where waterways link the interior of a country to the sea, the port area near the estuary will generally be a major city with a complex road structure. Barges slipping up river from a mother ship in the estuary avoid this congestion, taking goods inland to depots on the far side of the conurbation, where they may be trans-shipped to rail and road transport for the hinterland above the navigable part of the river. A really huge, interconnected river and canal network exists in Europe which enables goods to move by water from the Mediterranean to the Rhine and North Sea. Further improvements and extensions, planned or under construction, will eventually make possible journeys right across Europe and Asia.

4.4.4 Seaways

The sea is, of course, the best waterway of all – a huge, linking waterway between continental land masses, with continuous access to the interior of many countries along major estuaries. Its size enables higher speeds to be achieved than are possible on inland waterways, the wash created by the high speeds dissipating itself in the vastness of the waters. Vessels can be very large, and modern bulk haulage (see page 252) takes full advantage of this. For passengers the size of ships ensures comfortable accommodation and recreational facilities, but the slow speed has meant that some freight traffic and almost all passenger traffic has been lost to air transport. This has not been the case with cruise travel, where the ship can offer passengers who are not in a hurry a vacation which combines the advantages of foreign travel with those of a holiday at home. The ship may be of their own nationality, the crew speaking their own language, serving traditional food and yet calling at exotic places with strange-sounding names.

Modern ship canals built in the nineteenth and early twentieth centuries or so have greatly reduced the length of many voyages. If these advantages are to be enjoyed these canals have to be enlarged in order to accommodate modern vessels. In fact, there are some vessels which the Suez and Panama Canals cannot accommodate. The effect of ship canals on ports was beneficial to those on the new route and detrimental to those on the old route.

4.4.5 Airways

Like the sea, the atmosphere is a way which requires no artificial preparation, has no repair bills and no private costs. It is more universal than the oceans, since all parts of the world are equally accessible. It is no accident that the great continental powers, the United States, the USSR and China, have had to wait for the air age before reaching full stature in the world. Apart from taking off and landing, air transport is quite free of terrain, the topography of most countries lying far below the flight paths. Only one or two major land masses, the Rockies in North America and Andes in South America and the Himalayas in Asia, present obstacles to some flights, and even these may be taken advantage of by 'pressure-path' navigation in which the pilot seeks to fly in jet-streams created by the mountain patterns. Flights are largely free of climatic factors except at the times of take-off and landing. For the rest of the flight the plane is in the stratosphere, above the 'weather', giving a smooth journey for both goods and passengers.

The chief characteristic of air transport is speed. The aircraft is fast and follows the 'least time track'. This may not be as straight as the crow flies, but takes advantage of pressure patterns which vary from day to day. The short journey time offsets the high cost of aircraft, the expensive labour necessary and the costs of surveillance to ensure safe arrival. These can be considerable, but frequent journeys and the maximum utilisation of the airframe keep fares low.

It must be remembered that each nation has sovereignty over its airspace and most nations have cabotage regulations, which restrict internal flights to their own aircraft. (Cabotage is the practice of reserving internal traffic –

including coastal sea traffic – to national flag carriers. By air this also includes traffic between a mother country and its colonies.)

If a country permits the aircraft of other nations to use its airspace, it is entitled to specify air corridors, governing routes, heights and times of traffic, all of which will be monitored by ground control stations using radar.

Commercial aircraft are subject to what are known as 'the five freedoms'. These are:

1. The freedom of one nation's aircraft to cross another nation's airspace without landing.
2. The freedom of such an aircraft to land in the event of an emergency.

Although many nations adopted these first two freedoms the USSR until recently restricted its airspace. The advent of satellite 'eyes in the sky' over its territories meant that it could relax its restrictions and open up more direct ways on the Far East/Europe routes.

The other three freedoms are normally the subject of reciprocal agreements between nations.

3. The freedom to land passengers, mail and cargo loaded in the flag carrier's own country.
4. The freedom to load passengers, mail and cargo destined for the flag carrier's own country.
5. The freedom to land passengers, etc. from any third party state and load passengers, etc. for any third party state.

The other chief characteristic is referred to above – independence of topography and also of the hinterland infrastructure. This has already opened up many places formerly land-locked to commercial and tourist exploitation. Katmandu is as accessible as Bombay and one enterprising salesman did really sell refrigerators to the eskimos – to freeze a lake into a permanent runway all the year round. The airship with its huge carrying potential may yet have a great future in making land-locked resources accessible with minimum terminal costs (see Fig. 4.1).

In evaluating air transport the 'least total cost' concept has been developed. This holds that the ticket cost or freight charges – which are usually higher than other forms of transport – must be reduced by the benefits gained. Examples are the more efficient use of executive time where top management flies instead of going by sea, and the production benefits enjoyed when machinery, flown to its destination, is installed and working when it would previously have still been on its way by sea. Although air transport freight charges are nearly always more expensive this is not the case with passenger fares. Journeys may take several days or weeks by sea – the cost of feeding, service, entertainment, etc., over a much longer period, raises the cost of sea fares. Air transport is flexible,

Fig. 4.1 The Goodyear Airship 'Europa' (courtesy of Goodyear Tyre and Rubber Co. (Great Britain) Ltd)

since each flight is unique and cannot affect other flights. Finally, the majority of flights are international in character and require international co-operation and agreement if they are to proceed without interruption.

4.4.6 Pipelines

The pipeline is a unique method of transport. Of the four elements of transport – the way, the unit of carriage, the propulsion unit and the terminus – three are combined. The way, i.e. the pipeline, is also the unit of carriage and embodies at intervals along the way propulsion units (pumping stations), which are themselves part of the pipeline system. Only the terminus – for example, a tank farm – is separate.

The 'way' in transportation by pipeline is essentially an artificial way, constructed usually by a private user for his own particular purposes. The commonest examples today are crude oil and natural gas pipelines owned and operated by oil and gas companies. The capital costs are high, requiring the negotiation of way-leaves (permission to cross land belonging to others); the digging of a trench about one metre deep; the installation of the pipeline in the trench; and the construction of booster stations at regular intervals according to the requirements of the installations.

Particular problems have to be faced when the landscape is interrupted by ravines or other natural features, and in mining areas where subsidence is possible. In desert areas the pipeline is looped at intervals to allow for heat expansion by day and contraction by night. In such cases it is exposed on the surface and is therefore more vulnerable to terrorist attacks. Once established this route is inflexible in two ways: (1) as to direction, and (2) as to use. We cannot easily turn a pipeline off in another direction should the product no longer be required at its present delivery point, so that before we construct a pipeline we must be confident that the demand will be a continuing one. As to the use of the pipeline, it is inflexible in that the product to be carried can only be varied within certain limits. It does no harm to vary the product from motor spirit to aviation spirit or paraffin oil, but we cannot vary it to beer or milk. Where a pipeline is constructed by the user for his own particular purposes these are not serious disadvantages.

Once constructed, continuous flow transport replaces batch transport by ship, train or road vehicle, with 24-hour operation at high speeds. Pipeline transport is very competitive with other forms of transport over short distances, especially if full utilisation of the pipeline is possible at all times, but it cannot compete with long-distance batch transport by sea in very large bulk carriers. On overland routes, where environmental factors such as reduction of traffic congestion enter into the calculations, or where climatic conditions are unfavourable to other surface routes, the pipeline is competitive.

The pipeline is a very efficient method of ensuring safe arrival under normal circumstances, but a pipeline which traverses several countries is vulnerable to interruption for political reasons, and to sabotage by dissident groups. Most pipelines are also subject to leakages. There are many joints and welds in a pipeline and external and internal pressures quickly discover weak points.

Corrosion is a great problem and the presence of anaerobic bacteria can play a major part in a particular type of corrosion. For this reason glassfibre and asbestos wrappings have replaced jute and cotton, which provide a source of food for these bacteria. Electric currents passing between pipelines also cause serious corrosion, but only at the positive unit in any coupling. Nearly all pipelines therefore are protected by cathode voltages, i.e. negative potential of about 1 volt is applied at intervals along the pipe. Being at negative potential, corrosion due to electric currents cannot take place. An added advantage of cathodic protection is that the escape of these voltages into the earth, which can be detected, indicates that the insulation on the pipe has broken down – perhaps stones have penetrated the insulation or subsidence has caused abnormal pressure at some point. Such breakdowns are the chief causes of water rusting the pipes, at the point where the coal-tar wrapping has broken down. By carrying out a repair job on the pipe before it has a chance to rust the 'way' is preserved, and continued safe arrival is ensured.

Pipelines often work by gravity, e.g. the water supply of many towns is fed from a single watertower, which gives the necessary head of water. Occasionally, where pipelines for various services are laid close together in built-up areas, a leak in one can cause corrosion in others, with serious results, e.g. Guadalajara in Mexico, where a water main laid through a main street leaked and corroded an underlying petroleum pipeline. The subsequent explosion left a 7-mile gash through the town killing 228 people and leaving thousands homeless.

Pipelines are an essential feature in the loading and discharge of modern tankers, providing a link between the shore and either an artificial island or an SBM (single buoy mooring) often many miles offshore, where there is sufficient depth for a fully loaded VLCC (very large crude carrier).

4.5 Summary

1. The way is defined as the medium on or through which the transport unit travels in performing its function of carrying goods or passengers. There are three types of way: natural ways, natural ways artificially improved and artificial ways.
2. The natural ways are airways, seaways, navigable rivers, lakes, tracks and bridleways. Modern vehicles such as hovercraft can also traverse low-lying land, swampy land, etc. Some natural ways can be artificially improved, for example, with locks on rivers, or by dredging rivers, by levées and banks, etc.
3. Artificial ways such as roads, rivers, canals, tunnels and pipelines provide high-quality ways at considerable expense. However, once built they have long lives, and the capital cost can be recovered by tolls, taxation, etc.
4. Roads are usually publicly owned, ubiquitous (they are found almost everywhere), flexible (we can drive round most hazards) and durable. Many roads are free from controls except those designed to promote safety.
5. Railways are artificial ways, usually privately or nationally owned, subject to controls. Their original construction is difficult and costly, because of the need to reduce gradients by the use of embankments, cuttings, viaducts, etc. Their chief advantage is high speed and low labour costs – often a driver alone, or a driver and a guard.
6. Eurotunnel opens in 1994 with its variety of services to Continental Europe. These feature through-passenger and freight trains and shuttle-operated cross-Channel services for cars, coaches and heavy goods vehicles (HGVs).

7. Waterways such as rivers and canals give access to inland areas, but at relatively slow speeds. Seaways are the best waterways, giving access to much of the world, but the pace is too slow for passengers, apart from cruise services and ferry crossings. The vast majority of cargo still goes by sea.
8. Airways are universal ways to all parts of the world. Major continental powers can now realise their potential through air passenger and freight services at high speeds, above the 'weather' except at take-off and landing. The way is free, needs no servicing, but does require international co-operation to ensure free passage over territories of nation-states.
9. Pipelines are not very adaptable, and are best used for bulk liquids in strong demand, such as crude oil.

4.6 Questions

1. Define a way. Distinguish between natural ways and artificial ways. Refer in your answer to (a) free ways, (b) privately owned ways, and (c) nationally owned ways.
2. Discuss the case for building Eurotunnel when a 'free' way of travelling to Continental Europe by sea ferry already existed.
3. 'Road taxes in the United Kingdom are rarely spent on roads.' What types of road taxes are there, and why are they rarely spent on roads?
4. Compare and contrast roads and railways in the movement of goods and passengers.
5. 'The opening of Eurotunnel will reduce the number of heavy goods vehicles on UK roads.'

   'While the opening of Eurotunnel may reduce ferry movements between the United Kingdom and Continental Europe, it is unlikely to reduce the number of heavy goods vehicles on our roads; it may even increase traffic flows.'

   Comment on these opposing views of the impact of the opening of Eurotunnel.
6. What are the special features of pipelines as 'ways' for the movement of goods?

5 The physical components of transport: the terminal

5.1 Introduction

Traffic (i.e. goods and passengers) needing to use the way must be provided with places of access to vehicles operating on that way, and places where interchange between different vehicles of the same mode of transport or between different modes of transport can take place. These points of access and interchange are called terminals.

Confusion sometimes arises between the two words 'terminal' and 'terminus'. A terminus has been defined as the point where something (e.g. the way) comes to an end. A terminal formerly meant the same thing, and in many contexts still does, but in transport usage it has the much wider meaning given above. So the word terminus can be used to describe a terminal situated at the end of a way, but not one situated in an intermediate position.

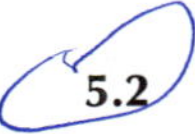

5.2 Functions of the terminal

A terminal has three main functions:

1. To allow access to vehicles operating on a specialised way.
2. To permit easy interchange between vehicles operating on that way, and on other modes of transport.
3. To facilitate consolidation of traffic.

People and goods to be transported are referred to collectively as traffic. A specific lot of goods sent forward at one time, by one consignor, for one consignee, to one destination, is called a *consignment*. It is not usual to refer to one passenger or group of passengers as a consignment, but for convenience when discussing traffic, consignment can be used in that way.

The arrival of a consignment will frequently not coincide with the availability of the unit of carriage. Even when it does, it is not usually efficient to transport that consignment on its own. Except where the consignment in itself constitutes a full load, it is necessary to combine it with other consignments until a vehicle load has been assembled. This process is called *consolidation*, and the length of time needed to achieve it depends upon the volume and characteristics of the traffic.

Terminals range in size from a simple roadside bus stop to the huge complex of a major port. The latter can be regarded as a single very large terminal, or alternatively as a series of separate terminals grouped together for convenience, efficiency and economy – each individual berth being considered as a terminal in its own right. Variation in the size and equipment of terminals is found between those provided for different forms of transport, and between passenger and goods transport. As with the time taken to consolidate traffic, the variation in the size and equipment of terminals is governed by the volume and characteristics of the traffic to be moved. Therefore before looking at terminals in detail, we should now examine the characteristics of passengers and goods, so far as those characteristics affect the type of terminal and the range of services which must be provided (see Fig. 5.1).

5.3 The effect of traffic characteristics on terminals

5.3.1 The characteristics of passengers

Generally speaking, passengers are self-loading and self-discharging and capable of moving themselves from one mode of transport to another. Unless the passengers are infirm or disabled, the transport operator needs to provide little assistance in loading and discharging; only where long distances, or changes of level are involved between the terminal entrance and the conveyance, or in interchanges between vehicles, does he need to provide ancillary transport. Moreover, passengers are capable of reading timetables and following instructions, and so can be in a sense self-consolidating. Whereas goods can be accumulated over a period of time and stored until a vehicle load is available, passengers 'store' themselves. If given a time and place and, where necessary, instructions detailing how to get there, passengers will present themselves, ready for transport. This relieves the operator from the task of collecting together the individuals that are to make up a vehicle load. Nevertheless, the extent to which passengers are self-consolidating has its limitations. The length of time a passenger is willing to remain in 'store', i.e. between vehicle departures, is shorter than the time that can be allowed to elapse between the dispatch of loads of goods on journeys of comparable distances. The longer the journey, the longer the interval between vehicle departures which will be tolerated by the passengers.

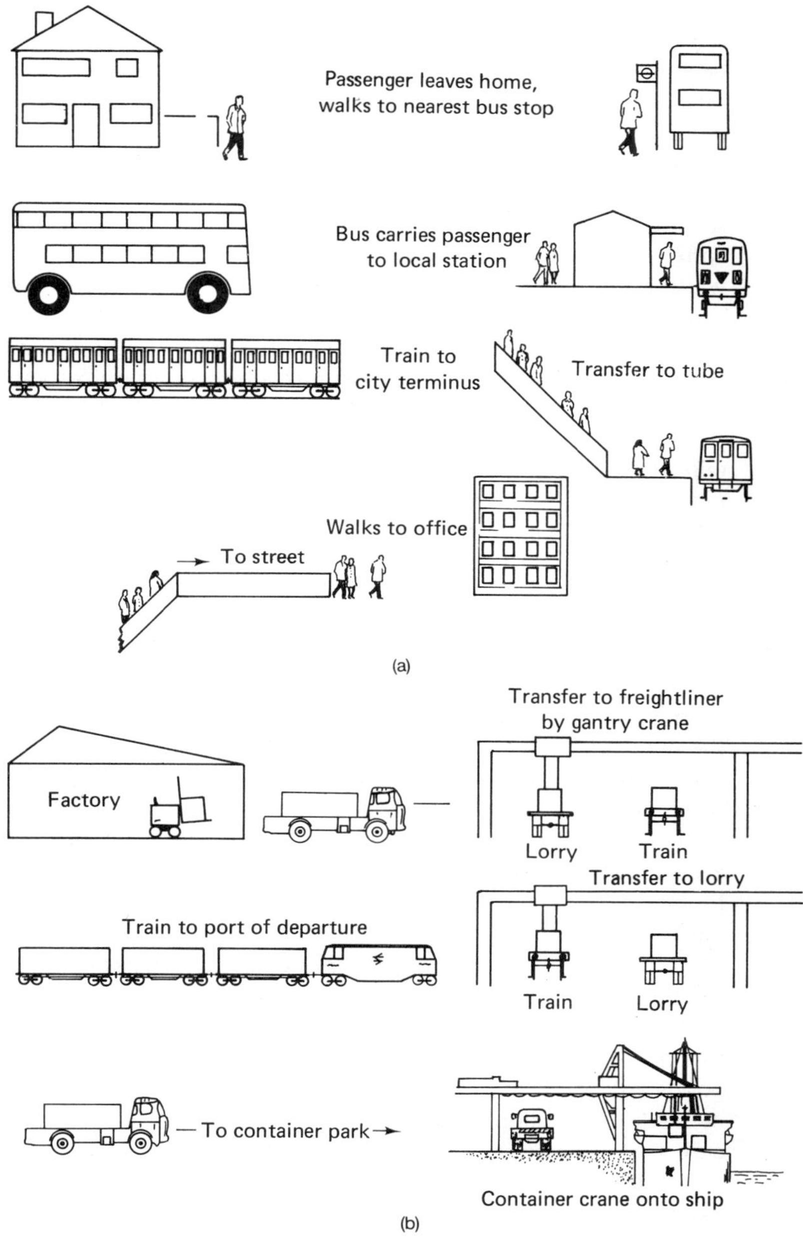

Fig. 5.1 The need for terminals (a) for passengers; (b) for goods

Few passengers arrive at the terminal at the precise time fixed for the departure of the conveyance. This may be due to personal preference, the timetabling of other forms of transport bringing them to the terminal, or because it is essential for operational, administrative and governmental purposes for them to arrive some considerable time before the vehicle is due to depart. Where interchange between vehicles and modes of transport is concerned, some time-lag is necessarily involved. First, there must be sufficient time allowed to enable the changeover to be accomplished, and second, additional time may be allowed to offset any delays to connecting conveyances. In addition to these deliberately built-in time-lags, some waiting time at interchanges may arise simply because it is impossible to timetable neat connections between all services.

During these waiting periods, the transport operator (or the terminal operator, if a different body) must provide certain services and facilities for the passenger. These services will vary according to the volume of traffic, the size of the carrying units, the length of journeys, the degree of comfort expected by the passengers, any special considerations peculiar to the mode of transport, and whether the journey is internal to one country or international. They will usually include seating, toilet accommodation and refreshment facilities.

5.3.2 The characteristics of goods

Goods, being inanimate, do not require the range of services necessary for the comfort and convenience of passengers, but present a different set of problems. Because goods are immobile it is essential to provide suitable mechanical handling appliances to facilitate the loading and unloading of vehicles, for sorting and for stacking and unstacking goods in the storage areas, and for transporting them around the terminal. Many of the goods to be transported will have been accumulated beforehand, and others having completed the major leg of their journey will need to be temporarily accommodated, pending collection, payment of dues and charges, customs clearance, etc. Adequate temporary storage space must be provided to permit these goods to be stored without creating congestion and avoiding the over-stowing of some consignments by others. At some terminals, goods will arrive in mixed loads, to be sorted, before individual consignments are consolidated with others bound for common destinations. Great care must be exercised in the design, layout and equipment of terminals where this type of operation is performed, to ensure that it is carried out expeditiously and efficiently.

It must be apparent from the foregoing that ample space and considerable forethought in the planning of terminals are essential prerequisites to efficient operations. Possible future expansion must be taken into account in the planning stage, for an efficient terminal can soon be crippled if the success of its operation generates additional traffic with which it cannot cope.

Recent developments in computerisation, e.g. SPARCS (Synchronous Planning and Real-time Control System), have transformed the work of terminals by enabling computer simulations of terminal procedure to be devised. Models of road vehicles, trains and arriving ships can be built up within the computer to show where each container is at present, and its ultimate destination. The route of a vehicle through the terminal can then be planned to enable unloading to be done at the most appropriate point. Movements can be arranged so that stacks of containers can be built up for loading onto vessels or distribution from vessels, trains, etc. These developments are referred to more fully later (see page 98), but clearly such sophisticated developments are highly desirable and give complete control of a container terminal.

5.4 The location of terminals

5.4.1 Road and rail

The planning and equipment of a terminal, important factors though they are, will be of little avail if the terminal is not in the right place. Terminals should be sited, so far as it is possible, in places convenient and readily accessible to those wishing to travel or to forward goods. This means close to concentrations of population or where large quantities of goods originate or are consumed. Towns and cities are by definition the places where we expect to find concentrations of people, and until the latter half of this century the greatest density of population would be found in the centre. Over the past few decades there has been a movement of people out of the centres of towns and cities, for residential purposes, but many of those who have homes outside the centre still work there. Moreover, in those places we will also find the greatest concentration of shops supplying goods for domestic use, as well as places of entertainment, and other essential community services, e.g. doctors, dentists, solicitors, estate agents.

Industrial activity presents a different picture. Extractive industries and those concerned with the production of basic raw materials, though attracting some build-up of population, rarely create a sufficient concentration of population to cause the industry to become completely surrounded, and eventually become the core of a large town or city. The opposite is often the case with manufacturing industry. Old, established industries are often found in the heart of towns and cities, surrounded by workers' houses. In this sort of situation the town has been born because the industry located there, and in an earlier era of poor transport people had to live within easy walking distance of their work. This necessity no longer applies, so that we find newer industries locating on the outskirts of towns and cities, where land is cheaper, but the sites are easily accessible to their workers, and close to the market for their products.

From this we can deduce that the centres of towns and cities could be important locations for terminals for some modes of transport, though not for all. However, these central sites may be unavailable to or unsuitable for the terminal operator, for various reasons:

1. Most land in or near the centre of a town or city is likely already to be occupied, and any vacant land will be very expensive.
2. Where there are no vacant sites, occupied sites might be acquired and redeveloped, but this would involve even greater expenditure than the acquisition of vacant sites.
3. The additional congestion created by road vehicles using the terminal may be unacceptable to the local authority and planning permission might be refused.
4. The environmental effects of noise, fumes, vibration and visual intrusion may be unacceptable to the community.

Points (1) and (2) are likely to make city centre sites economically unsuitable for goods transport, unless the site was obtained at an early stage in the city's development, when land was still relatively cheap. This is often the case with railway goods depots, and we find extremely valuable sites being used for activities which today would not justify their being acquired on either economic or environmental grounds. The high cost of land in the city centre and the non-availability of sites have given rise to a tendency for new industrial undertakings to locate on the periphery of the city, and road goods terminal operators tend to do likewise. By so doing, they get the benefit of cheaper land, proximity to younger developing industrial undertakings, yet remain near enough to be able to serve the industries and consumers located in the city centre.

The choice of location for road passenger terminals (bus and coach stations) is usually more straightforward because in most cases the town or city centre is the focal point for numerous road passenger services.

A model showing the pattern of road passenger services in a typical area would reveal the following:

1. Networks of local services within the city and within the large towns of the area.
2. Radial services connecting the city and the large towns.
3. Services connecting the large towns with their neighbours.

4. Radial and circular services linking the large towns with the smaller towns and villages.

In almost all cases, the focal points of the services will be the town and city centres, which act like magnets in attracting the surrounding population. Passengers demand to be set down within easy walking distance of their destinations, or if changing vehicles, that the interchange be made as convenient as possible. If these conditions are not satisfied, the result will be that many passengers will transfer to personal transport. Planners of new towns are well aware of this situation and endeavour to fulfil the conditions from the start, but in older, established towns this has not always been possible. However, it is now becoming necessary to redevelop the centres of many old towns, and where this is happening it often becomes possible to incorporate a bus station in or near the town centre, when the redevelopment of the area is planned.

Two towns in adjoining areas of Essex provide interesting illustrations of the two situations described, i.e. the provision of bus stations in new and old towns.

Basildon is a new town built since the Second World War, primarily to accommodate the overspill from London. Unlike many old towns which have main routes running through their centres, Basildon is located between two almost parallel arterial roads. The older London–Southend road, the A13, runs to the south, while the newer A127 passes to the north of the town. Wide roads link up the industrial area, residential areas and the main shopping and recreational area. The bus station is located close to the main shopping area giving good access for shoppers, and convenient for passengers to and from Chelmsford to the north, Southend to the east, and the Grays area and London to the west. The railway station at Basildon was not built until twenty years after the town was started, since the new town was built between two existing stations and good, convenient bus services to the nearest stations were therefore adequate. With the increased town size and the large number of people who commute to London to work, or travel there for other purposes, this became inconvenient and a town centre railway station was built.

Grays, an old town which has grown up over several hundred years, though chiefly in the nineteenth and twentieth centuries, presents an entirely different picture. The nucleus of the town was located on the north bank of the Thames where a chalk outcrop gave access, unhindered by marshes, to the river, and firm building land. Industrial development has spread along reclaimed marshland to the west and east and residential development to the north, so that the town has grown in a fan-shape from the nucleus. Until the First World War the town could be said to be bounded to the north by the A13 but subsequent growth caused the town to spread well beyond that boundary. Other residential developments on the outskirts of the town placed the residents some considerable distance from the main shopping centre and other services. The High Street was bisected by the London–Tilbury–Southend railway line, with a station and goods yard in the 'town centre'.

A large part of the working population, particularly white-collar workers, commute to London and many other workers travel daily to the factories and docks of industrial Thames-side. Those travelling to London depend to a large extent on bus services to carry them to and from the railway station and the surrounding towns and villages. Where shorter journeys to work are involved, buses and cars are the preferred modes of travel. For the bus users, this frequently means changing from one service to another in the centre of Grays. The lack of a bus station made it necessary for boarding and alighting points to be scattered some distance from each other, and the railway station, in various streets in the centre of the town. Passengers changing from one bus service to another, or from bus to train, had to proceed on foot for two or three hundred yards, and sometimes further. This was unpleasant in bad weather, and frustrating when delays to one mode of transport resulted in missed connections with another despite a frantic rush between two terminals. The town centre has been redeveloped, and a bus station has been provided alongside the railway station. This has removed many, though not all, of the bus stops from the principal streets and with the introduction of a one-way traffic system has greatly improved traffic flows.

In the United Kingdom the railway system has been long established and therefore consideration of where to locate new terminals rarely arises. In recent years the pattern has been to close many of the smaller goods depots and to concentrate facilities on larger central depots. The problem has therefore been not where to locate new terminals, but which terminals to retain and develop, and which to close down.

Before leaving the consideration of the location of road and rail terminals it is interesting to note that whereas it has become customary to locate road terminals in or close to centres of population, railway terminals have often in the past been responsible for creating centres of population and industry.

Although many early railways were built initially to link specific towns or to serve specific industries, a common effect was for some small communities situated along the line of the railway to develop into important towns, while other communities in the same area, but not similarly served by the railway, remained small and unimportant, perhaps even disappearing altogether. Industrialists seeking new locations for their factories appreciated the value of good transport facilities. In consequence they established their undertakings alongside the railways, close to the developing towns, and towns and industries prospered together.

5.4.2 Airports

The process of choosing a site for a new airport would seem at first to be comparatively easy – find a piece of flat land close to a large centre of population, and build it there. This may have been near the truth in the early days of flying, but the process has now become extremely complicated. Three sets of considerations must now be taken into account: (1) customer requirements, (2) operational requirements, and (3) community requirements – all of which are unlikely to be compatible.

Let us examine the requirements of each of these conflicting forces to see how and why the conflict arises.

5.4.2.1 Customer requirements

As already mentioned, the airport will need to be located close to a large centre of population, probably a city. Much of the traffic using the airport will originate from the city itself; other traffic, especially passengers, will be drawn from surrounding areas to road and rail terminals in the city centre. The customers will almost certainly have selected air transport because of its speed. They will therefore wish the terminal to be as near to the city as possible to reduce the journey time from the city to the airport, and to keep the overall transit time as low as possible. Passengers will demand good transport services between the city centre and the airport, while for freight traffic there must be good access for surface transport.

5.4.2.2 Operational requirements

The terminal operator will look for a site having the following attributes:

1. A large area of flat, well-drained land. As aircraft have become larger and faster, so the need for longer and more heavily constructed runways has increased. In addition, more space is required for aircraft parking and manoeuvring, and very large areas to accommodate the ancillary services.
2. It must be away from mountains or large hills, which would make approach and take-off difficult and could create dangerous air currents.
3. The site should, as far as possible, be free from fog.
4. It should not be surrounded by concentrated development. Since cities continue to grow, future development must be taken into account, otherwise there is a real danger that in a relatively short space of time the airport will be hemmed in, with no further land for expansion and hampered by restrictions imposed on operations in built-up areas.

5.4.2.3 *Community requirements*

Airports require very large areas of land, as we have seen, and these need to be located near to large centres of population. In countries not so densely populated as the United Kingdom, such sites may be readily available, but in this country suitable sites are few and have alternative uses. Those open spaces sufficiently large to be considered as airport sites that are to be found in the vicinity of our major cities, are either valuable agricultural land or areas set aside for recreational purposes. Even when not densely populated there are certain to be some scattered houses in the area, and probably one or more villages. We find, therefore, that any proposal to locate an airport in one of these areas must be measured against the value to the community of its alternative uses. Can we as a nation afford to sacrifice valuable farming land? If we give up open park land, where are town and city-dwellers to go for recreation? What is to happen to the people who have homes and jobs in the selected area? It may be possible to find them new jobs – indeed many new jobs may be created by the airport – but there is no guarantee that these jobs will fit in with the chosen way of life of those displaced. Similarly, it may be possible to rehouse people who have been forced to leave their old homes, but will this compensate for the loss of homes that have been cherished and which may have been family homes for generations? These questions have no easy answers; each case must be judged on its merits and whatever decision is reached, it is likely to be a compromise solution, not wholly satisfactory to any of the three conflicting forces.

It must be emphasised that these problems are particularly severe in the United Kingdom, which is so densely populated and where open space is at a premium. Other countries with much greater land areas do not have the same problems except where large conurbations have developed. Moreover, because of the much greater length of many inland journeys, air travel is much more commonplace. In the United Kingdom, while the percentage of the population using air transport is rising every year it is largely recreational rather than an intrinsic part of the life in the local community. Are we justified in appropriating a large open space for an airport, and subjecting the surrounding population to almost perpetual aircraft noise and heavily increased road traffic, simply to meet an occasional recreational need of a small section of the population?

If the airport is designed primarily to meet the needs of the local population justification may not prove too difficult and the facility may meet with general approval from the local inhabitants. If, however, the airport is to be primarily concerned with international traffic, resistance to the proposed siting may become very strong indeed. A country can only support a limited number of major international airports. Although some local people may use it, the majority of passengers and freight will have originated from or be destined for other parts of the country, or be merely passing through, in transit. It becomes very difficult in these circumstances to convince local inhabitants that their area should be used in preference to another. While most people will agree that an international airport is desirable, few will be happy to have it located in their own vicinity.

The Roskill Commission's report, and others, on the site for the proposed third London airport demonstrated the complexities involved in reaching an acceptable solution.

5.4.3 Ports

Because they represent the earliest form of transport terminal, a study of the location and growth of ports can be a fascinating exercise. Some ports established over a thousand years ago have continued to grow and to thrive; some, once flourishing, have faded into obscurity; while others have remained, little changed in size, for the past few hundred years. The enterprise of their owners or controllers may have had much to do with their success or failure, but often the result was due to their natural attributes, to changing patterns of trade or to technological developments. Before examining the factors which lead to the location and growth of ports, we need to establish clearly in our minds exactly what we mean by a port.

The word 'haven' is used in some countries to describe what we call a port, and 'harbour' is often used in a similar manner (some government reports refer to 'trade harbours'). In common with many other words used in the port industry, it is often difficult to distinguish between them with any degree of precision because the usage varies from place to place and according to the context in which they are found. Both haven and harbour indicate a place of refuge, somewhere that a ship may lie safely at anchor, protected from wind, wave and current. Generally it is true to say that whereas a haven can be a place of refuge fashioned by nature, a harbour usually indicates some degree of artificial improvement, though this is not always so. A port is something more than simply a place of refuge. Its Latin *portus* means a gateway, and that meaning roughly describes its function. It is the place through which passengers and goods pass from land transport to water transport, and vice versa. There are of course river ports and canal ports, but we usually employ the word port to mean seaport, and it is on that meaning that we shall concentrate. If we subscribe to the 'chain of transport' concept, then a seaport can be defined as 'that link in the chain of transport where sea transport is exchanged for inland transport'. The essential difference then between a haven or harbour and a port is that the latter is essentially concerned with the handling of passengers or cargo or both.

Let us now examine the factors which lead to the location and growth of a seaport, and seek to discover why some prosper while others stagnate.

5.4.3.1 *Shelter*

A ship at anchor is more at the mercy of the elements than one at sea, unless it is anchored in a sheltered spot. Faced with a violent storm at sea, and depending of course on the size of the vessel relative to the severity of the storm, a master can run before or head into it. What he would not choose to do would be to sail broadside on to the direction of the storm. If he did so, this would present the greatest surface area to the force of the wind and waves, with the biggest risk of damage and disaster. With present-day early warnings of typhoons, etc. it is not uncommon for larger vessels to leave port and try to run before the storm in the open sea. Where this is not possible in the case of up-river ports (e.g. in Bangladesh) we have often seen cyclones leave large vessels high and dry in rice paddies far from any deep-water channel. Should a storm strike suddenly when a ship is at anchor, there might be no time to alter its position so as to minimise the force of wind and waves. This could result in the vessel being pounded against the quay wall if tied up alongside, or if in an open anchorage possibly in the vessel capsizing. For this reason, as well as for ease in handling cargo or in embarking and disembarking passengers, it is essential that a port should give good protection from the elements.

This either is found naturally in land-locked bays, where the surrounding land affords protection, or in the estuaries of rivers, where it is supplied by the sides of the river valleys. Sometimes a site which in other respects may be admirable, is unable to give the required protection. In this case, it may be possible to create the necessary shelter artificially, for example by erecting breakwaters. These must not only be able to break the force of the waves, but be sufficiently high to give shelter from the wind. Dover harbour is a good illustration of a harbour with artificial breakwaters. Breakwaters are expensive and their construction is unlikely to be undertaken unless there is no better site in the area, or the port is long established but the existing protection is no longer adequate for the much larger modern vessels.

5.4.3.2 *Deep water*

Although small vessels, or vessels especially constructed with strengthened keels and hulls, may sit on the mud at low tide, most modern vessels do not have this facility and must 'remain always afloat'. Should a large modern vessel settle on the bottom it would almost certainly suffer severe structural damage unless by some freak chance it settled in a natural cradle so that all parts of the hull were equally supported. This is because the immense weight of a modern vessel bearing down on an unsupported section of the ship's bottom would cause distortion or fracturing of the structural steelwork. It follows that not only must there be a sufficient depth of water to enable a ship to enter port, but that there must be a sufficient depth of water to support it at all times.

We have already noted that the estuaries of rivers provide excellent shelter, and in Chapter 4 we saw that rivers were the principal means by which goods were conveyed before the advent of canals and railways. Rivers, on their way to the sea, cut themselves channels, deeper in the centre than at the sides, so that even at low water there may be sufficient depth in the centre of the channel for a vessel to remain afloat. The nearer the river gets to the sea, the greater the depth of water available. It is not surprising, therefore, that given shelter and deep water, many early ports were established in the estuaries of rivers.

Rivers were great highways, but they were also barriers. The nearer the approach to the mouth of a river, the wider it became and consequently more difficult to cross. It was likely, too, that as the river neared the sea, the speed of flow dropped and marshes formed on either bank, making crossing even more precarious. It would be necessary to travel some distance upstream before a point could be found where it was possible to ford the river. At this point early settlements usually developed, and as this was the farthest upstream that large vessels could safely penetrate, it was here that ports were established. Port and settlement developed together; as one flourished so did the other, each dependent upon the other. Most of the major ports of the world began like this, centuries ago. London is a prime example, a settlement and later a port growing up below a point where a gravel outcrop made it possible to ford the river.

In some estuarial ports, vessels moored in midstream and transferred their cargoes to and from shore in smaller craft – lighters, barges, etc. Sometimes quays and jetties were built along the banks, and by dredging the area around them vessels were able to lie alongside to load or discharge their cargoes. For many centuries the size and draught of vessels changed only very slowly, and such growth as there was in the size of ships could be accommodated by the majority of ports, especially if assisted by dredging. But gradually the growth in size of vessels and the demands of shipowners that their vessels should always remain afloat brought about the introduction of enclosed, impounded docks in many places.

Whether or not enclosed docks are necessary or desirable depends upon the following factors: (1) the depth of water available at all states of the tide; (2) the depth of the approach channel at low water; (3) the size of the ships using the port; (4) the tidal range, i.e. the difference between the depth of water at high tide and low tide.

The principal advantage of enclosed docks is that a constant depth of water can be maintained so that vessels remain always afloat. A further advantage is that the additional shelter provided makes cargo-handling easier than in rough, open water. Without enclosed docks the tidal differences mean that the level between the ship and the quay is constantly changing, and when a ship is using its own lifting gear this makes working very difficult.

The principal disadvantage is that where there is an insufficient depth of water in the approach channel, except around high tide, large vessels are restricted to a relatively short period before and after high tide during which they can pass into and out of the docks. Missing a tide can result in a delay of almost twelve hours and this can prove very costly where today's highly expensive ships are concerned. Even in the case of smaller vessels which have a longer period within which to negotiate the locks, the time wasted in waiting to lock in and out, and in passing through the locks, can be inconvenient and expensive, especially if the vessels are engaged in short-sea, ferry-type services.

As vessels have become so much more expensive and turn-round time consequently more important, this disadvantage has tended to outweigh the advantages of enclosed docks and wherever possible these are being avoided in favour of open berths.

A further important problem connected with lock entrances concerns their size. Dock installations in general involve very heavy capital expenditure and are built with an intended long life. In planning dock entrances, future possible increases in the size of vessels must be taken into account. If this is not done, entrances will be unable to cope with the new larger vessels which will be excluded from the docks with consequent loss of revenue if the trade is transferred to other ports. On the other hand, if an overestimate is made of the future increase in size of vessels and the lock entrance is made unnecessarily large, the extra capital expenditure incurred may prove a heavy financial burden to the port. Port planners in the past could not possibly have foreseen the tremendous growth in size of vessels which has taken place in the past two or three decades. The result has been that many ports have found themselves saddled with enclosed docks with insufficient depth of water and lock entrances too small to accept the new larger vessels, and have seen their trade lost to other ports with more suitable facilities.

5.4.3.3 Access

It is not sufficient that vessels should be able to lie at anchor sheltered from the elements; they must be able to reach the anchorage easily and safely. A harbour whose entrance is guarded by dangerous rocks or sandbanks is unlikely to prove popular with seafarers. But these obstacles are not insurmountable. Rock can, if necessary, be blasted away and safe channels can be dredged through the sandbanks, but it is important that any impediments are clearly marked by lighthouses, lightships, beacons, etc., and the safe channels clearly marked by navigational buoys.

On its way to the sea a river carries with it quantities of silt and debris, the amount varying according to the nature of the land through which the river passes, and whether or not it is subject to violent flooding. As it nears the sea, especially if it passes through an extensive coastal plain, its speed drops, and the material carried in suspension may be deposited in the estuary or the immediate surrounding sea areas. In this way sandbanks are created which may reduce the use of an otherwise admirable harbour. If the speed of flow of water is sufficient, natural channels will be formed through the river-made barrier which may be adequate for navigation. Where the river is sluggish, a delta may form with numerous channels the width and depth of which may make navigation impossible. The once important port of Chester on the River Dee is now completely defunct as a result of the silting up of the estuary, whereas the swiftness of its current saved the neighbouring estuary of the River Mersey from a similar fate. As a result, and helped by considerable engineering ingenuity, Liverpool developed into one of Britain's largest ports. (For an account of Liverpool's problems and how they were overcome, see *The Major Seaports of the United Kingdom*, by James Bird.)

Just as the growth in the size of vessels affected the depth of water that had to be provided to enable vessels to lie safely afloat, so it affected the depth and width of the approach channels that were necessary. Some dredging has always had to be provided in almost all major ports to prevent docks, anchorages and channels from silting up (maintenance dredging), but as vessels grew in size it often became necessary to dredge deeper and wider approach channels, or to cut entirely new ones (capital dredging). The cost of dredging has been a major item of expenditure for many ports and is reflected in the charges they make for the use of the port. Dredging cost can therefore be an important item in determining the competitiveness of two rival ports. For some ports blessed with deep-water approaches, very little dredging is necessary, sometimes none at all. This is particularly true of Ria-type (drowned valley) ports such as New York, Sydney or Bantry Bay. For others, the amount of dredging required could be so great that the financial returns from being able to accommodate larger vessels would be insufficient to cover the heavy cost involved. These ports, unless heavily subsidised, have had to resign themselves to their inability to accommodate vessels beyond a certain size. The most successful ports in this category are those that recognised their limitations early, and have concentrated on securing those traffics best suited to smaller vessels.

We have looked at the problem of access from the sea, and some of the ways in which difficult access can be improved. Equally important is access to the port on the landward side. A fine natural harbour, with deep water and good easy access from the sea, is unlikely to have developed into a major seaport if, on the landward side, cliffs rise almost vertically from the sea, or it is surrounded by extensive marshes. With today's technology, it would not be impossible to develop such sites, although the capital cost would be high, but in the past an alternative site would have been sought and developed. In all probability the chosen site would not have been so desirable from a seaward aspect, but the deficiencies could have been more easily overcome. This again illustrates the point made earlier that when selecting a terminal location, only on rare occasions does an ideal site emerge. Usually the chosen site represents a compromise between what is desirable and what is easily attainable.

A serious problem of access often arises in the case of long-established ports. The natural sequence is for a town or city to develop as the port develops, the growth of one feeding the growth of the other until the prosperity of each is dependent upon the other. Where this development has occurred over several centuries, as with many of the world's major ports, the port becomes enclosed in a built-up area that may extend to a depth of many miles. Some of this urban development will have taken place prior to the age of motor transport, and much of the remainder during a time when the present volume of motor transport seemed inconceivable. If this has resulted in the landward approaches to the port consisting of mile after mile of narrow congested streets totally inadequate for today's high-capacity road vehicles, port developers are faced with a problem over which they frequently have no control. Unless the port authority is also the municipal authority, the provision of a road system adequate to meet the needs of the port will be the responsibility of other bodies whose priorities may not coincide with those of the port authority. When this happens a situation may arise where the efforts of the port developers in providing up-to-date facilities in keeping with the demands of modern ocean transport and the 'through transport' concept are in part frustrated by inadequate road approaches. But whoever is the responsible road authority, clearing the way for wide new approach roads will be a very costly undertaking.

5.4.3.4 *Large flat land areas*

Earlier port developers probably did not consciously select sites which had large areas of flat land available for industrial development. They would, however, seek sites where land was available to build warehouses and houses for the community which would follow the port's establishment. In many cases the land available would be far in excess of their immediate needs or would have been viewed as favourable for agricultural development. The most successful ports would have attracted industries to them, and the availability of land would have assisted the industrial development.

Today, when economies of scale are well understood in both transport and industrial activity, port developers must search for large areas of land, capable of industrial development, and having access to deep water as sites for their new ports. These sites have been named MIDAs (Maritime Industrial Development Areas). Some may be associated with existing major ports, e.g. Rotterdam's Europort; others associated with what were relatively small ports, e.g. Dunkirk. Often it may be necessary to create the land area required, as with Rotterdam where large areas of land were reclaimed from the sea. In the developed countries MIDAs will almost certainly be associated with existing ports, for although there may be many sites having all the attributes previously mentioned as necessary for the establishment and development of major ports, they may lack the final necessary attribute, a flourishing hinterland.

5.4.3.5 *Hinterland*

One dictionary defines hinterland as 'the district behind that lying along the coast (or along the shore of a river); the back country', and it is in this sense that most people use the word. It has, however, developed an additional special meaning when used in connection with ports, i.e. the area from which a port draws its trade. This means the area from which it receives its exports and to which it sends its imports.

In order to be successful a port usually needs to develop a two-way trade. For this it needs people and industries to create a demand for imported goods, and to produce raw materials or manufactured goods for export. (The word 'industry' here is used in its widest sense, i.e. including agriculture, extractive industries, etc. and not merely manufacturing.) The exception to this rule is the port which predominantly imports or exports one or more bulk commodities in such quantities that it is a viable economic entity on the basis of that traffic alone. The majority of the world's ports are in fact one- or two-product export ports. There are actually very few similar import ports and these are mainly associated with the crude oil trade. Bantry Bay was one such port.

Ports, then, exist to serve people and industries; these are its hinterland, and without that hinterland a port cannot develop, no matter how ideal the site is in terms of its natural advantages. A good example of this situation is found in Scapa Flow. Scapa Flow is a 12 mile- (19 km) wide anchorage encircled by the South Isles of the Orkney Islands off the north coast of Scotland. It has good approaches and deep water and is sheltered by the islands that surround it. It was used as a naval anchorage in both the First and Second World Wars, and it has been said that the entire Allied fleets could have anchored there at the same time. Yet it has never become a major port, simply because the population of the islands is inadequate to support one – there is no hinterland.

The earlier development of Whiddy Island, Bantry Bay, in the south-west corner of Ireland seemed to contradict the proposal that a port could not flourish without a hinterland, for this was a recently established port in a sparsely populated part of Ireland. But this port was not established to serve south-west Ireland; it was located there because the 312,000 tonne tankers which used it require 100 ft (30.4 m) of water and were unable to enter the North Sea to deliver their cargoes of oil to Western European ports. The oil had to be trans-shipped in smaller tankers (80,000–100,000 t), but the economies of scale obtained on the long haul from Kuwait justified the trans-shipment costs. What seemed to be a port without a hinterland was really a port separated from its hinterland by the barrier of inadequate depth. However, problems associated with spillage and other potential hazards forced the closure of the port, but fortunately by this time other facilities capable of handling those vessels had been developed elsewhere.

The world's major ports tend to fulfil several roles simultaneously. They are at the same time bulk ports, often with industries processing imported raw materials in close proximity; transit ports concerned with the rapid exchange of goods between land and sea transport, to and from inland destinations; trans-shipment ports where cargoes are transferred in large quantities from large vessels to smaller vessels or to other modes of transport for onward transport to destinations not served by the major ocean carriers; and Entrepôt ports involved in the warehousing and marketing of imported goods. Because of this multi-role character of major ports they can be said to have not one hinterland but many, according to the particular aspect of the port's operations or the specific traffic that is being examined. Equally many inland areas comprise the hinterland of several competitive ports (e.g. the West Midlands of the UK is hinterland to Felixstowe, Ipswich, Liverpool, Tilbury and even Southampton). For example, it may be found that the hinterland of the port in relation to its bulk cargo operations extends only as far as those industries located in the immediate vicinity of the port. Where its transit and trans-shipment traffic is concerned, however, it may extend hundreds of miles in several directions. Today much of the European traffic to the east coast of India is trans-shipped via Singapore.

In earlier centuries, when inland transport was poor, ports tended to serve the needs of local communities. Much of the traffic was coastal, this being the easiest way of moving goods from one part of the country to another. Many ports would be involved in some degree of short-sea trade with not-too-far-distant countries while a few would establish reputations as starting points for voyages of discovery and trade with distant parts of the world. Where a country had a long, indented coastline, as in Great Britain, innumerable small ports would be established. As world trade developed, the better endowed ports attracted most of the trade and trans-shipped to other areas in coastal vessels and along inland waterways. The

Industrial Revolution brought changes in the pattern of population and industrial activity. Instead of the population being thinly spread throughout the country with relatively small concentrations of population in the towns and cities, much larger conurbations began to develop. These favoured the growth of those ports best situated to serve the new conurbations.

When shipping companies began to establish liner services they often based their regular calls on ports able to offer large quantities of 'bottom cargo', e.g. iron and steel, which were required for stability purposes. Regular calls at such ports attracted other traffic, and influenced the location of firms. Grangemouth and Middlesbrough were two such ports in the United Kingdom. Calls at other ports became less frequent, or were discontinued, the other ports being served by coastal shipping after transshipment. At the same time improvements in inland transport enabled importers and exporters to bypass the smaller ports in favour of those with more frequent sailings to and from a wider range of overseas ports. In this way the major ports extended their hinterlands at the expense of smaller ports located nearer to the origin or destination of the goods. This feature is particularly noticeable in connection with particular types of goods distributed on a world-wide basis, e.g. London would hardly seem to embrace Scotland with its hinterland, yet because it has more sailings to more parts of the world than any other port in Great Britain, it is a favoured port for the shipment of large quantities of Scotch whisky. Although London with its commodity markets and other capital features was not so reliant on a 'bottom cargo' facility, nevertheless cement was always available for this purpose.

An apparently paradoxical situation has arisen in recent years: some smaller ports have been attracting traffic away from major ports, while at the same time some major ports have been capturing trade from their rival major ports. This situation has been made possible first by the tremendous improvement in inland transport in the post-war years, resulting from the provision of motorways and the railway Freightliner services, and second by the growth of containerisation.

Failure on the part of major ports in this country to use effective techniques to establish the cost of handling specific commodities but instead relying on the principle of charging 'what the traffic would bear', placed them in a vulnerable position. It meant that some commodities handled in large quantities but requiring little in the way of specialised services, were subsidising the handling of other commodities whose handling costs were very much higher but which were not reflected in higher port charges. Other commodities carrying high port charges were being handled in obsolete, labour-intensive facilities in an economically inefficient manner. A number of small ports, on examining the charges schedules of the major ports, realised that they could offer much more attractive terms, which would outweigh the additional transport costs now that the improved inland transport services no longer placed them at a geographical disadvantage in terms of transit time. They were able to offer much lower charges because they were dealing with selected commodities rather than trying to supply a full range of services. This meant that their capital costs and overhead charges were much lower. Often their labour charges were lower and they did not suffer losses resulting from bad industrial relations. Finally, where necessary, they could provide modern facilities which could handle selected cargoes at a much cheaper rate than could ports with obsolete facilities. Typical of this type of resurgence were ports such as Shoreham and Sheerness.

The development of roll-on roll-off vessels and containerisation gave other small ports the opportunity they required. Provided they had good road and rail links, these new developments enabled many smaller ports to capitalise on their geographical positions relative to the mainland of Europe. The shorter sea distances between east coast ports and the ports of west and north-west Europe enable vessels to complete a greater number of voyages within a given period of time. Felixstowe, an outstanding example of small port growth in the post-war period, is so situated that to achieve the same frequency of service to Rotterdam, two vessels would be required to operate from London, compared with one from Felixstowe. This progressive small port has been so successful in attracting traffic from outside its former hinterland that it is not uncommon to see container lorries passing through London *en route* for Felixstowe and bypassing the country's premier port. These containers are not necessarily bound only for European destinations, for by being first in the field in providing facilities for specialised container vessels, Felixstowe succeeded in securing a considerable volume of deep-sea container traffic.

The decisions of various container shipping consortia, notably those in the Australian and Far East trades, to limit their ports of call to one port per country and to arrange inland transport to and from that port from all parts of the country with little difference in freight charges has led to some major ports losing large quantities of traffic to others. The charges were based on the cost of inland freight to Liverpool from areas in Scotland and the North, while charges to Southampton covered the rest. The decision to base Australian sailings on Tilbury has meant that London has gained at the expense of other ports. At the same time, London has lost some traffic due to the decision to base Far East trade on Southampton.

From the foregoing it can be seen that radical changes have taken place with regard to what were fairly well-defined hinterlands, due to changes in transport systems and organisation, and improvements in inland transport. Established ports have had to learn to adjust to these changes, and by offering modern facilities and efficient working to attract a reasonable share of trade. Some have succeeded better than others. In this country, with far too many ports for its size, port authorities now realise that the time has passed when they could rest comfortably knowing that traffic would come to them because of their geographical location. There is no longer any guarantee that in future the largest vessels will make direct calls to this country. Unless conditions are favourable, they could call at European ports, and trans-ship the British portion of their cargo.

Given the existence of competition between ports in different countries for the same traffic, the survival or growth of individual ports no longer rests on the natural attributes that we have discussed or on the foresight and energy of port authorities, but is affected by political decisions. Political consideration may decide which ports in a country are to be given government support and the extent and manner in which the support is to be given. The decisions may be based on a need to protect the national economy, to safeguard national security or perhaps simply to preserve national pride.

5.4.3.6 *Climatic factors affecting ports*

Mention has already been made of the need for shelter from storms but other climatic factors can play a key role in a port's development and on port working. With the advent of containerisation rain is no longer a major factor affecting port working, but nevertheless many anchorage ports in south-west India and west Africa close during the monsoon season, when on-shore, rain-bearing winds make them unsafe. Fog can play havoc not only with the movement of ships in and out of ports, particularly in enclosed docks, but also with road and rail traffic serving the port. Many of the world's ports are seasonal owing to ice, and even where icebreakers are used to keep a channel open, only ice-strengthened vessels can use them. The amount of tonnage that a vessel can carry on any particular voyage is also governed by climatic conditions reflected in the vessel's load line. Thus a vessel loading in west Africa for the United Kingdom can lift more than a vessel sailing in the opposite direction, since her weight loss due to use of water, fuel and stores during the inward voyage will give her the necessary load line lift for entry into northern waters, where wind and wave conditions call for a larger freeboard.

5.4.3.7 *Free trade zones (FTZ)*

The principle of free ports, or free trade zones, has long been accepted in many countries but until 1983 was not permitted in the United Kingdom. In that year the government announced that it was willing to consider schemes for the establishment of a number of free ports in the United Kingdom.

A free port or free trade zone (FTZ) is a port, or an area within a port, permitted to receive imported goods, usually raw materials or semi-processed goods, without payment of import duties. These goods can then be processed and subsequently re-exported without the need for tying up large amounts of capital in import duties and the time-consuming process of recovering these duties on re-exporting.

The essential feature of an FTZ is that goods received have not technically arrived in the United Kingdom. There is a security network thrown around the FTZ and goods can be landed, sorted, sampled, blended, manufactured, repackaged or displayed without payment of duty. As the goods have not entered the United Kingdom they are free of EC import duties, levies, quotas and import VAT. H.M. Customs only becomes interested in them as they pass through the security network to enter the country proper. If they leave the FTZ on the landward side, they become liable for duty. If they leave on the seaward side to be re-exported, they do not enter the country and consequently have never become imports. One final point is that goods may be 'shipped out' from any UK port or airport, and this also applies to Eurotunnel movements. Technically, such assignments do breach the security network and enter the country proper, but under controlled movements supervised by H.M. Customs. The point is, of course, that the new destination of the improved product may be more conveniently served by a port other than the free port, and certainly may be better served by rail-freight into the heart of Europe.

The government designated as free ports the seaports of Southampton, Liverpool and Cardiff, and the airports of Birmingham, Prestwick and Belfast. Only Liverpool and Southampton have actually started to operate. Liverpool has made a significant recovery after some years of decline because of a fundamental re-appraisal of its role. The west coast ports of Bristol, Liverpool and Glasgow benefited in Imperial times from their proximity to the Atlantic and the colonies and Commonwealth countries. When UK trade became dominated by EU trade these west coast ports suffered, and the ports in the south-east, which were close to Europe, developed. However, long journeys on poor roads in East Anglia were a disadvantage and added costs, which reduced the advantages of proximity to Europe. What no one had realised was that world trade into the European mainland could still use Liverpool once its facilities were updated and could land containers for an easy run on fast motorways to the short-sea ports in the south-east. Once Liverpool got its seaside and land-side activities sorted out – turning round major container ships in twelve hours on the seaward side and heavy lorries in forty minutes on the landward side – with return loads already arranged – the port began to recover. The designation of Liverpool as an FTZ raised the tonnage in

1991 – a recession year – to 25 million tonnes. The port has also been designated as a Eurotunnel terminal, which should see containers being landed onto trains – not lorries – and moved directly through Eurotunnel into the heart of the Continent.

The FTZ idea has now extended beyond the original six, for example Tilbury began to operate a free trade zone in 1992, and in 1993 reported very good first-year results.

5.5 Services and facilities required at terminals

Earlier in this chapter we looked at the main functions of terminals and the effect of traffic characteristics on terminals. We also noted the variation in size between terminals provided for different modes of transport, and for goods and passengers. All these things affect the range of services and facilities which need to be provided at the various types of terminal.

For passenger traffic, provision must be made for the orderly discharge and loading of vehicles and rapid and easy transfer of passengers between vehicles within the same or differing modes. It is not possible for all passengers to arrive at the terminal at the exact time of departure of the conveyance and some waiting time must occur. Where interchange is involved, unless precise connections can be arranged, some waiting time will result between disembarking from one vehicle and embarking on another. During these waiting periods, provision must be made for the comfort and convenience of passengers. The extent of this provision may range from a simple seat and shelter at a bus stop, to toilet facilities, restaurants, shops, cinemas and hotel accommodation at important international terminals. The facilities provided at the larger terminals will be available not only to incoming and outgoing passengers, but also to friends and relatives who may be meeting them or seeing them off. Where international traffic is involved, provision must be made for H.M. Customs and immigration officials to perform their duties, and for passengers to change currencies.

With goods traffic, the emphasis must be on the speed of turnround of vehicles and of rapid transfer of goods between modes. This, of course, means that the terminal must be designed to avoid congestion by vehicles. It must be amply equipped with mechanical handling appliances for general loading, discharging and transferring and with specially designed equipment for handling specific traffics. An example of such specialised equipment is the straddle carrier, used to pick up containers and carry them to stacking areas away from an unloading ship, or to feed a ship with containers when it is loading.

There must be adequate space for the temporary accommodation of goods prior to loading and after discharge, and for sorting goods where

Fig. 5.2 A straddle carrier, a skeletal chassis articulated vehicle and a Paceco-Vickers container crane (courtesy of the Port of London Authority)

consolidation and deconsolidation take place. As with passenger traffic, if international transits are involved, facilities for H.M. Customs and health authorities will need to be provided.

All vehicles, whether passenger or goods, require servicing and facilities for this are often provided at the larger terminals. Road and rail terminals are frequently located in the centres of towns, on high-cost sites where space is at a premium. Because of this, major servicing is often done at less expensive sites some distance from the terminal, though care is usually taken to ensure that the distance is not so great as to create heavy costs owing to empty running. Nevertheless, even at town centre terminals it is not uncommon to see some degree of servicing performed, e.g. refuelling and carriage-cleaning. The advent of containers has meant that in addition to servicing vehicles, provision must be made for the cleaning and repair of containers, and this is becoming an important service to be provided at those terminals handling a large volume of container traffic. It is also essential that the various mechanical handling devices, e.g. straddle carriers, forklift trucks, etc. are regularly serviced. A feature of transit sheds either in ports or at ICDs (inland clearance depots) is a charging bay for the overnight recharging of forklift batteries.

5.5.1 Road transport

5.5.1.1 *Passengers*

The simplest form of road passenger terminal is the roadside bus stop. In some country districts where buses stop when hailed, the stop may not even be marked with a sign, but may be a spot where by custom the local population elect to wait to be picked up. Usually, though, it will be indicated by some form of permanent sign affixed to a post or a building. The next step up is the provision of a shelter, with or without seats, for the protection and comfort of waiting passengers. The final stage is the provision of bus and coach stations of varying sizes in town and city centres. Depending on size, the following facilities are likely to be found: toilet accommodation, an enquiry/booking office and waiting rooms, with perhaps a bookstall or shop and some provision for light refreshments. At the larger terminals, especially those associated with long-distance coach journeys, greater provision for refreshment and shopping may be provided, depending on the distance to similar facilities in the town or city centre.

5.5.1.2 *Goods*

As with other modes of transport, the type of operation and the variety of traffic has a considerable bearing on the range of services and facilities which must be provided. But nevertheless certain basic facilities will be required at most road haulage terminals. Congestion is the enemy of efficient working, and therefore a large circulating area is necessary. Office accommodation will be needed from which to administer the business. The office block may well embrace other staff facilities such as rest rooms, locker rooms, a canteen, etc. Vehicles will need to be parked, garaged and maintained, and for these operations adequate space is needed. The emphasis of current regulations on quality licensing means that great importance must be attached to the provision of proper maintenance facilities, an aspect which did not always receive proper priority in the past. Finally, goods will need to be handled and this means providing a variety of mechanical aids.

5.5.1.3 *Long-distance haulage (full loads)*

This type of operation often consists of two parts: (1) the trunk haul, and (2) local collection and delivery, in which the separate parts are performed by different drivers using articulated vehicles. The loaded trailer is brought into the terminal by the local or shunt driver and is parked ready for pick-up by the trunk or long-haul driver, and vice versa. The operation calls for plenty of parking space for vehicles awaiting pick-up. Although it is not intended that loads should be transferred from one vehicle to another, vehicle breakdowns may sometimes make this unavoidable. With some loads the transfer could be done manually, but this is often impossible. Heavy individual packages and the increasing use of pallets and containers make the provision of mechanical appliances such as forklift trucks, mobile cranes and overhead gantry cranes a virtual necessity.

5.5.1.4 *Local and medium-distance haulage (full loads)*

This operation usually calls for the same vehicle and driver to pick up and deliver the load in the same day, without the goods passing through the terminal. On occasion, however, it is convenient for the load to be picked up, held at the terminal overnight and delivered the following day. Similar facilities as in the previous category are required.

5.5.1.5 *Consolidated loads*

Goods may be brought into the terminal by either local or long-haul vehicles and consist of a number of consignments, none of which is large enough by itself to constitute a full vehicle load or to warrant a vehicle to itself because of value or urgency. The loads are broken down, sorted according to destination and consolidated with other part-loads for either trunk haul or local delivery. For this kind of operation to be performed efficiently, a transit shed with a loading bank is essential.

5.5.1.6 *The loading bank*

This consists of a platform at tailboard height, against which vehicles can be backed for easy loading and unloading. The bank will usually be backed by a large shed or warehouse, with a canopy extending over the platform and vehicle to give protection from the weather. Sometimes, instead of an external bank, the raised floor of the shed acts as a platform, and vehicles are backed up to shuttered openings in the walls of the shed. A canopy is still necessary, but it need not be as large, since it need only cover the vehicle. A further variation consists of a large, raised, covered area, with open sides. This involves lower capital expenditure, but is less secure, gives less protection from the weather and is unsuitable for some kinds of goods, when the structure is also required to serve as a warehouse. Whichever system is used, it is essential that adequate room is provided for sorting, and that the area is well lit to enable work to continue expeditiously and safely at night. Because of the increased amount of handling required, particularly of smaller packages, compared with the previous type of operation, a greater variety of handling equipment will be needed. In addition to that already mentioned, this is likely to include: hand trucks, pallet trucks, platform trucks and belt conveyors. (For detailed descriptions of various mechanical handling appliances and conveyor systems, see Chapter 12.)

5.5.1.7 *Parcels traffic*

This will require facilities similar to those described in the previous category, with much greater emphasis on the space required for the sorting and temporary accommodation of goods awaiting consolidation. If the volume of traffic is sufficiently large, it may justify the installation of complete conveyor systems. These are designed to speed up the sorting process by minimising the number of individual movements and to lower costs by reducing the labour content of the operation. A parcels office will be required to facilitate the delivery to and collection from the terminal of those parcels for which local collection and delivery services have not been requested.

The various categories of road haulage operation which require terminal facilities have been dealt with separately, but in practice more than one and often all categories are dealt with at the same terminal. This enables considerable economies to be made in the use of vehicles, equipment and manpower. At the same time it calls for great care in planning the layout of the terminal and in selecting the most appropriate items of equipment or heavy losses due to congestion and unsuitable equipment can soon occur.

5.5.2 Rail transport

5.5.2.1 *Passengers*

Terminals range in size from small country stations to main-line stations which handle local, national and international traffic. At a country station, a simple shelter, lavatories and perhaps a ticket office are the only facilities likely to be provided. As stations get progressively larger, other facilities are added – waiting rooms, bookstalls and refreshment rooms – until at the largest main-line stations more extensive toilet facilities, restaurants, shops, banking and foreign exchange facilities, and provision for customs and immigration procedures are necessary. Passengers are mobile and capable of carrying small amounts of luggage themselves. The terminal operator must therefore concentrate on providing those facilities which promote passengers' comfort and convenience, rather than on physically moving them as is necessary with goods traffic. Nevertheless, he must not lose sight of the need to move passengers swiftly and without confusion through the terminal, especially where a large volume of commuter traffic is concerned, and to ensure that boarding and alighting from vehicles is carried out with the minimum of delay to vehicles.

Passengers undertaking long rail journeys are much more likely to have baggage with them than short-distance travellers. Where their stay is likely to be prolonged, the amount of baggage accompanying them may be more than can be easily carried, so that porters and baggage trolleys must be provided. During waiting periods, while taking refreshments, etc., or when breaking their journey, passengers need somewhere to deposit their baggage in safety, to permit them to move around freely. This generates a need for baggage lockers and baggage rooms.

The rail terminal is not generally within easy walking distance of the origin or destination of the majority of passengers, so that good access to and from other modes of transport must be provided. At the large city terminal with heavy commuter traffic a large proportion of the passengers will be transferring to and from buses and underground railway systems. Other passengers will be arriving and departing by taxis and private cars. For passengers transferring between surface and rail and underground systems escalators must be provided. To simplify transfer between rail and road, access for road vehicles should be as near to the rail platforms as possible.

The larger the station, the greater the opportunity for confusion. To overcome this, clear and reliable information and instructions must be given to the public. Traffic indicator boards, colour-coded direction signs, multilingual notices and regular announcements over public address systems are all ways in which this essential exercise in communication is carried out.

The increasing use of the private car has meant that greater numbers of passengers arrive at the station by this mode of transport. This is especially so with commuter traffic. The commuter uses his car for the short journey between home and the railway station, travels by rail over the long distance, and completes his journey by underground railway, bus or taxi. This means that car parking facilities have to be provided in or near the station premises. Failure to provide parking space results in lost passengers to the railway. This happens when former rail travellers decide to complete the whole journey by private car. Frequently, the car owner persuades other rail travellers to join him as passengers to share expenses, or where several car owners are concerned a rota system is established using a different car each week. If further restrictions are imposed on the use of cars in cities, greater provision of car parks will have to be made at railway stations (and bus stations) on the outskirts of cities, to enable car users to park and continue their journeys into the city centre by public transport.

5.5.2.2 *Goods*

As with road goods traffic, rail traffic can be divided into several categories: (1) train-load, (2) truck-load, (3) less than truck-load, (4) 'smalls', (5) Freightliner traffic. It is important always to remember that apart from private siding traffic, rail traffic will begin and end its journeys on road vehicles. Rail terminals must therefore be designed not just with the needs of railway operation in mind, but to facilitate the transfer of goods between road and rail.

Almost all full train-load traffic will originate from private sidings. If we apply our original definition of a terminal, i.e. places of access to vehicles operating on the way, it will be seen that private sidings fall within this definition. Most train-load traffic will be of a bulk nature, e.g. coal, ores, cement, oil, etc., although unit trains (i.e. operated for one consignor) of manufactured goods such as motor vehicles and parts, are becoming more common. Homogeneous traffic lends itself to handling by specialised equipment, and this we would expect to find at the private siding from which the goods originated, with corresponding facilities at the receiving end where this is a regular destination for a specific traffic. Typical equipment for bulk goods would be loading hoppers and conveyors, with truck-tipping mechanisms at the receiving end or elevated tracks for gravity discharge of trucks fitted with bottom doors. For motor vehicles conveyed by rail, end-loading and discharging ramps would probably be used.

Some truck-load traffic originates from private sidings, where separate trucks bound for different destinations may form part of a complete train-load destined for the nearest marshalling yard. Or it may be picked up as individual truck-loads, a truck here, two or three trucks there, by a local train collecting from small stations and private sidings on its way to the marshalling yard. Unlike road transport consignments of a similar size and weight, a truck-load on the railway cannot travel by itself from origin to destination, but must be linked up with other truck-loads to make up a train-load of trucks bound for a common destination or area. It is this process of consolidation, or marshalling into train-loads, that makes the marshalling yard so essential to a large proportion of railway goods traffic operation.

5.5.2.3 *The marshalling yard*

A marshalling yard consists essentially of a number of incoming or reception sidings from which fan out a large number of train assembly sidings. Incoming trains of mixed destination trucks are pushed towards the sorting point, where they are disconnected and dispatched to one of the sorting sidings, where they will be joined up with other trucks to form a train for a common destination. This operation is carried out either using shunting engines or by utilising gravity in connection with a hump (see Fig. 5.3). A 'hump' is an embankment or artificial hill. Incoming trains are pushed to the top of an incline, and as they pass over the top are released to run down the other side to the appropriate siding. The path to the correct siding is controlled by switching points operating from a control tower, and the speed of the truck controlled by retarders designed to check the downward rush of the trucks. Whichever method is used, and despite buffers fitted to trucks, this process causes violent shocks to the contents of the trucks and necessitates heavy packing, a disadvantage from which this mode of transport suffers. British Rail point out that the Old Margam marshalling yard gives a good idea of how 'the hump' operates. This system is no longer used by British Rail, though doubtless it is in use elsewhere around the world.

The assembled trains are then hauled to their final destinations (if there are sufficient trucks to make up a complete train for one destination) or to a marshalling yard in another part of the country. Here the train is broken down and resorted with trucks from other trains, into trains for local delivery. Some trucks will eventually reach private sidings where they will be discharged, others will be taken to railway goods terminals near to their final destinations, where their loads will be transferred to road vehicles.

5.5.2.4 *Less than truck-load and 'smalls'*

The facilities required for this type of traffic are comparable with the facilities required for similar goods carried by road, viz. a loading and sorting bank with plenty of space, good lighting and suitable handling appliances. Railway goods sheds are usually either through or dead-end types. In the former, trucks can pass right through the shed; in the latter they must be shunted in and out. In either case, platforms alongside the trucks will enable goods to be easily loaded, discharged and sorted, with access for road vehicles on the opposite sides of the platforms. Some older

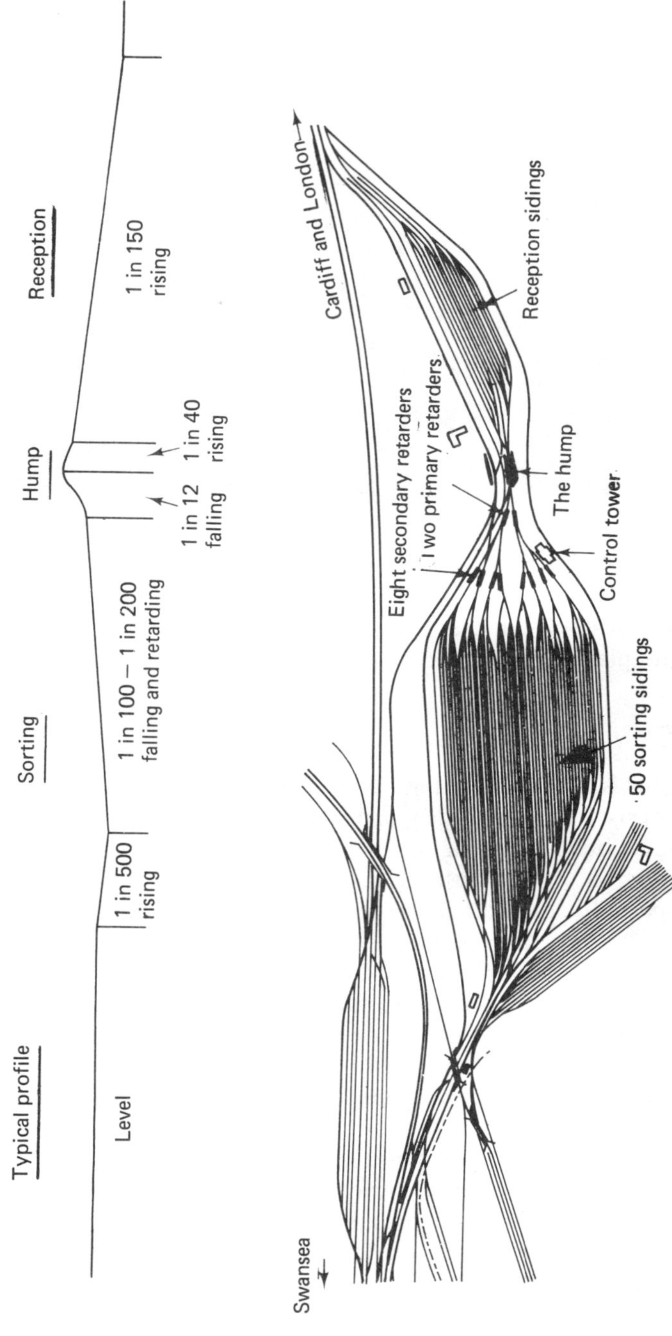

Fig. 5.3 Margam marshalling yard, showing profile and configuration (courtesy of British Rail)

Fig. 5.4 Freightliner terminal with gantry crane in operation (courtesy of Railfreight Distribution)

goods sheds may have the platform on the outside, with a canopy covering the platform and trucks, with access for road vehicles inside the shed.

5.5.2.5 *Freightliner traffic*

This is traffic carried in ISO containers on special unit trains. These trains consist of continuously coupled, standardised rail cars fitted to accept all ISO containers. The trains provide regular, high-speed services on a point-to-point basis, without marshalling, over high-volume routes between specially designed and equipped terminals. At these terminals the essence of the operation is the rapid transfer of containers between road and rail transport, and in some cases between one train and another. A feature of these terminals are the container cranes capable of lifting containers up to 40 feet (12 m) long and weighing 30 tons. These cranes, which are self-propelled along their own tracks, straddle several sets of rail tracks and roadways. They can remove a container from a lorry and place it on the waiting rail car, move along the track, pick up another container further along the train, return and load it on to the lorry, all in the space of a few minutes (see Fig. 5.4). Another feature of these cranes is that the driver can lift containers of various sizes from 10 feet to 40 feet (3–12 m) without changing the head, since the lifting head of these cranes can be automatically changed to fit the size of the next container, an essential feature where train-loads carry a mixed bag of containers.

Sometimes 'groupage' facilities may be found at Freightliner terminals. 'Groupage' is an expression now regularly used to describe the consolidation of less than container-loads into container-loads (and less than vehicle-loads into vehicle-loads in the case of international road haulage). Groupage services are usually supplied by freight forwarders – sometimes by a consortium of a number of freight forwarders, who operate regular services to specific destinations. As with any other transport operation concerned with less than vehicle-load traffic, a covered area with loading banks, mechanical handling appliances, etc., is required. In addition, because international traffic is likely to be involved, facilities must be provided for customs clearance. Figure 5.5 shows a typical Freightliner terminal layout.

It will be obvious that as Freightliner terminals are involved in the rapid transfer of containers, the greatest care must be exercised in the planning stage, to ensure the smooth flow of traffic through the terminal. Ample space must be allocated for the manoeuvring of road vehicles. Although Freightliner terminals have been dealt with under rail transport, road transport to, from and within the terminal must be given equal consideration if the terminal is to operate efficiently. Space must also be devoted to the temporary accommodation of containers awaiting loading on to road or rail vehicles, when direct transfer has not been possible (see Fig. 5.5).

However fast the rail transit, and no matter how quickly containers are transferred between modes, the benefits will be lost if documentation cannot keep pace with the speed of movement of containers, or if a lorry has a long wait for clearance at the office, or is delayed because a container cannot be located. This means that the systems for recording container movements and container locations, for transmitting information concerning container numbers, contents, ownership, etc., between terminals must be rapid and accurate. Many of these operations will involve the use of electronic equipment, which in turn means the need for well-trained staff, all housed in well-planned offices, if bottlenecks are to be avoided.

The documentation of transport is dealt with in Chapter 17, but it is perhaps worth mentioning here that in the United Kingdom, as far as export consignments and EU movements are concerned, British Rail has solved the documentation problem by doing the work itself. The official document is the CIM (Convention on International Merchandise) consignment note. The documentation has to be accurate and the documents must be checked if delays are to be avoided. If customers are forced to make out this documentation, they invariably make errors and it is necessary to train staff at every reception depot in the correct completion of these forms. An easier solution is to train a special team, with a suitable computerised system, to complete the form on an electronic master document layout. All the customer has to do is fax the necessary details to Dover, where the completion of the form is done by the team. The entire documentation for

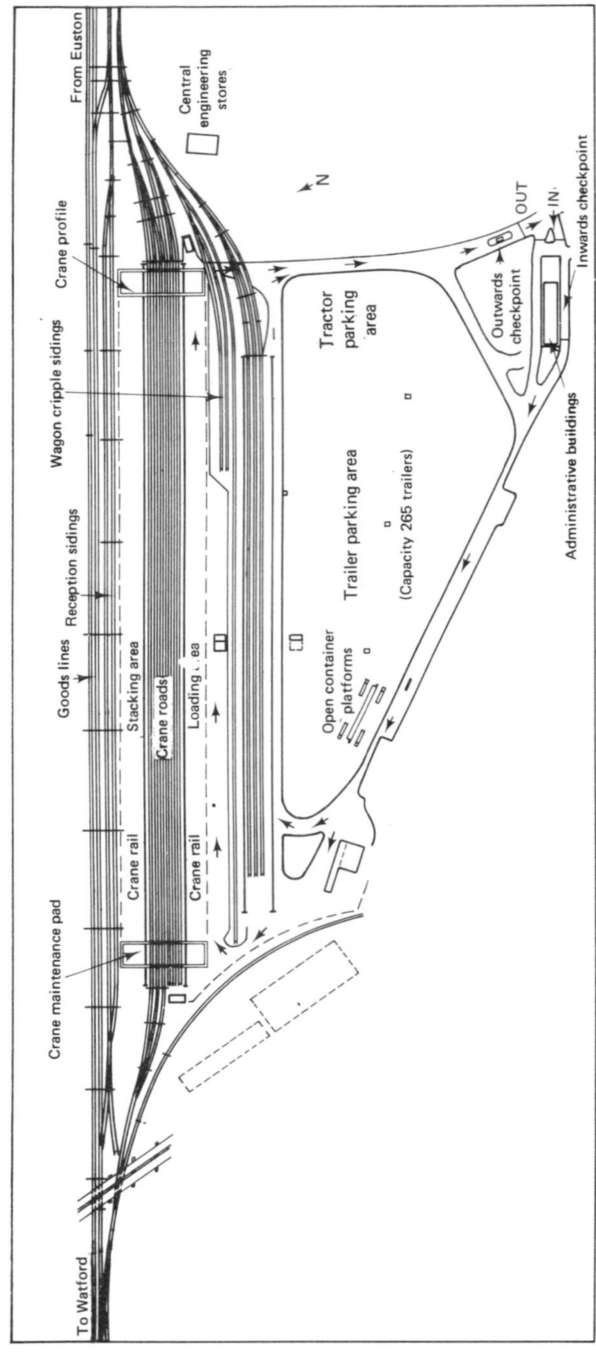

Fig. 5.5 Willesden Freightliner Terminal (courtesy of Freightliners Ltd)

all movements goes by electronic data interchange (EDI) to all parties concerned in seconds. The United Kingdom is the only country in the European rail network to send all its documentation in this way.

5.5.2.6 *A road and rail terminal – Le Shuttle*

By the time this book appears the unique road and rail terminals on either side of the English Channel (La Manche to the French) should be in operation. A short description follows based on the press releases made available just before the terminals were finally completed. The courtesy of Eurotunnel (whose trademark is Le Shuttle) is gratefully acknowledged. (For full information about the freight services available exporters and carriers should write to Le Shuttle UK and Eire Freight-Sales Office, Farthingloe Village, Folkestone Rd, Dover, Kent, CT17 9TU. Tel: 0303 273 300; Fax: 0304 209560. French operators should write to Head Office, Le Shuttle Freight Division, Eurotunnel, Operating Headquarters Calais, B.P. 69, 62231, Coquelles, France. Tel: 010 33 21 00 60 00; Fax: 010 33 21 00 61 59.)

Reference has already been made (see page 36) to the fact that Le Shuttle is a specialised way under the English Channel for road vehicles, with separate shuttles for freight vehicles and passenger vehicles (coaches and cars). The freight shuttles consist of twenty-eight special road-loading wagons each capable of carrying a 44 tonne vehicle. HGVs wishing to use the service will pull off the English motorway, the M20, and join the special 'freight' road, segregated from tourist traffic, to the toll booths. The toll booths are computer-linked to give a very rapid service, and payment can be made using a special 'rapid service' card, a fuel card, a credit card, cheque or cash. All formalities are completed at the access end, either in the United Kingdom on an outward journey or at Calais on the homeward journey. This has the advantage that after the crossing, the driver simply rejoins the vehicle, drives out of the shuttle, up the loading ramp and away on the exit road. The driver therefore passes through both UK and French passport controls at the access point to the system, and proceeds to an allocation area for loading. The loading process has already been described (see page 35).

The service is confidently expected to allow drivers to leave the UK motorway and join the French autoroute A16 within 80 minutes. Operations will be continuous, 24 hours a day, 365 days a year with up to three departures an hour (four an hour after 1995). Eight shuttles are available, each consisting of 28 carriers weighing 36 tonnes, each of which can easily carry a 44 tonne vehicle. The shuttle trains can operate at speeds of up to 87.5 mph (140 km/h). The loading staff position chocks on each vehicle once the driver has parked it. Drivers and co-drivers are then collected from their vehicles and taken to the Club Car, which has toilets and washing facilities, refreshments, air-conditioning and audio and visual information systems. On arrival at the far end the driver rejoins the vehicle, drives off the shuttle and is away.

5.6 Air transport

As with other modes of transport, air transport terminals can vary considerably in size from small airports concerned mainly with light passenger aircraft; to major international airports. If we study one of the latter, Heathrow, we can see the full range of facilities and services required, while bearing in mind that the former will be scaled-down versions with some of the refinements being dropped as we proceed lower down the scale.

The first regular air service to Europe began in 1919. In the following years air passenger transport has grown to such an extent that by 1969 Heathrow alone was handling over 13 million passengers and by 1990 this had grown to 43 million passengers a year. Goods traffic developed more slowly, but in the last decade has increased enormously. Again, citing Heathrow, freight has risen from 115,000 tonnes in 1962 to 698,000 tonnes in 1990. Peak traffic to date for all UK airports was 1,119,000 tonnes in 1990.

This enormous expansion in air traffic has posed many problems for airport authorities. As existing airports have become inadequate to deal with the growing traffic, new sites have had to be found. Ideal locations which will satisfy the requirements and objections of all interested parties are rare, as mentioned earlier in this chapter. Even when an apparently suitable site has been selected, the airport authority cannot be certain that it will be adequate for future needs. No one can forecast with any degree of certainty what the future growth of air traffic will be, or what new developments in aircraft design and size are likely to emerge in, say, 15–20 years. Meanwhile the airport will have created a fairly large conurbation (Heathrow supports approximately 250,000 people) and what was once an open site may now be a built-up area with no further room for expansion, or where further expansion is socially unacceptable. As aircraft grew larger and faster, longer runways were needed, and the introduction of much larger, heavier jets has meant that stronger runways have had to be built. These larger aircraft also need much more room for manoeuvring on the ground and occupy more space on the traffic apron. They require greater space separation between aircraft because of the increased blast from their more powerful jet engines.

The greater passenger capacity of new aircraft which are now coming into service in increasing numbers, and the even larger capacity aircraft being developed, may absorb some of the projected traffic increase, but there is still likely to be a trend towards increased aircraft movements at most major airports. This could lead to the airspace in the vicinity of existing airports becoming dangerously overcrowded, or air traffic control being stretched to breaking point. Even where sufficient space is available on the ground, new airports may have to be established to reduce the load on existing ones. At Heathrow in 1991, 360,000 aircraft landed or took off. In 1991 42 million passengers passed through the airport, and on an average day 40,000 vehicles were estimated to use the approach tunnel. These figures illustrate the magnitude of the problem, and show why airport planners must look well to the future in anticipating demand. A miscalculation in the level of future demand could lead to a potentially dangerous situation, or a curtailment in the growth of services in a particular area.

Because an aircraft cannot be brought to rest on its specialised way, unlike land and sea transport, the standards of safety and maintenance required must be more exacting than those required for other modes. These of course necessitate very frequent and meticulous maintenance schedules, and strict safety checks. Many of these require to be done between landing and take-off and so require facilities to be provided at the terminal.

Modern aircraft consume enormous quantities of fuel; for example, a Boeing 767 flying between Gatwick and Palma will consume, depending on weather and traffic conditions, between 5,160 and 5,860 kg of fuel. This must be loaded quickly to avoid unnecessary delay, yet, because of the potential hazard, with maximum regard to safety. At older airports, fuel is taken to the aircraft by road tankers, but at more modern airports permanent underground pipelines are laid from the storage areas to hydrants at the aircraft refuelling points, where it can be pumped aboard under pressure at high speed under strict safety control.

5.6.1 Passenger facilities

As would be expected from previous discussion on the facilities required by passengers at the major terminals of other modes, aircraft passengers would expect to find shops, restaurants and banking facilities. Because many long-distance flights involve overnight stops, and because aircraft are subject to delays due to weather, etc., hotel accommodation must be provided adjacent to or at the terminal. Heads of state, politicians, major figures in the commercial and industrial worlds, film stars, pop stars and other celebrities are usually accorded special facilities. The abbreviation VIP (Very Important Person) was probably coined by airlines to describe these categories of passenger, and it is customary to find VIP reception rooms set aside at major airports where important travellers can be

Fig. 5.6 Cres-Flight baggage claim conveyor at Perth (courtesy of Matthews Conveyor Co. Ltd, Canada)

received, interviewed or may wait in privacy. When strict security must be observed, special landing areas are sometimes set aside.

Apart from light hand baggage, passengers do not accompany their baggage to the aircraft. It must be checked (especially, from a security viewpoint), weighed, transported to the aircraft and carefully stowed so as to maintain the trim of the aircraft. At the end of the flight the procedure is reversed, with an additional customs examination where necessary. With some aircraft now taking hundreds of passengers on a single flight, and remembering the number of flights per hour that may be involved, this must be done speedily and efficiently if delays to aircraft and passengers are to be avoided. This requires the provision of extensive baggage handling systems (see Fig. 5.6).

5.6.2 Cargo facilities

An aircraft is designed to fly in a particular attitude; that is to say, with the tail in a particular position in relation to the nose when in normal flight at a given speed. If the plane is nose-heavy or tail-heavy it could result in the aircraft failing to take off properly or stalling when in flight. Therefore the trim of the aircraft must always be correct before it is permitted to leave the ground. To achieve this, great care must be taken to ensure that the weight carried is properly distributed. Many variables other than weight of cargo must be taken into account: the weight of the aircraft itself, weight of fuel which varies according to distance, weight of mail, the weight of aircrew and baggage, and, since a large proportion of cargo is carried on passenger aircraft, the weight of passengers and their baggage. All these factors, and others, including any special stowage requirements of the cargo itself, must be considered to guarantee a proper trim.

The detailed attention that must be paid to the stowage of an aircraft means that it is often necessary for cargo to be delivered to the airport transit shed 4–5 hours before take-off, even though the actual flight may only take the same length of time. During this pre-flight time, the cargo must be check-weighed, documented and labelled. Then a stowage plan, load sheet and trim sheet must be prepared, and the cargo loaded.

Since a large proportion of the cargo sent by air consists of small packages, much of it will be palletised in the airport transit sheds, particularly if it is to be carried in all-freight aircraft. To handle large quantities of small packages, sophisticated handling and conveyor systems are required, and these are a feature of the cargo-handling facilities at modern airports. The loading doors of large aircraft are often a considerable height from the ground and could present problems in loading. Sometimes direct access can be obtained by means of a ramp. In other cases, specialised pieces of mechanised handling equipment, such as scissor-lifts, have been developed to overcome the difficulty.

The total tonnage handled by airports is small by comparison with that handled by major seaports. Nevertheless if a comparison is made in terms of value of cargo, the picture is very different, and the high value of a large percentage of air cargo is clearly demonstrated. This has, in fact, seriously affected sea freight since it has denied sea freight the more valuable cargoes earning a higher freight. These were previously used to offset the lower freights charged on less valuable commodities; in effect, it has skimmed off the cream. On the basis of value Heathrow is the most important UK port, handling 16 per cent of the nation's total trade. Because of this high proportion of valuable goods, particular attention must be paid to security arrangements, and since much of the cargo is subject to customs or excise duty, extensive facilities must be provided for the temporary accommodation of dutiable goods. Fig. 5.7 shows the general configuration of Heathrow Airport.

The principal benefit derived from the use of air transport is speed of transit, but as air traffic increased there was some concern that this advantage would soon be lost by delays on the ground due to non-arrival of documents and slow customs clearance. The various agencies involved – airport authorities, airlines, freight forwarders and H.M. Customs – have devoted a lot of time, thought and effort over the years to the problem of

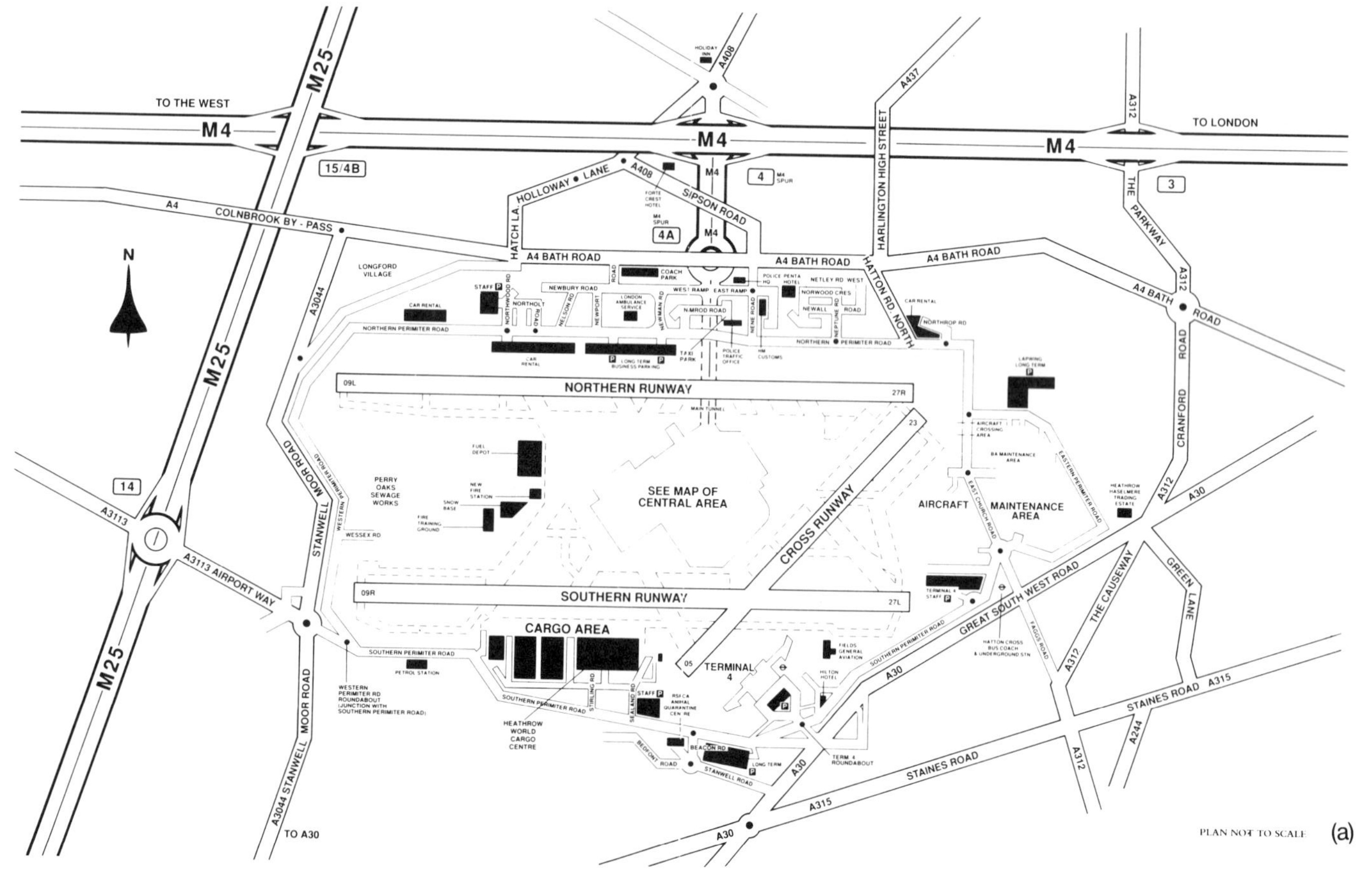
TO THE WEST
M4
M25
15/4B
TO LONDON
A312
THE PARKWAY
3
A408
4
M4 SPUR
4A
HOLLOWAY LANE
SIPSON ROAD
HATCH LA
A4
COLNBROOK BY-PASS
A4 BATH ROAD
HARLINGTON HIGH STREET
A437
HATTON RD. NORTH
A4 BATH ROAD
CRANFORD ROAD
N
LONGFORD VILLAGE
A3044
NORTHERN PERIMITER ROAD
09L
NORTHERN RUNWAY
27R
23
SEE MAP OF CENTRAL AREA
CROSS RUNWAY
AIRCRAFT
MAINTENANCE AREA
PERRY OAKS SEWAGE WORKS
STANWELL MOOR ROAD
14
A3113
A3113 AIRPORT WAY
09R
SOUTHERN RUNWAY
27L
CARGO AREA
05
TERMINAL 4
SOUTHERN PERIMITER ROAD
HEATHROW WORLD CARGO CENTRE
GREAT SOUTH WEST ROAD
A30
THE CAUSEWAY
GREEN LANE
STAINES ROAD
A315
A244
A3044 STANWELL MOOR ROAD
TO A30
PLAN NOT TO SCALE
(a)

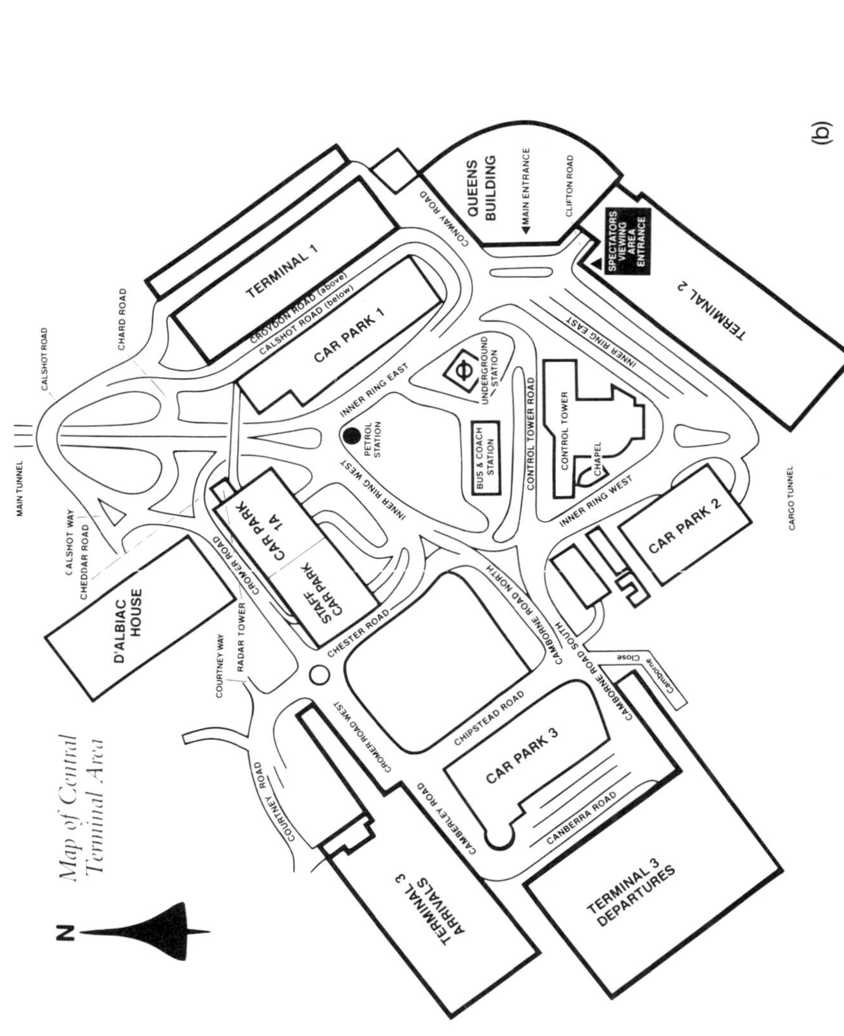

(b)

Fig. 5.7 (a) and (b) The general configuration of Heathrow Airport, London (courtesy of BAA PLC)

producing documentation and clearance systems which could keep pace with the reducing transit time.

The highly successful computerised system developed at London Airport and later used at sixteen UK airports – originally called ACP 80 (air cargo processing for the 1980s) and later ACP 90 – is now being replaced by a new system – the CCS-UK system – developed by BT Customer Systems. (CCS stands for Cargo Community System.) It provides users with a wide range of facilities, including document capture, data capture, data processing, consignment controls, customs entry and delivery control of exports, imports and transits. It also provides messaging facilities which give extensive inter-system communication. This system is described more fully below (see page 358).

5.7 Sea transport

The terminals for sea transport range in size from small, riverside wharfs capable of accommodating vessels of a few hundred tonnes in size, and perhaps built with strengthened bottoms to enable them to sit on the bottom at low tide, to huge complexes covering an area of many square miles. In fact what we often refer to as ports at the present time are not so much terminals for sea transport as industrial areas with port connections, in which the actual area devoted to purely port work is only a small part of the total complex.

It is not possible to deal with the various facilities and services to be found at ports of various sizes according to some ascending or descending ladder of size, for the number of steps on such a ladder would be almost as large as the number of ports themselves. Instead, as we did with airports, we will look at the provisions made by major ports and remember that these will be scaled down or dispensed with as the ports decrease in size and complexity.

We have already seen (page 56) the necessity for providing shelter, deep water and safe access from the sea. Immense capital expenditure will have been necessary to provide the fixed installations, viz. enclosed docks, lock entrances, quay walls, etc., where these are necessary; to provide extra protection in the form of breakwaters where extra protection is needed; or to dredge deeper channels to keep pace with the ever-increasing draught of modern vessels. After these provisions much more needs to be done. Maintenance dredging must be carried out on a continuous basis to preserve the depth of water, and a multitude of other services and facilities must be provided for the safe reception and handling of the vessel, its passengers and cargo.

First, the vessel must be brought safely to its berth. This may involve a tricky navigation from the outer limits of the port to a berth in an enclosed dock some miles upstream. Unlike aircraft, which for the most part operate in strictly controlled air lanes and are virtually handed on from one air control point to another, ships while on the high seas are free from regulation, and it is not until they reach the approaches to a port that they come under the jurisdiction of the port authority. Even then, the degree of control exercised by the port or harbour authority is much less than that which applies to aircraft. It has been said that a ship's master is 'Master under God'; that is, that in all matters relating to the safety of his ship, passengers, crew and cargo, he is the sole arbiter, and while port authorities may have statutory powers to 'regulate' the passage of his vessel, they do not 'control' it.

Some time before its actual arrival, perhaps a few days, perhaps weeks, sometimes even months before, the shipping company will have advised the port authority of the ship's intended visit. The longer the voyage, and the larger the number of ports of call, the more difficult it will be to give a precise arrival date and this may be adjusted several times as a more accurate picture of the vessel's progress emerges. When the vessel is a tramp rather than a cargo liner, its expected arrival date is likely to be more imprecise, because the loading of extra cargo will always take priority over the need to sail on a planned date. Unless the ship is destined for an allocated berth, i.e. one leased or rented for the exclusive use of a specific shipping company (or a specific stevedoring company in the case of many European ports), a provisional allocation to a common user berth will be made. This allocation may have to be amended several times before the ship actually arrives, depending on how the discharging and loading of preceding vessels has progressed – for example, whether the programme has been upset by the late arrival of preceding vessels, bad weather, breakdowns, labour disputes. Once *en route* to the port, the shipping company or its agents will give an ETA (estimated time of arrival) to the port authority. This will later be confirmed by the ship's VHF radio to the port navigation service, as the vessel draws nearer.

It will, it is hoped, assist the reader who has no knowledge of the workings of a large, modern port to understand the parts played by the many services and organisations if we follow the progress of a vessel from the time it arrives at the outer approaches to a port, until it reaches the safety of its berth. The description which follows of organisations and procedures is based loosely on those applicable to the Port of London, but they are not always identical and considerable variations will occur from port to port.

Long before the vessel reaches the outer limits of the port authority's jurisdiction it will require assistance in avoiding natural hazards such as rocks and sandbanks. Coastal lightships, lighthouses, buoys and beacons placed in position by the lighthouse authority will serve to guide the vessel safely on its way.

5.7.1 Lighthouse authority

The general lighthouse authority for England and Wales, the Channel Islands, the adjacent seas and islands and Gibraltar, is the Corporation of Trinity House of Deptford Strand, London. In association with the Commissioners of Northern Lighthouses and the Commissioners of Irish Lights, the Corporation controls and maintains the lighthouses and lightships on and around British coasts. To finance the construction, maintenance and administration of these and other seamarks, money is raised by means of special dues levied on shipping using the ports of the British Isles. These dues, called 'light dues', are collected on behalf of the Corporation by H.M. Customs, and the accounts are submitted annually to parliament. A number of other bodies having a limited local jurisdiction perform a similar service. In other countries this function may be performed by government services or departments, e.g. a 'Ministry of Marine' or a 'Coastguard Service'.

Having reached the outer limits of the port, especially an estuarial port such as London, the vessel may now face the problem of navigating a considerable distance before entering the actual estuary, and then many more miles of estuary and finally the river itself, before arriving at the lock entrance of the enclosed dock. From its surface the water gives little clue as to what lies beneath. To an experienced mariner 'broken water', i.e. where the surface appears very disturbed, may indicate rocks or shoals, but there can be little to indicate a difference in depth between 30 ft and 40 ft (9 and 12 m) and this may be critical to the safe progress of the vessel. The master needs to know where the safe channels lie. These will be marked by positioning navigation buoys (as opposed to mooring buoys) along the length of the deep-water channels. Each of these will be of a different shape or system of marking, will be named individually and recorded on the charts.

In most rivers these navigation buoys are suitable for both day and night navigation, but in some cases navigation can be done only in daylight hours (e.g. the River Swayle). A missed daylight high water can mean a day's delay or even more in winter, when daylight may be limited to 7–8 hours.

Navigation information for the port will give a detailed description of each one so that they can be easily identified and the ship's position accurately located even in conditions of poor visibility when shore marks may be hidden. The provision of these navigation buoys may be undertaken by the Port Authority or the Lighthouse Authority. In London, they are provided and maintained by the Corporation of Trinity House.

5.7.2 Pilotage

Buoys alone are not sufficient to ensure that the vessel can safely navigate in confined waters. Difficult currents, tricky cross-winds, speed of tide and ferry crossings are just a few of the hazards that create the need for the assistance of someone with extensive local knowledge. It is here that the pilotage service plays its part. Pilots operate under licences granted either by the Port Authority (which may be designated as the Pilotage Authority) or an independent Pilotage Authority. In London the Pilotage Authority is another department of the Corporation of Trinity House. Licences are granted to satisfactory applicants only after they have passed tests and gained experience in the work they will have to do, e.g. by a period of training under experienced pilots. In some ports possession of a Master's Certificate for Foreign Going Ships is a prerequisite for acceptance as a trainee, at others this is not required and the pilot progresses under experienced pilots, through several stages of competency to handle vessels of increasing size. In some ports the use of a pilot is compulsory, in others it is optional. Even in non-compulsory ports few masters will dispense with the services of a pilot, except where they are in command of a small vessel operating a very frequent service so that they have acquired an extensive local knowledge. In compulsory pilotage ports, the masters of small vessels that are frequent visitors will sometimes qualify as pilots so as to avoid the necessity of having to employ one each time they enter and leave the port. It is important to note that even where pilotage is compulsory, control of the vessel and responsibility for its safety and conduct remains with the master; the pilot acts in an advisory capacity only.

5.7.3 Towage

It is difficult for large vessels to navigate and manoeuvre in confined, congested waters without assistance. Even when barely moving, considerable power is required to halt the forward momentum of a large vessel, and the damage it can cause by a slight collision with a fixed structure such as a pier can be enormous. Imagine an elephant leaning gently against a garden shed and you can probably visualise the effect of a 100,000 tonne tanker still moving, though very slowly, bearing down on the steel structure of an oil jetty. Furthermore, a vessel which is hundreds of feet long finds it impossible to change direction quickly. A considerable time must elapse after the rudder has been moved before the vessel's head comes round. To counter these two difficulties, tugs must be used. These small, but immensely powerful vessels can pull, push and check the movement of giant vessels and enable manoeuvres to be performed with much more success than could be achieved by the ship's engines and rudder alone. Although Port Authorities themselves frequently maintain fleets of tugs for work in enclosed docks, towage on the river, in the estuary, and some dock work is usually performed by tugs belonging to firms of tug owners established in the port.

Many very large crude carriers (VLCCs) are fitted with thrusters each side of the bow, to help them to move sideways into the berth, and in order to combat the loss of steerage when moving at very low speeds an outboard motor behind the rudder helps create enough local water movement to give adequate steerage.

5.7.4 Port navigation service

Although by no means a universal feature, most major ports now have some form of navigation service. This, as its name implies, is a service designed to assist vessels in safely navigating the confined waters of a port area. Mention has already been made of VHF radio which permits easy communication between ship and shore. This enables the latest information regarding availability of berths, anchorages, weather conditions, temporary hazards such as dredgers working, etc., to be passed to incoming vessels. As vessels have grown larger over the years it has become necessary for Port Authorities to take powers to regulate and control water traffic in the areas under their jurisdiction. For example, at ports where the tidal range has necessitated the provision of enclosed docks and lock entrances, it may be vital to regulate the order in which vessels proceed upstream. This is to ensure that those vessels with the deepest draughts have the benefit of the deepest water when entering dock, i.e. their arrival will need to coincide with high water at the lock entrance. In this situation they may be required to remain at an appropriate anchorage in the estuary, and to proceed upstream, in sequence, on instructions from the navigation service. Other smaller vessels will be limited to entering the locks before and after the deeper draughted vessels, and their progress will be regulated so that they do not impede the larger vessels.

The reverse procedure will operate for vessels leaving the docks, and where the arrival of a number of large vessels coincides with the departure of others, strict adherence to a plan is necessary to ensure that vessels do not miss a tide. When very large tankers are turning in midstream to go alongside or leave riverside oil terminals, such manoeuvres would be very hazardous if other vessels were moving upstream or downstream at the same time. In this situation the navigation service would have to regulate the movements of other vessels, in the interests of safety.

Most readers will be aware that tide tables are published giving the predicted times and heights of high and low water for principal ports around our coasts. These predictions are usually based on official tide tables provided by the Liverpool Observatory and Tidal Institute, and are as accurate as science can make them. But it must be emphasised that they are only predictions and must be used with care. Meteorological conditions nearly always affect both times and heights of tides. For small and medium-sized vessels differences of a few feet and some fluctuation in the actual time of high or low water are unlikely to be serious, especially if even at low tide there is likely to be ample depth for them to navigate in safety. With larger vessels, and especially in the case of giant tankers, such discrepancies could be disastrous if undetected. For this reason a very careful watch must be kept on the height and timing of the tides when very large vessels are due to enter or leave the port. In London, for example, not only are there tidal gauges in the estuary and its approaches, but others are located on the coast many miles to the north and south of the mouth of the Thames. The readings from these automatic gauges are transmitted to visual displays in the Thames Navigation Service Centre at Gravesend. A higher or lower, or earlier or later, reading than that predicted will show up on these coastal gauges an hour or more before a similar reading would appear at the mouth of the Thames. This early warning of any deviation from the prediction will enable a very accurate estimate of the time and height of the tide in the Thames to be made. Such information is invaluable when dealing with vessels exceeding 100,000 tonnes deadweight, which may have only a few feet of water under their bottoms when proceeding upriver on a rising tide.

Lastly, the navigation service will almost certainly have shore-based radar coverage of the estuarial waters. The Thames Navigation Service is able to provide coverage from the Sunk and Tongue light buoys on the seaward limit of the Port upstream to Woolwich, a distance of 50 miles (80 km). A common question asked in connection with shore-based radar is: 'Why is it necessary when nearly all vessels have their own radar?' The answer is that radar cannot see round corners and a vessel proceeding upstream or downstream cannot tell what is around the next bend because the image will be hidden by the high banks of the river and any buildings or trees upon the banks. Additionally, the multiplicity of other ships, cranes and other shore equipment and buildings would present a confused picture. Shore radar has the advantage of being mounted on high buildings and towers; the equipment is probably more powerful than can be mounted on most vessels; and the operators have the advantage of local knowledge when interpreting the image. In foggy weather, shore-based radar can be of tremendous assistance to vessels enabling them to be guided into and out of the port and thus avoiding the delays which would occur if vessels were forced to drop anchor.

5.7.5 Berthing

If a vessel is passing through an entrance lock on her way to a berth she will need assistance in negotiating the lock. The operation of lock gates and raising the level of the water will almost certainly be performed by staff of the Port Authority's Dockmaster's Department (or some equivalent name). The handling of the ship's ropes when passing through the lock, and when she is finally secured at her berth, may be carried out by Port Authority staff, or by other men licensed to do this work. At river berths this will probably be performed by licensed boatmen and watermen. In some instances, e.g. the New Welland Canal, ship's crew are expected to handle the ropes while negotiating the locks.

5.7.6 H.M. Customs

At some point on the inward journey to her berth the vessel will be boarded by H.M. Customs officials who will search the vessel for hidden contraband. While this search is in progress, the master will be interviewed by a customs officer and will receive two very important documents:

- *Pratique*. This is the ship's health certificate, and is issued only if there is no infectious disease on board. Neither passengers nor crew may land pending issue of pratique. Should there be infectious disease on board, or if it is suspected, then the Port Health Authority will be called in.
- *Certificate of clearance inward*. The master supplies the customs officers with a list of dutiable goods declared to be in possession of each member of the crew. Duty is charged on these after a small allowance for personal use has been made. The master is given a certificate of clearance inwards after the bonded ship's stores remaining on board have been checked against the report and sealed up by the Customs. (After the ship has discharged, the bonded stores will again be checked and resealed and the master will be given a jerque note, in duplicate, one copy of which must be handed in at the Customs House before the ship can be given an outward clearance.)

5.7.7 Reporting inwards

Most people are aware that an entry must be made to H.M. Customs for all goods imported into the country, irrespective of whether or not they are subject to duty. But many are unaware that it is also necessary for all vessels from abroad to be 'entered inwards'.

As soon as possible after the arrival of the vessel, the master and his agent must report the vessel's arrival to H.M. Customs' Long Room. (Even if it is a square room or a round one, it is still called a Long Room, after the original one in London.) The master must report in person as he will be asked certain questions about his recent voyage, which only he can answer. When reporting the master must produce the Report, which contains details of the ship, its cargo, the name of the master, port of origin, present berth, dutiable stores, cargo intended for other ports, number and nationality of passengers, name of the ship's agent, and a declaration that the ship has not 'broken bulk', i.e. landed any cargo, since leaving the port of origin. Where a large variety of cargo is carried, this will probably be described on the Report as General Cargo, and a copy of the manifest will be attached to the Report. He must also produce the certificate of pratique, and where applicable, a pilotage slip, showing details of any pilotage done, a deck cargo certificate, a grain cargo certificate, and a tonnage dues slip showing the dues to be paid. Finally, the master will make a declaration of any unusual sightings, icebergs, wrecks, etc.

Before sailing, the reverse procedure is adopted except that the presence of the master is not required. Before outward clearance is given, the following documents must be presented at the Customs House:

1. Clearance Outwards and Victualling Bill, giving details of bonded and drawback stores on board.
2. Load Line Certificate.
3. Ship's Certificate of Registry.
4. Wireless Certificate.
5. Light Dues Certificate.
6. Safety Equipment Certificate.
7. Passenger Number Certificate.
8. Inward Clearing Bill (Jerque Note).
9. A certificate is required for the Department of Trade certifying that all necessary certificated crew members are signed on, including a certificated ship's cook.

On completion of these formalities the ship may leave port, but it is important to note that within six days of the clearance of the ship, the ship's agent must submit to the Customs House a copy of the ship's manifest and a list of the names of passengers carried.

5.7.8 Dredging

While not strictly part of a ship's progress into port, the activities of port authorities in the dredging and conservation of the river channel are vital to the movement of ships. Engineers make painstaking studies of the ebb and flow of tidal waters, in some cases using research models of entire estuaries. These models, which are very accurate representations of the topography of the estuary, its banks, bed and approaches, faithfully reproduce the effect of tidal variations and changes in the force and direction of the flow of water. Through the study of this model, and by constant monitoring of the actual channel, silting up and erosion can be detected and remedial measures taken. Sometimes the careful study of a tidal model will reveal that a realignment of a dredged channel will harness the self-scouring effect of the tides, to reduce or eliminate the need for dredging in the future.

It is not only the river which is affected by silting. Every time a ship passes through the enclosed locks, water carrying fine particles of soil in suspension is admitted. In the calm waters of the dock, this silt settles out and gradually builds up a layer of fine sand on the bottom of the dock. In London, this deposited spoil amounts to a million tonnes per year, which must be dredged out and pumped ashore to reclaim low-lying marshy land.

Many estuaries yield high-quality gravel and sand which can be sold after being dredged up or used in port developments as the basis of concrete for piles and jetties. Our ship, oblivious of this valuable work, proceeds to its berth through channels kept clear by the Marine Services Department.

5.7.9 Conservation

Estuaries must also be conserved in other ways. The problem of pollution is one that requires constant vigilance. Even to fall into some rivers is dangerous, not because you might drown but because you might swallow some of the water. Where River Conservators are appointed, as in the Port of London, to monitor oxygen levels and detect pollution as soon as it occurs, steps can be taken to prevent repetitions of pollution by offending factories, municipalities or agricultural enterprises. Similarly, river banks can be regularly inspected, flood prevention organised in low-lying areas, animal pests controlled, fisheries promoted, etc. Driftwood collection prevents damage to small vessels, and floating debris which would make banks and sea shores unsightly can be collected and destroyed.

5.7.10 Security

The security of any port area is vital. In the port we have a concentration of desirable commodities, ready to be pilfered, re-routed or stolen. Every conceivable kind of theft and malpractice has been tried at one time or another, from petty theft to major robberies. A port police authority, or river police authority, working in conjunction with other land-based police forces in the hinterland, preserves and safeguards this valuable collection of property. Unauthorised entry to dock areas is forbidden, and patrols must enforce this prohibition. Cargoes and vehicles must be checked at gateways, and only authorised movements permitted. Customs officers will be alert for unauthorised movements of goods seeking to avoid customs duty; will maintain records and checks on movements of vehicles through port areas where roll-on roll-off facilities make smuggling easier; and will watch for illegal entry of drugs and other prohibited articles. Immigration officials will check the movements of foreign nationals, exclude prohibited immigrants and detain for investigation those visitors whose documents are defective.

5.7.11 Health

The port medical officer will supervise the admission of people from areas where outbreaks of infectious diseases have been notified. Veterinary officers will quarantine animals which may be carriers of diseases, such as rabies, foot and mouth disease or swine vesicular disease. Similarly, infested cargoes which could spread pests like the colorado beetle may need to be fumigated or excluded.

5.7.12 Ship's services

A ship at sea is a self-contained unit, generating its own power, often distilling drinking water, baking its own bread, disposing of its own waste products, etc. In port the engines are still and the ship relies temporarily on shore-based services. It will almost certainly link up to shore power supplies to keep essential services going while in port. The ship will take on board, and pay for, a fresh water supply sufficient to meet most needs of the coming voyage. In taking on water some vessels have to differentiate between water for boilers and drinking water. In many overseas ports the water might be all right for boilers but unsuitable for drinking, while in Aden the reverse is true, due to the high lime content of the water.

The ship will be revictualled, and resupplied with countless items such as table linen, bed linen, cleaning materials, lubricants, paint, cutlery, etc. She will discharge accumulated waste products and dispose of rubbish ashore. She will link up to the public telephone network so that external calls can be made.

Shore-based services will be engaged to effect repairs of a major nature, and at times the facilities of the dry dock will be used. A dry dock is a basin which has an entrance mouth which can be closed by a floating plug called a 'caisson'. First, the dock must be made ready to receive the ship which is to be dry-docked, by preparing within it a cradle which will exactly match the configuration of the keel. Then the dock is flooded, the ship brought in, the plug is repositioned and sunk in the entrance by filling it with water. This seals off the basin from the main harbour. Now the dry dock can be pumped clear, the ship settling on to the cradle and being supported as the dock is emptied by suitable methods so that it does not fall over. The entire hull of the ship can now be cleaned and painted, and the cathodic protection renewed. Dry-docking is an annual event for passenger ships, and slightly less frequent for other vessels, but may also take place at other times for the inspection of damage. It does not take too long, and other refit work can be carried out at a wet berth to free the dry dock for other vessels.

5.7.13 Bunkering services

Today, bunkering is largely a matter of taking on oil. This is easily supplied by pipeline from shore-based pumps or from small tanker craft specially built for the purpose and can often be taken aboard while the cargo is being turned round. A chain of bunkering facilities around the world has made the task of refuelling a simple process, compared with the time-consuming, dirty business of refuelling with coal at special berths, which often entailed loading by basket.

Bunker prices vary considerably from port to port with a differential of some 3:1 between the dearest and the cheapest. Ports like Rotterdam with its enormous refinery capacity are able to offer cheap supplies, but additional bunkering at a cheap port is offset by lower cargo capacity and vessels have to strike a balance.

5.7.14 Cargo-handling facilities and services

Today, the vast majority of non-bulk cargo movements are containerised, and the day of the general cargo vessel has largely passed, although some general cargo movements will no doubt always be met in less sophisticated areas of the world. Conventional general cargo vessels carried heterogeneous cargo, manually stowed in the holds and loaded by traditional cranes or ship's derricks. Today, containerised cargo carried in unit loads has largely replaced conventional cargo, and a totally different procedure is followed for turning vessels round. It is therefore appropriate to deal with current practices first, leaving general cargo to be considered later.

5.7.14.1 *Container berths*

Vessels using purpose-built container berths will vary in size from those operating short-sea feeder services and carrying 30–40 containers, to large ocean-going cellular container ships capable of carrying up to 4,000 containers, including a large number of refrigerated containers. Where a berth is reserved solely for short-sea container services it is likely to be a multi-user berth, i.e. used by several shipping companies, operating high-frequency services. In consequence there may well be around 4,000 containers on the berth at any one time, either awaiting shipment or having been discharged, awaiting clearance and delivery. At deep-sea berths accommodation for 5,000–6,000 containers may be necessary. The following facilities are essential to the successful operation of a purpose-built container berth:

1. *Space*. A large area must be available to accommodate the large numbers of containers that will be present on the berth at any one time. A minimum of 15 acres (6 ha) was frequently quoted, but many port operators feel that with increasing numbers of larger vessels coming into service, 20 acres (8 ha) would be a more realistic figure.
2. *The stacking area*. This must be capable of supporting heavy vehicles, and containers stacked three high. Only 20 ft containers can be stacked three high; 40 ft containers can be stacked two high only because of the nature of the straddle carrier. If containers are to be stacked higher than this – which may be necessary in certain locations where space is at a premium – then a wind shelter with overhead gantry cranes is used. Empty containers may be block-stacked much higher, using tower cranes.
3. *Container cranes*. In the initial stages of trans-ocean container traffic many existing berths succeeded in handling container vessels through adaptation, utilising heavy lift cranes. As the volume of traffic increased this temporary measure proved inadequate and purpose-built berths and container cranes became essential. These special cranes must have gantries which can be raised to avoid collision with the ship's superstructure on arrival and departure. They must be self-propelled along their own tracks to permit correct positioning in relation to the cells or 'slots' on board ship. Single-lift cranes must have a lifting capacity of 30 tonnes (the maximum loaded weight of a 40 ft (12 m) container) and must have a fast working rate capable of sustaining a discharging/loading cycle of approximately 3 minutes. Twin-lift cranes will have a correspondingly higher lifting capacity.
4. *Handling equipment*. We must remember that unlike the days of conventional cargo, when ships were unloaded completely and the holds swept, container vessels are discharged and reloaded simultaneously. If a discharging/loading cycle of 3 minutes is to be maintained, it means that as a container is landed on shore, another must be in position to be picked up

(a)

(b)

Fig. 5.8 (a) View of Tilbury Docks showing container operations in progress (courtesy of the Port of Tilbury Ltd). (b) Aerial view of the Port of Felixstowe (courtesy of Felixstowe Dock & Railway Co.)

and loaded on board. Before the next container is landed the previous one must be taken away for stacking, and another for loading placed in position. This sequence of operations requires several shore-based vehicles to serve each container crane. These container handling vehicles may be straddle carriers, heavy-duty forklift trucks or other vehicles specially designed for rapid container handling.

5. *Container terminal control.* High-volume throughputs at container

terminals call for sophisticated systems of operation and control. There are many organisations around the world wrestling with these problems and developing systems which can handle them. Ideally, what is needed is a unified, world-wide system, or at least mutual compatibility of all the systems developed. Much has already been done to achieve this, and more will be said about this later (see page 203). Here we are describing the grass-roots problems of ports in receiving containers for export, unloading ships with incoming containers and loading them with export containers and then, after the ship's departure, sending the imported containers to their hinterland destinations. To show what happens in the modern situation we have been allowed to describe the procedures used by one of the leading companies in the field, Community Network Services Ltd (4 Brunel Way, Fareham, Hampshire, PO15 5TX). They provide the control and information system for Southampton Container Terminals Ltd, and are leading suppliers of direct trader input (DTI) systems in the United Kingdom. Over 1,000 users process more than 2.5 million customs entries a year via the CNS mainframe computer.

As far as the container terminal is concerned it is only interested in the unit (i.e. the container) itself, and not the contents of the container. There are two exceptions to this – hazardous cargoes and refrigerated cargoes. The terminal is interested in the contents of such containers because of the special arrangements that must be made. The terminal is responsible for the container from the time of its arrival by road, rail or ship to the moment of departure by ship, road or rail. To keep track of a unit during this time, extensive use is made of computer facilities, which operate 24 hours a day, 7 days a week. The CNS Ltd system is a real-time monitoring system. This means that it can be accessed at any time and knows where everything is at any given moment. The system can be accessed by anyone authorised and can provide information for all aspects of the terminal operation, including all the basic container data and even such matters as the stability calculations for vessels being loaded and unloaded. The main features are as follows:

- Initial input, which may be manual or by electronic data transfer, consists of information about each container which is stored until an export container physically arrives, either by road or rail.
- A model of the road vehicle or train with its associated containers is built up within the system.
- The route of the vehicle through the terminal is controlled by the system and instructions are produced for the working of its associated containers.
- In the case of trains, the flow of containers to and from the rail terminal is controlled by the system, to meet the train schedules.
- Containers entering the terminal are categorised automatically by the

system according to voyage, port, weight, size, etc., and a directive given for the placement of each container.

- In this manner a stack of containers is built up awaiting the ship.
- The ship planners consult this stack model and adjust it as ship arrival time approaches.
- A model of each ship is held within the system and the ship planner is responsible for transferring containers from the stack model to the ship model within the rules of ship loading and stability.
- After ship planning, the paperwork necessary for controlling the flow of containers on to the ship can be produced by the system.
- In the control room, the containers are moved on to the ship using a split VDU screen with the appropriate section of the ship on the upper half, together with the stack of containers on the lower half.
- After loading has been completed and the ship's tanks have been added to the model, the complete ship stability is calculated by the system.
- Finally, after the ship's departure, a list of the containers loaded by each region of each shipping line is produced. Some lines require this in printed format, but some find it more convenient to have a directly produced telex tape linked to a telex computer and, hence, the telex network.
- For import vessels a complete discharge profile is held in the computer.
- The containers are stacked by use of split VDU screen facilities showing the section of the ship to be discharged and available stacking space.
- On collection, the import containers are located in the stack and allocated to the appropriate vehicle.
- Various statistical printouts for shifts, days, weeks or voyages are produced by the computer.
- Charges associated with the movement of containers, including demurrage charges, are produced by the computer.
- Projections of forward utilisation are made to assist with management planning.

6. *Refrigeration equipment*. Where refrigerated containers are handled, facilities must be provided to maintain the refrigeration process on shore. These facilities may consist of points where containers can be plugged into an electrical supply, or when cold air is used for refrigeration the containers must be connected to a shore-based system similar to that used on board ship.

7. *Office accommodation*. This should be located at the rear of the berth to permit a clear working area as large as possible. Facilities for vehicle maintenance and container repair, if these are provided at the berth, should also be located at the rear. Consolidation depots, for the 'stuffing and unstuffing' of containers should not be located on the berth at all, but

some distance away to remove possible congestion. Where this is not possible, these facilities should be kept at the rear of the berth.

5.7.15 Timber berths

Most people will have heard or seen something of the revolution in transport which has been brought about by containerisation because of the wide publicity it has received and from the large numbers of containers moving on the roads. They are perhaps not so likely to be as aware of the revolution which has taken place in the transport of timber, although it is no less important to those involved. The packaging of timber, another form of unitisation, is what this revolution is all about.

Packaged timber consists of timber made up into sets of 'bundles', each containing pieces of the same length, breadth and thickness, weighing 2–4 tonnes, held together by wires or steel bands and remaining in that from throughout the journey.

To appreciate what difference this simple concept has made, we should first look at a berth for handling timber in the conventional or traditional form.

5.7.15.1 Traditional timber berth

When timber is shipped in the traditional manner, i.e. non-packaged, its discharge is a slow, time-consuming, labour-intensive process. This is because the stowage in the ship consists of layer after layer of random lengths in the holds, and often a considerable amount carried as deck cargo. Many of the vessels engaged in this trade are quite small, carrying only a few hundred tonnes. To discharge their cargo each piece must be picked up separately until the 'deal porter' has sufficient to carry ashore over plank runways. As discharge proceeds and the level of the timber gets lower in the holds, runways are no longer possible and the pieces must be bundled into sets and discharged by crane. Once ashore the timber must be sorted and carefully stacked in large, open-sided sheds. Where timber is to remain in the storage sheds for any length of time, the stack must be 'sticked', i.e. thin pieces of timber inserted between each layer, at right-angles to the length of the boards, to ensure proper ventilation. It may take over a week to discharge just a few hundred tonnes in this manner, whereas at a packaged timber berth rates of discharge between 3,000 and 4,000 tonnes per day are not unusual.

5.7.15.2 Packaged timber berth

Packaged timber vessels tend to be much larger than traditional timber ships, often exceeding 40,000 NRT (net registered tonnage) in size, and both vessels and cargo require different facilities from those required by their smaller counterparts.

1. Because of their size the vessels can only be handled at berths with deep water and if these are in enclosed docks, large entrance locks are necessary.

2. To accommodate very large cargoes, extensive stacking grounds must be provided.

3. To maintain a fast rate of discharge, and therefore a quick turn-round, this must not be linked too closely with the shore operations of sorting and stacking. It is customary to provide a very large quay apron which acts as a 'surge' area. This enables the vessel to maintain a fast rate of discharge, even when there is a temporary slowing down of shore operations, e.g. when handling vehicles are diverted to load road vehicles.

4. An ample supply of mechanical handling equipment must be available, e.g. forklifts, side-loaders and straddle carriers, to ensure that removal to the stacking ground can keep pace with the ship's discharge and, when necessary, load road vehicles simultaneously. Because of the extent of the parking area, and high stacks making vehicle location and control difficult, vehicles are frequently fitted with VHF radios to make communication easier.

5. Cranes. The method of discharge varies: sometimes quay cranes are used, but most bulk timber ships are fitted with their own discharging equipment. Where forestry products other than timber are also carried the cranes are frequently gantry type with interchangeable lifting gear for handling packaged timber, bales of pulp and reels of paper. Where vessels commonly using the berth are equipped with self-discharging gear, quay cranes are often dispensed with so as to leave the quay apron as clear as possible.

6. Where other forestry products, such as liner board, pulp, newsprint and plywood, are regularly carried temporary storage accommodation must be provided to protect them from the weather. Special handling equipment should be provided: for example, large pallets designed for use with straddle carriers enabling several bales or reels to be carried at one time, and squeeze clamps for fitting to forklifts for easier handling of reels and bales when stacking or loading.

5.7.16 Grain berths (usually called grain terminals)

Since the Second World War the pattern of grain imports to this country has undergone a rapid change. Where before the bulk of grain shipments arrived in parcels of 1,000 tonnes or so in general cargo vessels, with occasional shipments by relatively small bulk grain carriers, the pattern has reversed and the bulk grain carriers have increased in size. This increase in size, though small compared with the growth in size of oil tankers because of the much smaller total demand for grain, is nevertheless very considerable in its own particular sphere. The average size of bulk grain carriers is now 25,000 tonnes with the larger vessels around 60,000 tonnes. Facilities which a few years ago were adequate to deal with the generality of ships and their cargoes are no longer able to cope with the large modern vessels. Floating grain elevators, capable of discharging at a rate of a few hundred tonnes per hour, will not suffice when discharge rates approaching 20,000 tonnes a day are required, and grain silos capable of holding 20,000–30,000 tonnes are of little use when one ship after another follows in quick succession, each carrying cargoes in excess of 20,000 tonnes. As a result we have seen those ports which are able to accommodate the much larger, deeper draughted vessels and are willing to provide larger and faster-working shore facilities, capture the major part of the grain trade. The remaining ports are left with the smaller vessels and cargoes trans-shipped to them.

The most modern terminals incorporate the following features:

1. *The berth*: capable of accommodating vessels of 60,000 tonnes, with provision made for even larger vessels in the years to come.
2. *Elevators*: multiple-bucket elevators, each capable of discharging rates of 750–1,000 tonnes per hour, with supplementary pneumatic elevators for clearing the holds when there is insufficient grain remaining to feed the bucket elevators.
3. *Storage silos*: capable of holding 100,000 tonnes or more, with automatic equipment for weighing and delivery to bulk rail and road vehicles.
4. *Associated mills*: to reduce transport costs, millers are keen to locate new facilities alongside grain terminals, so that their mills can be fed directly by conveyors. Sufficient space must be available for a number of such mills.
5. *Trans-shipment*: all grain received will not pass directly to associated mills or to rail and road vehicles for inland carriage. Most mills throughout the country are located on waterways, some on major rivers, but many smaller mills are on quite small rivers where they were once fed by sailing vessels and now receive their supplies from small coasters and short-sea traders. A major grain terminal must therefore provide facilities for trans-shipment to these smaller mills. This can best be secured by arranging for the large bulk carrier and other smaller vessels to berth on opposite sides of a deep-water jetty (see Fig. 6.4, page 130).

There are many more examples of specialised berths which may be found at major ports and brief descriptions follow of a few of the more common ones. For more detailed descriptions, the student is advised to consult books and publications dealing solely with ports and port operations.

5.7.17 Oil terminals

Oil terminals frequently have long jetties extending into deep water to accommodate deep-draughted vessels with the minimum of dredging. At loading terminals pumping equipment at the tank farm must be capable of a very rapid rate of loading to ensure a fast turn-round for the vessel. Whether or not a receiving terminal is directly associated with a refinery, an extensive tank storage farm will be necessary to act as a holding facility until the very large cargo can be absorbed by the refinery or inland receivers.

5.7.18 Roll-on roll-off berths

These are equipped with loading and discharging ramps and require extensive vehicle parking areas for lorries and trailers awaiting shipment or awaiting collection after unloading. If vessels also carry containers and pallets, the berth will require heavy-duty platform trucks and forklift trucks for loading and discharge, and for handling loads in the stacking area (see Fig. 5.9(b)).

5.7.19 Side-loading berths

Side-loading vessels have ports or doors let into their sides instead of the more conventional hatch openings in the deck. Quay cranes are unsuitable for working this type of vessel and should be dispensed with, the quay apron being kept as uncluttered as possible. This will allow freedom of operation for the forklift trucks, which are used to pass cargo to and from the ship through the side ports. Electric trucks are most suitable for operation on board ship as they do not give off fumes, which would be undesirable in the closed space of a ship's hold. Recharging stations must be provided for the forklift trucks, whose batteries must be recharged after every shift (see Fig. 5.9(a)).

5.7.20 Fruit and meat berths

A feature of both meat and fruit traffic is the necessity to remove large quantities of cargo from the berth in a relatively short space of time. In most cases this will involve large numbers of road vehicles awaiting their turn to load. Provision must be made for several vehicles to be loaded simultaneously. To avoid congestion in the working area, lorry parks should be provided from which vehicles can be called forward in batches as required. Various forms of automatic discharging equipment may be installed to speed up the process of discharge and to simplify sorting. Where meat is concerned, cold store facilities must be available in the vicinity of the berth, or at not too great a distance from the port.

5.7.21 Bulk wine berths

Wine was traditionally shipped in barrels or in bottles. The increased demand in recent years, particularly for the lower-priced table wines, has led to the introduction of bulk shipment in tanks. The wine is pumped ashore for storage in glass-lined or glassfibre tanks. It is not necessary for the tanks to be situated on the berth itself but they can be housed in buildings to the rear of the berth, provided that suitable piped connections are installed. This frees the berth itself for the handling of other cargoes.

5.7.22 General or conventional cargo berths

By general cargo we mean cargo of a non-specialised nature, i.e. a heterogeneous collection of bags, bales, boxes, crates, cartons, drums, etc., stowed in the holds of a vessel as individual pieces or packages. Despite the revolution which has taken place in the transporting of goods in specialised ships, a declining part of the world's maritime trade is still carried out by smaller, conventional cargo vessels trading to less sophisticated ports around the world. Conventional methods are more labour-intensive than containerised and bulk cargo handling. The heterogeneous cargo has to be stowed manually in the holds.

The following are the essential requirements of a modern general cargo berth:

1. A plentiful supply of quay cranes. Although most general cargo vessels are equipped with their own cargo derricks, these are generally much slower working than quay cranes, so the latter will usually be preferred in the interest of faster working. The quay cranes will probably be of 5 tonne lifting capacity. A decade or so ago, a 3 tonne capacity was the more general rule, but the average weight of lifts has increased making the higher capacity necessary.

2. A wide quay apron (i.e. the space between the quay edge and the transit shed). The increasing use of mobile mechanical handling equipment has made this necessary to allow plenty of room for manoeuvring, and to avoid vehicles obstructing one another. In some ports rail trucks run along the quay apron, and at the rear of the transit shed. Where quayside tracks

(a)

Fig. 5.9 (a) General cargo berth, side-loading fruit. (b) Roll-on roll-off ship discharging at Felixstowe (courtesy of the Port of London Authority and Felixstowe Dock and Railway Co. respectively)

are still important (for example, where a country has a large railway network with economic long-distance rail haulage) it is important to have at least two sets of tracks with frequent crossovers, to avoid disrupting work along the length of the quay while shunting is in progress.

3. A modern transit shed. This should incorporate the following features:

(a) A roof of cantilever construction so that space inside the shed is unobstructed by supporting pillars.
(b) The roof should be extended at the rear and ends of the shed to give weather protection to vehicle loading and unloading. The canopy should be high enough to permit mobile cranes to operate beneath it.
(c) A strong floor, capable of supporting heavy loads when cargo is piled high.
(d) Loading platforms at lorry tailboard height at the rear and ends of the shed.
(e) Good natural lighting through transparent roof panels, and good artificial lighting both inside and outside the shed to permit safe and speedy working during the hours of darkness.

Fig. 5.9(b)

(f) Good ventilation so that fumes from mobile equipment and other vehicles working in the shed are quickly dispersed.
(g) Wide, high doors to permit easy access by mobile equipment.
(h) Lock-up facilities for bonded, valuable and pilferable cargoes.

4. An adequate supply of mobile equipment, e.g. forklift trucks and mobile cranes for handling palletised cargo and packages too heavy for manual handling. Wherever possible, non-palletised cargo should be made into pallet loads during the 'striking' operation, i.e. unloading goods from road vehicles. If this is done the palletised cargo can be taken into the shed by forklift trucks, stacked several pallet loads high to conserve space, and removed from the shed and lifted on board as complete units. This will minimise the number of individual handling movements, reduce the

amount of labour required, and speed up the whole process. Pallets used in this way will of course have to be returned from the ship to the shore, as stowage in the hold progresses. To ensure the success of this method of working, a plentiful supply of stevedore's pallets must be available.

5. Where a shipping company operates a pallet scheme, i.e. supplying pallets so that cargo can be loaded in palletised form, banding machines must be available for making up pallet loads of cargo received in non-palletised form. Alternatively, shrink-wrapping facilities may be used.

Unless a large number of heavy lifts (i.e. exceeding the capacity of the normal quay cranes) is regularly received at a particular berth, it is neither economical nor desirable from a space and congestion point of view to supply a heavy-lift crane at a general cargo berth. Instead it is better for these to be received at a specially designated heavy-lift berth. One such berth will satisfy the needs of a large number of conventional berths.

5.7.23 Heavy-lift berths

This will be equipped with a heavy-lift crane, possibly the Scotch derrick type, of sufficient capacity to cope with the generality of heavy lifts. Loading and unloading heavy lifts onto and off conventional vessels is usually accomplished by means of the ship's 'Jumbo' or heavy-lift derrick. This takes several hours to rig, and while it is in use other cargo cannot be worked. This means that to avoid continually interrupting the general working of the vessel, all heavy lifts on one vessel must be dealt with during the same period, or at worst in several batches. To make this possible, vehicles carrying heavy lifts must be timed to arrive at specific times during the loading or discharging periods and can be involved in long periods of waiting. Where a heavy-lift berth is used this problem is avoided. Heavy lifts for loading can be brought to the berth at a convenient time, removed from the vehicle and subsequently transferred to the loading berth in barges or on dock trailers at the appropriate time. The reverse process takes place with imported heavy lifts.

It is essential, when using ship's gear to handle heavy lifts, that both the quay and its approaches are capable of bearing the weight. It is also essential that an incoming heavy lift is placed onto some form of low-loader, be it road or rail. Once the vessel departs, the lifting facility departs with it, and a heavy load placed on the ground could not be lifted.

An alternative to the use of ships' derricks is the use of floating cranes provided by the Port Authority. These will invariably be used when very heavy lifts are encountered, the larger among them being capable of lifting weights of several hundred tonnes.

An interesting innovation in recent years has been the introduction of special heavy-lift vessels such as those used by the Central Electricity

Generating Board for the coast-wise transport of very heavy pieces of power station equipment. 'Heavy-lift vessel' is rather a misnomer, as these are a specialised form of roll-on roll-off vessel designed to accommodate road low-loaders complete with loads. Where these are used heavy-duty ramps must be provided.

Many conventional vessels carry a small number of containers, usually stowed on deck or in the square of the hatch. It is usual for them to be handled by ships' derricks directly to or from road vehicles or trailers. Where direct handling is not possible, they may be received and delivered through heavy-lift berths as described above, or at container reception depots, e.g. Freightliner terminals, and moved between berth and terminal by tractor-drawn trailers.

5.8 Pipeline transport

Terminals for pipelines take the form of pumping stations and tank farms. Each tank farm acts as a buffer zone, where cargoes arriving out of phase with the demand can be stored until required. Ships do not observe strict schedules – delays occur for a variety of reasons. Some days no ships will come in, and another day several may arrive together. Refineries miles away may be working at a steady pace. Supplies must be available at times when ships do not arrive and when several ships arrive together there must be tank capacity to unload the ships and turn them round. This is the function of the tank farm.

The pipelines themselves vary in size. From ship-to-shore tank units we have large diameter pipes to unload ships rapidly. On the exit side of the tank farm smaller capacity pipes will distribute the oil in a steady stream to the refinery.

Each pumping station has two or three pumps in series. They are often in the open air, with control instruments housed in buildings near by. A typical unit is shown in Fig. 5.10(b).

An interesting example of a pipeline system incorporating both termini and terminals is the pipeline from the Thames Refinery Complex to the Ellesmere Port Refinery Complex. Not only is there a terminus at each end, with 'both-ways' pumping facilities, but there are a number of spur pipelines off the main line which lead to terminals where distribution facilities and storage tanks permit the marketing of refined products.

Today many refineries are supplied with crude oil via land pipelines from remote oil terminals in deep water ports serving VLCCs and ULCCs (ultra-large crude carriers). For example, Finnart in Loch Long, north of Glasgow, can handle the very largest crude carriers. It is the starting point of an oil pipeline which takes crude oil across Scotland to a refinery at Grangemouth, near Edinburgh.

Fig. 5.10(a)

(b)

Fig. 5.10 (a) Getting ready to pull the pipe-string across the Duddon estuary (courtesy of Jim Harris, British Gas). (b) Pumps at work boosting pressures on the crude oil pipelines at Fahud (courtesy of Shell International Petroleum Co. Ltd)

Many of the original refineries were built in the days when tankers of 15,000 tons were the norm; e.g. Stanlow on the Manchester Ship Canal was formerly served by berths alongside the refinery. Subsequently, a pipeline connection to Tranmere permitted 60,000 tonners to serve the refinery and now a pipeline crosses the Wirral Peninsula and the Dee estuary and runs along the north Wales coast crossing the Menai Straits to Anglesey, where an SBM (single buoy mooring) off Amlwch handles VLCCs.

5.9 Summary

1. The points of access to the way, where goods and passengers can join the vehicles operating on the way, are called terminals. The functions of a terminal are to allow access to vehicles operating on a specialised way; to permit easy interchange between vehicles operating on that way and other modes of transport; and to facilitate consolidation of traffic.
2. People and goods to be transported are referred to as traffic. A specific set of goods for one consignee, sent by one consignor to one destination is called a consignment.
3. The characteristics of passengers are that they are self-loading, self-discharging and able to make their own arrangements to fill in time gaps between journeys – they do not have to be placed in stores or

safeguarded before departure, unlike goods. They require basic facilities such as seating, toilets and refreshment facilities.

4. Goods require storage space, safe custody, consolidation to ensure that they are transported in the correct vehicles to the correct destination, and possibly customs clearance.
5. Terminals should be sited in convenient places for passengers and goods, where adequate traffic is available. Congestion, adverse environmental effects, the price of land, etc. may be considerations when siting a new terminal. The operational requirements are vital to any decision about the siting of terminals.
6. For airports the chief considerations are a large area of flat, well-drained land, away from mountains or large hills, not liable to fog, and not surrounded by concentrated development, but close enough to a major conurbation to generate traffic of all sorts.
7. For ports, the chief considerations are shelter for shipping, deep water, easy access from both sea and land, a large flat area for container stacking, packaged timber stacking, flour mills, etc., a large hinterland generating traffic, good access by road for roll-on roll-off services, ice-free if possible and fog-free most of the year.
8. A free trade zone (FTZ) is a designated port area sealed off from the rest of the country where goods can be landed, sorted, processed and manufactured without having to pay import duties.
9. An efficient passenger terminal requires seating, escalators, walkways, toilet facilities, refreshment services, perhaps Customs Halls and immigration offices, bureaux de change and banks, loudspeaker services, etc.
10. An efficient cargo terminal requires mechanical handling devices, cranes, straddle carriers, plenty of space for stacking containers and other loads such as packaged timber, Customs, and health and security controls. Major forwarding firms will have offices, equipped with modern electronic communication systems and sheds for groupage activities.
11. Container terminals lend themselves to electronic modelling which enables computerised models to be developed of ships, trains and stacking yards. Arrivals and departures can therefore be pre-planned, with containers being off-loaded to designated stacks and on-loaded to vehicles, trains and cargo holds in the optimum sequence for future accessibility, and to maintain the trim of the vessels.

5.10 Questions

1. What is the function of a terminal? How would a main-line railway station fulfil these functions?

2. Explain how a vessel arriving at a major port would be handled by a computerised system in order to be turned round for the next voyage.
3. What are the requirements of a new airport if the site is to be satisfactorily developed?
4. What are the requirements of a good port? Illustrate your answer with references to any major port with which you are acquainted.
5. Explain what is meant by 'the unit load concept'. Refer in your answer to as many methods of making up 'unit loads' as possible.
6. Write short notes (6–8 lines) on each of the following:
   (a) straddle carriers
   (b) the trim of a vessel
   (c) the consolidation of passengers
   (d) heavy-lift berths
   (e) reporting inwards
   (f) the consolidation of goods
7. What are the duties of a lighthouse authority?
8. Compare and contrast the terminals used by (a) heavy goods vehicles; (b) freight trains.

6 The physical components of transport: the unit of carriage

6.1 Introduction

Every mode of transport must have a unit of carriage in which the goods or passengers actually move. This unit of carriage will be designed to suit the particular mode. Thus a supersonic aircraft will be designed to different specifications from an underground railway train, since it must encounter different stresses and strains. While there will be many points of similarity there will be countless points of difference between any two units of carriage reflecting the modified requirements imposed by the way, the motive power, the class of traffic to be carried and even the termini to be used. *The unit of carriage represents the response of transport engineers to the requirements of a particular class of traffic, moving on a particular way, powered by a particular method of propulsion across a particular pattern of interfaces.* Each particular solution to these problems will be a compromise, in which the engineer seeks to achieve the best of all possible worlds, but in fact inevitably falls somewhat short of this ideal.

6.2 Principles in the design of units of carriage

The chief principles the engineer will bear in mind in designing a unit of carriage are:

1. the need to embrace the widest possible market;
2. the requirements of the particular way;
3. the requirements of the traffic concerned;
4. ergonomic aspects;
5. cheapness.

A word or two about each of these aspects is desirable.

6.2.1 The need to embrace the widest possible market

Any unit of carriage has heavy design costs, which must be recouped out of sales. It will therefore most easily recoup the costs if it is able to sell in a wide range of markets to a variety of users. Thus we find the basic design for motor vehicles being used in a variety of models to appeal to different tastes and needs. It will have its basic and cheapest design for general use, its hotted-up version for the enthusiast, its estate version for the salesforce personnel or the family who need plenty of space. The container manufacturer will provide a range of containers covering a wide variety of markets, general cargo containers, top-loading containers, open-sided containers, tank unit containers, etc., all using standard parts to a considerable extent but appealing to different customers in particular details. The principles of simplification and standardisation are applied to the design of units of carriage so as to achieve the maximum number of alternative uses for a particular unit, which thus sells in a wide variety of markets.

6.2.2 The requirements of the particular way

The character of the way has a very great impact on the unit of carriage. A few examples will illustrate this point. Aircraft operate in a way, the atmosphere, which is unable to support them except when they are in motion. The aircraft cannot pull up and stop along the way, except for very specialised machines, e.g. helicopters and jump-jets, which can hover. Even then the pilot cannot step out to service the machine. Aircraft must therefore be perfectly manufactured, almost flawless in the excellence of their craftsmanship and meticulously maintained.

Unfortunately, in recent times there has been a growth of counterfeit spares of all types, which jeopardises the safety of aircraft. This is the result of a lack of regulation of the various agencies supplying aircraft spares, so that an essential washer, for instance, may be replaced by one of much poorer specification.

Throughout this chapter we shall see that the way imposes strict limitations on the size, shape and speed of the units of carriage which use it.

6.2.2.1 Air

Aircraft designers are forced by the constraints of the way into concentrating on either carrying capacity or speed. They cannot seek big improvements in both, simultaneously, without major increases in the size of power units. To do so would necessitate disproportionate increases in fuel consumption and render the aircraft uneconomic to operate. (This constraint does not necessarily apply to military aircraft, for which economic operation is not a prime consideration.)

To increase the carrying capacity of an aircraft not only must the size of the body be increased, but the surface area of the wings must be increased to create additional lifting capacity in proportion to the extra weight to be carried. To utilise the extra lifting capacity of the wings, more powerful engines are required to generate the forward speed necessary to create lift-off and sustain that speed as the aircraft climbs to operational height. More powerful engines will consume more fuel. The extra fuel will have to be carried and this means added weight. The extra weight will mean that greater lifting capacity will be needed, which will mean . . ., etc. Somewhere the designer must strike a balance. If the aircraft is to operate over relatively short distances it will require less fuel to reach its destination, and the saving in weight of fuel will permit more passengers or cargo to be carried. If the same aircraft is to operate over much longer distances, then passenger and cargo weight must be sacrificed to allow a greater weight of fuel to be carried on board.

To achieve faster forward speeds, the aircraft designer must produce a shape that offers the least resistance to forward movement, i.e. to minimise drag, and to incorporate more powerful motive units to thrust the aircraft along. The most suitable shape is a pointed, pencil-like fuselage, with minimal wings, for although large wings may be needed to enable it to leave the ground, once it has reached operational flight it no longer requires the same wing area to sustain it in forward flight. The so-called variable-geometry machines, by changing the shape of the aircraft, seek to improve the engineer's command over lift–drag problems which affect its operation. Pressurised bodies enable passenger and crew to breathe air at normal pressures and thus allow aircraft to fly in the stratosphere where there is less drag, and they can take advantage of jet-streams.

6.2.2.2 Sea

The problem of space versus speed also faces marine designers, though perhaps not to the same extent as it affects aircraft designers. Although the vessel relies on the water for support, and compared with land-carriage is relatively free from friction, as speeds increase bow waves build up and drag along the sides of the vessel, reducing its forward speed. This has been remedied by the use of the bulbous bow which projects in front of the vessel and throws the bow wave clear of the sides, thereby reducing drag. By constructing more and more powerful engines speeds could be considerably increased, but the cost of the extra fuel consumption involved in overcoming the increased water resistance encountered at higher speeds would far outweigh the benefits to be obtained from faster transit times.

Thanks to the buoyancy of water, no problems like those associated with 'lift' in aircraft arise, and enormous vessels can be constructed. However, the designer is still limited as far as size is concerned by the constraints of the way. Because the oceans, seas and rivers of the world are not of uniform depth he must take into account the depths available in those areas in which the vessel will operate, and the availability of terminals able to accommodate it.

Paradoxically, the problem of friction which must be overcome if economic speeds are to be achieved works in reverse as far as large vessels are concerned. The absence of friction which enables very large weights to be moved by water, with relatively small units of propulsion, creates problems when very large vessels seek to come to a halt. Sudden stops are impossible and the vessel must be slowed down gradually, and finally halted with the assistance of tugs. This lack of braking ability means that even in the open ocean large vessels may find themselves on a collision course while they are still half a mile apart.

6.2.2.3 *Road*

Roads are narrow ways, often carrying heavy flows of traffic which are not separated according to grade or speed of vehicles, and are often flowing in conflicting directions. They are also used by animals and pedestrians, except for motorway-type roads, and particularly in urban areas are often hemmed in by buildings, many of which were constructed decades or even centuries before road traffic developed to its present weight and intensity. Roads frequently pass under or over bridges which impose limitations as to the height and weight of vehicles. All these factors, some concerning the character of the way itself, others derived from the method of use, have resulted in limitations being placed on the size and speed of the units of carriage. These limitations, though arising initially from the character of the way, have been given the force of law through parliamentary and ministerial enactments. The designer must therefore operate within strict size and weight limits and very detailed regulations concerning construction, while the operator must observe speed limits and restrictions on use.

6.2.2.4 *Rail*

Railways are artificially constructed private ways, usually under the sole control of the undertaking. Despite this, they impose limitations on the vehicle designer. Like roads, they frequently pass over or under bridges, or through tunnels, which impose limitations on the height, width and weight of vehicles. Most railways were constructed in the latter part of the nineteenth century or the early part of the twentieth century, and the dimensions established at that time largely determine the dimensions of present-day rolling stock. Vehicles cannot be made wider because of vehicles on adjoining tracks, and their length is governed by the severity of the curves which they must negotiate. Similarly, their speeds are governed by the extent to which curves are present in any particular section of track and whether or not it has been designed and maintained for high-speed running.

6.2.3 The requirements of the traffic

While for marketing reasons the unit of carriage seeks to be as versatile as possible, it will often fail to capture a particular traffic unless it caters specifically for it. Specificity within a versatile general framework is what is aimed at. Thus a road tanker manufacturer might – from a standard design – offer specific vehicles for milk, petroleum products, corrosive liquids and bulk powders. The linings of tanks, internal construction and pumping mechanisms might vary, but a standard unit of carriage underlies all the types offered. Nowhere is the specific nature of vehicles more evident than in the problem of the 'empty leg' journey. For example, milk moves in tankers from the agricultural areas to big cities all over the advanced world. Yet what use is the vehicle on the return journey to the countryside? Clearly its specific nature renders the return journey an 'empty leg'. It cannot be filled with fertiliser for the farms, or with furniture for rural households. At least one big firm has found a useful solution to the problem of the 'empty leg' in the container-sized plastic bag. A huge plastic bag the same shape as a container is filled with fruit concentrate and transported in a container. On arrival it is pumped clear, cleaned and sterilised, and returned rolled up for re-use. The non-specific container sets off on its next, unrelated journey; the plastic bag returns at a very economic rate.

Other firms which have tried this solution have found that the cleansing and return of the plastic container is inconvenient and unsatisfactory for their purposes and have discarded the idea in favour of stainless steel-lined tanks. Using various solvents, detergents and high-pressure steam they can be thoroughly cleaned in a very short space of time. If the method is to be employed successfully, cleaning facilities must be available at a very large number of centres to avoid excessive empty mileage to and from cleaning stations. By arranging for reciprocal use of each other's facilities, a number of road haulage undertakings have established a chain of these centres throughout the country. It is now possible for a load such as lubricating oil to be carried on the outward journey and, after cleansing, for the vehicle to return loaded with bulk wine.

Such happy solutions to the 'empty leg' problem are rare and only possible if a suitable return load is available. Generally speaking, you must have a specific vehicle for a particular class of traffic and if you do not, you will not capture the market. 'Facilities create traffic' is an old rule in transport, and the unit of carriage catering specifically for a particular traffic will not only capture the existing market but divert traffic away from other less efficient units to increase its share of the market to the general benefit of the economy.

6.2.4 Ergonomic aspects

Ergonomics is the study of work and the way it is performed. It gives cost-saving benefits in the design, layout, maintenance and operation of units of carriage. For example, many units of carriage require someone to work in the unit of carriage, or in and out of the unit of carriage. Thus air stewards must perform their duties in the aircraft, moving up and down the gangway or gangways, with trays of food, liquid refreshments, etc. A baker's driver not only drives the unit of carriage but climbs in and out of it countless times a day.

A study of the work done by these employees of the transport and distribution industry will enable many useful features to be incorporated in the design of the unit of carriage. Access points can be varied to reduce strain. The delivery van which has direct access from the driver's cab to the unit of carriage enables the driver who has stopped the vehicle to leave the driver's seat and enter the unit of carriage to collect the order for delivery. Previously the driver had to get out, go round the back and get in again.

With units of carriage ergonomic aspects include two related studies. The maintenance of units of carriage in good order and condition is an enduring requirement. The accessibility of vital points to the maintenance engineer will be an important preoccupation for design teams. They will need to know how mechanics work to ensure that their activities are performed as quickly and effortlessly as possible. The other aspect is that the total operation of the unit of carriage must be socially and environmentally acceptable. The operation of units of carriage is an extension perhaps of ordinary work study, yet it may impose on the design staff requirements which modify the unit's size, speed and efficiency, in the interests of ensuring a wide sale unrestricted by official or public disapproval.

The provision of on-vehicle devices to assist the working of staff is a major development in recent years. Such devices as 'on-vehicle' cranes which can be operated by drivers to load and unload their vehicles are an immense advantage, since lifting devices are not always available at points where collections have to be made or deliveries unloaded. The frustration of waiting for a crane to arrive can be entirely avoided, and many a driver has earned a welcome tip by lifting a load of bricks to the precise point on a scaffolding where they were required. Similarly, tail lifts can ease the work of unloading heavy items such as furniture, DIY materials and palletised goods of every sort.

6.2.5 Cheapness

Henry Ford once defended his system of mass production with the following definition: 'Mass production is not buying cheap and selling dear. It is the focusing upon a manufacturing project of the principles of power, accuracy, economy, system, continuity, speed and repetition.' It is an enduring definition. Units of carriage lend themselves particularly to mass production for they are required in large numbers, by people who are not rich and therefore need a cheap unit. Even the most advanced technological units, like the airframes and engines of supersonic aircraft, are best produced in this way, for perfect components can only be made by people who repeat a small range of activities and thus acquire skill by repetition. Perhaps where aircraft are concerned it could best be called 'repeat production', since the techniques of the mass production-line are not quite applicable.

Had Ford been asked to give a full definition of the entire physical distribution process he would have included in his analysis two further sections. Before mass production can begin, design teams must prepare plans for the unit of carriage which embody the principles outlined in this chapter. The design of units of carriage requires us to focus attention on the needs of society, so that units are produced which are fit for the purpose of many potential customers; appropriate to the way on which they must travel and for the traffic they must bear; convenient to work with; easy to maintain and cheap to buy. After mass production has taken place according to the principles given in Ford's definition, the units of carriage must be cheap to operate, to service and to renew as and when required, they must conform with the law, and be socially and environmentally acceptable. If the result of all these activities is in the end the cheapest possible product to perform that particular class of carriage, the capital employed in its production will not have been wasted but will yield a satisfactory return based upon repeated orders from contented customers.

6.3 The unit of carriage and the unit of propulsion

Sometimes the unit of carriage embodies the unit of propulsion and with other systems they are separate. In so far as they form a single unit the flexibility of the system is reduced. The engine of the family motor car propels that unit of carriage only, and is of no use unless that unit of carriage is required. A tractor unit of an articulated vehicle is free from this inflexibility. When a trailer has to wait for some reason, such as customs inspection or the availability of space on a ship, the tractor unit can be uncoupled and proceed to other trailers.

A second point is that the tare of a unit of carriage (its unladen weight) relative to the payload is a vital point in the economy of operations. If the unit of propulsion is embodied in the unit of carriage it must be designed to reduce the fraction of tare weight to total weight, if operation is to be economic. A heavy tractor unit will represent a less serious problem, since its weight will pull many units of carriage and be proportionately less important in the tare weight to total weight fraction.

6.4 Units of carriage by road

6.4.1 Passenger units

Today the tram and trolleybus have largely disappeared from our roads, and the typical unit of carriage is the private motor vehicle. The 1992 figures for licences current show that there were 19,737,400 motor cars on the roads of Great Britain against 109,100 buses and coaches. Small wonder that those who use them complain that buses are few and far between. We have become a property-owning democracy, and the outward symbol of property is the motor car. It is in many ways an inefficient means of transport, with the propulsion unit embodied in the unit of carriage and unutilised when the unit of carriage is not required. It is an expensive user of space – both road space and parking space – but all such costs count as little compared with the convenience of personalised transport.

The bus is the general workhorse of public passenger transport, in the short-haul field. They may be single-decker or double-decker units of carriage, and of impressive length and size. They may offer seating to the majority of passengers, or seating to those travelling some distance, while the short-distance traveller crowds into a standing area. They may be operated by a driver and conductor, or by a single operator. Many single-operator buses have mechanical slot machines for payment on entry. In country areas where driver/conductor operation is prohibitively expensive, buses are either single-operated single deckers or mini-buses. The latter have between twelve and sixteen seats, and operate on routes where traffic is light. The development of post buses by the Post Office is an interesting use of its new powers, and of the grants available for this type of service. Briefly, the service implies the use of a postal vehicle to carry passengers on a once-daily trip to the local town and back. Usually a mid-morning bulk delivery of mail to outlying villages drops off mail on its outward run and on the return journey picks up passengers wishing to spend a day in town. The return journey for the passenger is in late afternoon, and is followed by the use of the bus to collect bulk mail from the outlying villages for sorting and onward transmission in the evening.

Coach services tend to be limited-stop services which operate on long-haul routes. The vehicles provide a greater degree of comfort and frequently require pre-booking of seats. Their wide use for tours in areas of scenic beauty has led to the provision of luxury coaches with wide-view windows, storage for hand luggage and capacious luggage compartments. Their ability to use motorways on the long-haul routes has made them an express form of transport competitive in price with railway travel, and very short journey times are possible with adequate facilities available for passenger comfort at motorway service centres. The unit of carriage embodies comfortable seating, ventilation facilities, toilet facilities, adjustable shades and personal lighting points for night travel.

6.4.2 Goods units

The responses of design engineers to the needs of road hauliers are legion, and no short paragraph can adequately describe the infinite variety of size, shape and facility made available. Certain broad classes, however, must be referred to here. The two basic groups are the *rigids* and the *articulated vehicles*. A rigid embodies the propulsion unit and the unit of carriage in a single vehicle, and is therefore less versatile than the articulated vehicle which has a separate motor unit (the tractor) which can be linked in a few minutes to the trailer or semi-trailer. This means, of course, that the trailer may be left at the loading bank or Customs depot pending loading or inspection, while the tractor is used elsewhere. A very important economy which can be achieved is the saving in driver's time, which becomes increasingly important as the 'permitted driving time' is reduced. The extension of the swap-body arrangement has increased the use of these vehicles, which can be used successively to load three or four bodies at a central dispatch point, take them to a regional transit point, demount them and pick up yesterday's empty bodies to return to the dispatch centre. The individual bodies are now picked up by local tractor units and taken off to do the deliveries. The local depot is eliminated, goods being supplied from the central dispatch point. The regional transit point only needs to be a piece of hard standing (concrete or tarmac parking space) large enough to carry out the switch. By arrangement with a suitable firm this exchange could simply take place at a nominal daily charge at the depot of some existing carrier; or reciprocal arrangements could be made.

The articulated vehicle is also very manoeuvrable, able to turn in a relatively small circle for a long vehicle. Rigids can only be made manoeuvrable if the body is short, with consequent increases in height for a given weight. This poses stability problems.

Within these general classes there are many sub-classes, of which the following are important:

1. *Covered vans*. These range from light vans and delivery vehicles up to pantechnicons for removals and bulk deliveries of furniture and equipment.
2. *Open trucks*. These have sides and tailboards, but are not covered in. They may be used for goods which do not spoil in wet weather.
3. *Tippers*. These are usually very large open trucks, used for carrying bulk deliveries of non-spoiling commodities such as aggregates, ores, etc., which can be easily discharged by tipping.
4. *Platform vehicles or 'flats'*. These have no sides or tailboard, and are used for containers or packaged timber, or crates and boxes stacked on the platform and restrained by ropes, chains and/or tarpaulins.
5. *Tankers*. These are usually of large size, with capacities up to about 5,000–6,000 gallons (22,000–27,000 litres) for the carriage of petroleum products, corrosive and other liquids, bulk powders like sugar and flour, or pellets and grains (see Fig. 6.1(a)).
6. *Hopper vehicles*. These are used for carrying bulk grains, cement and similar products (see Fig. 6.1(b)).

There are many more, and a particular feature of many of them these days is their independence of facilities at either end of the transit, since they are equipped with cranes, tail lifts, cylinder lifts and similar devices to assist loading and unloading (Fig. 6.2).

6.5 Units of carriage by rail

6.5.1 Passenger units

Railway journeys are of three types: long-distance, suburban and 'in-town' services. Railway carriages reflect the differing needs of these three types of journey. Long-distance journeys require comfortable carriages, insulated from outside atmospheric conditions at the limited number of stopping places. The number of access doors can be few, usually at the ends of the carriage and in the centre, so that passengers who are alighting or embarking do so with the minimum of discomfort to through passengers. Access to toilets and to restaurant cars requires a corridor train, and flexible connections between carriages from one end of the train to the other. In Pullman carriages tables are provided for the convenience of passengers, and luggage stowage is possible between seats or above the

(a)

(b)

Fig. 6.1 (a) Bulk sugar tipper. (b) Ready-mixed concrete vehicles building a 'continuous pour' silo (courtesy of Carmichael & Sons (Worcester) Ltd and Ready Mixed Concrete Co. Ltd, respectively)

backs of seats. Couchette-type seating is sometimes provided on long-distance trains, while sleeping cars for overnight journeys are also used.

Fig. 6.2 The HIAB lorry loader in operation (courtesy of George Cohen 600 Group Ltd)

Suburban services require more frequent stopping-places and consequently a greater need to disgorge passengers rapidly. This requires a door to every bank of seats, rather than at the ends of coaches only. Since toilet accommodation is less necessary the corridor can be dispensed with, and a multi-compartment carriage each with its own access doors be used instead. The standing room available is less convenient than in a corridor train, but rapid access and egress and the extra seating available compensate for this.

Many railway lines, particularly underground railways, have frequent stops very short distances apart. The time spent in stations must be reduced as much as possible, and so a large number of wide doors must be provided. To avoid harm to passengers in very crowded circumstances doors do not open inwards or outwards but slide into the hollow walls of the carriages. Operated electrically, they give rapid ingress and egress, and as a safety measure may be over-ridden in an emergency.

Today computer-controlled train systems of short units of carriage operating at very frequent intervals are beginning to be used. The most famous recent addition to this is the BART (Bay Area Rapid Transit) system in San Francisco, which is reducing very considerably the road commuter problems in that area. The computers send the fleet of carriage units round the circuit at intervals of 90 seconds. They anticipate peak loads, and adjust speeds to compensate for any delay caused at stations and to bring the carriages back on schedule. The multiple-journey tickets issued at electronic booths permit travel to the value of the money paid, the ticket being reduced in value on each trip. The journey across the bay has been cut to 9 minutes compared with the 40 minutes it takes by road, due to congestion at the road bridges.

6.5.2 Goods units

A full description of rail units of carriage for bulk transport is given in Chapter 13. The vast majority of goods rail traffic is now bulk haulage, which is most logically and effectively carried in company trains or on the Freightliner networks. Some general cargo travels on passenger trains, and a good many 'express' packages travel in this way. In former times most wagons on goods trains did not have separate braking systems, and hence the speed of trains had to be kept low. Today, most freight trains have pneumatic brake systems similar to passenger trains and this makes express freight services much more common. This is certainly the case with Freightliner services and company trains, and when really long-distance freighting becomes possible once Eurotunnel opens express freight services – with guaranteed movements of 185 miles (300 km) per day and often much more – should offer an excellent service to customers.

6.6 Units of carriage by sea

Ships are large, costly units of carriage, much less susceptible to standardisation than road and rail units. They tend to be built to a particular specification, and although there are economies to be achieved by producing sister ships of largely similar layout, few firms are large enough to order an entire fleet at one time, and the need to sell similar models to different owners results in their modification in major or minor ways to suit a particular need. Even apparently similar sister ships in the same fleet tend to differ in minor ways.

Ocean-going ships, as their name implies, sail the major ocean routes. They carry a wide variety of products on the long-haul routes. The short-sea trade routes by contrast are concerned with inter-European movements across the North Sea, the English Channel and Irish Channel and the North African and Near East traffics across the Mediterranean. Many of the units used on these short sea routes are roll-on roll-off vessels, though the roll-on roll-off type of operation has now also been proved to be economic with trans-Atlantic vessels.

Every ship, like any other unit of carriage, represents a response on the part of the ship-building industry to the needs of world trade. The last quarter of a century has been a very fertile period, with an immense variety of solutions to particular problems resulting in a very broad range of vessels being produced. These include a large variety of conventional-hull ships, hydrofoils and hovercraft. Some of these are referred to elsewhere in this book, and reference here is for the purpose of establishing a list giving brief descriptions of the more common types. The list includes:

- General cargo ships.
- Cellular container ships.
- Roll-on roll-off ships.
- Barge-carrying vessels.
- Very large crude carriers (VLCCs).
- LNG (liquefied natural gas) carriers.
- LPG (liquefied petroleum gas) and clean product carriers.
- Hydrofoils.
- Hovercraft.

A few details about these different units of carriage are appropriate at this point.

6.6.1 General cargo ships

The general cargo ship is still the chief type of vessel carrying goods around the smaller ports of the world, though the container ship and the barge-carrying vessel are making inroads into its traffic. Fig. 6.3 shows the SD14 class of general cargo ship built by Austin and Pickersgill. The SD14 is largely a mass-produced ship, and was originally conceived as a replacement for the utility Liberty ships built during the Second World War. It has now become a ship type in its own right, and more powerful versions are being developed to meet the evolving needs of shipowners.

The five spacious holds have fluorescent strip lighting and MacGregor single-pull mechanical weather-deck hatch covers to aid cargo working in port. All cargo spaces have smoke detectors and CO_2 firefighting equipment.

Among the other modern features of the ships can be included Marconi true-motion Radiolocator 16 radars with Seachart C echosounders and associated Seascape visual depth meters. The Radiolocator sets combine the latest in conventional radar technology with an almost total use of solid-state devices and advanced circuitry techniques, giving all normal marine radar facilities with picture auto-alignment, electronic bearing indicator and interference suppression devices.

Air-conditioned single-cabin accommodation is provided for the ship's complement of thirty-two officers and crew.

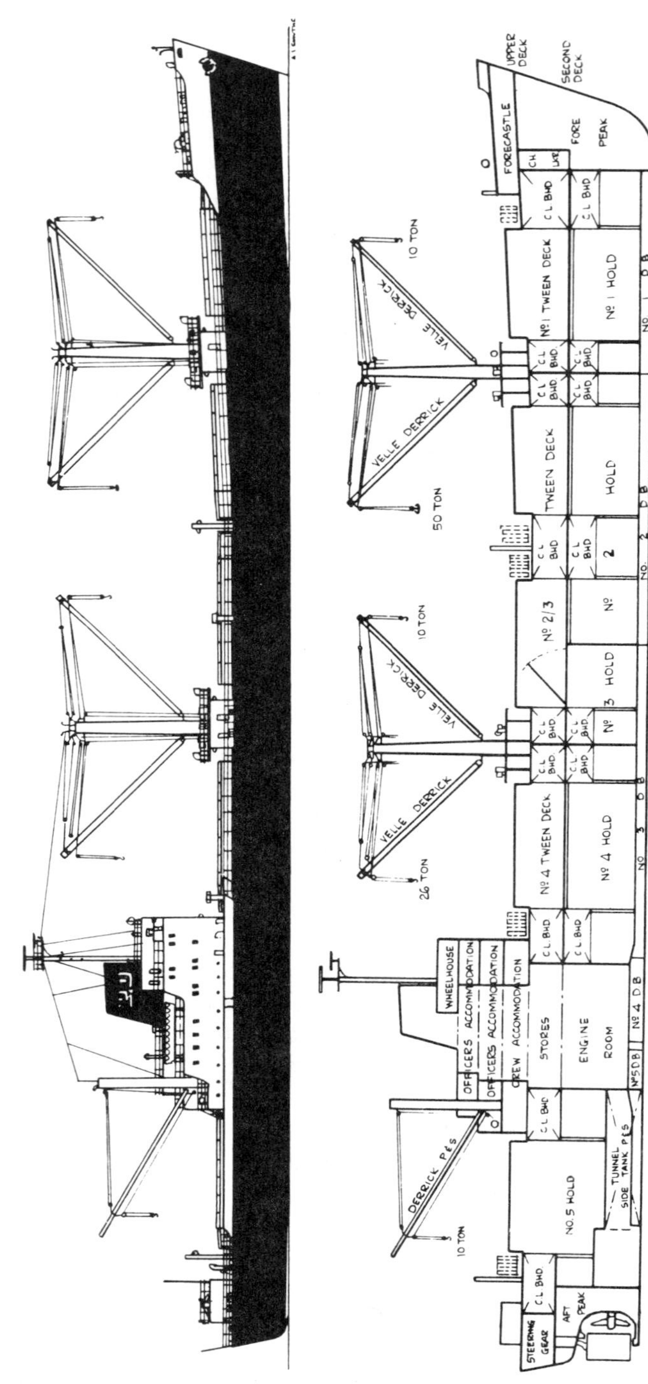

Fig. 6.3 Water line profile and view of cargo holds and cargo handling equipment of a modern general cargo vessel

6.6.2 Cellular container ships

The specialised container ship has largely replaced the conventional cargo liner on the major cargo routes of the world. The latest ships have holds designed to accommodate ISO 10 ft, 20 ft, 30 ft or 40 ft containers, which can also be stowed on deck. A typical ship of about 100,000 tonnes holds upwards of 4,000 TEUs (twenty-foot equivalent units), of which about 1,500 would be carried as deck cargo. About 250 containers of a typical cargo would be refrigerated. The ships may be provided with gantry cranes if they are likely to use ports inadequately equipped with heavy lift gear. They usually reach speeds of 25–8 knots and despite their much greater capacity, they spend only a fraction of their time in port as compared with their conventional forebears.

Because of their high volume, high speed and fast turn-round each ship of this type can carry about seven times the cargo in a year that a conventional cargo liner would carry.

In an age when fewer and fewer passengers go by sea the specialised cargo ship is clearly more economic. However, frequency of service is also vital, and the operators of large container ships, by operating in a consortium of ships from several countries, can offer customers regular fast services leaving every day or two for major trading areas of the world. Fig. 6.4 and Fig. 6.5 show container ships.

6.6.3 Roll-on roll-off ships

These ships enable vehicles to drive on to the vessel and then drive off at destination. They are usually bow- or stern-loaders. Roll-on roll-off ships have the disadvantage that cargo space is wasted between the deck of the ship and the lorry or trailer floorboard, but this loss is made up by the ships' many advantages. In many ways roll-on roll-off ships offer the purest form of inter-modal transit, in that the vehicle is not unloaded and no trans-shipment really takes place. They are very flexible in the type of load they carry, accepting everything from flat beds to tank units. The roll-on roll-off operator does not have to invest in vast numbers of containers (which are frequently not where they are wanted). His equipment inventories are quite small, and although he may carry containers on deck he has fewer expensive and under-utilised shore-based gantry cranes or Scotch derricks.

Cargo is carried in considerable safety, with a minimum of damage from weather or spray, while the greatest advantage of all is the speed of the ship's turn-round. This is most advantageous on very short sea routes, such as the English Channel crossing from Dover to Calais. Since roll-on roll-off services began in 1953 Dover has become the busiest passenger port in the

Fig. 6.4 The container ship 'Discovery Bay' passing Tilbury grain terminal (courtesy of Overseas Containers Ltd)

world, handling 17,940,121 passengers in 1992. 2,563,403 cars crossed the Channel in that year through Dover, and cargo movements, which are not seasonal like the passenger trade, rose to 13,111,417 tonnes in that year. The operation of large container ships, which tend to call at one big port only in each continent, has increased the traffic on the short sea routes, especially from the United Kingdom to the Low Countries and the Baltic. This has made the roll-on roll-off ship a viable proposition on all the routes serving this busy area.

The versatility of the roll-on roll-off ship can be increased by such devices as roll-on roll-off loading with packaged timber and similar products by straddle carriers belonging to the vessel. This increases the productivity of the long-haul routes by utilising the space wasted on normal roll-on roll-off operations. One group of ships which carries cars to Canada in one direction only has four car decks which she lowers into position from the deck-heads. The ships become vast floating garages for 2,000 auto-

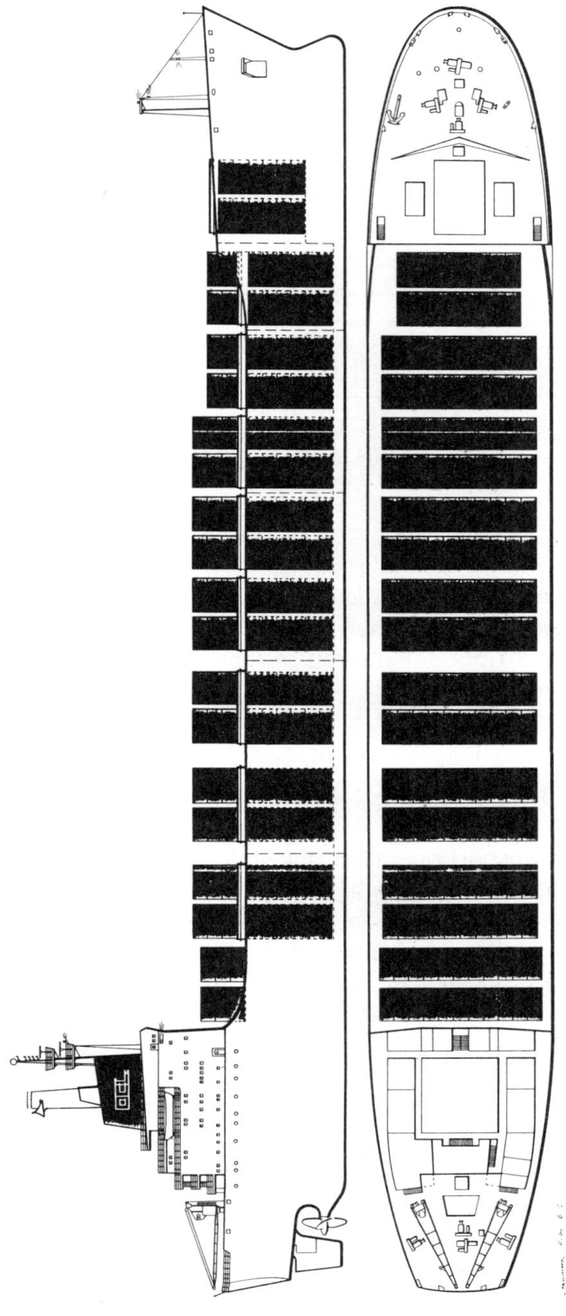

Fig. 6.5 A cellular container ship showing the stacking arrangements (courtesy of Overseas Containers Ltd)

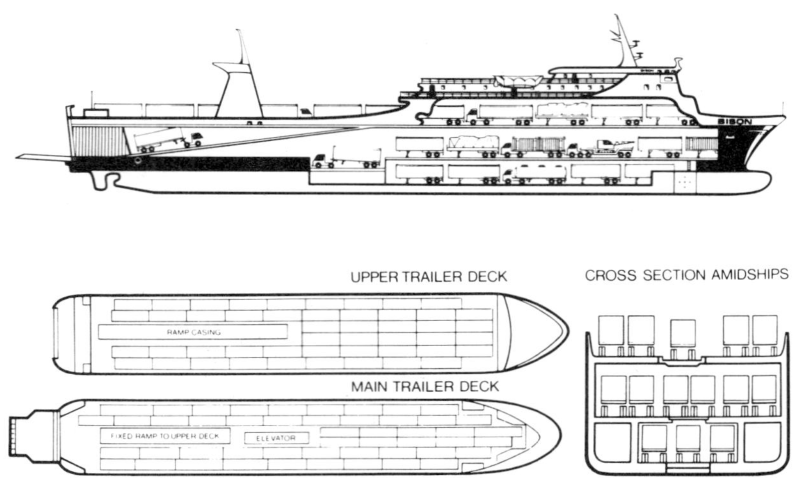

Fig. 6.6 A roll-on roll-off ship (courtesy of P. & O. Steam Navigation Co. Ltd)

mobiles, but on unloading, the car decks are raised and the huge holds are filled with forest products, newsprint and wood-pulp, loaded by the ship's own straddle carriers, for the return journey to Europe. Fig. 6.6 shows a typical roll-on roll-off ship.

6.6.4 Barge-carrying vessels

While some transport operators have been pressing ahead with containerisation, and others with bulk haulage, a further solution to the problems of securing efficient sea transport has been developed by a third group. The solution is a system consisting basically of a large vessel, carrying many smaller vessels which can enter river estuaries while the main vessel proceeds on her way after having lifted on board a further group of loaded barges for transit in the reverse direction. Two basically similar systems have evolved: the Lash system (Lash standing for 'lighter aboard ship'), first operated by the Norwegian firm T. Mosvold of Kristiansand, and the Seabee (sea-barge) system operated by Lykes Lines. The material in this chapter is drawn from literature made available by this firm.

The Lash and Seabee systems are both intended for trans-ocean traffic. A third variant of the Barge-on-Board (BOB) system as these have also been called, is the Baco-liner system which is described later in this chapter.

6.6.4.1 *Why use a barge-carrying vessel?*

The barge-carrying system combines the advantages of all the recent developments in cargo handling. The points borne in mind by Lykes Lines in devising their system were as follows:

Multi-port pattern. The Lykes Lines have traditionally operated from the Gulf ports. These stretch from Florida to Texas, a complex of nineteen ports all generating important agricultural and manufacturing produce. These Southern States are all experiencing rapid development as industry moves into the area. More than half of these new plants have access to waterways, and many of the rest are in existing port areas. While the container ship is best utilised where it can make one call at a major port area – unloading, reloading and sailing away – it is less useful in a region with a multiple-port pattern. In the Gulf area traditional ships call at as many as eight loading ports and offer services to several destination ports to attract an economic mix of cargo.

The diseconomies of large-scale ships. On the long haul between major port areas, such as the Gulf and Europe, large ships achieve economies of large-scale operation. Ideally, therefore, ships should be as large as possible – up to certain limits. Against this it is a regrettable fact that traditional break-bulk ships cannot exceed a certain size. The bigger a ship is the longer it takes to load by traditional methods. Therefore, large-size break-bulk ships must spend a greater proportion of total time in port. The need to call at several ports to collect an adequate mix of cargoes, and to stay at each port longer to load and unload its huge holds, means that the large ship is uneconomic for traditional break-bulk cargoes.

The nature of the cargoes to be carried. Not all cargoes are suitable for containerisation. This may be because the firms that produce them are small-scale firms and do not generate full container loads of traffic. The utilisation of containers then requires the development of groupage firms, who will assemble, and break, loads at either end of the transit. Many agricultural products are uneconomic to containerise, but time-consuming to load by traditional methods. The problem is to load these goods by traditional methods without wasting the time of a large ship. If this can be done, the final delivered cost of the product can be kept low, and competitive on world markets.

The need for flexibility. The container ship, which achieves economies of large scale, rapid cargo handling and rapid turn-round, does so at the expense of flexibility. It only calls at a limited number of ports, leaving multi-port areas to be served by a short-sea distribution network. Often these ports are big ports, with the shore facilities to unload and stack a large collection of containers in a very short period. The ship and the port are thus very specialised, while the cargoes handled are limited to those which are easily containerised. The problem was to build a ship which was large enough to achieve the economies of large-scale operation but which did not have to spend very long in port; which could be loaded by traditional break-bulk methods where these were cheaper and more convenient, while at the same time carrying containers where movements of pilferage-proof unit loads were advantageous.

6.6.4.2 The mother ship

The barge-carrying ship offers all the advantages of the container ship, the roll-on roll-off ship, the lift-on lift-off ship, the traditional break-bulk ship and the small tanker. It can be employed with almost any type of cargo. It is not so much a ship as a 'system' of transport. The Lykes Line 'Seabee' system has mother ships – barge-carrying hives of the Seabee system. Each mother ship is 875 ft (266 m) long and 106 ft (32 m) wide, with stabiliser systems which give 'passenger trade' size, stability and speed to the cargo trade. It is equipped with a 2,000 ton submersible elevator which can raise or lower two fully loaded 'Seabee' barges from deck to sea level. The three decks will accommodate 38 'Seabee' barges (out of a total fleet of 246 such units) stowed fore and aft. They can be taken aboard at a speed equivalent to 2,500 tons per hour, each barge holding 832 tons of freight.

The mother ship never enters dock or pulls in to a pier. She loads and unloads barges away from any port installation. It is the barge units which enter ports or estuaries, where they act as flexible extensions of the mother ship. They are of shallow draught and can reach wharves and jetties inaccessible to conventional break-bulk ships, let alone container ships. The 'Seabee' system thus restores the inland waterway network to importance, opening up connections to areas inaccessible for decades, and sometimes a century.

6.6.4.3 The barge units

Each barge unit is a cargo-carrying vessel of shallow draught, with double-hulled construction, watertight compartments and watertight hatch covers, which when removed reveal the entire cargo compartment. The cargo can thus be placed directly into its point of rest for the entire journey. This loading takes place in traditional docks, at riverside wharves and jetties far from the mother ship, which has proceeded on her way to other roadsteads where she will hive off yet more 'bees' and collect returning ones which have been filled at the leisure of the shipper. The barges are designed to accommodate pallets, containers and 'intermediate decks' for large units of pre-stowed cargo. The arrangements are entirely at the direction of the cargo shipper, who supervises the stowage in the barge unit which has been delivered to his own location, possibly under cover, since its size is small. Finally, containers may be carried on special support beams below the barge hatch covers, while in the case of those barges stowed on the upper deck of the mother vessel 16–40 ft containers may be stowed on top of each barge's hatch cover.

It is difficult to imagine a more versatile, flexible and economical system (see Fig. 6.7).

6.6.4.4 *Lash vessels (lighters aboard ship)*

Lash vessels carry 73 barges of just under 400 tonnes capacity giving an overall cargo capacity of approximately 27,000 tonnes. The barges are hoisted aboard by a travelling gantry crane fitted to the stern of the mother vessel. On discharge at an estuarial location, the barges which are block-ended and of shallow draught can be made up into barge trains and moved by giant pusher tugs into the port's hinterland. Barge trains of 50–60 barges, five abreast are to be found on the upper Mississippi with the pusher tug and an unmanned bow boat operated from the tug. The bow boat can be manned and used to move individual barges to and from the train.

Lash vessels can be converted swiftly to container carriers with a capacity of approximately 400 TEUs.

6.6.4.5 *Baco-liners (Barge-container liners)*

Another barge-carrying system which also carries containers is the Baco-liner system (see Fig. 6.8). Baco-liners have been specially designed for West African ports, though they could be used at any estuarial system where inland waterway traffic can operate. Baco-liner operations are unaffected by port congestion and no waiting time is involved in the smooth efficiency of this unique transport system. Each ship has three sets of barges, one being positioned in the loading port, one on board and one in the discharging port. Each barge is 75 ft (24 m) long, 30 ft (9.5 m) wide and 800 tons dead-weight capacity – just about twice the size of the barges described above. Their up-river journey continues using local tug facilities.

While the barges are completing the last leg of their journey the Baco-liner has already begun a new voyage.

The barges are suitable for inland waterways and river estuaries. The loading and discharge of the barges from the carrier is achieved within hours. Other floating items of a suitable size can be accommodated within the carrier's floating dock. Each floating dock is 470 ft (144 m) in length, 30 ft (9.50 m) in width and 30 ft (9.50 m) in height.

Fig. 6.7 A 'Skyfotos' picture of a Lykes Line Seabee barge-carrying ship (courtesy of Lykes Line Agency Inc.)

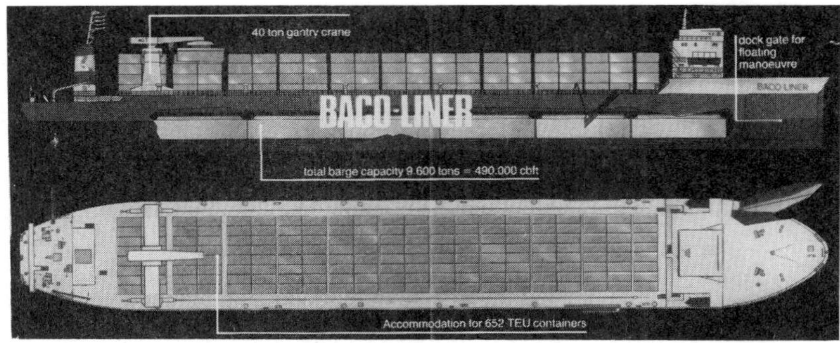

Fig. 6.8 The Baco-liner system (courtesy Baco-liner GmbH)

Additionally, 652 containers (TEUs) are accommodated four tiers high on the deck.

An outstanding control system guarantees careful and continual supervision of up to seventy-eight reefer containers.

The 'Loadmaster' computer on board ensures the correct positioning of containers, which can be loaded, discharged or restowed by operating the carrier's 40 ton gantry crane.

The ready availability of Baco's barges and containers means that transport and packing problems are reduced, and damage and pilferage risks are minimised.

Vessels currently in service operate between Europe and West Africa.

Baco-liner is an independent and economical shipping system which is a proven operational success. Owned by Baco-liner GmbH of Emden, the UK agents are Cowell Nicola Shipping Co Ltd (Tel: 081 514 3300).

6.6.5 Very large crude carriers

VLCCs have been referred to elsewhere (see page 254) but one or two interesting features of these particular units of carriage are worth mentioning here. First, the draught of the tankers may be as great as 81 ft (24 m) and this poses difficult navigational problems in the relatively shallow north European waters.

Many north European ports are at present unable to accept the very largest VLCCs afloat and can only accept those which are slightly smaller, with great difficulty. As even larger vessels become operational the position will become even more critical, except for a few ports blessed with deep water inshore and with deep-water approaches. For the present, a number of devices have been used to overcome this natural obstacle of inadequate depth.

Dredging is an obvious solution, and where there is deep water at a relatively short distance from the port, the approaches and berths can be progressively deepened to keep pace with the ever-increasing draught. However, as time passes and draughts become larger and larger, it may become necessary to extend the dredged channel further and further seawards until the cost of dredging is no longer economically viable and the port must forgo the revenue and prestige which would accrue from handling the largest ships.

An alternative is to utilise the very high 'perigee' spring tides, when the depth of water available will be at its greatest, to bring the vessel to its terminal. A peculiarity of the super-tanker is that it bobs up out of the water quickly as the load is reduced. Since most super-tankers can discharge at about 13,000 tonnes per hour, enough cargo can be discharged as the tide ebbs to leave them still afloat at low tide.

A second alternative is to dredge a hole at the terminal and in its vicinity deep enough to ensure that a loaded vessel, brought in on the 'top of the tide' could remain safely afloat at low tide, even without lightening her. This, of course, is much cheaper than trying to dredge the whole of the channel to the depth required.

In practice, a combination of all three of these possible solutions is used: channels and terminals being deepened until costs become prohibitive, very fast discharge being undertaken to lighten the vessel, and advantage being taken of high tides to bring vessels to their berths.

A fourth solution ignores the established major ports as far as the VLCCs are concerned and concentrates on providing discharging facilities in places where natural deep water exists, such as the SBM (single buoy mooring) at Amlwch in Anglesey, with pipeline connections to major ports with their established hinterlands. The deep-water facility at Bantry Bay formerly used for the discharge of VLCCs and trans-shipping their cargoes onwards has now been closed.

6.6.6 LNG carriers

LNG stands for liquefied natural gas. The first LNG carrier was called *Methane Pioneer* and began experimental deliveries of liquefied natural gas from the gasfields of Algeria to Canvey Island in Essex early in the 1960s. By 1974 there were seven main LNG schemes in operation: Algeria to the United Kingdom, Le Havre and Fos in France, Libya to Spain and Italy, Alaska to Japan and Brunei to Japan. Today there are almost 100 LNG ships in operation, many of them over 80,000 tonnes GRT (gross registered tonnage). The largest gas carrier (1982), the *Hoegh Gandria* 95,683 GRT, was built in 1977. There are proposals to improve pipeline facilities – for example, from Algeria to Europe – which may reduce the LNG fleets somewhat in the years ahead.

Over the years experience has shown that the best way to carry natural gas, which liquefies either under refrigeration or under pressure, is to use the refrigeration process and carry at −165°C. At this extremely cold temperature insulation between the tank and the hull of the ship is of vital importance. The insulation is of polystyrene. The tanks may be large spherical tanks of 9 per cent nickel steel or aluminium construction. Alternatively, the tanks may be double-walled, the inner one being a flexible corrugated stainless steel membrane. A third type, the MVT (multi-vessel tank), has a large number of relatively small, vertically positioned cylindrical units. These are safer from the point of view of damage to the ship – only those tanks actually damaged will leak – and the insulation problems are also easier when the tanks are small. Wherever possible the tanks are rectangular, to ease the problems of calibrating the tanks for content, but at the fore and aft parts of the ship tanks are shaped to suit the vessel. Difficult problems arise at 'custody transfer' points, such as shore-to-ship on the start of a voyage and ship-to-shore on delivery at the end of the voyage. The mere pumping of the liquid causes heat-inleakage and consequent vaporisation of the more volatile products. The resulting gas reduces the volume delivered and must be refrigerated again, or even burned off in a flare. There is also a constant vaporisation of the cargo during the voyage and the engines of these vessels have been adapted to run on this gas as a supplement to their normal fuel.

6.6.7 Clean product carriers and LPG carriers

Clean products, as distinct from crude oil, are carried usually at normal temperatures, being liquefied by pressure if they are not liquids at ordinary temperatures. They are not usually carried in such enormous quantities as LNG and ships can be quite small. They are consequently often called mini-bulk carriers. They may carry several different products, for different customers.

LPG stands for liquefied petroleum gas, usually propane and butane. Methanol, or methyl alcohol, can be prepared from natural gas and shipped at normal temperatures instead of in LNG carriers. Clean product carriers are rarely bigger than 26,000 tonnes and the vast majority are in the 1,000–5,000 tonne class, but ships of 60,000 tonnes and over are in use.

6.6.8 Hydrofoils

A hydrofoil is a ship fitted with foils, which operate very much like the aerofoil of an aircraft, i.e. pressure from below creates lift. (Aerofoils on racing cars operate in reverse, the shape of the aerofoil being designed to ensure that downward pressure is exerted so that contact is maintained with the road surface.) Perhaps a better illustration would be to liken them to water-skis. A water-skier starts off with his skis submerged in the water. As the tow-boat increases speed, the skis are angled and the pressure created by the water rushing underneath causes them to skim over the water, supporting the weight of the skier. When a hydrofoil is at rest or moving slowly, it floats with its hull partly submerged like any conventional vessel. As forward motion increases, pressure on the angled foils causes them to skim the surface, raising the hull clear of the water. This reduces drag and permits increased speeds. The wash of a hydrofoil is much less than an ordinary ship's wash. This is helpful in rivers and other enclosed waterways, where banks and other property can suffer damage from wave action created by fast-moving vessels.

6.6.9 Hovercraft

The hovercraft principle was originally developed by Christopher Cockerell around 1954, out of two coffee tins, with a space between them. Air was blown through this space with a small industrial drier and the lift he had predicted occurred. Since that date, after many trials and tribulations and with considerable help eventually from the National Research Development Corporation, a whole range of hovercraft types has developed, and wide industrial uses, particularly load removals, have been developed.

While the ordinary hovercraft has conquered the world, crossing Africa coast to coast and sweeping over South American jungle waterways, its most testing performances have undoubtedly been the cross-Channel services between England and France. These services are scheduled to operate 364 days a year and services are maintained in all but the most severe conditions. Such services represent an engineering maintenance achievement of no mean quality.

The hovercraft operates on a cushion of air built up inside the skirt by a powerful engine. Each Proteus gas turbine, for example, produces 4,250 h.p. at 12,000 r.p.m. The hovercraft is thus an aircraft and not a sea craft, although its basic design is that of a buoyancy raft and if the skirt fails it can in fact proceed at about 6 knots. In flight its normal speed is about 70 knots and it operates over land or water equally well, so that where appropriate it can take short-cuts across mud flats and sand bars. The stretched version of the SRN4 which operates the Dover service can take wave variations of up to 13 ft (4 m), and carry 424 passengers and up to 55 vehicles (Fig. 6.9). An American firm has developed a 2,000 tonne 'Surface Effects Ship', the skirts of which were made by the British Hovercraft Company. She is ten times as big as the Dover ferries.

6.7 Units of carriage by air

The aeroplane is the typical unit of carriage, but helicopters and airships are alternatives. The aeroplane is fast, safe and reliable, and since 1908 has moved from the Deutsch Archdeacon prize for the first officially observed flight of a single aviator around a circular course, to the carriage of millions of passengers over billions of flight miles. In 1992 Heathrow airport alone carried 45 million passengers. It has been estimated that at any given moment, 24 hours a day, one million of the world's citizens are in the stratosphere, going somewhere for business or pleasure.

The aircraft is a heavier-than-air machine, which is raised from the ground by the flow of air over the aerofoils or wings. This lifts the aircraft, partly by a build-up of pressure under the wing, but even more by the suction effect created above the wing due to the design. This increases the speed of the air above the wing and hence reduces its pressure. The unit of carriage and the engines are embodied in the same frame, but the engines have been placed in almost every conceivable position. The wings, nose, mid-fuselage, rear fuselage and tail plane have all borne engines in recent years. The comfort of passengers is certainly increased with modern high-speed aircraft if the engines are to the rear, as with the VC10.

All modern aircraft are pressurised to avoid the use of oxygen when flying at high altitudes. A non-pressurised aircraft can only be operated at about 10,000 ft (3,000 m) without oxygen. At the altitudes at which modern aircraft operate huge supplies of oxygen would be necessary. Pressurised cabins are the only practicable solution. They do mean that greater stresses are put upon the skin metal and careful examination for metal fatigue is necessary.

6.7.1 A typical unit of passenger carriage – the Boeing 747

It is impossible to describe fully all the many types of aircraft which are in operation around the world. The Boeing 747 is a typical aircraft in the sense that it is flying the major long-haul inter-continental air routes for many airlines today. It is an economic aircraft even in these days of high fuel costs giving about 60 miles (96 km)/gallon per passenger against the

(a)

(b)

Fig. 6.9 (a) A hovercraft leaving Dover and (b) a 'Sea Cat' catamaran (courtesy of Hoverspeed Ltd)

family car's 40 miles (64 km)/gallon per passenger on average. It is a US aeroplane, with four Pratt & Whitney JT9D-3D engines slung on underwing pods. These develop a thrust of 80,000 kg. The aircraft when fully loaded with its economy-class load of 496 passengers and 6,190 cu. ft (175 m^3) of cargo weighs 340 short tons (308 tonnes). Its wing span is 195 ft 8 in (59.5 m); its length 231 ft 4 in (70 m); its height 63 ft 5 in (19 m); and it carries 41,900 US gallons (158,609 litres) of fuel. It cruises at 565–600 mph (909–66 km) at altitudes of 30,000–45,000 ft (9,144–13,716 m).

The British Airways 747s have five cabins, one first class and four economy class. The walls are straight, the ceilings flat and high, seats are arranged in rows of nine in the economy class cabins, with two wide aisles intersecting the seating into groups of three. The first class cabin has seats in rows of four separated into two-abreast seating by a wide aisle. There is also an exclusive lounge bar, furnished with comfortable chairs and settees, where passengers can enjoy drinks and snacks. There are six galley areas, with automated ovens able to serve hot meals to all passengers, with a personal choice individual service for first-class passengers. Full-length feature films are shown, and there is a selection of audio entertainment.

6.7.2 Concorde – the supersonic unit of air carriage

Concorde has now been operating for several years and still arouses enormous interest wherever it goes despite the uneconomic nature of its operations at present.

The aircraft is supersonic, flying at a speed of 1,450 mph (12,330 km/h), which is greater than Mach 2. It operates at altitudes of 50,000–65,000 ft (15,000–19,800 m), and has a range of 3,910 miles (4,980 km), carrying 136 economy-class passengers. The great advantage Concorde offers is the speed at which travel is possible. It would reach Australia in 10½ hours, and although the Jumbo jets offer it severe competition where maximum time-saving is not all-important, there are many who believe that it could still have a valid part to play in aviation – for example a strategical role. The present operators, British Airways and Air France, are making a healthy profit out of it, but not of course a profit that would recover the enormous capital costs incurred in building it (see Fig. 6.10 (a)).

6.7.3 The air freighter

From the earliest times in aviation the cheap way to carry freight has been on the passenger aircraft. It has been a happy coincidence that while most passengers travel at weekends most goods travel on weekdays. It has thus

(a)

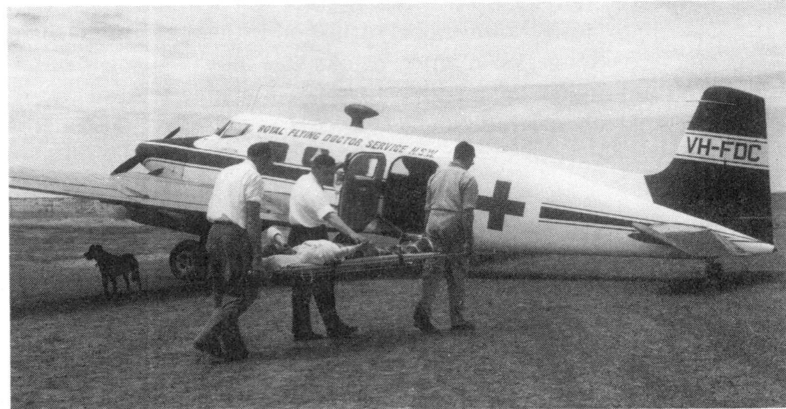

(b)

(c)

Fig. 6.10 (a) Concorde 02 touching down. (b) Australia's Flying Doctor Service. (c) Rushing a human kidney for transplant. (courtesy of British Aerospace (a), the Australia High Commission (b), and St. John Ambulance Brigade (c))

been possible to fill up the mid-week passenger planes with extra cargo in the freight holds. However, the growth of air cargo has now reached such proportions that many airlines now offer cargo movements by air freighters. London Heathrow's Cargocentre handled 661,000 tonnes of cargo in 1991, with eighteen aircraft stands and 94,000 m^2 of bonded warehouse space owned by thirteen airlines. There are two non-bonded sheds which provide agents and forwarders with over 12,000 m^2 of space for warehouses and offices. Seventy per cent of UK trade through airports was through Heathrow, and the total value exceeded £34,000 million. Specialised 'igloo' containers, special loading channels and scissors-lift devices have been developed to assist in the loading of air freighters, and extremely rapid transit times – two days from the United Kingdom to New Zealand is typical – have been achieved.

6.7.4 Other uses of aircraft

Because of their high speed and ability to ignore topography and travel as the crow flies, aircraft have always been of use in emergency situations. Their independence of ordinary hinterland infrastructures is of enormous importance in vast poorly developed areas such as the Australian outback, the Canadian tundra and in Africa (see Fig. 6.10 (b) and (c)).

6.8 Pipelines and tubes

The pipeline is a unit of carriage which is fully described in other sections of this book. It is both a way and a unit of carriage and requires no further description here. However, the use of pneumatic pipeline systems for the transport of freight, a king-size development of the pneumatic systems used in some department stores for centralised cash desk operations, is a distinct possibility. The Soviet Union claimed at one time to be developing a pneumatic freight pipeline which would move 10 million tonnes of freight a year over 30-mile (50 km) distances. Units of 25 tonnes were to be moved at 45 mph (72 km/h), in freight cars which fitted tightly into the pipe.

For many years a power station in the US Midwest was supplied by pipeline with a coal slurry mix, which was fed straight into the furnace, while another slurry mix of chalk for a cement works was operated at Northfleet.

Conveyor-belts, which like pipelines form both the way and the unit of carriage, are used to carry Peruvian iron ore from the mine to the ports. They are also used as an internal feature of some bulk carriers for discharge purposes to shoreside conveyors.

6.9 Summary

1. Every mode of transport has its particular unit of carriage. This unit of carriage represents the response of transport engineers to a particular class of traffic, moving on a particular way, powered by a particular method of propulsion across a particular pattern of interfaces. Each unit of carriage is a compromise which seeks to produce the best possible results from the particular set of circumstances.
2. The aim is to achieve the widest possible market in the most economical manner.
3. The way imposes serious limitations on the size, shape and speed of the units of carriage which use it. For example, air travel requires high speeds, relatively low weights, a streamlined shape, large wings at take-off to lift the plane off the ground – but variable geometry may reduce the wing size after take-off.
4. Other factors imposing limitations on the designers of units of carriage are: the requirements of the traffic to be moved, the needs of staff employed to work on the units of carriage, and the need to keep costs down to remain competitive.
5. Units of carriage by road are of two sorts: units for passengers and units for goods. The goods units feature a wide variety of general-purpose vans and lorries and a huge range of specialist vehicles, such as articulated lorries, tankers, tippers and ready-mixed cement vehicles.
6. Rail passenger and goods units of carriage display a similar variety to cater for particular traffic. On the goods side, bulk movements of ores, grains, cement, petroleum products, etc. are common and move at faster speeds now that braking devices are fitted to most wagons. Unit loads of containerised cargo travelling on Freightliner trains between major Freightliner terminals have improved the services offered by the railways. These should increase further with the opening of Eurotunnel in 1994.
7. Today, the general cargo vessel for carriage of goods by sea is rare, and specialised bulk carriers, tankers, LNG carriers and cellular container ships carry the vast majority of the deep-sea traffic. The growth of short-sea movements resulting from the development of free trade areas around the world – but particularly in Europe – has meant a huge increase in roll-on roll-off ships and ferries. Barge-carrying vessels enable the carrier to take advantage of fast ocean-going transport while still being able to enter estuaries and visit many ports – the barges being of shallow draught are able to collect up-river cargoes and deliver up-river supplies.
8. The aeroplane is the typical unit of carriage for air transport, but the helicopter and airships are alternatives. Although much cargo still

travels on passenger aircraft the air freighter carries an increasing share of total traffic, the equivalent of 7,000 fully loaded Jumbo jets in 1991.

9. The pipeline is, of course, both the way and the unit of carriage for the products which travel through it. While most appropriate for crude oil, natural gas and water, pipelines are also used for slurries of coal, chalk and other minerals.

6.10 Questions

1. What is a unit of carriage? Why is such a huge variety of units of carriage available in the world today?
2. Thinking only of rail passenger traffic, what are the common types of passenger trains and what are the significant differences between them?
3. Why are roll-on roll-off ships such a common feature of the European transport scene? What part has the use of container ships with fast turn-round times played in the development of roll-on roll-off ships?
4. What is a VLCC? What are the advantages of these vessels as far as world movements of crude oil are concerned? Why carry crude oil around the world when refined products would take up much less room and consequently would use smaller clean-product carriers?
5. What is an LNG carrier? What are the characteristics of LNG? How does the vessel take account of them?
6. List five different types of heavy goods vehicle. Considering them from the point of view of units of carriage, what are the distinguishing features of each?
7. Explain the thinking behind barge-carrying ocean-going vessels as a transportation system.
8. 'Aircraft are no longer just a means for carrying valuables and perishable cargoes. They now carry a significant proportion of world freight.' What are the advantages and disadvantages of the air freighter? Why are they gaining an increasing proportion of total trade?

7 The physical components of transport: motive power

7.1 Introduction

The modern transport scene is dominated by enormously powerful motive power units. Aircraft weighing 300 tonnes roar off into the sky, supertankers weighing half a million tonnes glide up estuaries to dock at oil terminals, streams of traffic start up within seconds of traffic lights changing colour and the Saturn rocket reaches an escape velocity of over 20,000 miles (32,000 km) an hour in less than a minute. Clearly we have moved a long way from the days of natural power, when becalmed mariners whistled for a wind, and a team of horses was needed to drag a single oak tree down the many 'timber log-lanes' that led to the naval dockyards. We still row our university boat races, we pedal our bicycles, we race our sailing dinghies in innumerable inlets and the prize for a man-powered crossing of the English Channel has been won by a pedal-driven microlight aircraft; but in the developed countries the world of transport has forgotten about natural power and is preoccupied with mechanised units of propulsion.

Before we too become preoccupied with the more sophisticated motive power units, we should pause to remember that in many underdeveloped countries animal and wind power are still very important. Bullock carts and horse and donkey carts are still used extensively in some of the poorer countries, and pack animals still persist in countries where poor roads, or absence of them, make wheeled transport difficult. Although their numbers have diminished in recent years, many sailing vessels still operate in the Middle and Far Eastern areas.

7.2 Types of prime mover

The term 'prime mover' is used to describe fundamental units of propulsion. Whatever variations of motion are achieved by gearing, belting, frictional contact or other means there must be a primary source of power to generate the original motion. The chief types of prime mover may be listed as follows:

1. the steam engine;
2. electric motors, which are of two types: series wound and shunt wound;
3. internal combustion engines, driven by petrol or liquefied petroleum gas (propane and butane);
4. diesel engines, or oil engines;
5. turbines;
6. jet engines;
7. linear induction motors.

7.2.1 Steam engines

The first prime mover was the steam engine, which for 100 years dominated both transport and production as the main source of power. Stationary steam engines drove the machines in the mills of the eighteenth and nineteenth centuries, pumped out the mines and even wound trains up hills on cables. Steam locomotives dominated the railways for more than a century from 1825 onwards. Steamships, independent of seasonal winds, could sail directly at a steady speed, permitting scheduled sailings on regular routes. The durability of steam engines gave them great 'inertia' as a form of prime mover. While nations less highly capitalised in steam than the United Kingdom turned readily to electrical and other forms of motive power, the United Kingdom hesitated to change because its steam engines continued to give good service. A further point is that the steam engine burned an indigenous fuel, coal, while the petrol and diesel engines required a foreign fuel supply.

7.2.2 Electric engines

The work of Michael Faraday in the years 1830–67 formed the basis of the modern electrical industry and when applied to transport gave us the series motor and the tramway, trolleybus and electric railway. The diesel electric motor operates on the same principles but uses power generated by a diesel engine instead of power from an external source of supply. There are also battery-operated vehicles like milk floats and forklift trucks, while a battery-operated motor car and battery buses have recently appeared.

The series motor has the merit of a very high-powered starting torque, which overcomes the initial inertia of a stationary vehicle. As the inertia is overcome the acceleration is extremely rapid under the enormous power of the series motor. As a safe operating speed is approached the power to the motor has to be reduced to conform with the reduced effective load now that the vehicle is moving.

Battery-powered vehicles have several disadvantages. They are not suitable for heavy work, or continuous work, and their rate of acceleration is low. The batteries have to be recharged at intervals, a slow process which means the machine cannot be used continuously unless a change of batteries is carried out. The renewable battery – one where the plates can be replaced by a new set for a further period of work – is being actively sought, especially as it would reduce the pollution problems inseparable from petrol and diesel prime movers. Such a development would influence very greatly the use of battery-operated electric vehicles.

The sodium–sulphur battery, which has as many as 49 cells using a sodium electrolyte, has enormous potential in this field. It lasts four times as long as a lead–acid battery, giving vehicles a range of about 100–140 miles (160–224 km), and should operate more efficiently and at lower capital cost than a lead–acid battery-driven bus or van.

7.2.3 Internal combustion engines

Internal combustion engines are more numerous than any other type of prime mover today. They are susceptible to mass production and are therefore relatively cheap. They are easily understood, suitable for small family vehicles, and relatively economical to run. They give good acceleration, high speed and are adaptable to many different types of transport. The range is convenient for most ordinary household or business purposes, and the capital cost is not great. Even the poorest families can advance up the trade-in range to the possession of a vehicle of reasonable quality.

Diesel engines operate on a slightly different basis from the internal combustion engine. The ignition is spontaneous once the engine is hot, and there are therefore no sparking plugs in use. There will be some device to start the engine from cold, but once warm the compression of the air in the cylinders heats it to the point where an injected jet of oil fires by itself. The diesel engine is very powerful, and best suited to heavy vehicles. It is an extremely efficient engine and converts about 40 per cent of heat energy to useful work. A steam locomotive by contrast would not convert more than about 5 per cent. The one disadvantage of diesel as a fuel is that it can freeze if the vehicle is stationary at low temperatures.

7.2.4 Turbines

A turbine may be one of two types: impulse turbines and reactor turbines – or a combination of both. The circular motion is achieved in the impulse turbine by a ready-made stream of air or steam which pushes the blades round. A reaction turbine has blades which are shaped so as to accelerate the flow, which results in a reaction which kicks the blades round. The refinements and developments of these basic systems are numerous, some applications being more suited to one mode of transport than others.

7.2.5 Jet engines

A jet engine consists of a shaft with a compressor at the front and a reaction turbine at the rear. There are a number of combustion chambers between. Air is drawn in at the front in huge quantities, compressed and fed into the combustion chambers where it is mixed with fuel vapour and fired. The gases produced are fed into the turbine, which operates the compressor, and pass from there into the jet pipe. The expansion that takes place then expels the gases at great speed, causing a forward thrust which propels the unit of carriage.

A later development, the bypass engine, only passes about half the compressed air through the combustion chambers. The rest bypasses the high-pressure compressor and combustion chambers. It is cooler and moving at a slower speed than the hot exhaust gases with which it mingles in the tailpipe. The resulting jet-stream is more efficient, less noisy and more economical of fuel. The Rolls-Royce Conway engine incorporating the bypass principle powers the VC10 and the Boeing 707.

The introduction of the wide-bodied jet aircraft, such as the Boeing 747, the original Jumbo jet, was made possible by the introduction of the turbofan engine of high bypass ratio. The JT9D engine which powers the Boeing 747 incorporates a fan with a diameter almost as great as the length of the engine. This giant fan handles many times more airflow than that passing through the 'core' engine. As a result, the engine develops many times more thrust than its predecessors and makes much larger aircraft possible, yet at the same time it is quieter and more economical than earlier engines.

7.3 Motive power and road haulage

Diesel engines are most appropriate for heavy haulage duties and a modern 6- or 8-cylinder diesel with an 8, 10 or even 12 speed gearbox is a powerful unit well able to move the plated weight it is designed to carry, with power to spare. Reliability and economy are a feature of the diesel engine, and developments like direct fuel injection and advanced piston combustion chambers mean clean combustion, free of fumes. Flame preheaters give starting from cold down to −19°C. Transmission from the engine is sophisticated, to give a smooth flow of engine power through the gearbox, dynamically balanced prop shafts and differentials to the wheel drive.

Typical power units for 32 tonne trucks give between 192 b.h.p. (the legal minimum necessary) and 335 b.h.p. for really heavy sustained motorway working.

By contrast the light vans on the market are usually petrol driven, and have engines which generate between 30 and 60 b.h.p.

Accessibility of power units for maintenance purposes is an important aspect, and many large vehicles have forward-tilting cabs to leave the engine clearly accessible.

7.4 Motive power and railways

In the United Kingdom the 1950s saw the beginning of the end of steam power and the switch to diesel power and electrified lines. Compared with the diesel, the electric traction unit offers greater power, greater acceleration (which is essential for commuter trains which stop frequently), greater reliability and cheaper operations. However, the capital costs of electrification are enormous, whereas a diesel locomotive operates on the traditional lines without major alterations. The modernisation of British Railways, which took place between 1955 and 1965, required a very considerable measure of dieselisation, since the supply of capital equipment for electrification was inadequate to push modernisation ahead at the rate envisaged in the plan.

There are two types of diesel: the diesel electric and the hydraulic diesel. The diesel electric uses the diesel engine to generate electricity, which is then used to drive the wheels through ordinary electric motors similar to those used by the electric traction unit operating on electricity from the national grid. The transmission to the wheels is thus an electrical transmission.

The hydraulic diesel, by contrast, transmits the drive to the wheels through a device called a torque-convertor which carries out the same function as a gearbox. An ordinary gearbox is unable to stand up to the high loads and fast speeds of railway traffic, but the torque-convertor transmits the motion through a fluid mechanism, much more smoothly and with greater power.

While it is true that the use of diesels was inevitable if fast, accurately timed services were to be offered in the modernisation years, the long-run aim of British Rail is to electrify all main lines. The electric traction unit is cheaper, it is available for almost continuous use, it is susceptible to computerised planning and control because of its predictable performance, and its high speed makes the return on capital invested very satisfactory.

The advanced passenger train (APT), which was originally powered by a gas turbine and gave a very favourable power/weight ratio and consequent rapid acceleration, is now to be replaced by a more conventional design, currently being built at Loughborough. The French have ordered nine of these, but at the time of writing the train is still being developed.

A recent development is Hyundai's successful launch of the magnetic levitation train, which finally makes use of that branch of science, so long experimental, known as the linear induction motor. The train floats on a magnetic field and moves frictionlessly on a monorail, free of noise and air pollution – an environmentally-sound technique. It should revolutionise mass-transit railway systems in the future.

7.5 Aircraft power units

The design of motive power units for aircraft, more than with any other unit of carriage, depends upon economic considerations. The performance of an engine is one thing; its performance as an economic unit is another. This means that before design begins, a clear picture of the background to the design must be built up. This picture is not easy to bring into focus, for many of the aims of the airlines who may eventually operate an aircraft are imprecisely stated, but as a rough guide we may mention three:

1. Safety and reliability are very important.
2. The economics of the power unit should be as good as possible.
3. The complete unit of carriage must be socially and environmentally acceptable.

By a series of optimisation studies the design engineer evaluates traditional ideas and well-established mechanisms against more recent ideas and proposals for turning them into practical reality. In the long run he must tell the manufacturer what to make and the airline what it can have and at what price.

Today, while petrol-driven piston engines are still important for club flying and small aircraft of many sorts, the jet engine reigns supreme for passenger and cargo aircraft. It is faster, quieter and more economical than any other type of engine, and its general performance has increased both the size and the economy of operation of commercial aircraft out of all recognition compared with other power units.

7.5.1 STOL and VTOL technology

Two aspects of aircraft design which are of great interest are the Short Take-Off and Landing (STOL) and the Vertical Take-Off and Landing

(VTOL) techniques. The high capital cost of airports for major civil airline operations is prohibitive in many parts of the world where the aircraft is a vital link in the national life yet the traffic to be carried is limited. Examples are the Canadian North and the Australian Outback. For these areas the STOL aircraft is ideal. Canada in particular has developed a range of STOL aircraft: the Beaver, Otter, Buffalo and Caribou and its latest De Havilland Canada 7 aircraft. These aircraft will operate from small airports in remote areas – even from frozen lakes (kept frozen all the year round by artificial refrigeration in some cases). They will also operate in and out of city centre airports without giving offence on noise levels. The Canadian Authorities say of the DHC-7:

> The DHC-7's main attraction for travellers is its ability to take off and land in busy city centres and designers have concentrated heavily on public reaction to this innovation. The craft is quieter than conventional planes. It is estimated that occupants of buildings will have difficulty detecting it flying overhead at 750 feet (228 metres), and in ascent and descent, the airplane's steeper angles will expose a much smaller area of land to noise. On a mile-to-mile basis, emission of pollutants will be one half that of the average automobile.
>
> The DHC-7's speed of 300 miles (480 km) an hour is slow by current standards but by eliminating time-consuming trips to outlying air terminals, it will deliver passengers to their destinations faster than more powerful planes. Frequent departures that will eliminate the need for reservations and reduce traffic bottlenecks in and around terminal buildings, are also expected to heighten the DHC-7's appeal.
>
> STOL promises even more important benefits for terminal authorities and carriers, particularly in countries where the public opposes expansion of existing terminal facilities and construction of new airports. Studies show that STOLports capable of handling five to ten million passengers annually – complete with runway and all necessary buildings and parking lots – can be built on approximately 40 acres (16 ha), or less than 1 per cent the area required by jetports.
>
> STOL runways can also be incorporated into existing facilities, thus delaying or eliminating new construction of conventional terminals. The shorter runways do not even require additional land acquisition and STOL's low noise output and steep flight profile permit greater activity without further disturbance to nearby communities.

The STOL principle does not of course depend only on the power unit – the whole design of the aircraft is vital – but the power units clearly have to be appropriate to the design.

With vertical take-off and landing aircraft the power unit is crucial. The ability of the engines to change their alignment so as to point downwards and thus give direct lift from the ground is an essential feature. As their fore and aft alignment is restored, the forward movement begins and ordinary lift from the aerofoils replaces the lift from the engines. This makes take-off from a landing pad a practical possibility but the chief use for VTOL aircraft at present is for military aircraft.

7.6 Motive power at sea

For centuries ships depended on the wind for their motive power. Then came the steam engine, which transformed marine transport and spelled the death of sail except for leisure purposes. At the end of the nineteenth century Charles Parsons took the principle of the steam turbine, which had been known to the ancient Greeks, and converted it to practical use. By allowing hot, high-pressure steam to escape past the curved blades of turbine wheels he created an engine far smaller but infinitely more powerful than the existing reciprocating engines.

Today only the biggest merchant ships are powered by steam turbines, because for small and medium-sized vessels marine diesel engines are more efficient and more economical.

Finally, there has been the development of nuclear power for ship propulsion. The advantage of this form of propulsion is that very little space is required for fuel and ships can have a very long range and high cruising speed. Despite the fact that nuclear-powered merchant vessels have been operational since the late 1950s, there has been no rush to switch to this form of propulsion and in many countries these vessels are regarded with suspicion and distrust and are refused entry to many ports for fear of nuclear hazards.

7.7 Motive power and pipelines

Piped products have to be driven along the pipeline by some sort of pump. The variety of pumps in use is very great, as is the variety of prime movers driving them. Reciprocating pumps and single-stage or multi-stage centrifugal pumps are the main types, driven by electric motors, diesel engines, gas engines and steam or gas turbines. The particular situation, the product to be pumped, the fuel available and the size of the installation are major factors in determining the responses of the engineer to the problems faced.

To double the volume of a fluid passing through a pipeline requires four times the pressure. Therefore a pipeline installed some time ago which, due to changes of demand, needs to take a bigger volume of traffic will need very much greater pumping power if it is to carry the load. Four times the volume would require sixteen times the pressure. It is better to install a number of pumping houses at intervals along the line and spread the increased work among them. In many cases pumping stations can be remotely controlled by an automatic sequence of operations, and sensing devices will shut down a pump which for some reason is malfunctioning.

7.8 Summary

1. A 'prime mover' is a fundamental source of power which can be used in any logistical situation. Since the industrial revolution began in the eighteenth century, we have seen steam power, electric motors, internal combustion engines, diesel engines, turbines, jet engines and linear induction motors acting as prime movers.
2. The mode of transport to some extent dictates the type of prime mover which is used. It is a case of 'horses for courses'; which prime mover is most suitable for a particular mode of transport.
3. We may give as examples the following:
   (a) The most suitable vehicle for the small motor car is the internal combustion engine. It is light in weight, powerful enough to give easy take-off from a stationary position and rapid acceleration, and it is economical to run.
   (b) The most suitable method of propulsion for a railway is the electric motor. It is powerful for taking off from a stationary position, but this power can be reduced as the train gathers speed. It is economical to run, and power can be picked up all the time on a journey, from overhead cables or a 'live' line. In many parts of the world trains are still pulled by steam engines, and in others, where the capital costs of electrification are too great, the diesel electric engine is the best alternative prime mover. It uses the diesel engine to generate electricity and then uses the power thus generated to drive ordinary electric motors to drive the wheels.
   (c) Diesel power is most appropriate for heavy goods movements. The engines are larger and more powerful than the internal combustion engine, and about 40 per cent of the heat energy is converted to useful work.
   (d) Turbines are rotary engines which are suitable for driving propeller shafts and are also widely used in the generation of electricity. The design of the engine is such that streams of air, or steam, impinge on blades which cause the rotary motion.
   (e) Jet engines depend on the generation of a jet-stream which arises from the expansion that occurs when compressed air is mixed with fuel vapour and fired. The expansion expels the gases at great speed causing a forward thrust, which propels the unit of carriage.
   (f) Piped products have to be driven along the pipeline by some sort of pump. There are many varieties of pump depending on the product to be pumped, the fuel available and the size of the installation. Where demand for a product increases and the pipeline has to be forced to carry more of it, greater pressure is required, and it is usual to install more pumping houses along the route to share out the work between them.

7.9 Questions

1. What is a prime mover? Refer in your answer to the historical developments of units of propulsion between 1760 and the 1990s.
2. Explain the principles behind the internal combustion engine. For what kinds of transport is it most useful?
3. At one time aeroplanes were pulled off the ground by a propeller driven by an internal combustion engine. Today they are pushed off the ground by a bypass jet engine. What is the difference between these prime movers, and why has the later method of propulsion largely replaced the earlier method?
4. What prime mover drives products through pipelines? Refer in your answer to (a) domestic water supplies; (b) petrol delivered to the carburettor of a car; and (c) crude oil from Iraq to the Mediterranean coast.

8 Logistics – the art of managing supply-chains

8.1 Introduction

The standard dictionary definition of logistics is 'the art of moving, lodging and supplying troops and equipment'. At the time that this definition was laid down almost the only vast movements of people and goods were military movements, and the word itself (from the French *loger* – to lodge) suggests that the biggest problem was billeting the troops from night to night as they moved through the countryside, eating their way across country, no doubt at the peasants' expense. Today, the word has little to do with finding lodgings, but it still serves to describe the activities required when vast numbers of people, or vast quantities of goods, have to be moved from place to place, often across frontiers. Imagine their amazement had those early military leaders, with their forced marches of 20 miles (32 km) a day and trains of donkeys carrying powder and shot in panniers, been able to envisage the tonnage that is carried every day on the roads of every country in the modern world. Many transport managers today are very Napoleons of logistics and never have to retreat from Moscow (or anywhere else).

We need a new definition of logistics. Before we devise one let us remind ourselves that we live in a world where people want things – food, shelter, clothing, medical care, education, entertainment, etc. These 'wants' lead to huge 'demands' for goods and services, for there are now almost 6,000 million people on earth. To meet the demands producers around the world must provide enormous quantities of goods and a vast array of services, each with its specialised requirements. It is these supplies which pose the logistical problems, for we must either move the goods to the consumers who require them or move the people to the places where the services can be enjoyed. It is the supply-chains for all these products and services which are the true subject-matter of logistics. The end of the logistical chain is when the finished product, available for immediate 'consumption' reaches the final 'consumer'. 'Consumption' and 'consumer' are in quotation marks to remind us that they have a special meaning in economics; they don't just apply to foods and beverages but to everything we use – from a Savile Row suit to a Japanese video. The full production–consumption cycle reads: wants; enterprise; production; distribution; marketing; exchange; consumption; satisfaction and back to 'wants' again. Consumption gives satisfaction, but in so doing destroys production and we're back to 6,000 million people who want things.

This is elementary stuff, but the way in which these 'wants' are satisfied in the modern, free enterprise world is far from elementary. The typical organisation in the free enterprise world today is the multinational company, engaged in multinational production. Manufacturing is rarely a one-site activity. Multiple-site manufacturing and assembly is the usual practice, and for the multinational company this means sites in a variety of countries spanning the five continents. Products may be designed in Japan; components may be manufactured in Taiwan or Singapore; sub-assemblies may be put together in Spain and the final product assembled in the United Kingdom and sold all over the European Union, North America, Australia and the Middle East.

All this dispersal of production may come about for a variety of reasons. It may be because of local resources; because of particular skills in a workforce; because labour is cheaper in a particular country; because quality is high in a particular field of activity. Often the spreading of production has to do with the requirements of governments, who will only allow an activity to go ahead if it brings some tangible benefits to the people of their country. They may require all activities to be by nominally local companies, with a home national in an influential position on the Board. Whatever the reason, this type of production requires logistical services to keep control of the many movements of raw materials, semi-manufactures, components and end-products which are on the move, often tied to tight deadlines. This is the subject-matter of logistics, which seeks to give control over all these movements while at the same time providing a system which is flexible and can respond to changes in demands, closures of routes and other interruptions of normal procedures.

8.2 A definition of logistics

Logistics is the art of maintaining control over world-wide supply-chains by a combination of transport, warehousing skills, distribution management and information technology. Transport bridges the geographical gaps in the complex pattern of manufacturing centres, sources of raw material supplies, depot locations and marketing outlets which are such ubiquitous features of the modern multinational company. Warehousing keeps goods of every sort, from raw materials to finished products, secure in the time gaps which separate 'production' from 'consumption'. Distribution centres accept and hold buffer stocks until required, and then route them to the factories, wholesalers and retailers that require them. Information technology keeps track of where everything is, alerts those who need to be informed of amended instructions, documents stocks, orders, transits, arrivals and departures and permits everyone who is authorised to do so to access its data banks, interrogate them and, if necessary, update them.

8.3 The logistics function

The logistics function in a major multinational company may be operated by an in-house department. More likely it will be either a specialist, wholly owned subsidiary charged with the responsibility of planning and implementing programmes for every aspect of the multinational's affairs, or it will be an independent, experienced logistics company with which the multinational has established a long-term relationship. The advantage of the last arrangement is that an outside firm which has wide experience of logistical activities will know beforehand many of the problems facing the firm that seeks its advice, and will have devised solutions to many of them. It will avoid the blind alleys down which a less experienced firm will be led by enthusiastic, commission-hungry sales staff. Different accounting practices, different operating procedures, different computer hardware and software all present problems to the firm trying to develop a viable system for a complex set of operations.

Until recently the term logistics was rarely heard in enterprises, except military enterprises. The term commonly used for the function we now call 'logistics' was 'physical distribution' and the person who personified the role was the physical distribution manager. This term was itself an advance on earlier terms in common use, such as transport manager, dispatch manager, export manager. It is not simply a question of taking a more grandiloquent name as the activities carried out become more professional – we are not turning 'rat catchers' into 'rodent operatives' or 'dustmen' into 'sanitation officers'. The point is that a new awareness of the importance of the management of supply-chains has developed in recent years, as the market has become increasingly important in the economic life of nations. We now operate in an atmosphere not just of multinational companies but of global companies, with outlooks which regard the whole world as the natural source of raw materials and labour and the natural marketplace for our end-products. The movements of primary goods, secondary manufactures and people are so enormous that we need a fully professional body of people not just to carry out the many activities required but to understand the whole procedure, to know what the objectives are and to keep the whole set of activities and procedures moving forward to achieve the objectives, and increase our competitiveness.

The word 'mission' has been used to describe the ultimate objectives for which the global company is striving, and it is a valid idea despite its overtones of 'Starship Enterprise'. It is for the Board of Directors of a company to consider and establish the 'mission' of the company. However, it is not enough to decide what the mission is; it is also necessary to promulgate it, to announce it to the staff, proclaim it to the world and to campaign actively for its achievement.

The importance of knowing what the mission is lies in the simple fact that every activity can then be judged by whether it helps to advance the achievement of the mission or retards it. There are always occasions in any business where different departments view things differently because they are judging the matter from different points of view. The Sales Department may be motivated by thoughts of the commission they will earn, while the Transport Department may be pondering whether they can do what the Sales Department wants and still get home by night-time. The accountant will be trying to reduce costs while the Export Department wants to oblige an important customer. If we know the underlying mission which the Board of Directors has decided on, we can promote the co-operation of departments because we can judge whether the attitude of a particular department is along the right lines, or if it is throwing a spanner in the works. To take a different example, it is very difficult sometimes to get an accountant to spend money, but you can do it if you can show that the mission requires it.

The increased interest in the activity called logistics has given us a new term for the person making these logistical arrangements – the logistician. If the true function of the logistician is to manage supply-chains with optimum efficiency so as to achieve the mission laid down by top management, then we know where the logistician is in the global company's total plan. He is there supervising everything to do with the supply-chain, keeping it free of bottle-necks, free of documentation difficulties, using the best equipment in the most efficient way, fast, cheap, economic, legal, environmentally friendly and, above all, on course to achieve the mission.

The 'mission' is for top management to conceive and publicise. To achieve it requires many, much more mundane activities, each of which has to be carried out smoothly and efficiently. All these activities, while they may not be much to do with logistics, in the long run will have logistical impact. For example, advertising is not a logistical activity but if it results in demand for our goods and services, it leads to our need to set up supply-chains.

There are three main supply-chains. There is the supply-chain that brings the raw material to the factory, the power to the blast furnace or the diesel fuel to the transport manager. There is the supply-chain within the business, or on a business-to-business basis, that moves components around from plant to plant and plant to depot. Finally, there is the supply-chain that will satisfy demand by moving our finished goods to the wholesalers and retailers who make them available at points convenient to the final consumer. If logistics is the art of managing supply-chains, its major concern is to manage the flows into, within and out of a business. The flows into a business are the supplies of raw materials and other goods which the business requires for its production activities. The flows within a business are the huge movements of goods which the global company moves between various production centres, assembly factories, depots and warehouses. The flows out of a business are supplies of finished goods on their way into the marketplace where they will become available eventually to the consumers who require them.

What are the links in the logistical chain for such a company?

1. The procurement and delivery of such raw materials as are required, in as optimum a condition as we can get.
2. The procurement and delivery of component parts, as required, from specialist suppliers or subcontractors, in such quantities as are necessary, while at the same time avoiding excessive stocks which will tie up capital to no useful purpose.
3. The procurement and delivery of capital assets of every kind; for example, machinery, tools, power plants, fixtures and fittings, motor vehicles, computers, office equipment, etc.
4. The procurement and delivery of all consumable items necessary to both factories and offices, such as lubricants, chemical products, packaging, packing materials, copying materials, etc.
5. It is necessary to assemble a labour force for both the production processes and the logistical operations. Good personnel are of the utmost importance. In both cases it is essential that all staff are made aware of the overall mission and the role expected of them in fulfilling it. Initially, we need to recruit staff in such numbers and of such qualities as are required for the variety of jobs we have to do. A nice mixture of theory and practice is required, so that both academic knowledge and on-the-job training are important. It goes without saying that a global company will take a global attitude to personnel, using nationals of a country wherever possible and a minimum of expatriates. Promotion opportunities must be available to all ranks and a high level of professional behaviour must be encouraged. This professionalism should include loyalty to the company, and both must be rewarded with appropriate pay levels and good conditions of employment. There may be some element of logistics in bringing the

labour force to the factory, although many of them may be prepared to arrange this privately, using their own personal transport. This does, however, require the provision of extensive car parking facilities at all production areas, and some supervision by car park attendants, security staff, etc.

6. The internal distribution of all these items so that they reach the right person, in the right place, at the right time, in mint condition for the purpose required.
7. The immediate clearance of production-lines as goods reach completion, and the tallying and safeguarding of the finished products.
8. The distribution of finished products by secure procedures either to appropriate warehouses and depots or to wholesalers and retailers, to fulfil orders already placed.
9. The final stage is the actual exchange of the finished products; their delivery to the final consumer in return for a monetary payment called the price.
10. Where the chain of activities is not concerned with goods but with services, it is the actual rendering of the service to the final consumer that is the final link in the chain. One logistical offshoot of this need to bring the customer to the service is the need to provide adequate car parking facilities at places such as hospitals, dental surgeries, clinics, etc., while free parking, cheaper petrol sold as a 'loss leader' and longer opening hours may favourably incline the local population towards a particular retail outlet.

8.4 The requirements of a logistical organisation

The task of the logistical organisation is to manage the flows of international trade around the world. Although there are many forms which the organisation could take, depending on its position within a group of companies, or on its status as an independent organisation working for a number of companies, we can say that we would expect to find some of the following characteristics:

1. A 'world-wide' organisation.
2. A sophisticated information technology (IT) system.
3. A complex pattern of transport facilities at the company's disposal.
4. Support services from other companies in the group, to offer a full range of logistical services.
5. A sophisticated network of management information services.
6. A high regard for the quality of its services.
7. A well-trained, co-operative and enthusiastic staff.

8.4.1 A world-wide organisation

The organisation must have a world-wide basis. True, for some companies the 'world' referred to might be rather more limited than the natural world. For example a UK multinational might have factories, plants, depots and marketing outlets in the United Kingdom, other European countries, Commonwealth countries and the United States. It could call itself a world-wide trader but in fact have no links with South America or much of Asia. When we say an organisation must have a world-wide basis we mean it must have not only an office in every region it deals with, but a network of offices in each region. One of these will be designated the regional office for that area, and will be in constant touch with International Head Office (IHO) and with all the sub-offices under its control. Such a regional office will control all the operations taking place in its region. It will ensure the quality of the service offered is high, will feed back problems to IHO and carry out IHO's policies in its region. Thus policies on human resource development call for training programmes which the regional office will organise and staff and will designate trainees to attend.

8.4.2 A sophisticated IT system

The company will have a sophisticated information technology (IT) organisation, giving instantaneous links with all sections of the company, outside organisations (such as H.M. Customs, banks, etc.) and with 'customers'. The word 'customers' therefore means not only outside firms which have asked to use the services available, but also subsidiary companies of the multinational or the Group, who rely on the Logistics Department for their logistical activities. One of the chief functions of this IT network will be to document all consignments correctly and to have this documentation in store in the computer, so that anyone requiring it can be sent copies electronically in seconds. It will almost certainly include DTI (direct trader input) facilities, so that departments and outside customers can access the computer to key in new information as it becomes available. The full information on any document cannot always be supplied at any one moment – it has to be built up over the course of a few days or possibly longer – by EDI messages keyed in from remote terminals. One of the important aspects of any EDI strategy is that there must be world-wide compatibility with customers, agents, carriers and customs authorities. The system therefore has to be designed to comply with such international specifications as UN/EDIFACT (the United Nations Electronic Data Interchange for Administration, Commerce and Transport). Unfortunately, there is no such thing as a fully-finished system of EDI. Progress is so rapid in the electronics field that all systems in use are constantly under examination with a view to upgrading them.

8.4.3 A complex pattern of transport facilities

The organisation must have a complex pattern of transport facilities at its disposal. We are talking about companies that need to move huge quantities of goods around the world, with multiple-site manufacturing and assembly, and multiple-outlet marketing. Such huge transport activities involve all modes of transport. The organisation needs either its own fleets of lorries, ships and aircraft or sound links with major hauliers, shipping lines and airlines. If it uses rail services, as may happen increasingly in the United Kingdom once Eurotunnel is open, it needs good links with its local rail depot and in some cases it will be worth building private sidings. It will need a variety of materials handling devices, forklift trucks, heavy forklift trucks, cranes and possibly overhead gantries.

8.4.4 Support services from other companies in the Group

The scale of the transport movements referred to in the last paragraph is likely to lead to the acquisition of specialist operators in various fields to perform many of these activities. In other words, the typical logistical organisation will be a group of companies acting as wholly owned subsidiaries of the holding company. There will also be more loosely linked arrangements, for example joint venture arrangements, links with finance houses and merchant banks and possibly mutual insurance arrangements as with P.I. Clubs (protection and indemnity associations) whereby those members who lose a valuable ship receive contributions from club members who have been more fortunate, and losses fall easily on many rather than heavily on one member.

8.4.5 A network of management information services

The rapid feedback of management information is a major feature of such large-scale logistical organisations. This chiefly comes from the excellence of the information technology (IT) available. Not only does such a full IT system give excellent opportunities for reporting back computer-detected problems (from simple stock re-order points and out-of-budget expenditures to very sophisticated number-crunching activities) but the e-mail links give instantaneous rapport between staff at all levels. E-mail means electronic mail, the ability to send messages at electronic speeds from one individual to another (to reply you only need to reverse the two codes for sender and recipient). One company claims that its staff get on average 160 e-mail messages every day – anything from detailed reports to rude remarks. One wonders how they find the time to answer them. It can be seen that such systems can alert top management to problem areas very quickly, which gives every opportunity to improve the quality of service being offered.

8.4.6 A high regard for the quality of its services

Mention was made earlier in this chapter of the 'mission' of the company to be fulfilled by staff. Quality of service to customers is an essential element in the objectives of a company and in the logistic field is of paramount importance, since the quality of service is very much on view. If goods fail to arrive because of vehicle breakdown, customs delays due to poor documentation or some similar fault, it will be obvious that the service is below par. The aim of the logistician is to comply absolutely with the agreed contractual arrangements made with the customer, for example as to safe arrival, delivery date, quality of product, etc. Where strict compliance cannot be achieved the aim is to advise the customer at once, explain the circumstances and propose corrective action.

It isn't just our service to the customers which needs to be monitored, we must equally monitor the service we get from the agents and suppliers who provide services to us. A systematic record of the services offered by airlines, contract carriers, shipping lines, etc., will establish how successful they are in meeting the promises they have made. Such suppliers of services are often called vendors; they are trying to sell us their services. If we know which suppliers regularly fulfil their promises, we shall establish them in our minds as 'preferred vendors' with a good track-record. We shall not lightly turn elsewhere when approached by their competitors with an attractive 'special offer'. We shall remember their track-record. Similarly, we shall be anxious for them not to turn to obliging someone else, rather than us. Thus we shall pay them promptly, in accordance with our agreed payments arrangements so that they will be anxious to retain our custom.

8.4.7 A well-trained, co-operative and enthusiastic staff

The final feature required in the logistics field is a happy, busy, contented workforce, who can be relied on to pull their weight in any emergency; to put the good of the company and its service to the customer first at all times, and thereby meet the requirements of the mission. They must be properly trained, from the moment of induction on joining the company, through a lengthy series of training activities to broaden and deepen the understanding of staff, leading ultimately to full professional qualification in the institute or professional body selected. The logistics field is not a line and staff organisation with strict military codes of discipline. Instead, it is a network, with each individual being joined up to other individuals in a network of communications, controls and authority. The point about this type of organisation is that knowledge can reside anywhere in the network at one time or another, and authority lies temporarily with the individual whose knowledge is most appropriate to the problem currently needing solution. Messages may arrive at any moment calling for urgent decisions about the switching of consignments, the recovery of loads; even the rescue of staff. No one should ever take the attitude 'That's not my worry – let someone else deal with it.' If it's only a matter of alerting someone with the required expertise that there is a problem, every member of staff must take action when things come to his attention. The rule is to act to advance the remedy and overcome the bottle-neck that is interrupting the logistical flow. It is also essential that members of staff who foresee a difficulty with a particular consignment, or have any work-related problem, should be able to air the problem with senior staff confident that they will be listened to and the problem resolved. Equally, staff with personal difficulties need to know to whom they can turn for advice and help.

8.5 BHP – a multinational conglomerate

Although logistics is concerned with the whole supply-chain from raw material supply through the production process to the final distribution to the customer, it too often manifests itself on the downside of the chain, as in the case of FMCG firms (fast-moving consumer goods), where the logistical activities are normally retailer led.

As an example of the whole logistical chain we turn to The Broken Hill Proprietary Co. Ltd (BHP), Australia's largest company, which nowadays has a world-wide diversity of assets and interests associated with the mining, steel and energy industries.

8.5.1 The early years

BHP started life in 1885 as a silver mining company at Broken Hill, which is in the outback area of New South Wales close to the South Australian border. Its initial wealth came not only from its silver but also from the associated lead and zinc ores. However, it later developed further mining interests in iron ore and after some years of trial activities it took a formal decision in 1911 to enter the steel industry. In 1915 the company opened its first steelworks at Newcastle, New South Wales. The years that followed saw the purchase of the company's first ship (an attempt to control transport costs) and the gradual development of its policy of vertical integration: integration from top to bottom of the industry, since under this policy value is added to basic raw materials at all stages of the supply-chain. For example, this policy gave rise to iron and steel industries at Newcastle and Port Kembla in New South Wales and at Whyalla in the Iron Knob area of South Australia, with coal moving westwards and iron ore moving eastwards, eventually using ships built in the company's own Whyalla shipyard (now closed as no longer viable). Other developments were in Tasmania, where limestone (a vital raw material for the steel industry) was quarried, and in the setting up of subsidiary steel product companies (more value-adding activities), mostly in the Newcastle area.

The company still produces a wide range of steel and associated engineering products both in Australia and elsewhere, continuing the vertical integration in that field.

8.5.2 BHP Petroleum

Oil was for many years the one major mineral which Australia lacked. However, in 1965 an offshore gasfield, and in 1967 an offshore oilfield, were found and developed in the Bass Strait, with BHP playing a 50/50 part. Subsequent finds of oil in the Torres Sea and natural gas on the North West Shelf (1976) spawned wider BHP interest in oil and gas exploration in other areas. In 1985 the company purchased the US petroleum interests of the Energy Reserves Group. In 1986 oil production began in the Timor Sea. In 1987 the majority of the shares of the UK firm Hamilton Oil were purchased (and the remainder were purchased in 1991). In 1989 the purchase of the USA Pacific Reserves Co. brought refining and other down-stream activities. The company's oil and gas interests are now as widespread as Papua New Guinea, the North Sea and Liverpool Bay. It also has offshore rigs in Vietnam, the Gulf of Mexico and in Argentina.

8.5.3 BHP Transport

BHP Transport began as a subsidiary shipping company in 1921. However, before examining its present-day role, it is as well to consider the transport infrastructure of Australia at that time.

Prior to the formation of the Australian Commonwealth in 1901, the separate Crown Colonies had each developed their own railway network, with no two adjoining colonies adopting the same gauge. Thus all inter-state freight movement was inevitably by coastwise vessels, while all intra-state traffic moved by rail to all parts of that state. The one exception was Broken Hill which, because of its isolation from the rest of New South Wales and its proximity to South Australia, established a cross-border link to Port Pirie where it established its smelters, using coal carried coastwise. Only governments were allowed to build and own railways, so the Company founded a tramway company, Silverton Tramway Company, to take the ore from Broken Hill over the border, to join up with the end of the South Australia railway line for transport to Port Pirie. This tramway line is considered to be the richest stretch of track ever built in Australia.

A similar tramway company was set up in South Australia itself to transport iron ore from the company's South Australia mines to Hummock Hill port (which later was renamed Whyalla).

Returning to our account of inter-state traffic, although nowadays the main cities are all linked by a through-rail service, the bulk of inter-state traffic, totalling many millions of tons, still moves coastwise by sea.

As a major indigenous mining and steel manufacturing company, BHP has been in a strong position to explore and develop the many and varied mineral products of this immensely mineral-wealthy continent. At the same time the advent of the bulk carrier and the increased world-wide demand for mineral products has brought Australia new world-wide markets, with Australian coal competing effectively in Western Europe, while many of its other mineral products find ready markets in the increasingly industrialised markets of the 'Pacific Rim' countries.

The present position of the Transport Group is explained in the next section.

8.5.4 The BHP Group today

Although today the company is not so intent on vertical integration and has diversified on a world-wide basis, the attached organisational diagram (Fig. 8.1) indicates its present structure. The diagram shows that the main component companies are BHP Minerals, BHP Petroleum and BHP Steel. The company's traditional interests in minerals have been extended at both national and international levels: limesands in South Australia (1966), manganese in Groote Eylandt (1966), iron ore at Mount Newman (1969), coal operations in Queensland (1976), the world's largest copper deposits in Chile (1983–4), gold at OK Tedi, Papua New Guinea (1984) and Syama (Mali) (1990) while New Zealand Steel was acquired in 1992.

The growth of the Company's oil and gas interests has been described above.

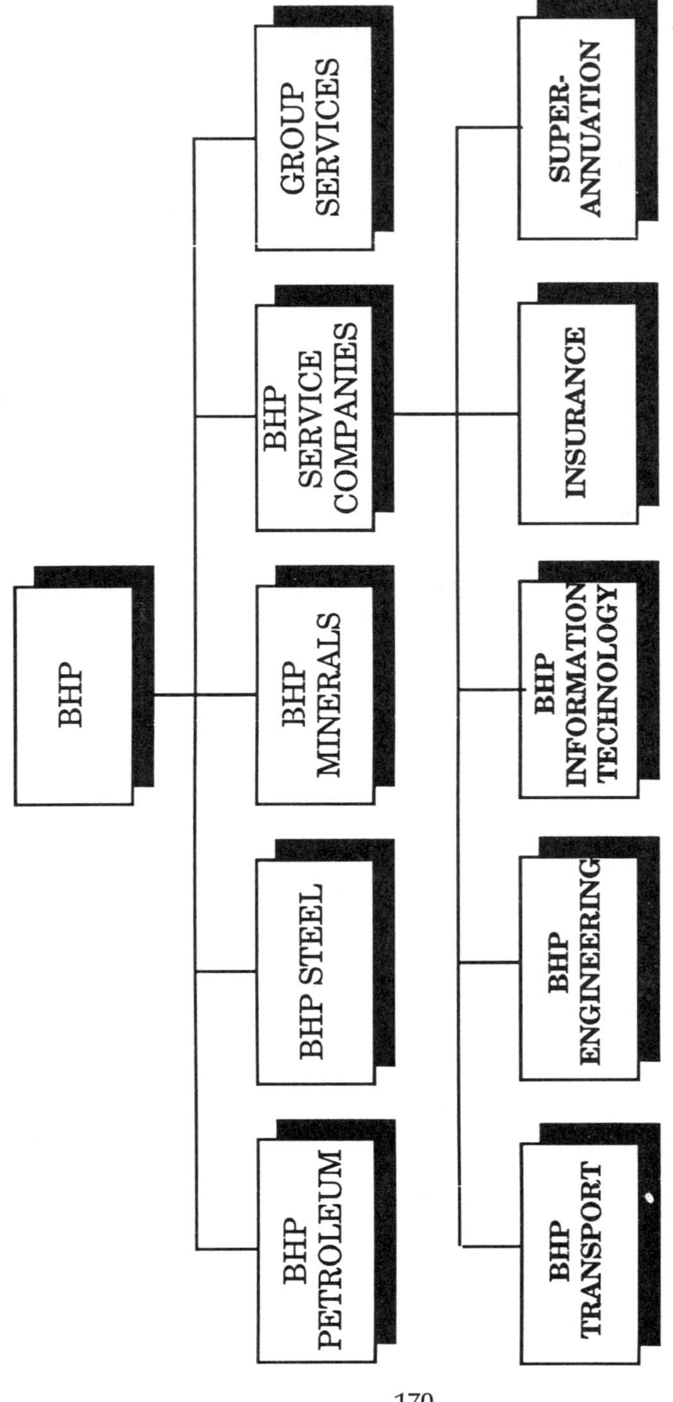

Fig. 8.1 Organisational chart of The Broken Hill Proprietary Co. Ltd

In its supporting role of providing the necessary transport for all these many and varied activities involving some 60 million tonnes annually, BHP Transport has a relatively small fleet of some 20 vessels under the Australian flag. This fleet comprises mainly bulk carriers, plus six tankers and two container vessels for the New Zealand Trade across the Tasman Sea. In addition its recently formed International Marine Transport subsidiary based in San Francisco operates a six-vessel liner service from the US West Coast to Australia, carrying containers, forestry products and machinery, with return cargoes of steel and minerals. A brand new four-liner service covering Australia, New Zealand, the United States, the Gulf of Mexico and Chile will carry not only containers, forestry products and steel but also bulk and break-bulk cargoes. To supplement its own vessels BHP has two chartering departments, which between them charter some 600 vessels annually. Although they occasionally use demise (bareboat) charters and there are currently some 15 vessels on time charter, their bulk cargo facility enables them to negotiate Voyage Charters on favourable terms, with the main responsibilities for such charters falling on the shipowners.

BHP Transport Ltd was hived off as a separate company in 1988. It is the largest Australian shipowner, and the largest single user of the nation's ports. In many of these ports it provides a wide range of services both for the vessels it operates and for non-BHP vessels. These services cover ship's agency, bunkering, tugs and stevedoring, with ship repair facilities available at Newcastle.

Ashore, BHP Transport Ltd is the largest single user of Australia's railways, accounting for some 25 per cent of all rail freight, although this would include traffic on their own mining lines in the Iron Knob area of South Australia, the iron and manganese mining area of north-west Western Australia and the line linking the coalfields of Queensland to Hay Point.

With some 8 per cent of all road traffic, BHP Transport Ltd uses contracted owner/drivers to tow their own trailers. Bearing in mind the competitive nature of road haulage and their strong cargo base, they are in a favourable negotiating position when arranging these contracts, which once again will tend to put the onus on the owner/drivers for such items as vehicle maintenance, return loads, etc.

In all their activities BHP Transport will have the advantage of cross-liaison with BHP's other service industries to provide them with the latest developments in transport engineering and information technology. Thus they are able to provide the main component industries with a strong representative in buying freight, which often represents a fairly significant percentage of total delivered costs. This strong bargaining position reduces Group costs for all BHP companies. Flexibility during peaks and troughs of activity is also provided by this bargaining power. Consolidated coverage is provided by the ancillary service firms as regards multi-modal operations, information technology and insurance. These wholly owned subsidiary ancillary industries cater not only for the needs of the main component companies but also for non-BHP customers. In the case of BHP Transport this is roughly on a 4/1 basis, with services such as ship's agency, tugs, bunkering, stevedoring and ship repairs being available to customer firms.

Often the main companies act as part of a consortium of international companies, e.g. in oilfield exploration and development. Furthermore, the company is prepared to diversify outside its normal sphere as far as investment is concerned. It recently became the largest shareholder in Foster's Breweries, of 'Amber Nectar' fame, perhaps better known world-wide than BHP itself.

From the logistical viewpoint we see therefore that BHP is able to achieve many economies by virtue of its large-scale operations. Co-operation between the various group companies and their service industries is close, and even when using outside firms, such as road hauliers, the railways and the charterers of vessels, the strong bargaining position of such a major company is a powerful weapon.

(We would like to thank The Broken Hill Proprietary Company Ltd for their co-operation in providing us with the necessary data used in compiling this summary.)

8.6 Summary

1. The traditional dictionary definition of logistics is 'the art of moving, lodging and supplying troops and equipment'.
2. A more modern definition of logistics would be 'the art of maintaining control over world-wide supply-chains by a combination of transport, warehousing skills, distribution management and information technology'.
3. The function of the logistician is to achieve the objectives of top management by supervising everything to do with the supply-chains into, within and out of the business, keeping them free from bottlenecks, breakdowns and documentation difficulties. Production today is rarely a one-site activity; raw materials, components and partially finished goods move from site to site in the course of completion.
4. It is the Board of Directors' job to establish the 'mission' of the multinational company and lay down the company's objectives. It is for the logistician to develop the information systems and the physical distribution network which will achieve the objectives and fulfil the mission.
5. The place of the logistician in the company's structure is to supervise everything to do with the supply-chains into, within and out of the

company – keeping them free of bottle-necks, free of documentation difficulties, fully safeguarded, moving in the best way; swiftly, economically, legally, in an environmentally friendly way and on course to achieve the mission.

6. The elements of a logistical organisation are:
   (a) A 'world-wide' organisation; but the word 'world' might only include those areas where the company is active. It implies a head office and a number of regional offices.
   (b) A sophisticated IT system which can keep track of everything being handled, with access to all offices of the company, H.M. Customs and similar bodies. Electronic data interchange (EDI) will enable all authorised parties to input data into the system and copy data from the system.
   (c) A complex pattern of transport facilities, either directly owned by the company or specifically contracted to perform certain operations, or (if public transport is used) generally contracted to handle the volume of traffic likely to become available for movement by that particular mode.
   (d) A well-trained, co-operative and enthusiastic staff, dedicated to the company's service, whose self-confidence is based on sound experience and training over a period of years, from the moment of induction, through a series of sideways movements to broaden knowledge of the industry, to junior management, middle management and senior management posts.

8.7 Questions

1. Why is logistics a feature of production by multinational companies? In your answer refer to any multinational company with which you are familiar.
2. Define logistics. Show how the main parts of your definition would apply to a company such as the Hyundai Corporation, which is active in automobiles, electronics, shipbuilding, engineering and construction, machinery and equipment, petrochemicals, trading and transportation.
3. What sort of supply-chains are met with in multinational manufacturing and trading?
4. What is information technology? Why has it such a large part to play in the logistical activities of major companies?
5. What are the elements of a logistical company? Why are they usually to be found as subsidiaries of major companies or independent organisations serving a number of major companies?

9 Just in time (JIT) strategies

9.1 The two sides to logistical strategies

If logistics is concerned with the management of supply-chains, there are two sides to logistical activities, and increased efficiency on either side of the divide will achieve economies, increase competitiveness and in time result in greater customer satisfaction. The dividing point is the wealth-creating site, whatever it may be. The typical site for wealth-creation is a factory site, but there are other wealth-creation centres. For example, farms are usually wealth-creating, and many offices which provide services are wealth-creating, but since logistics is chiefly about the management of supply-chains we will stick to the factory as the typical wealth-creation centre. On one side of the divide is the series of supply-chains which brings everything required into the factory. On the other side of the divide – the marketing side of the logistical activities – are the supply-chains which lead to customer satisfaction by bringing the products of the factory to the wholesalers and retailers who handle them and eventually ensure that they reach the customer.

In fact, of course, every supply-chain is a marketing supply-chain, because the complex nature of free enterprise society means that all the inputs illustrated in Fig. 9.1, which are being demanded by our factory, are being supplied by producers who are either primary producers (in the case of the raw material suppliers) or secondary producers working on intermediate products – products which are not marketed to final consumers but on a business-to-business basis for eventual incorporation in the finished product.

The unique feature of a JIT (just in time) strategy is that the management of the wealth-creating site achieves control of its suppliers by requiring them to deliver 'just in time' to meet the production needs of the factory. However, it isn't just a question of time, it is also a question of quality, because it is no good having a sub-standard component arriving just in time; the whole emphasis is on persuading the supplier to ensure

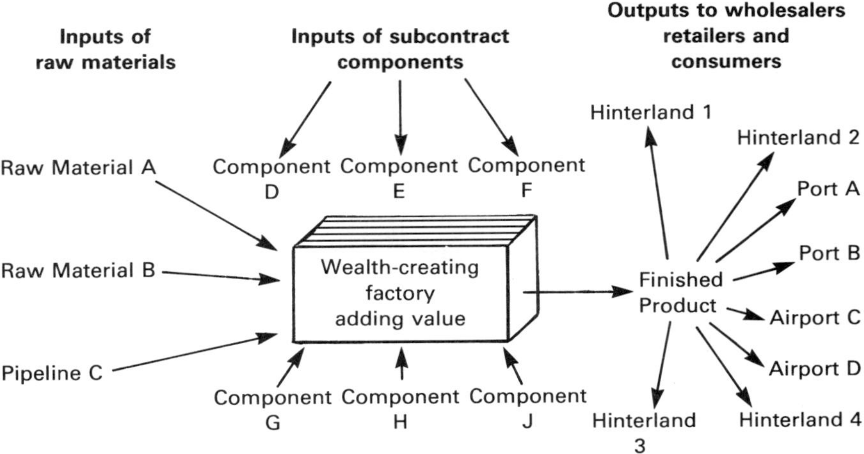

Fig. 9.1 The supply-chains that logistics seeks to manage

that the quality of the product is exactly right and according to specification. If the vendor – and all our suppliers are vendors to us of the goods and services we require – wishes to achieve the status of 'preferred vendor', and thus be ensured of regular daily orders and regular payments for the fulfilment of the orders, he or she must deliver JIT and with quality guaranteed.

9.2 What is a JIT strategy?

A JIT strategy is a strategy which seeks to ensure that, by careful planning and improved communication and ordering arrangements, supplies of products such as raw materials and components reach the production site just in time for the activities for which they are needed. The reason for the strategy is that if this can be done, enormous savings in both capital and revenue expenditure can be achieved. We do not need the expensive costing procedures which are necessary when supplies are taken into stock and then issued against requisitions from the factory floor. Such procedures require the keeping of records, the processing of documents and the double-handling of the supplies as they move in and out of stock. They also require premises, storage containers, handling equipment and other capital assets. If they arrive just in time, and go straight to the point where they are to be used, and are at once incorporated into the finished product, huge economies can be achieved.

One essential element in the rethinking of the industrial processes is the way in which supplies are ordered. Instead of setting stock levels and laying down EOQs (economic order quantities), all we need to know is how many units of output we intend to produce tomorrow. Having laid down very careful specifications for the materials or components we require, and having accepted test deliveries to ensure that the supplier understands the product exactly and can achieve the quality we need, all the supplier needs to know after that is how many to deliver, and when. Orders can be phoned or faxed through on a day-to-day basis, and the supplier is required to deliver direct to the factory floor where the goods are available for immediate use. There is no need to take anything into stock, or to issue it against a requisition from the department needing it. What is checked off on delivery is what passes into production that day. As far as all parties are concerned, production is 'to order' rather than for stock. Goods inwards come straight off the delivery vehicle to that point on the shopfloor where they are required. Layout of the shopfloor is carefully planned so that work flows from one process to the next with a minimum of re-routeing. Quality control procedures are strict, so that faults are discovered early to reduce spoilt work and waste, or reworking costs. Feedback alerts staff early to any defect so that machines can be adjusted and reset. Detailed allocations of costs for labour, raw materials, power, etc., are not required at cost centres since the whole process can be calculated backwards from the finished total costs. We know what materials are in the finished product, how much time the average process takes, and consequently what the labour costs will be. This process of estimating costs backwards is called 'back-flushing'.

The finished goods coming off the production-line are again being produced to order, rather than for stock. They can therefore be made into pallet-sized unit loads which can be shrink-wrapped if necessary and at once containerised into larger unit loads. They are therefore ready for dispatch to the wholesaler or customer who has ordered them. The savings in storage space, double-handling and security are enormous.

9.3 Preferred vendor status

Each subcontractor is viewed as a vendor of services who has undertaken to provide batches of raw material or batches of assemblies according to our specifications. Since we are only producing 'to order', the batches ordered will exactly fit our requirements and any defect of quality will mean that the order planned to be completed today will be subject to delay, or if sent forward will have to declare a shortage. This means extra cost and failure to fulfil our promises to our customers, although the fault lies with our supplier. In order to retain 'preferred vendor' status the supplier will therefore be forced to pay great attention to quality control; to the training of staff; to the inspection of work at every stage and to the elimination of faults. There is a pressure backwards from the main wealth-creation site to establish sound procedures by suppliers, and by those suppliers on their suppliers, so that the whole level of production is raised.

The size of batches has an important impact on the quality of the product. Imagine a subcontractor who produces the driver's seat for a particular model of a motor car manufacturer. Because production is 'to order' the subcontractor will not be making seats in an endless production process which could become boring and repetitive, with consequent loss of interest and lowering of quality. There are no stocks of seats being built up, waiting for orders. Once the batch is done work stops and attention can be given to proper maintenance, training, group discussion in the form of quality circles (see page 178 below), etc. This batch production gives more opportunity to look at what has been done (how it went, what snags arose, how they were solved, etc.) than continuous production for stock – where spoilt work may, in fact, be concealed for some time until it is almost impossible to allocate responsibility.

Vendors may complain that the JIT system forces them to hold stocks on behalf of the manufacturer, since the numbers ordered each day will fluctuate and they are bound to some extent to go on producing to make the best use of their staff and machinery. This may be true, but the onus is then on them to require their suppliers in turn to operate a JIT system too. Clearly, there may be some element of stock-building somewhere in the system, but the emphasis on quality control will ensure that any stocks that are built up will at least be of high quality.

9.4 The savings of a JIT system

The following savings may be achieved:

9.4.1 Savings in inventories (stocks) of raw materials and components

These arise because requirements are being delivered on a daily basis, in batches of small size. The manufacturer takes delivery of the goods at the factory gate and acquires title to them at that time. The manufacturer thus becomes liable for them at that moment, and does not acquire any stocks before they are needed. Smaller stocks (or the total elimination of stocks) reduces the capital required in a business and consequently raises the return on capital invested. This is one of the basic ratios in business. It is found by the formula:

$$\frac{\text{Net profit} \times 100}{\text{Capital invested at start}}$$

Clearly, anything that increases net profit, or reduces the capital invested at the start, will improve the return on capital invested. If a business produces for stock and holds large stocks of various items, it means capital has been wasted by ordering and paying for items before they were really needed.

9.4.2 Savings in costing procedures

Costing procedures are time-consuming and involve budgeting beforehand, cost allocation as jobs proceed and variance analysis (investigation of variations of actual costs from budgeted costs). These procedures can be short-circuited if 'back-flushing' is used – working backwards from the finished outputs and the total costs.

9.4.3 Reduced problems with work-in-progress

Work-in-progress calculations require us at certain times to value the work-in-progress, since it is part of stock. If we arrange for each day's work to be completed, there is no work-in-progress.

9.4.4 Reduced handling costs

Handling costs are a major cost of any production system and any reduction in them means more efficient and more competitive activities. We have already referred to the avoidance of double-handling by not taking goods into stock and then issuing them to staff; instead, they go straight to the point of production where they are required. Such activities as loading and unloading vans and stuffing and unstuffing containers can be major causes for delay. If these activities are carefully analysed, and special equipment in the form of forklift trucks, pallets, stillages, etc. are provided, considerable savings can be achieved.

9.5 Quality circles

A basic principle behind JIT operations is that it is always possible to improve the methods of working so as to make a component simpler and less costly. Everyone is welcome to contribute ideas to this end and to benefit from the savings achieved, possibly by some sort of direct payment like a team bonus, but in general by the improved prospects for the company as a whole. For example, security of employment is something that most employees appreciate, and improved efficiency and competitiveness encourage security of employment.

The changes that are to be achieved must be such as to save resources, or to save time, or to make more intensive use of the capital equipment, etc., provided.

A quality circle is a meeting which is held regularly – say, fortnightly or monthly – in which everyone is able to take part in a discussion about the work of the section, the products it is making and the methods used. There is usually a team leader, such as the section supervisor, and possibly a 'secretary' – a team member who makes notes of points decided. The matters for discussion may be the result of a customer complaint, a report from management, a vocal worker's complaint, etc. Such matters as excessive waste, poor quality, delays in material supply, etc. will be raised. The views of shopfloor workers are particularly valuable since they are closer to the scene of action and know what really happened. They are also pretty quick to detect a cover-up.

Sometimes the discussion may lead to enquiries into what happens in other departments, and it may be that the views of an expert – for example, a quality control specialist – will be needed. The company can appoint a 'facilitator' to liaise with the group, find out what is bothering them and bring in an appropriate person to explain the matter. The facilitator has to win the respect of the group by a willingness to listen, and to take their problem seriously.

The final result of a quality circle discussion (or possibly series of discussions) is a recommendation to management for a change in current procedures. This would almost certainly be adopted, or at least adopted for a trial period. If there is some good reason for top management's refusal to adopt the idea this should be carefully explained, by someone higher in rank than the facilitator, since otherwise the shopfloor may feel that no one is really listening 'up there', and they may lose confidence in the whole procedure.

9.6 The effect of JIT on manufacturing

One feature of JIT operations is that there is no intention to go on producing things that are not wanted yet anyway. Consequently, any breakdown in one department means that while the people in that area do their utmost to solve the problem the people further up the line stop production and do other things. This cuts across many of the 'trade' ideas prevalent in industrial labour forces. Thus the idea that only an electrician can change a plug, or only an engineer can tighten a bolt, are redundant ideas in the JIT context. If today's batch has gone through production, the workforce are left with time on their hands, which can be usefully filled by all sorts of activities so long as restrictive practices do not interfere. Some of this time can be filled with training, to raise the level of young staff or new staff, and teach them a range of useful skills. These skills need not be particular to any trade, but to the factory as a whole. This gives a more flexible labour force, who can apply their skills to a number of different tasks should absence or a change in market demand call for a different range of activities.

Another major use for this spare time is for general maintenance work on the system of production in use, and even changes of layout may be effected in this way. If everyone lends a hand, and demarcation disputes cannot interfere, much can be achieved without laying off idle workers. Of course, such activities will be under the guidance and control of design staff and maintenance staff who know what is required, but other staff will be able to play a useful part and earn their wages in the normal way.

9.7 The effect of JIT on distribution

We can see that if suppliers are being required to deliver in smaller quantities, more regularly and 'just in time', they are going to need a distribution system appropriate to the scale of their new activities. Similarly, if the day's output is cleared from the production-lines in unit loads for immediate dispatch to the customer who has ordered the goods, this again calls for regular deliveries and requires close communication links between suppliers, distributors and customers. The logistical problems must be considered in detail before the JIT system is introduced, and reliable solutions must be found. Whether the matter is to be handled by own-account vehicles, by contract hire, or by the use of public transport services, the procedures have to be thought through completely. JIT is usually introduced in a small area of a company's activities and is gradually extended to other areas. This gives the opportunity to develop the distribution system in the same way, curing problems as they arise and gradually developing sound solutions.

One thing that helps is reducing the number of suppliers, since the more suppliers we have delivering different items the more complex the distribution network becomes. Drivers can be delayed because other vehicles are blocking unloading bays. If suppliers can be persuaded to take over other ranges of components and extend their expertise to offer an increased share of the company's requirements, this will make it easier to develop a genuine partnership of interests and result in the conferment of 'preferred vendor' status on the supplier concerned.

Further simplification of the distribution system can be achieved by a careful assessment of a manufacturing company's centres of production and the location of its chief suppliers. We need rational arrangements which group production centres as closely as possible, and it may even be desirable to close production at an awkwardly placed site and redevelop the activity closer to other units. Similarly, important suppliers may be persuaded to relocate more conveniently where they become satellite locations of the main company, thus reducing distribution problems.

9.8 The effect of JIT on cashflow

Cashflow is an important factor in the economic conduct of any business, and if the parties are contracting together on fair terms, the movement of regular daily consignments should enable all parties to improve their cashflows. The tendency of large companies in recent years has been to extend the credit period they require from suppliers, and this has amounted to exploitation of the weak by the strong. It has caused considerable resentment, and innumerable bankruptcies of smaller firms, to such an extent that it seems likely that the UK parliament will legislate for a more favourable regime.

In the absence of such unfair treatment a JIT system promotes cashflow because all parties assume their responsibilities in a regular, repetitive way. The goods arriving JIT at the factory gate change hands and ownership at the same time, and an invoice passes from supplier to customer. In this case the factory is the customer, so to avoid confusion we will use the term 'value-adder'. The invoice passing from supplier to value-adder becomes liable for payment under whatever terms the parties have agreed, which ideally should not be longer than 30 days from invoice date. Similarly, the goods which have gone into production that day have been delivered (or at least sent on their way) that very day, so that an invoice from value-adder to wholesaler (or retailer) will also be dispatched. If this invoice is also payable within 30 days of invoice date the cashflows should soon begin which enable all parties to meet their commitments. Of course, a whole chain of commercial activities may be generating this cashflow – because the final consumer may pay on credit card or on hire purchase, so that banks and finance houses are involved – but the whole climate of business will be more optimistic, since the prospects of payment, and therefore of profitability, are improved.

9.9 The logistical implications of JIT

The implementation of a JIT strategy has profound logistical implications for the parties involved. Absolute reliability of delivery services is essential, and as suppliers will be responsible for this they must look to their transport arrangements to ensure they are absolutely reliable, so that they can comply with their contractual liabilities. If own transport is used it must be adequate for the purpose, and back-up cover must be available from reserve vehicles. If the delivery service is subcontracted to a specialist haulage firm, it must be fully informed about the new urgency of 'safe arrival', and its arrangements must be such as to provide adequate back-up, prompt notification of any problem and the need to take urgent steps to rectify the matter. It may be desirable to change to a recognised 'express delivery' service now that regular consignments with a clear deadline are available. If this is not deemed necessary, it may still be advisable to establish a link with such a company for agreed priority treatment on an emergency basis when problems do arise.

With inter-company movements, for example moving components to other 'value-adding' centres, full-load movements on a door-to-door basis have much to recommend them. They avoid double-handling as goods are switched from one mode to another, and they are under the personal supervision of drivers and mates at all times. This means customs delays can be reduced, pilfering and theft are less likely and usually time lost at interfaces is reduced to a minimum.

Against all these innovative attitudes to a changed production system, where production only supplies goods 'just in time', we must say that there are drawbacks as well as advantages. The whole idea of a mass-production system is that a plant is set up to achieve an optimum output, using a given combination of factor resources, land, labour and capital. If we abandon that optimum layout in order to fit in with a JIT approach, we lose the economies of large scale on which efficiency depends. On the other hand, at least the marketplace is giving the instructions under the JIT system. We have seen what happened to industry in the Soviet Union, where factories designed to make goods at optimum levels went on producing them even though the marketplace manifestly did not want them. An even better example is European Union agriculture under the Common Agricultural Policy, where farmers carry on producing even though the market can manifestly not afford these products at the inflated intervention price, giving rise to butter and beef mountains, wine lakes, etc. at even further costs for storage, cold storage, etc. If the market was dictating production, those mountains of grain and meat would not be accumulated.

One firm which is particularly interested in JIT arrangements, and which has the facilities for handling such deliveries and the information technology to expedite and keep track of consignments, is TNT Transport Systems. They are based at Garn Avenue, Righead Industrial Estate, Bellshill, Strathclyde, ML4 3JU (Tel: 0698 844602; Fax: 0698 740862) and have a nation-wide delivery service from about thirty depots.

Since JIT was originally a Japanese idea it is interesting to read what one

Japanese manufacturer, Toyota, has to say on the matter. We are grateful to be allowed to reproduce this extract from *Toyota Factfile*.

Just-in-Time

Just-in-Time production management makes sure that everything that takes place throughout the production sequence is a necessary and useful contribution to serving real, market demand.

A 'pull' system: Traditional mass-production systems were 'push' systems, where each process in the production sequence passed its output onto the next process regardless of the latter's actual needs.

In contrast, Toyota Production System (TPS) is a 'pull' system. Each process withdraws items from the preceding process only in the types and quantities needed, and at the time required. Each process only produces additional items to replace items the subsequent process has withdrawn. This arrangement helps prevent the accumulation of inventories and excessive production of any item.

Kanban: For just-in-time production to function smoothly, processes throughout the production sequence must operate in conjunction with each other.

Kanban, which means signboard in Japanese, are usually printed cards in clear plastic sleeves. These cards accompany every item or box of items which moves through the production system.

The kanban indicates vital information about the item it accompanies, such as the model number, the quantity and (on kanban for outside suppliers) bar-coded information for processing payments.

Toyota uses two main categories of kanban: withdrawal kanban, which convey information between processes, and intraprocess kanban, which circulate within a process.

An employee removes the withdrawal kanban from a set of parts when the first part from the set is used. The kanban is then returned to the preceding process to indicate the need to produce additional parts.

Continuous-flow processing: The ultimate purpose of TPS is to streamline the sequence from the receipt of a customer order to the delivery of a finished product into the shortest and smoothest possible flow.

The production processes are arranged into a single flow, with work moving one piece at a time through the sequence of processes. In work such as stamping with large press machines, manufacturers use the smallest possible amounts to make this practical. Handling items one piece at a time reduces inventories dramatically and enhances quality, since the time and circumstances in which a problem has occurred are immediately apparent.

Kaizen/Standardised Work: Standardised work and kaizen are two sides of the same coin.

Standardised work consists of the procedures that team leaders devise for their teams – usually comprising about eight members – to follow at their factory.

It is the framework that guides employees in performing their jobs.

Kaizen

Kaizen are the continuing improvements that the team members and their leaders make in these procedures to streamline the flow of work, enhance quality and improve working conditions.

Kaizen is the dynamic of continuous effort to make standardised work evermore efficient and enjoyable.

Although kaizen is usually referred to in relation to the production process it is a concept which applies to all aspects of Toyota's operations.

Voluntary employee participation takes place in quality control (QC) circles and through a Company-wide Creative Suggestion System. In 1990, Toyota employees in Japan contributed some two million suggestions for improvements. Of those, 97 per cent were implemented.

9.10 Summary

1. Logistical strategies are concerned with the management of supply-chains on either side of the wealth-creating site (the factory).
2. A JIT strategy is one which calls on suppliers to supply the goods we require just in time, at the moment we require to use them. Not only this, but the goods must be in perfect condition and of the very highest quality (commensurate with the specifications laid down).
3. A JIT strategy reduces the problems associated with stock-holding, of both raw materials and components, and the problems of warehousing finished goods. The goods we manufacture are manufactured to order and can be dispatched at once to the customer.
4. Costing procedures are reduced, since there are no stocks in store and no need to requisition stocks or allocate them to cost centres. The only need is to order each day what is required from the supplier, and any costs for particular products can be calculated, in so far as they are required at all, by 'back-flushing' from the total costs incurred and the output achieved.
5. Handling costs are reduced by the JIT system, goods being allocated an access point to the production-line and delivered to that point immediately on arrival. Double-handling does not occur, nor are any records necessary other than the invoice (advice note) arriving with the goods, which will be checked and passed to the Accounts Department.
6. Quality circles are group meetings which discuss the conduct of the section concerned, the problems that they have had to face, any suggestions from staff about any matter, but particularly about the working methods in use, etc. The result could be a recommendation to management, or a complaint. It is important that the views expressed are treated seriously.
7. The advantages of JIT include (a) the raising of the level of interest of staff in the importance of quality, in both workmanship and design and delivery; (b) the reduction of cost by the elimination of double-handling, waste, reworking of poor quality product and idle time due to disputes, breakdowns, etc.; (c) an improvement in cashflow and the

general profitability of activities, thus ensuring job stability and confidence in future employment.

9.11 Questions

1. Explain the 'just in time' concept. What economies could be achieved by a manufacturer who adopted this method of working?
2. Thomas, a component manufacturer, has been approached by a multinational, a manufacturer of pumps of all sizes, to become their 'preferred vendor' of a small control component. Their requirement is for him to tool up to produce the component, supplying 100 sample units for evaluation, and once any snags have been sorted out to supply such quantities as they require 'just in time' each week. No batch requested will be smaller than 500, or more than 5,000. What are the implications of such a request? Give your answer in the form of a list, writing a few lines about each point you make.
3. What is a 'quality circle'? How could it affect the quality of a firm's product, or the market share it achieves?
4. Traditionally, industry has always been production-oriented – Henry Ford once said that his customers could have cars of any colour they liked, so long as it was black. Today industry is market-oriented. Explain the term 'market-oriented' and explain why the 'just in time' movement is so appropriate to firms that are market-oriented.
5. Who is responsible for the logistical activities when a manufacturer switches over to JIT operations? Explain the logistical implications for the various parties in a JIT situation.

10 Physical distribution management

10.1 Introduction

'Physical distribution' is a basic logistical activity. Physical distribution management is the control of a wide range of activities which take place after goods have been produced and before they reach the consumer, or the next stage of production if they are part of a continuing process. These activities include materials handling, storage and warehousing, packaging and unitisation and freight transportation by all modes of transport. Related activities such as vehicle routeing and scheduling and vehicle maintenance are also included. The purpose of these activities is the bridging of gaps between the producer and consumer. They ensure the safe passage of goods from the point of production to the point of consumption, so that they arrive in perfect condition where they are wanted when they are wanted.

In performing such a wide range of activities in a world where specialisation is a major feature of the method of production, long geographical journeys will be inevitable. Vast quantities of raw materials and finished products move restlessly along the major trade routes, subject to attack by climatic changes, insect pests, desiccation, humidity, pilfering and theft. To counter such influences strategies must be developed and plans prepared. At the same time, these plans must be economically viable, because safe arrival over the geographical and time barriers will be fruitless if the final cost to the consumer is greater than he or she can afford. Goods must reach the consumer not only in the right quantity, the right condition, the right place and the right time, but also at the right price. A chief function of physical distribution therefore is to ensure economic operations.

10.2 Planning physical distribution – the total distribution concept

A company involved in distribution will be wise to draw up a strategic plan after examining the detailed requirements of its own or its customers' activities. The aim of this strategy is to achieve the most economic operations possible in the circumstances. The costs of moving goods about and of their storage are clearly interrelated, so that they must be viewed as complementary costs. Greater efficiency in movement will reduce storage, while greater warehousing efficiency will enable the goods to wait safely and economically while transport is organised. The plan must weigh up the total distribution problem from start to finish, and devise a system of operations which will achieve the desired result at the least possible cost. Factors such as market forecasting, materials handling, space utilisation, inventory control, natural wastage, damage during handling or storage, employee fatigue, employee motivation, safety, protective packaging, security, speed of transit, depot location, inter-modal handling, order processing and documentation and customer service will become part of the overall strategy, and the plan will aim to overcome the difficulties envisaged.

Physical distribution is concerned with demand satisfaction, whereas marketing seeks to create demand. In satisfying demand the aim will be to reduce the time between the receipt of an order and its actual completion by delivery. To reduce this time – called the *lead-time* – we must examine the procedures necessary to document the order, process and perhaps transmit it, pick out the goods at the warehouse (perhaps with a sophisticated computer selection system or order-picking lift trucks), pack, load and deliver it to the customer. Once each of these processes has been improved as much as possible we are left with a basic lead-time for the earlier activities plus the transit time for actual delivery which will reflect the distance to be travelled. However, one further factor – reflecting the company's policy on stocks – is the *percentage satisfaction* possible. Any item which we are unable to supply at once from stock necessarily generates a back-order. To attempt to fulfil orders completely is to offer the perfect service, but at an increasing cost as we approach perfection. Most firms will settle for something less than this – say, 95 per cent satisfaction. This rate of satisfaction is usually based upon the goods ordered, i.e. it tells us what percentage of goods ordered we were able to supply from stock.

It is, of course, in the changing attitude to stock-holding that such developments as JIT have their greatest effect.

10.3 Total distribution cost

Total distribution cost is the aggregate of the following costs:

1. In-plant movement and storage.
2. Plant-to-depot transport.
3. Depot operating costs.

4. Depot inventory costs.
5. Depot-to-customer costs.
6. Collection and distribution charges where the carrier is not operating a door-to-door service.
7. Customs duty and associated charges where these are levied on a CIF (cost, insurance and freight) valuation basis.

These costs will include such items as (a) packing, (b) insurance, (c) freight, (d) documentation, (e) interest on capital tied up in transit, and (f) terminal handling charges. Each of these will vary considerably depending on the route or mode of transport chosen.

The first of these – in-plant movement and storage costs – will be fairly uniform, however many depots are used, so long as there is no undue delay and storage in the plant. The rest will reflect very considerably the company's depot policy. A few large depots will be internally large-scale and efficient, but situated some distance from customers. A greater number of depots implies more sites and fewer economies of scale, but reduced distances to customers. The problem is to establish the best configuration of depots to achieve the least combined cost. Transport, warehousing and inventory costs will all vary with the policy, and trade-offs of one against the other will have to be estimated as the alternative policies are envisaged.

The range of costs envisaged under each of the headings 1–7 above will vary with other factors besides the depot policy. For example, the channels of distribution to be employed vary from own-account road transport through privately operated haulage services to nationalised road, rail or air transport. The number of lines to be offered, the degree of customer satisfaction aimed at and the minimum order size are other factors to be considered, while constraints such as warehouse space, inventory cost, vehicle utilisation and labour supply may require modifications in any plan.

Distribution is essentially a flow, and the preparation of a *flowchart* showing the distribution process will enable the centres of activity within the flow process to be isolated and costed. The contribution made by each activity within the overall process can be assessed, and the total system compared with alternative proposals envisaged along different lines. A new activity will be envisaged from different angles and viewpoints to ensure that the total distribution solution is the most economical possible under the circumstances.

In assessing cost, and seeking cost reductions, it is essential to review the activities carried on at present; quantify them in the light of current costs and volumes; consider viable alternative systems; cost them and select the best alternative; and finally compare this best alternative with the present system. A word about each of these aspects is desirable.

10.3.1 Evaluation of the present system

The following questions need to be answered:

1. What is the present pattern of distribution?
2. What are the centres of activity and what costs do they involve, including hidden costs such as stock deterioration, pilfering, etc.?
3. What is the present pattern of order size, order frequency, lead-time, percentage satisfaction from stock, etc.?
4. What is the pattern of demand for each item, and are there any seasonal fluctuations? If so, what is their nature, their duration and the volume required to meet the boom when it arrives – including growth trends?
5. Are there any marked geographical characteristics in the present pattern; if so, what is the cause of the disparities?
6. What are the existing management objectives; are they the proper objectives today, and to what extent have they been met?

10.3.2 Costs of the present system

1. Quantify the costs of each centre of activity in the present system, under such headings as packaging costs, handling costs, transport costs, storage costs, operating costs, documentation costs, personnel costs, capital costs, overhead costs, etc.
2. Integrate these cost-centre figures into total cost figures under each heading.
3. Analyse by finding average order-processing cost, rate of stock turn, storage cost per unit, handling cost per unit, etc.

10.3.3 What alternatives are available?

Here it is necessary to think carefully about the present system, posing questions which indicate weaknesses in it that could be solved by alternative systems.

1. Is the tonnage carried in each centre the most appropriate and economical? If not, what would the cost savings be by other methods?
2. What double-handling occurs, and what savings could be made by its elimination? Large cost savings can sometimes be made by the provision of materials-handling equipment of a new type, which may also increase the utilisation of warehouse space, freeing accommodation for other purposes and releasing capital by the disposal of properties no

longer required. Often double-handling can be eliminated by the use of through-transport or inter-modal transport.

3. Can customer service be reduced without loss of business? If the small order is disproportionately costly, can a contribution towards it be compelled from the customer?
4. Will high-speed but expensive transport save more money than its extra costs? For example, a decision to air-freight components may mean the closure of dispatch centres previously concerned with the provision of timber cases for transits by sea, or might eliminate the need for warehouse facilities at customer's end, now to be supplied with daily requirements by regular air transits.

All the above costing exercises come under the heading of *differential cost analysis*, in which we seek to analyse the differences of cost involved when various ranges of goods are distributed in different ways, i.e. different order sizes, different modes of transport, different depot locations, etc.

The answers to many of the questions given above may result at once in the implementation of improvements which save costs. The best solution to the problem may be obvious, but comparison must now be made with the present system.

10.3.4 Comparison with the present system

Today, computer simulations of proposed distribution systems can be tried out under a representative range of operating conditions. These techniques enable management to make decisions about future activities on a much sounder basis than formerly. These techniques should enable decisions to be made for effecting the greatest cost savings over the total distribution network.

10.4 An outline of the distribution process

There are a number of functions in the distribution process, not all of which will appear in every distribution system, but most of which will be present in any system. As management moves into a fully sophisticated control of physical distribution it embraces activities previously thought to be separate functions from physical distribution so that a full list now includes the following:

1. A purchasing function.
2. An 'assembly' activity.
3. A packaging and unitisation activity.

4. A storage function (warehousing).
5. Inventory management.
6. A transport function.
7. A depot activity.
8. A marketing function.

While the particular circumstances of a firm may be such that some of these functions may not be necessary, most of them will be necessary in all firms. A brief description of each is given here and a fuller account of some, and other related matters, is given in the succeeding chapters.

10.4.1 The purchasing function

This function procures for the business those items that it requires for the successful prosecution of its activities. For manufacturing concerns it will be raw materials, components and capital items like machinery. For wholesale businesses the purchase of stock for resale will be the major requirement. Haphazard and intuitive purchasing has probably led to more failures in business than any other weakness, and the purchasing function must be fully reviewed at regular intervals.

10.4.2 An 'assembly' activity

This will be less apparent in a factory manufacturing situation than in a farming or market gardening system. With many types of produce – fruit, vegetables, milk, poultry, etc. – there will be a process of collection to take place. Fruit does not all ripen on the same day, for example, and a succession of collections will be necessary during the season. The assembly function leads into a packaging and unitisation function.

10.4.3 Packaging and unitisation

This is a major feature of modern distribution. More than anything else the selling of pre-packaged, often perishable products has transformed the retail trade in recent years, breaking down barriers between retailers that have existed for centuries. The skilled trader who understood his or her merchandise and how to market it has been replaced by the self-service trader, whose sole function is to display and sell. The pre-packaging function is of great importance, and greatly simplifies distribution. Its compact units lend themselves to palletisation and modern mechanised handling, while bulk haulage by containerisation makes for economic transport over long distances.

10.4.4 Storage and warehousing

Storage is inseparable from distribution for a variety of reasons. Goods are often produced seasonally but consumed continuously. A notable example is wheat, and the bread we make from it. Others are consumed seasonally, but produced throughout the year, like Christmas decorations and fireworks. Others may be produced in batches – because the demand for a period can be produced in a few days. Almost any product may require storage at a particular time for reasons quite external to the product itself – a strike, or a dislocation of transport, or a minor depression reducing demand temporarily. The storage function may involve many types of expertise, often referred to as 'merchandising' knowledge. Every product has its peculiar properties, its own inherent vice which must be controlled by appropriate treatment.

10.4.5 Inventory management

Related to the purchasing function, but most obvious in the warehousing situation, is the question of inventory management. Stocks which are not turned over represent capital tied up without return. It must be a management function to control stock levels, in the interests of shareholders to ensure a good return on capital invested. It involves decisions about 'assortments', optimum ordering, maximum and minimum stock levels, etc. 'Assortment' is a term which refers to the variety of stock available. It is a matter of policy how wide a variety of stock shall be handled and what limitations shall be placed on the range of sizes, colours and qualities available.

10.4.6 The transport function

Transport alters the geographical position of the goods from the production point to the point of consumption. They can rarely go the entire journey in a single trip, because the economic load for the major part of the journey is usually greater than any single customer can use. In rare cases they might do so: for example, a road tanker might leave an oil refinery with a full load of petroleum for a single customer's garage. More usually some sort of depot network will be used as a buffer where the uneven nature of supply and demand can be accommodated. Sometimes a wholesaler will perform this function as an intermediary at whose premises bulk can be broken. A large organisation will use its depots as bulk-breaking centres.

10.4.7 Depot activity

The depot constitutes a local warehouse for temporary storage where merchandise is secure and properly cared for by staff who understand its characteristics. The depot acts as a buffer to accommodate excess of supply over demand, and a source of reserve for emergency requirements. It often provides an area stock of slow-moving items to reduce stocks held in branches, the slow-moving item being ordered up when required.

10.4.8 The marketing function

Marketing is the final link in the distribution chain. It puts the product into the hands of the consumer, or perhaps the retailer who serves the consumer. It is of enormous importance, bringing to fruition the activity commenced long ago when the production process started.

10.4.9 The logistician's approach to the various functions

Having listed the various elements which make up the total distribution function we can see that modern methods of transport and materials handling can achieve considerable economies in distribution. For example, the adoption of JIT techniques (described in Chapter 9) will have a considerable impact on the storage and warehousing activities, and may eliminate some aspects of them altogether. If goods are delivered to the production-line, used that day and sent on their way to customers, there will be no storage of either raw materials or finished products.

More important than JIT are the changes that have come over the industry as a result of 'third party logistics companies', in which a specialist logistics company with a sophisticated IT (information technology) system takes over the work of rationalising the distribution function and making it a servant of the marketing organisations rather than a servant of the production organisation. This is explained more fully below (see Chapter 14).

10.5 Packaging

No single aspect of production today has had more effect on physical distribution than the change to pre-packaged commodities which lend themselves to self-service marketing by 'non-expert' retail staff. This is not to suggest that retail staff today are less knowledgeable than those of former generations, but their skills are marketing skills rather than merchandising skills. A supermarket manager is not an expert grocer, knowledgeable about produce, but an expert in shop organisation, display and stock turnover.

This revolution began with the packaging of produce, which is a developing technique in its own right. It proceeded by unitisation (the conversion of many small packets into a single unit lift) to containerisation. We must examine these three types of activity in detail, starting with the packaging revolution.

Most manufactured articles require some form of packaging. The word 'container' was formerly used for these specialised packages, but it has now come to mean a standard-sized unit for major transport activities. To save confusion we will use the word 'carton' to describe the individual package in which such articles as motor vehicle components, household articles, etc., are sold.

The carton serves three purposes. It *contains* the object, altering its shape to a convenient packaging shape, a cube or cuboid. Internal packaging, either of corrugated cardboard or moulded polystyrene, assists in this modification of the real shape of the packaged object, and plays a large part in the second function of packaging, to *protect* the object packaged. This protection is against breakage, distortion and contamination. Finally the carton is a vehicle for the marketing organisation, which uses it for advertisement and *communication*, enabling the packaged article to be identified, and to appeal to the customer, while instructions and information can also be printed appropriately.

With many cartons the product has no intrinsic shape – beef suet, for example. These products are packaged in cartons designed to hold an appropriate quantity. The package is easily handled and stored, the product is free from contamination, the cube size is the minimum necessary – thus saving on transport costs – and pilfering is easily observed (one packet missing from an array leaves an obvious gap).

The packaging proceeds to a further level by the use of cardboard cartons which aggregate the small packs into a unit load of standard proportions. Many considerations enter into the use of cardboard boxes, and a packaging policy must be devised to take account of them. For example, protection should not be greater than is really necessary, since it requires thicker board and adds weight to the consignment. Strength may be necessary if boxes are to be piled one upon another, shrink wrapping may be appropriate to protect goods from moisture, rodents, insects and atmospheric pollution, and opaque wrapping which hides what is inside reduces pilfering.

Some major considerations in formulating a packaging policy include:

1. The nature of the goods; their fragility, their dangerous nature, their susceptibility to damp, sweating or other contamination, their pilferability and perishability.
2. The nature and duration of the transit, the mode to be employed and the constraints imposed as a consequence.
3. The value of the goods, and the relation between value and packaging cost. Clearly we cannot afford expensive packaging of very cheap goods. In the case of some products, e.g. perfumes and talcum powders, the packaging costs more than the product.
4. Statutory or other regulations relating to the transit of particular goods, or to their inspection *en route* for customs, insurance or other reasons.
5. Since packaging is part of the marketing impact it must take account of marketing factors. The motor trader who exported white motor vehicles to the Far East in blissful ignorance of the fact that to the Chinese white is associated with mourning was doomed to be disappointed about his turnover. Similarly green is a sacred colour to Moslems, and should not be used on profane things (such as fertiliser).

Even when packaging has been designed to suit the product and its proposed journey, it does not follow that the load is convenient to handle. Traditional movements by road, rail and sea tended to be movements of a haphazard collection of packets, crates and loose objects. Such goods cannot be handled cheaply or easily; they must be dealt with in a non-specialist way using small-scale methods. The docker with his hook for bagged goods and for easing crates on to hand barrows was a non-specialist, low-productivity jack-of-all-trades. Only in recent years has the professional approach of the logistician done away with traditional handling activities. The first step in any such improvement in physical distribution management is the unitisation of cargo.

10.6 Unitisation – the unit load concept

The concept of the unit load is that a collection of items is moved as a single unit. Thus if sixty tins of baked beans are put into a cardboard carton that is a small unit load. If twenty such cardboard cartons are put on a pallet in five rows of four cartons each, the forklift truck which lifts them as a unit load is lifting 1,200 tins. If twenty pallet loads are deposited in a container the gantry crane which lifts it on to a rail wagon is lifting 24,000 tins as a unit load. This will be a very economical lifting operation.

Unit loads may be of the following types:

1. *Work boxes*. This type of unit load is suitable for handling small components, such as metal castings, angle joints, bolts, washers, etc. Metal or plastic boxes designed to stack easily can be moved manually, or on conveyors or by forklift trucks.

2. *Cardboard cartons*. These are a protective packaging unit which can be stored on pallets or racks. If the contents have intrinsic strength, i.e. canned goods, light cardboard cartons will be enough. Stronger cartons will be needed for contents which might crush in transit.
3. *Sacks*. Sacks are made in a variety of materials, paper, jute and plastic being the commonest types. When properly filled and dry, paper sacks have considerable strength and can be easily piled one upon the other. They will not stand excessive amounts of handling in transit, but otherwise are cheap and appropriate for many goods such as cement, animal feedstuffs, fertilisers, etc. Designed to hold a designated quantity of product, they are easily tallied by storekeepers at both ends of a journey, and unlike some bulk methods of transporting powders do not suffer losses due to blowing away. Nowadays a pallet of sacks can be shrink-wrapped as a protection against damp.
4. *Stillages*. A stillage is a base-plate, usually of wood, with bearers to give a clearance between the platform and the floor. The clearance enables the forks of a truck – most probably of the 'ground-clearance' only type – to enter below the stillage, raise it clear of the floor and reposition it where required. Stillages cannot be stacked one on top of the other.
5. *Pallets*. The most versatile unit load system is the pallet, which is a wood or metal framework which can be picked up by a forklift truck or other mechanical device. Figure 10.1 (see pages 198, 199 and 200) illustrates several different types of pallets. Two-way entry pallets can be picked up from front and rear, a clear passage for the forks of the truck being left between the bearers. Four-way entry pallets, instead of bearers, merely have short blocks of wood to separate the top and bottom decks of the pallet, so that whatever angle the forklift truck approaches the pallet it can secure a sound lift from all four sides. There is also an eight-way pallet which can be lifted from all four sides and from all four diagonals. This is sometimes a convenience in restricted areas – for example, in container stuffing – but the extra expense hardly makes them worthwhile for most firms.

   The component parts of a pallet, as illustrated in Fig. 10.1, are thus as follows:

   (a) A top deck, on which the load rests.
   (b) Three bearers, usually of 3 × 2 in (7½ × 5 cm) wood, or smaller metal strips, which in the case of two-way pallets run the full length of the pallet, but with four-way pallets are reduced to nine mere cubes of wood to permit entry from all sides.
   (c) Stringers, which are horizontal members to join up the cubes of wood in four-way and eight-way pallets.
   (d) A lower deck (not always included). It gives extra strength and also is useful in stacking, since the lower deck spreads the weight of the goods above over the full area of the goods below. This

lower deck is, however, an inconvenience when the pallet truck (as distinct from the forklift truck) is being used, since these ground-clearance only trucks carry the weight of the pallet on 'load-wheels' which have to be introduced between the upper and lower decks, and positioned on the floor on the far side.

There are many other types of pallet which have their particular uses. A brief mention of each is desirable.

(i) *Wing pallets*. These have the decks extending out beyond the bearers to facilitate the use of spreader bar slings for crane hoisting.

(ii) *Skeleton pallets*. These have slatted decks for cheapness, where goods are lightweight.

(iii) *Stevedores' pallets*. These are very strongly built, reinforced with steel, and with steel lifting-eyes for use with slings in crane lifting.

(iv) *Expendable pallets*. Pallets are expensive, and securing their return is a great problem. Expendable pallets are used for goods which are travelling a long way, and where the return of the pallet is unlikely. They are as cheap as the activity they are to perform will permit and the recipient puts them to any use he can.

(v) *Post pallets*. Post pallets are pallets used for carrying fragile, awkwardly shaped or crushable items which for economy reasons need to be stacked. The posts provide a solid framework to support the pallet above. The posts usually have feet to locate on the pallet post below them, and thus form a solid, rigid stack. Similar devices, called convertors, can be removed from the pallets and folded flat for the return journey. These are usually patented by the firm which supplies them (see Fig. 10.1).

(vi) *Box pallets*. These are boxes with three sides or a fourth side which can be dropped for access. They are useful for safeguarding small objects which would otherwise fall out, or be pilfered perhaps. Wire netting sides are quite common, while many box pallets have drop bottoms to enable them to be used in production processes releasing the contents as free-flowing materials or parts.

(vii) *Paper pallets*. Paper pallets for light carton work consist of a single strip of 3-ply tarred paper which is wrapped around light carton work in such a way that the second layer of cartons overlaps each side of the bottom layer and enables lifting by forklift.

Other interesting aspects of pallets are as follows:

(a) *Materials*. Most pallets are wooden, but steel pallets and aluminium pallets are common, especially for collapsible pallets and pallets which have a very long life. Aluminium pallets are rustproof and light, but more expensive than steel pallets. A wooden pallet will cost between £7 and £12 with higher prices for steel and aluminium.

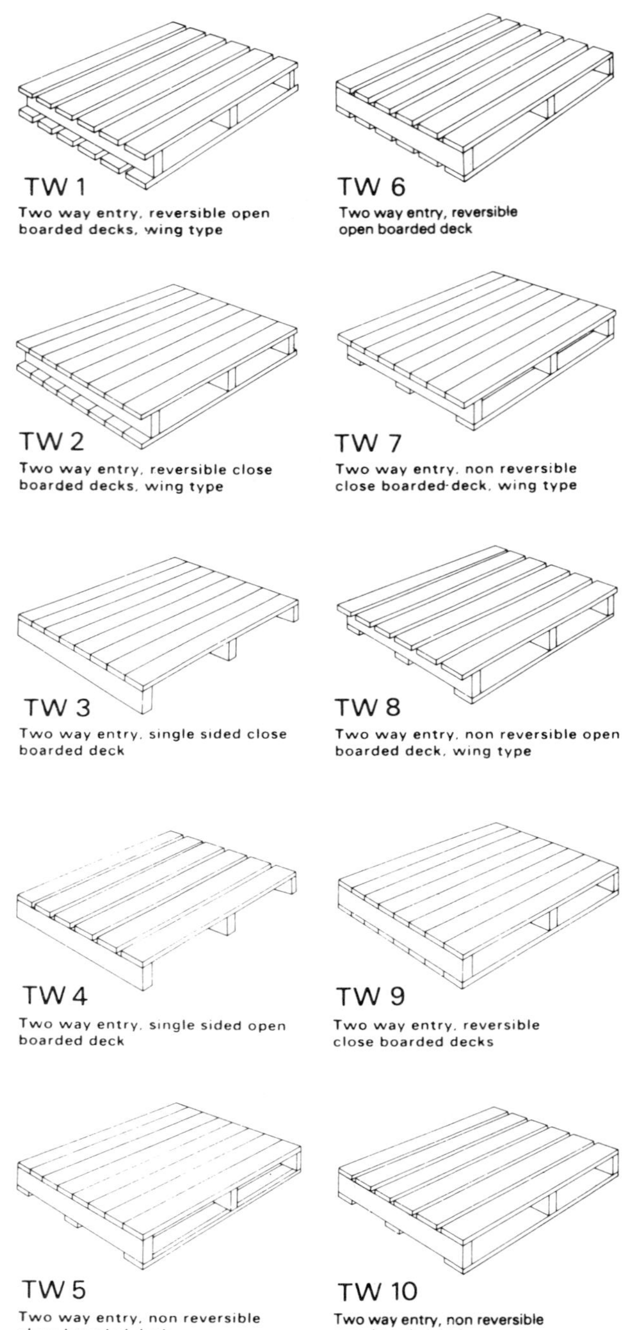
TW 1
Two way entry, reversible open boarded decks, wing type
TW 6
Two way entry, reversible open boarded deck
TW 2
Two way entry, reversible close boarded decks, wing type
TW 7
Two way entry, non reversible close boarded-deck, wing type
TW 3
Two way entry, single sided close boarded deck
TW 8
Two way entry, non reversible open boarded deck, wing type
TW 4
Two way entry, single sided open boarded deck
TW 9
Two way entry, reversible close boarded decks
TW 5
Two way entry, non reversible close boarded deck
TW 10
Two way entry, non reversible open boarded decks

Fig. 10.1(a)

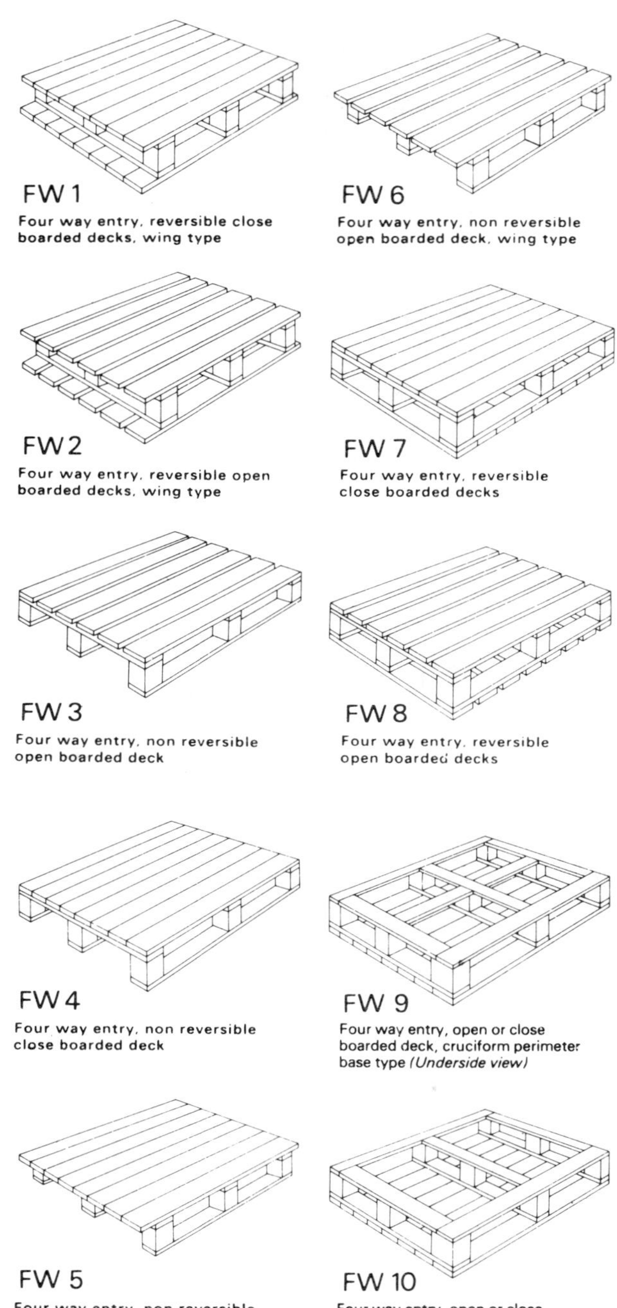

Fig. 10.1(a) continued

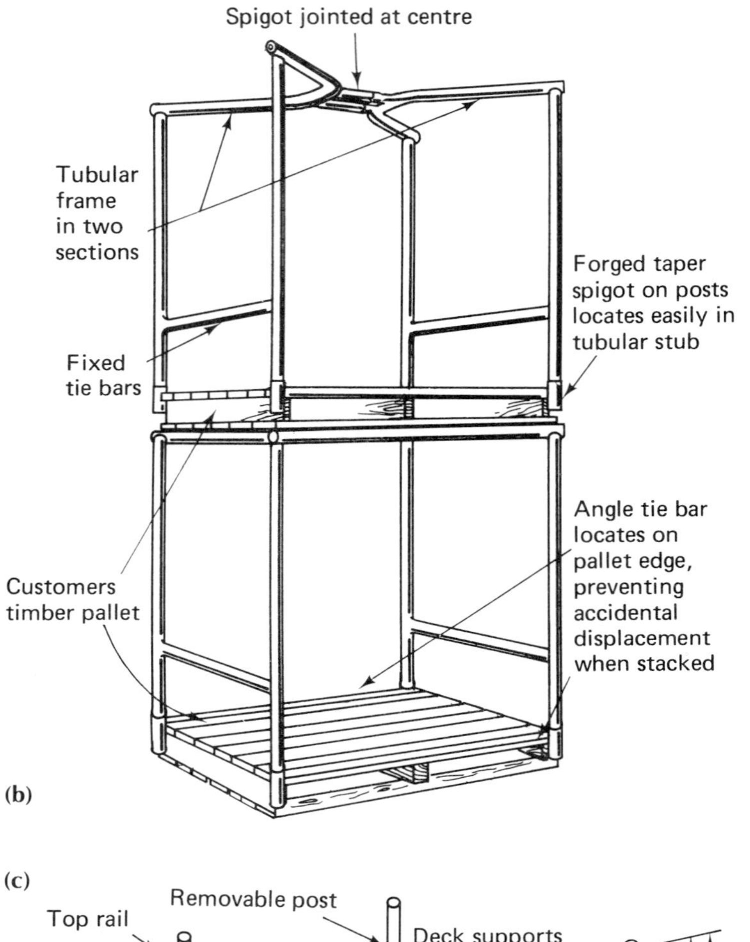

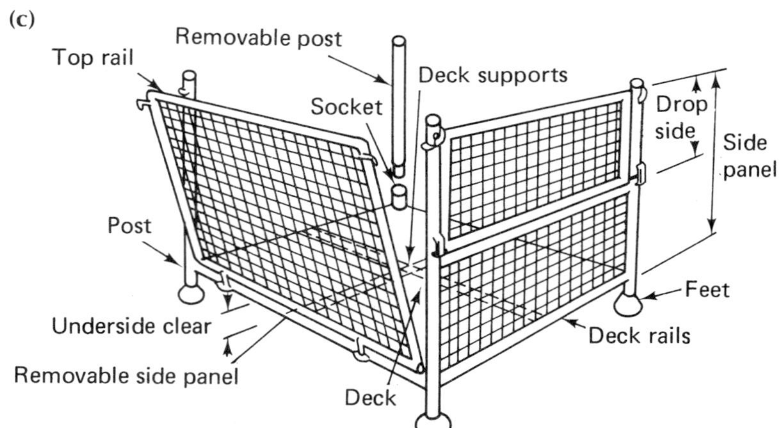

Fig. 10.1 (a) A variety of pallets (courtesy of Pallet Handling Ltd, Hildenborough, Kent). (b) Gibbons pallet convertor; (c) Gush and Dent collapsible pallet (courtesy of Gibbons Bros. and Gush and Dent Ltd)

(b) *Standardisation*. The use of standard-sized pallets has great advantages in many ways, especially if racking, vehicles, cartons and even warehouses were designed to accommodate them. The 1,200 mm × 1,000 mm pallet is popularly suggested, but no firm agreement has yet been reached, and most pallet manufacturers undertake to manufacture to customers' specifications.

The use of pallets for the stuffing of containers has led to pallets being developed which fit snugly into a standard container. This is why when pallets are going to be used, it is essential to supply a standard, general-purpose container rather than a reefer type of container with its smaller internal dimensions. Where this type of container is used for general-purpose-type cargo due to an imbalance in reefer traffic it is best to use it for non-palletised cargo.

Fred Olsen's pallet-carrying vessels were introduced in the fruit trade with the Canary Islands before full containerisation. They were side-loaders raising palletised cargoes to pass them through the hatches (see Fig. 5.9(a), page 106).

(c) *Pallet pools*. Once a pallet has been made, how does the owner compel its return or prevent its use by 'pirate' organisations who use it for their own ends? It is a difficult problem which led some time ago to suggestions for a national pallet pool. Regrettably, this has presented some major difficulties, but where a number of firms agree to co-operate and use one another's pallets, an increased utilisation rate would seem likely. Any increase in utilisation rates is highly desirable from the point of view of the physical distribution industry.

6. *Pallet-less unit loads*. The latest development in unit loading is the pallet-less unit load. This is achieved by special machines called 'load formers' which form unit loads automatically on the pallet principle but without the use of pallets. Layers of the desired pattern are formed either automatically or manually on a marshalling table, and are then moved on to a stripper apron from which they can be picked up by a lift section of the machine. This receives successive layers without the use of any pallet. A clamp-lift truck can collect as many layers as it requires from the stack using its squeeze clamps.
7. *Packaged timber*. The packaging of timber was one of the earliest forms of unit loads, before containerisation fully developed. It was an obvious saving to be able to handle a package of timber instead of the individual lengths of wood, manhandled through the hatches. Later the development of shrink-wrapping provided a package which was protected from the weather, as well as being bound into a unit load. The development of side-loader forklift trucks simplified movements of packaged timber around the stacking areas.

10.7 Containerisation – inter-modal transport

Although containers were first used as long ago as the 1920s, the container revolution may be said to have started in April 1963, when the first 'Sea Land' service opened from Puerto Rico to Baltimore. Two ships, the *Mobile* and the *New Orleans*, operated this service so successfully that Sea Land began construction of the first container terminal at Baltimore. Since then the use of containers has increased enormously, and the variety now available to freight forwarders demonstrates their versatility and popularity. Their use has had repercussions on the designs of ships, on the operation of the ports, on rail and road haulage and on warehousing. It has necessitated new attitudes on the part of both management and labour. It has led to the development of integrated transport systems offering depot-to-depot (or door-to-door) services on world-wide routes for both refrigerated and general cargo.

The revolution was essentially the provision of a door-to-door service from the point of inland origin to the point of inland distribution at destination, utilising more than one mode of transport, without having to break bulk. It is the *inter-modal* nature of the transit that is so important. Instead of traffic meeting delays at every interface, where rail or road reaches the sea, or where the sea transit again changes back to inland transport at the port of destination, the containers move easily off one unit of transport and on to another. The port ceases to be a bottle-neck, and becomes a smooth linking mechanism between the different modes of transport.

The enthusiasts for container transport confidently predicted in the late 1960s that eventually 80 per cent of all traffic would be containerised. Estimates of 50 per cent by the mid-1970s were not quite fulfilled, but in the late 1970s, the change to containerisation was so rapid that container manufacturers found it difficult to meet all needs. The initial stage of containerisation, from 1963 to 1970, was a period of trial and error with individuals experimenting with the new system and eventually reaching international agreement on a standard range of sizes. The second leg of the race to containerise was run between 1971 and 1975, with approximately 100,000 containers in circulation in Britain alone by the end of that period. By 1982 2 million container units were carrying 45 million tonnes of cargo, or 64 per cent of all non-bulk cargo. Container traffic peaked in 1990 at 2,700,000 units passing through UK ports. In 1991 (the latest figures available) traffic through UK ports was 2,691,000 units, of which 462,000 units were empty units being returned to their bases. This gives some idea of the imbalances of trade not anticipated, perhaps, by the early enthusiasts.

By comparison, in 1991, 3,415,000 road goods vehicles, no doubt most of them carrying containers, passed through UK ports. The tonnage of goods carried was 42,080,000 tonnes by the road haulage vehicles; 34,698,000 tonnes by the containers, a total of almost 77 million tonnes out of a grand total of goods passing through UK ports of 80,770,000 tonnes. It would appear that the 80 per cent of traffic figure has been realised, and that the container has fulfilled early predictions as the simplest way to carry international cargoes. This enormous throughput of goods has been aided by H.M. Customs permitting simultaneous loading and discharge of cellular vessels, as opposed to their general ruling that before a vessel can start loading all cargo for that port has to be discharged and a Jerque Note (inward clearing bill) issued.

10.8 What is a container?

A container is a steel-framed box, with a strong floor and panelled sides, end and roof. The doors at the open end can be secured and sealed giving good protection against pilferage. The steel frame must be strong enough to support other containers stacked above it, since in some ships they are stacked five high. The ISO (International Standards Organisation) containers have hollow castings at each corner with holes which engage with special T-headed twist locks on vehicles, whether lorries or rail freight wagons. These twist locks can be turned through 90° to clamp the container securely to the vehicle. They can also be used to clamp adjacent containers together for added security. The same hollow castings on the top of the container engage with lifting platforms lowered on to the container by container cranes and straddle carriers, so that the container can be lifted cleanly by all four corners at once to transfer it from road vehicle to rail, or from ship to shore and vice versa. The bottom frame also has hollow sections in the sides of the framework, which permit giant forklift trucks to operate, lifting it on to road and rail vehicles. Fig. 10.2 illustrates these features.

Since the weight capacity of a container's corner posts is 80 tonnes it is unsafe to stack them more than five high, assuming they are full or nearly full. In container depots (e.g. East India Dock) empties are sometimes stowed much higher, using tower cranes and they are also stacked in blocks to prevent wind damage.

The side, end and roof panels may be made of a variety of materials. Stainless steel is best, being rustproof and strong, but it is more expensive than aluminium, plastic or plywood. All these are more vulnerable than steel to damage or deliberate attack by thieves. Whatever the material, panels should be smooth rather than corrugated, thus facilitating their use for promotional advertisements. In some containers where full access to side-loading is desired, side panels can be demountable, slotting into position after loading to give weather protection and to restrain the load for greater security. The floor must be strong enough to take the weight of a fully loaded forklift truck. Many types of specialised fitting to suit the requirements of regular consignors are offered by the manufacturers, but of course their installation inhibits the use of the container for other traffic and makes it specific to the class of goods for which it has been designed.

10.8.1 ISO containers

The standard size of ISO containers was originally 8 × 8 ft (2.5 m × 2.5 m) cross-section, but nowadays 8 ft × 8 ft 6 in (in height) is more common. There are half-height containers for heavy goods. These are 8 ft × 4 ft (2.5 m × 1.2 m) cross-section, and reduce the weight of, and space occupied by, a container carrying dense material – for example, steel rod or steel plate. However, experience has shown that there is little point in having half-containers unless there is a significant volume of two-way traffic in heavy goods. This is rarely the case, and therefore it is better to half-fill a general-purpose container with heavy goods on one leg of the journey and it can then be fully loaded with lighter general cargo on the return leg. Lengths of containers are 10 ft (3 m), 20 ft (6 m), 30 ft (9 m) and 40 ft (12 m). The 20 ft (6 m) size is the most popular and container statistics are for this reason usually given in TEUs (twenty-foot equivalent units). Besides having standard dimensions, the ISO containers must be strong enough to be stacked five high fully laden, and meet stringent requirements about roof, wall and door strengths, and watertightness. Tare weight (the weight of the empty container) and maximum gross weight must be marked on the right-hand door and side walls. The owner's identification has to be marked on the front and on the roof, while on the sides a code indicates the type, size and country of origin. Exact details of ISO requirements may be found in *Specifications for Freight Containers*, published by the British Standards Institution.

10.9 Types of container

Apart from the ISO standards for containers, manufacturers are free to supply whatever types of container they like, with whatever fittings are most appropriate, bearing in mind the need to keep the container versatile. From the standpoint of thickness of skin – an important factor for some cargoes – there are three main types:

1. *Thin-skinned containers* of the general type already described. These give no real insulating effect as far as temperature is concerned, and merely protect against weather and pilfering.
2. *Insulated containers*. These have no system of temperature control but

are thick-skinned, having some sort of fibreglass or other material which reduces both heat loss, e.g. heated milk, or heat gain, e.g. meat, and work in conjunction with a blown-air refrigeration system within the ship and at special points on the quayside or on the container stack. It is essential that air can flow around the cargo and although the aluminium floor and the steel doors are designed to permit this, it is also essential that sufficient air space is left on top of the stow.

3. *Refrigerated (reefer) containers* are of similar build but have their own independent refrigeration unit, so that they can be set for a particular temperature. They need to be connected to an electrical supply. This may be supplied from the ship, or from a diesel generator in the container park. The refrigeration unit reduces the internal dimensions of the container, and may give rise to difficulties in restraining cargo.

The following types of container are also in use:

1. *General cargo containers*. These have access through the end doors, with internal securing points at appropriate places.
2. *Top-loading containers*. These are for use with large, heavy or awkward cargoes. The roof, and the header bar above the door, can be removed to allow cargo to be swung in through the door opening as well as through the roof.
3. *Half-height containers*. As mentioned earlier, these are for use with heavy, dense cargoes such as steel pipes and tubes. A full-height container stuffed with these dense materials would exceed the normal weight of a container.
4. *Open-sided containers*. Especially suited for hazardous cargo, this type of container is fitted with a fixed roof and there are open sides fitted with wire mesh.
5. *Flat rack containers*. These are basic 'flats' with removable slatted boards at each end. They are used to assist the movement of heavy and awkward pieces of cargo. There are lashing points for strapping down the goods in transit.
6. *Dry bulk containers*. These are for the carriage of granular cargo and dry powders. There are three loading hatches and a discharge door at the front end, which is used to empty the container by tipping it on a tipping trailer.
7. *Tank containers*. These enclose a tank within a standard frame of similar dimensions to a standard container.
8. *Igloo containers*. These are specially designed to fit into the hulls of specific aircraft. They are not inter-modal containers, but are designed for air transport operation only (see Fig. 10.3). With the very large aircraft now available ISO standard containers can be carried by air.
9. *Fantainers*. Fantainers are identical to the general-purpose container

and can be used as such but they have a hatch on the container door, which when fitted with an electrical extraction fan, makes them suitable for the carriage of cargoes subject to damage due to condensation. The fan requires an electrical supply and the cargo should be stored on pallets with a space above to allow a free flow of air which is drawn through a perforated front sill. A number of agricultural products, e.g. cocoa or coffee beans, are subject to sweat damage and require a ventilated container which has ventilators in the top and bottom side rails. They are designed to prevent water entering the container. Other perishables use *open-sided containers*, which have a fixed top but reinforced PVC curtains on each side to meet TIR requirements. (TIR is the system of long-distance haulage which permits cargoes to cross frontiers without inspection by Customs.) These open-sided containers can be converted to a general-purpose container by rolling up the curtains and closing the sides with side gates, which are stowed in the back end of the container when it is being used as a tilt. The rear door opening is standard.

Some of these types of containers are illustrated in Fig. 10.2 and Fig. 10.3.

10.10 The advantages of containers

These may be listed as follows:

1. They consolidate cargo, bringing into a unit load what was previously a number of smaller packages or crates.
2. This unitised cargo is handled more quickly and more easily, thus reducing loading and unloading time.
3. A very important advantage is that usually much less packing is required – the cost of timber to make cases and the labour involved can be very expensive. Less packing often makes possible the stowage of a greater quantity of actual goods as opposed to goods plus cases in the same space. It is important, however, to ensure that containers are carefully stowed, otherwise extensive damage can occur to lightly packed goods if excessive movement occurs within the container.
4. The goods are carried more easily, since they are better restrained than loose cargo. Of course, container vehicles do turn over if driven round bends at excessive speeds, but the traditional problems of shifting loads are not met with in a well-stuffed container.
5. The carriage itself is economic, since a fully loaded container represents an economic utilisation of that volume of cargo space, whether in a ship, or on a railway wagon or road haulage vehicle.
6. Pilfering is reduced. The sneak thief cannot pick up and walk off with a

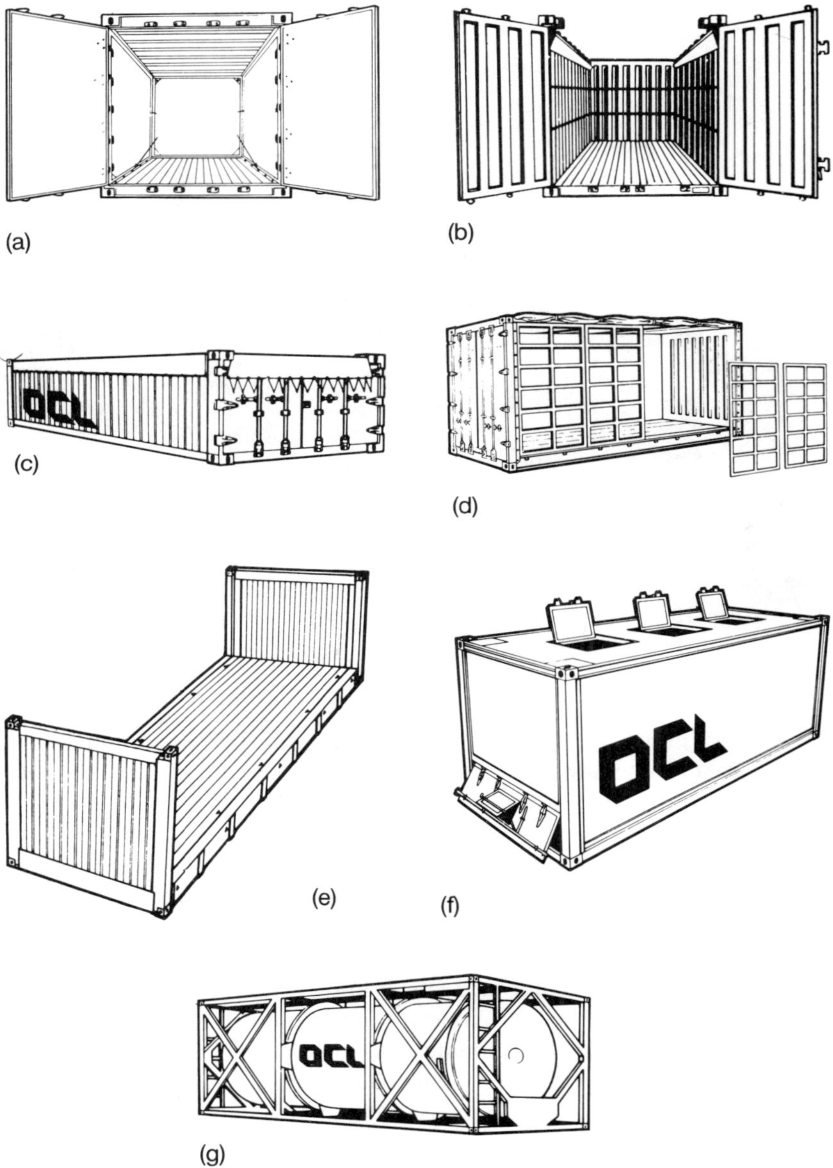

Fig. 10.2 (a) 6 metres general cargo container showing position of securing points. (b) Open-top container showing header bar removed. (c) 6 metres half-height container. (d) Open-sided container showing positioning of full-height gates. (e) 6 metres flat rack container. (f) Dry bulk container. (g) 6 metres tank container (courtesy of Overseas Containers Ltd)

Fig. 10.3 Loading igloo containers from a roller pallet van, via a scissors-lift (courtesy of Lufthansa)

container, as he can with loose cargo. Theft of containers is of necessity a large-scale operation, requiring conspiracy by a group of thieves. As conspiracy is more severely punished than mere theft, this is in itself a deterrent.

7. Simpler documentation can be achieved. A given volume of cargo requires much less documentation, even if it is going to a large number of eventual consignees. The groupage firm which specialises in unitising cargo from a number of small consignors will prepare documentation for the container as a single unit. It then assumes the responsibility of destuffing the container at the far end of the journey so that individual items reach the ultimate consignee safely.
8. Insurance costs are reduced, because individual packages no longer need to be handled separately, and the container offers good protection to its contents. In addition, once the container is sealed, losses due to pilfering virtually disappear, and the exterior markings give thieves little idea of the contents of the container. For insurance purposes an average loaded container is worth about £17,500 (1994).
9. Containers make through-transit the logical and economic way to forward cargo. We thus see the development of integrated door-to-door or depot-to-depot services by rail–sea–rail, rail–sea–road, road–air–

road, etc. We also see the development of documentation devices such as TIR carnets to speed goods through customs without examination.

Taken together, the points listed above present a formidable argument in favour of containerisation. Despite the problems inseparable from their use, the response of freight forwarding and shipping firms to their introduction is evidence that these advantages reduce costs and are reflected in cheaper freight rates. Let us now consider the problems involved.

10.11 Problems of containerisation

Any new mode of transport brings its problems. These are of many kinds: technical, operational and financial. Some of the more important may be listed as follows:

1. *Technical problems*. These have largely been solved in the twenty or so years that have elapsed since containers began to be widely used. The chief technical problems, which involved international agreement on standard strengths and sizes, were solved by the ISO agreements described above (see page 204). The responses of engineers and design staff to the needs of the freight-forwarding industry have been varied and interesting, yet new uses are being found every year for these versatile components. One shipping firm has now built containers into a permanent feature of the superstructure of its vessels, to give replaceable ship's galley facilities for each ship. The entire galley requirements for each voyage are collected into two refrigerated containers occupying a regular position on the deck of each vessel. On arrival in port the remaining supplies and all waste products are removed in the old containers, to be replaced by two new containers fully provisioned for the new voyage.

An important aspect of container operations is the need to design special ships, berths, container parks, handling facilities and vehicles. These have presented formidable technical and financial problems. Some of these units are dealt with more appropriately elsewhere in this book. Others are described on pages 212–14.

2. *Operational problems* have been numerous and varied, particularly in the early days when containers were used on vehicles not specially designed for them. The overall problem is to provide an integrated system, based on standard ISO containers, and maximising the advantages accruing to their use. Improvements in performance have been achieved with services such as the Seatrain land-bridge service from the United Kingdom and Europe to the East Coast of the United States which goes over the land-bridge to the Pacific Coast by special unit train and catches container ships for Japan. This type of inter-modal transport offers very considerable economies in operation to both European and Japanese shippers.

Similarly, the opening-up of the trans-Siberian routes has reduced the journey time from London to Japan by about three weeks – a very considerable saving.

While these types of integrated operation illustrate the economies of container transportation the capital costs of the facilities required are enormous, and many areas of the world must of necessity handle containers by less satisfactory methods. Typical problems concern the difficulties of unloading containers at ports which are without special cranes. The problem is best solved by putting the crane on the ship, making it independent of shore-based facilities. Such gantry cranes are, of course, very expensive; they are large and offer considerable wind resistance in passage, but they are of great service in many ports. The ship can actually be trimmed by positioning the gantry crane at the best point to trim the ship.

Securing the return of empty containers or getting as many as possible reloaded for the return journey is a major problem. Unfortunately, world trade is not evenly balanced: containerised cargo from Europe may be used to pay for oil from the Middle East which is shipped in bulk. There is then no return cargo for the container, and it makes an uneconomic return journey. Skilled traffic organisation is required to minimise 'empty-leg' journeys, and the growth in specialist forwarding agencies and specialist transport companies reflects their greater ability to fill containers on return journeys.

10.11.1 Who provides containers?

One operational aspect is the actual provision of the containers. They are not too expensive to build, costing between £1,000 and £1,500 each. The most obvious providers are the carriers, who in the early years built the majority of containers, leasing them out to shippers and other consignors. Before a major breakthrough was made in convincing operators of the practicality of the containers as a transport method, rates were very competitive. Container builders were forced to offer a wide variety of styles of container, and even to cater for special requirements. This was not a bad thing, since it finally convinced all sections of the freight market that this system was adaptable to their particular needs, but it was scarcely a profitable period.

Generally speaking, operators supply containers free of charge; they do not lease them to shippers. The charge for the use of the container is built into the freight charge. They do charge demurrage if the container is detained by a shipper or a consignee. Operators buy and own containers and they also lease containers. There are container leasing firms who are not themselves transport operators, but have a world-wide network of depots, agents, etc. In this system empty containers are returned to the nearest depot, and are then available for use on any shipping line's vessels on any route.

The significant development in the provision of containers came in the 1980s when specialist container leasing firms became the dominant force in the market. Today, at least half the containers in use world-wide are owned by leasing companies. Their ability to switch containers from one trade to another reduced the problems caused by the imbalance of trade and reduced the number of empty-leg journeys. Even so, as we saw above (page 202), one container in five is empty and simply being returned to the nearest depot from which it can once again be allocated to a customer. This ability to lease containers whenever they are required has reduced the major carriers' needs to invest in containers, without jeopardising their services to the customer.

Normally a mega-carrier will own some containers and use them as widely as possible in its various ships. It will probably have even more on long-term lease from a container leasing company to carry a good proportion of its regular requirements. It will lease others as and when required under a master-lease agreement. The bigger a mega-carrier is the more it will be able to switch containers between trades, and even-out the imbalances between trade in various directions. Similarly, carriers who normally co-operate with one another, e.g. conference members, operate container pools which go some way to providing more efficient use of containers.

With the development of the specialist freight forwarder, particularly the groupage firms, the shippers began to provide their own containers, if only to bring the containers under their personal control. Later still, large manufacturers shipping regular consignments found it practical to have their own containers. These could then be specially adapted to suit their own products, or even designed and constructed for their personal use. Containers became analogous to, but more flexible than, the 'own-account' fleets (owner-operated vehicles), with promotional advertising on the sides and ends, and standard packaging and dispatch procedures. Special contractual relations with other firms, often at very cheap rates, for return loads, helped to reduce 'empty-leg' journeys.

10.11.2 Financial aspects of containerisation

The container revolution has required enormous capital expenditure by all branches of the distribution industry. The port authorities have had to provide special terminals, cranage and other facilities. Shipping firms have had to design new ships. The railways and road hauliers have had to develop new terminals and vehicles to handle the new mode of transportation, while at every stage modifications in procedure, documentation, communication, etc., have been required. The total capital expenditure must exceed the cost of any previous transport revolution, but of course, the modern world is able to afford this capital cost more easily. Some idea of the costs borne by individual firms in the early days can be gathered from two examples: one firm in 1972 received delivery of its 20,000th container from a single supplier – a capital expenditure over ten years of £30 million on containers alone. Another international firm by the spring of 1975 had 100,000 TEUs or £150 million of containers.

The high cost of port facilities in particular has required the establishment in many countries of strict control over development finance. In Britain, with over eighty major ports, the National Ports Council was at one time used to control the capital invested in container berths, which otherwise might have been too numerous and fractionated for real efficiency. Although the National Ports Council has now been discontinued, and some proliferation of expensive port facilities has resulted, the utilisation of berths since containerisation has increased enormously, with very high movements per metre of quay compared with traditional berths.

10.12 Special facilities for containerisation

1. *Specialised ships*. These include cellular ships, roll-on roll-off ships and barge-carrying ships. They are described fully elsewhere (see page 129).

2. *Gantry cranes*. The essential feature of a gantry crane is that, having picked up its load, it can traverse with it to a suitable position for lowering the load on to another vehicle or vehicle route. Thus a container may be lifted from a road vehicle or railway wagon and traversed over the hold of the ship. At the same time, the gantry crane can move on its own tracks, under its own power, so as to line up with the precise 'slot' or 'cell' in the vessel. Here the container is lowered into the hold and secured. The gantry crane then picks up a container for off-loading from the ship, traverses with it back to the road vehicle or railway wagon and places it on the vehicle. If a vehicle is not being used it will off-load it on to the ground, where it will be collected by a straddle carrier. A container crane costs about £1.4 million and can carry out a typical on-off loading cycle in about three minutes. Vickers PLC's subsidiary, Jered Brown Brothers, are a major supplier.

3. *Scotch derricks*. Scotch derricks are heavy lift derricks with a very long jib, able to reach out and cover the holds of a ship to handle unit loads weighing as much as 50 tons. They are very useful in container operations, and commonly handle as much as 200,000 tonnes of cargo per year.

4. *Forklift trucks*. Very heavy forklift trucks, capable of lifting a fully loaded container, are now available to load containers on to road and rail

vehicles. The forklift engages with special apertures in the bottom frame of the container. The whole container can then be lifted to the required vehicle height and can be positioned on the vehicle. The forklift truck then backs away and the prongs disengage from the container. Special frames can be fitted over the forks to enable top-lifting where required. These are especially suitable for side-loaders, i.e. forklift trucks with the forks at the side instead of in front of the vehicle.

5. *Container parks.* Traditionally, quays have only needed to be big enough to enable road and rail vehicles to come alongside the ship to receive cargo. Container working requires much larger working areas, for the speed at which containers are landed is so great that other transport cannot be called forward fast enough. The protection formerly given by the transit shed is now provided by the containers themselves, which are parked upon open stacking grounds behind the quay apron. Part of the modernisation of an existing port usually involves the provision of huge parking areas, where containers can be stored, marshalled and sorted. Customs inspection may also take place there, or at special inland clearance depots.

6. *Inland Clearance Depots (ICDs).* An Inland Clearance Depot is a depot approved by Customs where goods may be packed in containers and sealed, or on arrival from foreign ports may be opened, examined and cleared. The use of an ICD ensures that the working of a ship is not delayed by the need for inspection of cargo by Customs. The sealed containers leaving the ship are transferred to the ICD, and sealed containers for export are received from the ICD. Approval depends upon certain requirements: convenient size to make the depot an economic customs control point; non-discriminating behaviour so that the depot is available to all firms in an area; and evidence of co-operation between commercial firms, port authorities and other interested parties. The concept of containerisation rests on the basic idea that goods should be containerised as close as possible to the point of origin, and decontainerised as close as possible to the point of destination. ICDs situated within major conurbations achieve these ends more effectively than container bases elsewhere. They are usually open for 16 hours daily, on a double shift basis, and may offer a wide range of groupage facilities.

7. *Groupage facilities.* Groupage is a system of container operations which groups together goods in such a way that maximum advantage is taken of containerisation. It can operate in several ways:

(a) A manufacturer shipping full container loads (FCLs) to foreign countries can have these full container loads broken up at destination by the groupage firm, which then transports the part-loads to the individual consignees.

(b) A manufacturer shipping small quantities only, less than container loads (LCLs) may hand them over to the groupage firm who will then containerise them with the goods of other firms, issuing a 'house bill of lading' as proof of shipment. The goods will be decontainerised by the groupage firm at the ICD in the country of destination, and distributed by traditional methods to the ultimate consignees.

(c) A consolidation of a multiplicity of cargo for a single consignee may be effected by the grouper in the exporting country. Thus a department store in Chicago buying European goods from countless European suppliers may have these goods grouped in London or Rotterdam for export to the United States as full container loads.

Groupage firms are able to take advantage of inter-modal world-wide operations in great detail, using road–sea, rail–sea, road–air–road, rail–air–road and similar combinations. For example, the use of the ice-free port of Halifax, Nova Scotia, as a link in the chain that joins the United Kingdom, Europe and the Mediterranean on one side of the Atlantic via the Canadian National Railway network and Vancouver, to Japan, Korea, Hong Kong, New Zealand and Australia is a typical world-wide example of inter-modal initiative.

10.13 Conclusion about unit loads

There is no doubt that unitisation has revolutionised physical distribution over the last few years, and made the whole distribution and forwarding industry aware of the economic advantages that accrue when many small lifts are converted to one big lift. In the years since trans-ocean containerisation began, the non-fuel container and roll-on roll-off traffic passing through UK ports has increased to about 3,000,000 units. About 50 per cent of this unit load increase has been with Europe, so that the short-sea routes have become very important. The development of unitisation has brought a significant growth in the understanding of exporters and importers of the need to choose least-cost methods for the movement of their goods. The ingenuity of the physical distribution and transport industries in finding cost-saving solutions to their problems has been remarkable. It has been one of the greatest periods in transportation history. However, as we shall see, the move into logistics, with third party specialist companies playing an increasing part in logistical activities is a further revolution in transport, which is only now beginning to make full use of the unit load principle.

10.14 Summary

1. Physical distribution management is the art of bringing goods over the gaps which separate producers and consumers. One gap is the geo-

graphical gap, which is bridged by transport. The other gap is the time gap, which is bridged by merchandising skills of various sorts. Goods must cross this gap without deteriorating in any way, and without being misappropriated.

2. The aim of physical distribution management is to bridge these gaps with the minimum total distribution cost. Managements will review their distribution strategies on a regular basis by examining such matters as the present pattern of distribution used, their depot locations, vehicle utilisation, security aspects, operating costs, etc. They will consider alternative systems and compare them with the present system.
3. Packaging is the procedure that precedes physical distribution. It prepares the good for marketing by placing it in an appropriate carton, which is both an advertisement of the product and a detailed explanation of its uses and qualities – in other words, it communicates useful information to the customer. This may then be consolidated into a reasonable pack of the product by the use of a cheap, strong, cardboard carton. It may then be further consolidated into a unit load by palletisation.
4. The unit load concept holds that goods are most easily distributed if they travel as a unit. The most basic unit is the carton, which may then be palletised to a larger unit, and a number of pallets may then be stuffed into a container to give an even larger unit load.
5. The variety of pallets includes stillages, wing pallets, skeleton pallets, stevedores' pallets, post pallets, box pallets, collapsible pallets and paper pallets.
6. A container is a steel-framed box with a strong floor and panelled sides, end and roof. They are of standard dimensions and varieties include thin-skinned containers, insulated containers (for chilled goods), refrigerated containers (reefers), top-handling containers, fantainers, dry bulk containers, tank containers and the igloo containers used on some aircraft.
7. The advantages of containers include the ease of handling of a unit load of such a size, the reduction in packing required, the economic use of shipboard space and the easy transfer from one mode of transport to another.
8. Containers may be provided in a variety of ways. Major exporters who ship goods regularly around the world may own containers outright. Many forwarding firms and groupage firms may own some containers. About half the containers used are leased out by specialist leasing companies, which assume the capital cost burden and the repair and maintenance charges in return for their leasing charges. The filling of 'empty-leg' journeys is a preoccupation for all who use containers.
9. Special facilities are required for the movement of containers. They include specialised 'cellular' ships, roll-on roll-off vessels and docks and barge carrying vessels, gantry cranes, Scotch derricks, heavy-duty

forklift trucks, large container parks, straddle carriers, inland clearance depots (ICDs) and groupage facilities where cargoes can be consolidated.

10.15 Questions

1. What is physical distribution management? How does it solve the transport and distribution problems of a major manufacturer of durable consumer goods?
2. What part does packaging play in the marketing of goods? How can packaged goods be made into unit loads?
3. What is a container? How can containerisation be described as a transport revolution?
4. 'One advantage of containerisation is that insurance rates are cheaper for containerised goods.'
   'We have refused to pay some very heavy claims on containerised goods because the damage was clearly caused by the fault of the consignor.'
   Explain why these two statements about containerisation are not mutually incompatible. What should a consignor do to ensure that he is not at fault when dispatching containerised goods?
5. Write short notes (6–8 lines) about *four* of the following:
   (a) fantainers
   (b) gantry cranes
   (c) stillages
   (d) eight-way pallets
   (e) heavy-duty lift trucks
   (f) container cranes
6. 'A container crane can execute a load–unload cycle in about three minutes.' Explain what such a cycle involves, and the co-operation that would be needed from other staff if it were to be achieved.
7. What is the unit load principle? How many ways are there of making up a unit load?

11 Physical distribution: warehousing and inventory management

11.1 The function of the warehouse

The warehouse exists chiefly as a storehouse where goods not currently required can be safely stored and cared for until required. It thus smoothes out fluctuations in supply and demand. These fluctuations may be influenced by natural events, political events, commercial practicalities, etc. For example, at times of political uncertainty a good deal of stockpiling of raw materials takes place in anticipation of possible interruptions of supply. Seasonal demand means that production must be stored until required. Batch production is often necessary to secure economic operations – perhaps a three-month supply of a particular component can be made in two weeks. The batch must be stored until required. Similarly, optimum order sizes often dictate a certain amount of storage of goods purchased at a cheap rate for a large quantity. Stockpiling against a possible interruption of production will ensure that sales can continue during the shutdown. We can therefore list the functions of the warehouse as follows:

1. To store flows of materials which are not in phase with production.
2. To store flows of finished products which are not immediately being demanded.
3. To build up stocks against possible interruptions in production.
4. To cater for seasonal demands, and seasonal supplies.
5. To assist economic batch production.
6. To assist economic purchasing.
7. To promote displays to customers.
8. To add value, by breaking bulk, sorting, blending, garbling, sampling, packaging and pricing.

Warehouses exist at many points in the distribution flow. Some form assembly-points in agricultural areas where produce is consolidated for shipment to distant markets. Others are located at factory premises where they receive finished goods for storage until distribution can be arranged. Unless journey distances are small to the final markets, manufacturers usually find the factory warehouse an inconvenient arrangement, and establish strategically placed depots to supply areas of the country.

This is too expensive for the small-scale manufacturer, who must rely on wholesalers to take his product and store, display and distribute it to retailers. The traditional pattern of three activities – manufacturing, wholesaling and retailing – has been considerably modified in recent years but is still commonly found operating alongside the direct selling by manufacturers and direct buying by multiple shops, chain stores, supermarkets, hypermarkets and consumer co-operatives. The wholesalers survive best in large countries where the depot system, if too widespread, places unbearable strains on managements of manufacturing enterprises, who therefore find that the specialist wholesaler still has a useful part to play.

As a general principle the rule 'first-in, first-out' applies to the storage of most items. To carry goods over time requires considerable skill; deterioration of some sort is almost inevitable. It is only prudent to remove and sell (or use) the item that has been in store longest.

11.2 Warehouse layout

For many years the typical warehouse was a single-storey structure of vast extent which enabled internal transport to operate horizontally at a single level. The multi-floor warehouse, with its need for expensive lifts or access ramps, strong construction and extra handling costs was deemed impracticable. In recent years the higher cost of sites and the development of specialist materials handling techniques has transformed warehouse design. By using standard turret trucks capable of reaching as high as 27 ft (8 m) and turning the load at right-angles to the direction of motion down the aisle, it is possible to stack up to seven racks high from a single ground floor. The actual racks can be used to strengthen the building and support the roof if necessary.

One constraint on excessively high racking is the difficulty of order-picking. Although order-pickers are available which will raise staff to pick orders from high racking, the raising and lowering speed is slow compared with horizontal movement. It is therefore better, if space is no object, to limit racking to about three racks high and have more order-pickers at work.

In designing a warehouse it is necessary to conceive the whole storage function as a handling system for particular commodities: the use of standard pallets; loads of uniform heights; racks of correct strength for the type of load being handled; aisle widths which are adequate for the reach trucks or turret trucks being used; order-picking trucks to take staff up to the height of the racks to select items required and computerised installations for the selection of the most popular items means that all these items are interdependent and part of a total warehousing concept. This concept seeks to ensure economy, system and security.

The warehouse is in many ways a terminal, where goods arrive and depart, but the interval between arrival and departure is a time of storage. While in storage the goods occupy non-selling space, and it may be possible to reduce this if design takes into account the need for customers to inspect merchandise. With many town centre sites space is at such a premium that shop display goods are not sold to customers, the order being fulfilled from storage stocks at some out-of-town depot. In others there is a shading-off between display and storage, some goods which are really in store being accessible to sales staff or even to persistent customers who are strong-minded enough to insist.

The layout of the warehouse must be such as to ensure location of any item that is in the warehouse when it is wanted. To this end we may have *fixed locations* for any item – perhaps in stock number order or alphabetical order. This fixed location system may be wasteful, in that it means the permanent provision of a certain fixed capacity of space for each item. At times when we have less than the normal stock, space is being wasted, while at times when for some reason we are carrying more than normal stock, space is inadequate. Some firms therefore adopt *random location* with goods being stored in the next available space. This is more economic in use of space but requires a check to be kept of location. Direct links to a computer facilitate this type of system. The computer is informed by electric keyboard of the arrival of goods. It then feeds back a location tag giving the goods a three-part location number, the first part giving the floor level, the second an aisle letter and the third a bin number. The goods are then stored in that location. When required an enquiry to the computer will trace the stock in seconds and feed back its location number.

11.3 Computerised warehouses

In the last decade computerised warehousing has made great strides, and the sceptical attitudes common when the idea was first proposed have been overcome. Specialist firms are now supplying complete and integrated services, from storage racks, stacking units and infeed systems to control equipment and programs to suit the needs of customers. The major cost savings are two: in the field of inventory control, so that capital tied up in stock is reduced; and in land use. One warehouse for a major motor manufacturer has racking 110 ft (33 m) high, at more than twenty levels, making a very economic use of space.

Horizontal transporters operate automatically at each level to store and retrieve unit loads. Pallets are often divided into two main sections, active stock and back-up stock. Active stock simply consists of a single pallet of each line in stock. This pallet will be called up to the order-picker as required, until it is empty, when the empty pallet will be expelled from the system and a full pallet brought forward from the back-up stock to the active stock. Transporters can also marshal pallets in correct sequence.

Many retrieval systems operate in three dimensions and have a two-command facility, which instructs the retriever to store one pallet and retrieve another by the shortest route in a cycle. Safety devices to prevent incorrect positioning, misalignment of the load and free-fall protection for the vertical carriage are incorporated in the retrieval system.

Direct on-line control of the system by a computer gives largely automated order-picking for high-user lines. This includes automatic keying to the computer of all goods on arrival. When demanded, the goods are retrieved and routed to a carousel or to a vertical closed-loop conveyor, where operators can select the number of items required for the order. One of the advantages the computer gives is in its choice of storage for particular lines. If a line is fast-moving it will be stored in a location close to the order-picking point; slow movers will be routed to more remote locations.

11.4 Warehouse equipment

Much will be said in Chapter 12 about materials handling and the equipment used in modern distribution. Basically, a warehouse requires racking of some sort to hold the goods; aisles between the racks in which lift trucks and order-pickers can operate; the necessary trucks and order-pickers; loose steps and ladders as required; and an internal transport system of some sort. A few words about each of these is required:

1. *Racking*. Racking may be of several types, and many manufacturers make similar equipment, so that evaluation of the types available is essential. The chief types of rack are *shelf racks*, *pigeon-hole racks*, *pallet racks* and *line storage racks*. Shelf racks are usually adjustable, and serviced by low steps or ladders. Pigeon-hole racks accommodate work-boxes of small parts or components, and are serviced by steps or small order-picking trucks incorporating different working levels and a main storage area where orders can be prepared. Pallet racks are skeleton frameworks serviced by turret trucks, and often as high as the building itself. Line storage consists of channelling with rollers to permit the movement of boxed or palletised materials, often under the influence of gravity.
2. *Trucks and order-pickers*. These will be fully described in Chapter 12.

3. *Steps and ladders.* Steps and ladders are likely to be the cause of accidents if they are not carefully designed. Strength and stability are vital; so is a good tread and, where possible, a container to receive the order being picked. Step-trucks are devices which not only provide steps for access to higher levels but also carry devices for the orders picked.
4. *Internal transport systems.* A circulating transport system which incorporates clip-on trolleys or trucks and some sort of sensing device which follows automatically a magnetic guide laid in the floor is essential for large warehouses. Control panels on the truck can direct it to off-load the truck at certain destinations.

11.5 Stockpiling of raw materials at factories

It is usual to think of warehousing as being mainly concerned with the safeguarding of finished goods when production is out of synchronisation with the demand for products. It can just as easily occur at the other end of the production cycle, before production really begins, when it features raw materials, components, consumable items needed in the production process and batched goods stored until required.

11.5.1 Raw materials

It frequently happens that raw materials are ordered in bulk, since that is the economical way to buy them. To keep costs low, bulk carriers are usually of large size and a delivery of thousands of tonnes of material cannot be immediately passed into production. The usual solution is to stockpile, though this may involve problems, depending on the type of material. For example, bulk powders may be blown away; some chemicals may react with the atmosphere and deteriorate; others may create a nuisance if they emit odours, wash into drainage systems or leach into rivers. Appropriate action must be taken to deal with such products both for economic reasons and to comply with regulations or environmental standards.

Raw materials are often stockpiled for strategic reasons – for example, wars and rumours of wars may lead to nervousness about the adequacy of stocks for future production and consequent stockpiling. The threat of a major strike affecting railways, ports or production of a particular component may lead to purchases in advance so that a plant can keep running.

11.5.2 Components

Although many factories are now using the JIT system for ordering components and do not expect to have stocks to handle, it is often necessary to warehouse components which come into the country from foreign factories. It may not be economically viable to send small, frequent loads of a particular component and a bulk supply will be sent which must be warehoused in the meantime.

11.5.3 Consumable items and batch-produced items

Frequently, manufacturing processes make use of a whole range of consumable items, such as solvents, powders, sweeteners and similar supplies. These can rarely be tied too closely to the production of the factory and some element of warehousing is essential. Similarly, where a component is small and easy to make, we may be able to make a year's supply in a day or so. We can set up the machine for the batch required, run them off and then take them into store. The storekeeper releases the required quantities as requisitioned by the shopfloor supervisor.

11.6 Warehouse operations

Warehousing overcomes the time-lag between supply and demand by holding stock in a secure and safe place. It can occur at various points in the production/distribution chain, ranging from the stockpiling of raw materials; through storage of components for production assembly, particularly where a firm like Ford is assembling cars from parts made in several of its European plants, as well as from ancillary industries; and finally, in the distribution of the finished product through the wholesale and retail network. At all these stages capital costs occur both for the purchase of stock and for premises, handling equipment, racking, etc. There are also other revenue costs for wages, security checks, stock deterioration, etc.

No doubt one of the reasons why the electrical power industry is turning from coal to gas is that whereas it is necessary to stockpile several months' coal requirements, gas provides a JIT fuel supply, with, furthermore, no residue for subsequent disposal.

Possibly because of its association with capital tied up, warehousing has been a Cinderella service, particularly where it is part of a production industry, rather than where it is provided by a specialist transport and distribution undertaking.

If a warehouse is to provide an efficient service, it is essential that once having determined the optimum size for the warehouse and the nature of the goods to be warehoused the premises are built to the highest specification as regards design, construction materials, wiring and lighting, ventilation, weight-bearing capacity of flooring and security. This equally applies to all the internal structures, e.g. racks, including their installation; the mechanical handling devices and the computer installation for monitoring the flow of stock. Although such high standards in the initial construction will be costly, they are necessary if you wish to provide your customers with a quality service.

These standards can, however, soon be frustrated unless:

1. There is a regular maintenance schedule to deal with the inevitable wear and tear on the infrastructure associated with the use of forklifts and other mechanical handling devices. This need for maintenance equally applies to the main structure of the building, as a broken window or a leaky roof can cause considerable damage to stock.
2. There is a well-trained and responsible workforce, who are not only competent in their handling of the equipment but are also well versed in the various procedures concerned with the receipt, in-house handling and delivery of stock. Staff training is therefore an essential feature.

There must be an area where goods inwards can be thoroughly checked to determine their nature and to ensure that they are the right quantity and quality, with adequate packing and marking for storage purposes. Any special requirements such as temperature control should be noted and acted upon, assuming that your warehouse has the necessary temperature control facilities. It is also necessary to check shelf-life limitations, and in this case the stock should be regularly monitored and the oldest stock delivered first. If turnover of such goods is slow and they begin to approach their shelf-life expiry date, this must be drawn to the owner's attention with a view to him arranging their disposal at a cheaper price.

As with a ship's stowage it will be necessary to ensure that goods which are incompatible with one another are kept well separated, and that goods liable to sweat are well ventilated. Valuable goods should be stored in a lockup facility, and so should highly pilferable goods. Odorous commodities should be kept separated and well ventilated, and as far away as possible from goods liable to taint. Hazardous goods should be warehoused separately. Suppliers' instructions, such as 'This way up', should be complied with. Any goods found to be damaged should be refused entry and if inadequate packing needs remedying, this should be charged for.

Once these checks have been made the goods should be allocated an identification number and put into storage. Their location and identification number should be logged into the computer, with a separate printout of this information, so that it is not entirely lost due to a computer malfunction or virus. While the goods are in store they should be regularly monitored by the computer as regards their turnover, especially if they have a limited shelf-life. Further control might include periodic physical inspections, where it is deemed necessary due to the nature of the goods.

On delivery it is essential to check that the goods are the right ones and of the required quantity. Any obvious damage, deterioration, shortages, etc. should be noted, the supplier should be immediately advised and the cause ascertained and dealt with.

If palletisation or further packing is deemed necessary in order to ensure safe delivery this should be done.

Although the ideal warehouse operation may appear to be costly it should ensure customer satisfaction. Bear in mind that if the warehouse keeper is acting as a bailee, he is responsible for making good any losses or correcting any wrong deliveries. The cost of such rectification will normally eventually outweigh the costs of installing and operating a quality service. (A bailee is a person who is in possession of other people's goods for some good reason – in this case to store them until required – and consequently has a duty of care to the true owner.)

11.7 Bonded warehouses (tax warehouses in the European Union)

Bonded warehouses fulfil a slightly different role, insofar as they are used by traders to delay the payment of duty and VAT, until such time as the goods are delivered into the market concerned. Thus the trader avoids tying up his capital until the goods are ready for sale in the market. Such warehouses are operated jointly by Customs & Excise and the warehouse keeper and are of two types:

1. Where the duty concerned is fairly negligible the warehouse keeper is required to keep strict ledger control of all inward and outward movements and Customs make sporadic checks of the actual stock to ensure that they match the ledgers.
2. In the warehouse for high duty goods both parties have keys to a dual locking system and Customs are in constant attendance during opening hours.

In both cases the warehouses have to be located in Customs-approved areas built to their specifications.

While goods are in such warehouses the trader is allowed to perform certain functions. These include storage for the maturing of spirits with an allowance made for natural ullage (loss by evaporation); breaking bulk, sorting, garbling (sorting good from bad) with duty liable on any bad goods disposed of; sampling; blending; repacking and displaying.

No duty is liable on any excise goods which are exported or the re-export of imported goods.

In all types of warehouse a battery charging bank should be installed for the recharging of forklift and other battery-operated machines. Battery-operated machines are best for enclosed spaces as they do not emit fumes, except during the recharging period, which is usually overnight.

11.8 The nature of stocks

The physical distribution concept is a wide-viewing continuous appraisal of the sum total of movements through time and space, from the first producer to the final consumer. It takes account of the distribution flow from raw materials to final sale. In the panorama the logistics manager sees many places where stages of production are out of phase with one another, and notes the accumulation of stocks to act as buffer zones adjusting for the uneven behaviour of supply and demand. Thus raw materials arrive in batches rather than daily requirements. When the ship comes in, or the lorry arrives, or the rail train shunts its trucks into the company siding, the stocks build up, only to run down steadily as production proceeds in the days and weeks that follow. These stocks are sometimes known as *replenishment quantity stocks*, ordered in optimum order sizes but used up as the cycle of production proceeds. A second type of stocks, known as *anticipation inventories*, are produced at steady rates in anticipation of a seasonal demand. *Safety stocks* are stocks accumulated to allow for sudden surges in demand, to prevent customer dissatisfaction. *Buffer stocks* are stocks of finished goods which pile up awaiting demand from wholesalers or depots. Rates of production cannot be varied easily, and a temporary fall in demand must be stockpiled if the complex production pattern is not to be disturbed. The time may come when everything is full to overflowing and we shall have to cut back, but until then the inventory, like a buffer, takes the strain.

To digress for a moment, the reader, who has recently read a long chapter (see Chapter 9) on JIT systems may feel that this sudden reference to stocks accumulating at every point in the supply-chain does not sound very much like the situation described in that chapter. It is a fact that some suppliers seeking to operate a JIT system have complained that the JIT manufacturer in effect forces them to accept the responsibility for stock-holding. There is some truth in this for if everyone adopts a JIT approach, they must lose the advantages that occur in production when we produce at the optimum level. Imagine a supplier who has an economic system of production and wishes to enjoy the economies it provides. An intermittent series of small orders from a customer ordering only his JIT requirements means that the rest of the output must be stockpiled, unless other customers are available.

The saddest tale of stockpiling and JIT operations occurred in the depression years of 1989–94, when the managing director of a famous brickworks to the north of London bewailed the state of affairs in the housing industry. Sitting in the middle of several artificial mountains of 350 million bricks, he said: 'We are as keen as anyone on JIT operations, and if we had our way we would not make bricks until they were needed. What can you do when there is a major recession and no one is building anything? At such times you must make bricks and stockpile or dismiss all your staff and mothball the plant.' Students of economics will recognise the case as one where an industry has specific assets, and it pays to go on producing if there is any prospect of an eventual sale.

Returning to the original thought, we can have stocks at all stages of the distribution network. What attitudes exist to stock? There are three chief attitudes to stock: the accountant's attitude, the salesforce's attitude and the production attitude.

11.8.1 The accountant's attitude to stock

To the accountant stock is only capital tied up to little effect. Profit can only be earned when stock turns over, and the ideal arrangement is to hold only enough stock to meet the demands of customers, replenishing it as and when required. The accountant is therefore interested in the rate of stock turnover, which may be found by either of the formulae given below.

$$\text{(1) Rate of stock turn} = \frac{\text{Cost of stock sold}}{\text{Average stock at cost price}}$$

$$\text{(2) Rate of stock turn} = \frac{\text{Sales}}{\text{Average stock at selling price}}$$

These formulae are more helpful in wholesale and retail trade than they are in other areas – for example, inventories of partially finished goods waiting to be completed do not throw up any helpful figures to calculate a rate of stock turn, but in general the accountant's attitude is to keep stock to a minimum wherever possible. This is the very reverse of the salesforce's idea of stocks.

11.8.2 The salesforce's attitude to stock

To the salesman or woman, with an eye on commission, the unpardonable thing is to be out of stock. If there are no stocks customers must be kept waiting, the lead-time between order and customer satisfaction increases and customers may be lost to other firms. The salesforce therefore likes full shelves irrespective of the capital tied up. Between the accountant's viewpoint and the salesforce's viewpoint comes the viewpoint of the production staff.

11.8.3 The production manager's attitude to stock

The production manager regards stocks as an incidental aspect of the general production problem. He or she will generally seek the optimum production from his or her own point of view, which means that 'batches' of parts will be produced with fairly long production-runs to cut down other costs such as rejigging machines too frequently. These batches must be stored, so that inventories are inseparable from production, but the idea of cost centres is such a natural one for production engineers that they are generally aware of inventory costs and will not produce excessive batches if it is clearly uneconomic. They therefore come closer to the accountant's viewpoint than the marketing viewpoint.

To reconcile these conflicting viewpoints in a dynamic situation is not easy. The dynamic nature of modern business life presents an endless variety of situations. Communication these days is instantaneous; a president sneezes and bankruptcies follow; natural disasters, political upheavals, military coups and guerrilla activities immediately affect inventory calculations. It is a lucky distribution manager who can keep ahead of the field in the daily assessment of requirements. However, the acknowledged techniques of inventory management can do much to assist in the decisions which must be made, and can significantly reduce inventories to the satisfaction of the accountant, without significantly reducing sales or raising production costs.

11.9 Inventory management by objectives

A management will achieve the best control over inventories if it has set appropriate inventory objectives. These will usually include the following aims:

1. A balanced inventory, operating at minimum costs within an inventory budget appropriate to the company's level of activity.
2. A prescribed level of customer satisfaction, say at 95 per cent of popular lines and rather less than this with other lines.
3. Secure control of stock positions by the adoption of a quantitative approach to inventory problems, which lays down clear guidelines to action in re-ordering, and in the alerting of management to exceptional situations.
4. The development of an adequate body of expertise by a training

Table 11.1 Sales analysis ABC, etc. order

	Units sold	Unit price	Total sales figures	Percentage of total sales figure
A	1,000	£48	£48,000	48
B	500	£72	£36,000	36
C	200	£50	£10,000	10
D	50	£40	£2,000	2
E	50	£40	£2,000	2
F	50	£20	£1,000	1
G	4,000	£0.25	£1,000	1

programme for both administrative and operative staff in the techniques of inventory control, so that there is the fullest understanding of, and sympathy for, the management's objectives.

We shall now examine these techniques.

11.10 The techniques of inventory management

11.10.1 Deciding what is important, or ABC analysis

Sometimes called volume analysis, this technique consists of arranging the various products handled in an ABC order, with A allocated to that product which represents the highest contribution to sales turnover, B to that product which comes next, etc. Having arranged items in this way, we can immediately see the items which should represent the major part of our inventory and those items of less importance. Thus the figures shown in Table 11.1 might be discovered.

It is clear that there is no point in spending time and effort upon items which have a negligible effect upon profits earned, and it might even be desirable to discontinue certain lines altogether.

11.10.2 Deciding how much to order – or EOQ analysis

The recommended formula for finding the economic order quantity is:

$$EOQ = \sqrt{\frac{2CoD}{Ch}}$$

where: EOQ = economic order quantity (basic order quantity, whenever re-ordering is required).

Co = costs per order (i.e. delivery and administrative costs of each order).

D = the annual demand.
Ch = capital and handling (storage) costs per unit per annum (usually expressed as a percentage of the cost per unit).

11.10.2.1 *Example*

Imagine an article costing £2.50 per item, the capital and handling charges for which are estimated at 20 per cent on cost. Other details are:

Cost of ordering = £15 (Co)
Annual consumption = 1,500 units (D)

Capital and handling (Ch) costs per unit per annum = 20% of £2.50 = £0.50

$$EOQ = \sqrt{\frac{2CoD}{Ch}} = \sqrt{\frac{2 \times £15 \times 1{,}500}{£0.50}} = \sqrt{\frac{£45{,}000}{£0.50}}$$

$$\sqrt{90{,}000} = \underline{\underline{300}} \text{ units}$$

Since the annual demand is 1,500 units and the EOQ is 300 units this means we shall re-order five times per year.

11.10.3 Deciding when to order

A common method is to designate a fixed re-order point based on the lead-time – the time between the placing of an order and its satisfaction. This period will require a certain stock, based upon the weekly sales. Thus a four-week lead-time requires us to have a four-week stock in hand. In practice, a safety margin would also be allowed – say, a further week's stock – and when stock fell to a five-week stock we will order the EOQ.

11.10.4 Depot replenishment

When depots or branches are delivering stock to customers their inventories fall day by day. How can we ensure that they do not run out of stock? The answer is to replenish supplies in some economic way, and often replacement on a one-for-one basis is adopted. Data supplied to head office of invoices to customers notify them of the quantities delivered. These can then be integrated into economic loads, preferably full container loads, and stock will be replenished when this point is reached.

11.10.5 Conclusion

Inventory control is a sophisticated process today, and computerised refinements of the basic concepts described in this chapter give modifications to take account of variations in the rate of usage; adjustment of replenishment procedures to take account of slow-moving items which are not very influential contributions to sales; alterations in lead-times, etc. The reader is urged to seek in-company advice if inventory control is important. Only in an in-plant situation can a really detailed answer be given to the question 'How does this company control inventories and ensure replenishment of stock for resale?'

11.11 A case study: Richardson Sheffield Ltd – a bar code system using a radio data terminal

(The authors are grateful to David Kennedy, the Purchasing and Materials Systems Manager of Richardson Sheffield Ltd, for permission to draw on this article in preparing this section.)

Richardson Sheffield Ltd are manufacturers of kitchen knives and scissors, based on two sites within 1 mile of each other in the centre of Sheffield. Each week some 750,000 blades are made at Blade Division and moved from there to Product Division for assembly, packaging and dispatch to customers around the world. Each day some 2,500 separate transactions in Product Division's stores produced paperwork which required punching into the company's stock control and material issue system. This was driven by an IBM AS 400 processor. The punching process was relatively slow and with the best will in the world the 2.5 operatives could not keep up. The best they could do was to be 7–10 days behind. Both Purchasing and Stores needed immediate and accurate data, which simply were not available.

11.11.1 The solution: a radio data terminal system

At the end of 1992, the company decided to look at a bar code-based system as a solution to this problem. It was felt that such a system would offer greater accuracy and throughput of data as well as the possibility of real-time downdating and updating of stock records.

One of the leading companies in bar code technology was contacted and briefed to produce a system proposal.

After several visits and discussions, a radio data terminal system was decided on (see Fig. 11.1). Conventional bar-coded systems rely on scanned data being downdated into a main system via PCs. A radio-based system not only gives direct, real-time access it also represents a significant saving over PC-based ones.

Stores personnel use hand-held radio terminals, with laser scanners attached, to perform stock movements, order-picking and other routines. The information scanned is transmitted to a base station and is then sent to

Fig. 11.1 Stores records being read by a hand-held radio terminal (courtesy of Mark Rodgers Photography, Sheffield and Richardson Sheffield Ltd)

the AS 400 processor via a modem link. A terminal access controller allows the hand-held units to interface with the existing AS 400-driven computer system and to function as and with the same processing power as an

IBM 5251 terminal. The main constraint is that in common with many terminal controllers, the terminal access controller unit can only control seven units. It was decided that five units was the optimum number for system implementations. Finally, a bar code decoder, with wand, is wired into an existing terminal in the goods-inwards office to allow the scanning of receipts.

The system is configured to read code thirty-nine format bar codes. The format is completely 'open' and gives the necessary flexibility required for a large component warehousing operation.

11.11.2 Stages in the implementation of the system

A team for the project, jointly co-ordinated by the Purchasing and Materials Systems Manager and the Computer Systems Manager included data processing staff, stores and production personnel. The following activities were needed to implement the system.

1. Ordering, delivery and installation of the hardware.
2. Writing the necessary programs.
3. The existing numeric locations in the stores were bar-coded.
4. The existing stock items in the bulk store were labelled with their bar codes. A 'carrier ticket' file had to be created to link the bar-coded labels with particular components.
5. Incoming goods had to be labelled with their bar codes as a matter of course on arrival.
6. Slow-moving stock in the 'Picking Store' had to be labelled.
7. Programs had to be tested and training undertaken in the new procedures.
8. The key suppliers of goods had to be persuaded to send goods with one bar-coded consignment label per delivery. In the event many suppliers not only bought the necessary software to produce the required consignment labels, but began to investigate the use of bar codes in their own manufacturing systems and supply-chains.

11.11.3 The lessons and benefits

David Kennedy lists these as follows:

11.11.3.1 Lessons

1. *Flexibility*. The company demonstrated its ability to respond positively to change and to adapt existing internal supply-chains in order to improve delivery to customers.

2. *Understanding*. The experience of specifying the system and the consequent scrutiny of existing procedures and routes within Product Division, has taught the valuable lesson that no part of the internal production chain works in isolation and has emphasised the need for greater exchange of information.
3. *Reliability*. The system has highlighted the need for true partnerships with suppliers to ensure not only reliable deliveries but also accuracy of information, e.g. their lead-times and the company's own forecasts.
4. *Mutual sophistication and enthusiasm*. The company's commitment to the use of the latest technology has encouraged many of its suppliers not only to invest in the appropriate software for producing the specified consignment labels but also to investigate the possible application of bar-coded systems to their own manufacturing and supply-chains.

11.11.3.2 *Benefits*

1. Real-time recording.
2. Improved accuracy.
3. More time for data management and interpretation.
4. Scanning allows for quick, accurate perpetual inventory routines: each time an item is picked the relevant location can be scanned and checked.
5. These perpetual routines should impact on stocktaking and reduce the need for three a year to one at the financial year-end.

His general conclusion is that the availability of timely and accurate data promotes efficiency and reduces stocks. Previously, because they did not know the exact stock position it was necessary to hold excess stocks. The uncertainties of business life had to be 'buffered out' by stocks. With the new system of real-time records that necessity has largely been removed.

11.12 Summary

1. The function of the warehouse is to carry goods over time until they are wanted, either for use in production (if they are raw materials or components) or by retailers and consumers (if they are finished goods).
2. Warehousing also caters for seasonal demands, and for surpluses to present requirements acquired in the course of economic batch production, economic purchasing or for strategic reasons.
3. The general rule for merchandise is first in, first out (FIFO) – it is only prudent in most situations to remove and sell, or use, the item that has been in store longest.

4. Warehousing operates most effectively when the layout is standard, and an item can be found in its usual place. When stocks are low this wastes space, and therefore some systems operate on a basis which places new stock in the first available space, but a tracing system – preferably computerised – keeps track of where every item is.
5. Sophisticated order-picking systems enable stocks to be retrieved electronically, pallets being moved on transporters and elevators to the order-picker and then restored to their original place in the system.
6. Warehouse operations are most easily arranged in purpose-built premises, constructed to high specifications and kept efficient by regular maintenance. Stocks require careful supervision by trained staff who know the merchandise and can supervise it to ensure prime quality, compatibility with other stocks and complete security.
7. Bonded warehouses (now called tax warehouses in the European Union) permit the breaking of bulk, sorting, garbling, sampling, blending, repacking and displaying of goods without the payment of duty or tax, but under strict control of the warehouse keeper (and in the case of high-value goods, H.M. Customs itself).
8. Different attitudes to stock are displayed by accountants, sales staff and production staff. These attitudes influence the regimes used in various warehouses. It is often not possible to achieve 100 per cent customer satisfaction (i.e. we are never out of stock). We have to settle for something less than that. Techniques for ensuring a reasonable inventory regime are management specification of the objectives to be achieved and rules to be observed in the warehousing field; ABC analysis (deciding on priorities), specifying economic order quantities (EOQs) and re-order points for each product.

11.13 Questions

1. Why is warehousing an inevitable activity in many industries? What are the problems of warehousing?
2. Where should warehouses be sited? Refer in your answer to (a) imports, (b) consumer durables for home sales, and (c) components for future production.
3. Write short notes about each of the following:
   (a) order-pickers
   (b) bonded warehouses
   (c) ABC ranking
   (d) bar codes
   (e) racks for warehouses
   (f) stockpiles
4. Distinguish between fixed locations and random locations in warehouses.

5. Compare the attitude to stocks of (a) the accountant, and (b) the sales manager. How could they best arrive at an amicable arrangement about the volumes of stock to be held?
6. What is an EOQ? How can an EOQ promote the efficient ordering of stock?

12 Physical distribution: materials handling

12.1 Introduction

The total distribution concept assumes that management will seek the cheapest and most efficient solutions to their physical distribution problems. It is therefore axiomatic that they should investigate rigorously all devices suggested or developed by design staff in the materials handling industry so as to obtain the equipment most suitable for the handling of their products. The materials handling industry has shown enormous ingenuity in the last thirty years, and has provided many interesting and economic pieces of equipment. They come under five main headings, which may be listed as follows:

1. Lift trucks.
2. Mobile cranes and lorry loaders.
3. Conveyors.
4. Holding aids.
5. Ancillary equipment.

A full understanding of the range of facilities available cannot possibly be given in this book. Many firms specialise in the analysis of storage and distribution requirements, and will design and install layouts of complete warehousing and distribution systems. Without partiality towards any particular manufacturer's equipment they will seek the solution that gives maximum efficiency of operation, tailoring the systems to meet the needs of the firm they are serving. The great advantage of using the services of such specialist firms is that a team of experts has been built up with the necessary types of expertise, able to deal with the varied aspects of the work involved, from nuts and bolts assemblies to sophisticated computerised control engineering. They will invariably be members of the professional body, the Institute of Logistics, which exists to foster and encourage the fullest development of this important science, and holds regular exhibitions in pursuit of these aims. The reader is strongly advised

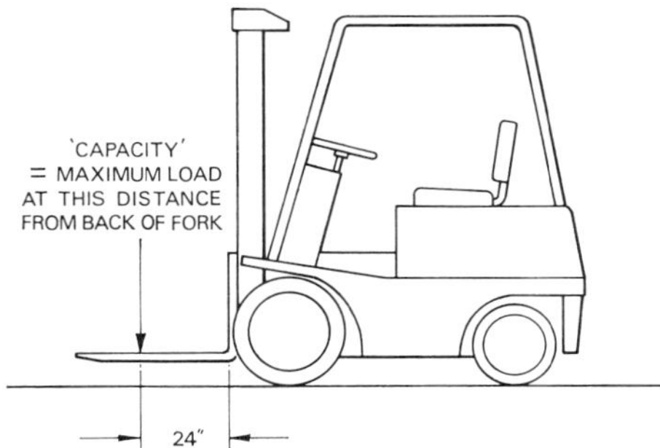

Fig. 12.1 The 'capacity' feature of a counterbalanced forklift truck (courtesy of Lansing-Bagnall Ltd)

to visit such an exhibition and see the equipment. Here it is only possible to outline the chief types of equipment.

12.2 Lift trucks

The handling of many small items individually is a tedious and time-wasting process. Wherever possible such cargo should be unitised. The effect of this process is to make one big lift of a number of little lifts. The problem then arises: can the warehouse keeper or stevedore lift them? The solution to the problem is the lift truck. Most lift trucks have forks to raise the load. Others use platforms or clamps. A brief description of the characteristics of a forklift truck is helpful at this point.

12.2.1 Characteristics of the forklift truck

In size the forklift truck may vary from the manually propelled truck, through the battery-driven truck with a lifting capacity of a few tons, to the very large, heavy-duty vehicles powered by internal combustion engines and capable of lifting loaded containers weighing up to 30 tonnes.

The forked platform can be raised (1) to free the goods from the floor for transit, and (2) to place them on shelves or vehicles.

Most trucks – the so-called counterbalanced trucks – can move with the forked platform raised to any height, provided that basic aspects of stability are borne in mind. The centre of gravity of the load must be kept within the specified number of inches of the heels of the fork, i.e. a '2 tons 24 inches' truck will be stable with a load of 2 tonnes if the centre of gravity is within 24 inches of the heels of the fork. The higher the truck is to lift loads the more tilt-back there must be on the fork ramps, and the lifting of heavy loads is made more difficult. The capacity of the truck is illustrated in Fig. 12.1.

The small wheel-base makes them very manoeuvrable.

If operating into and out of sheds or departments problems arise with (1) fumes, (2) doors, (3) draughts, (4) door frames. These difficulties are explained below.

Trucks may be manually operated (i.e. you push it yourself), electrically-operated by a battery-powered motor, or driven by an internal combustion engine, driven by either petrol, diesel or liquefied petroleum gas. Battery-driven trucks have the advantage that the battery is heavy and provides much of the counterbalance weight required to counterbalance the load. They take 8–12 hours to recharge, and thus are less economic for shift working unless a battery change is undertaken. Changing batteries is an inconvenient operation due to their weight, and it is usually preferable to plug them in for recharging while still on the vehicle, at purpose-built recharging stations. Where many vehicles are required spare vehicles may be provided to give an overlap while others are being recharged. Petrol engines give off poisonous carbon monoxide fumes and are therefore only suitable for outdoor use, in countries where petrol prices are low enough to make them economic. Diesel engines give off less toxic fumes than any other internal combustion engine, but when badly maintained they do give off very unpleasant fumes, the unpleasantness arising from unburnt hydrocarbons. Sheds where diesel lift trucks are used must therefore be well ventilated and trucks should be well maintained. Liquefied petroleum gas is conveniently bottled, and the exhaust from gas engines is less toxic than exhaust from petrol engines. More importantly, engine wear is reduced and the servicing costs are therefore lower than for diesel engines.

When forklift trucks are used it is obvious that door frames must be flush with the floor; trucks cannot jump over steps. Also, loads are likely to catch on door frames and do damage to both the load and the framework of the building. If draughts are not to be unbearable some type of door must be devised which opens as the truck drives at it. These are often of overlapping rubber, but even then a safety problem arises. Any member of staff standing in the doorway is liable to be hit by a door giving way before a loaded truck entering from the other side.

12.2.2 Types of forklift truck

There are many types of forklift trucks. The chief types are described briefly below, but any reader who is selecting trucks is strongly advised to consult the leading manufacturers, who will gladly give guidance in the best type for a given purpose. Some of these are illustrated in Fig. 12.2 and a description of the chief types is appropriate at this point.

1. *Pallet trucks*. These are usually pedestrian-operated trucks, which roll under the pallet or stillage and raise it sufficiently to free the load from

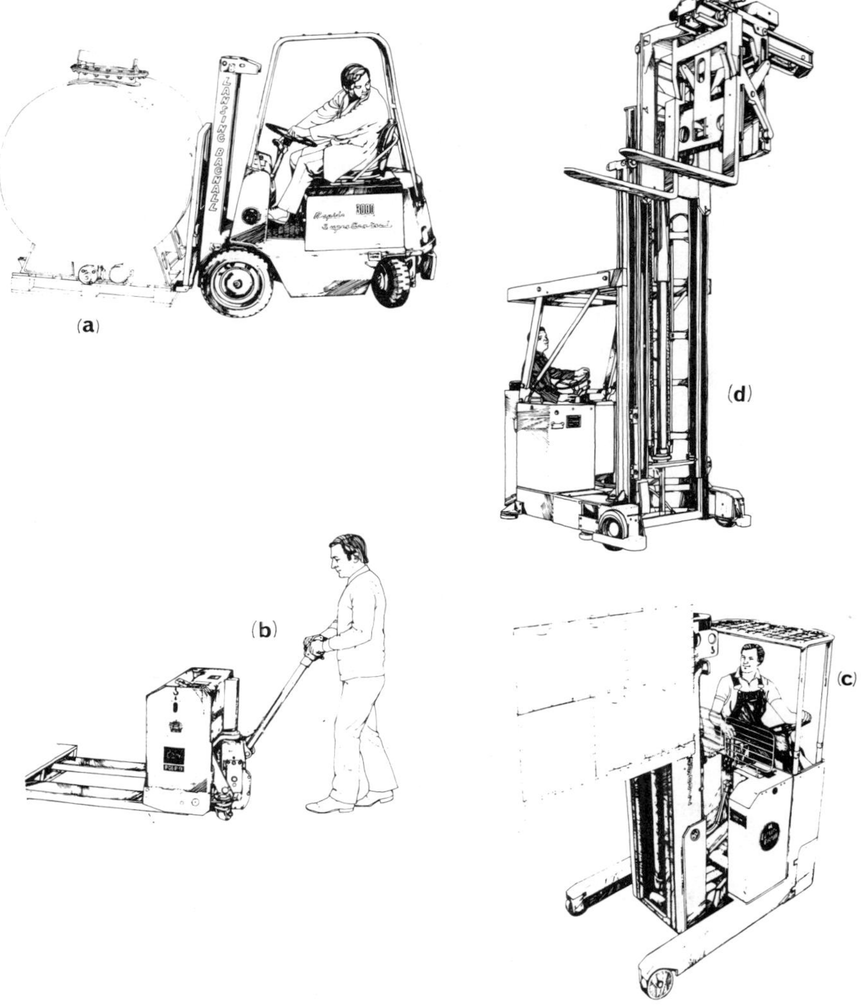

Fig. 12.2 Types of lift truck: (a) counterbalanced battery-driven truck (b) a pallet truck (c) a narrow-aisle reach truck (d) a turret truck (courtesy of Lansing-Bagnall Ltd)

the floor. It can then be moved to a new warehouse position, but the load cannot be raised for stacking. These are essentially load-transporting trucks. Another type of pedestrian truck is the pedestrian high lift truck, which can raise loads as high as 10 ft (3 m).

2. *Counterbalanced trucks*. The characteristics of these have already been

described above. They are the types of truck most commonly seen by the ordinary public, for much of their work is done in the open air. They can lift, raise and stack palletised loads, and a variety of attachments is available for specialised handling (see descriptions below).

3. *Narrow-aisle trucks (reach trucks and turret trucks)*. Narrow-aisle trucks are either reach trucks, which can move the load forward of the truck to place it upon shelving either side of the aisle, or turret trucks, which travel over a guide-rail down very narrow aisles but have the facility to turn the turret head to left or right to place pallets on racking. Special models can reach as high as 68 ft (20 m) which gives many rows of shelving in a warehouse, and consequent capital saving on warehouse space. The reach trucks may operate either by a scissors-like motion of the forklift pantograph, or by moving the whole mast-assembly forwards.
4. *Heavy-duty side-loaders*. Side-loading forklift trucks are used for picking up long loads such as packaged timber or containers. The forks are positioned at the side of the vehicle, between two solid platforms. They have a reach-action, moving forward in front of the platforms to pick up the long heavy load. They then raise it above the platforms, retract inwards and lower the load on to the platforms. The truck now moves off with the long load supported not on the forks but on the strong platforms at either side. On arrival at the destination – say, a waiting road haulage vehicle – the forks again take over the load by raising it off the platforms, move it out and lower it on to the flat surface of the vehicle. By carrying the load along the length of the vehicle, rather than at right angles across the front forks, much narrower gangways are possible. For example, a 20 ft (6 m) long package of timber would require a gangway at least 25 ft (8 m) wide, whereas a 12–15 ft (4–5 m) gangway would suffice if side-loaders are used. Anyone who has seen road vehicles moving timber stacked three high, two abreast and three long, will appreciate the economy achieved with the side-loading forklift truck. Before this method of handling packaged timber, planks were moved individually at enormous labour cost.
5. *Rough-ground trucks*. These are for use on building sites and other rough ground. The forklift is part of a tractor-like vehicle with large wide-tyred wheels.
6. *Order-pickers*. An order-picking truck does not raise goods, but raises stores personnel to the level of the stacked produce in a warehouse. A control platform on the forklift can be raised or lowered to enable the storekeeper to reach and select items from storage to fulfil orders for customers. The order-picking operator can control the truck movements along the aisle and be raised and lowered with the trays or pallets on which orders are being assembled for dispatch.
7. *Cold-store trucks*. These are adapted to work in temperatures of −30°C.

Fig. 12.3 A heavy-duty front-loading forklift truck (courtesy of Lancer Boss Ltd)

8. *Hazardous-area trucks.* These are enclosed to prevent any spark or overheating causing explosions. They may only be operated on the authority of the factory inspectorate.
9. *Heavy-duty lift trucks.* As their name implies, these trucks are capable of lifting the heaviest loads. The most celebrated name here is Lancer Boss, a firm which makes a complete range of trucks but is particularly successful in the heavy lift truck field. Their latest model, the world's biggest ever front-lift truck, has 58 tonnes' capacity. For duties in steelworks, foundries, shipyards, terminals and ports, the K130/48 has 20 tonnes' more lifting capacity than previous trucks in the range. Features include a braking system that automatically applies the inner service brakes during a full-lock turn, independent fork positioning, hydraulic sideshift, a six-cylinder diesel power unit and powershift transmission (see Fig. 12.3).

12.2.3 Special attachments for forklift trucks

There are a number of attachments which enable a forklift truck to deal with loads which would otherwise be inconvenient. Some of these are illustrated in Fig. 12.4. The commonest attachments are:

1. *Drum tines*. This attachment slips over the forks and replaces them by three drum tines. The drums, which must have been stacked horizontally, settle between the tines.
2. *Drum claws*. These are used for drums stacked vertically.
3. *Drum grips* are also used for vertical drums.
4. *Side clamps* are used for picking up baled cotton, cartons, drums, etc., the particular type of clamp being designed to suit the object to be lifted. Side clamps do not need pallets, since the object itself is picked up, and hence recently developed methods of pallet-less lifting use this kind of attachment.
5. *Timber grabs* are able to embrace logs and lift them with an arm-encircling action.
6. *Overhead block clamps* fit down over the top of a stack of blocks and embrace them firmly from above.
7. *Paper roll clamps* similarly embrace the roll of paper from above and are contoured to give a good grip on the roll.
8. *Crane attachments*. These give a gallows-like structure which enables the forklift truck to pick up members hung on the gallows by a hook. It is convenient for lifting heavy members of constructional platforms, etc.

Attachments are a mixed blessing. They tend to be more specific in their use than the forklift, and consequently reduce the truck's versatility. On the other hand, a firm which has a full-time use for a particular type of attachment can gain enormous benefits from a truck specially adapted to its needs. Once again, the industry is keen to supply and discuss the design of special attachments for particular purposes.

12.3 Mobile cranes and lorry loaders

Besides the wide variety of lifts made possible by the lift trucks, materials handling firms have need of cranes able to lift materials both on sites and in industrial premises. A wide range of mobile cranes is now available with an impressive range of mountings, reaches and attachments. Many of these are hydraulically operated, with fully slewing superstructures, mounted on vehicles ranging from small solid-tyred manoeuvrable platforms for in-plant use to four-wheel drive vehicles with broad tyres for site operations.

Perhaps the most useful of all are the lorry loaders, which render a vehicle independent of lifting capacity at either end of a transit. The HIAB

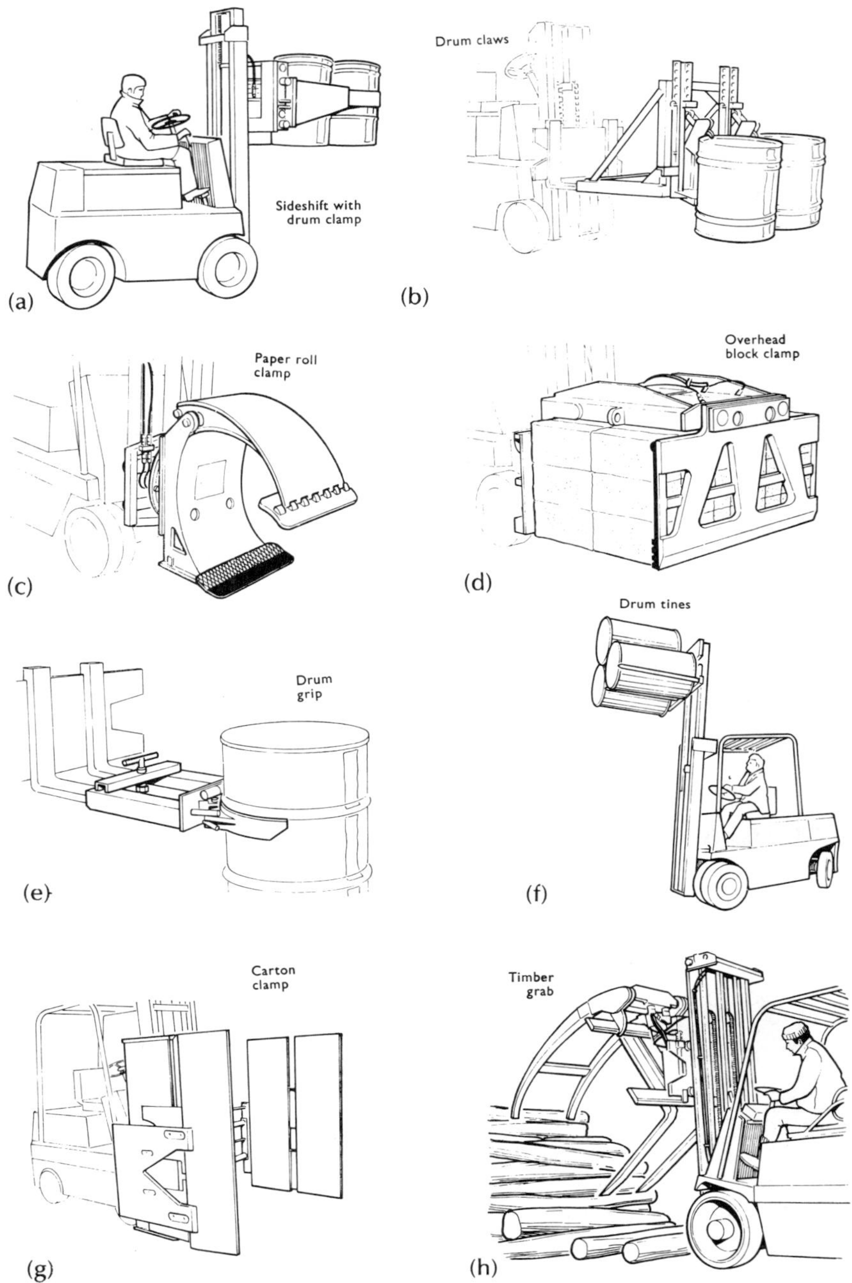

Fig. 12.4 (a) Sideshift with drum clamp (b) Drum claws (c) Paper roll clamp (d) Overhead block clamp (e) Drum grip (f) Drum tines (g) Carton clamp (h) Timber grab (courtesy of Lansing-Bagnall Ltd)

lorry loaders reproduced in Fig. 6.2 (see page 125) and Fig. 12.5 (see opposite) illustrate the reach, variety of attachment and neat stowage of this type of crane. A co-operative driver of such a vehicle will place site materials in convenient packs exactly where they are required on the site, thus eliminating much post-delivery movement. It is just as easy to deliver materials on a scaffold 10 ft (3 m) up as to leave them at ground level.

12.3.1 Pallet loaders for lorries and containers

A pallet loader is a device which fits into channel tracks laid in the floor of lorries, containers or ordinary premises. Once a forklift truck or tailboard lifting device has placed a pallet on the tail of a vehicle it can be raised off the floor by the pallet loaders through the action of simple tommy bars. Once free of the floor, the load can be rolled forward to the head of the vehicle. It cannot crash the headboard because a safety device operates, nor can it overrun the tailboard on the return journey when unloading or de-stuffing the container. Each pair of pallet loaders can lift 1.5 tonnes, and is rustproof, rugged and portable for transfer from one vehicle to another. On reaching its final position the tommy bar is turned to the lowered position, leaving the pallet firmly positioned on the floor. The pallet loaders are now below floor level in their channel tracks and can be rolled back to pick up the next pallet.

12.4 Conveyors and elevators

Conveyors are used for a wide variety of activities, from manufacturing projects to luggage conveyance at busy airports. The essential feature of a conveyor is that a product is moved from A to B either on a continuous belt or in a continuous tube impelled by friction with the belt itself, by the force of gravity, or by compressed air. Conveyors frequently include some element of elevation to raise products to floors or levels where they are required. Some have lifts which automatically tip up at the top of their travel to tilt products on to a further conveyor.

Conveying equipment has become very sophisticated with electronic and on-line computer control. Horizontal transporter units will bring up unit loads for order-picking; transfer back-up stock to active stock; discharge empty pallets from the system; deliver documents to correct work stations and store; accumulate, rearrange and group carriers as desired. Many carriers will move horizontally, vertically up or down and across inclined planes. Many conveyors for granular materials and powders have bucket-type transit vessels which can be automatically tipped into hoppers or on to

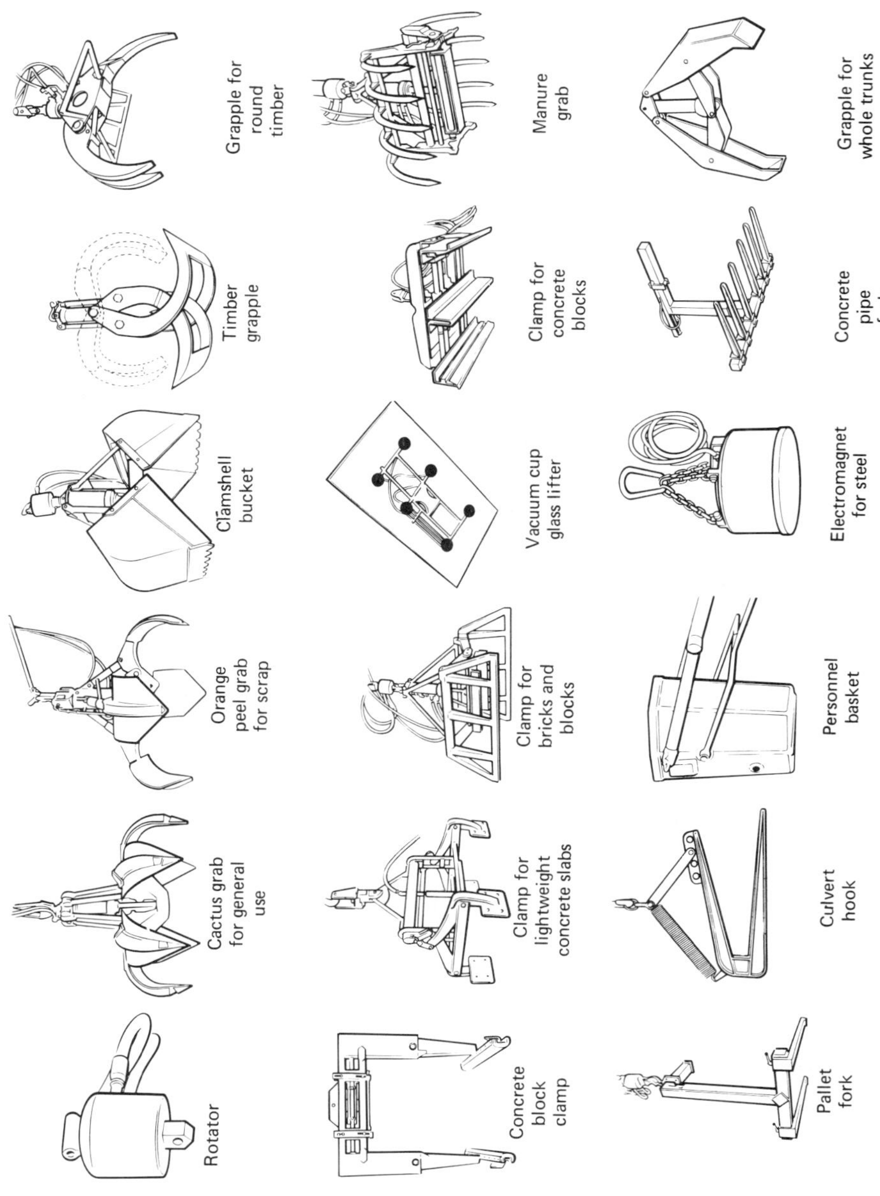

Fig. 12.5 Attachments for lorry loaders (courtesy of George Cohen 600 Group Ltd)

belt conveyors. Other conveying equipment uses gravity or powered rollers and tubs into which orders can be picked manually or automatically on the larger volume lines. Others have screw conveyors. Conveyors for food products may be of stainless steel and incorporate hose-proof motors and switchgear to facilitate cleaning. Figure 12.6 shows a zig-zag overhead conveyor of a type used in manufacturing. It is made from standard parts which can be assembled into complete conveyors to customers' specifications.

A wide variety of *elevators* is available, both for integral installation in a conveyor system or as free units which can be moved into position to suit the materials handling situation and capable of handling a variety of goods, including boxes, packages, bags, cartons and bottle crates.

12.5 Holding aids

Modern materials handling requires that warehouse shelving space shall be available as cheaply as possible, yet it must be strong and adaptable. There are many types of angle iron and interlocking racking which give adjustable storage, often in combination with pallets, tote trays, bins or containers, assembly benches, shelving, order-picking stepladders and elevators. Dense storage is possible in mechanised bins and drawers, mounted on roller bearings and with variable internal partitions. Some systems are mobile, gangways being reduced because hydraulically operated racks can open a gangway up at a speed of 6 in (15 cm) per second.

The variety of racking and other holding aids is enormous, many of them boltless systems where parts click together to give strong, space-saving installations to customers' requirements. A typical system, which in this case is boltless, is illustrated in Fig. 12.7.

12.6 Ancillary equipment for materials handling

The ancillary equipment used in materials handling is diverse, and varies with the system adopted and the components selected for that system. Materials handling is essentially a 'better mousetrap' world, where established firms, firms wishing to diversify into the materials handling field and countless engineers actually operating equipment are alert to the need to improve products. There is hardly a component that is not under constant consideration and the subject of regular reports on performance. This constant surveillance leads to prompt detection of faults, research into the difficulty and the development of a new piece of ancillary equipment, or optional extra or standard component in due course. Some of the available equipment is described in the following paragraphs.

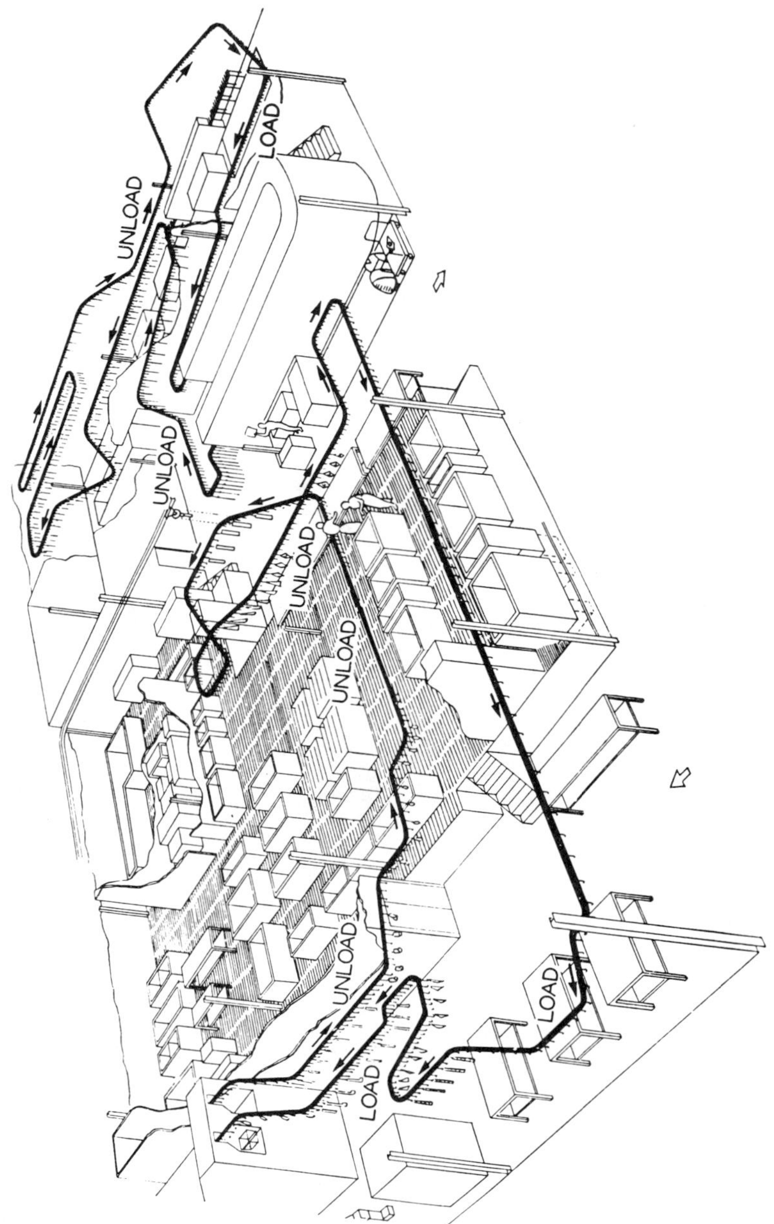

Fig. 12.6 An overhead conveyor system (courtesy of Brockhouse Finspa Handling Ltd)

Fig. 12.7 Boltless XL Pallet racking for warehouse storage (courtesy of Boltless Systems Link 51 Ltd)

12.6.1 Automatic battery chargers

Electric forklift trucks need fully charged batteries for each shift. They take 8–12 hours to charge up, and are discharged in about the same period. This constant charging and discharging is a great strain on any battery, but the strain can be reduced if the charging is carefully done. Automatic battery chargers allow the battery itself to dictate the rate of charge. The battery charge controllers automatically monitor the requirements of the battery, which when fully charged will not need to be immediately disconnected, but simply shuts down and is ready for use when required.

12.6.2 Tyre protectors

Lift trucks and other mobile plant operating in industrial conditions are prone to high puncture rates. Tyre protectors are cord-reinforced rubber interlays which fit between the outer casing and the tube. Any sharp object piercing the outer cover is deflected by the interlay, saving as much as 85 per cent of punctures.

12.6.3 Urethane tyres

Industrial trucks often operate in conditions where rubber tyres are a disadvantage. Spillages of chemicals increase the wear of rubber tyres. Urethane tyres are dilute acid and alkali-resistant. They are stronger, cut- and tear-resistant, and as they roll more easily they sustain battery life.

12.6.4 Runway systems

These are useful for moving heavy objects like engines around in workshops. An overhead runway with lifting devices enables components of up to a tonne or more to be moved about. Similarly, scrap iron can be fed by magnetic lifts into furnaces.

12.6.5 Slings and grabs

Innumerable types of slings are available from specialist manufacturers to suit particular needs. For example, where the outer surface must not be damaged by chains or ropes; when varying sizes and circumferences are constantly being handled; when the headroom is limited, etc. The wide variety of grabs available with cranes has been illustrated in Fig. 12.5 and specialist firms will design such attachments for any system or requirement.

12.6.6 Dock levellers

Dock levellers are devices which adjust differences between heights of vehicle tailboards and loading banks. Most of them allow for variations of about 0.5 m up and 0.25 m down. They accelerate the flow of goods into and out of the warehouse.

12.6.7 Automatic weighers

Many materials require to be weighed at some point in the incoming–outgoing cycle. Automatic weighers, often custom-built, are available for most types and sizes of products, and give documentary evidence of the weight registered.

12.7 Summary

1. The problems of logistics are largely solved by having a range of materials-handling devices capable of moving unit loads of reasonable size, to give economic loads at every stage of the journey from producer to consumer. Such handling devices are especially required at interfaces where goods move from one mode of transport to another.
2. The five chief types of handling devices are: lift trucks, mobile cranes and lorry loaders, conveyors, holding aids and ancillary equipment of many types.
3. Lift trucks are devices which can lift goods from a floor, platform, shelf or vehicle and raise or lower them to a different position. The basic problem with the design of forklift trucks is stability, especially if the vehicle is to move with the forks and their load in the raised position. Problems also arise with fumes, doors, draughts and door frames.
4. The chief types of truck are pallet trucks, counterbalanced trucks, narrow-aisle trucks, side-loaders, order-pickers, hazardous-area trucks and heavy-duty trucks.
5. Attachments include drum tines, drum claws, drum grips, side clamps, timber grabs, paper roll clamps, overhead block clamps and crane attachments.
6. Mobile cranes may be independent vehicles or lorry-mounted cranes. They can have a wide variety of attachments including grabs for scrap metal, clamps for lifting blocks, bricks and packaged timber, personnel baskets, clamshell buckets, pipe lifters, etc.
7. Pallet loaders are devices for rolling pallets, placed on the tailboard of a vehicle, forward to the front of the lorry, and vice versa on unloading.
8. Conveyors are used in a wide variety of situations, particularly in industrial situations but also at airports for passenger luggage. They may have on-line computerised controls, and be capable of moving horizontally, vertically or on inclined planes.

12.8 Questions

1. Explain the use of a pallet truck. Where is it most likely to be used? What is the difference between a pallet truck and a pedestrian high-lift truck?
2. What is a narrow-aisle truck? Where is it used and what are its advantages?
3. Explain the sequence of operations when moving packaged timber with a side-loading forklift truck.
4. Write short notes about *four* of the following:
   (a) timber grabs
   (b) personnel baskets
   (c) lorry loaders
   (d) slab clamps
   (e) block clamps
   (f) glass lifters
5. What is an automatic battery charger? Why do some firms prefer electric forklift trucks rather than machines powered by diesel or liquefied petroleum gas?
6. What sorts of job can conveyors do in the logistics field?

13 Physical distribution: bulk transport

13.1 Introduction

Containerisation apart, the increase in bulk transport is the most significant development in land and sea transport in recent years. During the Second World War, American Class T.2 tankers of 16,500 dwt were regarded as outsize giants. Today the 477,000 tonne tanker is sailing and the million tonner is on the drawing boards – but with the present overcapacity in world tanker tonnage it is unlikely to be built for the foreseeable future. Oil is a natural choice for bulk physical distribution, but the significant advance is not only in the size of bulk carrier of the ULCC (ultra large crude carriers) type. The variety of products now carried in bulk is also important. At sea we have bulk carriers for oil, methane, ores, grain, chemicals and other specialised carriers. On land we have petroleum, liquid gases, powders, chemicals, milk and countless other products moved in bulk. What are the advantages of bulk transport?

13.2 The advantages of bulk transport

Transport is peculiarly susceptible to the achievement of *economies of scale*; great benefits can be derived from large size. Although at very large sizes certain diseconomies do begin to creep in they do not arise until certain critical sizes have been reached. Thus the million tonne ship would face operating problems not faced by the 250,000 tonner and the 44 tonne lorry is environmentally less acceptable than the 38 tonner. Below these critical sizes there are strong arguments for increasing the size of ships and vehicles to achieve economies of scale.

Obvious examples of operating economies are the capital cost per unit carried, the crewing costs per unit carried, and maintenance and servicing costs per unit carried. If we double the size of a ULCC we do not have to double the number of radar units or double the crew, or to service the ship twice as frequently. Most important of all, we do not have to double the amount of motive power and the quantity of fuel used. In road haulage, where for congestion reasons the number of possible journeys between depots is necessarily few in a day, it makes good sense to increase the size of the tanker and thus achieve a maximum advantage from each completed journey.

Other economies are in the safety and training fields. If we move products in bulk, the number of transport units required is reduced, as are the chances of collisions or incidents at sea or on land. Many products moved in bulk are dangerous; such as petroleum, liquid gases, acids and alkalis. Not only will the number of incidents be reduced but the reduced number of personnel required can be specially trained to meet the increasingly stringent requirements of a pollution-conscious world. Yet another economy is achieved in the administration field. The documentation for a large consignment is much less than for many small consignments, while it also becomes worthwhile to fit a large vehicle with sophisticated measuring equipment and other devices which promote administrative control.

Another major factor in the growth of bulk transport is the political stability of advanced nations compared with developing nations. In earlier times industrial complexes were built close to the sources of raw materials, and only the finished manufactured products were actually moved. This was clearly more economic than moving the crude material including all the impurities. This was certainly the case with the early iron industry. However, where political instability means that plants or oil refineries are likely to be expropriated – as in Iran and Indonesia in the years following the Second World War – it becomes more economic to move the raw material, however crude, and refine it in the advanced country. It is also true to say that the more intensive industrial exploitation of the crude reduces the waste to a very small proportion of the total crude.

Where ores are concerned, sometimes partial refining takes place to produce pellets of concentrate, which makes more economic use of the bulk carrier. Thus bulk carriage by sea tends to be of unrefined, untreated products, while bulk carriage on land by road or rail tends to consist of internal movements within a country of refined and processed products or semi-manufactured products on their way to factories where manufacture will be completed. Hard-and-fast lines cannot be drawn, however, and within a group of nations of similar development many bulk movements will occur as if only a single politically stable unit existed. Only the severest political stress is likely to interrupt such movements.

13.3 Bulk transport by sea

Bulk transport by sea has been the major development in maritime transport in recent years. In a single day Port Hedland, a previously little-known Australian port serving the grazing industry, loaded four bulk ore carriers with 417,213 tonnes of iron ore and pellets. The port had been developed during the 1960s to take ships up to 160,000 tonnes, at a cost of $A75 million. The ore carriers using the port are fed by ore trains from Mount Newman and Goldsworthy Mining. These ore trains are themselves one of the most spectacular examples of bulk rail haulage in the world.

Bulk carriers by sea tend to be specialised ships, owned by particular international companies or chartered to them for long periods. The chief types are VLCC vessels (very large crude carriers), ULCCs, OBO (ore–bulk–oil) vessels, grain carriers, methane carriers and specialised carriers for such cargoes as caustic soda and bananas. The container ship is considered separately elsewhere in this book.

All these ships incorporate special design features to suit their purposes. Oil tankers have extensive bulkheads to divide the ship into separate compartments which prevent surging of the liquid cargo as the ship rolls and pitches. Engines are at the rear of the vessel so that the propeller shaft is short and need not pass below the cargo as it would do with engines in the amidships position. Tankers suffer from the great disadvantage that crude oil is essentially a one-way traffic, and the tanker must spend much of its time in ballast. It is also specific to one product. The ore–bulk–oil ship is more versatile, though slightly more expensive to build. It has alternative uses so that it is more likely to be chartered at times when there is surplus tanker capacity available. On the other hand, most other bulk products tend to move from primary producing countries to advanced secondary producing countries so that the problem of the return load has not been entirely eliminated.

Bulk carriers now include a very wide range of ships that are not necessarily of enormous size. While the ULCC ranges up to 500,000 tonnes, many products benefit from shipping in rather smaller ships. Thus bulk carriage of refined petroleum products is very economical in 20,000 tonne ships, and products such as solvents, agricultural products, fishmeal, caustic soda, etc., are often carried in mini-bulk carriers ranging from 2,000 to 26,000 dwt. Specialist Belships, or heavy-lift ships, are in use today for carrying indivisible heavy loads, both on deck and below deck.

13.4 Bulk haulage by rail

Railways are particularly effective for bulk haulage. A fully loaded bulk haulage train manned by a crew of three is a very economic form of transport. We therefore find trainloads of tank wagons leaving oil refineries at regular intervals with motor spirit, and bulk ore trains delivering ore to ports for shipment. A thousand tonnes is easily moved in this way, compared with a maximum 44 tonnes by road haulage. Safety is much greater, speeds are higher, regularity of service to industrial customers is excellent and the cost is low per tonne of product carried. The usual criticism of railways, that there are delays in terminals, does not affect bulk movements which go from door to door in their service to major industrial customers.

The types of wagon available in a modern railway system are numerous, and designs are available for all sorts of traffic. Often these are built by the railway company to customers' specifications so that they are specific to the product concerned. Such tailor-made wagons can be purchased outright, leased over long periods or hired as and when required. The 'angle of repose' of the bulk commodity is vital if it is to be unloaded easily, and steep valley sides within the vehicle prevent materials sticking. Linings are designed to suit the product – for example, where corrosion is a possibility stainless steel, or coated steel, or aluminium may be used. Internal fittings can be supplied to prevent packages shifting, overall dimensions adjusted to suit palletised cargo exactly, heat shields can be provided for refrigerated cargo and fibreglass coatings reduce heat losses to protect low-temperature cargoes. The list below gives some idea of the versatility of the transport engineers in designing specialised units of carriage. These include:

1. Tank wagons for petroleum products, petrochemicals, carbon dioxide, ammonia, china clay slurry, cement powder, acids, alkalis, molasses, etc.
2. Tipping ore wagons for iron ore, coke, coal, limestone, clay, aggregate, etc. (see Fig. 13.1 (b)).
3. Side-discharge vehicles for aggregates, wheat, fishmeal pellets, etc., with gravity loading and discharge.
4. Side-loading vans for bagged and other products, such as fertiliser, cement, zinc blocks, palletised cargo, etc.
5. Hopper wagons for salt, lime, wheat, aggregates, etc.
6. Insulated and refrigerated vehicles for meat, frozen foods, ice-cream, etc.
7. Car-carrying wagons fitted to receive and restrain motor vehicles (see Fig. 13.1 (a)).

Typical capacities of these units of carriage would be 25–100 tonnes. Filling can be by gravity, pressure or forklift truck; emptying by bottom door, side door, pressure or forklift truck. Speeds of 60 mph (96 km/h) are normal and transits are usually by special train or liner train with guaranteed delivery times so that factory schedules can be met.

(a)

(b)

Fig. 13.1 (a) A 'Cartic' company train carrying cars for export. (b) Quarried stone in 37-tonne hopper wagons (courtesy of British Rail)

A rapid switch to rail freighting of bulk commodities is confidently expected with the opening of Eurotunnel in 1994. For example, aluminium ingots from British Alcan's Lynemouth smelter in Northumberland are regularly sent to Bressica in Italy by rail, and this type of transit will become much easier when Eurotunnel opens. Similarly, ore trains, coal trains, car-carrying trains, meat, bulk wine, and many other products will be able to travel in through-freight trains in both directions. A large fleet of multi-modal railfreight wagons has been built for these trains.

Total cross-Channel freight in 1992 was about 135 million tonnes, of which about 35 million tonnes is the unitised and bulk traffic so appropriate to rail movements. Of this, about 2 million tonnes only was carried by rail; about 6 per cent of the total. It is confidently expected that this will rise to about 18 per cent within a year of the tunnel opening, about 6.3 million tonnes.

13.4.1 Company trains and Railfreight Distribution (RfD) services

The wide variety of rail wagons described above has created a large 'company train' traffic, rail freighting bulk requirements on a regular daily basis (e.g. Ford Motor Co cartrains), loading and unloading at specialist terminals. The chief traffics are petroleum products, iron ore, limestone, cement, petrochemicals, chemicals and steel. The routeing of such trains has been made simpler by the completion of the rapid transit Freightliner network. Freightliner is the trade mark of Railfreight Distribution.

The Freightliner concept is the use of high-capacity containers carried on high-speed wagons run as fixed-formation trains. They give fast, reliable services at low cost over medium and long distances. A network of lines links forty-two terminals in all parts of the country, where containers are accumulated in trainloads, being transferred from road to rail or ship to rail by gantry cranes. This enables a national and international inter-modal service to be offered to customers.

Freightliners Limited is an independent subsidiary of British Rail. The company's services run 200 trains daily, over some 75 routes and handle over 600,000 containers a year.

As shown in Fig. 13.2, the network includes 42 terminals and 14 port terminals, linking every major container port in the country. Trains are of 15 wagon length, able to carry 45 containers to a maximum weight of 915 tonnes per train. It owns 5,500 containers, 450 road vehicles and 1,100 trailers – the second largest vehicle fleet in the United Kingdom. There is 'on-line' computer control linking all depots and ports.

The advantages claimed for the Freightliner system are as follows:

1. Fast transits and reliable scheduled deliveries enable stocks to be

Fig. 13.2 The Freightliner network (courtesy of Freightliner Ltd)

minimised, i.e. the amount of money tied up in distribution is minimised especially where intermediate warehousing can be reduced. This is clearly of great importance to those interested in physical distribution management.

2. Complete container trains with high payloads running to fast schedules over medium and long distances give scope for competitive trunk haul

charges to hauliers and traders and to shippers a rapid accumulation or dispersal capacity at container ports.

3. Complete door-to-door prices over medium and long distances for the transport buyer who requires an overall service.
4. Flexible charging policy based on customers' requirements, designed to encourage a regular pattern of business, making possible high utilisation of equipment.
5. The container offers a high degree of security against pilferage as well as freedom from damage associated with shunting and trans-shipping piece by piece in a depot shipping shed, or ship loading in a similar manner. Containers carry no labels and, therefore, their contents are known only by a few people.
6. Freightliner containers are designed for easy loading and the majority are to world ISO standards.
7. The system is simple, as is the documentation, which is minimal.

13.5 Bulk haulage by road

Bulk haulage by road gives some of the advantages accruing to bulk haulage generally as well as the usual road haulage advantages, i.e. personal control of the consignment and door-to-door delivery. Once again the responses of motor vehicle designers to the needs of customers and traffic have resulted in a wide variety of specialised vehicles for bulk road transport. The movement of containers is a special class of road bulk movements, dealt with elsewhere (see Chapter 10). Apart from containers the main types of vehicles used are as follows:

1. *Tankers* carrying petroleum spirit and hydrocarbon oils, latex, acids and other chemicals, beer, wine, spirits, molasses, milk and other liquid foodstuffs. Powders such as flour, sugar, fertilisers, cement, lime and sand are major cargoes, while grains and pellets such as fishmeal are increasingly important. Liquids and powders are loaded and off-loaded by a variety of methods – gravity, pumping under pressure or sucking by vacuum the chief means. They move easily under pressures of about one atmosphere.
2. *Flats* (vehicles or trailers simply providing a flat base). The commonest goods moved in this way are packaged timber, bricks, tiles and other building materials, steel rod, pipes, etc.
3. *Articulated vehicles*, tractors drawing tankers or flat trailers, are particularly useful since they combine a low centre of gravity with good manoeuvrability. To achieve the same manoeuvrability with a non-articulated vehicle the design must give as short a vehicle as possible. This tends to raise the centre of gravity of the load, with consequent instability.

Special features of bulk road vehicles include those complying with statutory requirements on safety. Since the chances of collision and vehicle failure are much greater than in rail haulage, and pollution problems (for example, liquid cargoes which escape nearly always enter water courses) are also potentially serious, special legislation has been passed to ensure the minimisation of these hazards. With inflammable cargoes fire prevention precautions include fireproof screens between the cabs and tank units, transverse exhausts on the cab side of this screen, marking of the vehicle with a 'flame' symbol and training of staff in fire prevention and control. Similarly, corrosive products are specially marked with a corrosive symbol. Some countries exclude tankers from certain roads where particular hazards to the environment exist; for example, water reservoirs nearby might lead to such a ban.

13.6 Bulk movements by pipeline

Pipeline transport has already been referred to (see Chapter 4) as a unique form of transport in which the way, the unit of carriage and the propulsion unit are combined. The result is a bulk movement of unwrapped product. The chief points about pipelines are most conveniently made in this chapter.

13.6.1 Advantages of pipeline transport

The advantages of pipeline transport are as follows:

1. Low operating cost.
2. No packaging or return of empty containers.
3. No return-journey load problems.
4. No trans-shipment problems.
5. No congestion.
6. High speed.
7. 24-hour operation.
8. Indifference to terrain.
9. Indifference to weather.
10. Submarine pipelines are widely used.

A word of explanation of some of these is necessary.

1. *Low operating cost.* Once constructed, the pipeline has low operating costs relative to other methods of transport. Many booster stations can be made fully automatic, with safety cut-out devices controlled by sensors able to detect excessive pressures in the pipelines, or abnormal temperature changes. The sequence of activities of starting up pumps, etc., can be remotely controlled, or self-monitoring and adjusting feed-back systems

can be incorporated. The cost of these systems is offset by the reduced labour cost of employing staff, whose presence at booster stations in unpleasant Arctic or desert conditions can be expensive. Apart from these costs the chief operating costs are way-leave rentals negotiated during the capital construction stage and renewable at intervals, inspection and maintenance of the pipeline and the labour and fuel charges for the pumping stations.

2. *No packaging or return of empty containers*. Clearly a product which is piped to its destination requires no packaging. Only the product itself moves, the pipeline providing the necessary protection of the product. There are no empty containers to be returned and no packing or unpacking problems at the start and finish of the journey.

3, 4 and 5. These points are self-explanatory.

6 and 7. *High speed for 24 hours per day*. Speeds of 62.5–94 mph (100–150 km/h) are quite common in pipelines. As they operate for 24 hours per day the speed is quite extraordinary compared with other forms of transport. For example, in railway transits 187 miles (300 km) per day is regarded as fast transit: 1,870 miles (3,000 km) per day is quite possible by pipeline.

8. *Indifference to terrain*. Overland transport is usually bedevilled by terrain. Railways face particular problems in mountainous territory; road vehicles suffer abnormal wear and tear in hilly country and ever-present possibilities of accidents. Pipeline engineers of course face problems in constructing pipelines in difficult country, but once these constructional problems have been overcome and the pumping stations have been designed to deal adequately with the volumes to be transported the actual transport of products is relatively free from difficulties. This is a great advantage over the life of any particular pipeline.

9. *Indifference to weather*. Weather presents few problems to products moving through pipelines. In desert conditions contraction and expansion of pipelines in the night-time and day-time cycle are accommodated by loops in the pipeline at intervals, while the friction of oil passing through Arctic pipelines is sufficient to raise the temperature and prevent freezing.

10. *Submarine pipelines*. Offshore drilling fields are served by submarine pipelines to carry away gas and oil, and they also serve to link SBMs (single buoy moorings for ULCC tankers) to the shore. There are few problems, but vulnerability to enemy action in war-time, or to terrorist action, is a security aspect.

13.6.2 The uses of pipelines

Pipelines are only suitable for the delivery of particular materials from one point to another on a long-term basis. The demand for the good must be steady and enduring if pipelines are to be economic. They have long been used for water supply, town gas supply and sewage disposal. In recent years the chief use of pipelines has been for supplying crude oil and natural gas, and 2,000,000 km of pipeline are already in use for these purposes. Some notable developments have taken place since the early 1980s. A major Siberian gas pipeline has been completed to supply gas to Eastern Europe, and a second pipeline is being planned. A natural gas pipeline from the Norwegian Troll gasfield started to deliver gas on 1 October 1993 to Zeebrugge in Belgium. This pipeline is at present the longest undersea pipeline in the world. Some idea of the complex network of pipelines on the Norwegian side of the North Sea can be gathered from Fig. 13.3.

The following account of the Middle East pipelines is interesting because it also shows how the enormous capital costs involved can be frustrated by military actions or political unrest. More cheerfully, it also shows how pumping can be resumed once peaceful conditions return.

There are seven major pipelines for crude exports from the Arabian Gulf countries. These are:

1. *Trans-Arabian Pipeline (Tapline)*, which runs from Saudi Arabia's Ghawar oilfield to the Mediterranean, originally to Haifa and later re-routed to Sidon. It was completed in September 1950 but has been shut down since 1975. It had a capacity of 500,000 Bbls/day, is still largely intact and could be recommissioned in the light of the Israeli–Palestinian *rapprochement* of 1993.
2. *Petroline* runs across Saudi Arabia, carrying crude from the Abqaiq and Ghawar fields to Yanbu on the Red Sea. Originally built with a capacity of 1.85 million Bbls/day (MMBPD), it has since been expanded to 3.2 MMBPD in 1987 and to 5.0 MMBPD in 1993.
3. *Sumed* runs from Ain Sukna on the Gulf of Suez to Sidi Kerir, just west of Alexandria, on the Mediterranean. The pipeline was established in 1976 as a joint venture between Egypt (50 per cent), Saudi Arabia, Kuwait and the United Arab Emirates (each 15 per cent) and Qatar (5 per cent). The capacity of the line is being increased from 1.6 MMBPD to 2.4 MMBPD by early 1994. The pipeline enables crude from the Arabian Gulf and the Red Sea to be delivered in up to 500,000 dwt tankers at Sidi Kerir, to be picked up 4–5 days later in up to 350,000 dwt tankers in the Mediterranean. This results in considerable savings as against voyages around the Cape of Good Hope or via the Suez Canal, which is limited to 150,000 dwt tankers (180,000 dwt by end of 1993).
4. A rival to Sumed is the Israeli *Tipline*, which runs from Eilat on the Gulf of Aqaba to Ashkelon on the Mediterranean. Built 35 years ago with 50:50 Israeli–Iranian ownership, the pipeline was shut down for most of the 1980s, but is now in active use, shipping mainly Iranian and

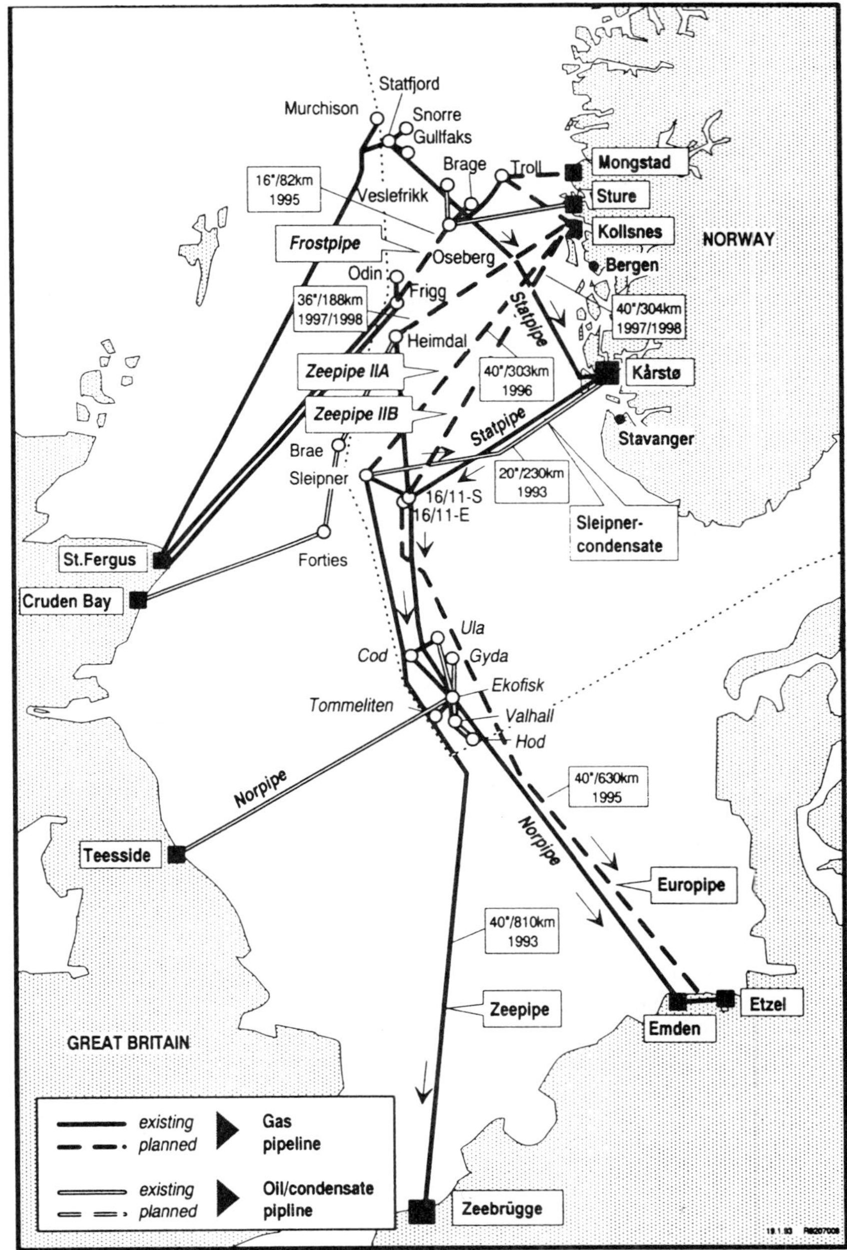

Fig. 13.3 Transportation systems on the Norwegian side of the North Sea (courtesy of the Norwegian Petroleum Directorate)

Egyptian crudes. Plans are under way to increase capacity from 900,000 BPD to 1.2 MMBPD.

5. Iraq has three major crude export pipelines, all of which are, of course, currently (1993) shut down. The oldest is the 1.4 MMBPD *Banias* line which runs from the Kirkuk field in northern Iraq to the Mediterranean ports of Banias and Tartus in Syria and Tripoli in Lebanon. This has not been used for a number of years owing to the political differences between Iraq and Syria. The other two major export pipelines, shut down as a consequence of the Gulf War, are the 1.5 MMBPD *Dortyol* line, carrying Kirkuk crude to the Turkish port of Dortyol on the Mediterranean, and the 1.7 MMBPD pipeline from the southern Rumaila oilfield. This line runs south and west across Saudi Arabia to Yanbu on the Red Sea.

Further developments are under active consideration. For example, the major crude line under discussion is designed to bring oil from around the land-locked Caspian Sea to world markets. One possibility being promoted by a group consisting of the Oman government and the republics of Kazakhstan, Azerbaijan and Russia would run from the Russian city of Grozny to Novorossiysk on the Black Sea. This would be fed by existing pipelines to Grozny from Tengiz in Kazakhstan and Baku in Azerbaijan. The initial capacity of the system would be 300,000 BPD, with an ultimate capacity of 1.5 MMBPD.

An alternative proposal, backed by Chevron, would route crude from the giant Tengiz oilfield to a Black Sea export terminal in Turkey. The Tengiz crude would flow via the existing pipeline to Azerbaijan and then be pumped with Azerbaijan crude through a new pipeline to Turkey via either Armenia (stalled by the Azerbaijan–Armenia conflict) or Iran (opposed by the US government).

Similar proposals for gas pipelines are under discussion including one long-distance under-sea pipeline from the Gulf states to supply India.

Other major pipelines are the dense networks of gas and oil pipelines in the United States and Canada; the Russian pipelines from the Urals to the East European countries, the Trans-Siberian pipeline and the south European pipelines taking Mediterranean oil via France and Italy to refineries in eastern France, Switzerland, south Germany and western Austria.

Besides crude oil and natural gas, pipelines are used extensively, particularly in the United States and Canada, to distribute processed products to major centres. Refined motor spirit, aviation spirit, liquefied petroleum gases (propane and butane), paraffin, diesel oil and other products are sent to depots in major centres by multi-user pipelines. The products are separated by one or two ‘pigs’ – piston-like objects of steel with rubber plunger ends – which are inserted into the pipeline at the point where products change. A special device removes the 'pig' when it comes to a pumping station and short-circuits it round the pump, reinserting it at the same point in the supply after the pump has been passed.

Solids are being moved increasingly by pipeline, usually in the form of a slurry with 40 per cent liquid to 60 per cent solid. Coal is moved in this way in America over distances of 100 miles (160 km) or more. It is particularly useful where the liquid used is water (because water is cheap) and where this water does not interfere with the subsequent processing of the product. For example, cement is manufactured in kilns from a slurry of limestone and clay. Huge tanks are used for mixing the slurry at the clay, limestone or chalk sites. It is then pumped to the kilns in slurry form. While this type of pipeline is for the sole use of a particular owner, and highly specific, it will be very economic as cement works themselves have a long life and the demand is continuing. Also, the solid products, clay and chalk or limestone, are difficult to scrape out of road vehicles or rail trucks, and travel much more readily in slurry form.

Pipelines are extensively used for transporting hot, molten products over short distances, and special problems have to be faced. One of the main ones is the 'freezing' of the product in the pipe due to heat losses. This is even a problem in ordinary pipelines in winter-time with some products like diesel fuel, and pipelines are often provided with electrical heating, which can be switched on in cold weather.

13.7 Summary

1. Bulk transport achieves the economies of scale; in other words, the economies of large size. There are operating economies, such as crewing costs, maintenance costs and servicing costs, and administrative economies in safety, training, documentation, etc. when large units of transport replace several small units.
2. The move to super-tankers began when the political instability of many Third World oil-producing states made it desirable to build refineries in the home state (such as the United Kingdom) and ship crude oil to the refinery, rather than refining it at the well-head.
3. Sea transport is particularly appropriate for bulk movements, as the floating vessel is weightless. The ships are usually designed for specific cargoes, and incorporate design features which are appropriate to the product. This does rob the ship of versatility – for example, oil cargoes tend to be mainly one-way, and the return journey has to be made in ballast.
4. Rail haulage is particularly appropriate for company trains – such as petroleum products moving from oil refineries to major tank installations – ore trains and containerised cargoes. The opening of

Eurotunnel should see a big shift from road haulage to rail, especially by this class of unitised goods. Special wagons have been designed for this traffic, including car carriers, tank wagons, side-loading wagons, hopper wagons and insulated and refrigerated vehicles.

5. The road haulage industry has catered for the bulk haulage of many products by developing specialised vehicles. Such vehicles include tankers for petroleum products, bulk wines, spirits, milk, molasses, flour, sugar and cement. Other bulk movements are on 'flats', such as packaged timber, containerised cargo and palletised cargo such as bricks. Chilled foods in insulated vehicles and refrigerated cargoes in reefer containers are also important loads.
6. The bulk movement of products through pipelines is very economic for those products which are suitable, giving high speeds of transit, low operating costs, no packaging or return of empty containers and complete indifference to terrain and climate.

13.8 Questions

1. What are economies of scale? Explain the economies that are achieved when two tankers of 450,000 tonnes replace a fleet of tankers holding 16,500 tonnes each.
2. Write short notes about *four* of the following:
   (a) methane carriers
   (b) powders (such as flour)
   (c) zinc pellets
   (d) ULCCs
   (e) OBO ships
   (f) clean product bulk carriers
3. Why is carriage by sea most appropriate to bulk movements of raw materials? What major cargoes move in this way?
4. What are the advantages of rail haulage over road haulage? In that case why has the growth in road haulage in the United Kingdom been so great, while rail haulage has declined? What is the likely impact of Eurotunnel on this situation?
5. The ingenuity of the road haulage industry's designers has been demonstrated again and again as they have catered for different types of traffic. Write an account of some of the vehicles which have demonstrated this ingenuity.
6. For what types of cargo are pipelines an appropriate means of transport? List the advantages of pipeline transport and show how the cargoes you have mentioned benefit from the advantages you have listed.

14 Third party logistics firms and the distribution industry

14.1 Economies of large scale in the distribution industry

Economists have always believed that there are economies to be achieved by operating on a large scale, and for a couple of centuries after the industrial revolution began in about 1760 they sought these economies of large scale in the production field. They were eventually found to be achieved best by a switch to mass production, through simplification, standardisation and specialisation. Popularly known as the three S's, they sought economies in production by the design of products, and partial products like components, in as simple a manner as possible, each part being designed to do its job as economically as possible. Asked whether he was worried just before blast-off, one US astronaut replied: 'If you were lying on your back on top of a piece of machinery with ten million parts the contract for each of which had been given to the cheapest tenderer, wouldn't you be worried?' Not only was each product as simple as possible, it was designed to be a standard part, which would be used in many different products (for example, the same carburettor in many different motor cars). This meant long production-runs of each unit, and the consequent reduction in costs per unit as the design and development costs could be spread over enormous numbers of units. Finally, this endless repetition of tried-and-tested products meant specialisation could play its full part. Automation, and eventually computerisation, turned out a flood of perfect units and made us into a throw-away society, where it was cheaper to throw away an item needing repair, and buy a new one. In the end, manufacturing reached such a peak of efficiency that there were no new economies to be achieved in it, and we had to look elsewhere. The next place to look was the distribution field.

The distribution industry had up to that time – say, the 1950s – been the handmaiden of production – it was production-driven. The task of the distribution industry was to clear the production-lines so that the endless flood of products coming off the lines would not be obstructed. Goods were cleared into warehouses and similar stockpiles, where they could be held pending demand from the wholesalers and retailers who would actually make them available to consumers. Production was king, because it aimed at the optimum production level, the best level to achieve the economies of large scale. Distribution was a safety-valve. Like a flood relief scheme, it absorbed excessive supplies coming off the production-line and funnelled them into a safe area where they could wait until demand from the public caught up with supply.

Unfortunately, distribution and storage were not cost-free. There were all sorts of problems associated with them – merchandising problems, which were different for each product. Storekeepers had to know their merchandise and its particular flaws. Food rots, iron rusts, clothes become unfashionable, furniture loses its polish – and everything, absolutely everything, is attractive to criminals and presents a security problem.

The search for economies in distribution began with the detailed examination of what was actually done in the distribution and storage industries, and the search for greater efficiency in store labour and inventory management (SLIM). It so happens that this search for better systems of operation in the distribution field began at the same time as the computer was beginning to make its impact on business systems of every sort. The new technology was ideally suited to examining the workings of supply-chains, and developed into a series of powerful tools to investigate various aspects of marketing activities. The emphasis on the marketing side of supply-chains was to lead eventually to a widespread system of information technology which was to change the emphasis from a production-oriented system to one that was increasingly market-oriented. The new situation was one where the large-scale retailer, seeking ever lower operating costs and ever higher efficiency, would bring the products of the world to market, so long as they represented a response to market demand, rather than production's idea of what people should be provided with.

14.2 Information technology – the computer as a network

The computer has much to recommend it as a stand-alone facility for business users to perform such activities as accounting, payroll, inventory control and countless other specialist activities. Its use in the logistics industry is at a higher level altogether. Here it acts as an intelligence-gathering network, and its responses to the intelligence gathered stimulate the distribution activities. Fig. 14.1 gives some idea of what we mean by a computer network. The network, and the way it works, are described in the notes that accompany Fig. 14.1. Before studying the figure the following introductory points may help.

14.2.1 Mainframes, mini- and microcomputers

To run such a system we need a fairly powerful computer. Originally, this meant a mainframe computer, a powerful machine with a very large capacity of memory and backing store. However, in recent years the miniaturisation of computers has meant that smaller machines, the so-called minicomputers, which cost around £50,000 could do all that the mainframe computer could do. Later still, the microcomputer, also known as the PC (personal computer), could do almost as much as the mini-computer, and certainly was entirely adequate for the small, stand-alone jobs that the small business required, such as accounts, payroll, etc.

To operate a computer network we need a host computer; that is, a computer at the centre of affairs able to accept data from numerous points. It may be a mainframe, it may be a mini-computer, or it may be a microcomputer, or a series of microcomputers.

14.2.2 Inputs

In order to receive data a computer must be able to understand the data, in other words the data must be in machine-readable form. To keep a network up to date (and we are really talking about split seconds of time) it must be possible for anyone who has information to input it into the computer from some sort of terminal. A terminal is usually a keyboard, but access could be provided to other devices, such as bar code readers, or cheque readers, which read MICR (magnetic ink character recognition) lines off the bottom of cheques. The details of the cheque are encoded in magnetic ink along the bottom of the cheque, showing the cheque number, the branch number, the account number and the amount of the cheque. The cheque reader can read cheques at the rate of 3,000 per minute. Other devices are punched tag readers, which read tags off garments sold in the clothing industry, and OMR and OCR readers (OMR means optical mark recognition; and OCR means optical character recognition). These machines read such things as census forms, examination papers, etc.

14.2.3 On-line inputs

To input this sort of data the terminal must be on-line to the computer and be able to access it at any moment. Suppose there are just two seats left on a plane to New York and a booking clerk accesses the computer to book them. The computer confirms there are just two seats left and the clerk's agreement to take them closes off the aircraft for any further bookings on that flight. One second later another booking clerk asks about seats on the flight, but the computer now shows the flight as fully booked. Without a network there would be a grave chance of double-booking and much distress and aggravation on the day of the flight.

An on-line computer is always available for inputs of new information. Equally it is always available to put out whatever information is required.

14.2.4 Outputs

The logistics industry's networks are some of the most fabulous from the point of view of the outputs they provide to the various parties interested in information. For example, think of the split second it takes in a supermarket for a bar code reader to read the code for the item we are purchasing, relay it to the host computer, instruct it to search its memory for the item, deduct one item from the stock records because it has been sold and relay back an instruction to the point of sale terminal to print the item and its price on the sale voucher, while at the same time displaying it for the customer to see on the cash register's display panel. Yet this, to us, almost instantaneous response is not the only thing that the computer has done. It may have discovered that the sale of that item reduces the stock level to the minimum order point, below which an order to replenish stock must be made. It will therefore trigger an order-placing activity, which will call for the generation of an order to that particular supplier for a fresh supply, which means finding the full details, name and address of the supplier, code and exact name of the product, the agreed supply price, the economic order quantity, and so on. In a busy supermarket with twenty check-outs the computer is dealing with all twenty simultaneously without getting them muddled.

The really significant thing with large-scale retailers today is that their on-line networks mean that ordering is store-based, the result of bar code readings of sales made, and replenishment of stocks is achieved by daily, multiple-deliveries from composite warehouses strategically placed to serve a large group of retail outlets. This end of the supply-chain is called the 'front-end', from the regional distribution centre to the supermarket shelf. The computerisation of the rest of the distribution chain is less well developed. Before considering this the reader is advised to study Fig. 14.1 and the accompanying notes.

14.3 Third party logistical contractors

A third party contractor is a firm or company that offers to take over a particular role within a major organisation and assume entire responsibility

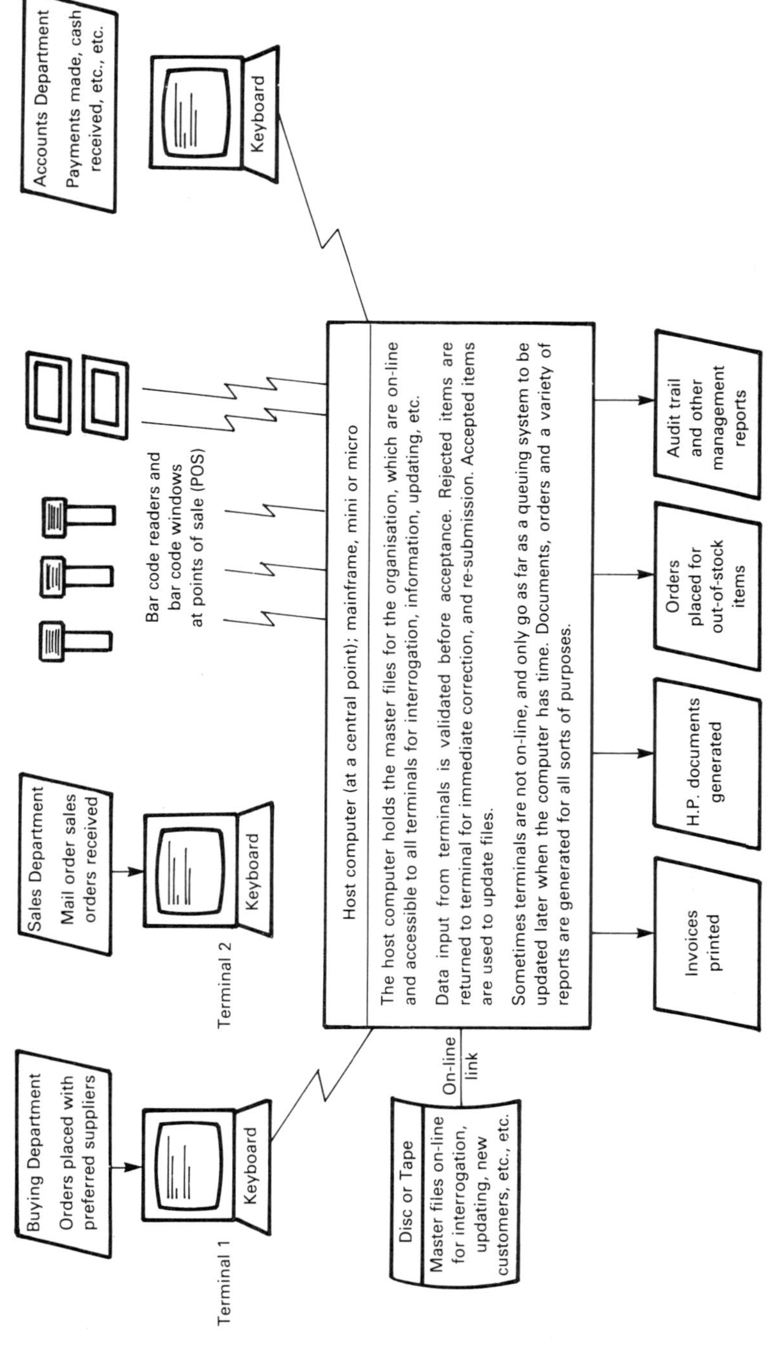

Fig. 14.1 A network of terminals around a host computer

for it. The commonest form of this arrangement is the logistical side of the organisation's activities. It is therefore commonly a service provided by a transport company which already has wide expertise not only in the sort of physical distribution management referred to in the previous chapters but also in the information technology field. This information technology will not only take care of the front-end services – bringing daily supplies into the retail outlets from a regional distribution centre – but it will also devise tailor-made systems for the entire distribution network – that is, the movements of goods from suppliers to the regional distribution centres. It is not just a question of putting another item on the shelf to replace the one sold yesterday. It is also a question of anticipating the demand. Thus changes of taste and fashion, cold snaps and warm spells, new regulations and financial concerns may mean changes in demand and supply. For example, the decision to impose VAT on gas and electricity in the United Kingdom in 1993 caused a huge surge in the sale of insulation materials, double glazing and even central heating systems, as householders sought economies to offset the increased costs.

The logistical company is in an ideal position to develop tailor-made software to deal with the needs of its client companies, because it is in the middle between suppliers and the regional distribution centre, and again between the regional distribution centre and the retail outlet. Close co-operation between these parties can reduce stockholdings, lower distribution costs, improve quality and reinforce control over all sections of the retailer's activities. Electronic data interchange, electronic mail, sophisticated import activities and JIT stock replenishment make the third party's role an indispensable one.

14.4 Electronic data interchange

Electronic data interchange (EDI) is the interchange of information in electronic form over ordinary telephone lines, or better still, over glass-fibre cables. Eventually (but it may be years away), the world's entire telephone networks will be glassfibre cables which can move information at the speed of light and handle an incredible capacity in the process. One of the earliest uses of EDI is in the export field, because it enables the documentation that is required for export transactions to be sent round the world in seconds. This ends the problems arising from documents which have not arrived, so that ship's masters will not release cargoes which have reached their destinations, because the documents which prove who is entitled to receive the goods have not arrived. This is explained more fully in Chapter 17, on the documentation of logistics.

Here we are concerned with third party firms and the services they can give to all parts of the supply-chains. EDI is a system where the computerised records of parties who are interested in a particular activity are available to all. Anyone who is entitled to know about a particular consignment can access the information, wherever it is, and see the present status of the transaction. He can add to it, update it, leave messages about it, give instructions, notify problems, enter it at Customs, or do whatever has to be done to record his view of the matter. Electronic mail (e-mail) is person-to-person communication fed over the same lines to give instantaneous information and seek an equally rapid response.

It follows that a company that can offer this kind of facility to other parties in the supply-chain can offer them an operation which will integrate all their logistical activities. It can monitor trends to alert retailers to changes of taste, fashion, business climate, etc. For example, if all these movements are taking place with less and less stock in the system (no margin of stock to allow for the unexpected), then many suppliers will be receiving orders which do not represent a viable load. In that case the distributor has to consolidate supplies from several suppliers to make a viable load. There is already a sense in the industry that dedicated warehouses are at a disadvantage because they cannot easily consolidate small loads with goods from other suppliers. Shared facilities would be better, because each warehouse user could help the others.

14.5 The advantages of contracting out logistics to third parties

The advantages of contracting out logistics operations to a so-called third party are as follows:

1. A company which does so can concentrate on its own core business but knows that it is not falling down on the transport and distribution of its products.
2. On the contrary, its customers will be getting improved levels of service because they are in the hands of an expert who has vast experience in the logistics field.
3. Contracting out is nearly always cheaper than going it alone, because the do-it-yourself firm inevitably makes costly mistakes, which the third party would have avoided.
4. Going it alone requires capital, and may require a firm to get into debt or set aside funds which would mean reductions in the core activity.
5. The third party can provide specialised management expertise which would be difficult to build up in house and might easily be attracted elsewhere – there is a shortage of skilled logisticians.
6. The third party can almost always supply added-value services which make extra profits for any management which has contracted to use their services.

14.6 Logistical services

The essential thing about appointing a third party firm to handle the logistics for your company is to avoid making a firm commitment until the package of services to be offered is clear in the minds of both parties. If disputes arise later and we become embroiled in a series of legal actions, we are in a worse position than when we started. It follows that the company with whom we are negotiating must be fairly large, because even preliminary negotiations take time and cost money and we have to choose one that has enough resources to go into our requirements in detail, make detailed plans and provide the resources we require from the start of the contract. There are, of course, a number of leading companies in this field, and some of them have been featured elsewhere in this book. At this point we have decided to feature Christian Salvesen Distribution, who list the services they can offer as shown below. Their UK address is Salvesen House, Townsend Drive, Nuneaton, Warwickshire, CV11 6TW (Tel: 0203 350707; Fax: 0203 350935). They particularly feature the concept of 'added value to logistics', a term which is explained below.

Christian Salvesen Distribution has a long-established reputation in the field of temperature-controlled supply-chain management, bringing deep-frozen, chilled and ambient products to major retailers in the United Kingdom, Europe and the United States. Ambient products are products which do not need temperature control but are best kept at the ordinary temperatures which surround them. From this base Christian Salvesen have moved into providing cost-effective logistical solutions for other sectors of industry, notably the garment industry, hi-tech industries and general distribution.

Their logistical packages, tailor-made to the requirements of individual customers, may include any of the following:

1. Temperature-controlled supply-chains (e.g. facilities for most high street retailers).
2. Time-critical supply-chains (e.g. JIT supply-chains to manufacturing industries).
3. Quality control systems in complex industries, such as the food trades, the garment trades and the computer industry.
4. Tailor-made handling, packaging and processing, including pre-retailing. These services are essentially added-value services, in that they reduce bulk supplies (for example, whole cheeses) into retail packs to suit different classes of customers, with weight, price per kg and value indicated clearly. Properly designed facilities for such activities ensure product quality, conformity with regulations, minimum waste, etc.
5. Contract vehicles and support services (a complete package based on Christian Salvesen's own distribution network, including, if necessary,

the design of special vehicles). For example, the company designed in co-operation with Haagen-Dazs, the ice-cream manufacturers, a fleet of special vehicles capable of operating at temperatures down to −40°C.

6. Warehouse and distribution facilities in dedicated composite warehouses for the majority of high street retailers.
7. Research and project consultancy (reviewing the operations of customers in view of changing circumstances).
8. Waste management and recycling, including resource recovery, environmental controls and compliance with regulations.
9. Hi-tech distribution (e.g. office equipment removal, storage, transport and installation).
10. Bespoke information systems, designed to control logistics operations, warehouse management, vehicle routeing and inventory control.

The concept of added-value holds that anything that is done to a product to put it into a form which makes it readily acceptable to customers, and makes them willing to pay more for the product, means increased profit for the retailer. Thus the pre-retailing activities of breaking bulk, slicing meats, slicing cheeses, bagging up potatoes and countless other activities are adding value to the product. Even such things as weighing, pricing, labelling and packaging products are part of adding value. If these services are to be carried out somewhere along the logistical chain, we might as well let the third party handle them in large-scale, dedicated, properly equipped premises, because the total charge will be less than we would have incurred doing it ourselves in a less well-organised, smaller-scale way, seeking to comply with regulations with which we are not familiar, etc.

Finally, the point is that both the third party and the manufacturer or retailer with whom the third party contracts are seeking a long-term working partnership, which is mutually beneficial, and quality-driven.

14.7 Summary

1. A third party logistics company is a company which is not a party to the actual contractual arrangements made between suppliers and wholesalers or retailers, but is engaged to manage the logistical side of their arrangements, including warehousing, transport, consolidation of loads and added-value activities where these are deemed desirable.
2. Almost invariably such logistics companies are large-scale organisations with expertise in transport and distribution, but also with a highly developed system of information technology.
3. One of the chief preoccupations of such a partnership between suppliers, logisticians and retailers is increased efficiency in all work areas, and the elimination of inventory within the system. The chief way of

Fig. 14.2 Loading vehicles for High Street deliveries by a third party contractor (courtesy of Christian Salvesen)

eliminating inventory is to develop a market-driven system which calls stock up to the supermarket shelf as required rather than taking what the manufacturer hopes to supply.

4. An information technology system is one where a central host computer which knows all there is to know about products, prices, suppliers, customers, etc. is accessible by all grades of staff for interrogation, updating, credit approval, etc. Access is provided via a large number of terminals, and point-of-sale equipment.
5. The advantages of appointing third party logistical contractors is that the business has the help and support of a large-scale operator in the logistics field, who knows the problems, has the equipment and vehicles to manage all aspects of the movements required, has the storage facilities available and can deliver a tailor-made system at an economical price.
6. Added-value activities are activities which make products more readily acceptable to customers. They include all sorts of pre-retailing activities, and such matters as weighing, pricing, packaging and wrapping goods. Because of these services customers are prepared to pay a higher price, and the retailer's margins are greater even after paying the logistics firm for its work.
7. The essential point is that customer satisfaction, profits and market share can all be raised even though the logistical firm has to be rewarded; a mutually beneficial, long-term working partnership can be developed.
8. From the IT point of view a new Croner Handbook, 'Croner's Guide to IT', is a valuable reference work (Tel: 081-547-3333).

14.8 Questions

1. What is information technology? How does it help in logistics?
2. What economies can be achieved in the logistics field?
3. What are the advantages to a retailer of making arrangements with a third party to run the logistics side of his retailing activity?
4. Explain the use of bar codes in supermarkets. What part does a host computer play in the use of bar codes?
5. What is added value? How can a logistical firm add value to its customer's product? How does added value benefit the retailer and the logistical organisation?
6. What is a tailor-made package in IT? How would a trader unfamiliar with IT arrange for such a package to be drawn up?

15 Transport aspects of logistics

15.1 Introduction – the choice of transport

An important part of the transport manager's or transport and distribution manager's job is to decide which mode (or modes) of transport is best suited for moving the company's traffic. He or she will be guided by a knowledge of the advantages and disadvantages of the various modes. At times this choice will need to be altered to take into account changes in circumstances, e.g. larger or smaller quantities to be transported, and the degree of urgency of a particular transit. The following are some of the characteristics the transport manager will need to bear in mind in inland and international transport. We have thought it best to include an account of the advantages and disadvantages of each mode of transport, since the choice available is very wide, but no account can be complete because of the improvements being implemented month by month in this dynamic and restless field.

15.2 Inland transport

15.2.1 Road transport

Advantages

(a) Ubiquity. Collection and delivery can be arranged without transshipment wherever a motor vehicle can travel. It is this characteristic more than any other that accounts for the pre-eminence of road transport over all other forms of inland transport: for example, in the United Kingdom there are 226,000 miles (362,000 km) of roads compared with only 12,000 miles (19,000 km) of railway, giving direct delivery advantage over rail in the vast majority of cases.

(b) Flexibility. Although the occasional hold-up does occur, the ability of vehicles to drive round an obstruction and the ability to divert traffic by using the complex network of roads available does make the road system a flexible way, not only in emergencies but at all times when loads become available at short notice, and drivers can be diverted to collect them.

(c) Promptness and controlled delivery. Fairly precise times for collection and delivery can be arranged. This is important for JIT deliveries, and where labour must be arranged for loading and unloading and where the arrival of goods must be arranged to suit the needs of manufacturers, construction work and consumers. Delivery can be specified for a particular time of day or at a specified rate, e.g. tonnes per day.

(d) Packaging. Frequently, less packing (or even no packing at all) is required, as compared with other forms of transport. For example, garments can be delivered hung on rails covered by a light, polythene sheet.

(e) Loads. There has been a steady increase in the size of vehicles, which in the United Kingdom has reached 38 tonnes for articulated vehicles with five axles and 44 tonnes for vehicles being driven to a railhead. Higher limits are proposed, and in many European states the limit exceeds 40 tonnes. The number of HGVs over 38 tonnes rose eight times in the period 1981–91.

Disadvantages

(a) Prompt discharge essential. Vehicles must be discharged promptly. Unexpected arrivals of vehicles may mean that labour for loading or unloading must be diverted from other work, or alternatively the vehicle and driver must stand idle until labour is available. This may be avoided with containerised cargo by off-loading the container, permitting the vehicle to move. However, demurrage may be payable if the container is retained unreasonably.

(b) Expenses. For less than full loads a minimum charge related to vehicle capacity will usually have to be paid, irrespective of the weight or quality of goods carried.

(c) Misdeliveries. Where a number of part-loads are sent by the same vehicle, crossed deliveries may occur unless careful attention is paid to labelling, etc.

(d) Pilfering and theft. Road vehicles are liable to pilfering and hijacking if they are left unattended.

(e) Low capacity. Compared with rail or waterborne transport capacity is low. This may render it uncompetitive in situations where there are good rail or canal connections.

(f) Traffic density. Traffic is growing all the time. It is predicted that cars will increase from 24 million in 1993 to 51 million by the year 2025. Traffic congestion is already a problem, especially during bad weather and at peak periods.

15.2.2 The merits of a self-owned fleet compared with alternative methods

Because of its inherent advantages, and its role as a link with other modes of transport, all transport managers will employ road transport to a greater or lesser degree. At some time it may be necessary to decide whether or not to rely on public hauliers for all road transport needs, whether to hire on a contract basis, whether to operate a company-owned fleet or to what extent a combination of two or more alternatives is desirable. A fourth alternative (discussed in Chapter 14) is the use of a third party logistics company to take over the logistical side of a company's activities.

The lists of advantages and disadvantages that follow demonstrate that economics alone may not be the sole factor in reaching the decision.

15.2.3 Public hauliers

Advantages

(a) The lowest haulage rate. By 'shopping around' the lowest haulage rate may be secured for each delivery.

(b) A wider choice of vehicle sizes and types is available: thus the vehicle best suited for a specific delivery can be obtained.

(c) Deliveries can be arranged without reference to return loads.

(d) Avoids idle vehicles. The problems of idle vehicles during slack time and shortage of vehicles during peak periods are avoided.

Disadvantages

(a) No user loyalty. A user who is known to 'shop around' generates no loyalty from hauliers, and if his peaks coincide with those of other users in the area, he may find his transport needs unfulfilled or subject to delay.

(b) Urgent loads not catered for. For similar reasons, urgent loads may not always be easily catered for, since the haulier will satisfy the needs of his regular customers first.

(c) Lack of control. The user has little control over the driver, and should a conflict of interests arise he is likely to put his employer's interests first.

(d) No advertising value. No advertising value accrues from vehicles not in the firm's livery and diseconomies may result from shabby vehicles and uncooperative drivers.

15.2.4 Contract hire fleet

Advantages

(a) Control. Gives complete control over drivers and the operation of vehicles.

(b) Livery. Vehicles painted in the company's livery provide valuable advertising.

(c) Haulier's responsibility. No garage or maintenance facilities have to be provided by the company – these are the responsibility of the haulier.

(d) Costs are known. There are no hidden costs, as can happen with own-account operations, and except where provided for in the contract, will not be subject to fluctuation according to market demand, inflation, etc., during the term of the contract.

Disadvantages

(a) Return loads are difficult to organise: hence a high proportion of light running will occur.

(b) Length of contract. The hired fleet must be fully employed for the currency of the contract.

(c) More expensive. It is more expensive than running an 'own fleet' or using public hauliers (but remember there are no hidden costs).

15.2.5 Self-owned fleet (own-account operation)

Advantages

(a) Complete control over drivers and operations.

(b) Valuable advertising: from smartly turned-out vehicles in company's livery.

Disadvantages

(a) Return loads are difficult to organise: hence a high proportion of light running will occur.

(b) Garaging and maintenance facilities must be installed.

(c) Expense. It is expensive to provide a fleet big enough to cover peak periods and this means that hiring must be done at busy periods.

(d) False cost impression. It often happens that the full capital cost, overheads and operating costs are not debited and a false impression of transport costs results.

(e) Demands on fleet. Unless very carefully controlled by the transport department, other departments will make uneconomic demands on the fleet 'since it is there to be used'.

15.2.6 Use of a third party logistics firm

This has already been discussed in Chapter 14. While there is much to be said for such a third party arrangement, such logistics companies are usually large-scale organisations and may not be interested unless the proposed volume of work is fairly large. In the FMCG (fast moving consumer goods) field (e.g. grocery products) it is likely to be the retailer who uses a third party logistics firm.

15.2.7 Load and route planning

Another routine daily procedure, which can be greatly improved thanks to computerisation, is the load and route planning of vehicles, particularly if new customers have traditionally been fitted into existing route schedules, as best as possible.

As customers are directly affected by this activity, which might involve both delivery and collection, it is essential to determine their exact requirements, both as to their demands on our services and any time constraints they may have (e.g. no deliveries to be made during shops' rush hours or on early closing afternoons). Do they require daily, weekly or some other frequency of calling? Their co-operation should be sought to complete a questionnaire from which the computer programmer can not only quantify their needs, but also determine their exact location and their degree of flexibility as to delivery or collection.

It is also essential to get the co-operation of the haulier's staff, as staff tend to look askance at any new development, especially if it could lead to redundancies or smaller commissions for drivers. It is essential to impress on them that a more efficient system giving greater customer satisfaction can lead to increased demand and even higher commissions. Having delivered and subsequently collected the customers' completed questionnaire, the drivers' own opinions should be sought. Such matters as average turn-round times, delays resulting from queuing for their turn to deliver and ease of access to customers' premises are very important. Police restrictions on unloading and loading outside customers' premises and the co-operation or non-co-operation of customers' staffs are also factors to be taken into account.

Another important consideration is the make-up of your lorry fleet; its total capacity and the percentage utilisation of that capacity on a day-to-day basis. Is there a seasonal demand? Equally important is the mileage travelled daily by each unit and the customer sequence on each route. The permitted drivers' hours must also be considered.

Initially, a pilot programme should be put into effect and feedback from both customers and drivers used to make any amendments. Experience shows that once these critical procedures are completed and a computerised overall load/route scheduling program is instituted, considerable savings in time, mileage and consequent costs are possible. Equally important is the greater efficiency achieved and therefore the greater level of customer satisfaction.

15.2.8 Conclusions

It is most likely that no single selection will be made, but that a flexible system will be selected. Depending on circumstances, this could result, for example, in a small own-account fleet, a contract fleet and occasional hirings to meet peak demands. The contract fleet operator is likely to have vehicles other than those operating on contract, and the provision of extra vehicles is unlikely to prove difficult.

Whatever decision is finally reached, the following factors will need to have been taken into account.

1. Is there a regular flow of traffic, and does it follow a particular pattern?
2. Can return loads be arranged for many of the journeys?
3. To what extent is the advertising value of vehicles important?
4. Can garage and maintenance facilities be provided without heavy capital cost?
5. Does the company possess or can it attract administrative and operational staff of the right calibre to ensure efficient operation?

15.2.9 Rail transport

Advantages

(a) Quick delivery over long distances between important towns and cities, e.g. London and Glasgow. This characteristic, true even for conventional rail traffic, has been accentuated by the development of the Freightliner system. It is even more true of movements through Eurotunnel, where times like 'London–Milan in 33 hours' are projected. It is well known that over 200 miles (320 km), the advantage as far as speed of transit is concerned lies with the railway.

(b) Convenient: where the receiving point has a private siding; even more so where both ends have private sidings.

(c) Demurrage. Goods can be left under load for one day exclusive of the day of arrival, without payment of demurrage. This is most useful for the economic deployment of labour for discharging purposes, as unloading can be performed at slack periods for other work, or between arrivals of road vehicles.

(d) Large capacity. Rail transport is convenient for the regular receipt of large quantities because of the much greater capacity compared with road transport. Company trains, i.e. those specifically allocated to one company, have become increasingly important in recent years, and special rates and 'tailor-made' services can be negotiated with Railfreight Distribution.

(e) Nationwide. A countrywide service is available for 'smalls' traffic.

Disadvantages

(a) Slow delivery. Away from main lines, services are infrequent and traffic has to wait in sidings.

(b) Trans-shipment. Except with private sidings, the beginning and end of transit must involve road transport. This can result in increased damage due to extra handling, loss of time in the trans-shipment process and greater overall transit times, where road and rail schedules do not coincide.

(c) Pilferage. Greater susceptibility to pilferage, especially where boxes or cartons are small and portable, and sent in less than truck loads. These require multiple handling, and goods are not constantly under the control of one person as with a road transport driver.

15.2.10 Water transport – inland waterways

Advantages

(a) Convenience. Where loading and discharging points are on canal sites and wharf facilities are available.

(b) Cheapness. Large capacity makes the mode of transport particularly cheap for bulk low-value goods.

(c) Environmental. Inland waterways avoid congestion of roads and built-up areas and may be suitable for hazardous goods such as petroleum, fragile goods such as glass and pollutants as with the transport of toxic waste through urban areas. Also arrivals do not congest factory sidings or roads.

Disadvantages

(a) Slow delivery. Speeds on inland waterways must be kept low.

(b) Limited mileage of way. The inland waterway has limited application due to very small mileage of canals available (350 miles (560 km)) in the United Kingdom. BACAT vessels (Barges Aboard Catamarans) were introduced in the 1970s to use the UK canal network. They were rendered uneconomic by the actions of dockers at Hull, who did not like the barges shortcircuiting the dock facilities and sailing straight into the canal system. Now that the Dock Labour Scheme, which gave the dockers a monopoly power, has been abolished the BACAT system could be reintroduced.

(c) Specialised terminals and equipment. Cranes, etc., are necessary for loading and discharging.

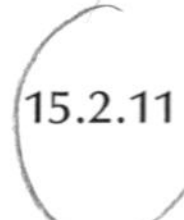

15.2.11 Estuarial transport

Advantages

(a) Uncongested transit: between points on the same estuary, but entry into, or exit from, enclosed docks may be limited by tidal conditions or priority given to ships at high water.

(b) High capacity. This means low-cost transport.

(c) Dock dues. Dock dues are not payable on overside deliveries to and from import and export vessels in enclosed docks.

(d) Demurrage. Free time is allowed before the incidence of demurrage and this permits economical use of labour.

(e) Inter-modal transits. Where estuarial transport forms part of an international transit, advantage can be taken of through systems such as Lash, Seabee, BACAT and Baco-liners. This will mainly occur where the estuary is the gateway for a large river system such as the Mississippi or the Rhine–Danube.

Disadvantages

(a) Minimum tonnage. High minimum tonnage per barge may have to be paid for, making it unsuitable for small lots. In many cases barges are carrying containers for general cargo.

(b) Specialised terminal equipment. Unless wharf facilities and equipment exist, high capital costs may preclude their provision unless regular traffic makes it worthwhile in order to take advantage of much lower transport costs.

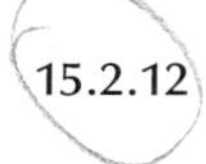

15.2.12 Coastwise transport

Advantages

(a) Low cost. The low cost of bulk transport by water makes this a cheap form of transport for lots of over 100 tonnes for journeys in excess of 150

miles (240 km), where loading and discharging points have access to or are near water.

(b) Awkward loads. For very heavy or large indivisible loads coastwise heavy-lift vessels may provide a better alternative to road or rail, provided that loading and discharging points are convenient to a port. Nowadays such loads are more likely to be moved on a roll-on roll-off-type vessel, e.g. the vessel used by the Central Electricity Generating Board for the movement of boilers for power stations.

Disadvantages

(a) Specialised terminal facilities must be available.

(b) Slow. Compared with road or rail, coastal transport is slow, except perhaps for heavy or indivisible loads.

(c) Additional transport costs. Additional costs may be incurred unless private access to a waterway is available.

(d) Weather. Coastal transits are subject to delays due to bad weather.

(e) Tides. These can also cause delay.

15.2.13 Air transport

Air transport is unlikely to be relevant except for very high priority transits, e.g. emergency drugs and plasma; vital parts during breakdowns, etc. (see International Transport below). The exception to this rule is the use of helicopters to gain access to otherwise inaccessible sites, or to off-shore rigs.

15.3 **International transport**

15.3.1 Sea transport

Because of its very high capacity relative to the motive power employed, water transport – in particular deep-sea transport, which can benefit most from economies of scale – can offer cheaper transport rates per tonne/km than any other form of transport. It will almost always, though not invariably, be cheaper than its competitor, air transport.

Advantages

(a) Low freight rates.

(b) Very high capacity.

(c) Continuous operation. On a 24-hour basis, partly offsetting the speed advantage of air transport over shorter distances.

(d) The way is free. Also vessels are not subject to political restrictions once they leave coastal waters and get outside the 12 mile limit (or other restricted zone).

(e) Turn-round time. Now that most traffic is containerised the turn-round time of a vessel is very quick, and may even be faster than the turn-around of an aircraft. This is because the ship can load and discharge simultaneously once an empty 'cell' is available, whereas an aircraft must be fully discharged before reloading begins.

Disadvantages

(a) Relatively slow speeds.

(b) Roundabout routes: compared with air transport, although this is offset by the greater capacity of the ship.

(c) Frequency. Services are less frequent today than in former times.

(d) Weather. Shipping is affected by adverse weather conditions, and this is evidenced by the load line, which takes account of adverse wind and wave conditions world-wide, on a seasonal basis. Unlike air transport, which offers a smooth passage, a ship is affected severely by rolling and pitching. Vessels in port are affected by fog, especially if they are in enclosed docks, and even at sea can only keep going thanks to radar.

15.3.2 Deep-sea transport

15.3.2.1 *Chartering a vessel*

With deep-sea transport the customer is offered a choice between the charter market and the liner trade. The charter market is essentially concerned with the carriage of relatively low-cost bulk cargoes, e.g. coal, iron ore, grain, fertilisers, etc., although nowadays there are specialist vessels for the carriage of cars and others for the carriage of livestock, particularly to the Middle East markets. Vessels are usually chartered on the Baltic Exchange in London, although due to terrorist action in 1993 the Exchange is temporarily housed in the Lloyd's building in Lime Street. The charter document is called a charter-party, and contains the terms and conditions of the contract between the shipowner and the charterer.

When chartering, the transport or distribution manager has a choice between a voyage charter, a time charter or a demise charter.

15.3.2.2 *Voyage charters*

In the case of voyage charters the shipowner undertakes to carry a specific quantity of a particular commodity between two named ports at a fixed freight per tonne or other unit. The freight rate is determined by market conditions, i.e. the availability of tonnage of the right type and size of vessel for use at the loading port. The shipowner must also consider the cost of any ballast movement to the loading port and the possible need for a ballast voyage after discharge.

He may also need to take into account any canal dues *en route*. All costs are for the shipowner's account, except possibly the stevedoring costs.

The charter-party may stipulate 'Liner Terms', in which case the loading and discharge costs are covered by the freight. Alternatively, the terms may be FIO (Free In and Out), which means that loading and discharge are for the charterer's account. This is quite often the case since in many instances the charterer owns the terminuses at each end.

In the case of a voyage charter-party it may be for a full cargo or a part-cargo. In the latter case the shipowners will have arranged for the carriage of other part-cargoes under separate charter-parties. Any shortfall in the amount of cargo delivered to the ship will result in a charge for dead freight, but this charge will possibly make some allowance as regards loading and discharge costs on the agreed rate if the charter-party was on liner terms.

Another feature peculiar to a voyage charter-party is laydays. If a vessel is chartered with laydays 2/20 August, then if it presents itself ready to load in every respect before 2 August, charterers are not obliged to start loading, and if it fails to present itself by 20 August (the cancelling date), then the charterer can cancel the charter-party. However, even if the vessel is obviously going to be later than the cancelling date, the shipowner must still present it at the port and only when he gives notice of readiness to load is the charterer obliged to cancel. If the market rates have risen in the meantime he will normally go ahead with the charter-party, but if they have declined he will cancel the original charter-party and negotiate a lower rate. Laydays are the time allowed for the ship to load and discharge.

They can be expressed in a variety of ways, some of which favour the shipowner while others favour the charterer. For example running days (sometimes called consecutive days) of 24 hours, midnight to midnight, including Sundays and holidays favour the shipowner, while others, e.g. Weather working days, SHEX (Sundays and holidays excluded) favour the charterer. If the charterer exceeds the permitted laytime, the shipowner is entitled to demurrage as specified in the charter-party and once this commences it is continuous, even if any subsequent delay is not the fault of the charterer, e.g. a seamen's strike. On the other hand if the charterer does not use all the laytime, he is entitled to despatch money which is normally calculated at 50 per cent of the rate for demurrage.

15.3.2.3 Time charters

Time charter-parties give the charterer more control over the vessel although the master is appointed by the owners, who are responsible for all costs appertaining to the running and manning of the vessel, plus overheads and depreciation. The charterer pays for all port charges, stevedoring, canal dues, pilotage, dunnage, ballast, water for the boilers, fuel and cleaning of the holds.

The vessel is hired out for a specified time at a rate based on its summer loadline deadweight capacity, irrespective of where it is to be used, and it is up to the charterer to use it to his best advantage. The hire charge is payable monthly in advance.

Shipowners may stipulate certain restrictions (e.g. no scrap metal to be carried), particularly if the vessel is new. Another restriction is 'not to be used in areas covered by the Institute Warranties', which are concerned with ice conditions.

15.3.2.4 Demise charter-parties

Finally, we have the demise charter-party, where the charterer takes control of the vessel for a long period and absorbs it into his own fleet. He appoints the master, subject to the owner's approval, and is responsible for all costs appertaining to the running of the vessel, while the owner is only responsible for depreciation, possibly insurance and survey costs depending on the terms of the charter-party. The owner is responsible for the brokerage payable to the shipbroker. Once again, the hire charge is based on the vessel's summer loadline deadweight capacity and as with time charter-parties, payment is due monthly in advance.

There is thus a similarity of choice in shipping as occurs in road transport although because of the bulk nature of the goods the transport or distribution managers in this case are more likely, although not invariably, to be looking to the import of their raw materials rather than the export of their finished products.

15.3.2.5 *The liner trade*

Nowadays the liner trade is virtually all containerised, and although there are some exceptions – e.g. Bank Line break-bulk services to the Pacific Islands – even here they are dealing with an ever-increasing number of containers. Certain national lines are limited in respect of containerisation by the lack of a sophisticated transport infrastructure inland from the ports.

Containerisation was initiated by liner operators formed into consortia to meet the enormous initial expense, and being conference members (see Glossary) they originally based their rates on the old commodity-based tariff. This led to competition from non-shipowners using chartered vessels, who offered a 'freight all kinds' (FAK) tariff similar to airline rates. Thus today the movement of goods in containers is shared between VOMMOs (Vessel-owning multi-modal operators) and NVOMMOs (Non-vessel-owning multi-modal operators). Today a simplified conference tariff is only the basis for bargaining, on which operators give considerable discounts to shippers on the basis of their tonnage. Both types of operators are prepared to offer a Combined Transport Bill of Lading by which they are prepared to be responsible for the movement on a door-to-door basis or from the point where they initially accept the cargo to the point of their delivery to the consignee or his agent. In view of this acceptance of through responsibility a shipped-on-board bill of lading, which used to be considered essential, is no longer necessary, but unfortunately, banks will still not accept 'received for shipment' bills of lading.

As we have seen in Chapter 10, there is now a wide variety of specialist containers to cater for the carriage of most types of cargo. Originally the ship operators owned the containers themselves, but today container leasing companies provide about half of all containers. There is nevertheless still a problem of trade imbalances, especially for specialist containers and the carriage of empties is a common feature. Furthermore, although a computer allocates each container to a vessel as soon as it is accepted by the carrier and then arranges the stowage of the vessel, there is nevertheless a certain amount of over-stowage, resulting in otherwise unnecessary handling of some containers at destination ports.

15.3.3 Land bridges

Where land masses make sea routes very much longer than direct distances, combined sea–land services have been developed with the object of providing faster services. Although land transport is more expensive than sea transport on a tonne/km basis, the reduced distance may bring the total freight charges closer together. This, combined with the time saving, may make the service very competitive: for example, the route over the US land bridge to Japan. Careful comparison of freight rates, times and the needs of the cargo must be made to determine correct choice.

15.4 Choices of transport from the United Kingdom to Continental Europe

Until the opening of Eurotunnel these routes were called short-sea routes. Now we have the choice of using Eurotunnel and this will become one of the logical routes to choose, and possibly the most logistical. More of this later. First let us remind ourselves that the traditional method of sending goods to Europe was by the conventional break-bulk vessel. Such vessels have virtually disappeared, to be replaced by road ferry (roll-on roll-off) vessels, rail ferries – though whether these will survive the opening of Eurotunnel is unknown at the moment – and short-sea container services of a lift-on lift-off type. There is the possibility that BACAT (barges aboard catamaran) services could start up again.

15.4.1 Eurotunnel

The opening of Eurotunnel in spring 1994 offers a unique opportunity for the return of the UK railway network to profitable operation, after almost a century of difficulties and at least half a century of subsidisation by central government. The trouble has been that railways are only really economic for full-load operations over 200 miles (320 km), and these kinds of movement simply do not exist within the United Kingdom. The link through Eurotunnel is going to add 240,000 km of pan-European railways to the 16,000 km of British lines. This opens a whole range of long-distance hauls to Railfreight Distribution (RfD) and should make the whole network much more viable. It is true that arrangements for the opening of the new routes have not been helped by the UK government's preoccupation with privatisation, but RfD has deliberately ignored these background discussions and instead has concentrated on getting things ready for Eurotunnel's operations, whoever finally owns the railways in the closing years of the twentieth century. The aim is to get an extra 4 million tonnes of goods off the lorries and onto the cross-Channel Freightliner networks in the first two years. At present RfD moves about 2 million tonnes of goods annually. To raise this to 6 million tonnes will be a good start for Eurotunnel, and make environmental sense both in the United

Kingdom and on the Continent. It is then planned to increase the traffic to 9 million tonnes (half as much again) by the year 2000.

The aim is to offer the road haulage industry the opportunity to trunk haul by rail and deliver and collect locally by road. The only sensible way to use the railway network is to carry containers on the trunk routes to a terminal close to the point for the content's eventual destination, and let road haulage collect and deliver the goods to destination, if necessary breaking bulk at an appropriate depot at or near the terminal.

One problem that had to be overcome was that of gauge clearance. The width between the tracks is the same on both sides of the Channel, but Continental trains are broader. To upgrade all UK track to mainland European Berne gauge would have cost £3000 million. Instead, an intermediate gauge – Swapbody Two – has been built which can carry 95 per cent of swapbody traffic. However, this will not carry pickyback traffic – where the lorry chassis and rear wheels are carried on the wagon. The use of pickyback traffic on the Continent has begun to decline for economic reasons. It is wasteful to have lorry bodies travelling on trains when they could be on the roads earning money.

As regards the freight services that will become available, the RfD brochure says:

15.4.1.1 *Channel Tunnel Freight Services*

Railfreight Distribution, in partnership with SNCF and other European railways, plans to operate a network of express freight services between the main regions of the United Kingdom and strategic European mainland destinations.

Nine regional Channel Tunnel inter-modal terminals will be the main focal points on the network. These will be at:

- Birmingham
- Cardiff
- Middlesbrough
- Mossend (Strathclyde)
- Normanton (near Wakefield)
- Seaforth (Liverpool)
- Stratford (East London)
- Trafford Park (Manchester)
- Willesden (north-west London)

These terminals will be complemented by the existing ferry wagon terminal network (see Fig. 15.1), company private sidings and three automotive distribution centres. Research undertaken by RfD has shown that more than 60 per cent of international traffic will be generated from locations north and west of London.

In certain regional locations the Channel Tunnel terminals will be the hub of a freight 'village' designed to act as the focus for distribution and manufacturing activity. The result will be a comprehensive range of facilities, creating some thousands of new jobs, which will complete the transport process and, more importantly, reduce the customers' workload.

Transit times between UK terminals and those on mainland Europe will be significantly faster than existing rail freight services and, in most cases, quicker than road transport. For instance, the door-to-door transit time between Manchester and Stuttgart will be 30 hours, and between London and Avignon, 20 hours. The Channel Tunnel will provide a direct link between BR's network of 10,000 route miles (16,000 km) and mainland Europe's 150,000 route miles (241,000 km). RfD will take advantage of rail's natural strengths in moving large volumes over long distances. Trains operating these services will be capable of running at speeds of up to 87.5 mph (140 km/h) and carry payloads of up to 1,000 tonnes.

Prices for RfD's Channel Tunnel freight services will be market-based and, in many cases, negotiated with individual customers.

Day-to-day operational control of the international freight service through the Channel Tunnel will be the responsibility of the Freight Control Centre based at Lille in northern France. This centre will be jointly managed by RfD and SNCF personnel, who will closely monitor freight train movements to ensure that service quality is maintained to the highest standards.

Goods originating within the EC will be subject to the new, streamlined customs procedures planned for introduction by 1993. This will mean that traffic will move smoothly direct to traders' premises, on a spot-check system. For non-EC goods, however, Willesden in north London will be used as an inland clearance depot by Customs. This traffic is expected to account for only a relatively small proportion of the total.

The terminals are shown in Fig. 15.1, while a view of the tunnel itself is given in Fig. 15.2. The actual terminal for the tunnel itself is at Dollands Moor, near Folkestone.

Apart from the building of the terminals work has also gone ahead in providing the new rolling stock and locomotives required. Forty-six Class 92 locomotives are in production and a stream of inter-modal wagons are in production at Loughborough and Douai in France and another French wagon construction company is building 300 totally enclosed car-carrying wagons. Freight will move in containers and swapbodies. Three specialist inter-modal companies have been set up to act as intermediate 'wholesalers' of train space, who will buy train space and sell it to customers (e.g. forwarders) who – perhaps – only need to send one swapbody a week through the tunnel. The plan reads:

> To initiate this system two specialist inter-modal companies have been established over the last two years.

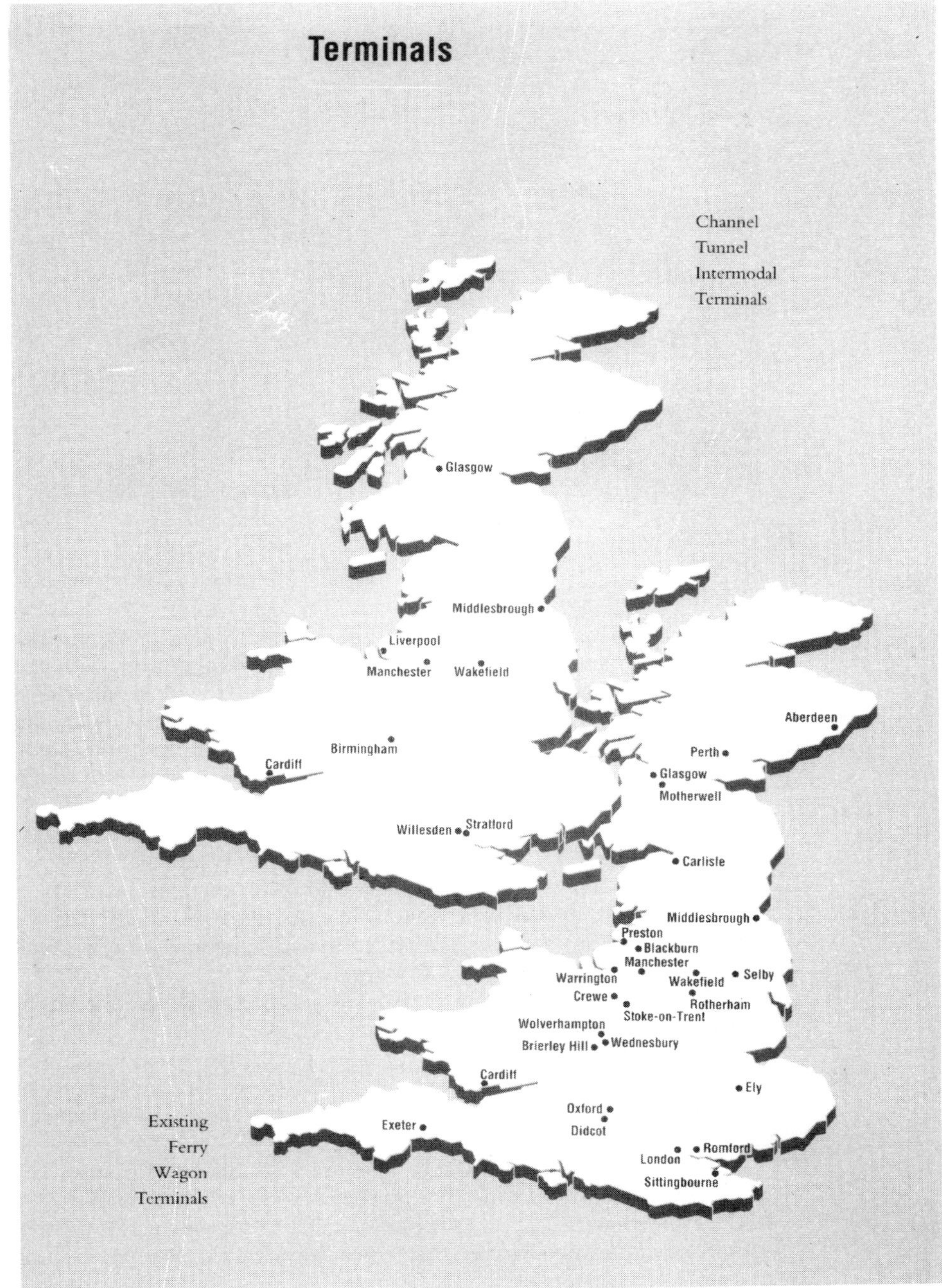

Fig. 15.1 UK terminals for the Channel Tunnel

Fig. 15.2 A view of Eurotunnel itself

First, CTL, Combined Transport Ltd, is a consortium of Continental inter-modal companies and major UK road transport operators with the Road Haulage Association and RfD. CTL has its background in the Union International Rail-Route (UIRR) companies. The predominant shareholding is by road hauliers who combine to gain access to rail for the trunk haul. UIRR companies traditionally focus on the swapbody but now cater also for container traffic.

Secondly, ACI – Allied Continental Inter-modal – was launched as a joint venture between RfD, SNCF and Intercontainer in September 1992. ACI seeks to build on existing strengths in the pan-European container market.

UNILOG is a further joint venture created by RfD, the SNCB – Belgian Railways, and Ferryboats of Zeebrugge to access the unique opportunities the Channel Tunnel offers the Low Countries.

Thus commercially, marketing channels are in place generating business well ahead of the Tunnel opening.

Wholesalers like CTL and ACI will then sell train space to various freight forwarders and international transport operators. It is at this level that the one swapbody a week forwarder can enter the market and enjoy the benefits of the Channel Tunnel rail service.

A third tranche of activity will be initiated by Haulmark European Transport, buying space from ACI or CTL – whichever is the more competitive. Formerly RfD's Freightliner Europe retail operation Haulmark will operate as an independent company owned by the British Railways Board pending its progressive transfer to the private sector.

Thus at one end of the scale, the needs of full train capacity are answered. Whilst the part-train and spot market are accessed too.

Whilst ensuring the product translates smoothly to the end-user RfD, working out the other side of the matrix, has been engaged in negotiating transit agreements with the other participating national railway organisations. Thus the group is now in a position to outline likely cost hypotheses on trans-national inter-modal freight flows.

Importantly these structures are operational now. When the Tunnel opens the Channel Tunnel Train Control Centre will be in place at Lille. A corresponding Freight Management Unit at Euston is also fully operational. The FMU – staffed by RfD and SNCF personnel – will oversee the commercial pathing of international freight trains through the Tunnel. British locomotive drivers are already training in France. RfD International Freight Services Managers will shortly take up their positions in Lille Centre Control du Fret.

The high level of co-operation between SNCF and RfD from driver to director is perhaps the most eloquent testimony to the benefits of international railways.

Railfreight Distribution brings to the Channel Tunnel a connectable international freight railway, ready now to run international freight trains across Europe as the market dictates. The foundations are in place. The implications for export, manufacturing and transport industry are those of speed, efficiency, safety, and distance.

Note: The authors are grateful to Railfreight Distribution for permission to reproduce this section of their bulletin on Channel Tunnel freight opportunities.

15.4.2 Roll-on roll-off movements

These are especially suitable for loads which would not benefit from or are unsuitable for containerisation, or for containerised goods originating from, or destined for, locations not well served by the Railfreight Distribution and Eurotunnel systems. Roll-on roll-off is also appropriate where it is desirable for the driver to accompany the goods from origin to destination, or for a driver belonging to an associated European company to complete the transit.

15.4.3 Short-sea container services

Suitable for container traffic as in roll-on roll-off and for trans-shipment traffic to and from feeder ports to connect with ocean-going vessels calling at major ports. Also used for traffic to and from ports not used by roll-on roll-off or rail/container ship services.

15.4.4 Rail/container ships

Especially suitable for containerised traffic which can benefit by Freightliner UK services and their Continental counterparts, but do not wish to use the Channel Tunnel. Precisely scheduled arrival times can be determined in accordance with rail timetables.

15.5 Air transport

Advantages

1. The universal way is free, and without maintenance costs.
2. Direct flight is possible to all parts of the world, within ground controlled flight paths.
3. Speed: much higher than any other mode of transport.
4. Lighter packing may be possible than for other forms of transport.
5. Cheaper insurance because goods are at risk for a shorter period and there is a good 'freedom from damage' record for this mode.
6. There is a great saving of interest on capital tied up in lengthy transits with other modes.
7. In many instances airports are much nearer source and/or destination, resulting in lower collection/delivery costs, although in the case of near continental destinations the trans-shipment involved may give the advantage to direct road haulage.

Disadvantages

1. High freight rates, but note that savings on packing, insurance, interest on capital, early delivery, inventory cost, etc., may cancel these out.
2. Susceptible to delays due to bad weather, particularly fog at take-off and landing.
3. Restrictions on size and weight may operate, but larger all-freight aircraft are making this less important.
4. Freight costs per tonne/km are higher by air, but the important point is that it is overall costs which have to be taken into account, and these may often be less than on surface routes.

Finally, we should say that it is usual these days for air forwarders to handle an increasing volume of air traffic leaving the airlines to concentrate on the actual flying of the aircraft.

15.6 Some case studies in transport and logistics

The range of enterprises with a logistical problem that needs to be solved is simply enormous. They range from 'around-the-town' deliveries by local retailers to trans-world activities by major importers and exporters. Some examples are given below, and permission to refer to these solutions to logistical problems is greatly appreciated by the authors.

15.6.1 British Road Services (BRS) schemes

Basically, BRS schemes are of two types, which may be modified to meet the particular requirements of a customer. The two types are illustrated in Fig. 15.3 (a) and (b).

It must not be thought that BRS are alone in providing these sorts of services. Other hauliers, large and small, are providing distribution schemes to firms whose products are distributed on a national or regional basis, but BRS, because of its nationwide network, was selected as ideal for illustrative purposes.

15.6.1.1 Case study no. 1: Boots (the Chemists) Ltd

The problem. In the Hampshire and Dorset area, the company has seventy-one retail outlets, located on 'high street' sites. The high rental value of such sites makes it imperative to utilise the maximum amount of space for the selling function, and keep storage space to a minimum. This in turn necessitates frequent replacement of stock. Apart from Boots' own products, those of many other manufacturers are carried as standard items among the many hundreds of lines sold by even their smallest stores. Storage space apart, direct delivery from each of the manufacturers would be impractical, and direct delivery by Boots after central consolidation would be uneconomic.

The solution. Boots and other manufacturers deliver in bulk to one BRS trans-shipment point in the area. Here, vehicles are unloaded and the various items placed in racking in coded order. Daily orders for individual shops can be 'picked' from the racks in code sequence and placed in special nesting bins for delivery. Most of the daily deliveries to the shops are transferred directly from the bins to the selling space, avoiding double-handling via the stockroom. Each store receives only one vehicle per day, with the whole of its intake. This scheme, which has been in operation since 1966, currently handles some 4 million packages annually.

15.6.1.2 Case study no. 2: Shell-Mex and BP Ltd

The problem. The company is involved in selling lubricants and grease, totalling approximately 750 product lines in a highly competitive market.

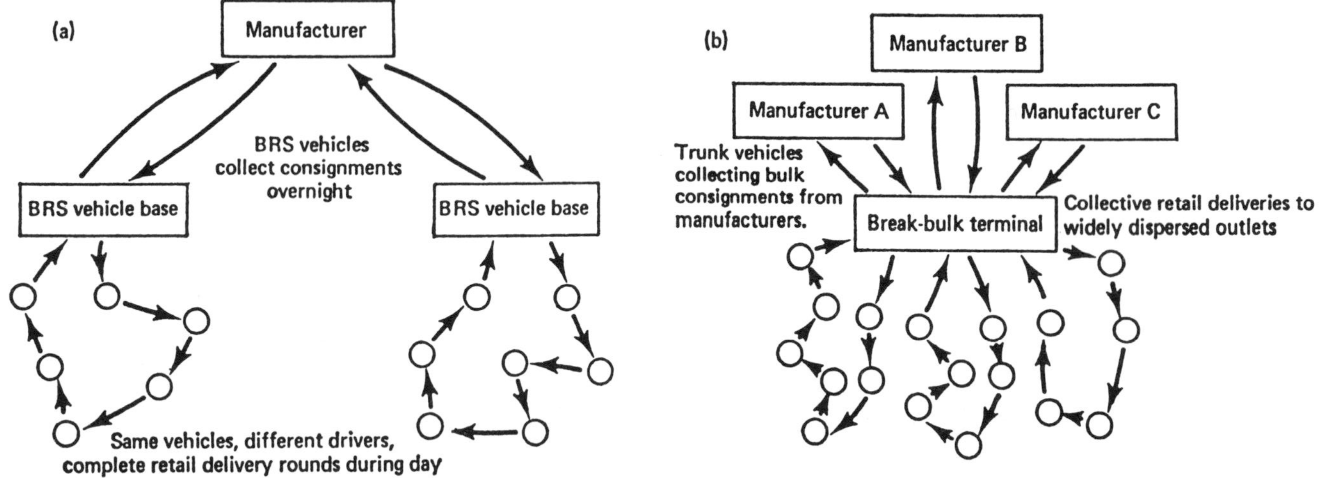

Fig. 15.3 Two BRS solutions to the transport problem (a) replacing regional stock depots by direct delivery through a BRS vehicle base, (b) delivery in remote areas direct from the manufacturer via a BRS break-bulk terminal

Notes to Fig. 15.3

Basic scheme (1)

(a) The regional stock depot, maintained by the customer, is replaced by a regional BRS vehicle base.

(b) Overnight trunk deliveries to the base from the manufacturer's premises bring full loads of the manufacturer's products into the region for distribution.

(c) Without trans-shipment the trunk vehicles are taken over by daytime drivers who deliver the goods to customers in the area.

Basic scheme (2)

This is particularly suitable for remote or scattered delivery areas, where no manufacturer has sufficient orders to merit the use of Scheme 1.

(a) Bulk delivery to a break-bulk BRS terminal – from several manufacturers.

(b) Consolidation of various products from various manufacturers into loads for local delivery. The loads on any vehicle must be compatible.

(c) Local delivery by BRS drivers.

Quality of service, and efficient stock control are essential requirements. The area to be covered consists of part of South Wales and the South-West. Deliveries are mainly to garage forecourts, with some deliveries to industrial users. The former are frequently limited in storage space and require stock replacement at short notice.

The solution. Bulk deliveries are made to the BRS depot at Avonmouth. On arrival the vehicles are unloaded by forklift trucks, some fitted with specially designed rim clamps enabling large drums to be handled two at a time. Slower moving products in large drums are stored in purpose-built drum racks, while faster moving products in large drums are stored in pallet stocks. Products in retail packaging are kept in multi-tier racking, palletised for forklift handling. As orders are received, delivery rounds are compiled for local deliveries. Two night-trunk deliveries are made to two other depots, where again local delivery rounds are compiled. Any point in the area covered can receive deliveries within 24 hours. Thirteen vehicles are used, all fitted with tail-lifts, for ease of handling the products at customers' premises.

15.6.1.3 *Case study no. 3: Jeyes Ltd*

The problem. This company and its subsidiaries manufacture disinfectants and other sanitary products, amounting to several hundred product lines (taking into account different sizes of the same product). Deliveries are mainly to 'cash and carry' wholesalers and to supermarkets. Direct delivery by Jeyes would be uneconomic, much of it involving empty or light running.

The solution. Bulk deliveries are made to Avonmouth from various sources, and stored in multi-tier racking. While many vehicle loads consist solely of Jeyes products, deliveries which on their own would be uneconomic can frequently be made in combination with the lubricants and greases mentioned above. Basing distribution schemes for compatible products on one depot provides a neat solution to a situation where the delivery of one company's products on their own would be a very unprofitable undertaking.

15.6.2 Logistics solutions at work in new hi-tech warehouse

Christian Salvesen has recently opened a new distribution centre in the north of The Netherlands. Dedicated to Iglo-Ola, a Unilever subsidiary and the sales organisation for frozen food and ice-cream in The

Netherlands, the site at Hoogeveen has been designed to store the main part of Iglo-Ola's national bulk and distribution stocks. Retail distribution from Hoogeveen covers the retail requirements of the north of The Netherlands and all of the central depot deliveries in the country. The retail requirements of the south are handled by the Salvesen site at Rotterdam.

A fleet of vehicles in Salvesen livery make deliveries to retail outlets, while a subcontractor takes care of the transportation to central depots.

The latest logistics solutions have been applied to this high-density storage and distribution warehouse. The core of the logistics operation is the interactive warehouse control system, which not only controls the flow of goods throughout the warehouse by issuing standard instructions, but also generates actions to take in case of exceptions.

From the moment the pallet is unloaded at the bay, its every movement is controlled by the real-time system. This significantly increases labour efficiency.

Deciding where to store the pallet is the responsibility of the system's instant location selection – based on a preferred location hierarchy – and the status of locations at that particular moment. The best use of warehouse space is guaranteed, as locations are released into the system immediately a pallet is physically removed.

Hi-tech radio interfaces and infra-red systems ensure that the pallet-carrying forklift truck communicates simultaneously, via an on-board terminal, with the stock management computer and the mobile racking, thereby optimising product movement, ensuring safe operation procedures have been followed and permitting the next load/unload cycle to commence.

The intelligent mobile racking system responds to the pickers' requests for additional product in the picking zone, by directing the reach truck drivers to the correct warehouse co-ordinates. Only after verifying that the current aisle has been cleared and that the main gangway safety light beams have not been broken, will the racking be moved to open the aisle which provides access to the replenishment stock. That action means moving 2,360 tonnes of product in less than a minute with one single operation!

What is perhaps more remarkable about the operation is the timescale in which it was built. The design of the operation started in mid-1990 and the contract was agreed with the client at the end of April 1991. The actual construction started in August the same year and the first pallets were delivered in mid-April 1992.

'Undoubtedly, the partnership approach adopted after the first few meetings with the client has resulted in a first-class distribution operation,' claimed Luc Moens, managing director of Christian Salvesen (Netherlands). 'Using an experienced and well-motivated team and ensuring all staff completed a thorough pre-operation training programme has resulted in an extremely successful opening period in which Iglo-Ola has broken all sales records.'

15.7 Summary

1. The choice of transport for a particular consignment must take account of the characteristics of the cargo concerned, and the modes of transport available to move it. Each mode has its advantages and disadvantages.
2. Roads reach every corner of the United Kingdom and are therefore convenient, direct, flexible (we can drive round obstructions) and it is easy to control the delivery of loads, now up to 44 tonnes. On the other hand, road consignments are vulnerable to accidents, misdelivery, pilfering and theft. Traffic density is a problem and so are the rush hour periods.
3. There is a choice of own-account transport, contract hired vehicles and the use of private carriers (who hold themselves out as willing to carry for the public at large). Own-account transport gives complete control of the vehicle and its driver but the owner must suffer under-usage to some extent, empty-leg journeys and the full costs of insurance, maintenance, capital costs, etc. With contract hire and the use of an independent carrier the consignor has less control over the vehicle and its operation, but has less expense.
4. The use of a third party logistics firm removes the whole burden of transport and distribution from the client firm and places it in the hands of an expert in the field, but such firms can only be attracted by a reasonably large-scale operation.
5. Rail transport offers quick delivery on very long-haul routes (for example, through Eurotunnel) but as few firms have private sidings they do become inter-modal activities at either end of the journey. Rail transport can handle bulk consignments with ease, and containerised traffic, but is less suitable for small parcels and 'retail' activities, which tend to be uneconomic. There is less control over small-scale rail movements, and consequently pilfering and theft are easier.
6. Deep-sea transport can handle large capacities at low freight rates, with continuous operations round the clock and fast turn-round times for containerised cargoes. The disadvantages are that speeds are low and journeys less direct than air movements. Vessels may be chartered on the Baltic Exchange, or privately. Voyage charter-parties give use of a vessel for a full cargo or a part-cargo. Time charters give use of a vessel for a stated period and demise (or barebones) charters give the use of a vessel for a long time, and allow it to be incorporated into the charterer's own fleet.

7. Today the liner trade deals almost exclusively with containerised goods, usually in specialised cellular ships which give easy loading and unloading cycles. Information technology is used to plan the loading and unloading movements.
8. In UK – Continental movements the opening of Eurotunnel is about to make a strong impact on both rail and road haulage. For the first time the UK railways will have the advantage of journeys in excess of 200 miles (320 km), which should make most journeys economic. Road haulage vehicles will have access to the Shuttle service through the Tunnel, avoiding a sea crossing.
9. Roll-on roll-off movements are especially suitable for road vehicles not using Eurotunnel, and give access to many ports remote from the tunnel exits. They give driver-accompanied transits, or unaccompanied transits may be met by drivers at either end of the sea voyage if firms have made mutually helpful arrangements.
10. Air transport is fast, direct, independent of topography, smooth and unaffected by weather, except at take-off and landing. Its high freight rates are offset by other savings – cheaper insurance, saving of interest on capital as a result of shorter journey times, cheaper packing and handling costs.

15.8 Questions

1. What is the likely impact on containerised road haulage to European destinations of the opening of Eurotunnel? Refer in your answer to (a) railfreight expansion; and (b) shuttle movements.
2. What are the advantages and disadvantages of own-account transport?
3. What is a charter-party? Explain the responsibilities of the shipowner and the charterer in a voyage charter in which the charterer has agreed to load a full cargo.
4. What advantages are gained by sending goods for Portugal on a roll-on roll-off vessel to northern Spain rather than by a Dover–Calais ferry?
5. 'Air freighting is too expensive for our machines.' Criticise this statement made by an American manufacturer of machinery for the hosiery industry, when discussing a movement of twenty machines to Hamburg.
6. What are the advantages of coastwise traffic? Who might make use of such transits today? Why have they declined so much in the last half-century?

16 Legal aspects of transport

16.1 Transport as a contractual arrangement

Transport and distribution are ancient activities and they have a very old legal background. The origins of *charter-parties* and *bills of lading* can be found in Greek and Roman times, while in the United Kingdom the concept of the common carrier, carrying by the *ancient custom of the realm* is still basic to the law of carriage. Another enduring feature of transport is its international character, so that a *conflict of laws* is inseparable from transport activities, especially today where nations are dependent on one another for so many basic requirements. In recent years these legal conflicts have tended to be resolved by *international conventions*, which have laid down mutually agreed rules for the carriage of goods and passengers by air, sea, rail and road. The most recent of these – concerned with the *law of combined transport* – has not yet been adopted by nations. This chapter can do little more than outline the general thinking behind the legal relationships in transport, which are now largely contractual, but you are urged to pursue your study of transport law as rigorously as you pursue the study of transport itself.

16.2 The common carrier

A common carrier in English law is anyone who holds him or herself out as willing to carry for reward. You must carry as a regular business, not as a casual operation. You may limit the extent to which you are willing to carry, both as to the type of goods and as to the distance and direction you are prepared to go. If you hold yourself out as a carrier, by announcing the fact on public notice boards, advertisements in the press, stationery, etc., then the law regards you as a common carrier, with a legal duty to carry.

Ancient custom of the realm regards the carrier as *prima facie* suspect for he goes 'over the hills and far away' with other people's property. Who can tell what tricks the carrier is up to when out of sight? English law therefore very early on placed a very onerous responsibility on carriers, that they were liable for every loss that occurred. This is often expressed as 'the liability of an insurer', but the idea precedes the idea of insurance by many centuries. The common carrier bore the heavy responsibility of compensating anyone who suffered loss, irrespective of whether or not he was at fault. If A's cart was overturned by B's cart whose horse had bolted, A must compensate the owners of any goods in his cart which were damaged, seeking indemnity from B, the owner of the other vehicle. Gradually the courts developed some 'common law exceptions' to the severity of this rule, and a common carrier who could prove that the loss occurred through one of these common law exceptions could escape responsibility. They were:

1. Act of God.
2. Act of the Queen's enemies.
3. Inherent vice.
4. Fault of the consignor (usually faulty packaging, addressing, etc.).
5. Fraud of the consignor.

The enduring nature of the concept of the common carrier is best illustrated by the railways. These were held to be common carriers right up to 1962, when the Transport Act 1962 – recognising that the heavy losses on railway operations were partly caused by the railways' status as common carriers – declared them to be private carriers from that time on.

16.3 The private carrier

A private carrier is anyone who is not a common carrier. He or she only holds himself or herself out as being a private carrier. That is to say, he or she announces in public notices, advertisements, etc., that he or she is not a common carrier, but only carries under private 'Conditions of Carriage', which form a contract between the carrier and the customers. In practice these sets of conditions of carriage are often drawn up by the trade associations, such as the Road Haulage Association or the Institute of Freight Forwarders Ltd, and readers are advised to obtain such a set of Conditions of Carriage and read them carefully. They form part of a body of contracts called 'Standard Form Contracts'. A word about the abuse of standard form contracts is desirable.

16.4 Standard form contracts and the privity of contract

Standard form contracts are to be found in every area of commercial activity, in sale of goods, in hire purchase and especially in carriage.

Typical examples are the conditions of carriage issued by the Road Haulage Association (the 1991 rules), the British Railways Conditions of Carriage (BR 18793), and the Conditions of Carriage of the Institute of Freight Forwarders Ltd. Naturally these bodies issue such conditions of carriage as a protection for their members, and embody in them the considered advice of their lawyers. Irrespective of the area they covered these documents could at one time be criticised from one point of view: they made the contractual agreement between the parties very one-sided. English law has always held that a contract is a private arrangement between two parties, both of whom are deemed to be equally knowledgeable, equally sophisticated, equally alert to the implications of the contract. The use of standard form contracts makes a mockery of this concept, for the housewife who asks a carrier to take goods from one part of the country to another has little knowledge of the law, or of contracts, and is forced to accept the terms and conditions offered. In many cases the carrier is a monopolist, perhaps even having a statutory monopoly, and no alternative mode of transport is available to the customer. In these circumstances, in years gone by, carriers abused their position by having onerous clauses inserted into their standard terms and conditions. Conflicts between customers and carriers have frequently arisen; parliament itself has intervened – sometimes to little effect – and only recently has the situation finally been brought under control, so that it no longer gives cause for concern.

The Act that brought about this desirable improvement in the law was the Unfair Contract Terms Act 1977. Not only did this Act require all clauses in sets of standard conditions to pass a 'test of reasonableness', but it also empowered the Director-General of Fair Trading to supervise the revision of such standard form contracts. In a lengthy procedure, during which the carriers were forced to concede more reasonable terms in each branch of the carriage of goods, the situation was finally brought under control.

16.5 Inland carriage and international carriage

Within the boundaries of any state or territory carriage of goods and passengers will be governed by the laws of the state concerned. It follows that a 'conflict of laws' can easily arise where goods and passengers cross frontiers, as they inevitably do in sea carriage and often do in carriage by air, carriage by road via roll-on roll-off ships, and continental rail carriage. The conflict of laws arises because the parties concerned, living in different countries, are free to bring their complaints in the courts of their own countries. Of course, the courts of both countries may reach the same conclusion about a particular matter, so that no conflict arises; the case is more difficult where the laws of the countries are different. What is permissible in one country may be illegal in another, and hence a conflict of laws is inevitable. How shall such conflicts be resolved?

The answer to this problem has been found in the convention system. An international convention is held at which the representatives of both sides in each nation are present. The two sides referred to are the carriers on the one hand, i.e. the shipowners, airlines, road hauliers and railways, and the consignors or passengers on the other hand. The consignors are chiefly the shippers or forwarders of goods, represented by their Chambers of Commerce. Passengers, a less well-organised group, tend to be represented at these conventions by their respective governments in some official way. The first of these international conventions was the *Convention Internationale de Marchandises*, which was originally signed in 1914. This was a railway convention, signed at a time when all merchandise travelling internationally went by either sea or railway. It was designed to provide a body of rules for European rail carriage. These rules are known as the *CIM rules*.

The United Kingdom, because of its island status, was not a signatory to the 1914 Convention but is since 1983 a full signatory of the modern version of this convention, the COTIF Convention. (COTIF means 'the Convention on OTIF', and OTIF are the initials for the French words for the Intergovernmental Organisation for International Carriage by Rail.) More than thirty countries are signatories to the Convention, and are called the 'contracting parties'. The aim of COTIF is to establish a uniform system of law for the international carriage of goods by railway, and two sets of rules, the CIM rules and the CIV rules apply. (CIM stands for the Convention on International Merchandise moving by rail, and CIV stands for the Convention on International Voyagers (travellers) by rail.)

Later conventions included the International Conference on Maritime Law, held in Brussels in October 1922. This convention drew up a set of rules which became known as the *Hague Rules*. The nations which ratified this convention then enacted statutes in their own countries embodying the convention in their own national laws. Thus the convention became law in all the leading maritime countries. In the United Kingdom the relevant statute is the Carriage of Goods by Sea Act 1924, later replaced by the Carriage of Goods by Sea Act 1971, which embodies modern amendments to the original convention. The rules are now known as the Hague–Visby Rules. More recently the United Nations has taken an interest in these conventions and a new body of rules – the Hamburg Rules – awaits ratification. These rules will then replace the Hague–Visby Rules. They are marginally more favourable to Third World countries. However, therein lies a problem. Because the United Nations has a preponderance of Third World countries it is all too easy for it to write into conventions like the Hamburg Rules terms which will never be conceded by the really powerful nations conducting the majority of world trade and transport. Even if such a set of rules is ratified by the necessary number of countries, it does not follow that it will have any impact, because nations that have not signed will not comply. They may even leave the Third World nations worse off by refusing to carry goods to them, because of the impracticality of the rules.

As regards air transport, in 1929 a Warsaw Convention laid down rules for international carriage by air. The relevant statute in the United Kingdom was the Carriage by Air Act 1932, subsequently replaced by the Carriage by Air Act 1961. These rules for the settlement of disputes about air carriage are called the *Warsaw Rules*. A new version of these rules, the Montreal Version, awaits ratification.

Finally, road haulage was the subject of a convention, the *Convention de Marchandises par Route*. When enacted into British law this convention became the Carriage of Goods by Road Act 1965. The rules are known as the *CMR Rules*.

One further draft convention, the TCM convention, drawn up by the Institute of Unification of Private Law (Unidroit) at Rome, and the Comité Maritime International, is about the legal rules on combined transport; that is, transport using more than one mode, e.g. road–sea–road, or rail–sea–road transits.

This is not a law book, and the reader must turn elsewhere for full details of these conventions, but Table 16.1 shows the main points made in the conventions, in tabular form (see pages 310–13).

16.6 Summary

1. Traditionally, transport in the United Kingdom has been subject to the common law of England, and to contract law, as it developed out of common law. In other words, the parties made their own arrangements, and the law only came into the matter if a dispute arose.
2. The common carrier is liable for every loss that occurs, unless it can be established that one of the five common law exceptions applies. These are Act of God, Act of the Queen's enemies, inherent vice, fault of the consignor and fraud of the consignor. To escape the rigours of common law, carriers make it clear to all the people for whom they carry, that they are not common carriers, but private carriers, carrying under private contracts with their customers.
3. In international carriage conflicts of law arise and to overcome these conflicts the convention system was developed. This means that all the leading parties (shippers, carriers, consignors and consignees) are represented at an international convention at which a set of rules is worked out and agreed. They then go home and persuade their home governments to enact the rules into their own domestic law. In this way,

Table 16.1 Comparative tables on the international carriage of goods

Basic concepts

Aspect of law	CMR (International road haulage)	COTIF Convention (International rail carriage)
Basis of legal relationship between the parties.	Statutory – by the Carriage of Goods by Road Act 1965 which enacts the CMR Convention. Later amended by the Carriage by Air and Road Act 1979.	Contractual – the CIM Rules of the COTIF Convention are adopted by the designation CIM on the rail consignment note.
The definition used for 'international' carriage.	The Convention applies to every contract for the carriage of goods for reward by road haulage where the place of taking over the goods and the place of delivery are in two different countries of which one at least is a country which has adopted the Convention.	The carriage of goods consigned under a through consignment note for carriage by rail over the territories of at least two contracting states and exclusively over lines declared under Article 10 of the Convention.
Extent of carrier's liability.	The haulier is liable for total or partial loss or damage to goods between takeover and delivery, but not where he can prove fault of the plaintiff, inherent vice, or circumstances beyond his own control. He is also liable for unreasonable delay, and for failure to collect COD charges.	The railway is liable for total or partial loss of the goods and for damage thereto between takeover and delivery unless it can prove fault of the claimant, inherent vice or circumstances beyond its own control. The time of transit is calculated on one of four formulae. Exceeding this time of transit leads to liability for delay.

Table 16.1 *(contd)*

Hague–Visby Rules 1971 Carriage of Goods by Sea Act, also Hamburg Rules awaiting ratification	Warsaw Rules (Carriage by Air) Montreal version awaiting commencement order	ICC 298 (Uniform Rules for a Combined Transport Document)
Statutory – a clause paramount is not required under the Hague–Visby Rules but will be required under the Hamburg Rules.	Statutory – by the Carriage by Air Act 1961. The Montreal version of the rules is enacted in the 1979 Carriage by Air and Road Act but awaits a commencement order.	Contractual – the Uniform Rules are adopted contractually whenever a combined transport document is issued.
The carriage of goods by sea in ships from any port in Great Britain or Northern Ireland to any other port whether in or outside Great Britain or Northern Ireland – provided a bill of lading is issued and goods are not live animals or deck cargo. These rules will change slightly when Hamburg Rules commence.	Carriage between a place of departure and a place of arrival which are in the territories of two different High Contracting Parties (states which have ratified the Convention), or carriage between two places in the same state if there was an intermediate stop in any other state whether a high contracting party or not.	The carriage of goods by at least two different modes of transport from a place situated in one country to a place designated for delivery situated in a different country.
The shipowner must exercise due diligence in providing a seaworthy and cargoworthy ship. He must properly load, handle, stow, carry, keep, care for and discharge the cargo. He is not liable for errors in navigation or management of the ship, nor for fire, perils of the sea, and a long list of exceptions. There are to be major changes in the Hamburg Rules awaiting ratification.	The operator is liable for loss, destruction or damage to cargo during the carriage by air (whether in an aircraft or an aerodrome or in the event of a forced landing anywhere else). Not liable if he can prove that he took all necessary measures, or that it was not possible to take such measures. Not liable if he can prove fault of the claimant. (Montreal version increases these immunities.) Liable for delay.	The CTO (combined transport operator) is liable for loss or damage to the goods from time of takeover to time of delivery caused by his own, his servants' or his subcontractors' acts. Liable for delay.

Table 16.1 (*contd*)

Comparison of rules

Aspect of law	CMR (International road haulage)	COTIF Convention (International rail carriage)
Official document	CMR consignment note	CIM consignment note
Does it have a 'paramount clause'?	The consignment note bears a large sign 'CMR' and the words 'International consignment note'	Consignment note bears the sign 'CIM'
Limitation of Liability (Note i. Liability never exceeds the total value. Note ii. Gold franc consists of 65.5 mg of gold of millesimal fineness 900. Note iii. SDR unit recalculated daily by IMF)	8.33 SDR units of account per kg of gross weight	17 SDR units of account per kg, converted to currency at the rate prevailing on the date that payment is made
Jurisdiction of the courts	Action may be brought (*a*) anywhere that is agreed (*b*) where the defendant is resident, or has his principal place of business or an establishment where the contract was made or (*c*) the place where the goods were taken over by the carrier (*d*) in the place of delivery	The plaintiff must select the railway he wishes to sue, under the rules of Article 55, and must bring his action in the courts of the state to which the railway belongs
Time limit on legal action	One year, extended to three years if wilful misconduct is alleged	One year normally, but by mutual consent this may be extended

Table 16.1 *(contd)*

Hague–Visby Rules 1971 Carriage of Goods by Sea Act, also Hamburg Rules awaiting ratification	Warsaw Rules (Carriage by Air) Montreal version awaiting commencement order	ICC 298 (Uniform Rules for a Combined Transport Document)
Bill of lading	Air Waybill (1961 Act). Air Consignment Note (1932 Act)	Combined Transport Document
The 1971 Act makes no mention of a paramount clause. The Hamburg Rules when implemented do require a paramount clause	It bears a warning that if the carriage is international carriage the Convention will apply and limit the carrier's liability	Yes, the Uniform Rules say it must bear the heading 'Negotiable combined transport document' issued subject to Uniform Rules for a Combined Transport Document (ICC Publication 298) or 'Non-negotiable, combined etc., etc.'
10,000 francs per package or 30 gold francs per kg whichever is higher. Under the old Convention £100 per package still applies. The Hamburg Rules will change these limits to 835 SDR units per package or 2.5 SDR units per kg of gross weight	250 gold francs per kg unless a higher value has been declared and a supplementary charge paid. The Montreal version will change this to 17 SDR units per kg and for baggage 1,000 SDR units per passenger	30 gold francs per kg unless a higher value has been declared by the consignor
The Convention does not mention jurisdiction – so the court would decide whether it was competent to hear a case and which law should be applied. The Hamburg Rules give very clear instructions about jurisdiction	Action must be brought, at the option of the plaintiff in the territory of one of the High Contracting Parties either (*a*) where the carrier is ordinarily resident or (*b*) has his principal place of business or (*c*) has an establishment where the contract was made or (*d*) at the place of destination	The Uniform Rules are silent about jurisdiction and therefore it will be for courts to decide whether they have jurisdiction in a particular case
One year normally, but by mutual consent this may be extended	Two years	Nine months after (*a*) delivery or (*b*) date when the goods should have been delivered or (*c*) date decided by Rule 15 (which says goods are deemed lost 90 days after a reasonable time for delivery has elapsed)

all countries who ratify the rules have the same laws, and conflicts of law cannot apply.

4. The rules for railway transit are called the CIM rules and the Convention is called the COTIF Convention (from the French words for the organisation for international carriage by railway).
5. The rules for sea transport are the Hague–Visby Rules.
6. The rules for road transport are the CMR rules (CMR stands for the Carriage of Merchandise by Road-hauliers).
7. The rules for air transport are the Warsaw Rules.
8. There is also a set of Uniform Rules for a Combined Transport Document, which is contractually adopted by the parties in any contract for multi-modal transport.

16.7 Questions

1. What is a common carrier? What are his or her liabilities at common law?
2. What is a private carrier? Explain the legal basis of his or her activities.
3. Why are a carrier's trading terms called 'standard conditions of carriage'? What is the general objection to standard form contracts?
4. What is a 'paramount clause'? What are the implications of such a clause in an international contract of carriage?
5. What are the main points in any convention on international carriage?
6. A UK carrier's standard trading conditions declare: 'The carrier will not be liable for any loss, howsoever caused, and neither will his servants, agents or subcontractors.' The carrier's vehicle is wrecked in France and the cargo is a total loss. What is the legal position, if it is established that the driver was not only careless, but reckless in the way the vehicle was handled?

17 The documentation of transport

17.1 Introduction

The documentation of transport is a very ancient activity, and two documents, the charter-party and the bill of lading, have their origins in Greek and Roman times and possibly even earlier. The charter-party, as we saw in Chapter 15, concerns the use of sea-going vessels, and the bill of lading concerns the ownership of goods which are on the high seas. In these days of instantaneous communication ships are never really out of touch with their home ports, but in former times they were, and the development of the bill of lading permitted the purchase and sale of goods on the high seas. If you purchased the bill of lading you effectively purchased the goods. Of course, this is still true today.

The evolution of documentation for inland transport was less well developed, since it was based on the ancient custom of the realm and contract law as it developed in the years after the Norman Conquest. Gradually, more formal arrangements came to be made, with such documents as delivery notes, consignment notes and waybills, but the chief developments were in international transport, by land, sea and air. The chief documents, apart from the charter-party which is a rather special type of contract, are as follows:

1. The bill of lading (for goods moving by sea).
2. The CIM note, for goods moving by rail.
3. The CMR note, for goods moving by road.
4. The air waybill, for goods moving by air.

Of almost as great importance is the development of electronic data interchange (EDI), which enables these documents to be computerised and sent around the world as a stream of data, to be reconstituted into a printed document at any time, wherever they are required. Naturally not everyone in the transport and logistics field has the latest and most sophisticated equipment for handling documents electronically, but the use of EDI is spreading rapidly and we need to know all about it.

In this chapter we first set out the current situation about the various documents in use, and then explain how these documents are computerised.

17.2 Aligned documentation

The amount of documentation required whenever goods or passengers move is considerable, and in recent years some hard looks have been taken at documentation procedure, so that wherever possible documents are *aligned*. This means that the information required by various parties is placed in the same position on a standard-shaped piece of paper, often of A4 size. For example, nearly everyone – consignor, carrier, Customs, consular officials, chambers of commerce, port authorities and the consignee – will wish to know the address to which the goods are to be sent. There is no reason why this unit of information, the consignee's name and address, should not be placed on the same spot on each document – the invoice, shipping note, bill of lading, air waybill or whatever document is in use. If this is done, and if all similar pieces of information are similarly placed in a standard spot on the page, then a master form can be prepared giving all the required information in the correct positions. From this master document, *once it has been thoroughly checked to ensure complete accuracy*, we can then run off copies of any document required, using modern reprographic techniques – for example, a plain paper copier or a more sophisticated device such as one of the Rank Xerox Docutech Publishing Models.

The master document referred to was originally drawn up as a result of international negotiations between the major trading nations under the auspices of the United Nations. The UK representative at all such meetings is the SITPRO Board (The Simpler Trade Procedures Board). The SITPRO Board is the authority on aligned documentation and publishes a loose-leaf collection of forms called 'Topform', all of which can be run off from the SITPRO Master Document once it has been completed with all the facts about a particular consignment. The point is, though, that not all documents will require all the information, so there has to be some way of masking off the items on the master document that are not required on each particular form. A system of masking sheets enables the operator to exclude from any particular document information on the master which is not required on that document. For example, it may be considered unwise to let the lorry driver know the value of the goods he is delivering, and the invoice copy which is used as a delivery note would be masked off at the point where the value is shown. The whole set of documents will be as accurate as the master, and need not be checked in any way, since only the information on the master can possibly come out on the documents; they have not been individually prepared so there is no danger that figures have been copied incorrectly. Also, every copy will be as good a print as the next. Before aligned documentation was developed, a typist producing several copies of a document using carbon paper could not fail to have fainter and fainter copies at the back of the pack. With aligned documentation all copies are equally clear. The file full of documents, now ready for processing, is then passed from the duplication department to the appropriate clerk in the freight forwarding office.

Once installed, an aligned documentation system enables transport and distribution activities to go ahead without difficulty, but a constant review of procedures is desirable. In particular, inter-firm liaison and liaison with other interested parties like foreign civil service organisations is essential. In any new procedure – for example, the imposition of special deposits for imports by some foreign country – we cannot just let the clerks in that country design a form for the collection of the special deposit. Their form, whatever they require on it, must fit into the aligned system. On the master form shown (see Fig. 17.1) there are certain areas shown as 'free disposal' areas. These can be used for any new procedure, a space being allocated by mutual agreement in those areas. The SITPRO master document is reproduced in Fig. 17.1 and deserves close study at this point. We will then look at the main documents that can be produced from it.

17.2.1 Completing the master document

As the boxes are not numbered the reader must be guided by the subheadings. If a copy of the master document can be obtained, it is best to have a copy available when reading each paragraph below, so that constant turning of pages to locate a particular box on the document is not necessary.

17.2.1.1 Exporter

Insert the exporter's full name and address, including the post code and country. If you pre-print this on your master or forms, we recommend that you include your STD telephone number and telex and fax numbers. If you include purchase orders or forms classed as correspondence in your system, the registered office, company registered number, and VAT registered number will be required by law. The VAT numbers should be shown in the space provided.

You may not be the actual exporter or shipper in, for example, ex-works sales, and you should be sure to reflect the facts correctly in completing this box. Thus the top left-hand box may be labelled 'Exporter' on a standard shipping note, 'Shipper' on a bill of lading and 'Seller' on an invoice.

©SITPRO 1992

MASTER DOCUMENT

Exporter VAT reg. no.	Invoice no.		Customs reference/status
	Invoice date	Carrier's bkg. no.	Exporter's reference
	Buyer's reference		Forwarder's reference
Consignee VAT reg. no.	Buyer VAT reg. no.		
Freight forwarder VAT reg. no.	Country of despatch	Carrier	Country of destination code
	Country of origin		Country of final destination
Other UK transport details	Terms of delivery and payment		

U N I C

Vessel/flight no. and date	Port/airport of loading		
Port/airport of discharge	Place of delivery	Insured value	EUR 1 or C. of O. remarks

Shipping marks; container number	Number and kind of packages; description of goods *	Item no.	Commodity code		
			Quantity 2	Gross weight (kg)	Cube (m³)
			Procedure	Net weight (kg)	Value (£)
			Summary declaration/previous document		
			Commodity code		
			Quantity 2	Gross weight (kg)	Cube (m³)
			Procedure	Net weight (kg)	Value (£)
			Summary declaration/previous document		
			Commodity code		
			Quantity 2	Gross weight (kg)	Cube (m³)
			Procedure	Net weight (kg)	Value (£)
			Summary declaration/previous document		

* DANGEROUS GOODS:
Refer to IMDG, ADR, IATA, CIM and UK regulations as appropriate and specify: proper shipping name; hazard class; UN no.; flashpoint °C

LIMIT OF SAD BOX 31 ▷

Identification of warehouse	FREE DISPOSAL	Invoice total (state currency)	
		Total gross wt (kg)	Total cube (m³)

Freight payable at	Signatory's company and telephone number
Number of bills of lading Original Copy	Name of signatory
	Place and date
	Signature

J468/001

Form No. 810

Published and Sold by FORMECON SERVICES Ltd., Gateway, Crewe CW1 1YN Tel. 0270 500800 Fax. 0270 500505

SITPRO Approved Licensee No.21

Fig. 17.1 The SITPRO 1992 master document (reproduced by courtesy of the SITPRO Board)

17.2.1.2 Consignee (and consignee's VAT number)

This is the party to whom the goods are to be consigned in the transport document and will usually be the person taking delivery of the goods. It could, on occasions, for example, be the importer's clearing agent or port office. It is not compulsory to insert this item on the EUR1, but H.M. Customs recommend that it be shown and it often helps forwarding agents to relate the document to the correct consignment.

17.2.1.3 Freight forwarder (and freight forwarder's VAT number)

The full name and address should be inserted. If you are selling ex-works or FOB to a UK-domiciled export house or other intermediary, this is the appropriate box in which to insert their name and address, as the party attending to shipping formalities. The full name and address should be shown.

17.2.1.4 Invoice number and invoice date

These are purely references for correspondence purposes.

17.2.1.5 Carrier's booking number

This reference is given by the Port Authority to cut down lorry queues and call cargo forward in the right order for loading.

17.2.1.6 Customs reference/status

This box has been fully described in the section on Customs. If a firm is using the simplified Customs procedure this box will contain the export consignment identifier – a number made up of a five-figure CRN (Customs registered number) plus up to nine characters of a commercial reference. *Do not* insert an ECI for any consignment which is not using the simplified procedure.

If an ECI appears in this box, H.M. Customs will expect a full post-shipment declaration to arrive in due course. Other consignments should show the customs status, not the ECI. These might read: PRE-ENTRY SAD, LVXXX, NON-STAT or CAP Schedule.

17.2.1.7 Exporter's reference

The consignment reference number used by the party shown as 'Exporter' should appear here. It will conveniently appear in a blank space on the EUR1 not used for other purposes. If this consignment reference can also be made to serve as export order number and export invoice number, it will avoid confusion on the part of those not so familiar with your system as yourselves. There is room for nine characters when the typewriter pitch is ten characters per inch, or ten when the pitch is twelve per inch. This number is *most likely* to be the container seal number on the seal put on the container by the export packer.

17.2.1.8 *Buyer's reference*

This is merely a reference number to remind the buyer of his order and who is handling it.

17.2.1.9 *Forwarder's reference*

The reference of the party shown on the form as 'Freight forwarder' may appear in this box. This information, though optional, is useful in practice.

17.2.1.10 *Buyer (and buyer's VAT number)*

If the buyer is not the consignee, the invoice will need to make this clear. The export cargo shipping instruction may also need to contain this information but the box is then headed 'Other Address' so that if preferred some other address, such as place of delivery or a separate 'Notify Party' could be inserted here.

17.2.1.11 *Country of despatch*

This is self-explanatory.

17.2.1.12 *Carrier*

Insert here the name of the shipping line, airline or combined transport operator.

17.2.1.13 *Country of destination code*

This is a customs code which complies with H.M. Customs computerised control of movements. The necessary codes are given in Notice No. 37, obtainable free from H.M. Customs.

17.2.1.14 *Country of origin*

Use of the EUR1 form is confined to goods of EC origin and invokes the complex origin rules set out in H.M. Customs & Excise Notices 810 and

810A, *inter alia*. At present, this item of information is pre-printed on EUR1 forms and need not be reproduced from the master document.

The country of origin is usually but not always required to appear on the export invoice. If so there will be varying origin criteria and you should consult your *Reference Book for Exporters*.

17.2.1.15 *Country of final destination*

Show the country of final destination of the goods.

17.2.1.16 *Other UK transport details*

Insert here any other details about the UK transport movement, such as dock, container base or airport where the consignment is to be loaded on the carrying vessel or aircraft; the name of any pre-carrier, place of receipt by pre-carrier to take to dock, airport, ICD, etc.

17.2.1.17 *Terms of delivery and payment*

These should be indicated either by reference to Incoterms (i.e. the thirteen three-letter codes) or by an accurate description of the applicable terms. Details of time of delivery, currency, etc., can also be included in this box (e.g. 'FOB Incoterms Liverpool, Documentary Sight Draft').

17.2.1.18 *Vessel/flight number and date*

The intended or actual name, flight or voyage number should appear, if known. The requirements of the shipping note and insurance certificate can be met by indicating the name of the *intended* vessel – the latter document is not invalidated in any way by a subsequent change of vessel, although your broker should be notified as there could be a resulting change in premium. This information is optional on the EUR1, but when appearing on this and/or the export invoice, difficulties may occur if a change of vessel is not duly notified to recipients of the documents.

17.2.1.19 *Port/airport of loading*

Show the name of the port or airport from which the goods are exported on board the 'Vessel/Aircraft' shown alongside.

17.2.1.20 *Port/airport of discharge*

Enter the port or airport at which the goods are to be unloaded abroad from the 'Vessel/Aircraft'. This may not necessarily be the final destination, nor even in the country of destination, e.g. goods unloaded at Dar es Salaam for on-carriage to Lusaka.

17.2.1.21 *Place of delivery*

This box is mainly intended to indicate the extent of any on-carriage in *through* bills of lading. It should also be used to specify on the insurance certificate the destination of the goods for warehouse-to-warehouse insurance purposes. These two places may be different (e.g. if the consignee is arranging transport from the ICD) and you should be careful to ensure that each document carries the appropriate item of information.

17.2.1.22 *Insured value*

This value need only be inserted in figures (words are not required as well) but the currency must be clearly stated.

17.2.1.23 *EUR1 or C of O remarks*

The EUR1 contains this box where exporters can declare the status of the goods for which they are seeking a preferential rate of duty. The most common remark is 'Article 21.1 satisfied'.

The new version of the certificate of origin has a 'Remarks' box in the same place, which may be used to insert such details as the Chamber of Commerce might require to be inserted on the certificate of origin for a particular consignment with a particular origin.

17.2.1.24 *Shipping marks; container number*

Marks are one of the essential means of identifying cargo and documentation and linking them to each other. In view of their importance as an identifier, marks and numbers should be as simple as possible, and identical on packages and documents. Any container number (and sizes and type if relevant) should appear in this area.

17.2.1.25 *Number and kind of packages/description of goods**

These details are required on many forms but the layout is particularly directed at completion of the single administrative document (SAD). Although the use of the SAD is now much reduced it still has a part to play as the statistical export declaration. The UK version of this document is Form C88. The EUR1 requires a horizontal line to be drawn under the sole or last item in the box and the unused space to be crossed through with a line in the shape of a 'Z'.

Packages should be described precisely, e.g. '10 pallets each holding 10 cartons' or '100 cartons loaded on 10 pallets' rather than simply '10 pallets'. Incorrect description of packages may affect the insurance premium and validity.

Goods may be described in general terms for most documents but must appear in detail item-by-item on export invoices for pricing purposes. Your system would need to be designed to accommodate these special requirements. The items should be numbered 1, 2, 3, etc., in the section headed 'Item No.'.

17.2.1.26 *Commodity code*

This box is used in pre- and post-shipment declarations. Enter the appropriate commodity code as listed in volume 2 of the tariff applicable to the goods described in 17.2.1.25. Enter the first eight digits in the first subdivision. Enter the ninth digit in the second subdivision. The other subdivisions are to be left blank unless volume 2 of the tariff says that an additional four-digit code applies, in which case enter the code in the fourth subdivision.

17.2.1.27 *Quantity 2*

The units of quantity required to appear in the boxes labelled Quantity 2 are shown in H.M. Customs & Excise Tariff and are for statistical purposes. This same area may be used in the export invoice as all or part of the invoiced 'Quantity' column, but in this event it may call for information different from that supplied for the SAD.

17.2.1.28 *Gross weight (kg)*

Metric weight should be used. A separate gross weight is normally given for each item shown under 'Description of Goods'. It may also be convenient to show the total gross weight, but the shipping note requires this item to appear in a different place.

17.2.1.29 *Cube (m^3)*

Insert the measurement of packages in cubic metres and indicate whether any pallet dimensions are included, e.g. 'Pallet dims. inc.'.

17.2.1.30 *Procedure*

This refers to the type of use to which the form is being put. Enter in the first subdivision the first four digits of the appropriate customs procedure code (CPC) from the list in appendix E1 of volume 3 of the tariff. Enter in the second subdivision the final two digits of the same code.

17.2.1.31 *Net weight (kg)*

Enter the net metric weight. National regulations may specify a particular unit of weight for export invoices – consult your *Reference Book for Exporters*.

17.2.1.32 *Value (£)*

This is the FOB value for H.M. Customs statistical purposes only, and may require certain adjustments compared with the FOB value as commercially interpreted. See H.M. Customs & Excise Tariff and Notice No. 276.

17.2.1.33 *Summary declaration/previous document*

This box is used where goods have been dealt with by Customs under one procedure and are now to be dealt with by a different procedure – for example, inward processing relief. The box relates the present document to the documents previously used.

17.2.1.34 *Identification of warehouse*

This box is used on the export cargo shipping instructions form, and also on charges advice notes to identify the area where goods are held.

17.2.1.35 *Free disposal*

As with all aligned documentation, areas on a master document which are not required by any of the forms in the aligned series may be used by firms for their own purposes to improve their in-house documentation. When a box is labelled 'Free Disposal' the exporter is invited to make use of it in any way he likes. Other documents in the aligned series will have other areas designated as free disposal, because they may not need some of the information on the master document. The unwanted areas will be masked off in the reprographic process, or left blank on an electronic document and consequently available for any use. Such free disposal areas are often used to give instructions about the completion of a form – or for advertising purposes.

17.2.1.36 *Invoice total (state currency)*

This figure is self-explanatory.

17.2.1.37 *Total gross wt (kg)/total cube (m^3)*

These boxes are self-explanatory.

17.2.1.38 *Freight payable at*

Mainly used for bill of lading and shipping instruction purposes, this stipulates the point at which ocean freight is to be paid.

17.2.1.39 *Number of bills of lading*

This item shows the number of negotiable bills of lading to be signed by/for the ship's master, 'one of which being accomplished the others shall stand void'. There is a sensible and increasing tendency to reduce the number of negotiable bills of lading issued for a consignment. The box also allows room for the number of copies to be recorded.

17.2.1.40 *Signatory's company and telephone number*

This facilitates contact with responsible persons in any emergency or difficulty.

17.2.1.41 *Name of authorised signatory*

Signatures are frequently illegible. The typewritten name inserted here assists officials attempting to contact the signatory for any reason.

17.2.1.42 *Place and date of issue*

The alignment of these items on the form does not mean that the dates will be the same on all documents. Whichever date is applicable will go in the space.

Certificates of insurance issued under open cover marine policies are not invalidated by their post-dating the commencement of transportation. The terms of a letter of credit may, however, stipulate the dating of insurance certificates and other documents, so that a post-dated certificate would not be acceptable.

17.2.1.43 *Signature*

A facsimile signature reproduced from a manually signed master document is acceptable on shipping notes, insurance certificates, SADs (by arrangement with the long rooms concerned), and some export invoices (consult your *Reference Book for Exporters*). The EUR1 requires an original manual signature on page 1 (in addition to that on the reverse).

17.3 The invoice

An invoice is a business document which is made out whenever one person sells goods to another. It is an important document because in law it is evidence of a contract between the two parties who are dealing with one another. If one gets to the point of making out an invoice, the court believes that the parties have struck a bargain and therefore intended to enter into legal relationships with one another. The invoice bears the name and address of both parties involved in the transaction, the date of the transaction, the quantity of goods, their unit price and total value, and possibly other details. Some reference to the method of delivery is usually included. It follows that this document is the most basic document of all, and all the facts required on it must be included when preparing the master document illustrated in Fig. 17.1. From this master we then prepare whatever other documents are needed for international trade.

SITPRO have produced three layouts for commercial invoices. If invoices are based on the design guides in the SITPRO leaflet they will fit into the aligned series and if relevant certificates are incorporated they will be accepted in many countries as certified invoices. Firms dealing with particular overseas states are strongly advised to submit their proposed layouts to the national authorities concerned to ensure their acceptability.

Two of the suggested layouts are in 'portrait' style (i.e. normal A4 size with the shorter side as the base). One is in 'landscape' style (i.e. the A4 sheet is used with the longest side as the base).

It frequently happens that an export order is made up in cases or containers holding several items. Thus, while the master document headings 'Marks and Numbers', etc., are appropriate for such documents as bills of lading and insurance certificates, the invoice requires different details, in particular, lists of the commodities enclosed in the crates. This can be achieved, using one of the technical tricks of the trade, so that detailed invoices are prepared while at the same time other master document details which are required still appear on the invoice.

Occasionally, invoices produced by reprographic means from a master document are queried because they appear to be photocopies. This is not the case as a 'photocopy' implies that somewhere there is an 'original' hand-typed invoice. In the event of such a query, SITPRO recommend that you explain that the invoice is not a photocopy, but an original invoice produced from a master document. Authenticity can be usefully emphasised if invoices are signed in a contrasting colour, say blue or red (if a manual signature is required). For some countries, stamping one of the invoices 'ORIGINAL' in a contrasting colour may also be helpful.

For the sake of convenience of the reader the invoice shown in Fig. 17.2 is a portrait style invoice with space for a list of items/packages. The reader should compare this layout with the master document shown in Fig. 17.1.

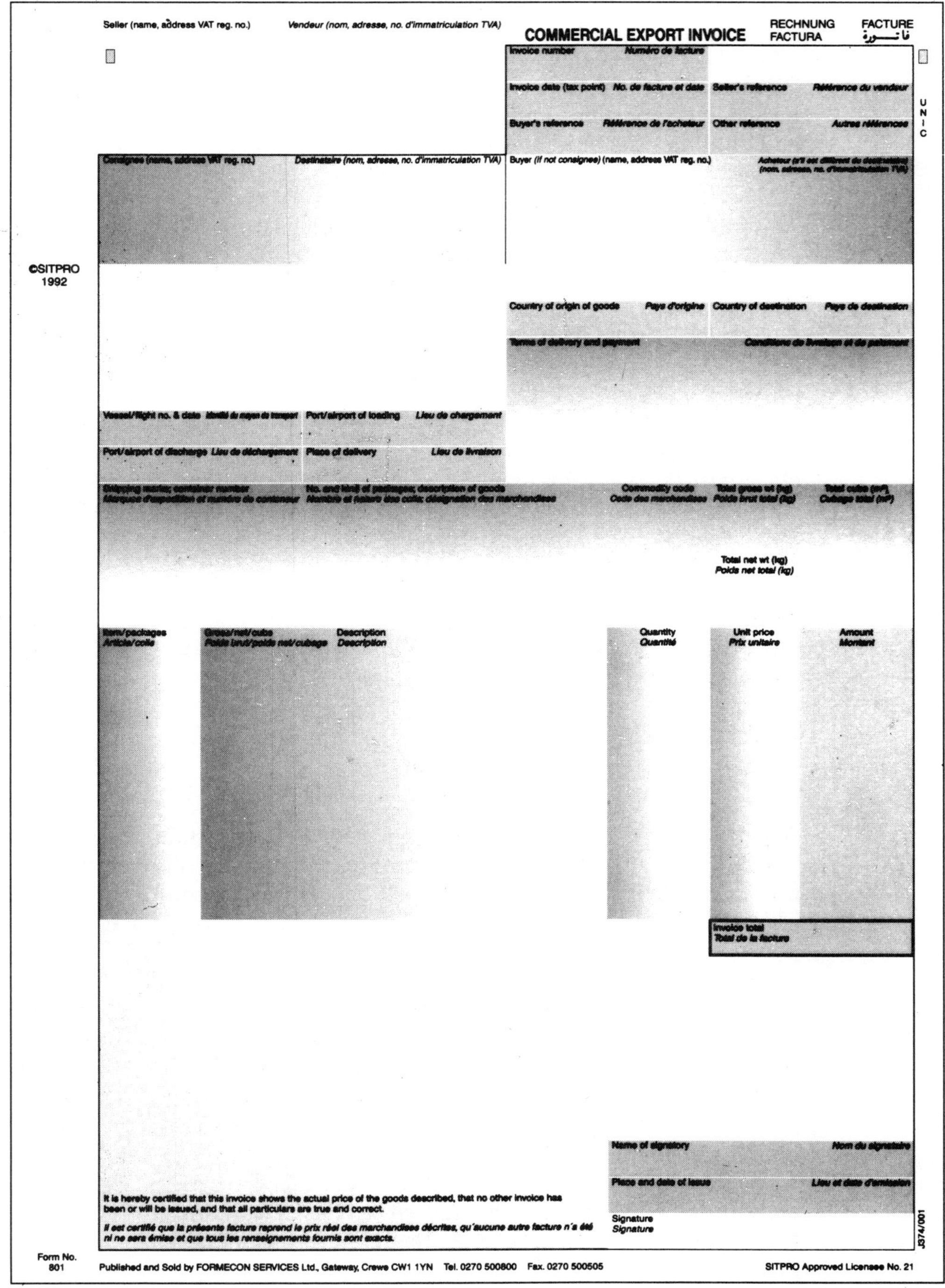

Seller (name, address VAT reg. no.) *Vendeur (nom, adresse, no. d'immatriculation TVA)*

COMMERCIAL EXPORT INVOICE RECHNUNG FACTURA FACTURE فاتورة

Invoice number *Numéro de facture*

Invoice date (tax point) *No. de facture et date* | Seller's reference *Référence du vendeur*

Buyer's reference *Référence de l'acheteur* | Other reference *Autres références*

U N I C

Consignee (name, address VAT reg. no.) *Destinataire (nom, adresse, no. d'immatriculation TVA)*

Buyer (if not consignee) (name, address VAT reg. no.) *Acheteur (s'il est différent du destinataire) (nom, adresse, no. d'immatriculation TVA)*

©SITPRO 1992

Country of origin of goods *Pays d'origine* | Country of destination *Pays de destination*

Terms of delivery and payment *Conditions de livraison et de paiement*

Vessel/flight no. & date *Identité du moyen de transport* | Port/airport of loading *Lieu de chargement*

Port/airport of discharge *Lieu de déchargement* | Place of delivery *Lieu de livraison*

Shipping marks; container number *Marques d'expédition et numéro de conteneur* | No. and kind of packages; description of goods *Nombre et nature des colis; désignation des marchandises* | Commodity code *Code des marchandises* | Total gross wt (kg) *Poids brut total (kg)* | Total cube (m³) *Cubage total (m³)*

Total net wt (kg) *Poids net total (kg)*

Item/packages *Article/colis*	Gross/net/cube *Poids brut/poids net/cubage*	Description *Description*	Quantity *Quantité*	Unit price *Prix unitaire*	Amount *Montant*

Invoice total *Total de la facture*

Name of signatory *Nom du signataire*

Place and date of issue *Lieu et date d'émission*

It is hereby certified that this invoice shows the actual price of the goods described, that no other invoice has been or will be issued, and that all particulars are true and correct.

Il est certifié que la présente facture reprend le prix réel des marchandises décrites, qu'aucune autre facture n'a été ni ne sera émise et que tous les renseignements fournis sont exacts.

Signature *Signature*

J374/001

Form No. 801

Published and Sold by FORMECON SERVICES Ltd., Gateway, Crewe CW1 1YN Tel. 0270 500800 Fax. 0270 500505

SITPRO Approved Licensee No. 21

Fig. 17.2 A portrait invoice (reproduced by courtesy of the SITPRO Board)

There are no real difficulties in completing this form from the master, provided the portions not required are masked out, and the details to be added in the lists of items/packages are made available on a suitable sub-master.

17.3.1 Consular invoices

A consular invoice is often required when goods are exported to foreign countries. This may be because of a language difficulty; the country concerned requiring true copies of invoices in its own language – say, Spanish or Arabic. The reason may be concerned with the country's need to control foreign exchange, to ensure that only essential goods are imported. By requiring invoices to be approved by its consular officials a country ensures that its own citizens do not infringe regulations by purchasing goods for which foreign currency is not available. The approval also confirms to the exporter that the order placed with him will be honoured by the foreign exchange authorities when the payment comes to be converted into sterling on the foreign exchange market. Legalisation of invoices can be charged as a percentage of the invoice price, and thus represent a very important cost to exporters.

17.3.2 Certificates of origin

A certificate of origin is a document required in certain circumstances where preferential tariff arrangements are made between countries. For example, if British goods may enter Germany free of tariff, but US goods may not, attempts to evade the tariff might be made by American firms if they could ship the goods to Britain first.

Under an international convention of 1923 it was agreed that in order to simplify customs formalities each nation should nominate certain official bodies, which should have the sole right to issue certificates of origin. In Britain the bodies nominated are the major Chambers of Commerce affiliated to the Association of British Chambers of Commerce. For a fairly nominal sum they will certify the origin of goods declared to be of British origin, provided evidence of their manufacture in the United Kingdom is available and a suitable declaration to that effect is made and signed by an appropriate person in the applicant firm. This declaration reads: 'I declare that the goods specified in the Schedule are of United Kingdom origin, production or manufacture.' The certification by the Chamber of Commerce reads: 'The undersigned, duly authorised by the . . . Chamber of Commerce (incorporated) hereby verifies the declaration made below by the Exporter specified above, in respect of the goods to be dispatched to the Consignee specified above.' Generally, the Certificate of Origin will be a separate document, but where the regulations of a country require the commercial invoices to be certified, the Chamber of Commerce will certify the actual invoices.

With the development of aligned documentation, the SITPRO Board has negotiated the combination of invoices, certificates of origin and certificates of value (which are also sometimes required). This means that a single document can be made to serve all three purposes.

17.3.3 Certificates of value

Here the intention of nations may vary. Some wish to prevent profiteering by foreign suppliers and call for a breakdown of costs charged to their importers – including the charge for the goods, the value of packing, the freight, insurance and other charges paid. Others wish to restrict imports of goods to those not manufactured in their own country, and therefore require a certificate that goods are properly described and that no alternative invoices are being issued to evade regulations. With others the intention is to avoid 'dumping' – the sale of goods to a foreign country at a lower price than is paid in the home market by a country's own citizens.

There are innumerable ways of dumping goods – the intention being to earn foreign exchange at any price. Thus, a factory making an article at £100 might achieve profitability by selling half its output at £200 to home consumers and the other half at £50 (a dumping price) to foreign customers paying hard currency. A profit margin of 25 per cent has been earned by selling at the differential prices, the home consumer subsidising the foreign consumer but, in the process, competing unfairly with the industry in the foreign country which can only make the product at a price higher than £50. Certificates of value may call for a clear declaration of the various costs incurred in the manufacture of goods, and a guarantee that, taking freight and other costs into account, the goods are being sold at the 'same' price in the home country as in the foreign country. If this is not established a tariff may be imposed to bring the price up to a fair level, or to one which will virtually exclude the goods in order to discourage the practice (see Fig. 17.3).

17.3.4 Invoices and letters of credit

It cannot be emphasised too strongly that when a letter of credit is in use it is essential that the invoice complies exactly with the requirements of the

FEDERATION OF NIGERIA

Combined Form of Certificate of Value and of Origin and Invoice for Goods Exported to the Federation of Nigeria **C.16**

.... 19 ....
(Place and Date)

(1) State here general nature or class of goods.
(2) Full name and address of manufacturer, supplier or exporter.
(3) Full name of business and address (not P.O. Box or Private Mail Bag) of the importer.

INVOICE of [(1)] consigned

by [(2)]

to [(3)]

to be shipped per

Order Number ....

Country of Origin	Marks and numbers on packages	Quantity and description of goods	Selling price to purchaser	
			@	Amount

Enumerate the following charges and state whether each has been included in or excluded from the selling price to purchaser:-

	Amount in currency of exporting country.	State if included in above selling price to purchaser.		Amount in currency of exporting country.	State if included in above selling price to purchaser.
(1) Cartage to rail and/or docks .... (2) Inland freight (rail or canal) and other charges to the dock area including Inland insurance .... (3) Labour in packing the goods into outside packages . (4) Value of outside packages .... (5) If the goods are subject to any charge by way of royalties			(6) OCEAN FREIGHT .... (7) OCEAN INSURANCE .... (8) Commission, establishment and other charges of a like nature .... (9) Other costs, dues, charges and expenses incidental to the delivery of the articles		
State full particulars of royalties:-					

I, ... (1) .... of (2) ....

of (3) .... *manufacturers/suppliers/exporters of the goods enumerated in this Invoice amounting to ....

hereby declare that I have the authority to make and sign this Certificate on behalf of the aforesaid *manufacturers/suppliers/exporters and that I have the means of knowing and do hereby certify as follows:-

1. That this invoice is in all respects correct and contains a true statement of the price actually paid or to be paid for the said goods, and the actual quantity thereof.
2. That no different invoice of the goods mentioned in the said invoice has been or will be furnished to anyone.
3. That no arrangements or understanding affecting the purchase price of the said goods has been or will be made or entered into between the said exporter and purchaser, or by anyone on behalf of either of them by way of discount, rebate, compensation or in any manner whatever other than as fully shown on this invoice.

ORIGIN

1. That all the goods mentioned in this invoice have been wholly produced or manufactured in ....
2. That all the goods mentioned in this invoice have been either wholly or partially produced or manufactured in ....
3. That as regards those goods only partially produced or manufactured,
   (a) the final process or processes of manufacture have been performed in ....
   (b) the expenditure in material produced and/or labour performed in .... calculated subject to qualifications hereunder, in the case of all such goods is not less than 25 per cent of the factory or works costs of all such goods in their finished state. *(See Note below.)
4. That in the calculation of such proportion of material produced and/or labour performed none of the following items has been included or considered:-
   Manufacturer's profit or remuneration of any trader, agent, broker or other person dealing in the articles in their finished condition; royalties; cost of outside packages or any cost of packing the goods thereinto; any cost of conveying, insuring, or shipping the goods subsequent to their manufacture.

Dated at .... this .... day of .... 19 .....

Signature .... Signature of Witness ....

(1) Here insert Manager, Chief Clerk, or as the case may be. (2) Here insert name of firm or company.(3) Here insert name of city or country.

NOTE. 1. The person making the declaration should be a principal or a manager, chief clerk, secretary or responsible employee.
2. The place or country of origin of imports is that in which the goods were produced or manufactured and, in the case of partly manufactured goods, the place or country in which any final operation, has altered to any appreciable extent the character, composition and value of goods imported into that country.
3. In the case of goods which have at some stage entered into the commerce of, or undergone a process of manufacture in a foreign country, only that labour and material which is expended on or added to the goods after their return to the exporting territory shall be regarded as the produce or manufacture of the territory in calculating the proportion of labour and material in the factory or works cost of the finished article.
4. *Delete the inapplicable.

Form No. 731(OS) Published and Sold by FORMECON SERVICES Ltd., Gateway, Crewe CW1 1YN Tel. 0270 500800

Fig. 17.3 An invoice with a certificate of origin and value (reproduced by permission of Formecon Services Ltd, Gateway, Crewe, CW1 1YN)

letter of credit if payment is to be released. The description of the goods must be exactly right, since even a spelling mistake may disqualify the invoice; packing and other details must also be correct.

It is important too that the appropriate type and number of invoices are forwarded, since the customs authority of the importing country may require several copies.

17.3.5 Other points about invoicing

17.3.5.1 *Packing lists*

A packing list may be required if the goods are packed in more than one crate. This saves time at destination since the customs officer will usually only open a statistical sample, i.e. three cases out of eight. If the three are in order he may conclude that the other five are also in order.

17.3.5.2 *Use of a factoring organisation*

When a supplier is using the services of a factoring organisation the commercial invoices may be made out by the factor and prior warning should be given to the buyer that he will be dealing with the factor's agent. On the other hand, the invoices may be the supplier's invoices but stipulate that payment is to be made to the factor and not the supplier. In the export field, payment is usually made to the factor's agent in the foreign country.

17.3.5.3 *The ultimate destination of the invoice*

The ultimate destination of the invoice is the foreign customer, but in many cases it will accompany the bill of lading and other documents to the bank, which will either release payment (against a confirmed letter of credit) or collect payment from abroad on the exporter's behalf if the letter of credit is unconfirmed, or if payment is on 'documents against payment' or 'documents against acceptance of a bill of exchange' terms.

17.4 The bill of lading

The bill of lading is the major shipping document in the liner trades but in chartering it is governed by the terms of the charter-party which is the actual contract of affreightment and therefore the paramount document. A bill of lading is shown in Fig. 17.4.

Page 2

1 Shipper

PHILIP GREENAVON (CAMBRIDGE)LTD
1758 CAMSIDE
CAMBRIDGE
CB4 1PQ

CONTAINER BILL OF LADING No.

Container No.:

Type:

F.C.L./L.C.L./F.C.L./L.C.L.

Seal No.:

2 Consignee

AL HEBRON TRADING Co LTD
P.O.BOX 175076
MUTTRAH
MUSCAT, SULTANATE OF OMAN

or order

3 Notify address

NECOL

NEAR EAST CONTAINER LINES

a joint service of
DEUTSCHE NAH-OST LINIEN
(see Clause 1)
and
KNSM-KROONBURGH B.V.

4 Vessel	5 Port of loading	6 CARRIER subject clause 31
THULE EXPRESS	FELIXSTOWE	AL KALIFA AGENCY
7 Port of discharge	8 to be forwarded to final place of delivery	9 Agents at port of discharge

10 Marks and Nos.	11 Number and kind of packages, description of goods	12 Container Tare Kilos	13 Gross weight	14 Measurement
OR/2385/83 AL HEBRON MCT CTIU 1213079 INTU 2253773	2 X 20'CONTAINERS STC 2800 CARTONS PACKED ON 36 PALLETS "FREIGHT PAID"	G.W. N.W.	43668 KGS. 41142 KGS.	

HOUSE / PIER / HOUSE / PIER

Carrier not to be responsible for quality or quantity of contents, nor for description of packages, same not having been examined. If in addition to the number particulars concerning the weight have been furnished, this Bill of Lading only constitutes a presumption as to number not as to weight loaded. In such case the weight is always presumed to be unknown. Weight also unknown if cargo has been received unweighed, the Carrier having no means to check merchant's weight declaration, especially bulk cargo.

cbm à	p cbm	DM
kos à	p to	DM
Collection Fee 5 %		DM
Disbursements		DM
Collection Fee 5 %		DM
		DM
Primage		DM
		DM
		DM
	Total	DM

SHIPPED on board in apparent good order and condition unless otherwise stated and to be discharged at port of discharge or so near thereto as the vessel may safely get and be either always safely afloat or safely aground.

Weight, measure, marks, numbers, quality, contents and value, condition although declared by the Shipper in the Bill of Lading, are to be considered unknown unless the contrary has been expressly acknowledged and agreed to. The signing of the Bill of Lading is not be considered as such an agreement.

In accepting this Bill of lading the Merchant expressly accepts and agrees to all its stipulations, exceptions and conditions, on both pages, whether written, printed, stamped or otherwise incorporated as fully as if they were all signed by the Merchant.

One of the Bills of Lading must be surrendered duly endorsed in exchange for the goods or delivery order.

IN WITNESS where of the Master or agent has signed the number of original Bills of Lading, stated above, all of this tenor and date, one of which being accomplished the others to be void.

15 Freight payable at	16 Place and date of issue	
FELIXSTOWE	BIRMINGHAM	10 NOV....
17 Number of Original Bs/L	18 Signature, for the master	
3/THREE		

43

Fig. 17.4 A bill of lading (reproduced by courtesy of West House Freight Services Ltd)

The bill of lading has three roles as follows:

1. It is the carrier's receipt for carriage of goods by sea.
2. It is *prima facie* evidence of the contract of affreightment and as such often incorporates the carrier's conditions of contract on the reverse side. It is of course issued after the contract has been made, which occurs either on the acceptance of the shipper's booking or when the goods have been physically shipped.
3. It is the document of title to the goods. As such it is quasi-negotiable. This means that the title of the holder is only as good as the title of the previous holder; the transferee does not get a better title of the document than the transferor had – which is the case with a fully negotiable document. Bills of lading are made out in sets with either two or three originals and a variable number of copies which are not negotiable. The number of originals must be shown in writing on the bill of lading and the presentation of one of them renders the others void.

Nowadays bills of lading conform to the SITPRO design and can be run off from their master document, suitably masked to exclude unnecessary items of information. Of course, bills of lading are commonly handled electronically as part of electronic data interchange (EDI).

17.4.1 'Received for shipment' bills of lading and 'shipped bills of lading'

Most letters of credit, on which exporters rely to ensure they get paid for the goods they have sent abroad, call for the release of the credit only when a suitable shipped bill of lading has been presented, along with other documents such as the commercial invoice, the insurance certificate, etc. The word 'shipped' recognises that the goods have actually been loaded. If a bill is only a 'received for shipment' bill of lading it is less satisfactory since the master of the vessel has not admitted that the goods have been physically placed on board.

Today the multi-modal operators of container vessels have a system where a received for shipment bill of lading is printed by the computer immediately the container has been allocated to a vessel. This is subsequently overstamped 'shipped' once the container has actually been loaded. With containerisation, which today accounts for over 90 per cent of all liner shipments, the CTO (combined transport operator) on receipt of the container either at the shippers' premises, at an ICD, or at the ship's side, will issue a computerised 'received for shipment' bill of lading. Technically, since the CTO is now fully responsible for the container, this should suffice for letter of credit purposes as far as the banks are concerned. Unfortunately, the banks have failed to grasp this and still insist on a 'Shipped on board' clause, which delays their receipt of the documents. Of course, received for shipment bills of lading and sea waybills are perfectly acceptable when the banks are not involved.

17.4.2 The combined transport bill of lading

Many container operators who are, by the very nature of container transport, collecting goods from exporters, carrying them to the port of destination and then delivering them to the consignee are now offering combined transport documents such as the combined transport bill of lading (see Fig. 17.5). There are special implications of such operations which may be listed as follows:

1. The general framework of such operations is described in a special publication of the International Chamber of Commerce. This document, UNCTAD/ICC Rules for Multi-modal Transport Documents ICC 481, is the result of international discussions on these matters. Whether an operator contractually adopts these uniform rules into his own conditions of carriage or not, he is likely to offer something fairly like them.
2. Since the operator assumes responsibility for the goods as soon as he takes control of them, the shipper and consignee enjoy a considerable degree of protection throughout the entire transit. They should therefore be willing to allow the container operator a degree of flexibility so that he can achieve the best possible use of his resources in the most flexible manner. For instance, there is little point in a letter of credit specifying that a 'shipped' bill of lading is to be provided. The CTD (combined transport document) is equally reliable 'shipped on board' or 'received for shipment', since the CTO is liable as laid down in the rules, or in his conditions of carriage. Overseas Containers Ltd advise that the letter of credit should call for a 'shipped on board bill of lading or combined transport document'. Similarly, there is little point in specifying a named port of loading or discharge. If the container operator has difficulty with a particular port because it is strike-bound, for example, but is free to use another port which is available, then he should do so in order to keep the exporter's goods on the move. The letter of credit should therefore show the term 'UK port', unless the buyer wishes to cover a possible port-to-port situation in which he can specify the ports of his choice but add 'or if Combined Transport Bill of Lading is used any UK port'.

   The restriction 'no trans-shipment' was designed to prevent trans-shipment because this always, under break-bulk conditions, meant extra handling at the trans-shipment port, from ship to lorry, lorry to shed, lorry to ship, etc., increasing the chances of pilfering and damage.

With containerisation such problems do not arise. If the CTO wishes to trans-ship the goods to expedite their passage he should be free to do so.

3. The points listed above emphasise that the exporter must discuss the terms of any letter of credit that is to be opened in the course of preliminary negotiations on an export contract, so as to ensure that the wording is appropriate to the type of combined transport he intends to use.

Note that in Fig. 17.5 the clause which reads: 'Above particulars as declared by Shipper, but not acknowledged by the Carrier (see Clause 11)' is a 'said to contain' clause. This is a clause which draws attention to the fact that the CTO, having received a container which he has not packed himself, has no real knowledge of the contents, or of their state, packaging, etc.

17.4.3 Order bills of lading

These have no named consignee, the word 'Order' being inserted in the 'Consignee' box while the intended consignee is shown as a 'Notify Party' immediately underneath. Before forwarding the bills of lading through the banking system under a documentary collection, the shipper must blank endorse the originals by signing his name and putting his stamp on the reverse of the bill. He will then give instructions for the collecting bank to release the bills of lading only against payment (documents against payment) or against acceptance of his accompanying bill of exchange (documents against acceptance). In this way he can retain title to the goods if the buyer refuses to accept them. Furthermore, since the buyer is only a notify party, he cannot lay claim to the goods without producing the bills of lading to the carrier. It is possible for a named consignee to do this under the laws of certain countries.

In view of the above it may seem odd that irrevocable letters of credit often call for order bills of lading blank endorsed, bearing in mind it is the buyer who is asking for the letter of credit. It is in fact a 'belt and braces' exercise on the part of the issuing bank which, having become a party to the letter of credit, insists on this method of safeguarding its interests.

17.4.4 Through bills of lading

A through bill of lading is used when goods are being trans-shipped. It covers both legs of the journey. It is issued by the major carrier but will have an accompanying local bill of lading, with the major carrier shown

Bill of Lading for Combined Transport shipment or Port to Port shipment

Shipper

B/L No.

Booking Ref.:

Shipper's Ref.:

P&O Containers

Consigned to the order of

Notify Party/Address (It is agreed that no responsibility shall attach to the Carrier or his Agents for failure to notify of the arrival of the goods (see clause 20 on reverse))

Place of Receipt (Applicable only when this document is used as a Combined Transport Bill of Lading)

Vessel and Voy. No.

Place of Delivery (Applicable only when this document is used as a Combined Transport Bill of Lading)

Port of Loading

Port of Discharge

Marks and Nos; Container Nos;	Number and kind of Packages; description of Goods	Gross Weight (kg)	Measurement (cbm)

Above particulars as declared by Shipper, but not acknowledged by the Carrier (see clause 11)

*Total No. of Containers/Packages received by the Carrier

Movement

Freight and Charges (indicate whether prepaid or collect):

Origin Inland Haulage Charge.. ... ...

Origin Terminal Handling/LCL Service Charge.. ...

Ocean Freight ... ...

Destination Terminal Handling/LCL Service Charge...

Destination Inland Haulage Charge... ... ...

Received by the Carrier from the Shipper in apparent good order and condition (unless otherwise noted herein) the total number or quantity of Containers or other packages or units indicated in the box opposite entitled "*Total No. of Containers/Packages received by the Carrier" for Carriage subject to all the terms and conditions hereof (INCLUDING THE TERMS AND CONDITIONS ON THE REVERSE HEREOF AND THE TERMS AND CONDITIONS OF THE CARRIER'S APPLICABLE TARIFF) from the Place of Receipt or the Port of Loading, whichever is applicable, to the Port of Discharge or the Place of Delivery, whichever is applicable. Before the Carrier arranges delivery of the Goods one original Bill of Lading, duly endorsed, must be surrendered by the Merchant to the Carrier at the Port of Discharge or at some other location acceptable to the Carrier. In accepting this Bill of Lading the Merchant expressly accepts and agrees to all its terms and conditions whether printed, stamped or written, or otherwise incorporated, notwithstanding the non-signing of this Bill of Lading by the Merchant.

Place and Date of Issue

ICS
CT B/L
April 78

Number of Original Bills of Lading

IN WITNESS of the contract herein contained the number of originals stated opposite has been issued, one of which being accomplished the other(s) to be void.

For the Carrier:

CANCELLED – SPECIMEN COPY

164019

P&OCL B/L2 3/92

Fig. 17.5 A combined transport bill of lading (reproduced by courtesy of P&O Containers)

as either consignor or consignee for the other part of the transit. Nowadays, the standard SITPRO bill of lading has provision for its use as a through bill of lading.

Trans-shipment traffic occurs either because there is no direct route or in order to get a faster transit. It covers the whole spectrum of commodities and at the time of original shipment the final destination of a consignment is known, so that it is possible to make out a through bill of lading.

It is not to be confused with entrepôt traffic, which is essentially limited to raw materials and foodstuffs dealt in by the commodity markets operating in the entrepôt port. At the time of original shipment its destination is the entrepôt port and its final destination will depend on its sale in the market.

17.4.5 Cover bills of lading

Where cargo is short-shipped from an earlier consignment (sometimes by accident, the cargo being left in a shed in error) it has to be sent on by the first available ship. This may be the first ship of the line in question, or a different line may be used in order to preserve goodwill with the exporter or the customer abroad. In such circumstances bills of lading to cover the consignment will be made out addressed to the first carrier's agent in the port of delivery. They will be specific in that they explain the problem and the action taken to rectify the matter. Freight will normally have been paid on the original bill of lading. Such cover bills of lading would only be met in the case of conventional break-bulk shipping, which, although still present in trade with less sophisticated areas, is steadily declining in importance.

17.4.6 Clean, dirty and stale bills

Bills of lading may be clean, dirty or stale. 'Clean' indicates that at the time of shipment the hatch tally which records the physical conditions of the goods as they are loaded had no clause indicating shortage or damage to the goods or insufficiency of packing. A clean, shipped-on-board bill of lading is the normal requirement of a letter of credit.

'Claused' or 'dirty' bills have clauses relating to shortage or damage to the goods or insufficient packing and as such are not normally acceptable under the letter of credit. In the past this often gave rise to shippers requesting the shipping company to issue a clean bill of lading against a *letter of indemnity*, under which they undertook to indemnify the carrier against all claims arising from the consignment. It has been established in the case of *Brown Jenkinson & Co.* v. *Percy Dalton (London) Ltd* (1957) that such an undertaking is not valid in law. The issue of a clean bill in such circumstances is a fraud on anyone buying the bill of lading, believing that he is buying goods 'when all he is really buying is lawsuits'. The agreement is therefore against the public interest and void by illegality.

A more limited letter of indemnity may be perfectly acceptable. Thus where a bill of lading is claused on some particular point (say 'secondhand packing materials used') a letter of indemnity covering that specific point would probably be acceptable. The implication is that the consignor believes the use of secondhand materials for packing will make no difference at all to the condition of the goods on arrival, but if it was found to be otherwise the consignee would be indemnified for any loss suffered.

'Stale' bills of lading are bills of lading that do not arrive before the goods. In these circumstances the importer cannot claim the goods and difficulties may arise in clearing the vessel. One solution is another example of the use of a letter of indemnity – usually in this case backed by a banker's guarantee. The named consignee may undertake to indemnify the carrier against any subsequent claim by any party with a better title to the goods. In return, a delivery order will be made out enabling the consignee to take delivery of the goods.

A bill can also become technically 'stale'. This occurs if it is presented under a letter of credit more than twenty-one days after the date of issue.

17.4.7 Sea waybills

These are non-negotiable documents made out to a named consignee and, providing the latter can give proof of identity, he may claim the goods from the carrier without producing the sea waybill. They therefore overcome the problem of stale bills of lading and are particularly useful for shipments sold on 'open account' terms. 'Open account' terms are used where exporter and importer deal with one another on a regular basis, and with complete confidence that payment will be made. There is no need to use any system which ensures payment is made before the goods are released, such as a 'letter of credit' system, or a 'document against payment' system. Instead the customer is treated like an ordinary debtor in the home trade, and is rendered a 'statement of account' at regular – often monthly – intervals.

The growing trade between parent and subsidiary companies also makes use of sea waybills. Since there is no intention at any time to sell the goods in transit to a third party, the quasi-negotiable properties of a full bill of lading are not required and a sea waybill is adequate for the purpose.

17.4.8 The ship's manifest

The manifest is a summary of all the bills of lading and sea waybills on a vessel, the bills being numbered in order according to each destination port. The Customs and Port Authority at the port of shipment each require a full manifest of cargo and, similarly, each port of destination is provided with a complete manifest, plus a number of copies of its section of the manifest together with a copy bill of lading for each consignment. The other copy bill of lading required by the carrier is the one used for freighting and checking the shipment and is retained in the freight department, along with an extended copy of the manifest which includes details of the freight. Another extended freight manifest is held by the accounts department.

Today manifests are transmitted to interested parties, such as the Port Authorities in destination countries, by electronic data interchange (EDI). Such computer-to-computer interchanges are virtually instantaneous and the information can be accessed by interested parties at any time.

17.4.9 The mate's receipt

Before issuing a shipped bill of lading for cargo which has been loaded direct overside from craft, the carrier will require the shipper to hand over the mate's receipt. This is a receipted lighterage note. If this was not surrendered the shipper would have two receipts signed on behalf of the master for the same goods.

17.4.10 Freight

In the liner trades freight is normally pre-paid and a clause to the effect that freight is deemed 'earned on shipment', whether the cargo or the ship be lost or not lost, is incorporated in the carrier's conditions. If freight is payable at destination, the total freight should be shown on the bill of lading which should be clearly marked 'freight payable at destination'. Some countries now insist that details of freight are shown on the bill of lading.

17.4.11 House bills of lading

With the development of groupage by sea consequent upon containerisation, the house (or forwarding agent's) bill of lading is increasing in importance. Like the carrier's bill of lading it has a negotiable original and non-negotiable copies. Obviously these can only be issued against a carrier's shipped bill of lading taken out by the forwarder and consigned to his agent at destination. The forwarder then issues separate house bills to the various consignors, to be forwarded to their consignees, who then apply to the forwarder's correspondent agent for delivery of the goods at destination. Banks are not prepared to accept such bills of lading under the terms of a letter of credit, unless specifically authorised to do so in the credit. If you are using a groupage forwarder ask your customer to word the letter of credit accordingly.

As previously stated, the bill of lading is technically a carrier's receipt for the carriage of goods by sea. However, with the development of inter-modal services carriers are offering a door-to-door service involving other modes of transport and this has led to the development of the combined transport bill of lading (see section 17.4.2).

17.4.12 The non-negotiable waybill

The bill of lading has a long history of useful service, but it was designed for use in situations where the exporter wished to retain a title to the goods, which he could assign to others at an appropriate moment. There are many situations today where this is unnecessary. For example, when dealing on open account terms, or when operating as a multinational company, the question of maintaining title does not arise. Carriers are therefore beginning to offer a non-negotiable liner waybill as an alternative document to the bill of lading.

The essential features of a liner waybill are that it is non-negotiable and title to the goods depends upon the normal rules for the passing of title. The carrier will deliver the goods to the named consignee or his agent at destination on proof of identity, and the waybill need not even be sent to the consignee. There is therefore no chance of delay, demurrage charges or warehousing costs due to the non-arrival of documents at destination.

It is essentially a 'received for shipment' document though it may be endorsed as 'shipped on board' if required. Some shipping lines are making all their waybills 'shipped' waybills, whereas others are prepared to issue a 'shipped' waybill if required.

The document is a 'short form' document, in that it is only printed on one side, and does not bear on the reverse side the detailed fine print conditions of carriage to be found on the ordinary bill of lading. Instead, a standard clause on the face of the document incorporates the carrier's conditions of carriage into the contract. These will be supplied on request.

The popularity of the non-negotiable waybill has led SITPRO and the General Council of British Shipping to introduce a non-negotiable sea waybill which has been acknowledged by a number of major shipping lines as acceptable in place of bills of lading (see Fig. 17.6). This standard waybill has been provisionally accepted as adequate evidence of exportation for VAT purposes, and also by the Intervention Board for Agricultural Products as evidence of shipment provided it is a 'shipped' waybill. The Export Credit Guarantees Department have accepted it with certain reservations in the case of buyer credit financing and claims under a shipment policy, in which case they require a certificate of shipment if it is only a received for shipment waybill.

17.4.13 Procedure

The exporter, or the forwarding agent, may run off the waybills from the master document if SITPRO aligned documentation is being used. If it is not being used, copies may be purchased from authorised stationers and, after completion, the waybills must be checked for accuracy. If banking transactions are being used, unless a full bill of lading is specified, it is still possible to use the waybill system. The goods, with bank permission, are consigned to the bank at destination or some reliable third party. They will then be released to the foreign importer on payment (or acceptance of a term bill of exchange), by giving written authority to the carrier. If letters of credit are being discussed with a view to an export contract and the use of waybills is envisaged, the letter of credit must be worded so as to render them acceptable.

17.5 The air waybill

Perhaps the most important document these days with the increase in air freight is the air waybill. Its position is interesting, since at present it is non-negotiable and the goods are released to the consignee as of right when they reach their destination. We may conceivably see the introduction of a negotiable air waybill, and it is significant in this respect that Article 15 of the new Warsaw Convention on the Carriage of Goods by Air specifically states: 'Nothing in this Convention prevents the issue of a negotiable air waybill.'

The air waybill is not completely aligned with the SITPRO aligned documentation series, though it does follow largely the original UN layout. Because of its increasing importance as a freight forwarding document a detailed analysis of the boxes to be completed is advisable. These have to be understood in accordance with IATA (International Air Transport

©GCBS
1979/1987
/1992

Shipper　VAT reg. no.

NON-NEGOTIABLE SEA WAYBILL

SWB no.

Shipper's reference

Forwarder's reference

Consignee　VAT reg. no.

Name of carrier

Notify party and address

The contract evidenced by this Waybill is subject to the exceptions, limitations, conditions and liberties (including those relating to pre-carriage and on-carriage) set out in the Carrier's Standard Conditions of Carriage applicable to the voyage covered by this Waybill and operative on its date of issue; if the carriage is one where had a Bill of Lading been issued the provisions of the Hague Rules contained in the International Convention for unification of certain rules relating to Bills of Lading dated Brussels, 25th August, 1924, as amended by the Protocol signed at Brussels on the 23rd February, 1968 (the Hague Visby Rules) would have been compulsorily applicable under Article X, the said Standard Conditions contain or shall be deemed to contain a Clause giving effect to the Hague Visby Rules. Otherwise the said Standard Conditions contain or shall be deemed to contain a Clause giving effect to the provisions of the Hague Rules. In neither case shall the proviso to the first sentence of Article V of the Hague Rules or the Hague Visby Rules apply. The Carrier hereby agrees: (i) that to the extent of any inconsistency the said clause shall prevail over the said Standard Conditions in respect of any period to which the Hague Rules or the Hague Visby Rules by their terms apply, and (ii) that for the purpose of the terms of this Contract of Carriage this Waybill falls within the definition of Article 1(b) of the Hague Rules and the Hague Visby Rules.
The Shipper accepts the said Standard Conditions on his own behalf and on behalf of the Consignee and the owner of the goods and warrants that he has authority to do so. The Consignee by presenting this Waybill and/or requesting delivery of the goods further undertakes all liabilities of the Shipper hereunder, such undertaking being additional and without prejudice to the Shipper's own liability. The benefit of the contract, evidenced by this Waybill shall thereby be transferred to the Consignee or other persons presenting this Waybill.
Notwithstanding anything contained in the said Standard Conditions, the term Carrier in this Waybill shall mean the Carrier named on the front thereof.
A copy of the Carrier's said Standard Conditions applicable hereto may be inspected or will be supplied on request at the office of the Carrier or the Carrier's Principal Agents.

*Applicable only when document used as a Through Sea Waybill

Pre-carriage by*	Place of receipt by pre-carrier*
Vessel	Port of loading
Port of discharge	Place of delivery by on-carrier*

Particulars declared by shipper

Shipping marks; container number	Number and kind of packages; description of goods	Gross weight	Measurement

Freight details; charges etc.

RECEIVED FOR CARRIAGE as above in apparent good order and condition, unless otherwise stated hereon, the goods described in the above particulars.

GCBS
SWB
1987

Ocean freight payable at

Place and date of issue

Signature for carrier; carrier's principal place of business

Form No. 481

Fig. 17.6 A non-negotiable sea waybill (reproduced by courtesy of the SITPRO Board)

Association) definitions, many of which are referred to below. Every air waybill has an identifying number in several parts, the first part being the IATA airline code number – in Fig. 17.7 it is 107.

Air waybills may be completed in English, French, German or Spanish. There are twelve copies, of which three are designated as originals. Each original or copy is marked with its number and the person to whom it is addressed. Thus, the first original copy is marked 'ORIGINAL 1 For Issuing Carrier' and is coloured green.

The pack of air waybills (usually abbreviated to AWB) is made up with either one-off carbon paper or NCR (no carbon required) paper. They are best drawn up on electric or electronic typewriters which have an impression control to ensure that all copies are clear even though there are twelve sheets and eleven carbons to type through.

The distribution is as follows:

Original 1	For issuing carrier (airline) – green copy
Original 2	For consignee – pink copy
Original 3	For shipper – blue copy
Copy No. 4	Delivery receipt – yellow copy
Copy No. 5	For airport of destination
Copy No. 6	For third carrier
Copy No. 7	For second carrier
Copy No. 8	For first carrier
Copy No. 9	For sales agent
Copy No. 10	Extra copy for carrier
Copy No. 11	Invoice
Copy No. 12	For airport of departure

Not all these forms will be used in every consignment but the extra copies are simply discarded.

The air waybill is the carrier's receipt by air and *prima facie* evidence of the contract of affreightment. It is almost always non-negotiable and as a result is not a document of title, despite the fact that it must be made out to a named consignee, who is the only party to whom the carrier can deliver.

Normally AWBs are completed by an air forwarder, although the airline itself may do it. The layout of the AWB has recently been improved and although the various boxes are basically the same, the nature of the document is such that an explanation of some rubrics is essential. The first one which might give rise to problems is the *consignee* rubric, since it is essential that there be a named consignee with a full address and, if known, the telephone number as an optional extra. There is no equivalent to an order bill of lading but a consignor can safeguard his interests by naming the correspondent bank as consignee, providing the bank has previously agreed.

107 LHR 00000011 X 107-00000011

Shipper's Name and Address | Shipper's account Number

EAST ANGLIA FORWARDING LTD
25 CROWELL ROAD
CAMBRIDGE GB
CB1 3ED

Not negotiable
Air Waybill
NEUTRAL AIRWAYBILL
issued by MEMBER OF IATA

Copies 1, 2 and 3 of this Air Waybill are originals and have the same validity

Consignee's Name and Address | Consignee's account Number

EAST ANGLIA FORWARDING CO
JFK INTL AIRPORT
NEW YORK US

It is agreed that the goods described herein are accepted in apparent good order and condition (except as noted) for carriage SUBJECT TO THE CONDITIONS OF CONTRACT ON THE REVERSE HEREOF. THE SHIPPER'S ATTENTION IS DRAWN TO THE NOTICE CONCERNING CARRIERS' LIMITATION OF LIABILITY. Shipper may increase such limitation of liability by declaring a higher value for carriage and paying a supplemental charge if required.

Issuing Carrier's Agent Name and City
EAST ANGLIA FWDG. 25 CROMWELL ROAD
CAMBRIDGE. GB.

Accounting Information

Agent's IATA Code: 9147028 0005 | Account No.

Airport of Departure (Addr. of first Carrier) and requested Routing: LHR

to	By first Carrier	Routing and Destination	to	by	to	by	Currency	CHGS Code	WT/VAL PPD	WT/VAL COLL	Other PPD	Other COLL	Declared Value for Carriage	Declared Value for Customs
JFK	BA						GBP		X		X		NVD	500.00

Airport of Destination: NEW YORK | Flight/Date: BA001 02 | For Carrier Use only | Flight/Date | Amount of Insurance

INSURANCE - If carrier offers insurance, and such insurance is requested in accordance with conditions on reverse hereof, indicate amount to be insured in figures in box marked 'amount of insurance'

Handling Information
ADD AND INVOICE REF KC001
SEC CODE AT-1-ER

No of Pieces RCP	Gross Weight	kg lb	Rate Class / Commodity Item No.	Chargeable Weight	Rate / Charge	Total	Nature and Quantity of Goods (incl. Dimensions or Volume)
1	10	K	M		50.00	50.00	ELECTRICAL EQUIPMENT
1	10.0					50.00	

Prepaid	Weight Charge	Collect
50.00		
	Valuation Charge	
	Tax	
	Total other Charges Due Agent	
	Total other Charges Due Carrier	
13.00		
Total prepaid 63.00		Total collect 0.00
Currency Conversion Rates		cc charges in Dest. Currency
For Carrier's Use only at Destination	Charges at Destination	Total collect Charges

Other Charges
CLEARANCE-HANDL ORG DUE CARRIER 13.00

Shipper certifies that the particulars on the face hereof are correct and that insofar as any part of the consignment contains dangerous goods, such part is properly described by name and is in proper condition for carriage by air according to the applicable Dangerous Goods Regulations.

Signature of Shipper or his Agent

01APR93 LHR CAMBRIDGE. GB.
Executed on (Date) at (Place) Signature of issuing Carrier or its Agent

107-00000011

ORIGINAL 3 (FOR SHIPPER)

Fig. 17.7 An air waybill (reproduced by courtesy of East Anglia Forwarding Ltd, Cambridge)

Where goods are being forwarded in advance for subsequent collection, they should be dispatched to the airline's agent at destination and marked 'to await arrival', with an estimated time of arrival (ETA). This type of consignment also requires a contact address with telephone number for use in case of non-collection and this information would be one of the items appearing under the *handling information* rubric.

Most large air forwarders are recognised IATA agents and as such can enter into contracts with IATA members to issue and sign AWBs on their behalf. Their name would thus appear under *issuing carrier's agent, name and city* and they would subsequently sign and date the AWB on behalf of the carrier. Their number would also appear under *agent's IATA code*. The airports of departure and destination are shown in full but references to other airports in the routeing or under RCP (rate construction point) use the airport's three-letter code. Similarly, the first carrier is shown in full but others are referred to by their codes.

The *accounting information* rubric is used to enter instructions to the airline regarding non-routine charges, such as when the airline is to be responsible for clearing and delivering goods at destination.

The *currency* entered under that rubric must be used for all calculations and values on the waybill, up to the *total pre-paid* or *total collect* point after which the carrier may convert to the destination currency.

Charges can either be pre-paid or collect and should be indicated by marking an X in the relevant boxes. They will then appear on the relevant side below the rubrics (e.g. *weight charge*, etc.), at the foot of the page. Although the *weight and valuation charges* must both be either pre-paid or collect, other charges such as cartage, insurance, AWB preparation, etc., might be different from the weight/valuation charge, e.g. if the latter is collect, they might be pre-paid.

The *declared value for carriage* rubric is used when the value is high and the customer wishes to increase the carrier's liability accordingly. If he enters a value here it will be the basis of a surcharge calculation which gives a valuation charge which is additional to the weight charge. This may be compared with an *ad valorem* surcharge by sea. If he does not wish to increase the carrier's liability he enters NVD (no value declared) in the box. The latest edition of the AWB has a separate *value for customs* rubric, whereas previously this was one of the items under *handling information*. The *amount of insurance* rubric does not appear as a separate box on some air waybills but would be entered under other charges. It is only completed if the shipper wishes the first carrier to effect cargo insurance on his behalf. The conditions and premiums will vary between carriers and the carrier must be notified of any special risks so that a fair premium can be agreed.

We have already mentioned earlier one item that appears under the *handling information* rubric. Other items include marks and numbers, method of packing, a list of attached documents and any special handling instructions (e.g. 'This way up').

Immediately under *number of pieces* is the rate construction point (RCP) which is denoted by the three-letter code for the airport over which the rate is constructed. Constructed rates occur where, by taking advantage of a specific commodity rate with its larger quantity discounts for part of the journey and then adding the 'on carriage' rate, which may well be a domestic cabotage rate, it produces a through rate which is cheaper than the direct quantity discount rate. It must be borne in mind that the rate may be constructed over an airport actually on the route flown, or another scheduled direct route, or even on a hypothetical route, where transshipment would be necessary if the goods actually moved that way. Rate class is denoted by various capital letters as follows: M = minimum, N = normal, Q = quantity discount, R = rebated goods, S = surcharge, C = specific commodity; X, in addition to one of the above, indicates that an IATA registered container is used and a discount is claimed.

Commodity item no. refers to specific commodity rates.

Chargeable weight can be any of five as follows:

1. Minimum.
2. Gross weight.
3. Gross weight rounded up to next quantity flat rate.
4. Weight measurement equivalent.
5. Weight measurement equivalent rounded up to next quantity flat rate.

Next follows the rate to be charged and then the total weight charge. The description of the goods should be in sufficient detail that they can be readily identified, both for customs clearance and also in determining whether or not a *specific commodity rate* is applicable. The dimensions of the individual packages and the total volume should also appear. The extra charges such as insurance, cartage, air waybill preparation, etc., are shown separately under *Other charges* with a C or an A to indicate whether it is a charge due to the carrier or agent. These charges are then shown in either the 'Pre-paid' or 'Collect' column and added to the weight and valuation charge to give a total overall.

17.5.1 House air waybills

Just as a consolidator may issue house bills of lading, it may be necessary to produce house air waybills. SITPRO has now designed a standard form for house air waybills, based on international standards. It is clearly desirable that consolidators should be able to have house air waybills integrated into their mechanised or computerised systems.

17.6 The CMR consignment note

The CMR consignment note is the result of an international convention called the *Convention de Marchandises par Route*, which may be freely translated as the Convention on Merchandise carried by Road Hauliers. This convention was held to attempt to resolve some of the difficulties arising in international road haulage by the different legal systems under which hauliers operate. For example, English law permits the haulier to strike any sort of bargain in his contracts, so long as the other party agrees. So English hauliers, before the convention, often refused to be liable even for their own negligence. An account of the legal effects of the convention is given in a companion volume, *Elements of Export Law*, but here all we need to say is that the general conclusion of the convention was that hauliers ought to be liable for the things they do wrongly, but ought not to be liable for things which were not their fault, such as strikes.

Most hauliers carrying goods internationally now use this consignment note, since they are bound by the rules laid down in the Convention under the Carriage of Goods by Road Act 1965. Some foreign countries insist that UK hauliers use this consignment note which is compulsory for Continental hauliers. It is more acceptable everywhere than an ordinary waybill and therefore difficulties are usually smoothed out at the mere sight of the conventional document.

The form is reproduced in Fig. 17.8. Members may obtain supplies from the Road Haulage Association and the Freight Transport Association.

17.7 The CIM consignment note

The CIM consignment note meets the requirements of the *Convention Internationale concernant le Transport des Marchandises par Chemin de Fer* – freely translated as the Convention on International Merchandise carried by Rail. The first CIM Convention was held before the First World War, when the only international movements of goods apart from sea transits were international rail transits. The problems of goods crossing frontiers in those days were the same as the present difficulties – caused by the conflict of laws that might arise. The United Kingdom was not very interested in those days, and did not ratify the convention for about fifty years, but, as explained earlier, the situation is now very different and the opening of the Channel Tunnel will make international rail haulage the logical way to move long-distance freight. British Rail now completes all CIM documentation, and the only requirement for exporters is to get the data to Dover where the documents are produced. This is best done by electronic data interchange (EDI) or fax. The convention is fully described in a companion volume, *Export Law*.

LETTRE DE VOITURE INTERNATIONALE (CMR) **INTERNATIONAL CONSIGNMENT NOTE**

COPY 1 SENDER
COPY 2 CONSIGNEE
COPY 3 CARRIER

Approved by FTA/RHA/SITPRO UK 1981

Sender (Name, Address, Country) Expéditeur (Nom, Addresse, Pays) 1

Customs Reference/Status Référence/désignation pour mise en douane 2

Senders/Agents Reference Référence de l'expéditeur/de l'agent 3

Consignee (Name, Address, Country) Destinataire (Nom, Addresse, Pays) 4

Carrier (Name, Address, Country) Transporteur (Nom, Addresse, Pays) 5

Place & date of taking over the goods (place, country, date)
Lieu et date de la prise en charge des marchandises (Lieu, pays, date) 6

Successive Carriers Transporteurs successifs 7

Place designated for delivery of goods (place, country)
Lieu prévu pour la livraison des marchandises (lieu, pays) 8

This carriage is subject, notwithstanding any clause to the contrary, to the Convention on the Contract for the International Carriage of Goods by Road (CMR)
Ce transport est soumis nonobstant toute clause contraire à la Convention Relative au Contrat de Transport International de Marchandises par Route (CMR)

*NB FOR DANGEROUS GOODS

INDICATE
1. CORRECT TECHNICAL NAME (PROPER SHIPPING NAME)
2. HAZARD CLASS
3. UN NUMBER
4. FLASHPOINT (IF ANY)

Marks & Nos, No & Kind of Packages, Description of Goods* Marques et Nos, No et nature des colis, Désignation des marchandises* 9

Gross weight (kg) 10 Poids Brut (kg)

Volume (m^3) 11 Cubage (m^3)

Carriage Charges Prix de transport 12

Senders Instructions for Customs, etc Instructions de l'Expéditeur (optional) 13

Reservations Réserves 14

Documents attached Documents Annexés (optional) 15

Special agreements Conventions particulières (optional) 16

Goods Received/Marchandises Reçues 17

Signature of Carrier/Signature du transporteur 18

Company completing this note Société émettrice 19

Place and Date; Signature Lieu et date; Signature 20

730

Fig. 17.8 The CMR consignment note (reproduced by courtesy of the SITPRO Board)

As far as the document is concerned the layout is similar to the CMR consignment note in many ways and is largely self-explanatory to readers who have already considered the SITPRO master document in detail. The CMR document is reproduced in Fig. 17.8.

17.8 The standard shipping note

The standard shipping note (SSN) was the first form produced in the SITPRO aligned series and replaced a multiplicity of non-aligned forms supplied by UK ports. It enables goods to be supplied to any port, airport or container depot on a standard form which incorporates all the details required, most of them from the master document already described.

Most additional details required on the form may be reproduced from a master document by utilising some of its free areas. Other static information, as in box 12 of the standard shipping note (which refers to special stowage arrangements) can be incorporated in the film overlay. As snap-apart sets of standard shipping notes use carbonless self-copy paper, they are not suitable for processing in semi-dry dyeline machines or plain paper copiers. Loose forms are available for spirit machines or firms may make their own under licence.

The standard shipping note (see Fig. 17.9) is rapidly gaining ground in its use for shipments of general cargo via any UK port. It is sent to the dock with the goods, except for the Port of Liverpool, where a special arrangement exists. The purpose of the shipping note is to acquaint the port authority with the nature of the goods being handed into its care, their destination, the vessel on which they are to be loaded, and any special stowage features. It is also used to calculate the port rates payable.

One copy of the shipping note is sent to the carrier's head office to notify the delivery of the goods to the dock. After shipment the tally details are incorporated in the other two copies, one of which is retained in the dock. The other is sent to the head office as a *dock return*, linking the persons physically handling the cargo with the *bill passer* who is then able to complete and sign the bill of lading on the master's behalf. Usually the sixth copy of the SSN is used on delivering the goods to the road haulier to obtain a signature acknowledging the number and condition of the packages. The fifth copy is similarly returned to the haulier as a receipt from the port authority.

17.8.1 Procedure

The shipping note is most easily run off from the master document of a SITPRO aligned system. If it is to be typed up separately it may be

© SITPRO 1991

STANDARD SHIPPING NOTE – FOR NON-DANGEROUS GOODS ONLY

IMPORTANT USE THE DANGEROUS GOODS NOTE IF THE GOODS ARE CLASSIFIED AS DANGEROUS ACCORDING TO APPLICABLE REGULATIONS SEE BOX 10A

Exporter 1

Customs reference/status 2

Booking number 3

Exporter's reference 4

Forwarder's reference 5

6

Freight forwarder 7

International carrier 8

For use of receiving authority only

Other UK transport details (e.g. ICD, terminal, vehicle bkg. ref., receiving dates) 9

The Company preparing this note declares that, to the best of their belief, the goods have been accurately described, their quantities, weights and measurements are correct and at the time of despatch they were in good order and condition; that the goods are not classified as dangerous in any UK, IMO, ADR, RID or IATA/ICAO regulation applicable to the intended modes of transport. 10A

Vessel/flight no. and date — Port/airport of loading 10

Port/airport of discharge — Destination 11

TO THE RECEIVING AUTHORITY - Please receive for shipment the goods described below subject to your published regulations and conditions (including those as to liability).

Shipping marks — Number and kind of packages; description of goods; non-hazardous special stowage requirements 12 — Gross wt (kg) of goods 13A — Cube (m³) of goods 14

FORMECON SERVICES LIMITED
SITPRO Approved Licensee No. 21

For use of shipping company only — Total gross weight of goods — Total cube of goods

PREFIX and container/trailer number(s) 16 — Seal number(s) 16A — Container/trailer size(s) and type(s) 16B — Tare wt (kg) as marked on CSC plate 16C — Total of boxes 13A and 16C 16D

DOCK/TERMINAL RECEIPT Received the above number of packages/containers/trailers in apparent good order and condition unless stated hereon.
RECEIVING AUTHORITY REMARKS

Name of company preparing this note 17

Haulier's Name

Vehicle reg. no.

Date

DRIVER'S SIGNATURE — SIGNATURE AND DATE

(Indicate name and telephone number of contact)

630 Non-completion of any boxes is a subject for resolution by the contracting parties.

Standard Shipping Notes and Dangerous Goods Notes obtainable from Formecon Services Ltd 0270-500800 — SSN J.094

Fig. 17.9 The Standard Shipping Note (reproduced by courtesy of the SITPRO Board)

purchased as 'snap-apart' sets from authorised stationery suppliers. It must be checked carefully to ensure accuracy and conformity with other documents. (Note that the aligned system saves all this checking of individual documents – once the master is right every document prepared from it will be right.) In the Port of Liverpool (not Seaforth Container Terminal) it is lodged with the Port Authority in advance of the goods. With all other ports and container depots it is sent to the dock with the goods.

17.9 The export cargo shipping instructions

These days freight forwarding is such a specialist occupation that many exporters find it both convenient and economical to use the services of a freight forwarder. In designing an aligned document to assist exporters in instructing freight forwarders, SITPRO have liaised fully with the Institute of Freight Forwarders Ltd, the leading trade association in this field. The result is a document which, while being largely run off the master document, contains the following additional sections which can be completed by a sub-master:

1. A 'documentation' section, which may be completed by the exporter requesting the documents needed, and giving instructions for their disposal once they have been prepared.
2. A 'charges payable by' section, which indicates how the various charges are to be allocated.
3. A section which gives full instructions on any hazardous goods.
4. An undertaking by the exporter to agree to the freight forwarder's terms and conditions.

It is, therefore, a most efficient and carefully designed document, as may be seen from Fig. 17.10.

17.9.1 Procedure

The export cargo shipping instructions are most easily run off from the master document of the SITPRO system, the special details for instructing the forwarder being run off from a sub-master at the same time. If prepared separately on a non-aligned form they must be checked carefully to ensure that the instructions are correct and clear. If a letter of credit is involved, it is wise to send the forwarder a copy of it so that he can ensure complete compliance.

With air transits it is usual to hand the instructions to the driver who collects the goods (after checking his credentials). With surface movements

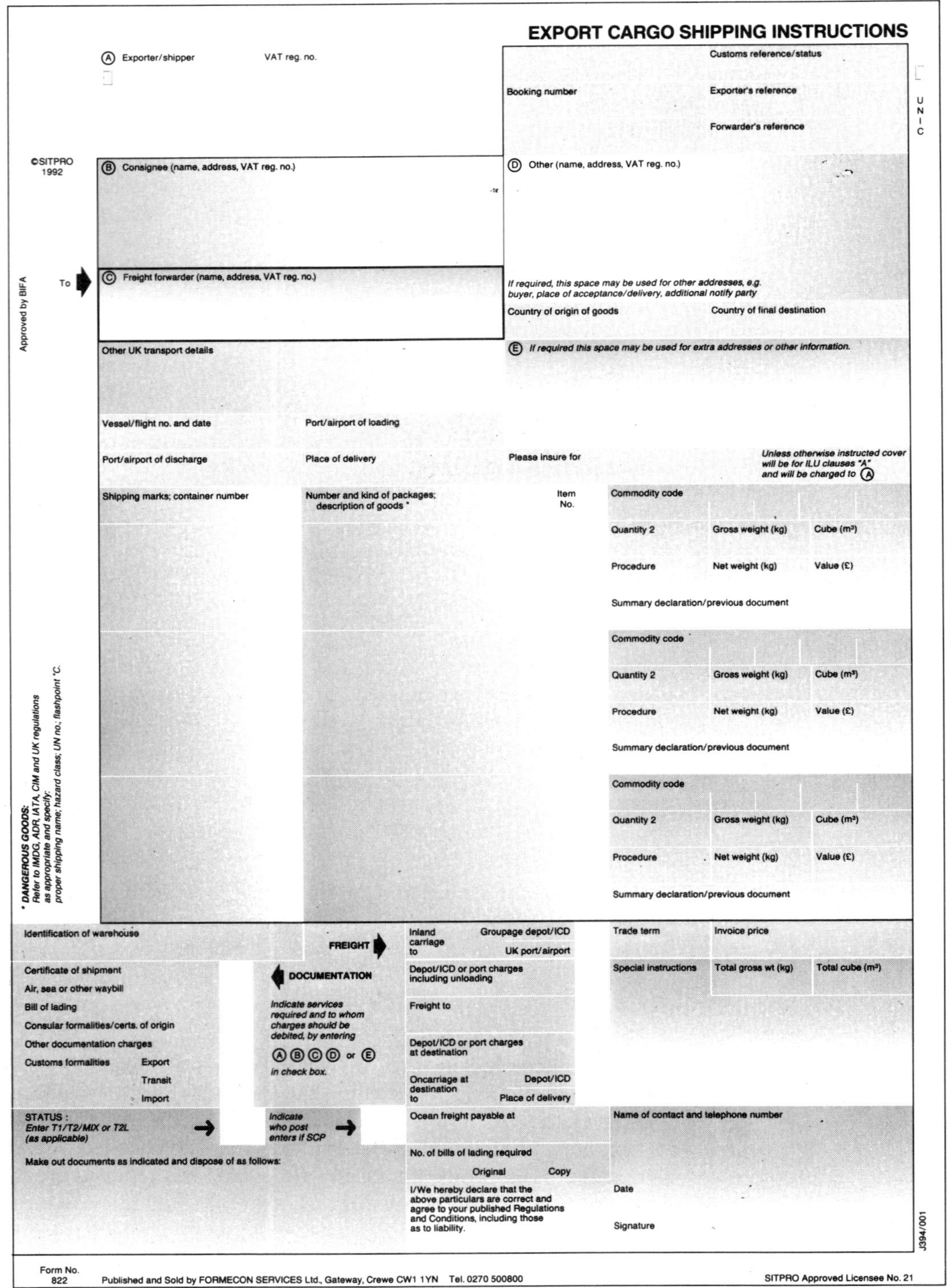

EXPORT CARGO SHIPPING INSTRUCTIONS

Ⓐ Exporter/shipper — VAT reg. no.

Customs reference/status

Booking number — Exporter's reference

Forwarder's reference

UNIC

©SITPRO 1992

Ⓑ Consignee (name, address, VAT reg. no.)

Ⓓ Other (name, address, VAT reg. no.)

To ➡ Ⓒ Freight forwarder (name, address, VAT reg. no.)

If required, this space may be used for other addresses, e.g. buyer, place of acceptance/delivery, additional notify party

Approved by BIFA

Country of origin of goods — Country of final destination

Other UK transport details

Ⓔ *If required this space may be used for extra addresses or other information.*

Vessel/flight no. and date — Port/airport of loading

Port/airport of discharge — Place of delivery — Please insure for

Unless otherwise instructed cover will be for ILU clauses "A" and will be charged to Ⓐ

Shipping marks; container number — Number and kind of packages; description of goods * — Item No.

Commodity code

Quantity 2 — Gross weight (kg) — Cube (m³)

Procedure — Net weight (kg) — Value (£)

Summary declaration/previous document

Commodity code

Quantity 2 — Gross weight (kg) — Cube (m³)

Procedure — Net weight (kg) — Value (£)

Summary declaration/previous document

Commodity code

Quantity 2 — Gross weight (kg) — Cube (m³)

Procedure — Net weight (kg) — Value (£)

Summary declaration/previous document

*** DANGEROUS GOODS:**
Refer to IMDG, ADR, IATA, CIM and UK regulations as appropriate and specify: proper shipping name; hazard class; UN no.; flashpoint °C.

Identification of warehouse

FREIGHT ➡

Inland carriage to — Groupage depot/ICD — UK port/airport

Trade term — Invoice price

Special instructions — Total gross wt (kg) — Total cube (m³)

Certificate of shipment

Air, sea or other waybill

Bill of lading

Consular formalities/certs. of origin

Other documentation charges

Customs formalities — Export — Transit — Import

⬅ DOCUMENTATION

Indicate services required and to whom charges should be debited, by entering Ⓐ Ⓑ Ⓒ Ⓓ or Ⓔ *in check box.*

Depot/ICD or port charges including unloading

Freight to

Depot/ICD or port charges at destination

Oncarriage at destination to — Depot/ICD — Place of delivery

STATUS:
Enter T1/T2/MIX or T2L (as applicable) ➡

Indicate who post enters if SCP ➡

Ocean freight payable at

Name of contact and telephone number

Make out documents as indicated and dispose of as follows:

No. of bills of lading required — Original — Copy

I/We hereby declare that the above particulars are correct and agree to your published Regulations and Conditions, including those as to liability.

Date

Signature

J394/001

Form No. 822 — Published and Sold by FORMECON SERVICES Ltd., Gateway, Crewe CW1 1YN Tel. 0270 500800 — SITPRO Approved Licensee No. 21

Fig. 17.10 The export cargo shipping instructions (reproduced by courtesy of Formecon Services Ltd)

it is better, if postal services are normal, to send the instructions ahead of the goods by post.

17.10 The single administrative document (SAD)

The single administrative document is a customs document drawn up by the Commission of the European Union (formerly the European Community) for use throughout the Union. Originally designed (as its name implies) to fulfil the functions of former export, transit and import documents its use has been limited to a certain extent by the introduction of the Single Market on 1 January 1993. Under these new arrangements the controls formerly exercised over cross-border movements within the Union have largely ceased, and the use of the SAD reduced. However, it still has some part to play in export movements to non-Union states and in controls over certain types of movements still subject to control within the EU. The document is illustrated in Fig. 17.11.

17.11 The EUR1 and EUR2

These forms are used when goods are exported from the European Union to certain trade areas with which the Union has established preferential tariff arrangements. These areas include the EFTA countries, Israel, etc. The EUR1 constitutes a declaration that the goods exported come within the terms of the preferential trade agreements. The conditions of the agreements and their rules of origin are explained in customs notices. The EUR1 is illustrated in Fig. 17.12.

EUR1 requires customs certification, but EUR2 is for consignments of lower value sent by post and certification is not required.

17.12 Electronic data interchange (EDI)

Electronic data interchange is the interchange, in electronic form, of information, formerly provided on documents, between interested parties. This revolutionary method of dealing with the many facts (data) that need to be passed between logistical firms, exporters, customers, agents, carriers and control authorities such as H.M. Customs has such advantages that it is certain eventually to be universally adopted. The difficulty is that a high degree of standardisation is necessary for what will be a world-wide system, and although considerable progress has been made many details have yet to be finalised.

EUROPEAN COMMUNITY

1 DECLARATION

A OFFICE OF DISPATCH/EXPORT/DESTINATION

1 6

2 Consignor/*Exporter* No

3 Forms | 4 Loading lists

5 Items | 6 Total packages | 7 Reference number

Copy for the country of dispatch/export

Copy for the country of destination

8 Consignee No

9 Person responsible for financial settlement No

10 *Cty 1st dest/ last consig* | 11 *Trad/Prod country* | 12 *Value details* | 13 *CAP*

14 Declarant/Representative No

15 Country of dispatch/*export* | 15 C disp/*exp* Code a| b| | 17 Country destn Code a| b|

16 Country of origin | 17 Country of destination

18 Identity and nationality of means of transport at departure/on arrival | 19 Ctr

20 Delivery terms

21 Identity and nationality of active means of transport crossing the border

22 Currency and total amount invoiced | 23 Exchange rate | 24 Nature of transaction

25 Mode of transport at the border | 26 Inland mode of transport | 27 Place of loading/unloading

28 Financial and banking data

1 6

29 Office of exit/entry | 30 Location of goods

31 Packages and description of goods | Marks and numbers — Container No(s) — Number and kind

32 Item No | 33 Commodity Code

34 Country origin Code a| b| | 35 Gross mass (kg) | 36 *Preference*

37 PROCEDURE | 38 Net mass (kg) | 39 *Quota*

40 Summary declaration/Previous document

41 Supplementary units | 42 *Item price* | 43 *VM Code*

44 Additional information/ Documents produced/ Certificates and authorisations

A I Code | 45 *Adjustment*

46 Statistical value

47 Calculation of taxes

Type	Tax base	Rate	Amount	MP
		Total:		

48 Deferred payment | 49 Identification of warehouse

B ACCOUNTING DETAILS

50 Principal No | Signature

C OFFICE OF DEPARTURE

represented by

Place and date

51 Intended offices of transit (and country)

52 Guarantee not valid for | Code | 53 Office of destination (and country)

D/J CONTROL BY OFFICE OF DEPARTURE/DESTINATION | Stamp

Result

Seals affixed: Number:

identity

Time limit (date)

Signature

54 Place and date

Signature and name of declarant/representative

C88A L.T. Printing 051-647 8006 SITPRO Approved Licensee No. 11

Fig. 17.11 The Single Administrative Document (SAD) (Customs 88) (reproduced by courtesy of the SITPRO Board)

MOVEMENT CERTIFICATE

1. Exporter *(Name, full address, country)*

EUR1 No. Q 766731

See notes overleaf before completing this form.

2. Application for a certificate to be used in preferential trade between
THE EUROPEAN ECONOMIC COMMUNITY
and
....
(Insert appropriate countries or groups of countries or territories)

3. Consignee *(Name, full address, country) (Optional)*

4. Country, group of countries or territory in which the products are considered as originating
EEC

5. Country, group of countries or territory of destination

6. Transport details *(Optional)*

7. Remarks

(1) If goods are not packed indicate number of articles or state "in bulk" as appropriate.

8. Item number: marks & numbers | Number and kind of packages (1): description of goods

9. Gross weight (kg) or other measure (litres, cu. m., etc.)

10. Invoices (Optional)

(2) Complete only where the regulations of the exporting country or territory require.

11. CUSTOMS ENDORSEMENT
Declaration certified
Export document (2):
Form..............................No. ....
Customs office ....
Issuing country or territory:
UNITED KINGDOM
Date..............................
....
(Signature)

Stamp

12. DECLARATION BY THE EXPORTER
I, the undersigned, declare that the goods described above meet the conditions required for the issue of this certificate.

(Place and date)
....
(Signature)
....

C 1299 CD 0322/2/N3(3/88)

Printed in the UK for HMSO. 5.88 Dd. 8121057. C420. 53031

Fig. 17.12 The EUR1 form (reproduced by courtesy of Her Majesty's Stationery Office)

The chief benefits to be derived from EDI are as follows:

1. *Reduced paperwork*. EDI gives hope for reduced paperwork and its replacement by computer-to-computer interchanges at electronic speeds. The administrative costs of handling documents are great, and the possibilities of error are legion, whereas with computer-to-computer transfers there is a great saving of double-handling and rekeying of information. The idea of paperless trading has often been mooted, but today it is within everyone's grasp if prejudices around the world can be overcome.
2. *Improved accuracy*. There is no need to check and cross-check information once data have passed the initial validation procedures built into the software. An incorrect entry from a terminal will be detected in the validation process, and will be returned to terminal for investigation, correction and rekeying. Once validated that information is available in its correct form to any interested party in the network.
3. *Faster receipt of information*. There are enormous savings to be made in such areas as the stuffing of containers, groupage, the allocation of cargoes to holds, clearance through Customs, scheduling of vehicles, etc. as a result of computerisation. The computer can keep track of the location of cargoes, supervise stowage to preserve the trim of the vessel, trace shipments required for particular ports, etc.
4. *Control of transportation*. The computer can plan routes, avoid congested areas, divert vehicles and ships in emergencies, update documentation, etc. In railway (CIM) movements the carrier now makes out the documents, and all that is necessary is for the exporter/forwarder to make sure that the data are supplied to the location near the south coast where the CIM document is produced.
5. *Moving at electronic speeds*: documents such as invoices arrive immediately and move up the queue for payment as a result. A faster invoice–payment cycle brings financial economies, reduced borrowing levels and smaller interest payments.
6. *Parties to transactions are linked through EDI*: a more stable relationship thereby exists for trading on a regular basis. There is less temptation to move to competitors, especially if the EDI link will lost by doing so. Higher volumes of movements are possible, for an EDI link cannot easily be overloaded – it always has spare capacity as far as any individual trader is concerned.

17.12.1 The basic principles of EDI

The basic principle of EDI is the transfer of structured business data from computer to computer to eliminate the need for paper documents. By 'structured business data' we mean any typical body of information that would traditionally have meant the use of a document – especially an aligned document. Thus purchase orders, invoices, shipping instructions and many other documents can easily be converted into an equivalent EDI form (albeit highly coded), giving the same information to any end-user who has access to the system. An electronic document is called a 'message format' and is in standard form. These standards have been built up over the years, and the world standard for international trade is UN EDIFACT. The SITPRO office is prepared to supply further information on UN EDIFACT.

Under the EDI system the usual procedure is for each trader to be linked to a 'store and call-forward' network run by a major operator such as BT, AT & T, GE1S, etc. The trader has the ability to send messages at any convenient time to suit his or her business, and to call forward any messages waiting in the electronic mail box. Eventually, direct trader-to-trader links will be possible.

17.12.1.1 *Standard message formats*

If we agree to move over to EDI we must all agree on two main points:

1. Which pieces of information are needed for a particular business activity – such as a shipping instruction or an air waybill?
2. Which sequence shall we all agree on so that the computer knows which bit is coming next and where it should go on its records?

The UN EDIFACT system lays down certain rules for putting pieces of information together. Since these are rather like the rules for putting sentences together in a language they are called 'syntax rules'. It also maintains groups of bits of information (segments) and whole messages which deal with a particular function (called 'standard messages'). All people who adopt a particular standard message for a particular function can exchange information with others who use the standard.

The problem is that a world-wide network is the real solution to the problem of world-wide trade, yet the establishment of such a network is only possible to very large organisations, which invariably are based in different countries and exist in a climate of friendly (or perhaps unfriendly) rivalry. While the UN may be able to set the standards for syntax and standard messages, the actual establishment of networks to link traders around the world requires these big operators to allow access to their systems by customers of other systems, in a truly global network of services. This is easy enough to say, but more difficult to arrange. To illustrate the thinking behind the system, as well as the system itself, we have chosen the new airport cargo processing system, which grew out of ACP 90 (Air Cargo Processing for the 90s) used by all UK airports until 1993, when the new CCS-UK system was introduced.

17.12.2 The CCS–UK system

Mention has been made above of the way this new system developed out of the ACP 90, the air cargo processing system in use at UK airports. The problem was to extend the intercommunication of business partners in the trade and transport fields to the fullest extent, while at the same time protecting the investments already made by the various firms in a huge variety of computerised systems. A major strategic study was started by British Telecom to identify the features of a system which would meet the whole range of needs in this complex of industries, while at the same time enabling those who had already invested to utilise existing equipment for its working lifetime. The concept was one of 'controlled migration', the gradual moving over of all end-users to a truly international system as the normal course of fair wear and tear rendered their existing equipment inefficient and ready for replacement.

The focus of a successful strategy proved to be inter-computer communications by an EDI messaging infrastructure. The essential starting point for an international system is the laying down of standards for a message-based system. The end-users had to be able to join the system with their existing technology, maintain full visibility of their consignments from start to finish and secure from the system those solutions to their ordinary business problems which they were entitled to expect if their businesses were to prosper. Of course, new firms coming into the system could start with the new technology, rather than migrating to it at some later date, but would also need to be inducted into the system. The full success of an EDI system depends on incoming messages being responded to by reliable and meaningful information provided by carriers, forwarders, exporters and importers. New users have to learn that everyone in the network has a part to play if the desirable level of efficiency is to be achieved.

The BT strategy study revealed the following key factors:

- The need for the new system to enable users with in-house computer systems to exchange information with each other.
- Conformity to international standards.
- Assured connectivity to other community systems world-wide.
- Protection of existing investments in systems and technology.
- Ease of use and access for new EDI users.
- The provision of a range of functions to enable users to implement their business requirements in a fast, secure and reliable communications environment.
- The need for all aspects of development to be driven by business needs.

The prime requirement emerged unchanged. The system should offer tangible business benefits, giving all members of the user-community a real service edge, and promoting profitable growth of the market overall.

17.12.3 The main components of the CCS-UK system

The main components of the system are the following:

1. *Message switching*. This core system component conforms to the IATA C-STAR standard to give a high-performance message and switching service.
2. *End-user distributed systems*. As far as the end-user is concerned he wants the system to carry out a range of in-house activities irrespective of the wider EDI facilities. These must be provided, but then the EDI gateway to the wider trade community provides the whole range of BT network services.
3. *The intelligent network*. While the end-user has a basic set of facilities through the central switch and end-user systems there is optional access to the BT global network service (GNS).
4. *International gateways and external customers*. Finally, these systems give access to other global systems in use around the world such as EDI*NET in North America. As EDI messaging increasingly becomes the preferred method of data interchange, end-users will be in direct communication, both nationally and internationally, with all those active in the field of international trade, cargo handling, distribution management and international payments.

17.12.4 The development of CCS-UK from ACP 90

The following account of how CCS-UK has developed from the ACP 90 system has been taken from their journal, *ASM News*, by courtesy of Agency Sector Management (UK) Ltd, who designed the ASM 2000 software (ASM 2000 is the component of CCS-UK which is end-user software for use by freight agents).

17.12.4.1 How will ASM 2000 differ from ACP 90?

Agents currently use personal computers to access the ACP 90 mainframe computer in Hemel Hempstead, using datalines (telephone lines adapted to carry computer data). In the same way that a telephone converts your voice into electronic signals, ACP 90 PCs convert your keystrokes into signals, which are acted upon by the ACP 90 computer. ACP 90 PCs are, in effect, communication terminals. ASM 2000 has been designed as an application software package tailored to take advantage of the power offered by PCs. It will include communication capabilities similar to the terminals currently used on ACP 90; however, ASM 2000 will do much more. Under the new system the personal computers using ASM 2000 will take over many of the processing tasks that are currently done by the ACP 90 mainframe computer.

For example, when goods arrive and the transit shed operator (TSO), or airline, input a post-arrival air waybill, the record will be sent to the agent's PC, where it will be processed and stored. Once this is done, the agent will simply access his own PC and create a customs entry without needing to access a mainframe computer. In fact, there will be no mainframe computer to access once ASM 2000 goes live.

17.12.5 The new CCS-UK system

Figure 17.13(a) shows the CCS-UK system which will replace ACP 90. For the sake of simplicity, we are showing only one agent, one TSO and one airline. In reality, the CCS-UK system will serve all the contracting agents, TSOs and ASI airlines in the United Kingdom. (An ASI airline is an airline with a system in-house, which has been connected into the general computer system by accredited software.)

This type of redevelopment or 'distribution' of air cargo processing will embrace all users of the current system. In addition to the work being done on ASM 2000, similar design and development work is being undertaken for ABS 2000, the independent TSO bureau system (which is currently part of the ACP 90 mainframe operation). The central database will incorporate customs local processing (currently operated in the ACP 90 computer). CHIEF (customs handling for import and export freight) and the ASIs will be accessed directly via the CCS-UK message switch in a manner similar to that in which ASIs and DEPS (The Departmental Entry Processing System of H.M. Customs) are currently accessed via ACP 90.

By separating and distributing the functions which are currently centralised in ACP 90, an entirely new sort of communications capability is being adopted: interactive electronic data interchange (Interactive EDI). This system of exchanging messages is being designed to ensure that all the computers on the system are able to communicate and interact responsively. An example of this is outlined in Fig. 17.13(b).

In Fig. 17.13(b) an entry clearance message is issued by CHIEF (Message 1) and sent to the community database via the CCS-UK switch. The database receives the message and updates the consignment record, which will have been previously created by an ASI or ABS 2000. Message 2 is immediately issued from the central database to that airline or TSO. This automatically updates the ASI or TSO record and initiates further processing. Another message (Message 3) is also issued immediately to the nominated agent's PC where the record on his ASM 2000 system is

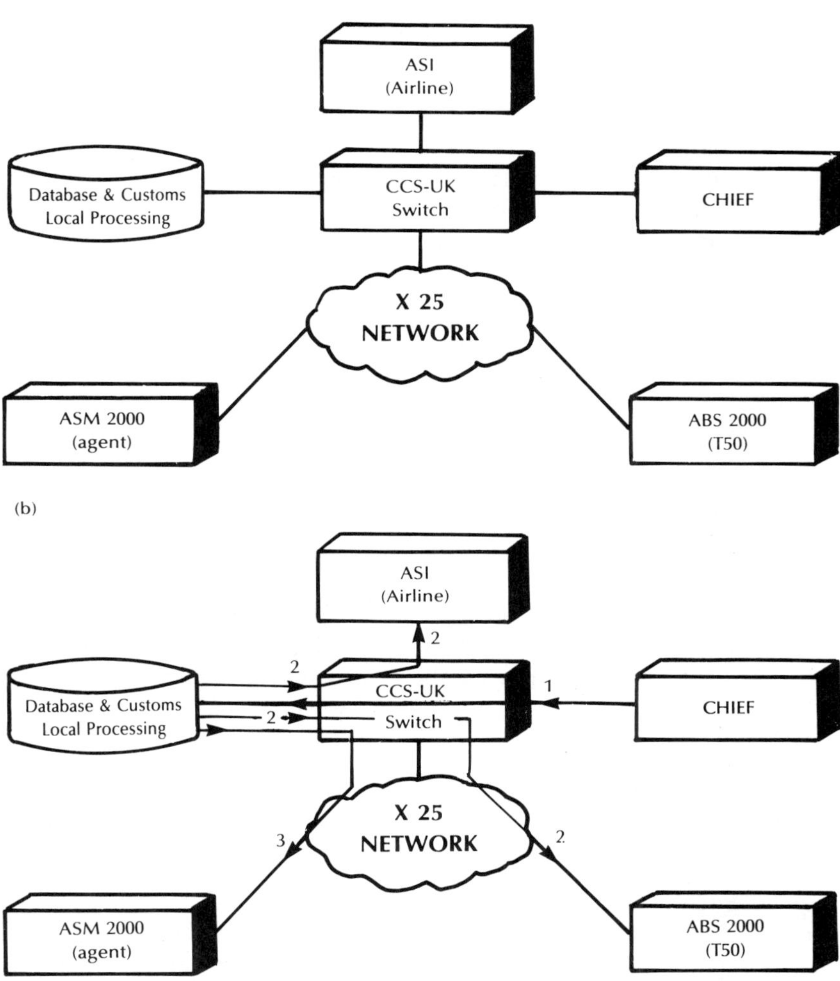

Fig. 17.13 (a) The new CCS-UK system. (b) Updating all concerned with a CHIEF message (see page 360) (courtesy of ASM (UK) Ltd and BT Customer Service who developed the CCS-UK system)

updated and the agent is notified. This is to happen within seconds of the initial message from CHIEF being issued.

Of course, the new system will do much more than this. Multiply this sort of process by thousands of clearances per day and you will begin to see a piece of what the new design will provide. This new system is being created to carry out all the basic functions of ACP 90 while preparing the way for new features and growth and a flexible way of accommodating future changes.

17.12.6 Conclusion on EDI

Reference has now been made several times to the very wide uses being made of EDI and other computerised systems in the transport and logistics field. It is regretted that the coverage is inevitably patchy. We cannot do more than hope that these references will encourage students and other readers to keep an open mind on such systems and to call in the expert firms offering these systems to see what can be done in their own particular logistical situations.

17.13 The dangerous goods note

The European Agreement on Dangerous Goods by Road (ADR) came into effect in 1968 and was designed to ensure the safe packing and carriage by road of dangerous items. The dangerous goods note reproduced in Fig. 17.14 is a declaration by the shipper of goods that dangerous goods have been properly declared; their true nature revealed; their packing carried out in accordance with regulations, etc. Naturally, dangerous goods travelling by road become even more hazardous when taken on board a vessel such as a ferry or container ship, and it is essential to stow them in such a way that they can be disposed of in emergencies.

17.14 Charter-parties

As explained elsewhere in this book (see pages 288–91) a charter-party is a contract for the hire of a vessel or part of a vessel by a shipper of goods. Such a contract is usually negotiated on the Baltic Exchange, although charter-parties can be negotiated privately. There are several types of charter-party, and some typical standard charter-parties are published by BIMCO (the Baltic and International Maritime Conference – Copenhagen). A typical uniform General Charter is reproduced in Fig. 17.15. Other BIMCO charter-parties are the Gas Voyage Charter-party (code name Gasvoy), the Uniform Time Charter (code name Baltime 1939), and the Standard Bareboat Charter (code name Barecon '89'). Altogether there are more than a hundred BIMCO charter-parties and related documents.

17.15 Tachographs

Under the Passenger and Goods Vehicles (Recording Equipment) Regulations 1979 most goods vehicles over 3.5 tonnes gross plated weight require

DG DANGEROUS GOODS DECLARATION, SHIPPING NOTE & CONTAINER/VEHICLE PACKING CERTIFICATE

DANGEROUS GOODS NOTE

Special Information is required for (a) Dangerous Goods in Limited Quantities (b) Radioactive Substances (class 7) (c) Tank Containers and (d) In certain circumstances a weathering certificate is required

SHADED AREAS NEED NOT BE SHIPPER COMPLETED FOR SHORT SEA, RO. RO, RAIL

Exporter 1

Veh. Bkg. Ref 2

Customs Reference/Status 3

Exporter's Reference 4

Exporter / Freight Forwarder — Port Charges Payable by* 5

Fwdr's Ref 6

SS Co Bkg No. 7

Consignee 8A

Other (Name & Address)

Name of Shipping Line or CTO 8

Port Account No.

Freight Forwarder 9

For Use of Receiving Authority Only

Receiving Date(s) — Berth/Dock/Containerbase etc 10

Consecutive no. or DG reference allocated by shipping line or C.T.O. (if any) 10A

Vessel — Port of Loading 11

TO THE RECEIVING AUTHORITY
Please receive for shipment the goods described below subject to your published regulations & conditions (including those as to liability)

Port of Discharge — Destination Depot 12

Name of Receiving Authority 13

Marks & Numbers; No. & Kind of Packages; Description of goods.†
INDICATE: HAZARD CLASS, UN NUMBER, FLASHPOINT °C 14

Receiving Authority Use

Gross Wt(kg) of goods 15

Cube (m³) of goods 16

Net Wt(kg) of goods 16A

MUST BE COMPLETED FOR FULL CONTAINER/VEHICLE LOADS:—

†CORRECT TECHNICAL NAME, PROPRIETARY NAMES ALONE ARE NOT SUFFICIENT.

CONTAINER/VEHICLE PACKING CERTIFICATE 17
It is declared that the packing of the container has been carried out in accordance with the provisions shown overleaf:—

Name of Company FCL

Signature of person responsible for packing container — Date

DANGEROUS GOODS DECLARATION
I hereby declare that the contents of this consignment are fully and accurately described above by the correct technical name(s) (proper shipping name(s)), that the shipment is packaged in such a manner as to withstand the ordinary risks of handling and transport by sea, having regard to the properties of the goods to be carried, and that the goods are classified, packaged, marked and labelled in accordance with the requirements of the Merchant Shipping (Dangerous Goods) Regulations 1981 as currently amended. I further declare that if appropriate the goods are classified, packaged and marked to comply with the requirements of the European Agreement concerning the International Carriage of Dangerous Goods by Road (ADR) and of Annex 1 (RID) to the International Convention concerning the Carriage of Goods by Rail (CIM) or special arrangements made between the contracting parties to these Agreements.

The shipper must complete and sign box 19.

Total Gross weight of goods

Total Cube of goods

Prefix & Container/Vehicle Number 18 — Seal Number(s) 18A

Container/Vehicle Size & Type 18B

Tare wt (kg) as marked on container 18C

Weight of container and goods (kg) 18D

Received the above number of packages/containers/trailers in apparent good order and condition unless stated hereon
RECEIVING AUTHORITY REMARKS

Haulier's Name

Vehicle Reg No.

DRIVER'S SIGNATURE — SIGNATURE & DATE

Name of Shipper preparing this note & tel. no. 19

NAME/STATUS OF DECLARANT

DATE

Signature of Declarant

890 — LONSDALE BUSINESS FORMS LTD 0933 228855

* Mark 'X' as appropriate. If box 5 is not completed the company preparing this note may be held liable for payment of port charges.

Fig. 17.14 A Dangerous Goods Note (courtesy of the SITPRO Board)

Adopted by
the Documentary Committee of the General
Council of British Shipping, London
and the Documentary Committee of The Japan
Shipping Exchange, Inc., Tokyo

RECOMMENDED
THE BALTIC AND INTERNATIONAL MARITIME CONFERENCE
UNIFORM GENERAL CHARTER (AS REVISED 1922 and 1976)
INCLUDING "F.I.O." ALTERNATIVE, ETC.
(To be used for trades for which no approved form is in force)
CODE NAME: "GENCON"

Part I

1. Shipbroker	2. Place and date
3. Owners/Place of business (Cl. 1)	4. Charterers/Place of business (Cl. 1)
5. Vessel's name (Cl. 1)	6. GRT/NRT (Cl. 1)
7. Deadweight cargo carrying capacity in tons (abt.) (Cl. 1)	8. Present position (Cl. 1)
9. Expected ready to load (abt.) (Cl. 1)	
10. Loading port or place (Cl. 1)	11. Discharging port or place (Cl. 1)
12. Cargo (also state quantity and margin in Owners' option, if agreed; if full and complete cargo not agreed state "part cargo") (Cl. 1)	
13. Freight rate (also state if payable on delivered or intaken quantity) (Cl. 1)	14. Freight payment (state currency and method of payment; also beneficiary and bank account) (Cl. 4)
15. Loading and discharging costs (state alternative (a) or (b) of Cl 5; also indicate if vessel is gearless)	16. Laytime (if separate laytime for load. and disch. is agreed, fill in a) and b). If total laytime for load. and disch., fill in c) only) (Cl. 6)
	a) Laytime for loading
17. Shippers (state name and address) (Cl. 6)	b) Laytime for discharging
	c) Total laytime for loading and discharging
18. Demurrage rate (loading and discharging) (Cl. 7)	19. Cancelling date (Cl. 10)
20. Brokerage commission and to whom payable (Cl. 14)	
21. Additional clauses covering special provisions, if agreed.	

It is mutually agreed that this Contract shall be performed subject to the conditions contained in this Charter which shall include Part I as well as Part II. In the event of a conflict of conditions, the provisions of Part I shall prevail over those of Part II to the extent of such conflict.

Signature (Owners)	Signature (Charterers)

Printed and sold by Fr. G. Knudtzon Ltd., 55, Toldbodgade, Copenhagen, by authority of The Baltic and International Maritime Conference (BIMCO), Copenhagen.

Fig. 17.15 The BIMCO uniform General Charter (courtesy of BIMCO, Copenhagen)

tachographs. A tachograph is a device which is installed in the driver's cab to record a variety of traces automatically during the 24-hour day – or from start to finish of the working day. It is essentially a clock mechanism which is also connected to aspects of the vehicle's movements, distance travelled, speed, etc. These aspects provide traces which enable the vehicle's movements to be carefully monitored. Sometimes referred to as a 'spy in the cab', the tachograph is not primarily designed for that purpose. It can be the best possible evidence for a driver that he has operated his vehicle in a proper manner, and reveals exactly when, where and at what speed he was travelling at any time of the day or night. The illustration provided in Fig. 17.16 shows the traces clearly and is largely self-explanatory.

17.16 Summary

1. Documentation of sea transport through charter-parties and bills of lading is a very ancient activity. Documentation in more recent times centres on the convention system, which seeks to overcome conflicts of law by agreeing a convention document, which is then enacted into the laws of all states and thus gives all states the same law.

   Any transport activity involves movements between consignors and consignees and probably a series of related contracts involving other parties, especially freight forwarders, insurance underwriters, bankers and various classes of carriers. These contracts are generally distilled down into documentary form, the use of a particular document witnessing the establishment of certain contractual relationships between the parties.
2. In order to reduce errors such as copying errors, spelling mistakes, etc., a system of aligned documentation has been prepared by the Simpler Trade Procedures Board (SITPRO). The word 'aligned' implies that on every document the same information is in the same place. All documents can then be run off from a single master document. The master document is completed, carefully checked and is then used to run off the other documents using masks to obscure any parts of the master not required on a particular document.

   Documents may also be prepared by electronic means and input directly into the computer networks of interested parties through the system known as electronic data interchange (EDI). Obviously such documents should be carefully checked on screen before input to other people's computer systems, but the advantages of aligned documentation still apply since, for example, an item like the exporter's address only needs to be input once and checked, and it will then appear automatically on every document related to that particular consignment.

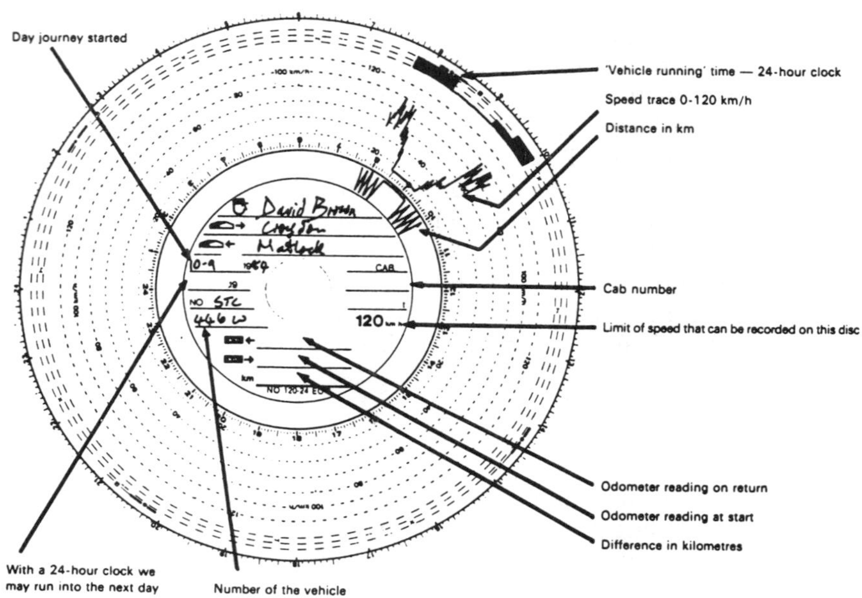

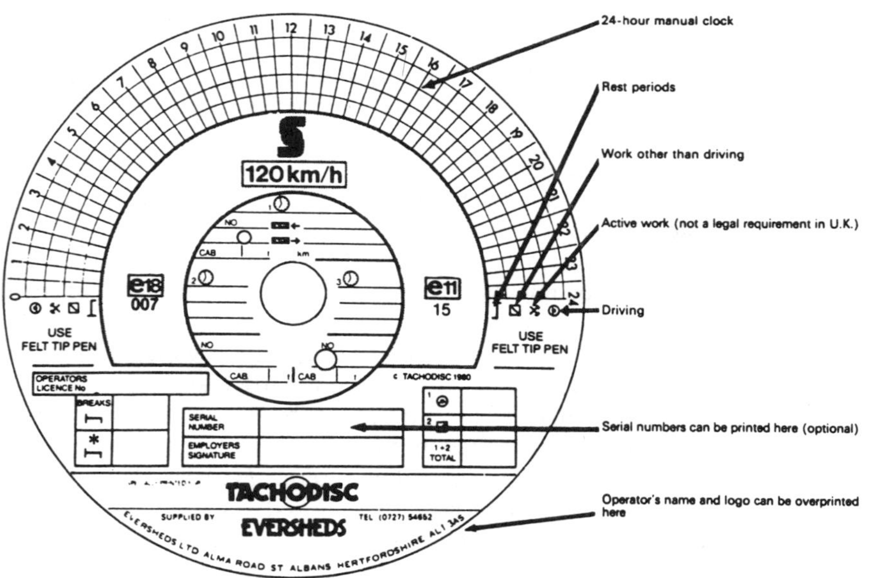

Fig. 17.16 A tachograph disc (courtesy of Tachodisc Ltd, Warrington, WA2 8RE)

3. The invoice is the basic commercial document, made out whenever one party supplies goods, or provides services to another party. It must contain the names and addresses of both parties to the contract, a detailed description of the goods sold or services rendered, and many other details. They may be combined with certificates of origin and certificates of value and may be legalised by consuls to ensure approval by foreign governments of the transactions taking place.
4. Bills of lading are the most important documents in the carriage of goods by sea. They have three functions. They act as a carrier's receipt for the goods; they are a document of title evidencing ownership of the goods and may be assigned from one owner to another, and they are evidence of the contract of affreightment. As far as banks are concerned they should preferably be 'shipped on board' bills of lading rather than 'received for shipment' bills of lading. However in the case of containerised traffic, which now forms 90 per cent of all liner traffic, an RFS bill of lading is just as good as a shipped bill of lading since the CTO is fully liable. Waiting for the goods to be actually shipped and then for the bill of lading to be returned to the shipper only causes unnecessary delay.
5. Similar documents in the carriage of goods are the air waybill, the combined transport bill of lading, the CMR note in road haulage and the CIM note in rail carriage. All these documents are the subject of control by agreed international conventions.
6. Other documents described in this chapter are the standard shipping note, the export cargo shipping instructions, the combined transport document and the single administrative document (SAD).
7. Electronic data interchange (EDI) is paperless communication between traders, computer-to-computer. It has many advantages, since it features direct trader input (DTI) into a common computer network which is accessible by all accepted persons who may consult the records on any consignment, generate hard copies as required, trace movements, charge for services rendered, etc.
8. The basic principle of EDI is the structuring of data into standard message formats capable of being received by the computer, and updated as procedures develop. The trader is linked to a 'store and call-forward' network which enables him to send messages at any time and access data he is entitled to see including messages waiting in an electronic mailbox dedicated to his personal use.
9. One of the basic systems to ensure a standard procedure is the UN EDIFACT, electronic data interchange for administration, commerce and transport. This lays down the syntax rules for putting electronic messages together and turning ordinary data into 'standard messages'.
10. The CCS-UK system is British Telecom's development of EDI from ACP 90 which is the chief cargo processing system for the 1990s for all

UK airports. Its basic elements are a message-switching system, an end-user system for in-house operations at the user end, an intelligent network and international gateways to give a world-wide service.

17.17 Questions

1. An export transaction involves a variety of contracts with numerous parties involved. Explain, referring in your answer to a cargo of heavy machinery exported by a forklift truck manufacturer to the port authority of an Arab state in the Middle East.
2. What is aligned documentation? Explain why aligned documentation is more efficient than a non-aligned system. Even if a firm is satisfied with its own documentation, why would it be well advised to adopt an aligned system?
3. What is a bill of lading? What are its functions? A, who is interested in purchasing a cargo aboard the *Peerless* from Calcutta, is negotiating for the purchase of the bill of lading. What will happen to the document if he does purchase it, and how will he eventually obtain physical possession of the goods?
4. Draw up a list of documents necessary in moving goods by sea to a foreign customer and securing payment against documents.
5. Write short notes (8–10 lines) about *four* of the following:
   (a) commercial invoices
   (b) air waybills
   (c) certificates of origin
   (d) standard shipping notes
   (e) charter-parties
   (f) the SAD
6. What is a CMR consignment note? Why is it used in roll-on roll-off haulage?
7. When goods are sent by rail internationally what is the appropriate document? Why was this form developed?
8. What is EDI? Explain the principles behind it and the advantages it brings.
9. A freight forwarding firm asks you whether it would be a good idea for them to commission a local computer specialist to write some software for them to computerise their operations. What would you advise?

18 Logistics and the environment

18.1 The environmental problem

Increasing environmental awareness and consequent tougher regulations on the environment by the International Maritime Organisation (IMO) and similar regulatory bodies provide a wide field of study for logisticians, covering many aspects of the supply-chain. These include not only transport, a major polluter, but also waste disposal, raw material supplies, packaging, site locations, hazardous cargoes including marine pollutants, and the need to prevent the spread of insects and other pests to areas (e.g. Australia and New Zealand) which, due to their natural isolation, are as yet free of such bugs.

The environmental problem presents itself in two main ways. First, there are the problems which are of a global nature where matters of principle have to be decided, such as questions of global warming, the ozone layer, noise pollution, air pollution, acid rain, the conservation of the countryside, the conservation of the great outdoors, the preservation of such innocence as is left, etc. These are matters largely handled at inter-governmental levels – but they involve wide discussions at a high level, and the logistics industry must be a major participant in that sort of discussion, for the economies of whole nations depend on the outcome. Second, there are the problems which are more localised than these global considerations and impact directly on the activities of the freight forwarding and logistical industries. These are the problems which arise directly from the day-to-day activities of transport, and bring environmental criticism from our fellow citizens. We are not thinking here of criticism from those groups which have been satirised by one American commentator as the 'eco-wackos', who take an extreme view of 'green' problems. Rather, we are thinking of criticism from the vast majority of 'right-minded citizens' who wish to see responsible behaviour by everyone about environmental matters and expect an important industry like the logistical industry to play a leading part.

Table 18.1 Passenger transport by mode 1952–91 (billion passenger km) (courtesy of *Transport Statistics in Great Britain*)

		(of which)					
Year	All road	Cars & motorcycles	PSV*	Cycles	Rail	Air	Total
1952	158	54	81	23	39	0.2	197.2
1962	226	152	65	9	37	1.1	264.1
1972	410	355	51	4	35	2.2	447.2
1982	468	421	41	6	31	2.9	501.9
1991	646	596	45	5	38	4.9	688.9

* PSV = Public Service Vehicle.

Table 18.2 Domestic freight transport by mode (billion tonne km) (courtesy of *Transport Statistics in Great Britain*)

Year	Road	Rail	Water	Pipeline	Total
1976	95.7	20.6	26.4	5.7	148.4
1986	104.1	16.5	51.4	10.4	182.4
1991	130.0	15.0	56.0	11.0	212.0

Note: Airfreight movements on domestic routes amounted to only 27 million tonne/km in 1991 and are therefore negligible in these statistics.

If these matters are addressed properly, they need not be an extra cost factor but rather a source of sound commercial practice, giving a competitive advantage to their proponents.

18.1.1 The United Kingdom's current transport situation

In the United Kingdom private and public transport, both passenger and freight, is dominated by road transport. The reasons are outlined below, but the actual data are given in Tables 18.1 and 18.2.

The reasons for the domination of road transport are as follows:

1. The private or business car or lorry is the most flexible form of transport. The entire journey from start to finish is under the driver's control, and subject to immediate change to meet personal, family or business requirements. When, where and how the journey is made is of

no concern to anyone but the driver and the employer, if it is a business vehicle.

2. The motor vehicle is also the cheapest vehicle if the capital cost is left out of the calculation and regarded as a 'sunk cost'. It is usual, with both private and business-owned vehicles, to disregard the cost of the vehicle and price each journey on the marginal costs, which are almost negligible. Of course, this cannot happen in public service vehicle use or freight transport, but from the environmental viewpoint it means that the family car is unhesitatingly used even for long journeys where rail traffic would be more efficient from all sorts of viewpoints, but cannot compete on price terms.
3. Freight transport moves from door to door, without any need for intermodal transfers. It offers close control over the time of delivery (subject to the exigencies of everyday life) and with today's sophisticated tracking systems, firms can know where their vehicles are at any time.

Against these enormous advantages must be set the disadvantages that arise from the growth of road transport – the congestion, pollution, the particular combination of these that constitutes the rush hour at mornings and evenings and the huge capital costs of road and motorway construction, which in the past have fallen on the general taxpayer rather than on the motorist and freight forwarder. That situation is of course changing, but the link between capital cost and burden carried is not made clear, because there is no true costing of infrastructure which makes the cost situation apparent to the everyday user of roads.

The statistics given in Tables 18.1 and 18.2 show clearly how the demand for road transport has grown over the years, and continues to grow. In doing so it places increasing pressure on the environment and leads to disputes with particular local communities and with the environmentally conscious general public. The resolution of such disputes is a complex, intricate process, involving many personal tragedies (one man's bypass is another person's bankruptcy as the passing trade is diverted elsewhere). A balance of advantages must often be struck.

18.1.2 'The polluter pays'

In former times the adverse environmental effects of industrial activity were borne as a social cost by the entire nation. Smoke-begrimed houses, polluted air, bronchial infections, etc., were inseparable from industrial activities in the Victorian era, and one has only to go to Eastern Europe to see the same conditions today. The social costs of East German and former Soviet industrial production are clear for all to see. Today, the concept that 'the polluter pays' is enshrined in the environmental policies of such states as the European Union countries. This could bring extremely heavy burdens to companies that do not put their environmental houses in order. Fines levied on polluters would enable the governments and local authorities to clean up the problems and compensate those who suffered.

18.2 Types of environmental pollution

Although it could be argued that environmental pollution is in many ways much reduced since former times – when, for instance, the area around Birmingham was called 'the Black Country' because of its smoke-begrimed appearance – the pressures on the whole eco-system are today simply enormous. Much of this is due to the growth in population. A world that, in 1832, had 1,000 million inhabitants now has 5,000 million. World population is growing at 1,000 million every ten years. It is not just the numbers of people, but their increased expectations which are the problem. It has been estimated that if the Indian and Chinese populations took to washing their hair once a week with modern shampoos the Indian and Pacific Oceans would rapidly be polluted. Increased expectations mean increased agriculture, manufacturing, personal transport, logistical activities, etc., and further deterioration in the environment. What are the major sources of pollution?

18.2.1 Emissions

Emissions of gases occur from many processes. Some of them are natural processes – from volcanic eruptions to the breath of cows and other bodily processes. The internal combustion engine and other machines and processes cause severe pollution from the combustion of fossil fuels. The chief of these are:

1. Carbon dioxide – which contributes to global warming.
2. Carbon monoxide – a deadly poison caused by the imperfect oxidation of fuel. Fortunately, it readily oxidises to carbon dioxide, which is harmless apart from its global warming aspects, but in a confined space this cannot happen and many people die from inhaling it.
3. Sulphur dioxide, from fossil fuels and in particular coal-fired power stations. It combines with water to produce sulphurous acid which falls as 'acid rain' and kills trees, many of which cannot live in acid soil.
4. Various oxides of nitrogen, which again combine with water to make acid rain.
5. Particulates (small particles of smoke and dirt which can be carcinogenic). They are released by diesel engines.
6. VOCs – volatile organic compounds emitted by vehicles, which produce

ground-level ozone – which is a major cause of respiratory diseases and asthmatic conditions.

18.2.2 Global warming

The United Kingdom is responsible for about 3 per cent of the global CO_2 output, which is the cause of the 'greenhouse effect'. This is so-called because it acts like the glass in a greenhouse – the gases trap the heat of the sun and keep the earth 30 per cent warmer than it otherwise would be. It is this extra warmth that makes life possible, but any increase in global warming poses problems because the melting ice caps will raise ocean levels and threaten much low-lying land – a lot of it densely populated and intensively farmed. Transport contributes about 20 per cent of the UK's CO_2 output.

18.2.3 Air pollution

Air pollution results from the emissions referred to above. It can be improved if emissions are reduced by the use of catalytic converters.

The chief ways of reducing emissions are to reduce fuel consumption, to use cleaner fuels and to change the way we travel – using the lorry less and the railway more, for example, or using the car less and our two feet, and perhaps the bicycle, more. Catalytic converters reduce pollution, while the drive to produce an effective electric car is largely inspired by the need to reduce emissions.

18.2.4 Noise pollution

Noise is a major pollutant, as those who live alongside busy roads or near major airports will know. Logisticians are well aware of the problems and should take every care to consider the likely noise from each new vehicle. A research programme to discover the 'Quiet Heavy Vehicle' was being carried out in 1993 and is proposing an 80 Db (decibel) limit for the heaviest vehicles.

18.2.5 Marine pollution

Marine pollution is chiefly a matter of oil pollution after accidents at sea, or the deliberate discharge of pollutants in the process of washing tanks.

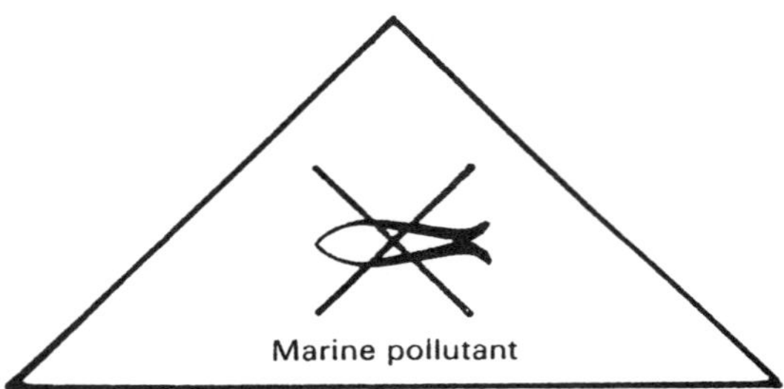

Fig. 18.1 Mark for marine pollutants

Other problems are chemical pollutants resulting from the loss overboard of containers or deck cargoes of chemicals, fertilisers and similar products. While these are mainly incidents calling for official action by central government or local authorities, the logistics manager is concerned to ensure that such incidents are kept to a minimum. Clearly, proper training procedures should ensure not only sound navigational practices but also correct documentation about the carriage of hazardous cargoes, an understanding of the risks such cargoes constitute and a clear understanding of how to restrain such cargoes and how to deal with spillages. Incidentally, nowadays, substances which have been identified as marine pollutants have to be documented in the same way as dangerous goods and marked with a triangular sign like the one shown in Fig. 18.1, even though they may be non-hazardous in other respects.

18.3 An environmental audit

Every logistical operation is going to contribute to environmental pollution of one sort or another, and consequently will result in criticism from one party or another from time to time. It is essential to have an environmental policy which is regularly reviewed and to this end a standing committee on environmental problems would serve as a body to whom all criticisms could be referred. The task of such an environmental committee would be to conduct an on-going environmental audit of the company's activities. In this way environmental problems would be anticipated – for example, with any new workload that developed, or any switch to different modes of transport. By viewing each new job, commitment or business relationship from the objective viewpoint of an outsider the committee should be able to make proposals to management about any matter that appears to have an adverse environmental impact. Hopefully, it would be possible to modify the arrangements so as to avoid the adverse effect. At worst, if nothing could be done to prevent it, the Public Relations Department would at least be forewarned of the problem.

If we attempt an environmental audit of our company's activities and the various forms of transport we use, we can see which are the most desirable modes from the environmental point of view and consequently decide to what extent we should influence transport choice in the interests of the environment and people's enjoyment of it. These will not always be the deciding factors for any particular development, but if they are constantly borne in mind, they should produce a favourable marginal switch into modes other than road transport. They might even cast doubts on the location of a particular plant, depot or other installation. A standing committee such as the environmental committee mentioned above could easily undertake such an audit, and roll it forward for consideration on a regular basis – say, at six-monthly intervals – so that the proposers of all new developments automatically consider the environmental aspects of the plans under discussion. Clearly, these would not necessarily override other considerations such as economic considerations, but they would effect a marginal improvement in many respects. This would give eco-consciousness a chance to develop in the organisation as a whole. It has been found that where a company embraces these issues it has often led to their suppliers and/or customers following suit, which in the latter case speaks of increased customer satisfaction.

Environmental issues are one area where the boardroom must make a positive contribution by making environmental awareness an integral part of its policy and performance. It will require the preparation and adoption of a training programme involving all levels of staff, to make them aware of environmental issues and to monitor their subsequent performance. This is an area where quality circles might be introduced so that all members are encouraged to make their contribution.

18.4 Some examples of environmental problems

The following specific cases of action being needed to take account of environmental aspects are interesting.

18.4.1 Hazardous cargoes

Although the carriage of hazardous cargoes by sea and air have been subject to regulations for many years (i.e. the Board of Trade Blue Book and IATA rules) it is only in the last quarter-century that road haulage has been covered with the advent of Hazchem, a purely UK regulatory body and the ADR (1963) regulations covering the carriage of hazardous cargoes in Europe, including the United Kingdom. Prior to that it was common for goods to be carried cheek by jowl on the tailboard of a lorry through busy high streets, which under Blue Book regulations by sea could not even be carried in the same hold.

Nowadays, besides the above-mentioned road regulations, all forms of transport have strict regulations regarding the notification, packing, marking and stowage of all hazardous cargoes laid down by their respective regulatory bodies, i.e. IMO regulations for sea carriage, IATA and ICAO regulations for air and RID regulations for rail. In the UK drivers carrying hazardous goods in tank vehicles operate under the Hazchem regulations with three marker boards on the vehicle, one at the rear end and one on either side. The one at the rear indicates the nature of the hazard, and has coded instructions giving advice to emergency services in the event of an accident. The driver must also carry written emergency instructions. On international journeys ADR regulations must be followed, with hazard warning panels at the front and rear of the vehicle. The driver must carry a Trem (transport emergency) card giving details of the hazard and actions to be taken. The Trem card is increasingly used on national journeys in place of Hazchem cards.

18.4.2 Waste disposal

This is an obvious area of environmental concern. If given some thought a considerable part of waste can be recycled providing the recycling facilities are drawn to the staff's attention. One firm recently paid an employee £1,000 for a suggestion that the cost of disposing of packing material should be saved by returning the material to its Belgian subsidiary in the empty containers for re-use with the next consignment. Companies should always encourage employees to come forward with helpful suggestions. In industrial firms it has been the practice for many years to find some use for waste materials, which with a little ingenuity may be turned into a further product. With the distribution industry there has not been the same thought given to the re-use of waste, particularly packing material.

18.4.3 Packaging

Packaging is a possible source of considerable savings. In fact, a manufacturer could do worse than employ a packaging consultant at the design stage of his product to see if, by some simple adaptation, a considerable reduction could be made in both the cubic measurement of cargo and the actual packing material used. It is possible to reduce both the packaging used and the freight and other distribution costs. It must be remembered that so far as the final customer is concerned, packaging normally ends up as waste, and since such waste is included in the final price, reduced packaging means the price can be that more competitive.

A prime example would be the Prestige pressure cooker, where a detachable handle, easily fitted by the customer using a screwdriver, can be tucked into a corner of the carton while the reversed lid fits snugly into the top of the cooker.

Another good example of cubic reduction was the replacement of half-inch boards top and bottom of a bale of hardboard by covers of paper which protected the boards from the wire banding. In this way a standard bale of board was reduced from 133 ft^3 to 99½ ft^3, a reduction of 25 per cent. All such reductions in cubic measurement not only save on packing material and subsequent waste, but also save on freight and handling charges and on warehousing and retailing space. If we think solely in terms of the last of these, a trip around the supermarket would indicate that there are numerous products – particularly cereals and soap powders – where considerable savings could be made without any need to jeopardise their product advertising on the package. There are also many instances where manufacturers have been penny wise and pound foolish, skimping on packaging costs to the detriment of their product during transit, and consequently damaging their customer relationships and their competitiveness.

18.4.4 The ozone layer

With the increasing depletion of the ozone layer due to the release of CFC gases, these latter are being phased out as refrigerants and all new reefer containers are using a new CFC-free refrigerant R134A. The Montreal Protocol requires all CFC refrigerants to be phased out by 1995 and therefore many existing reefer boxes are having their CFC gas withdrawn and captured. They are being retro-filled with R134A. Ships now keep records of all CFC gases released into the atmosphere.

18.4.5 The importation of pests

Due to their geographical isolation, which has meant that they developed different species of fauna and flora, Australia and New Zealand have long operated very strict regulations against the possibility of infestation from the rest of the world. They have thus imposed very strict rules regarding packaging materials; in particular timber, which might introduce insect infestation. All packing material, containers, dunnage, etc. must be certified as having been treated according to their regulations. Straw is yet another packing material, which is banned in many countries, especially banana-growing areas, which have suffered in the past from crop disease attributable to imported straw.

18.4.6 Harmful emissions and discharges

With increasing environmental legislation emanating from the EU a new important factor in determining the location of industry has appeared. No longer can factories pollute the air and the local environment with their noxious fumes, harmless but nevertheless obnoxious smells (e.g. palm oil) and fall-out, or poison the nearby river with their waste discharges. In the past it has not only been the local environment which has been damaged. Areas many hundreds of miles away, e.g. the forests and lakes of Scandinavia, have been poisoned by fumes from power stations, giving rise to acid rain. Our geographical position relative to the prevailing wind conditions meant that we were a major polluter of Scandinavia. We, and many other nations, were polluted by the radiation leak from the Chernobyl disaster, while marine pollution from our own and Continental rivers has damaged fish stocks in the North Sea. Ireland complains of pollution of the Irish Sea by discharges from the nuclear power station at Sellafield. It is only in recent years with the creation of the National Rivers Authority that any real overall attempt has been made to clean up our sewers and coastal waters, although to be fair, the Port of London Authority had already done a good job in cleaning up the Thames.

Road transport can be made 'greener' and more efficient in several ways. Fuel consumption can be reduced by fitting speed limiters and by training drivers in correct driving techniques, which incidentally also reduce accidents. Considerable further savings in fuel consumption can be made by reducing drag, through the development of more aerodynamic vehicles. Greener fuels can also be used and one of these, which is only at a pioneering stage, is the development of a lorry engine powered by natural gas, which has a less harmful emission than normal fuels.

The monitoring of correct tyre pressures for both vehicles and trailers will considerably reduce wear and tear and give better traction. A recent survey found that a very large percentage of both vehicles and trailers had tyres which were seriously under-inflated, while another large percentage were over-inflated, which also seriously reduces tyre mileage.

In the field of sea transport new water-based, rather than solvent-based, paints are being used for both the interior and exterior of containers; to date trials have proved successful. A new paint is also being used for boot-topping the hulls of vessels below the waterline, which is TBT (Tributyltin)-free, self-polishing and not harmful to aquatic life.

A less obvious form of 'discharge' is the disposal overside of waste from ocean-going vessels. Thor Heyerdahl, the Norwegian explorer of ancient sea routes, told with dismay how, crossing the Atlantic in a vessel made of papyrus in the ancient Egyptian style, he and his crew had their illusions shattered by the trail of waste products, food containers, disposable cups, etc. jettisoned by the crews of deep-sea vessels. This practice can be ended by the provision of an onboard incinerator for all garbage disposal. A record is kept of all such disposals by a senior engineer officer, designated environmental officer. Where a ship does not carry its own incinerator garbage is kept on board, and most ports offer disposal facilities.

Both on land and sea companies which have adopted a 'green' policy are now using wood from managed forests to meet their need for tropical hardwoods in the construction of container and lorry flooring, both of which are subject to excessive wear and tear. P & O Containers Ltd are currently experimenting with a container flooring containing layers of tropical hardwood and rubber wood, which would considerably reduce their demand for the former. Paperless trading, through the increasing use of EDI, will have a green effect in reducing the demand for forest-produced cellulose. In fact, any elimination of waste will have two beneficial effects: it will reduce the need for waste disposal, and the demands on the world's natural resources will diminish.

18.4.7 Noise emissions

Noise emissions are yet another factor in pollution and particularly affect transport, in that depots, with their virtually round-the-clock activity, should be excluded from dormitory locations. Noise is, of course, more important as a factor in determining the location of new airports and limiting night flights at existing ones.

In this book we can only give a brief insight into this complex and important subject, but the Institute of Logistics have compiled a three-volume publication *Logistics and the Environment*, which is regularly updated and can be obtained from the Corby Office, Douglas House, Queens Square, Corby, Northants, NN17 1PL.

18.5 Summary

1. Many of the major environmental issues – global warming, the destruction of the rain forests, acid rain, etc. – are the subject of inter-

governmental negotiations and are likely to affect firms and companies in a regulatory way, rather than as a matter of in-house policy.

2. At the same time many customers are eco-sensitive these days and so are employees. A company should therefore have a clear, sensitive policy on environmental matters, and preferably a standing environmental committee with wide staff representation to keep such matters under review.
3. One of the activities of such an environmental committee should be to conduct an environmental audit of all the company's activities to pinpoint weaknesses in the company's behaviour, and propose remedies to each problem. Such an audit should be rolled forward every six months to review the progress made, consider the environmental impact of new contracts, new procedures, etc. and anticipate criticisms so that their cause can be eliminated before problems arise.
4. The chief types of emission pollutions are of carbon dioxide, carbon monoxide, the various oxides of nitrogen, VOCs (volatile organic compounds) and particulates. They may be reduced by reducing the use of road transport, using cleaner fuels, fitting catalytic converters, etc.
5. Other pollution problems are noise pollution, marine pollution and global warming. The movement of hazardous cargoes is always a potential source of pollution and requires companies to train staff in the observance of the regulations, and to deal defensively with all such consignments.

18.6 Questions

1. What is an environmental audit? List five aspects of a firm's activities which could be the subject of an environmental audit, bringing out in each case the adverse situations which might be studied.
2. 'The rise in asthma cases in recent years can be linked to harmful emissions from industrial and logistical activities.' Explain the term 'harmful emissions'.
3. What is noise pollution? Where would it be met, and what are the likely effects?
4. Explain the terms 'Hazchem' and 'ADR regulations'.
5. What are the chief causes of marine pollution? To what extent can the logistics industry prevent them?
6. What is meant by the term 'the polluter pays'? Is this a desirable policy? What problems does it pose?

19 Transport, logistics and the European Union

19.1 Introduction

The European Economic Community was founded by the Treaty of Rome, which originally had six signatories: France, Germany, Italy, The Netherlands, Belgium and Luxembourg. The intention was to establish a free trade area and eventually a political and monetary union. The Community was enlarged on 1 January 1973, by the accession of Britain, Denmark and Eire. Greece became the tenth member in 1981, and Spain and Portugal were admitted on 1 January 1986. Later renamed the European Community and now called the European Union, the institutions are shown in a rather simplified form in Fig. 19.1. The emphasis has been placed on transport matters in this figure, but the institutions of the Union study all aspects of the life of the community and attempt to harmonise them so far as possible. The reader is urged to study this figure, and note how the five major institutions are related to one another. These are: (1) the Council of Ministers, (2) the Commission, (3) the European Assembly, (4) the Court of Justice, and (5) the Committee of Permanent Representatives (COREPER).

When the Treaty of Rome was signed in 1957 the parties agreed, by Articles 3e and 74, to adopt a common policy in the field of transport. It was felt that a 'free trade' area, where goods were free to circulate within the Community boundaries, could only be developed if coherent Community transport arrangements were introduced. Accordingly, the Treaty required the progressive introduction of measures which reduced discrimination against carriers of other member states. In the early years fairly rapid progress in harmonisation was achieved, but this period ended in 1966, and since then the Common Transport Policy has made slower progress. The objectives of the 'Transport' section of the Treaty (Articles 74–84) still remain the basis for action to achieve a common policy. We must first see what these provisions require.

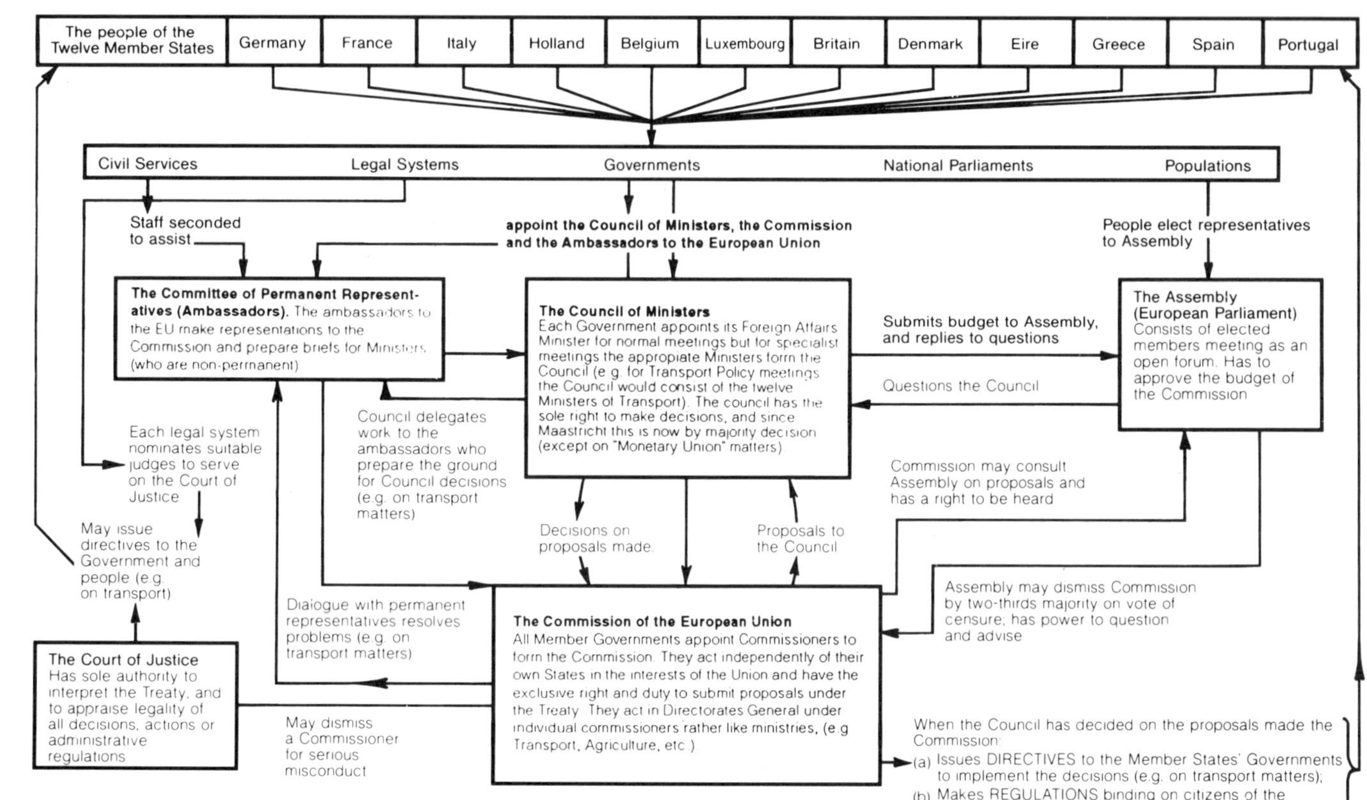

Fig. 19.1 The institutions of the European Union

19.2 The 'transport' provisions of the Treaty of Rome (Articles 74–84)

- *Article 74:* provides that member states shall pursue the objectives of the Treaty of Rome within the framework of a common transport policy.
- *Article 75:* in order to implement Article 74 the Council of Ministers shall lay down common rules applicable to international transport between the territories of member states, and the conditions under which non-resident carriers may operate transport services within member states. These rules, and any other appropriate provisions, would be based on proposals submitted to the Council of Ministers by the European Commission, and would be subject to unanimous agreement in the early years, and a qualified majority later. In fact, this use of a qualified majority to overrule a member state is never used if the member state makes it clear that it regards the matter as vital to its national interests.
- *Article 76:* prohibits member states from introducing legislation which discriminates against the carriers of other member states, pending the introduction of common rules for inland transport.
- *Article 77:* provides that where a member state gives assistance to transport firms this shall be compatible with the Treaty if the aid given is for the purpose of promoting transport co-ordination or for providing facilities which constitute a service to the public. This might, for example, cover the operation of uneconomic bus routes in country districts.
- *Article 78:* provides that measures taken which affect rates and conditions of carriage shall take account of the economic state of the transport industry.
- *Article 79:* prohibits discrimination by carriers on grounds of country of origin or destination.
- *Article 80:* prohibits aid being given to support rates so that goods and services are carried below economic cost, unless authorised by the Commission.
- *Article 81:* requires member states to reduce charges for frontier procedures and formalities, so that the sums recovered are close to the true cost of the procedures.
- *Article 82:* a special provision permitting the Federal Republic of Germany to adopt special measures to compensate certain areas which suffer disadvantages due to the division of Germany.
- *Article 83:* provides for the setting-up of an expert Transport Consultative Committee to advise the Commission.
- *Article 84:* limits the application of these rules to inland transport until such time as the Council decides what common transport policies shall be applied to sea and air transport.

These clauses operate within the general climate of the Treaty of Rome, which holds that in a free trade area any interference with free competition is *prima facie* undesirable; therefore, state aid apart from that permitted by Article 77 is generally prohibited.

19.3 Development of the Common Transport Policy

The underlying principle, originally laid down in the Commission's proposals in 1961, was that the advantages of competition should be more fully realised for the mutual benefit of transport users and transport undertakings. This principle embodies traditional economic thinking which holds that the world will be richer if nations concentrate on doing those tasks at which they have the greatest comparative advantage. Transport facilities should be provided by the most efficient carriers, irrespective of nationality. In fact, it has not been possible to develop this policy very far. Transport is inextricably bound up with the whole economic life of a nation, and nationalism prevents the development of a truly free market in transport. This is not surprising, since transport in many areas is uneconomic and must be subsidised in one way or another. Although Article 77 recognises this, it is not easy to get agreement on aid to particular services or areas, and nations are unwilling to surrender rights in order to sustain the 'free trade' principle.

The Commission is charged with the duty of preparing proposals for transport which are in the interests of all countries in the Community. When it submits these proposals to the Council of Ministers for decisions, it often finds that they are unable to agree on the adoption of the Commission's schemes. Instead, they usually abstract certain parts of the proposals and implement these more limited measures. This slows down the work of developing a meaningful transport system based on an overall approach to problems. A note of desperation can be found in some of the Commission's communications to the Council, appealing to that body to institute dialogues between itself and other institutions such as the European Parliament and the Economic and Social Committee to resolve the national differences which are delaying the Common Transport Policy.

There has been a marked expansion in transport in Europe since the Community began. The specialisation envisaged in the Treaty of Rome is only possible if more and more transport takes place. If all transport is included, then it forms 15 per cent of the total gross national product of the Community; while it is 6 per cent if we leave out private cars and own-account transport. This compares with agriculture, which only creates 5 per cent of the total wealth. If such a large share of total wealth is to play its proper part in benefiting the European people, the Common Transport

Policy must be agreed. The Commission has therefore recently reformulated the policy and redefined its aims.

19.4 Objectives and scope of the Common Transport Policy

The objectives of the Common Transport Policy are as follows:

1. To remove impediments to the free circulation of transport services.
2. To harmonise the framework of laws and regulations within which the different modes and undertakings operate.
3. To devise controls limiting extreme competition where this is found to be harmful.
4. To devise guidelines which will enable transport to play its part in achieving the objectives of the Paris Summit of 1972. This conference attempted to put a more 'human' face on the Community, and the socio-economic aspirations of its people.

These objectives can only be achieved if transport plays a major role in other Community policies. Transport is an essential element in almost all aspects of community life, and the following particular cases illustrate its importance.

1. *Regional policy*. Regional policy is concerned with the solution of problems in particular regions which are either underdeveloped or are suffering from declining industrial activity. Transport can improve the accessibility of these areas; it can enable populations to move where necessary; it can develop their resources or promote schemes for their reclamation and rehabilitation.

2. *Social policy*. Social policies envisage the harmonisation of standards of living, working conditions, health and social security benefits, industrial safety, etc. Transport forms a large part of social life, and employs several million Europeans. It is desirable that employees in the same sort of transport services should have similar working conditions and rewards, while transport services to other citizens should be as uniform as possible in the different countries. Thus transport aspects of programmes of social action in environmental fields, in ambulance and similar services, and in education and training should be comparable.

3. *Fiscal policy*. Inevitably, vehicles and their fuels attract taxation. The demand for transport is inelastic so that taxation levied on transport is inescapable and the yield to the Treasury is high. It is very desirable that taxation in this field should be harmonised, so that all operators face similar costs. Variations in tax could affect the relative competitiveness of operators, giving unfair advantages to countries which have less severe taxes.

4. *Industrial policy*. Transport bridges the gap between producers and

consumers. It follows that industrial concentration and specialisation is increased when the transport system is efficient. The gaps can be bridged more easily, and the economies of large-scale operation are achieved.

5. *Environmental policy*. Transport is a major factor in environmental problems, especially those of noise, atmospheric pollution, traffic congestion and accidents: 60,000 people are killed and 1,500,000 injured every year in the Community. The Common Transport Policy aims at reducing these social costs.

6. *Energy policy*. A drastic rethinking of energy policies has been taking place since the 1973 Middle East conflict. Transport policy must be influenced by energy policy and the utmost economy in energy must remain a feature of transport design for the conceivable future.

7. *External policy*. The Community is part of a greater world, on which it relies for resources, services and markets. The transport system has a major part to play in promoting international links, in developing the Third World, and in defence.

19.5 The role of the public authorities in transport

The public authorities are expected to play a much fuller part in future transport policy than they have in the past. This is because the creation, extension and continuous adaptation of the transport network is to take place within the framework of the Common Transport Policy. Such activities were considered at the time the original Treaty was drawn up as being best performed by public bodies. This does not necessarily mean bodies of the EU, but national authorities taking action along lines laid down in EU directives. The chief aim of such directives would be to harmonise transport policies along the lines described in objective (4), page 385. The public authorities would, in particular, be responsible for shaping the transport infrastructures. Firms, by contrast, would be responsible for planning their own investment in vehicles, installations and equipment.

Whether everyone would still agree, in 1993, that such matters are best performed by public bodies is debatable, but to be fair there is certainly something to be said for the proposition. The ease with which the French have found the capital and the drive to get their side of the Eurotunnel infrastructure finished compared with what has happened on the UK side must be some sort of evidence for the central planning of infrastructure facilities. It is never easy to find the capital for an infrastructure development from the private sector, and a nationalised industry can be hamstrung by an unsympathetic government attitude, closing off the purse-strings with every setback.

The original intention of the Common Transport Policy was that the cost of the infrastructure should be calculated in such a way that each branch of transport could be charged with some appropriate share of the burden. These costs should be imputed with a view to achieving the best possible allocation of resources. Other public authority measures may also be used; priority for public transport, controls over routes, prohibitions of certain types of traffic, etc.

The public authorities charged with the implementation of the Common Transport Policy looked carefully into the following matters:

1. The preparation of forecasts of transport supply and demand.
2. The preparation of a master plan for the infrastructure network which will best serve the whole community. This plan should promote the exploitation of the comparative advantages of each particular mode of transport, and the development of inter-modal systems.
3. The development of committees to ensure co-operation about, and finance for, all projects which go beyond the national frame of reference.
4. The allocation of costs, using the charging system proposed by the Commission. This charging system is based on marginal social cost and the need to balance the transport budget. This means that charges for the use of the facilities provided would be greater if the social cost was great (for example, road use in town centres) but smaller if the social cost was small (for example, utilisation of an existing railway system in a depressed area). At the same time, the overall cost of the facilities should fall upon the users of the facilities, i.e. the transport budget should balance. While the Commission expected some difficulty in costing out this system properly, it was confident that the system would become more precise as knowledge of the true costs improved.

Although the European Community (now the European Union) may have envisaged the full development of a strategic plan for transport in the Community in general, and at a national level within each member state, the UK government has been dilatory in the extreme. There may be a reason for this. The logical focus of a nationalised transport system is the railway network. In continental Europe the railway has always made more sense than in the United Kingdom because of the need to have average journeys exceeding 200 miles (320 km) if railways are to be viable. Paradoxically, at the very time when Eurotunnel is about to make the UK rail network more viable, the UK government is obsessed with privatisation, even though no one is prepared to buy the whole network and whatever parts of it are privatised must inevitably be less than the viable whole.

In the United Kingdom the lack of any real common transport policy is nowhere more obvious than in the decline of shipbuilding and the merchant navy fleets. An island nation whose prosperity was built on sea power and a huge merchant navy has declined to almost total insignificance. We have allowed a once thriving shipbuilding industry virtually to disappear, and our national fleet owners have been forced to use foreign yards, some of them within the EU, whose governments were prepared to subsidise the industry. Many of them have had to turn to foreign flags of convenience, and much of our trade is carried by foreign vessels which have poor records for safety and are often subsidised. They may be cheaper, but what makes economic sense today could be strategic nonsense tomorrow.

19.6 The future of EU transport

The history of transport gives many illustrations of transport systems appropriate to their own era but forming a vested interest resistant to future change. Examples are the canal system in Britain and the railway systems of almost every nation in the world. The Common Transport Policy, with its recurring review of the whole transport network and its clear principles, should ensure that the European Union is served by a transport system which promotes the best interests of the transport users. A sound transport infrastructure serving the entire Union; a transport market operating in conditions of healthy competition; a well-trained and competent transport profession enjoying harmonised working conditions and rewards; these are the objectives of the Common Transport Policy. At the same time little progress has been made in defining a policy for sea and air transport. If the Union is to become an outward-looking body, rather than an introverted continental group, it must soon implement Article 84 and decide on a policy for shipping and air transport. The United Kingdom would presumably hope that such a policy would be a positive, vigorous one, based on the freedom of the seas and the air, enabling established transport firms to compete effectively in world transport.

The progress made to 1992 in achieving the aims of the Treaty of Rome for the harmonisation of transport regulations and the achievement of a 'common market' – let alone a Union – in this field was disappointing. Transport policy has been described as the Union's 'greatest failure', with the various nations pursuing independent transport policies to a very considerable extent, and vested interests with powerful home lobbies doing their best to continue to enjoy the monopolistic practices to which they have so long been accustomed. However, the creation of a Single Market on 1 January 1993, and the virtual elimination of hold-ups at frontiers, has done much to ease traffic flows, and the opening of Eurotunnel in 1994 should do much to improve not only British but also European rail services as a large part of heavy goods traffic leaves the roads and uses the railways instead. This will improve the viability of all railways. Looking at the various aspects of transport in turn we find the following situations.

19.6.1 Road transport

During the 1970s and 1980s the growing road haulage industries of all the EC countries were beset by the problems of licensing and quotas arranged on a reciprocal basis. With the advent of the Single Market much of this interference with the free movement of vehicles has ended, except for a simple process of authorisation designed to certify that a particular road haulier does run a proper business paying due attention to the EU rules about the use of tachographs, the servicing of vehicles, etc. The abolition of the quota system means that road haulage companies are now free to make as many journeys as they like, to any destination, and to seek such return-loads as they can find. One effect of this will be to reduce the number of lorries on the roads, since about one-third of all movements before the Single Market were empty-running vehicles, unable to get a return-load without a permit.

Much has already been said about the effects of the opening of Eurotunnel (see pages 292–7). This will not only divert a lot of lorries through the tunnel, on Le Shuttle, but even more will move many containers onto the railway proper, where they will complete the major long-haul part of their journey, only leaving the railway at an appropriate point for their final delivery by road in the immediate home area of the consignee. The further the goods have to travel, the more likely it is consignors will opt for rail transport. This is going to mean some reduction in long-distance road haulage fleets in the years ahead, but this effect will be offset by the usual tendency of traffic to grow where road haulage predominates (the short-haul movement of goods) and by the development of the single internal market in road haulage now that restrictions have been removed.

19.6.2 Rail transport

While the United Kingdom is chiefly preoccupied with the opening of Eurotunnel and the fundamental reappraisal of long-distance haulage that should follow from it, the Commission has other interests. The Continental powers have always known what an advantage they have in their long-distance rail networks, but have been slow to realise their full potential because of narrow, national interests. The Commission is keen to develop a truly international rail network, and is calling for a radical restructuring and linking of national routes. Such a link-up would be a unifying change, which would break down barriers between nations and forge the real European Union which is required. This requires the breakdown of existing national monopolies and the creation of a European railway system which will promote international passenger and freight services.

How this would come about remains to be seen, but it is unlikely to be achieved by privatisation, for such a huge network surely requires some sort of central planning by representatives of the major countries concerned. This makes it all the more worrying that the UK government is so besotted with privatisation – it looks as if all it will be able to bring to the conference table is a piecemeal collection of small-scale private operators, none of whom would be capable of representing the United Kingdom in any meaningful way.

19.6.3 Air transport

Since the early days of the EEC, attempts to devise a common transport policy for air travel have been frustrated by a narrow nationalism which was only in 1993 beginning to break down. The difficulty has been partly that governments are essentially transitory, whereas such rights as airspace are enduring – even eternal. In reaching agreement on matters of airspace the governments tended to hand over responsibility to the actual operators in the air transport field, and as these were all nationalised industries in the early days, it did not seem illogical to negotiate in this way. However, monopolists are hesitant to surrender their monopolies, and concessions were largely made on a reciprocal basis, the arrangements made being mutually beneficial to the operators, and totally regardless of the consumers. The nominal controls envisaged by such bodies as parliament over the national carrier – for example, British European Airways at one time – were largely reduced to one 'supply' day in the year, when the affairs of the industry were debated and the accounts put before parliament. By convention, when the Opposition deemed that the affairs of the industry were non-controversial it could instead give notice of some other topic which it wished to discuss on the supply day set aside for air transport. This was often done; so much for parliamentary control. Sometimes reciprocity between any two nations reached such a pitch that the two airlines in any particular arrangement set prices in such a way that costs and a generous profit would result, and shared the revenue earned by both parties on a 50:50 basis. Such an arrangement is hardly conducive to competition.

To offset the manifest absurdity of such policies the use of charter aircraft and eventually charter airlines developed, and although these became well-established in the travel and tourism field, they could not break the stranglehold of the scheduled airlines on ordinary air transport, particularly business travel, with half-empty planes flying the scheduled routes. The sole beneficiary of this policy was the air freight system, and it became a rule that the logical place for goods travelling by air was in the cargo bays of passenger aircraft. Eventually, the deadlock was broken by the European Court, which ruled that domestic airlines were not exempt from Treaty obligations to devise a common transport policy. This, coupled with the Commission's determination to achieve the same end, began to produce changes. A policy of discounted fares and deep-discounted fares was agreed, and began to be implemented in the late 1980s, but these are grudging concessions to the spirit of a Common Transport Policy rather than a wholehearted acceptance of the principle.

A major consideration in air transport was the reluctance of member states to relax control over their national airspace. This reduced the air traffic control system to a patchwork of twelve systems. After much discussion and endless delays in peak holiday periods, a system of central control based on the Dutch organisation Eurocontrol was finally agreed, and a much fuller harmonisation of air traffic control has resulted. There is not yet, and there may not be for a long time, any unified system comparable with the system for the United States, but there is now very close co-operation in this field, and there has been a real reduction in delays.

The situation in 1993 was that there was increased freedom for independent air carriers on major European routes, and the privatisation of some nationalised airlines is further emphasising this trend. At the same time even a privatised, former state airline can be a difficult competitor for a new airline seeking to break into an established market. The many restrictions placed on new developments in air transport by environmental requirements do not ease the problems of new entrants, while in long-distance movements negotiations for landing rights can be lengthy and expensive.

19.6.4 Sea transport

The European Union's impact on sea transport, and the devising of a Common Transport Policy for sea transport, has been slight to date. The developments in sea transport have been described elsewhere (see pages 64–5), and their chief effect is the change to containerisation and the tendency to call at only one big port in Western Europe, where everything is off-loaded and a new return cargo loaded. Sea distribution of the containers that are landed and the inward movements of containers for export are handled by the short-sea routes, either as roll-on roll-off or lift-on lift-off movements. Other containers may, of course, be taken direct by road or rail into the hinterland of the base port chosen, or assembled from the hinterland to await the arrival of the ship. The growth of short-sea movements has developed to meet market demand, as part of the reaction of entrepreneurs to a developing situation, and without any real direction from the EU authorities.

Similarly, in deep-sea movements, the highly competitive influence of carriers registered with flags of convenience, or state-run subsidised merchant fleets from the former Communist states, has meant that the European Union has been able to wield little influence. No real harmonised policy has been developed.

Another area where harmonisation of transport policy was similarly not well developed was in coastal cabotage. (Cabotage is the practice of reserving to a nation the right to its own internal and coastal trade.) In the EU this means the right to pick up and set down goods or passengers within a country, and in road haulage until the Single Market came in, it was occasionally conceded to foreign hauliers by reciprocal arrangements. Such reciprocal arrangements were not as willingly conceded with the coastal trade, and for a long time the United Kingdom, Ireland, Belgium and The Netherlands were the only countries which conceded unrestricted rights to other EU countries' vessels. Since the implementation of the Single Market these restrictions on the part of such countries as Germany and France have been conceded and freedom of access has become possible for UK coastal vessels.

19.7 The European Conference of Ministers of Transport (ECMT)

At the time of writing (early 1994) attempts continue to devise an effective transport policy, not only for the EU but also for the wider 'Europe'. A European Conference of Ministers of Transport (ECMT) was set up by a protocol signed on 17 October 1983. It constitutes a forum for the Ministers of Transport of nineteen European countries – Austria, Belgium, Denmark, Finland, France, Germany, Greece, Ireland, Italy, Luxembourg, The Netherlands, Norway, Portugal, Spain, Sweden, Switzerland, Turkey, the United Kingdom and Yugoslavia. (Australia, Canada, Japan and the United States are present as associated countries.) The work of the Council of Ministers is prepared by a Committee of Deputies who, for convenience, are based at the OECD office in Paris but are in fact a separate organisation.

The purposes of the conference are:

1. To take whatever measures may be necessary to achieve, at general or regional level, the most efficient use and rational development of European inland transport of international importance.
2. To co-ordinate and promote the activities of international organisations concerned with European inland transport, taking into account the work of supranational authorities in this field.

This brief is wide enough to cover most aspects of European transport, though once again air and sea transport do not appear to be matters for discussion, as has happened in the EU itself. The list of problems under study includes:

> transport policy; the financial situation and organisation of railways and road transport; problems concerning inland waterway transport and combined transport; development of European trunk lines of communication; problems concerning urban signs and signals; traffic trends and long-term traffic forecasts. (ECMT official publication)

It also organises round tables and symposia about transport matters at which expert reports can be presented and informed discussion can take place. These may lead to proposals for ministerial decisions.

One of the first discussion papers to be produced dealt with the fundamental problem of regulation versus liberalisation in the transport field. Regulation seeks to control transport developments to ensure a sound, integrated system of transport which makes use of existing assets at a sound level while permitting developments to occur where they are manifestly advantageous. The forces in favour of regulation, and the barriers to reform, are numerous. Shippers in principle are in favour of a more competitive system of transport but even they recognise that an unbridled free-for-all may be undesirable in the long term and involve social costs by excessive bankruptcies and waste of capital when market forces are misjudged. The transport entrepreneurs, the manufacturers of transport equipment, the bureaucrats and the trade unions are generally in favour of regulation.

This particular round table heard no voice in favour of rate regulation – which was universally held to be too inflexible for the wide variety of influences at work in deciding the price of particular services. Instead, it was felt that regulation through costs should be the method adopted.

Aspects of this method include:

1. The internalisation of external costs. This means that the social costs to be borne by the community in terms of noise, pollution, accident problems, policing, etc. should be carried by the transport industry in some acceptable form – taxation imposed to provide funds which would then be used to reimburse local authorities, accident victims, etc.
2. Regional aid was agreed to be necessary, but the delegates argued for 'transparency' of aid – in other words, aid should not be by covert subsidies but by open, properly justified allocations of resources for social reasons.
3. While rail transport must inevitably be supported, it was urged that its best role – heavy movements over long distances – should be emphasised and substitution encouraged in this particular area so far as possible.
4. The impact and objectives of official infrastructure policy need to be the subject of very close study. Trunk line routes do not improve the infrastructure if minor roads in peripheral areas are not improved to promote accessibility.

The general conclusion of the round table was that a more liberal and competitive framework was desirable, but was unlikely to be achieved on a European basis – each nation should seek to reduce regulations in line with the general principle. The proposed measures were as follows:

- *Capacity*. A gradual return to freedom was envisaged, with transport licences continuing for some time and any relaxation related to short-term economic trends.
- *Prices*. Reference rates could take the place of compulsory tariffs, which presumably means that the parties could agree, in the light of particular circumstances, to reduce or increase the rate payable.
- *Market structure*. Monopolistic or oligopolistic distortions of the market should continue to be rigorously opposed.
- *Harmonisation of costs*. Those transport modes using a 'free' way (i.e. road hauliers) should be charged for social costs imposed upon the community generally as explained at (1) above. As explained at (4) above, investment in the infrastructure should be carefully reviewed for its impact on the system of transport.

The rather conservative conclusions reached by such a round table emphasise the difficulties of harmonising transport arrangements. At the same time such top-level reviews of fundamental problems must be helpful.

19.8 Summary

1. The European Union (EU) is the new name for the European Community (EC), which was originally known as the European Economic Community (EEC).
2. The twelve current member states in the Union are: France, Germany, Italy, Belgium, Holland, Luxembourg, the United Kingdom, Eire, Denmark, Greece, Spain and Portugal.
3. The chief institutions are: the Council of Ministers, the Assembly (i.e. the European Parliament), the Commission, the Committee of Permanent Representatives (COREPER) and the Court of Justice. The duties and powers of these bodies are summarised in Fig. 19.1 (page 382).
4. The transport provisions of the Treaty of Rome are set out in Articles 74–84. The aims of these provisions are: to remove impediments to the free circulation of transport services, to harmonise the laws and regulations dealing with transport, to prevent excessive competition where this would be harmful, and to assist in the development of regional policies, social policies, fiscal policies and industrial, environmental and energy policies. It is also aimed at promoting international links, including the development of Third World countries, and defence.

5. Slow progress was made in developing a Common Transport Policy until the advent of the Single Market on 1 January 1993, when many of the old restrictions were finally abandoned and the European Union became a Single Market with free access to trade and transport by road, rail and short-sea vessels. Greater harmonisation was also achieved in air transport, particularly in the opening of airspace through Eurocontrol, based in Holland. Freer competition in air transport is developing slowly, but carriers, whether nationalised or privatised, are not keen to cut fares, holding that the public are not best served by very cheap transport if it means lowering of safety standards, and loss of viability by some airlines.

19.9 Questions

1. Write short notes on *three* of the following:
   (a) The Council of Ministers
   (b) COREPER
   (c) The Court of Justice
   (d) The European Assembly
   (e) The Commission
   (f) The European Union
2. What is meant by the Common Transport Policy? Thinking of the railways, once Eurotunnel has opened, what sort of influences would be at work in any attempt to secure a common railway policy throughout the European Union?
3. 'The Single Market has largely resolved the problems of securing a common transport policy in road haulage.' Would you agree? What does this mean for the proprietor of a small road haulage business with only one long-distance lorry and a couple of vehicles used for local deliveries?
4. 'The Commission is calling for a radical restructuring of national railway systems and a truly international rail network.' Explain this sentence and discuss what needs to be done to implement the Commission's policy.
5. Why has the European Union had little success in devising a common transport policy for deep-sea transport? Refer in your answer to (a) the types of deep-sea traffic; (b) the types of deep-sea carriers; (c) the competition facing deep-sea movements.
6. 'We are in business to make profits – so why should we cut fares?' Discuss this remark by the chairman of a major European airline, in the course of an investigation into European air fares, and their comparison with fares in the United States.

20 Financial aspects of transport and logistics

20.1 Business finance for transport and logistics

The field of business finance is wide, and the problems for management in successfully launching, developing and controlling any firm are very numerous and complex. We live in an era of sophisticated financial techniques, where extremely rapid evaluations of alternative projects can be made. To convince investors of the merits of a transport firm, the private entrepreneur must prepare conclusive evidence that the envisaged prospects of profitability are in fact real enough. The managers of public corporations do not face the same tests, but the scrutiny of auditors, the Public Accounts Committee or other scrutinising body, and the legislature itself are daunting. Whatever the results achieved by public bodies, criticism can be expected from one quarter or another.

Financial problems come under the following headings, each of which will be examined in detail:

1. The risks involved, and the sources of finance available.
2. The flow of income and expenditure, and the management of these funds by budgetary control.
3. Depreciation and obsolescence of transport facilities.
4. The control of costs by budgets and control procedures.
5. The return on capital invested in private enterprise firms, and the allocation of profits.

It is difficult in a general book of this type to deal with the financial problems of the huge range of firms and institutions to be found in transport, and more specialised reading should be undertaken by those particularly concerned with finance. They should also read the current literature, trade journals, etc., in their own specialist field, with particular attention to anything likely to affect the financial plans of their own firms. The professional institutions publish reading lists for students.

20.2 Risks involved in transport

There are as many types of uncertainty which have to be faced in the conduct of a transport firm as there are in life itself. These risks can be divided into insurable risks and non-insurable risks. Insurable risks are those where it is possible to calculate the probability that the risk will occur, so that a fair premium can be proposed which will enable a pool to be set up for compensating unfortunate contributors. Non-insurable risks are those that are not susceptible to calculation, so that insurance companies are unwilling to attempt to set up a pool for compensation. Even where a risk is insurable it does not follow that the business person can afford the necessary cover. Certain insurances – for example, the insurance of road vehicles against damage to third parties – are compulsory, and the transport firm will *have* to afford them, but many other forms of cover available may be so expensive that there is no alternative but to carry the risk personally. A table of uncertainties is given in Table 20.1.

20.3 Sources of finance available

The sources of finance available to transport and logistical firms – as to other firms – are as follows:

1. Personal savings.
2. Ploughing back of profits from a previous period.
3. Private borrowing from friends, banks or other institutions.
4. Partnerships.
5. By issuing shares, either as a private company or as a public company.
6. By issuing debentures, either privately or publicly.
7. By public loans, or state loans, to bodies set up by Act of Parliament as statutory bodies, municipalities or nationalised undertakings.

Only a brief look at each of these is possible in this book, and the reader with a particular interest should consult specialist books on finance.

20.3.1 Personal savings

In those fields of transport and logistics where it is possible to enter the field with relatively little capital, the personal savings of the proprietor make the most important contribution to the start of the enterprise. The purchase of a first vehicle from savings, or partly from savings and partly by hire purchase, has brought many a firm into existence. It is difficult to borrow money unless security can be offered, but banks will often lend relatively small sums without security, and slightly larger sums against a life insurance policy. Thus a business project which appears to a bank to offer

Table 20.1 Uncertainties in transport and logistics

Type of uncertainty	Examples in transport	Insurable or non-insurable	Avoidance action
1. Natural hazard	Flood, fire, frost, storms, gales, subsidences, rockfalls, static electricity.	Insurable	(*a*) Insure premises, contents, vehicles (compulsory), employer's liability (compulsory) and where applicable goods in transit. (*b*) Train staff in insurance aspects of their duties (e.g. duty of assured to minimise risks, take proper details of all accidents, obtain names of police, etc. attending, etc.).
2. Human uncertainty	(*a*) Death of key staff.	(*a*) Insurable	(*a*) Insure key personnel, for the benefit of the business, not the dependants.
	(*b*) Transfer of employment by key staff.	(*b*) Non-insurable	(*b*) Train up substitutes with good staff training programme. A 'grow your own' policy for the future.
	(*c*) Vandalism, theft, embezzlement, etc.	(*c*) Insurable	(*c*) Insure under contents policy, but take out fidelity bonds on key staff handling funds of any sort.
	(*d*) Lack of capacity in the owner or entrepreneur.	(*d*) Non-insurable	(*d*) Be cautious before embarking. Lay down clear contractual arrangements before commencement of any partnership or company.
3. Economic risks	(*a*) The risk that conditions of demand may change so that demand at the price envisaged is smaller than expected.	Both non-insurable	None – the uncertainty must be borne by the business owner.

	(*b*) The risk that conditions of supply may change so that supply at the price envisaged proves to be impossible.		Be conservative in all plans, expecting the worst scenario rather than the most favourable. Have contingency plans ready for alternative policies and approaches.
4. Technical risks	(*a*) Risks that the project may prove technically more difficult than anticipated. The more technical the project the more risky it is.	Non-insurable	Careful preparatory work with built-in safeguards as to price and delivery dates.
	(*b*) Risks that new developments may render existing equipment obsolete. Premature obsolescence is a feature of transport and logistical operations.		Try to arrange high-volume contracts which fully utilise assets before they become obsolete. Adequate provisions for obsolescence with the creation of sinking funds not available for other purposes.
5. Political risks	Risks that the project may prove politically unpopular or that pressure from environmental, domestic or foreign political interference, wars and riots may render it impossible.	Mostly non-insurable	Careful cost–benefit analysis can rebut ill-informed criticism. Caution in international arrangements. ECGD cover can be arranged for particular projects. Clear environmental policy, with a special environmental audit for major new projects, desirable.
6. Monetary risks	Risk that inflation/deflation, etc., may adversely affect calculations.	Non-insurable	Caution in preparatory work, with possible hedging transactions on foreign exchange market, or contracts expressed in units of account (EUAs or SDRs) to avoid inflationary problems.

prospects of profitability provided the future owner keeps living may lead a banker into suggesting to the would-be borrower that if he goes away and insures his life, the bank will then lend against the security of the life assurance policy. This is a risk to the bank, since life assurance policies of the type described only have a very small surrender value in the early years, though they do pay out at death. However, the venture may fail for other reasons. Illness may prevent the success of the business but the bank will not get compensation apart from any small surrender value. It is therefore vital for the would-be transport entrepreneur to save the maximum sum possible before embarking on any venture.

20.3.2 Ploughing back profits from a previous trading period

Once a business has begun, the ploughing-back of profits by the owner is the best source of finance for the expansion of the firm. The more profitable a firm is, and the more frugal the standard of living of the proprietor, the more it is likely to grow, to the eventual enrichment of the owner. Even with a public company, whose shares are owned by the general public, the ploughing-back of profits is a major source of new capital for the firm. Of course, the shareholders in such cases do not receive such a large dividend, since the profits are being retained in the business, but the price of the shares on the Stock Exchange will rise because the value of the business is increasing. An individual shareholder wishing to enjoy the extra value as income can usually sell his or her shares and take the profits at the expense of losing a stake in the company.

In order to plough back profits it is essential to charge a good margin of profit on the work done, and this will be easier if a record of absolute reliability can be established on such matters as safe arrival and strict compliance with contractual obligations. In short, complete customer satisfaction must be the aim. At the same time, we cannot satisfy the customer with rock-bottom competitive prices simply to get a larger and larger share of what – for us – is a totally unprofitable market. We cannot generate profits for future development unless we are able to add a reasonable profit margin above costs. The more we add value to a product while it is in our possession, the easier it is to charge a reasonable profit margin – we are able to share in the added-value we create. This is why the logistics company which carries out value-adding processes like breaking bulk, packaging, weighing, pricing, etc. can make good profits, while at the same time preserving its customer base. The customer hesitates to break the established bond, for to do so would be to lose the valuable services, including the IT links, with its preferred supplier.

Why is the ploughing-back of profits such a desirable method of growth?

It is because whatever profits accrue from the increased size of the business are ours, and ours alone. If we borrow money to expand, the profits resulting from the expansion are creamed off by the lender, be it the bank or any other creditor. What is more, the creaming-off process goes on year after year, even if the terms of trade move against us and margins decline. Those who borrow in good times at high rates of interest go bankrupt in bad times when earnings decline but repayments do not.

20.3.3 Private borrowing from friends, banks and other institutions

Borrowing is often helpful when a firm for some reason hits a patch of illiquidity (i.e. it has little cash available). If the illiquidity is foreseen, and can be justified to the person or firm making the loan, then it can usually be arranged to borrow the money on reasonable terms. For example, a firm purchasing new vehicles which will make it more competitive, or able to tender for a new class of work, will be sympathetically listened to when it asks for an overdraft. A firm which is in financial difficulties because its trade is declining or because incompetence has led it into financial difficulties is less likely to be able to borrow at reasonable rates.

Most lenders require some safeguard from the borrower, and the most usual form this takes is a mortgage on the title deeds of the land and buildings. This type of security is not available to businessmen or women who do not own the freehold or leasehold of their properties, but are in rented accommodation. It is also possible to borrow against the security of other assets: vehicles, for example, or plant and machinery. The paradox arises that it is easiest to borrow money when you have plenty of assets and can offer good security. This is usually the very time that you do not need to borrow money. This paradox is a sad fact of life which would-be entrepreneurs must bear in mind. Government assistance is available under a scheme called the Loan Guarantee Scheme, which is operated by the banks and other participating institutions. It guarantees 80 per cent of approved loans, repayable over 2–7 years, to a limit (at the time of writing) of £75,000.

Second mortgages are sometimes available. Here the firm which has already borrowed money on a mortgage of its landed property, borrows a further sum, usually from a different source, as a 'second' mortgage. The second mortgagor cannot get any benefit from the mortgage until the first mortgage has been settled and consequently is running a bigger risk. The rate of interest is therefore higher, and borrowers are well advised to keep away from such borrowing if possible. Legislation is in preparation to control the worst abuses of second mortgages, but even this legislation envisages a true interest rate of 20 per cent or more as a 'fair' rate of interest – a sobering thought for any borrower.

Second mortgages apart, more than one person has found that a generous lender of funds has, in the end, replaced him as the owner of the business. The astute lender, seeing a business which is viable but which is in difficulties due to the inexperience of the owner, uses funds to secure control by helping the original owner to get into debt at higher rates of interest than the business can afford. By creaming off the top 15–20 per cent of profit so little is left for the original owner that the enterprise ceases to be worthwhile and falls an early prey to the big fish waiting to swallow it.

Small businesses experiencing real difficulties in finding finance from the normal institutions such as banks and finance houses may find the specialised consortia operated by the clearing banks (with some assistance from the Bank of England) helpful. Under a general umbrella called Investors in Industry PLC a number of specialist organisations operate to assist in particular directions. Investors in Industry's address is 91 Waterloo Rd, London SE1 8XP.

Grants, small loans and other assistance are also available from COSIRA (Council for Small Industries in Rural Areas), the Enterprise Allowance Scheme, the Loan Guarantee Scheme for firms having difficulties in raising funds and the various employment subsidies. The Enterprise Initiative may be helpful – their hotline is: 0800 500 200.

20.3.4 Partnerships

Partnerships are formed for a variety of reasons, but the provision of the necessary finance almost always enters into the partnership agreement. A partnership agreement is best expressed in a formal *partnership deed*, in which the parties lay down the terms on which the business will be conducted. It is not essential to have such an agreement, but where it exists the provision of the capital, the proportions in which profits will be shared, the rate of interest to be paid on capital, if any, and the rate of interest to be charged on drawings, if any, will be specified in the agreement.

Partnerships in the transport and logistical field are chiefly found in small-scale enterprises, such as minor road haulage firms. They do not represent a significant part of the total industry, since the limited liability company has such advantages over partnership as a form of organisation in a competitive industry.

20.3.5 The issue of shares by limited liability companies

Practically all the major firms in the transport and logistics field are limited liability companies, and many small firms also adopt this form of business organisation. The reason is that the limited liability company gives at least some safeguard to those who form the company, or buy shares in the company, that their liability is limited to the amount of money that they put into the company. They do not, like sole traders and partners, have unlimited liability and run the risk of losing their homes and personal goods and chattels should the business get into difficulties.

It was not always so. In the early days of the Industrial Revolution – say, 1760–1855 – those who contributed capital to dig mines or build canals and railways were held to be partners in the enterprise and hence liable for any losses suffered by the business. Since many of these early industrial activities were highly speculative many who contributed capital to them lost all their material possessions, which were seized to pay the debts of the business. Often the speculators themselves who floated the original company had sold their own shares at a good profit before the collapse of the company. Such bitter experiences meant that others who had capital to spare would not risk investing it, but hoarded it unused, against some future 'rainy day'. Only when the Companies Act 1856 gave the privilege of limited liability could the funds necessary to finance new capital projects be tempted out onto the market.

Today, the limited liability company is the most popular form of business organisation. You can buy a company 'off the shelf' for about £120, and by a simple registration process change its name, registered directors, etc., at very short notice. There are about 1½ million companies in the United Kingdom. Recently one of them with a capital of only £2 was used to purchase a multinational company worth £1,500 million. Clearly, it had to borrow a lot of money to do so, but it shows how much can be borrowed if the directors have a viable proposal.

Every limited company issues shares, since the shares represent ownership of the company, but for many private companies the capital is very small. A private company is one the shares of which may not be sold on the open market, but may only be held by the directors and their friends or business acquaintances who agree to take shares. The name of the company must end in the word 'Limited' (or its Welsh equivalent). This is a warning to those who do business with the company that the proprietors have limited liability, and creditors can only look to the amount of the original capital for reimbursement should the company get into difficulties. Since the vast majority of private companies have capital of £1,000 or less, there is not much for the creditors if difficulties arise.

The issue of shares as a means of raising capital is chiefly confined to the public companies who are granted a quotation by the Stock Exchange Council so that their shares may be dealt in on the Exchange. Under two new schemes called the Venture Capital Scheme and the Business Expansion Scheme individual investors can obtain some guarantee of security in new ventures and this has made them more willing to take a shareholding in new enterprises. One approaches such investors through professional advisers on finance, such as accountants and banks.

New issues of shares are usually made with the assistance of specialised banking houses called Issuing Houses, who are almost always members of the Issuing Houses Committee. These houses may 'place' the shares privately with institutional investors such as insurance companies and trade unions. With issues of shares in private companies there is often an understanding that the company will apply for quotation at a later date, when a favourable opportunity arises. With publicly quoted shares the Issuing House will assist in the preparation of the application to the Stock Exchange Council, and arrange the necessary publication of the prospectus of the company. Discussion of the variety of rules and procedures required is inappropriate here. The final result will be the availability of the capital required, after deduction of expenses, underwriting fees for the issue, etc. The minimum capital for a public limited company is £50,000, but usually shares are issued for much larger amounts, depending on the project to be financed. A public limited company's name ends in the words 'Public Limited Company', or its abbreviation 'PLC'. An underwriting fee is a fee paid to an Issuing House for underwriting an issue. This means that if the public do not buy the shares the Issuing House will itself buy them, thus ensuring that the issue is successful and the company is able to start trading. The Issuing House will hold the shares and sell them off gradually as the company makes progress and is seen by the public to be a 'good buy' after all. Table 20.2 shows in tabular form the various types of security issued by limited companies.

20.3.6 Debentures

Companies, if permitted to do so by their Articles of Association, may borrow money by the issue of debentures. Debentures are a charge on the assets of the company and give debenture holders a trust deed, which entitles them to step in and seize either the general assets or specific assets should the company appear likely to be unable to pay the interest on the due date. They are therefore a very safe form of investment, and are popular with the more conservative investor unwilling to risk the loss of savings, and with institutional investors investing money collected from the public, as part of a balanced portfolio. They may be of three types:

1. *Fixed debentures*, secured on the fixed assets of the company, i.e. the land, buildings, plant and motor vehicles.
2. *Floating debentures*, secured on the stock in trade. Some firms have few fixed assets, but much stock in trade. This type of debenture might be

Table 20.2 Securities issued by companies (courtesy of Butterworth-Heinemann from *Commerce Made Simple*)

Type of investment	Reward earned	Degree of risk	Who buys them	Who issues them
Ordinary shares	Equal share of profits; hence so-called 'equity shares'	Carry the main risk	(*a*) Well-to-do investors who want big returns. (*b*) Institutional investors, for a balanced portfolio. (*c*) People interested in capital gains, rather than revenue profits.	Private and public companies
Deferred ordinary shares (founder's shares)	Share of profit after ordinary shares have had some (say 10%) profit	Same as ordinary shares	They are taken by the vendor of a business when he sells it to a company, as an earnest of goodwill	Public companies chiefly, but also private companies
Preference shares	Definite rate of dividend (say 7%), but only if profits are made	Less than ordinary shares as they *usually* have a prior right to repayment	Investors seeking security rather than large dividends	Public and private companies
Cumulative preference shares	As above, but if profits are not earned in one year the dividend accumulates and is not lost	As above	As above	As above
Participating preference shares	After taking the fixed rate (say 7%) these shares earn extra dividend if the ordinary shares get more than 7%	As above	As above	As above
Debentures (loans to companies; debentures are not really shares)	Fixed rate of interest (say 6%), payable whether profits are made or not	Very small	Institutional investors and others seeking a secure investment	Public and private companies, if permitted by their Articles

issued, for example, by a motor trade parts dealer, but would not be issued by a road haulage firm providing services.
3. *Naked debentures*, issued without security, and therefore, as the name implies, more exposed. They could only be issued by firms with excellent reputations.

Debentures have a prior claim on the assets of a company, ranking for repayment before the shareholders and before other unsecured creditors should the firm get into difficulties. For this reason it would be most undesirable for debentures to be issued secretively, so that shareholders and creditors did not know that they had come into existence. Therefore companies are required under the Companies Acts to register their debentures, i.e. record them on a 'Register of Charges' in their company records at Company House. Since these records are open to the public for a very nominal charge, anyone doing business with a company can inspect the register and see whether there are 'secured creditors' likely to step in and seize all or part of the assets should the firm get into difficulties. Secured creditors are creditors who have a legal document, a security such as a debenture deed, which entitles them to prior payment of the moneys owed to them.

Debentures earn a fixed rate of interest which is lower than other investments because the lender is running little risk of losing any money. Many of them are redeemable either at a specific time or at the discretion of the company, whose directors may repay the loan when they feel its usefulness has declined and profits in cash form are available to repay it.

20.3.7 Finance for statutory bodies

Many transport organisations are set up not as limited companies registered under the Companies Acts but as public corporations authorised by an Act of Parliament to perform certain transport activities. Often this involves the nationalisation of firms currently offering services to the public. In other cases the process stops short of nationalisation. For example, with the Port of London Authority, in 1908 Parliament thought fit to solve the problems of the port by taking over the activities of the various enclosed docks and placing them in the hands of a public body established for the purpose. While not actually run as a nationalised enterprise, the autonomous Port Authority acts in the interests of all parties using the port: shippers, shipowners, lighterage firms, trade unions, etc. The finance is arranged for autonomous bodies by the issue to the public of stock, which entitles them to interest at an agreed rate and to redemption of capital at a future date. Clearly, different terms of issue of such stock are possible, and the range is too wide to discuss here.

In recent years the wisdom of nationalising major industries has been called into question, and a great deal of privatisation, or partial privatisation, has taken place. Thus while the Port of London Authority still exists, it is mainly concerned with the waterway – the River Thames and its various facilities such as buoys, radar networks, channel, etc. The major dock still dealing with export cargoes has been privatised as the Port of Tilbury Ltd, and many other riverside wharves and berths are privately owned and operated.

20.3.8 The provision of capital by government agencies and other bodies

In transport economics, as in all economic activities, we are faced with the problem of scarcity. There is never enough of any resource available to satisfy all demands, and this is true of capital more than most resources. Generally speaking, the flow of capital will be controlled by market forces, where certainty of return on capital invested and security of the capital itself are the chief influences at work. This means that capital will flow most readily to those industries which are certain to be successful. Unfortunately, the rich and powerful multinational firm is most likely to meet this requirement, while the inventor struggling to produce a revolutionary product or the innovator endeavouring to launch a new service is starved of capital. Such growth points in industry often need to be helped from official sources, where a longer-term view of profitability can be taken. In this way the more serious risks of new enterprises can be carried partly by society as a whole.

The specialist bodies available to finance this type of project are under the general direction of the Department of Trade and Industry (DTI). Advice should be sought from DTI local offices (see your local telephone directory under 'Trade').

For smaller firms a number of minor schemes for the provision of capital are now available in the United Kingdom. They include the Venture Capital Scheme, the Loan Guarantee Scheme, grants from COSIRA (the Council for Small Industries in Rural Areas), the Enterprise Initiative, and other schemes. Further information is available from Freephone Enterprise Initiative. Old schemes decline and new schemes are brought forward at regular intervals, so the reader should consult his local Enterprise Agency or the freephone service.

Besides these official bodies various independent private sector groups have been set up by consortia of banks, industrial entrepreneurs, etc. Such a group is Investors in Industry, an umbrella organisation owned by nine

London and Scottish banks, with a 15 per cent stake held by the Bank of England.

20.4 The calculation of initial capital requirements

The capital requirement of a new firm is often underestimated by the promoter of the enterprise. It is easy to forget that the return of funds as payment for services rendered is often delayed for some considerable time. It is quite usual not to render accounts until the end of a month, and then to give 30 days for payment. This may mean that as much as two months elapse before payment is received. Many larger firms demand much longer, often three months, and will not take on a transport contractor who cannot wait for this period. Such major firms are valuable customers and absolutely reliable if you can meet their conditions, but the initial waiting period can be difficult for the contractor. The authors know of one firm, handling a major contract for a reputable manufacturer, which had done £9 million worth of forwarding before the first payment arrived. This had only been possible because of firm backing by a merchant bank.

The following fictitious example will illustrate the initial capital requirements of a small firm.

Example

1. The three Wills Brothers will set up in business as road hauliers using three vehicles which will cost, second-hand on 1 January 19.. £38,000, £18,000 and £12,000, respectively. They have initial capital of £1,000 each.
2. It is hoped to do £18,000 of business a month for the first two months and £24,000 thereafter: 20 per cent of this is expected to be for cash, 40 per cent payable in 30 days, and 40 per cent in 3 months.
3. Apart from the cost of vehicles, outgoings will include rent of £1,000 per month, other fixed expenses of £2,200 per month and variable expenses of 40 per cent of the business done.
4. The three brothers expect to draw £1,200 a month each for personal use.

The cash budget over the first six months is shown in Table 20.3.

Clearly, the total finance required before the cash flows into the business making the firm viable is £83,000, far more than the original cost of the vehicles, which was £68,000. A bank manager approached for a loan with which to buy three vehicles, costing £68,000 will react coolly to the idea until more facts are known. A bank manager presented with the cash budget shown in this example will have a greatly improved view of the likely situation of the business in the months ahead. Astute questions will be asked. Readers should consider what questions they would ask were they a bank manager. Likely questions might be:

Table 20.3 Summary of cash position

Receipts	Jan. £	Feb. £	Mar. £	Apr. £	May £	Jun. £
Original capital	3,000					
Earnings						
Cash for services	3,600	3,600	4,800	4,800	4,800	4,800
Monthly credit	–	7,200	7,200	9,600	9,600	9,600
3-monthly credit	–	–	–	7,200	7,200	9,600
Total (A)	6,600	10,800	12,000	21,600	21,600	24,000
Expenditure						
Motor vehicles	68,000	–	–	–	–	–
Rent	1,000	1,000	1,000	1,000	1,000	1,000
Other fixed expenses	2,200	2,200	2,200	2,200	2,200	2,200
Variable expenses	7,200	7,200	9,600	9,600	9,600	9,600
Total	78,400	10,400	12,800	12,800	12,800	12,800
Drawings	3,600	3,600	3,600	3,600	3,600	3,600
Total outgoings (B)	82,000	14,000	16,400	16,400	16,400	16,400
Net cash flow						
In + (A–B)				+5,200	+5,200	+7,600
Out – (B–A)	–75,400	–3,200	–4,400			

1. What customers have you sounded out to make these estimates of £18,000 business in the first two months and £24,000 thereafter?
2. What items do you include under fixed expenses?
3. What grounds have you for believing that one fifth of your work will be for cash, and two-fifths for firms prepared to pay within 30 days?
4. Do you consider that these second-hand vehicles can be kept serviceable, so that business is not interfered with by maintenance activities? How many days per month do you think a vehicle can be on the road?
5. When your cashflow eventually turns favourable (in April), what proportion of the balance are you prepared to use to repay the loan and interest?

Budgets of this sort are clear plans for the future activities of the firm. No one is going to get into too difficult a situation if he or she watches the firm's activities from month to month and compares the actual achievements with the budgeted achievements. The budget 'rolls forward' ahead of the business, being adjusted as experience shows. If, in fact, three-fifths of the customers pay within 30 days the cashflow position will improve and the budget will be adjusted to account for this change. Management must keep an open mind, exploiting favourable situations as they arise and getting the best results possible in the circumstances from adverse situations.

20.5 Keeping capital intact – depreciation and obsolescence

Any transport or logistics firm must be at pains to preserve the assets it creates or buys in as good a condition as possible. Inevitably, vehicles, equipment, installations and buildings decline in efficiency with the passage of time. To fail to renew and repair as and when necessary is to consume one's capital. Every accounting period must provide not only the reward to the investor but sufficient funds to keep the original investment in good heart. This is done by charging all repairs and renewals to the profit and loss account so that the profit available for distribution is reduced. Where an asset declines in value over a period of years, it is usual to provide for this by a process known as depreciation. Special account must also be taken of obsolescence.

A more difficult problem arises in times of inflation, when the cost of new assets rises year after year. To put away a sum of profit each year which is based on the cost price of the present facilities means that when the replacement time arrives there will be insufficient funds available to purchase the new asset at its higher price. This leads us into considerations of what is known as 'inflation accounting'. We shall now consider these three problems: depreciation, obsolescence and inflation accounting.

20.5.1 Depreciation

Depreciation is the reduction in value of an asset as a result of fair wear and tear. As an asset loses value we reduce the book valuation of it in line with our estimate of the loss. There are several ways in which depreciation can be calculated. The accounting principle which motivates accountants to try different methods of depreciation is that they are seeking in their accounting to achieve a 'true and fair view' of the position of the business. As far as limited companies are concerned in Great Britain, this is positively required by law. The Companies Acts 1985–9 require all businesses to keep accounts in such a way as to give a 'true and fair view' of the company's affairs. This requires two things:

1. The assets must be valued on the Balance Sheet at a fair value so far as we can estimate it.
2. If a loss has been suffered it must be charged against the profits – to do otherwise would overstate the profitability of the business.

Applying these two rules to the problem of depreciation, we see that if an asset wears out, the loss suffered as a result of wear and tear must be written off the profits. At the same time, the asset will be reduced in value to show only its present value now that it has been partly worn out.

A common method adopted in transport firms is the 'straight-line method', which has the merit of being simple to understand. In any case,

Table 20.4 Leaving the asset on the books at cost price

Motor Vehicles Account

19. .		£
Jan. 1	Roadworthy Ltd J.1	22,800

Provision for Depreciation on Motor Vehicles Account

19.1		£
Dec. 31	Profit & loss A/c	4,500
19.2		
Dec. 31	Profit & loss A/c	4,500
19.3		
Dec. 31	Profit & loss A/c	4,500
19.4		
Dec. 31	Profit & loss A/c	4,500

whatever system is used assets wear out or become obsolete for so many reasons that no method can be exact.

20.5.2 The straight-line method of depreciation

The accountant first calculates the amount of the annual charge for depreciation necessary to reduce the asset to its scrap value, or residual value, over the lifetime of the asset. To do this we use the following formula:

$$\text{Annual charge} = \frac{\text{Cost price less scrap value}}{\text{Estimated lifetime in years}}$$

Example

A motor vehicle is purchased from Roadworthy Limited for £24,800 of which £2,000 is the value of the tyres, leaving a vehicle value of £22,800 on 1 January. It is estimated that it will need replacing in four years, and will then fetch £4,800. Using the formula, we have:

$$\text{Annual charge} = \frac{£22{,}800 - £4{,}800}{4} = £4{,}500$$

The asset will be depreciated by four equal instalments of £4,500 each. Each year the sum of £4,500 will be written off the Profit and Loss Account as a loss due to depreciation, and this will be collected into a special 'Provision for Depreciation on Motor Vehicles Account', as shown in Table 20.4. The value of the asset at any given time is therefore the book-value (i.e. cost price), less the accumulated depreciation to date. In this case by the end of year 3 it would be:

	£
Cost price	22,800
Less depreciation	13,500
Present value of asset	9,300

20.5.3 The diminishing balance method

A further method of depreciation is the *diminishing balance method*. Under this method the asset is depreciated by a fixed percentage every year on the diminishing balance of the account. This is a very simple method since recalculation is not required when additions or sales take place during the year.

Using the same example as before, a motor vehicle valued at £22,800 and depreciated at 25 per cent per annum on the diminishing balance would be depreciated as follows (calculations to the nearest pound):

Year 1	Depreciation	£5,700	Balance at year end	£17,100
Year 2	Depreciation	£4,275	Balance at year end	£12,825
Year 3	Depreciation	£3,206	Balance at year end	£9,619
Year 4	Depreciation	£2,405	Balance at year end	£7,214

It so happens that this method is very similar to the method used by the Inland Revenue when giving capital allowances. Although companies have a statutory duty to write off a fair amount of depreciation, as explained earlier, in fact for the purpose of calculating profits and the tax due on them, the system is to ignore the firm's own calculations (adding back to the profits whatever they deducted for depreciation). Instead they are given a capital allowance of 25 per cent on any asset purchased during the year, and in subsequent years 25 per cent of the balance, which is said to be a 'pool' of assets. This puts everyone on the same footing, but the day does come when an asset is disposed of and the two values (i.e. the firm's valuation and the Inland Revenue's valuation) have to be reconciled. This simply means an adjustment for the depreciation figure in the year of sale. It need not bother us here.

20.5.4 Sinking funds and depreciation

There is an anomaly about depreciation which some people find hard to understand. Compare depreciation as an expense of the business and any other expense, such as telephone expenses. When we pay our telephone bill the cash goes out of the business and so naturally we can see that it is sensible to deduct this loss from the profits of the business as an overhead expense. When we deduct depreciation (say, £5,700 as in Year 1 of the last example) from our profits the money has not gone out of the business, but is left in the system. The shareholders cannot have the £5,700, because it has to be retained to buy a new vehicle when the present one ends its useful life. The £5,700 is 'loose' in the system, and someone who notices it in the bank account may use it, for whatever purpose. We must prevent this, and the best way is to invest the £5,700 in an investment which will not only keep the money safe but will earn interest or dividends until we need the new vehicle. This is called a sinking fund – we sink the money out of sight in a portfolio of shares or debentures. Any interest earned, or dividends received, are similarly invested and added to the portfolio. Finally, when we need the new vehicle the shares, etc. are sold on the Stock Exchange and the cash realised is used to buy the new asset.

20.5.5 Obsolescence

Obsolescence occurs when technical developments render an asset uneconomic in use, and it has to be prematurely replaced. It effectively reduces the lifetime of the asset, and represents an abnormal loss in value. Such abnormal losses have been particularly common in the aviation industry, where rapid advances in technology have made aircraft obsolete before their full working life has elapsed. For example, the introduction of the 747 Jumbo Jet some years ago caused the premature retirement of smaller aircraft. When such abnormal losses are likely to occur it is common to establish a Provision for Obsolescence Account, where sums written off the profits can be retained to meet any abnormal decline in value which may occur in the years ahead.

If proper allowance is made for depreciation and obsolescence, the capital will be preserved at its original value and the business will be kept in good heart.

20.5.6 Inflation accounting and historical cost accounting

The Company Acts 1985–9 require companies to publish annual accounts for their shareholders. These accounts must give a 'true and fair view' of the affairs of the business. This has traditionally meant that the original cost of assets must be shown, less the total depreciation to date, to give their present value on the books. At the same time, in the Profit and Loss Account, the total receipts must be shown, set against the total expenditure incurred in earning these receipts. The difference will be the profit, or loss, of the venture. In times of stable prices this picture does give a 'true and fair view' of the affairs of the business. In inflationary times the picture may be far from true, and even absolutely misleading. This is because the

Table 20.5 Costs of vehicles

	Historical cost (£)	Cost at present-day prices (£)
10-year-old vehicle	16,500	32,600
6-year-old vehicle	19,800	32,600
4-year-old vehicle	22,600	32,600
New vehicle	32,600	32,600
	£91,500	£130,400

sums of money spent over the years, i.e. the 'historical costs', are in fact sums of money of different values. The reader will understand this most easily if a simple example is taken.

Imagine a road haulier who has purchased four similar lorries over the years, one of them ten years ago, one six years ago, one four years ago and one this year. The historical costs and current costs are roughly shown in Table 20.5.

When we provide depreciation for road vehicles we deduct the depreciation from the Profit and Loss Account, thus reducing the profits available for distribution. This amount of money is then invested until such time as the lorries require to be replaced. But if the amounts put away are based on historical costs, even with interest they will not provide enough funds to buy new lorries at today's inflated prices.

Every transport firm is faced by the problems of inflation. These problems may be listed as follows:

1. Prices are always rising, so that both running costs and the costs of new assets to replace worn-out assets increase all the time.
2. £1 put away for future use in purchasing new assets will, by the time it is put to use, have declined in value so that it buys less. This means that in depreciating our assets we need to put away more than the ordinary fraction of its original cost; we need to put away the same fraction of its eventual new cost. It is not easy to guess what this will be.
3. If we do not use inflation accounting the following results ensue:
   (a) Profits will be overstated, and hence will give a false appearance of well-being to the firm.
   (b) This false appearance will lead investors to expect a distribution of dividends in excess of what is really desirable, since in fact the profits were overstated.
   (c) Labour will demand a higher share of the rewards available to the industry; that is, pressure for wage increases will follow higher profits, although in fact these profits are illusory.

There is plenty of evidence to show that all these results have followed the continued use of historical accounting in the last few years. The 'true and fair view' given by historical cost accounting is used to justify higher dividends and higher wages, although in fact it is not 'true', and not 'fair'. The higher the rate of inflation the more the distortion of the true position, and the higher demands of both labour and investors, leaving firms short of finance for the replacement of assets.

Some years ago the accountancy authorities did their best to persuade accountants to adopt an approved system of inflation accounting, but it was highly technical in nature and eventually was 'more honoured in the breach than in the observance'. Instead, more straightforward arrangements for recognising the effects of inflation were adopted. The 'true and fair view' we need the auditors to certify is the fact that the capital has been kept intact in real terms, before profits have been declared. The final accounts which are to be published need simply to be revalued in terms of current costs and prices. If this is done and we realise that the depreciation calculated on the historical cost is inadequate to provide the funds needed for replacement of the asset concerned, we simply base our calculation on the current cost, not the historical cost. This puts more funds in the sinking fund account and reduces the profits available for distribution. If this is done, then the following desirable effects ensue:

1. Profits are reduced to their true level, and this reduces demands for the distribution of dividends.
2. Trade union pressure is reduced and wage negotiations are pursued on a more realistic basis.
3. Changes in the valuation of shares occur as Stock Exchanges take account of the true profitability of firms.
4. Amalgamations and takeovers are reduced, since the number of firms getting into financial difficulties is reduced.

20.6 The financial statements of an established enterprise

It is now appropriate to consider the accounts of an established enterprise. Before looking at the actual accounts of an important transport body we must consider the principles governing the accounting records of such an enterprise. Every enterprise has two aspects of finance to consider: the capital aspect and the revenue aspect. Let us examine these two aspects in some detail.

20.6.1 Capital receipts and capital expenditure

Capital receipts and capital expenditure refer to the following matters:

1. The collection of the original capital necessary to start the enterprise.
2. The provision of additional capital during the course of its activities, whenever expansion of the firm or institution requires it.

3. The expenditure of this capital in creating the capital assets of the firm, from the purchase of the geographical site or sites, the erection of buildings, installations and plant to the provision of furniture and equipment, motor vehicles, etc.

An annual presentation of the current capital position is made in the Balance Sheet, a document which lists the assets and liabilities in some simple format to present a true and fair view of the affairs of the enterprise, for the benefit of interested parties. This document always shows the capital employed and the sources from which it was obtained. Against this, under a heading 'Financed by', are listed all the assets of the business which have been purchased with the capital made available by investors and creditors. These assets represent the capital in actual physical form and can be viewed, valued and appraised by interested parties. Such a Balance Sheet for a major logistical company is shown in section 20.6.3.3 below.

20.6.2 Revenue receipts and revenue expenditure

Revenue receipts and revenue expenditure refer to the following matters:

1. The revenues earned by the firm's activities, from all sources such as sales of trade goods; sales of manufactured articles; payments for services rendered and for facilities provided; fees for professional advice; commissions and other profits; rents from land or premises; leasing of facilities, premises and plant and other revenues such as licensing of other firms to use patents, etc.
2. The expenditures incurred in earning the revenues listed above, including wages and salaries; running expenses of every kind; fixed charges such as rent, rates and taxes on vehicles; losses such as bad debts, insurance premiums, loan interest, etc. Depreciation charges are also included in these expenses and make possible the purchase of new assets to replace worn-out or obsolete capital items.

The difference between revenue receipts and expenditure will be the profit or loss of the firm or institution. Profits will be used to pay the dividends to which shareholders are entitled. Alternatively they will be ploughed back into the firm for expansion purposes and will appear on the Balance Sheet as reserves. Losses will represent a decline in the total value of the capital and will appear as such on the Balance Sheet.

20.6.3 Financial statements

At one time when enterprises were small and proprietors conducted their own affairs, financial statements were not necessary to the conduct of an enterprise. Today they are essential. Not only are they required to satisfy the Inland Revenue who wish to levy income tax or corporation tax on the business, but business is so competitive that proprietors who do not have some regular and effective check on expenditures and incomes will find themselves in difficulties. For limited companies they represent an opportunity for the shareholders to review the activities of the directors and for the public corporations they present a similar opportunity to Parliament to review the industry's work.

This book will be read by readers with a wide range of experience – some of whom will be extremely knowledgeable about accountancy and others who will be quite ignorant of the subject. To give a reasonable picture of the accounts of logistical companies the authors have therefore presented two sets of accounts. The first is a simple set of 'final accounts' of a small road haulage business run by a sole trader. The second is a highly sophisticated set of 'final accounts' of a fictitious major logistical firm. To keep things as clear as possible, the two sets of accounts are produced in similar styles, but to bring the more sophisticated set into a format as near as possible to the published accounts of major companies this set has been re-presented in 'vertical style'. In reality there are no real advantages to the vertical style of presentation, but accountants have developed this style over many years, and even Parliament has sanctioned its use to some extent. This is really regrettable, for the vertical style is more difficult for the layman to understand, and also makes it rather easier to hide 'creative accounting' – i.e. any accounting trickery which disguises what the directors are actually doing. All such activities are illegal, for the Companies Acts require the published accounts of a company to give a 'true and fair view' of the affairs of the business. Parliament hoped that this wording would encourage the Boards of companies to produce sets of accounts which comply with the spirit of the law. However, there are always people who prefer to pretend that complying with the letter of the law will be good enough for them. We read every week in our financial press of companies that have failed, some from incompetence, some from over-enthusiasm and some from downright fraud. When we remember that they all have accountants and they all have auditors, we can see that compliance with the spirit of the Companies Acts is not high on everyone's agenda.

The reader is now recommended to consider the three sets of Final Accounts presented below. A set of final accounts is a set of accounts drawn up on the last day of the financial year. Such sets of accounts are drawn up in different ways, according to the type of activity carried on. The main types are:

1. *Trading businesses, which buy and sell goods*. These have a Trading Account, followed by a Profit and Loss Account, and ending with a

Balance Sheet of assets and liabilities as at the last moment of the last day of the year. The Trading Account reveals the *gross profit* on trading, the Profit and Loss Account reveals the *net profit* (clean profit) after the overheads have been deducted from the gross profit. The net profit is available to the proprietors (but if it is a company tax will be levied first).

2. *Manufacturing businesses*. These have first of all a Manufacturing Account, and this may, if desired, throw up a manufacturing profit. The goods manufactured are then passed to the Sales Department and we have a Trading Account, Profit and Loss Account and Balance Sheet as in (1) above.
3. *Service businesses*. These do not manufacture or trade, but offer a service. They have a single account called a Revenue Account, in which the revenues received are set against the expenses incurred, to produce a net profit. Our sets of accounts are of this type where all that is needed is a Revenue Account, followed by a Balance Sheet of the business as at the end of the financial year.

20.6.3.1 *Accounts of a small road haulage firm*

M. Marlow

Revenue Account for year ended 31 December 19..

Administrative expenses	£		£
Postage	182	Fees received	230,026
Rates	1,560	Discounts received	852
Light & Heat	540	Commission received	12,700
Telephone expenses	2,156		243,578
Salaries	36,941		
Depreciation	2,304		
Stationery	425		
Distribution costs			
Wages	34,944		
Insurance	12,956		
Repairs	11,280		
Petrol & oil	16,250		
Tyres	7,904		
Depreciation expenses	15,640		
Loan interest	3,300		
Total expenses	146,382		
Net profit	97,196		
	£ 243,578		£ 243,578

Balance Sheet as at 31 December 19..

Fixed assets	£	£			£
			Capital A/c (M. Marlow)		
Premises		122,590	at 1 Jan.		165,310
Fixtures	23,040		*Add* net profit	97,196	
Less depreciation	9,732		*Less* drawings	36,800	
		13,308			60,396
Motor vehicles	78,200				225,706
Less depreciation	19,640				
		58,560	*Long-term liability*		
		194,458	Loan		22,000
Current assets	£		*Current liabilities*		
Debtors	26,420		Creditors	7,200	
Fuel, etc.	10,272		Salaries due	1,650	
Bank balance	25,166				8,850
Cash in hand	240				
		62,098			
		£ 256,556			£ 256,556

Notes

1. The net profit for the year was £97,196.
2. This net profit belongs to the proprietor, but some of it has already been drawn on as 'drawings for personal use'. Therefore, only the net amount of £60,396 is transferred to the proprietor's Capital Account, raising it to £225,706.
3. The balance sheet has been presented in correct European style with the assets on the left and the liabilities on the right.

20.6.3.2 *Simplified accounts of a major logistical company*

A Forwarder PLC

Revenue Account for year ended 31 December 19..

	£m		£m
Distribution costs	241.1	Fees received:	
Hire fleet expenses	89.0	Distribution	276.2
Costs of food services	55.1	Vehicle hire	117.4
Manufacturing costs	27.9	Food services	67.5
Other costs	35.1	Manufacturing	30.7
Interest paid	5.1	Other receipts	36.2
	453.3		
Net profit	74.7		
	£ 528.0		£ 528.0

Appropriation of Profit Account

	£m		£m
Goodwill written off	10.8	Balance at 1 Jan.	162.1
Corporation tax	21.0	Profit for year	74.7
Dividends paid	22.7	Profit on foreign exchange	12.0
Balance to next year	206.3	Funds from sale of subsidiary co.	12.0
	£ 260.8		£ 260.8
			£m
		Balance to next year	206.3

Balance Sheet as at 31 December 19..

	£m	£m	£m			
Intangible asset	Cost	Deprec.	Value	*Ordinary Shareholders'*		£m
Goodwill	30.7	(10.8)	19.9	*Interest in Co.*		
				Ordinary Share Capital		75.6
				Premium on Shares		27.8
Tangible assets				Profit and Loss A/c Balance		206.3
Land & Buildings	201.4	(60.4)	141.0			309.7
Vehicles & Plant	452.6	(219.2)	233.4			
Other Assets	3.5	(0.2)	3.3			
			397.6	*Long-term Liabilities*	£m	
Current Assets		£m		Loans	89.3	
Stocks		43.0		Other Creditors	17.7	
Debtors		138.1		Deferred Taxation	19.6	
Cash at bank		51.5				126.6
Cash in hand		1.3		*Current Liabilities*	£m	
			233.9	Trade creditors	159.5	
				Ordinary dividend	13.4	
				Corporation tax	16.8	
				Short-term loans	5.5	
						195.2
			£ 631.5			£ 631.5

Notes

1. The accounts above are shown in the same style as the simplified accounts of M. Marlow, and not in the way that is required by the Companies Acts 1985–9.
2. Once the profit has been worked out in the Revenue Account it has to be transferred into an Appropriation Section of the Profit and Loss Account, where there is already a balance from the previous year. One or two other unusual profits (such as a profit on foreign exchange dealings) are joined with it to give a total of £260.8 million profit.

3. Some of this is used to write off goodwill, which is an intangible asset – we don't get much for our money except people's good opinion of the previous owner. It is usually written off over four years.
4. After paying corporation tax and the dividends there is a balance of £206.3 million left in the business.
5. Note that on the Balance Sheet the assets are set against the liabilities. Notice that the original capital of £75.6 million has now risen to £309.7 million (the total ordinary shareholders' interest with all the profits ploughed back). The value of each £1 share is therefore £4.10 on the Stock Exchange (although, of course, the actual price may be a little different from this if the market is 'bullish' (optimistic) about the prospects of the company, or 'bearish' (pessimistic) about the company's future).

20.6.3.3 *Published accounts of a major logistical company*

Note: This is not a proper set of published accounts because the requirements of the Companies Acts 1985–9 are many and varied and most public limited companies need a whole booklet to display all the figures. All these accounts can show is the vertical style of presentation. Readers, and especially students, are recommended to send off to any major public limited company in the transport and logistics field and they will make a copy of their final accounts available to you.

Published Accounts of A Forwarder PLC (£ million)

for year ended 31 December 19..

		£m
Turnover of the business		528.0
Less costs incurred in achieving this turnover		(453.3)
Net profit for year		74.7
Add balance from previous year		162.1
Add other profits (sale of subsidiary, etc.)		24.0
		260.8
	£m	
Less Goodwill written off	10.8	
Corporation tax provided	21.0	
Dividends paid	22.7	
		(54.5)
Balance on Profit and Loss Appropriation A/c (profits ploughed back)		206.3

Balance Sheet of A Forwarder PLC as at 31 December 19.. (£m)

			Cost	*Depreciation*	*Value*
Intangible asset – Goodwill			30.7	(10.8)	19.9
Tangible assets			657.5	(279.8)	377.7
	£m				397.6
Current assets	233.9				
Less					
Current liabilities	(195.2)				
Net current assets (working capital)					38.7
					£ 436.3
Financed by:					
Ordinary Shareholders' Interest in the Co.					£m
Ordinary shares of £1					75.6
Capital reserves					27.8
Revenue reserves					206.3
Ordinary shareholders' equity					309.7
Long-term liabilities		£m			
Loans and other financial creditors		107.0			
Deferred taxation		19.6			
					126.6
					£ 436.3

Notes

1. The one advantage of the vertical style is that there is more room to display the figures across the full width of the page.
2. Much of the detail is left out of the main display and given in notes later in the report. That is why we need a whole brochure to publish the Final Accounts.
3. It is usual to deduct the current liabilities from the current assets to give a net figure for 'working capital'. Working capital is the money you have left over to run the business once you have purchased the fixed assets. In this example there is £38.7 million. Lack of working capital is one of the commonest reasons for the failure of a business – you must have working capital to pay wages and to pay your suppliers (your creditors). Failure to do so is an 'act of bankruptcy' and can lead to bankruptcy if no one is prepared to provide extra cash for working capital.

20.7 Costing transport and logistical activities

20.7.1 Definition of costing

Costing is an accounting process which allocates expenditure to particular activities or operations, so that their likely or true cost can be discovered.

If the costs are being forecast, then the cost accountant is said to be preparing a budget for future activities. If the costs have already occurred, and they are simply being allocated to the particular activities which caused them, we say that the accountant is preparing 'historical' costs. In most firms both processes will be carried out.

20.7.2 Budgets

Budgets represent an intelligent and informed forecast of the expenditure to be incurred and the revenues to be earned. As the operations get under way and 'actual' costs are incurred, it becomes possible to compare the actual costs with the budgeted costs. Any variance between actual costs and budgeted costs will be analysed to discover the reason. This process is called 'variance analysis'. It may reveal price trends which would otherwise be overlooked; errors in calculations; even dishonesty, embezzlement, or theft of fuel and spare parts. The resulting action varies from dismissal of the dishonest employee to corrective action to make the budget more realistic in view of current trends in prices of supplies, labour and other resources.

A *capital budget* is a forecast of capital expenditure under particular headings for a forthcoming period, and the sources of finance available. The budget will be scaled down to what seems possible in view of the current financial position, postponing until a later date those projects which are least necessary. These marginal projects will usually be those with smaller prospects of profitability.

A *revenue budget* is a forecast of expenditure and receipts from a particular activity. By adding together the budgets for all these activities we can arrive at a total budget for the firm. Help in the preparation of budgets can often be obtained from trade associations which make available tables of costs, updated from time to time. For many industries specialist accounting firms have devised special systems of cost records. These can be very useful to firms in the industry.

The road haulage revenue budget given in Table 20.7 refers to a single vehicle, but in practice would be prepared in columnar form for all vehicles to give a budget for the total fleet.

The total budget for the whole fleet per week would then be compared with the actual weekly costing statement shown in Table 20.6. This statement would be produced as soon as the figures became available. Actual figures would be used for the revenue earned and the wages, while the running expenses would be based on the budget for the actual mileage run. The rest of the figures would be based upon the budgeted figures.

Table 20.6 Weekly costing statement for 5-day week ending . . .

Revenue earned (actual)		£—
Expenses		
Wages (actual)	—	
Running costs (based on actual mileage)	—	
Licences/Insurance (as per budget)	—	
Depreciation (as per budget)	—	
Overhead expenses (as per budget)	—	
Total expenses		—
		£——
Profit for week		—

20.8 The return on capital employed

Every enterprise can be judged according to the return it brings to the investor. Such returns are best calculated as a percentage return on capital employed. The formula is:

$$\frac{\text{Net profit}}{\text{Capital employed}} \times 100$$

Unfortunately, as with all formulae, we must define our terms carefully or we shall arrive at different answers, or answers which are less useful than they might be. Let us consider limited companies first.

20.8.1 The return on capital employed – companies

With limited companies the true capital employed is found as follows (some imaginary figures have been inserted):

		£
1. Ordinary shares issued	=	100,000
2. Reserves retained in previous years	=	40,000
Ordinary shareholders' interest in the company	=	140,000
3. Preference shares issued at the start of the year (7%)	=	28,000
4. Debentures issued at the start of the year (6½%)	=	32,000
Capital employed	=	£200,000

		£
True figures are:	Net profit (say)	31,720
	Debenture interest paid	2,080
		£33,800

$$\therefore \text{Return on capital employed} = \frac{33,800}{200,000} \times 100$$

$$= 16.9\%$$

Table 20.7 Budget for road haulage operations (January–June 19. .)

Details	Costs & revenue Vehicle No. 1 for period		Costs & revenue Vehicle No. 1 per working day	Further vehicles would appear in columnar form
Vehicle no.	2123 ABC			
Date of purchase	1.1.19. .			*Notes*
Capacity	44 ton			(*a*) Since tyres are regarded as a running expense it is usual to deduct these from the value of any vehicle purchased.
Cost	£32,500			
Less tyres	£ 2,500	(*a*)		
Net cost	£30,000			
Running costs per km (p)		(*b*)		(*b*) These costs are based on current prices at the time the budget is prepared.
Fuel and oil	8.425			
Tyres	5.325			
Repairs/Maintenance	1.230			
	14.980p			
Estimated km	40,000	(*c*)	320	(*c*) This estimate is based on previous experience, and 125 days' operations.
Estimated revenue	£42,000	(*d*)	£336.00	(*d*) As above
Deduct				
Estimated costs				
Wages	£14,150		£113.20	(*e*) As above
Licence/ insurance	£ 1,840		£ 14.72	(*f*) Factual at the time the estimate is prepared.
Depreciation	£ 3,000		£ 24.00	(*g*) Straight-line method.
Overheads	£ 2,215		£ 17.72	(*h*) Allocated on vehicle tonnage basis.*
Running costs	£ 5,992		£ 47.94	(*i*) Based on estimates above.
Total expenses	£27,197		£217.58	* Note on (*h*) above:
Profit	£14,803		£118.42	Total vehicle tonnage = 880 tonnes
	£42,000		£336.00	*Total overheads* = £44,300
				This vehicle = 44 tonnes
				$\frac{44}{880} \times £44,300 = £2,215 \quad £2,215 \div 125 = £17.72$

Notice that although this return on capital was earned by all the capital employed, some of it was rewarded with a much smaller figure than 16.9 per cent. The debenture holders only received 6½ per cent and the preference shareholders only received 7 per cent, so that in fact the ordinary shareholders received rather more than 16.9 per cent. Of course, it does not follow that they actually received anything like this percentage in actual dividend, since it is up to the directors how much is given away as dividends to the shareholders. A Board which is expanding the affairs of the company may retain most of the profits to finance expansion.

20.8.2 The return on capital employed – sole traders and partnerships

With sole traders and partnerships there is a modification required if correct ideas are to be formed about the profitability of the firm. Since the proprietors are usually working in the business, it would not be right to regard the net profit earned as being entirely 'profit'. Some of it should be regarded as wages of the proprietor. The reader who has studied economics will know about 'opportunity cost': the cost of any resource is the value of the lost opportunity we sacrificed of employing it in the next best situation. If the proprietor had not been running his transport firm he might instead have been employed elsewhere, perhaps as a manager in some other firm. We must therefore deduct from the net profit earned the probable wage he could have been earning elsewhere – say, £12,000. Similarly, had the capital not been employed in this business it could have been employed in some safe investment earning, say, 6 per cent. This would be 6 per cent on £140,000 if we imagine a firm of similar size to the company above. Of course, such a firm would not have preference shareholders or debenture holders but it could have borrowed money from external sources such as banks and building societies. Therefore, if we imagine the same amount of capital employed we have:

Return on Capital employed =

$$\frac{\text{Net profit} - (\text{Estimated wage elsewhere} + \text{interest elsewhere})}{\text{Capital employed at the start of the year}} \times 100$$

$$= \frac{\pounds 33{,}800 - (\pounds 12{,}000 + \pounds 8{,}400)}{200{,}000} \times 100$$

$$= \frac{\pounds 13{,}400}{200{,}000} \times 100$$

$$= \underline{\underline{6.7 \text{ per cent}}}$$

This return is the *extra* return earned by working in *this* industry.

20.9 Costs in distribution – analysis and control

In distribution, as distinct from transport, there has been insufficient thought given in the past to the true analysis of costs. A full analysis may therefore result in salutary decisions affecting the performance of the company. These may include alterations to the product range, resiting of depots, new inter-modal handling methods, etc. A complete reappraisal starts with the preparation of a list of distribution centres of activity and cost. These may be listed as follows, but an individual firm may not have all of them in its organisation.

20.9.1 Distribution cost centres

1. Collection and storage of raw materials.
2. Collection and storage of components from subcontractors.
3. Finished goods storage at the factory.
4. Dispatch centre costs at the factory.
5. Transport to the depot.
6. Depot handling and inventory costs.
7. Inter-depot transfer costs.
8. Depot dispatch costs.
9. Depot to customer transport costs.
10. Administration and documentation costs at each of the above cost centres.

Many of the true costs of distribution are hidden away in the accounts of many companies, disguised in other costs. Thus costs (1) and (2) will often be found included in manufacturing costs, and costs (8) and (9) will often be included in sales costs. The true distribution costs are often therefore much greater than at first thought, due to poor definition and analysis. A true estimate of distribution costs is likely to be about 30 per cent or even 40 per cent of total costs. The chief difficulty in controlling costs is that the only true guide to the performance of a company is the return on capital invested, so that a simple procedure of always reducing costs as much as possible will not necessarily produce the best result. This is why the concept of minimum total distribution cost is so important – it alone brings the best return on capital invested. To cut out a distribution process simply because it was expensive might result in greater total costs if the expensive item was more effective, and therefore its removal only caused other costs to rise.

20.9.2 Allocating costs to products or activities

Very often existing costing systems list costs under expense categories, such as labour, fuel, light and heat, occupation, administration, etc. This system of allocation lends itself to the examination of variances in expense categories – we can see whether fuel costs rose this month and do something about investigating them. What it does not help us to do is to evaluate the worthwhile nature of a particular product in its contribution to the return on capital invested. If these costs are allocated to products – so that occupancy reflects the time goods are in storage – we shall soon see whether it is worthwhile keeping a slow-moving item in stock. If the return on that item is less than the cost of storage and handling, we can either raise our margin of profit on it or phase it out as a line of stock.

Having identified the true costs of distribution, and allocated them to particular products or services, the accountant can examine them with a view to reducing total distribution costs. Streamlining of many activities may be immediately highlighted, particularly in the administrative field. It may become apparent that certain customers are given services which are uneconomic, while others are given services, which, while uneconomic viewed on their own, are marginally profitable because they are make-weight services thrown in while serving other customers with whom it is profitable to trade. Some simulation of these activities on a computer may be very helpful here in analysing ultimate profitability.

Example

Consider the case of a UK exporter who receives an order for twenty computerised machines to be used in the manufacture of garments in a land-locked African country. The letter of credit calls for shipment through an East African port, in Mozambique. By this route the machines would need export packing and would take three weeks to get to the Mozambican port (partly because of calls elsewhere). There would also be a further two-week delay due to the infrequency of shipping to Mozambique. The journey from Mozambique to the hinterland would be by rail, through an area subject to bandit activity with extra 'war risk' insurance costs.

The exporter proposes to the customer that the letter of credit be amended to permit air freight direct to the capital of his own country. The air freight will be greater than sea freight, but packing costs and insurance would be less, a built-in element for the use of capital tied up during transit would be reduced, and delivery would be the day after dispatch. This would mean the machines were in use some five weeks earlier and would produce some 20,000 garments in that period. In the exporter's opinion this factor alone would far outweigh the extra freight costs.

Unfortunately, this chapter cannot deal adequately with the analysis and control of distribution costs, but the subject is of great importance and readers concerned with this particular field are recommended to pursue its study. Mention made earlier of JIT procedures (see Chapter 9) in manufacturing reduces the importance of detailed analysis of costs in that field, but total distribution costs still need to be kept under review – for example, when JIT demands call for smaller volumes to be delivered we have already seen that to keep loads viable it may be necessary to consolidate deliveries from several suppliers.

20.10 Summary

1. Financial aspects of transport and logistics include the risks inherent in the enterprise, the type of business unit proposed, the flows of income to be generated and the expenditure to be budgeted for, the control of costs, the conservation of capital and the return on capital employed in the enterprise.
2. The chief risks involved are natural hazards, human uncertainties (such as the death of partners or vital staff), economic, technical, political and monetary risks. Many of these are insurable risks, and some of these we must insure against, such as employers' liability and third party cover on vehicles. Because a risk is insurable does not mean we can afford to insure it and where insurance is not compulsory we may decide to carry the risk ourselves. When a risk is uninsurable it means that there is not sufficient evidence for insurers to be able to estimate probabilities – for example, we cannot usually insure against a lack of demand for a product.
3. The sources of finance begin with personal savings, self-financing from profits earned in a previous period and borrowing from friends, banks and other institutions. Partnerships can usually command more capital and public limited companies can appeal to the general public to subscribe for shares. Debentures are securities issued by companies to acknowledge loans made to them by parties who have funds to spare but do not wish to buy shares. The debenture is secured, usually, on the fixed assets of a company but sometimes (a floating debenture) on the current assets as well, i.e. the stock. If the interest on the debenture is not paid, the floating debenture 'crystallises' over the stock and freezes its sales, to safeguard the debenture holders. A certain amount of official finance is also available under the 'Enterprise Initiative'.
4. Government agencies and public corporations are usually financed by grants from the Exchequer or from local authorities, but they may generate income from the services they provide.
5. A business can only be kept in good heart if its assets are renewed as and when required; this requires funds to be put away so that they are available when required. The procedure is to charge each year's accounts with a fair amount for depreciation, thus reducing the profits available for distribution to the proprietors or shareholders. This amount is then invested in a sinking fund investment which will provide

the funds required when vehicles, premises, etc. need to be replaced. The two chief methods of depreciation are the 'straight-line method' and the 'diminishing balance method'. Allowance should be made for inflation if prices rise. The amount to be put away in the sinking fund should be based on the likely replacement price, not on the historical cost of the vehicle, machine, etc.

6. The final accounts of a business are made out at the end of each financial year. They should give 'a true and fair view' of the affairs of a business, which means that the accounts should include every penny of income received in the year, set against every penny of expense incurred in earning the income. The difference will be the profit (or loss) on the year's activities. The Balance Sheet which follows will then give a true and fair view of the assets and liabilities of the business.
7. Costing is a series of procedures by which costs incurred are allocated to particular activities, to discover the true cost of any particular product or service. Budgeting is a similar process in which we envisage future costs for the various activities we perform, so that we can see the likely total costs to be incurred and can make arrangements to provide the finance required. A cashflow budget is particularly concerned to discover where a shortage of funds is likely to occur so that help can be arranged if necessary.
8. The return on capital employed (ROCE) in a business is found by the formula:

$$\text{ROCE} = \frac{\text{Net profit}}{\text{Capital employed}} \times 100$$

Suppose an ordinary investment would return, say, 7 per cent, it is clear that a business activity using the same funds would need to earn much more to be an attractive investment, because of the risks being run in the process.

20.11 Questions

1. Distinguish between insurable risks and uninsurable risks in business. Give five examples of insurable risks that would be run every day by a major logistical company. Give three examples of non-insurable risks that would be carried by the same company.
2. How does a public limited company obtain the funds it requires? In your answer refer to ordinary shares, preferred shares and debentures.
3. What is meant by self-financing? Why is self-financing the best way to expand the activities of a profitable enterprise?
4. What is depreciation? Why is it important? How should we ensure that the profits retained in the business to replace worn-out assets are used for that purpose and not for any other reason?

5. From the figures given below, work out the revenue account of T. Harper, road haulier, and a balance sheet as at the end of the financial year, 31 March 19.. Fees received £333,538; Discounts received £1,235; Commission received £18,415; Postage £264; Rates £1,559; Light & heat £783; Telephone expenses £3,126; Salaries £53,564; Depreciation £3,341; Stationery £616; Wages £50,669; Insurance £18,786; Repairs £16,356; Petrol & oil £23,562; Tyres £11,462; Depreciation £22,678; Loan interest £4,785.

   Balance sheet figures were: Premises £177,755; Fixtures £33,408 *less* depreciation £14,111; Motor vehicles £113,390; *less* depreciation £28,478; Debtors £38,309; Fuel, etc. £14,894; Bank balance £36,491; Cash in hand £348; Capital at 1 April £240,204; Drawings £53,360; Loan £31,900; Creditors £10,440; Salaries due £2,392.
6. Consider the likely costs involved in shipping wine-making machinery to Adelaide, Australia by container on a cellular ship. Compare this with the likely costs and benefits of sending it air freight.

21 The control of transport

21.1 *Laissez-faire v.* control of transport

The doctrine of *laissez-faire*, which drew its force from the eighteenth-century activities of the early capitalists, holds that the state should not interfere with the activities of private individuals who are showing enterprise, but should leave them to do as they see fit. It holds that in doing what is best for themselves, entrepreneurs will also do what is best for society at large, for their activities will utilise natural resources, give employment to their fellow citizens, create wealth, and – as far as transport is concerned – create the utilities of space which will be of great benefit to society.

It soon became apparent that in reality the doctrine was less applicable to transport than to other fields of enterprise. The entrepreneur, in aiming at the greatest personal profit, was likely to exploit the general public, especially in view of the monopolistic nature of many early transport enterprises. The pursuit of minimum business costs might result in excessive social costs, be it in pollution of the atmosphere, an excessive accident rate, dumping of unsightly or noxious waste material, etc. From the very earliest times, therefore, we find statutory regulation of transport, local bye-laws to control abuses and a running conflict between government and the transport industry.

There are a number of reasons why society must exercise control over transport:

1. The basic operations of any transport system need to be regulated in the interests of public safety.
2. Transport is in many cases a natural monopoly. It is impractical to lay down two railways to Birmingham just to give people the benefit of competition in ticket prices.
3. In other cases transport is so competitive that cut-throat price competition could lower standards of safety and service, and reduce wages to exploitation levels.

4. Transport is not static but dynamic, and new transport modes developed alongside existing modes cause capital to be wasted and levels of service to be reduced on the outmoded transport network. The result is that some subsidy or encouragement may be necessary in the public interest.
5. The social costs of transport are great and control must be exercised to keep them within reasonable limits.
6. Transport often has international implications that require official agreements which are best conducted at governmental levels, and then imposed as a body of rules upon the operators of each particular nation.
7. A comprehensive, efficient, internal transport system is a strategic necessity.

Some illustrations of controls introduced over the years in the United Kingdom with regard to each of these aspects of transport may be appropriate at this point.

21.1.1 The regulation of basic operations

Any transport system requires basic regulations in the interest of public safety. We may decide to drive on the left or on the right, but we cannot leave it to the general public to please themselves. A basic framework of rules must be laid down and enforced. We must agree on the types of sign to be used to signal hazards or notify compulsory regulations, and their exact meaning must be laid down. Offences must be delineated and punishments prescribed. These regulations may be of general application to the ordinary public or only known to the specialist operator, but the regulations will be numerous and far reaching in their effects.

21.1.2 Controlling monopolies

Transport is a natural monopoly in many ways but particularly in the case of transport where very heavy capital costs are involved. The best examples are the canals of the eighteenth century and the railways of the nineteenth century, but the forerunners to both of these were the turnpikes built between 1663 and 1760 and on into the industrial era. It was found in all these cases that no entrepreneurs were prepared to put up the capital for a project unless they could be assured of a return on the investment, and this required the granting of a monopoly for a period of years. Since any such transport undertaking required the use of other people's land, which had to be compulsorily acquired, and also needed the privilege of limited liability if it was to collect the capital, a private Act of Parliament was necessary to confer the requisite powers. The Act was also a convenient medium for conferring the monopoly, usually for a period of years. Even in recent times the same device has been adopted: for example, to build the Dartford–Purfleet Tunnel under the Thames. The original idea was that the company formed to do the work should be allowed to charge tunnel-users for twenty-one years, but after that the tunnel would revert to an ordinary 'free' facility. In fact, long before the first arrangement came to an end the tunnel had to be doubled to give two lanes each way, and soon afterwards a four-lane bridge had to be built to give four tunnel lanes one way, and four bridge lanes the other way.

When we say that transport is a natural monopoly we mean that it is obvious from the very nature of the project that it will be uneconomic to build two motorways, or two railways, or to cut two canals from A to B. If we confer on one company the sole rights to build a facility, we are giving it the opportunity to exploit a monopoly position. We will therefore incorporate as many safeguards or controls as we can. A common safeguard which does not always prove practicable is to say that anyone who wishes to do so may use the facility. Thus the early canal builders were required to accept other people's barges on their canals, and the early railways were forced to accept other people's trains. Frequent accidents soon put a stop to that, but even in the Pipelines Act 1962 the minister has the power to insist that other people may use any pipeline that is constructed to prevent a proliferation of applications to construct pipelines. Probably that is not a very practicable idea in many cases. A whole string of Railway Acts from 1845 to 1894 wrestled with the abuse by railway companies of monopoly powers. Such ideas as the 'Parliamentary Train', which required the railways to run at least one train in each direction every day which stopped at all the stations, ensured that the general public had at least a minimum service. The Cheap Trains Act required railways to offer cheap fares before 7.00 a.m. so that workers could travel cheaply to work. Above all the requirement that railways must not show any undue preference in offering their services was designed to give equal opportunity to all wishing to move goods by rail.

21.1.3 Controlling excessive competition

Cut-throat competition is a feature of those transport modes which do not have excessive capital costs. It was therefore most commonly encountered in the road haulage industry, but air transport has also suffered from it. It was also the reason why nineteenth-century shipowners formed themselves into conferences. In a world where tramp steamers would go anywhere to get a cargo, especially if it was a cargo that would take them home to the United Kingdom, the conference liners often found that their homeward-bound cargoes had been diverted onto cut-price tramps. The conference had a long memory and when shortages of space did occur would get their own back on the cargo-owners who had used the cheaper vessels on past occasions. The free enterprise system has much to recommend it and it might therefore seem unnecessary to control competition, but in fact cut-rate charges invariably lead entrepreneurs whose profit margins are being reduced to cut back on costs.

The most likely costs to be cut are wages and maintenance costs. The first of these actions – cutting labour costs – will vary in its impact depending on the economic climate at the time. During periods of high unemployment, when workers are fearful of losing their jobs, it can result in reduced wage rates and excessive hours being worked. During periods of full employment only incompetent, less qualified staff would be prepared to accept such conditions. Better staff would soon seek work elsewhere and a deterioration in efficiency would result. Reduction in maintenance costs – highly desirable if the same standards can be maintained – could, where reduction of costs was the sole criterion, result in reduced safety standards, a higher incidence of breakdowns, and more frequent accidents.

There is a third type of waste: the waste of capital entailed when there are more than enough vehicles to carry the goods and passengers available, i.e. surplus capacity. This capital could have been used for alternative purposes and is therefore a squandering of the nation's resources. To solve such problems both quantity licensing and quality licensing have been used in the past. The term 'quantity licensing' implies a restriction of the quantity of transport made available, usually by the licensing of services. A licence is granted to an efficient operator, who is then given protection from competition. The licence is renewable at intervals provided the operator continues to conduct the service in a proper manner. Additions to existing services will only be sanctioned on clear proof of increased public need, and against objections lodged by existing operators. New applications to enter the industry would be similarly opposed. This type of quantity licensing was used in the United Kingdom from 1930 to 1970 for controlling goods vehicles, and even longer in the passenger-carrying services. When the controls on buses were removed in the late 1980s a large variety of small bus services were rapidly developed, but already many of them have gone out of business – a clear waste of capital which might have been used elsewhere. There hasn't been quite the same decline in servicing, or in wages paid, because of a wider appreciation of the need for safety, but no doubt bankruptcy came all the sooner, and led to job losses.

Quality licensing requires that the licensing authority shall be satisfied as to the ability of the licensee to maintain and service the vehicles or aircraft properly, and that the staff are adequately trained for whatever functions they are required to perform. There may also be particular controls over the operations of vehicles and aircraft. This type of licensing is that used today in road haulage, where the 'operator's licence' certifies the ability to maintain and operate the vehicles, but not the number of vehicles the operator will operate, although the operator must declare how many will be used. Failure to continue to meet the required standards (for example, when spot-checks disclose poor maintenance, overloading or other infringements) may result in the licensing authority reducing the permitted number of vehicles, or revoking the licence altogether. If the operator is using a vehicle over 3.5 tonnes, he, or a member of his staff, must have passed the relevant Certificate of Professional Competence, if the vehicle is used for 'hire or reward' activities.

21.1.4 Controls necessitated by 'structural' changes in transport

'Structural' changes refer to changes that come about as a result of changes in taste or fashion, or as a result of technical innovation. Thus petrol and diesel engines have changed the face of transport in the twentieth century, and rendered rail and inland water transport less attractive to many freight forwarders, although company trains are becoming more common and very attractive to some users. Similarly, air transport has practically eradicated the seaborne passenger trade, except for the cruise trade and the car ferry. When such changes occur, the pattern of influences at work is complex, and controls may be introduced which, though seemingly desirable in the short term, may have debatable long-term effects.

It is difficult for policy-makers to extract the best policy from the welter of opinions, pressures from vested interests, etc. Old systems in decline rally their supporters to preserve the dying industry and the proponents of the new techniques, facing problems in proving their technology, may be less vocal and less politically active because of their involvement with those problems. The resulting policy may rivet an obsolete system on the nation for a considerable time, until inescapable economic pressures force its final rejection.

The nationalisation of road haulage in 1947 was an example. It brought all methods of transport under a single control, the British Transport Commission, with 943,000 employees – the largest enterprise ever to be set up in the United Kingdom. Pursuing an 'integrated system of transport', it was under very strong influence from the railway lobby, with its well-organised trade unions. The road haulage system – the logical new system of transport for a small country – was temporarily strangled by the vested railway interests.

Although this was largely undone in 1953, and no attempt was ever made to renationalise the section of road haulage denationalised in the Transport Act 1953, the accelerated switch from the railways to road haulage which occurred between 1953 and 1962 would have occurred earlier but for the nationalisation of transport in 1947. Only when it became clear that 943,000 employees were too unwieldy a labour force for anyone to control, and that enterprise and talent were being strangled by the attempt to plan and integrate all movements, did parliament step in to free the roads from the railways. The attempt to restore controls in 1968 to provide an integrated system was good in some ways – for example, in raising the quality of vehicles – but by then the railways were much weaker and the road haulage industry much stronger – and market forces were playing a much greater part than theoretical ideas like the integration of transport.

Nationalisation is an extreme form of control, but it has some place in solving problems of structural change. Where an area of activity has become hopelessly run down, with obsolete facilities and a demoralised staff, we can have a situation where the replacement of the obsolete facilities and the provision of new capital assets and infrastructure can only be achieved by a super-authority with funds provided by central government. There is a cost, which must be borne by the taxpayer, since private enterprise is not willing to undertake the work. It could be argued that this was precisely the position of British Rail in 1993 and that no amount of tinkering to persuade private enterprise to come forward would be of any help. What was needed was resolute government action to put 2p on the income tax for a year or two and provide the funds to revitalise the network.

21.1.5 Controlling the social costs of transport

Free enterprise activity aims at profitability. Profits can be achieved in three ways: by keeping costs low, or by keeping prices high, or by a combination of the two. The ability to impose high prices is limited by competition and the degree of flexibility of demand. This means that cost-reduction probably offers the best solution to the problem of maintaining a high level of profitability. It has therefore been a common practice of entrepreneurs to avoid costs wherever possible, often without regard to the social consequences. Without positive legal sanctions to compel entrepreneurs to pay fair wages, contribute to training costs, install seat belts, insure third parties, eliminate noxious exhausts or pay fair contributions to road repairs, many would feel no obligation to do so. Unless these costs are imposed on transport operators, they are likely to evade them and leave society to supplement the inadequate wages, subsidise training courses, bear the cost of accidents and workmen's compensation, hospital care and relief for the victims of accidents, endure the smogs and diseases inseparable from unclean air, pay for the repairs to roads, etc. To the extent that these increased costs are passed on to the consumer, they must still be borne by society in general, but even so the costs are borne more fairly, for the average cost of safety devices is low and general, while the costs of injuries sustained by individuals are expensive and personal.

The development of a proper appraisal of social costs in recent years has done much to allocate the costs where they ought to fall, and has inevitably imposed many controls on transport. These controls have increased the costs of transport firms, but have reduced costs overall and have shared them more fairly. They have also helped us to make wiser decisions about which forms of transport to develop and which to restrict.

21.1.6 International implications of transport

Transport is frequently international. Aircraft must fly over other countries if they are to utilise 'least time tracks' adequately. Ships finish their journeys in foreign ports and inter-modal transits finish up on the roads and railways of foreign states. Countless problems arise as a result. There are conflicts of laws inherent in national attitudes to what is and is not permissible or fair. There are problems of infestation, disease and virus control and quarantine. There are problems of liability for accidents in roadsteads, harbours, airport approaches, and on rivers and road and rail networks. All these matters are the subject of discussions at inter-governmental level, and lead to conclusions embodied in conventions, which have to be enacted as laws in the individual states. These laws are imposed on and enforced among the citizens operating in the particular field concerned. This gives a very broad system of control.

For all these reasons the control of transport is an important aspect of the total transport scene. The reader who hopes to understand and participate in transport must know what the particular regulations are and observe them carefully.

21.2 The development of transport control

Although the history of transport is too great a study to be dealt with fully in this book, a brief outline of the main policy threads over the years is worth a place here. In very early times the chief concerns of those seeking to control transport were twofold: (1) to control charges so that they reflected a fair price for the services rendered, and (2) to raise revenue from what was largely considered to be a luxury pastime for the well-to-do. In a nation which practised self-sufficiency to a very considerable degree, the movement of goods was largely confined to luxuries, furs, silks, wines, etc. Personal travel for pleasure was limited to the rich. Poor people walked.

Conditions have now changed. We are far from being self-sufficient, and transport is essential for the distribution of all those goods regarded as the necessities of our present mode of living and to enable people to go about their daily business. Yet transport is still regarded by governments as a lucrative source of revenue. Revenue is raised from transport in many ways, particularly from the private motor car, and severe criticisms could be made of the ways in which this revenue is levied. We do not usually regard this as a feature today of the control of transport. The problem is that the demand for transport is relatively inelastic with respect to price. Students of economics will understand this term. It means that if the Chancellor of the Exchequer imposes taxation on motor vehicles and on petrol, it will not reduce the demand very much for motor vehicles or petrol. People will still demand them because the demand is not at all responsive to changes in price. All that will happen is that the Chancellor will collect a lot of money. So you cannot control transport by taxing it. You have to control it by other methods – by regulations of one sort or another.

The mechanisation of transport made the control of transport much more necessary and shifted the emphasis to control in the interests of public safety. This emphasis has endured down the years, and is still a major preoccupation of the Ministry of Transport and other transport bodies. Many of the controls to be looked at later in this chapter are controls designed to ensure the safety of the general public in their roles as transport users, transport employees and innocent third parties. There is a host of Acts of Parliament, EU Council Regulations and subordinate legislation to ensure the proper maintenance and operation of transport facilities, the proper training and fitness of staff and the adequacy of supervision.

A second aspect of control, which developed alongside the mechanisation of transport, was the drive to secure comprehensiveness and standardisation. This was not appreciated at first in the original parliamentary sanctions given to those transport innovators, the Turnpike Trusts. Only when the miseries of a patchy road system made it obvious to all did Parliament begin to insist on a comprehensive road network rather than the making-up of lucrative sections of road only. There was more awareness of the need to develop through-lines at the start of the railway era, and some members of parliament openly campaigned for parliament to refuse to sanction piecemeal developments. It is true that their cries went unheeded to some extent, but Acts like the Gauge Act 1846 did much to remedy the problem. The needs to secure standardised systems of working and co-ordination and even integration of the total transport system have been an enduring feature of control which is still of major importance.

The third thread in the control of transport was the control of charges to prevent the abuse of monopoly powers. This control is still an important aspect of the control of transport today, but it tends to be less a matter of setting maximum levels: such a policy is only effective in times of stable prices. Today it is more usual to find the control of charges consisting of a continuous, or at least frequent, monitoring of proposed price increases to ensure that the prices charged do reflect the increased costs incurred and conform to general government policy about prices.

The control of transport by nationalisation might seem at a first glance to be the ultimate form of control. In the United Kingdom this has not proved to be particularly rigid control, since the nationalised bodies have largely been left as autonomous units operating on a commercial basis with a duty to achieve a balanced budget taking one year with another. Included in this balance has been an element for a normal return on capital invested, and for the provision of capital for further expansion. Parliament, in attempting to achieve the best results from the nationalised industries, has modified its policies again and again, and has written off some heavy railway deficits. This has resulted in the original aims of a completely integrated transport system not being realised, and perhaps experience shows that they cannot in fact be realised without surrendering entirely traditional British ideas of what is desirable in terms of control. We have refrained from attempts to impose on transport any rigid system of operations which might only inhibit new developments in an extremely dynamic sector of the economy.

In the years since 1979 we have heard more calls for privatisation than for nationalisation and it does appear that privatisation has much to offer in the road transport field, where enterprises are relatively small and many occupy niche positions where they can fulfil the needs of a particular customer or sector of the industry. Even a big logistical organisation can make decisions much more quickly than a nationalised body, and this is especially true of capital projects, where money can be borrowed in seconds which would take months to organise if it had to be budgeted through official channels.

The arguments for privatisation centre on the dynamic nature of transport, which has experienced a revolution in methods in the last quarter of a century. Dynamic developments cannot be controlled by official channels, which are by their very nature bureaucratic and cumbersome. We have to take a *laisser-faire* attitude – let the thing work itself out. Let those who are prepared to risk their capital in the hope of enriching themselves have a go. As Adam Smith said long ago in the *Wealth of Nations*, hopefully they will enrich the rest of us too.

The pattern of control in transport is so complex and there are so many aspects to keep in mind that the authors have presented this section as a modal review of controls applicable to particular forms of transport. Where a full description has been given elsewhere in this book a cross-reference has been given, and the reader is urged to read the relevant pages.

21.3 The control of road transport

The principal Acts of Parliament still in force relating to the control of road transport are as follows:

- The London Hackney Carriage Act 1831
- The Highway Act 1835
- The London Hackney Carriages Act 1843
- The Town Police Clauses Act 1847
- The London Hackney Carriage Act 1850
- The Locomotive Act 1861
- The Town Police Clauses Act 1889
- The London Cab and Stage Carriage Act 1907
- The Roads Act 1920
- The Road Traffic Act 1960
- The Road Traffic Amendment Act 1967
- The Vehicles and Driving Licences Act 1969
- The Road Traffic (Foreign Vehicles) Act 1972
- The Greater London Council (General Powers) Act 1974
- The Road Traffic Act 1974
- The Public Service Vehicles (Arrest of Offenders) Act 1975
- The Transport Act 1980
- The Public Passenger Vehicles Act 1981
- The Transport Act 1981
- The Transport Act 1982
- The Road Transport (Driving Licences) Act 1983
- The Road Transport Regulation Act 1984
- The Road Transport (Parking) Act 1986
- The Motor Vehicles (Wearing of Seat Belts by Children) Act 1988
- The Road Traffic Act 1988
- The Road Traffic Offenders Act 1988
- The Road Traffic (Consequential Provisions) Act 1988
- The Motor Vehicles (Safety Equipment for Children) Act 1991
- The Road Traffic Act 1991

Acts of this type are amended regularly and are reinforced by a host of pieces of delegated legislation, Ministerial Orders, etc. It is difficult for the transport manager to keep abreast of changes that occur. There are several firms which publish updating circulars about transport operations at very reasonable prices. For an annual subscription, the transport manager receives a current loose-leaf folder containing the present situation on every aspect of the law affecting road haulage operations, and monthly, a packet of amended pages, designed so that the obsolete page may be removed and the up-to-date page substituted for it. Perhaps the best system is by Croner's Publications Ltd; readers who are in road transport are strongly recommended to become subscribers. There are two manuals, *Croner's Road Transport Operation* and *Croner's Coach and Bus Operations*. In view of the more limited changes in passenger operations the revision packages are only sent quarterly. This handbook also includes a European section.

Some of the implications of these Acts for the transport operator will be developed in the sections which follow.

21.3 The regulation of road traffic in the interests of public safety

Road traffic presents enormous problems of control to the police in their everyday affairs. The sheer volume of road transport and the relatively high speed at which it operates require clear directives to be given about the use of roads, early signalling of hazards and controlled areas, speed limits, the proper maintenance of vehicles and the fitness of drivers. These and many other directives are incorporated in the various Road Traffic Acts. The current Act is the Road Traffic Act 1991, but minor sections of earlier Acts are still in force. The main provisions of the Acts deal with driving offences, construction and use of vehicles, driving licences, etc. For the convenience of the ordinary public many of these rules are embodied in the Highway Code, a small pamphlet which lists several hundred rules, illustrates the chief signs used and the principles behind the design of signs, and gives a list of the enactments which confer powers on the police in dealing with offenders. Every transport manager should have a copy, and buy new editions as they appear. A booklet entitled *Test Yourself on the New Highway Code* is available from Shaw and Sons Ltd, Shaway House, 21 Bourne Park, Bourne Road, Crayford, Kent, DA1 4BZ.

Driving offences include causing death by reckless or dangerous driving, driving in a manner or at a speed dangerous to the general public, driving without due care and attention, and driving under the influence of alcoholic drink or drugs. More general offences include failure to obey a police officer directing traffic or in the performance of his or her duties, and parking a vehicle in a dangerous position. There are rules about accidents and what to do when one occurs, about the manning of certain vehicles, about the minimum age for driving and the licensing of vehicles and drivers.

21.3.2 Construction and Use Regulations

This body of rules is of very great importance to both the designer of road vehicles and operators, because vehicles must conform to the construction

Fig. 21.1 The symbols for inflammable and corrosive loads (courtesy of Hazchem Signs Ltd)

rules and be used in the manner laid down. The Secretary of State for the Department of the Environment has the power to make regulations about the width, height and length of motor vehicles and trailers, the diameter of wheels, the condition of tyres, the emission of smoke, fumes, sparks, etc., the weight, laden and unladen, the braking, steering and lighting and the loads to be carried.

Vehicles must be examined at an approved centre within one year of purchase to ensure that they conform with the construction and use regulations.

If they do, the operator will be issued with a *goods vehicle test certificate* and a *plating certificate*. The former confirms that the vehicle has been inspected and is in accordance with the Construction and Use Regulations. The latter records the 'plated weights' at which the vehicle may be operated. This plate must be attached to the vehicle at all times and spot-checks are held on the roads of any vehicle suspected of being operated at an excessive weight. A free *Guide for Vehicle Operators* is available from the Department of the Environment on the plating and testing of vehicles.

Certain vehicles carrying hazardous cargoes must be marked with internationally recognised symbols and with plates giving instructions on what to do in an accident. Two of these symbols are illustrated in Fig. 21.1.

21.3.3 The licensing and insuring of HGV drivers

It is an offence to drive or to employ a person to drive unless the driver has first passed a test conducted by an official supervisor to prove his or her competency to drive that particular class of vehicle, and has received the appropriate driving licence. Licences may be revoked or suspended in certain circumstances.

All users of motor vehicles must either be insured against third-party risks with an authorised insurer; alternatively they must deposit £500,000 with the Supreme Court as a security against claims made by aggrieved third parties. This sum covers more than one vehicle.

21.3.4 Control of heavy commercial vehicles

The Heavy Commercial Vehicles (Controls & Regulations) Act 1973 empowers local authorities to draw up proposals for lorry routes through their areas, and to restrict heavy vehicles to these routes. It may also prohibit them from entering certain roads or zones in their areas. It also prohibits parking of heavy commercial vehicles on verges, footpaths and land situated between two carriageways. There are exceptions in emergencies or with police consent, or for unloading purposes provided the vehicle is not left unattended.

21.3.5 Quality and quantity licensing

Under the Transport Act 1968, the quantity licensing which had existed in Britain since the 1930s was abolished and the system of quality licensing by 'operator's licences' replaced it. This system has permitted the expansion of competent operators but an element of quantity licensing was retained to the extent that a maximum number of vehicles is usually stated in the licence. An operator purchasing extra vehicles is bound to notify the Licensing Authority of their purchase within one month, and must not exceed the limit set in his licence, which presumably reflects the Licensing Authority's opinion of the number of vehicles the operator's facilities can adequately maintain.

21.3.6 The control of road haulage to achieve co-ordination of transport

Co-ordination and integration of transport are two ideas which have constantly recurred in the transport debate since 1945. The 1947 Act aimed at integration, bringing all inland transport under the control of a single organisation – the British Transport Commission. In the event it proved an unwieldy affair, particularly at that time when the nation was slowly recovering from the effects of the Second World War. The result was that measures to reduce the centralised control of transport began to be discussed before the industry had really had a chance to see what integration could achieve. The less centralised system – the co-ordination of transport arrangements by willing co-operation between the various branches of the industry – was pursued instead. Both the 1953 and the 1962 Acts reduced centralisation and the scale of the institutions, each mode becoming independent of the others.

The 1968 Act restored the emphasis to integration, particularly the integration of long-distance rail and road haulage. For a few years the co-operation between road and rail operators was good, but the changing pace of transport and the refusal of central government to provide funds to finance deficits on purely social grounds eventually led to further tensions within the industry. The move towards privatisation has also reduced any tendency to integrate services.

21.3.7 The control of road haulage to conform with international requirements

The Carriage of Goods by Road Act 1965 requires that where road haulage activities involve international carriage, the goods shall be carried under an international consignment note which conforms to the International Convention on the Carriage of Merchandise by Roadhauliers (the CMR Convention). The consignment note automatically embodies the Convention as a part of the contract of carriage and overrides national laws on the carriage of goods. This means that a very much fairer contract exists between the parties than would be the case under many of the sets of conditions of carriage permitted by English contract law. Some brief details of this Convention are given in Table 16.1 (see pages 310–13), but a full study of the Act is the only way to gain a real understanding of its implications for the consignors and carriers of goods.

The European Agreement for the International Carriage of Dangerous Goods by Road (ADR) came into force in July 1969, and permits the carriage of dangerous goods provided that they are packed and labelled in accordance with the Agreement and carried in vehicles complying with the Agreement. Special tests of vehicles and tanks are conducted by the Department of the Environment inspectors at Heavy Goods Vehicle Testing Stations. They will be tested for corrosion, cracking of attachment points, valve connections, wiring and electrical connections, etc. Fire extinguishers and tool-kits must be carried, as well as flashing emergency lights independent of the vehicle to be placed 10 metres ahead and 10 metres behind the vehicle when it is halted on roads at night or in bad visibility.

A similar agreement, the ATP Agreement, covers the international carriage of perishable foodstuffs by road.

21.4 The control of rail transport

The Railways Act 1993, which came into force on 1 April 1994, changed the way railways have been run in the United Kingdom as a nationalised industry, British Rail. Apart from a few narrow gauge railways, and one or two privately run railways rescued by enthusiasts when the network was reduced in the 1960s under Dr Beeching's proposals, the network has been nationalised since 1947. Prior to this the railways had been privately run, and during most of the nineteenth century they were extremely profitable. For most of the nineteenth century Parliament sought to control the railway companies because they were powerful monopolies which did not hesitate to exploit their monopoly position. By the time Parliament had controlled the monopolists, the railways were beginning to face severe competition from the roads, and the monopoly was continuously eroded in the first four decades of the twentieth century.

A second reason for the control of railways was the overriding need for safety in rail operations; an insistence on proper maintenance, signalling and manning was imperative. Many of the requirements imposed costs upon the railways, and repeated attempts were made by Parliament to monitor railway operations. Not that Parliament was always right. The drive by the railway companies to amalgamate lines in the interests of economic operations was opposed at every turn by a Parliament suspicious of such moves as a further tightening of the monopolists' grip. Only when the railways were taken over during the First World War and run as a unified group was it fully appreciated that the economies of amalgamation were indeed real and desirable.

Although the return of the railways to private enterprise in 1921 was achieved by forming four large-scale regional companies, the economic climate of the 1920s and 1930s was not one where they could expand and grow. Uncontrolled road haulage and road passenger transport in the 1920s and the severe depression of the 1930s combined to depress the railways and reduce their share of the limited business available. Its strongly unionised labour force, whose syndicalist co-operation with the seamen and the miners in the first quarter of this century was finally defeated in the 1926 General Strike, believed strongly that only nationalisation could really solve the railways' problems, and was powerfully influential in the Labour government, which finally nationalised transport in 1947. Since 1947 parliament has enacted eight Transport Acts – the 1947, 1953, 1962, 1968, 1978, 1980, 1981 and 1982 Acts. These Acts were respectively concerned with outright nationalisation, partial denationalisation (1953 and 1962), integration of transport (1968) and since then the emphasis has been on privatisation of various parts of the system.

This urge to privatisation has finally led to the Railways Act 1993. It was a controversial Act, bitterly fought in both Houses of Parliament, first because it seemed to those that know about railways that it was being pushed through in the name of an abstract concept, privatisation, at a most unfortunate time. What made the moment so inopportune was that Eurotunnel was about to open, and would at once transform the railway scene. What has made British Rail a rather poor prospect ever since nationalisation (and even before 1947) is the fact that 200 miles (320 km) is the minimum journey at which rail haulage can compete adequately with road haulage. British Rail's weakness has had something to do with nationalisation, but even more to do with the limited hinterland in which it had to operate. Had the government waited even a year or two, it might not have been necessary to privatise British Rail at all. Instead the government has chosen to try a system of privatisation that seems doomed to failure. Unable to find a buyer willing to operate the system as a whole, it has opted to hand the system over to a body, 'Railtrack', which will run the system, but the trains will be operated by private concerns which will be licensed to operate particular services, and will pay for the use of the lines. Way back at the dawn of the railway era they tried this system, and it was a failure. It remains to be seen whether it can be made a success the second time around.

Will a sufficient number of entrepreneurial rail enthusiasts appear to provide the services? If not, British Rail itself will no doubt bid to operate the sections which are not appealing to outsiders, and the service will then be as before. Perhaps the entrepreneurs will see the sense of using Eurotunnel and will bid for the long-haul routes – and in the process cream off all the profits which, had the government only waited, would have made the whole network viable.

21.4.1 Parliamentary control and the railways

Parliament has the right to introduce a new Act whenever it likes, and as the previous section reminds us, it has not hesitated to do so in the last fifty years. A revisionary Act is clearly the most far-reaching type of control that is possible of a nationalised industry. The general rule for day-to-day activities is that Parliament should not control or attempt to control such matters, since the industry is expected to operate generally on commercial lines. It should not be expected to undergo an Annual General Meeting every day at 'Question Time'. Theoretically, Parliament debates these matters on 'Supply Days', which are traditionally at the disposal of the Opposition. As the Opposition often has more vital matters to debate, it usually does not choose to use the Supply Days for these matters, and the government has to make time available instead. The railways therefore are usually debated in government time as part of a general transport debate shortly after the Annual Report has been submitted to the minister and the accounts to the Public Accounts Committee. Even so this only happens about every other year as a full debate is rarely necessary more frequently.

The Railway Inspectorate was set up in the nineteenth century as part of governmental attempts to control the railways. It still functions as part of the Department of the Environment. Its investigations and formal inquiries into accidents are an important feature of its work, which also includes technical advice to the Secretary of State on railway affairs.

21.4.2 Control of the railways to conform with international requirements

As explained in Chapter 16, the United Kingdom showed little interest in international rail movements when these first became of importance to the continental powers. Today, the position is very different, and the opening of Eurotunnel will make British Rail a major player in rail transport with much to gain from rail haulage and much to offer the continental railways in terms of traffic to and from mainland Europe and even to the Far East and Pacific fringe countries. Its ratification of the COTIF Convention places it in an excellent position for co-operation with its fellow signatories, and with the European Commission in its bid to establish a truly Union-wide rail network unrestricted by national rulings about rail activities. Interference by the UK government in the affairs of a revitalised British Rail should decline rather than increase in the future, but we must wait to see what is the full impact of the Railways Act 1993.

21.5 The control of sea transport

Sea transport operates in the highly competitive field of international trade and is less susceptible to control by national governments than most other forms of transport because it operates over a way which is free to all, and beyond the control of a single nation. At the same time, most nations exert control over their own shipping, and in Britain this has taken the form of a series of enactments which tend generally to ensure that ships are operated safely and that crews are treated fairly.

The major Act is the Merchant Shipping Act 1894, which specifies what a British ship is and how it is to be surveyed, marked, registered and measured. It outlines the master's powers, duties and position, deals with crews, their payment, rights and duties, it provides for medical inspection and other health aspects, and it lays down rules on loadlines, wrecks, fire, the carriage of dangerous goods and the liability of shipowners. A subsequent minor Act, the Merchant Shipping Act 1958, extends some of the protections given to shipowners in the 1894 Act to their crews.

To the extent that its sea transport is controlled by each nation as it thinks fit, a ship's competitiveness in world markets may be affected if governments impose strict manning requirements, safety standards, or prescribed levels of wages. This may encourage the use by shipowners of flags of convenience, which involves registering the ship with a foreign nation such as Panama, Liberia or Honduras. The chief advantage of such registration is fiscal, for taxation in these countries is at very nominal rates. The other advantage of the use of flags of convenience is that for much of the routine seafaring work crews can be Third World residents, less highly unionised than British seafarers and therefore commanding lower wages all round.

Although flags of convenience, known by their American initiators as 'flags of necessity', do enable unscrupulous shipowners to bypass manning and wage levels, nevertheless there are many new vessels representing many millions of pounds sterling or US dollars investments registered under such flags and these vessels are not only properly maintained and manned but their crews also enjoy wage levels in excess of UK levels. This is because the owner cannot afford to jeopardise his investment.

21.5.1 Voluntary controls in sea transport

The advent of steam vessels in the mid-nineteenth century which enabled ships to sail in a more or less direct line, irrespective of winds, meant that liner trades could develop. Liners provided regular services calling at scheduled ports at stated times. They faced severe competition from tramp vessels, who had no schedules to stick to, but were prepared to wait for cargoes. The liner owners therefore developed the 'conference' system as a way of protecting the liner trade from this competition. Members of a conference allocated the trade between them on the basis of their existing tonnages and offered shippers a regular service calling at scheduled ports at stated times, irrespective of whether or not they had a full cargo. The conference determined a common freight tariff for all its members and this applied to all shippers irrespective of their tonnage. Shippers who undertook to give all their trade to conference members were allowed either a deferred or an immediate rebate. If another shipowner attempted to enter the trade, the conference would use a fighting ship with lower rates to undercut him. An example was the Far East conference war with Mitsui Line in the 1950s.

They justified their virtual monopoly by the fact that they offered the same reliable service to all shippers at the same rates, irrespective of tonnage, and to be fair most shippers approved of the system.

The establishment of new independent nations following decolonisation in the 1950s and 1960s meant that new member lines, representing these newly independent countries, had to be admitted into conferences serving those countries, e.g. India. This led to over-tonnaging and the adoption of a pooling system whereby individual sailings were allocated a certain tonnage and the freight on anything carried in excess of that tonnage, less a disbursement allowance for loading and discharge, was put into the pool and used to compensate a vessel which failed to fill its allocation. Other problems arose with the Soviet fleet, which with all the resources of the state behind it could undercut the conference rates and could not be fought in the usual way. The Trans-Siberian railway also posed a threat to the Far East conference, since although it did not offer a faster service, its rates were considerably cheaper.

The advent of containerisation saw the amalgamation of existing liner companies into consortia to meet the very high initial costs of containerisation but in the deep-sea trades the conference former rates still applied. However, competition arose from non-conference multi-modal operators many of whom were non-shipowners (NVOMMOs – non vessel-owning multi-modal operators) who were prepared to offer shippers FAK (freight all kinds) rates. The conferences have thus had to modify their tariffs considerably and these are now only the bases from which individual shippers are allowed varying rebates dependent on tonnage and loyalty. The 'conference' idea is still in use to some extent and amounts to a voluntary arrangement to maintain good standards in sea transport by ensuring steady business for reputable shipowners.

In Appendix II the activities of many transport organisations are described. One of these is the Baltic and International Maritime Council, an organisation of some three thousand owners, brokers and club members, with a registered tonnage of 360 million GRT (gross registered tonnage). BIMCO is perhaps the best example of a shipping organisation where representatives of sea transport examine mutual problems.

21.5.2 Control of sea transport to meet international needs

There are almost a hundred international conventions on sea transport currently in operation. They deal with such matters as the safety of life at sea, loadlines, maintenance of lighthouses, construction and use regulations, oil pollution, nuclear ships, collisions, hazardous materials, etc.

In most cases the conventions become binding on shipowners and shippers in one of three ways. They may be formally enacted by the legislatures of the countries adopting the convention, thus becoming laws of the countries concerned. They may be complied with as a result of a requirement for membership of some voluntary body such as a shipping conference or freight conference. Finally, they may be required by the insurers, who will not offer cover unless the terms of the convention are complied with.

IMO (International Maritime Organisation), described in greater detail in Appendix II, acts as a forum for member nations to exchange information and discuss problems of control over maritime matters. As a specialised agency of the United Nations, it is frequently responsible for initiating international conventions on maritime matters.

21.6 The control of air transport

Air transport in the United Kingdom is controlled by the Civil Aviation Authority (CAA), an independent public corporation, separate from the government, which was given powers under the Civil Aviation Act 1971 to control almost all aspects of aviation. It consists of a chairman, a deputy chairman, four full-time members and seven non-executive members. The Authority was set up as a direct result of the recommendation of the Edwards Report, 'British Air Transport in the Seventies'. It recommended that the new Authority should take over all the civil aviation functions previously undertaken by the Air Transport Licensing Board, the Air Registration Board, the Department of Trade and Industry and the National Air Traffic Services. The Authority is therefore both a public service enterprise and a regulatory body. Its responsibilities include:

- Air safety, both airworthiness and operational safety, including the licensing of flight crew, aircraft engineers, air traffic controllers and aerodromes, the certification of UK airlines and aircraft and the maintenance of air traffic control standards.
- The National Air Traffic Services, both air traffic control and telecommunications, in conjunction with the Ministry of Defence.
- The economic regulation of the civil aviation industry, including air transport licensing, the licensing of air travel organisers, the approval of air fares and the setting of certain airport charges.
- Advice to the government on civil aviation matters, both domestic and international.
- Consumer interests; private aviation requirements; economic and scientific research; the collection and publication of economic and scientific data; and consultancy and training for overseas administrations.
- The CAA also owns a subsidiary company, Highlands and Islands Airports Ltd, which manages and operates eight airports in Scotland.

The Authority's 'Mission Statement' reads:

- The CAA's primary purpose is to maintain and where possible improve existing standards of safety. It will:
  - provide and manage a safe air traffic control system in the UK
  - set standards for and monitor the airworthiness and operational safety of all UK registered aircraft
  - ensure the maintenance of high levels of safety in the operation of UK aerodromes, the licensing of UK aircrew, air traffic controllers and maintenance engineers and in the UK design, manufacture or overhaul of aircraft, engines and equipment.
- In operating the air traffic control system it will exploit up-to-date technology so as to:
  - allow all users of British airspace to fly in safety at an acceptable system cost
  - provide for future traffic growth for as long as possible.
- It will aim to secure for the air transport user travelling on UK airlines:
  - a choice of service in terms of both quality and frequency
  - the lowest prices consistent with efficient and profitable airline operations taking into account the interests of other users of UK airspace, and the efficient use of airports and the capacity of the air traffic system.
- It will advise the government on:
  - the actions needed to achieve these aims where they lie outside its own powers
  - the priorities to be adopted if the capacity of the air transport system is insufficient to meet the needs of all potential users.
- It will collaborate with other European authorities in order to maximise safety and ensure the efficient use of European airspace.

The organisation chart (Fig. 21.2) is helpful in understanding how such a public body organises its activities.

21.6.1 Economic regulation of air transport

The Civil Aviation Act 1982 gave the CAA the duty of ensuring that British airlines satisfy public demand in a way that is consistent with the sound development of the industry. Since the completion of the Single European Market on 1 January 1993 the Authority now conducts these functions within the much wider framework of the European Union. Aspects of economic regulation are as follows:

- Before a British airline can offer a scheduled or a charter air service it has to obtain a CAA air transport licence and satisfy the Authority about its finances.
- The CAA is also responsible for approving scheduled international and domestic air fares.
- The CAA issues Air Travel Organisers' Licences (ATOLs) to applicants who can show they are fit to hold a licence and who have adequate financial arrangements. They must also lodge a bond with the Authority.

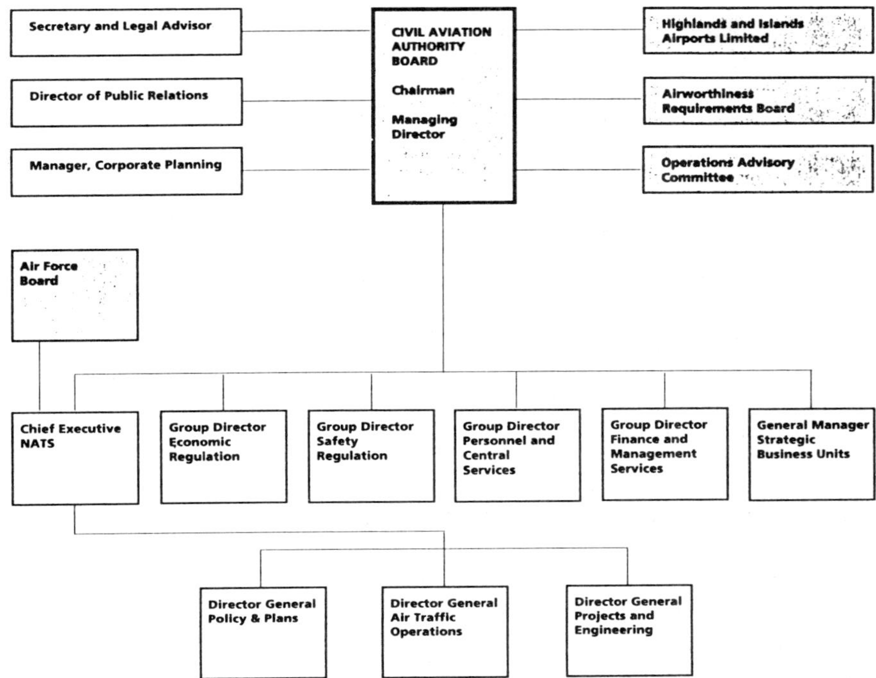

Fig. 21.2 An organisation chart (courtesy of the Civil Aviation Authority)

This is a sum of money which can be used to repatriate passengers stranded abroad should the licence-holder cease to trade. It will also be used as far as possible to compensate those who have paid in advance for tickets.

- The Authority regulates the landing and other charges at British airports.
- The Authority collects and publishes statistics on air transport; it established an Air Transport Users Committee and it investigates complaints from users of both passenger and freight services.

21.6.2 Regulation of air transport in the interests of safety

The Authority develops and enforces safety standards applicable to every aspect of civil aviation, from public air services to crop spraying. The Group Director Safety Regulation is a member of the Authority, charged with responsibility for airworthiness standards and operational safety. There is an Airworthiness Requirements Board to advise the Authority on all aspects of design, construction and maintenance. No aircraft registered in the United Kingdom operating for public transport is permitted to fly unless it holds a current airworthiness certificate issued by the Airworthiness Division of the Authority. The Division is also responsible for the safety of hovercraft.

The operator of any aircraft must also hold an Air Operator's Certificate, which signifies competence to secure the safe operation of aircraft. The Authority's Flight Operations Inspectors investigate management structure, operational planning and control, training and testing of flight crews, operating instructions for pilots, premises, equipment and records. The Authority has a Civil Aviation Flying Unit (CAFU) which examines pilots for flying ability and tests navigational aids. All pilots have to be tested initially by CAFU – subsequent tests are delegated to suitable company pilots.

21.6.3 The National Air Traffic Services

The National Air Traffic Services is a joint civil and military body supervising Air Traffic Control. It reports to both the Civil Aviation Authority and the Ministry of Defence. It maintains a network of navigational aids, air traffic control centres at West Drayton, Preston and Prestwick, and operates the enormous telecommunications system. In 1972 more than one million flights were contacted and advised by the three traffic control centres.

ICAO and IATA (described in detail in Appendix II) are the two international associations responsible for the control and regulation of international air transport. ICAO is an association of member states, while IATA is an association of air transport operators. The former is concerned more with legal problems, safety, constructional problems, etc., while the latter has jurisdiction over more commercial matters.

21.7 The control of pipelines – The Pipelines Act 1962

Pipelines are of greatest importance to continental powers with large inland areas remote from ports. It follows that a system of control for pipelines is more necessary to continental powers than to countries like Britain.

A standard procedure for pipeline development in Britain was not introduced until fairly recently; the traditional system of legislation by private Act of Parliament being adequate for the pipelines laid down before the 1960s. Such private Acts gave authority for a particular project. The 1962 Act is a general Act, regulating and facilitating the construction of any pipeline, and ensuring that they are not unduly proliferated. The chief points covered by the Act may be listed as follows:

1. No cross-country pipelines are to be constructed without the authority of the Minister of Power (now the Department of Energy), who has discretion to grant an application or refuse it. Local pipelines do not normally require authority, but sixteen weeks' notice of the intention to construct a local pipeline must be given to the minister, with plans and full particulars of the route, material to be conveyed, duration, maintenance procedures, etc. The minister may then rule that authority is required if he deems it necessary. He may require the pipeline to be of such a size that others may use it too, to prevent the proliferation of pipelines by a multitude of applications.
2. For safety reasons the minister may impose certain methods of construction, use of appropriate materials, etc., on the constructors of pipelines. He may order the performance of remedial work to protect a pipeline endangered by any building or other work, and in default he may even carry out the work at the expense of the parties concerned.
3. The minister has power to order inquiries into any accidents relating to pipelines. The owner of pipelines is bound to notify any explosions, collapses or the ignition of any substance in or from a pipeline.
4. Owners of pipelines are required to keep local authorities and the minister informed about changes of ownership, use and disuse of pipelines, and to inform police, fire brigades and other authorities of any escapes, fires, etc.
5. Inspectors may be appointed by the minister to test, inspect or take samples from any pipeline, and are vested with authority to inspect documents, enter upon land, etc.
6. Certain powers are conferred upon the minister to ensure the preservation of amenities, the prevention of water pollution and the restoration of agricultural land.
7. The Act does not apply to drains, sewers, heating installations, refrigerating plants, domestic and many factory pipelines, gas, electricity or Atomic Energy Authority pipelines, and pneumatic dispatch tubes.

21.8 Summary

1. It is essential to control transport from many points of view, but it is important not to make regulations so burdensome that they discourage enterprise. The chief reasons for regulations are to promote the safety of the public, to prevent the abuse of monopoly situations and to avoid cut-throat competition. It is also important to ensure that transport costs are not passed on to the general public as 'social costs' – for example, as pollution, noise, accident damage, etc.

2. Many transport facilities are natural monopolies, and monopolies can be abused. Parliament seeks to control monopolies by such measures as price regulation and requirements to give impartial treatment to all.
3. Excessive competition can be harmful because it leads to cost-cutting in many areas, such as vehicle maintenance, reductions in services offered, reduced amenities, etc. It may be desirable to introduce quality licensing to ensure all operators reach a required standard.
4. As transport is a dynamic and capital-intensive industry we can have new methods driving out old methods and making them obsolete, or at least less profitable than in the past. The older methods become vested interests keen to preserve what they can of their markets in the face of aggressive new techniques. It is not easy to preserve a balance between the old – but still useful – systems and new systems seeking to expand.
5. Nationalisation is the expropriation of all the assets in a particular industry and their operation by a public corporation, to provide an integrated system where central planning ensures that assets are used in the best possible way. The nationalisation of transport in the United Kingdom in 1947 proved to be a bureaucratic nightmare and within six years the process of privatisation had begun. This process reached its final conclusion on 1 April 1994 when the railways were finally privatised by the Railways Act 1993.
6. Road transport is controlled by a number of licensing schemes for drivers, vehicles and road transport operators. The system of quality licensing is the best for road haulage – the operator is given a licence when he proves he has a proper structure for his business and adequate financial resources for the size of business envisaged. There is also an international convention, the CMR Convention, which overcomes conflicts of law when goods move by international road haulage.
7. Rail transport is now controlled by the Railways Act 1993 which has privatised the track to be run by an organisation called Railtrack. It has also made the track available to entrepreneurs prepared to run trains over the system. How successful this proves to be remains to be seen, but the opening of Eurotunnel to make Europe-wide journeys possible means that the railways should become viable on long-haul routes and therefore should attract private operators. The international rules of the COTIF Convention on Rail Traffic apply to all international movements of goods and passengers by rail.
8. Sea transport is less susceptible to control than other methods of transport, but the requirements to be met by British registered ships are many, in the interests of safety. There are many agreed conventions on sea transport to which the United Kingdom has acceded and the Hague–Visby Rules control the legal arrangements between the various parties in the carriage of goods by sea.
9. Air transport is controlled by the Civil Aviation Authority, which is

charged with the general supervision of the whole industry with particular reference to safety, airworthiness, the licensing of crews, the operation of aerodromes, the economic viability of the whole system and the control of air traffic.

10. Pipelines are controlled by a general Act, the Pipelines Act 1962. Control is exercised today by the Department of Energy, with a view to avoiding excessive proliferation of pipelines. The minister may impose regulations about materials for construction, etc., may order inquiries into accidents and may appoint inspectors to test, inspect, take samples, etc.

21.9 Questions

1. What is meant by the statement: 'Transport is often a natural monopoly'? What is the problem with natural monopolies in transport and how may the problem be overcome?
2. In the early years of many transport activities powers were provided by a private Act of Parliament. Later, a 'general Act' would be passed to cover all future developments. How does a general Act work? Refer in your answer to the Pipelines Act 1962.
3. Why is excessive competition harmful in a transport industry? How can we prevent excessive competition, and what are the dangers if we try to do so?
4. What is quantity licensing? What is quality licensing? Which is better and why?
5. What aspects of aviation are controlled by the Civil Aviation Authority? From where does the Authority derive its powers, and how can it ensure that its orders are carried out?
6. Do you support a nationalised system of transport, or do you prefer privately run transport organisations? Argue the case for the system you prefer.

I Appendix: Glossary of transport and logistical terms

Introduction

In transport and logistics there are countless abbreviations and specialised terms which are full of meaning to those who use them because they define precisely the relations between various parties or have legal implications which are well understood. In drawing up this chapter it seemed best to use a 'Glossary of Terms' format and arrange items in alphabetical order. Inevitably there will be omissions, but we hope the reader will find most of the terms here that are used in the logistics industry.

Glossary of terms

AAD (Accompanying administrative document) This is a document that accompanies goods sent to EU destinations from another EU country where excise duty is payable. It enables Customs to keep a check on the cargo until the duty is paid.

Act of God A concept in English law which relieves the common carrier of liability for losses suffered as a result of events so unusual as to seem to be the result of a supernatural power. Thus, to be struck by lightning or a tidal wave would be an act of God. It is one of the 'common law exceptions'. Since the concept does not occur in some other systems of law the courts have considered that the use of this term in a contract of carriage implies that the parties intended the English courts to have jurisdiction.

ACV (Air-cushion vehicles) Vehicles which ride on a cushion of air. Though the principle has been applied to both land and sea vehicles, the best-known example is the marine hovercraft.

ADR This is the European agreement concerning the international carriage of dangerous goods by road. It lays down standards for packing and labelling of the goods and also special conditions covering the vehicle, some of which, e.g. tankers, have to be certified to say they have been built and maintained to ADR standards.

Ad valorem According to value: a method of charging customs duty on high-value goods. There is also an optional *ad valorem* surcharge by sea, whereby the shipper raises the carrier's liability to a declared value, on which the shipper pays a surcharge. This also applies to carriage by air.

Air waybill A document made out for the carriage of goods by air. There are twelve copies of which the most important are the three signed copies; one for the consignor, one for the carrier and one for the consignee. Under the 1975 Montreal version of the Warsaw Rules it may also exist as an electronic record in a computer memory bank. In the United Kingdom the vast majority of air waybills are now computer-generated.

Aligned documentation A system of documentation based on standard designs for forms. The essence of the system is that the same information will always appear in the same place, whichever form is being used. A4 paper is used and each geographical area on the form is designated for a particular piece of information. A master document can then be prepared, with the correct information in each box. All the completed documents required in connection with a particular consignment may be produced by running off copies from the master copy, using various masks to blank out any information not required on a particular form. The object is to avoid the time-wasting process of copying information from one document to another, and to avoid the likelihood of omission or error inherent in such a process. Aligned documentation can also be produced electronically, the various boxes on the form becoming part of a databank that can be called up when required.

Appointment The process of nominating someone as agent to act on our behalf. Appointment may be formal (by deed), oral or in writing.

APT Advanced Passenger Train.

ATA An international customs agreement under which samples, professional equipment and goods for exhibitions can be temporarily imported without payment of customs duty, if accompanied by an ATA carnet (Carnet de Passage en Douane pour L'Admission Temporaire).

ATC Air traffic control.

ATP The European agreement covering the international carriage of perishable foodstuffs by road.

Average From the Arabic *awariya* – damaged goods. A general term for losses at sea.

Average adjuster A specialist in preparing statements relating to maritime losses and apportioning them among underwriters.

AWB see *Air waybill*.

Baco-liner A barge carrier operating Europe–West Africa. It carries twelve barges of 24 m × 9.5 m and 800 dwt capacity plus up to 500 TEUs, including some reefer. It has its own 40 ton gantry crane for loading heavy-lifts or containers on deck.

BAF (Bunker adjustment factor) A plus or minus percentage freight adjustment to reflect the current cost of bunkers.

BART (Bay Area Rapid Transit) The San Francisco computerised train service.

Bay Plan A container vessel's equivalent of a stowage plan.

Bill of entry A shipper's detailed declaration of the nature and value of goods moving through Customs.

Bill of lading This is a document made out in the carriage of goods by sea. It has three functions: it is a receipt for the goods shipped; it is evidence of the terms of the contract of carriage, and it is a quasi-negotiable document of title to the goods. This means that it can be used to transfer ownership of the goods listed in it while they are still on the high seas. The one who holds the bill of lading can claim the goods from the master of the vessel at destination. It is said to be quasi-negotiable (almost negotiable) in that it is easily transferable but it does not – like a true negotiable instrument – transfer a better title than the giver of it had. The transferee only gets the same rights as the transferor had.

BIMCO (Baltic and International Maritime Council) Shipowners' organisation based in Copenhagen. It provides advisory services; represents their interests and prepares standard shipping documents, e.g. charter-parties.

Blue Book The Department of Trade's regulations covering dangerous goods carried by British vessels, or any vessel in British ports. To a large degree superseded by the IMDG Code to which it refers.

Bonded warehouse A warehouse for goods stored under customs control pending payment of duty. In the EU they are now to be called tax warehouses.

Box Colloquial term for container.

Box time A standard BIMCO charter-party for a container vessel.

Break-bulk cargo Another name for general or conventional cargo, i.e. non-unitised and non-bulk.

BSI (British Standards Institution) The body authorised to lay down national standards in the United Kingdom.

Bunkering Replenishing a ship's fuel supplies.

CABAF (Currency and bunker adjustment factor) A combination of CAF and BAF.

Cabotage The practice of reserving internal or coastwise traffic to national flag carriers. By air this has been extended to cover traffic between the mother country and colonies. By road it means that a foreign haulier can pick up a return load for an overseas destination but cannot carry internal traffic. Also a foreign driver cannot move another foreign load internally, while awaiting clearance of his own load, while an imported container cannot be used for internal loads.

CAF (Currency adjustment factor) A plus/minus percentage of freight to reflect currency fluctuation.

Capacity tonne-kilometres The capacity of the vehicle multiplied by the number of kilometres travelled (see *Load factor*). A 10 tonne capacity vehicle travelling 100 miles has travelled 1,000 capacity tonne-kilometres. This measurement is used as a unit of output to form the basis of a costing and rating system.

Carnet A pad or set of international transport documents, as used in TIR transport, to provide two copies for every frontier crossing.

Carriage forward A delivery system where goods are carried on the understanding that the carriage charges will be paid to the carrier on arrival at destination.

Carriage paid Goods are supplied at a price which includes charges for delivery to the buyer's premises.

C/B (Container base) A UK container freight station with transit shed facilities for stuffing/stripping containers and often with a Customs Long Room.

CCC (Customs Co-ordination Council) An organisation to obtain co-operation between the various Customs authorities around the world and reach some degree of uniformity and harmony in their approach.

CCS-UK (Cargo Community Systems–UK) The new air cargo distribution network replacing ACP 90, which interfaces with Customs' CHIEF and also acts as the EDI network for air cargo movements.

C & D Collection and delivery between customers' premises and a container freight station.

Cellular ships The name given to container ships with holds fitted with vertical steel guides so that each container can be slotted in to a particular space, slot or 'cell' by the crane driver, without any assistance from shipboard labour.

Certificate of analysis A certificate required for the shipment of drugs.

Certificate of origin A document certifying the place of growth or manufacture of an article for export. The certification is done (for a fee) by a Chamber of Commerce, on proof of the true facts about production of the goods.

CFR (Cost and freight) Formerly known as C&F this is one of the 1990 Incoterms. The seller must pay the costs and the freight as far as the port of destination, but the *risk* passes to the buyer as the goods cross the ship's rail in the port of shipment. Insurance costs are not included, and the buyer must insure.

CFS Container freight station.

Chargeable weight In air transport the chargeable weight can be one of the following five different weights:

1. Minimum.
2. Gross weight.
3. Gross weight rounded up to next quantity flat rate.
4. Weight measurement equivalent.
5. Weight measurement equivalent rounded up to next quantity flat rate.

CHIEF (Customs handling of import and export freight) The new computer system for H.M. Customs, which replaced the DEPs system for the 1990s. There are four Community systems which interface with it. They are CNS, MCP, DHP and CCS-UK. Two other related data processing procedures are HCI and EPUs.

CIF (Cost, insurance and freight) The seller is in the same position as in CFR but in addition has to provide marine insurance during the carriage. The risk passes to the buyer as the goods cross the ship's rail, and the insurance policy then covers the buyer's risk.

CIM (Convention on International Merchandise) Drawn up in 1914 and renewed from time to time, this convention is about international carriage of goods by rail. It makes the railways liable for loss, damage and delay. Before 1914 many railway companies excluded liability for such losses. The Convention is now called the COTIF Convention – the French acronym for the Convention on Carriage of Goods and Passengers by Railway. The term CIM has been retained for the CIM Rules which cover the carriage of goods. There are also CIV Rules which cover the movement of passengers (*voyageurs*).

CIP (Carriage and insurance paid to) The same as CPT but the seller also has to insure the goods for all modes of transport to destination. The risk transfers to the buyer when the goods are given into the custody of the first carrier, and the buyer then has the cover of the insurance policy.

CIT The Chartered Institute of Transport.

CIV (Convention Internationale de Voyageurs) The international agreement on the carriage of passengers and their luggage by rail.

Closing date The last day on which a Port Authority will accept general cargo through the transit shed for a particular liner vessel. It does not apply to deck cargo delivered direct over quay, or overside cargo delivered by lighter.

CMR (Convention Marchandises par Route) The international agreement on the carriage of goods by road, embodied in UK law by the Carriage of Goods by Road Act 1965.

CNS (Community Network Services) A network of services which interfaces with Customs' CHIEF. (It is described in detail on pages 98–100.)

Code of practice An agreed code of behaviour, usually drawn up by a trade association in agreement with the Director-General of Fair Trading, to ensure that members of the association, in their dealings with the general public, behave in a proper manner, deal with complaints, etc.

COI The Central Office of Information, in London.

Combined transport operator A transport operator who uses multi-modal transport for international carriage (e.g. road–sea–road, road–sea–rail) to deliver goods door-to-door. He or she undertakes responsibility for the entire journey, thus simplifying legal problems. The customer whose goods are lost or damaged is compensated by the CTO, who then discovers where the actual trouble arose and seeks to recover from the carrier actually at fault.

Common carrier A carrier who holds himself out as ready to carry for the public at large. He is liable in law for every loss that occurs apart from the five common law exceptions. These are: Act of God, Act of the Queen's enemies, inherent vice, fraud of the consignor and fault of the consignor. Many carriers make it clear in their contractual documents that they are not common carriers but private carriers.

Community transit A system of transit documents for intra-Community use in the EC. There are two procedures: those under 'movement certificates' and a full 'T form' transit procedure. Movement certificates are used when goods move directly into the destination country or by air and signal the status of the goods. T forms are used when they have to cross other frontiers before reaching the country of final destination. Since the Single Market these forms are not required in many inter-member movements, but are still in use for movements of non-EC goods and in one or two other situations.

Conditions of carriage A set of conditions devised by a trade association or by a firm itself laying down their terms for carrying goods or passengers. It is incorporated into their contracts and is binding upon customers, providing the terms pass the 'test of reasonableness' in the Unfair Contract Terms Act 1977.

Conference An organisation of shipowners engaged in the same trade which sets a common tariff and enters into contracts with shippers. It represents the owners' interests with governments and other bodies. Although less influential in the present era of multi-modal transport it is premature to say that the conference idea is obsolete.

Consignee The receiver of goods.

Consignor The sender of goods.

Consortium An organisation of combined transport operators (CTOs) engaged in the same trade. Members agree to allow slots for other members on their own vessels. They may not all be conference members and some may be NVOMTO (non-vessel owning multi-transport operators).

Contract A legally binding agreement between two persons, or more than two persons, by which one party supplies goods or performs services for the other, in return for either a money payment or some reciprocal supply of goods or services, or for some forbearance. To be legally binding there must be a clear offer, validly accepted, and valuable consideration must pass between the parties – unless the bargain is made under seal, where the formality of the promise makes it binding without valuable consideration.

Cost per freight tonne-kilometre A costing unit found by the formula:

$$\frac{\text{cost of operating the vehicle}}{\text{no. of freight tonne-kilometres carried}}$$

COT Customers' own transport to or from container freight station.

COU Clip on unit, i.e. a portable refrigerating unit.

CPT (Carriage paid to) Another Incoterm. The seller pays the freight or carriage to the named destination but the *risk* passes to the seller once the goods are delivered to the first carrier, whatever the form of transport used or the multi-modal nature of the transit.

Cranage Charge for the use of cranes operated by the Port Authority.

CRN (Customs registered number) A number allocated to an exporter or freight forwarder for use when exports are to be entered under SCP (Simplified clearance procedure).

CTD (Combined transport document) The CTO's bill of lading.

CTO See *Combined transport operator*.

Customs collections H.M. Customs is divided into a number of 'Collections' each administered by a collector who is responsible for the collection of both import duty and excise duty within his area. His staff also carry out duties for other government departments where H.M. Customs is conveniently situated to exercise official controls of various sorts (e.g. over firearms, drugs and veterinary matters).

CY (Container yard) A collection and distribution point for FCL containers. If it has Customs clearance facilities it is an ICD (inland clearance depot).

DAF (Delivered at frontier) One of the Incoterms of trade. The seller bears all the costs and all the risks until the goods arrive at the named frontier, but before they go through the 'Customs border'. The buyer clears the goods through the import frontier, paying the duty (if any) and bearing the risks. It applies to all modes of transport.

DCA (Differential cost analysis) A system of cost analysis which compares probable costs under alternative systems of distribution and hence seeks to find the best financial solution to a particular distribution problem.

DCF (Discounted cashflow) A method of evaluating capital expenditure by calculating the likely net cashflow to be earned by the new asset in years to come, and discounting it back to represent present-day receipts. If the earnings exceed the costs, when both are in present-day terms, it will be worthwhile proceeding with the investment.

DDP (Delivered duty paid) An Incoterm. This is the maximum commitment for the seller and the minimum for the buyer. The seller delivers to the buyer after paying the duty on import to the country of destination. However, it is possible to deliver 'DDP exclusive of VAT and/or taxes'. (The term *franco domicile* is now obsolete, and the term DDP is used for delivery at the buyer's premises.) Applies to all modes of transport.

DDU (Delivered duty unpaid) An Incoterm where the goods are delivered to customer's premises, or other named point. Although the exporter is not liable for duty or taxes he is responsible for costs and risks of carrying out Customs formalities. Applies to all modes of transport.

Dead freight Freight claimed on cargo-space not used by a charterer who has undertaken to load a full cargo but has not done so. (An allowance is made for the reduction in costs of loading and discharge resulting from the shortage.)

Deadweight tonnage The total load-carrying capacity of a ship measured in tonnes weight. It is the difference between the vessel's unladen displacement weight and her displacement weight when she is down to her relevant loadline, which varies according to voyage and season. The difference must account for bunkers, water and stores as well as payload.

Demurrage A charge made to a shipper or charterer for delay caused to ships, barges, etc. Once commenced it is continuous, irrespective of the cause of any further delay. In the case of containers/trailers it is a charge for keeping them at a CFS for longer than allowed in the tariff.

DEQ (Delivered ex quay) An Incoterm. The seller bears all the costs and risks until the goods are on quay at destination. These include the duty due on entry to the country unless otherwise specified. Buyer takes delivery and assumes risk from there.

DES (Delivered ex ship) An Incoterm. Seller bears all costs and risks of bringing the goods to the port of destination, where they are passed to the buyer. The buyer bears the risks when unloading and in the onward transit.

Despatch A chartering term referring to the reward given to a charterer if he completes his loading and/or discharge in less than the stipulated laytime. Normally it is rated at half the rate of demurrage.

Detention A charge raised for detaining containers/trailers at custom premises longer than agreed in the tariff.

Deviation Diversion of a ship or road vehicle to call at places other than the agreed destination. It has important legal consequences, since it is not permitted in common law, and therefore a deviation clause may be inserted into contracts by carriers to make it permissible.

DGN (Dangerous goods note) A SITPRO document similar to SSN except that it is printed in red on white and has a hatched edge. It accompanies goods throughout transit and besides the dangerous goods declaration giving such details as the correct technical name, hazard and UN number, it incorporates the container/vehicle packing certificate signed by the packers and countersigned by the shipper, declaring that the goods have been packed and stowed in compliance with IMDG Codes.

DHB (Dover Harbour Board) A network service that interfaces with Customs' CHIEF (see above).

DOT Department of Transport.

Down-stream analysis Concerned with the final customer's requirements. The manufacturer will seek to meet these requirements, and in order to be competitive a manufacturer needs to apply the same criteria by looking at his own performance from the customer's point of view.

DRP (Distribution Resource Planning) This is concerned with the planning of distribution on the bases of current and past information. It is to be hoped that computers will enable future planning to be more accurate.

DTI Department of Trade and Industry.

Dunnage Comprises a variety of materials (including timber, tarpaulins, bamboo frames, coir mats, old tyres, straw and airbags) used in stowage for many purposes including securing, separating, ventilating, safeguarding cargo against contact with areas of condensation, making a flat and spreading a load.

DVLC (Driver and Vehicle Licensing Centre, Swansea) Issues ordinary driving licences and vehicle excise licences and maintains the national computer records of these.

ECSI (Export cargo shipping instruction) Document sent to carrier at time of booking advising him of who is to pay freight charges; relevant information for bill of lading; quarantine declaration, where required, and also enables shipper to ask for ancillary services, e.g. completion and lodgement of customs entries.

EDI (Electronic data interchange) An electronic system whereby structured data can be transferred from one computer to another, and can be processed, accessed, etc., by all interested authorised parties.

EDIFACT (Electronic data interchange for administration, commerce and transport) The organisation responsible to the United Nations for the development of standard messages in these three fields.

EDISHIP An organisation responsible for exchanging data between carriers and merchants by electronic means, e.g. booking, shipping instructions, bills of lading and freight invoices. Banks could also fit into the system.

EHA (Equipment handover agreement) Incorporates contract under which equipment is taken over and returned to carrier. Includes signatures evidencing condition at time of take-over and return.

EPOS (Electronic point of sale) A terminal used in retail trade to accept payments by credit card with instant verification of the creditworthiness of the cardholder.

EPUs (Entry processing units) A data processing system which is local to traders and away from ports and airports.

ETA Estimated time of arrival.

ETD Estimated time for departure.

Exclusionary clause Any clause inserted in a contract which seeks to exclude liability on the part of one party to the contract for any event, breach of contractual duty, or failure to comply with a statute. The rule of interpretation *contra proferentem* holds that all such clauses must be interpreted strictly against the one who drew them up.

Export house A commercial house which specialises in making purchases for foreign customers and in exporting the goods.

Export licence The Department of Trade and Industry issues such licences for export of items over which control is exercised, e.g. *objets d'art*, armaments, etc.

EXW (Ex works) Another Incoterm. The seller's only responsibility is to make the goods available at his works or factory. The buyer bears the costs and the risks from that point on, including loading onto the vehicle (unless otherwise agreed), and the entire transit to destination. 'Ex works' terms are therefore the minimum obligation for the seller and the maximum obligation for the buyer.

Face vet An initial scan of an entry by an experienced customs entry clerk, who will reject the entry if he or she notices anything amiss.

FAK (Freight all kinds) System where charge is made for each container carried irrespective of its contents. Equally applies to most air freight.

FAS (Free alongside ship) An Incoterm. The seller's obligations cease when the goods are placed alongside the ship on the quayside, or in lighters. The buyer bears all the costs and risks of loss or damage from that moment, and even the responsibility of clearing the goods for export.

FCA (Free carrier (named point)) An Incoterm for all modes of transport. Seller responsible for delivery of goods to a carrier at a named point. This could even be at the seller's premises, or at an airport or container depot. Buyer responsible for risks and costs thereafter.

FCL Full container load.

Fiscal charges on road vehicles Taxes imposed by certain countries on foreign international haulage operators travelling through their country. In most cases UK hauliers are exempted under bilateral agreements but not in every case (e.g. Austria, where a lorry tax based on the weight is charged).

Flowchart A physical distribution chart showing how goods move from the point of production to the point of consumption. It pinpoints cost centres and enables the physical distribution manager to appraise them and compare present costs with those likely to be incurred by the use of alternative methods. A flowchart may also be used to show the path documents take through an export department.

FMCG (Fast moving consumer goods) A sector of business dominated by large-scale retailers, and shelf-driven – where the main preoccupation is the calling-forward of stock items each day to replace sales made.

FOB (Free on board) An Incoterm. The seller is responsible as far as loading the goods on board ship at the port of departure. The risk passes as the goods cross the ship's rail. The buyer bears the loss if they fall upon the deck.

Freeport facility A designated enclosed area within the port wherein goods may be landed, stored, sorted, garbled, sampled, blended, repacked, displayed and manufactured so that their subsequent Brussels Nomenclature category is altered. It is only in this last respect that it differs from the alternative bonded warehouse system. The Customs are not concerned with the goods until they attempt to enter the hinterland, in which case they are liable to entry and duty in the normal way. Such a facility is favourable to both transshipment and entrepôt traffics.

Freight account The document sent by a shipowner to a shipper for freight due on his goods. The document is a debit note, making the shipper a debtor for the amount.

Freight forward Freight to be paid by the consignee. The carrier has a lien on the goods until the freight is paid and the freight should be clearly shown on the bill of lading.

Freight/tonne A unit of weight measurement, based on a tonne of 1,000 kg or $1m^3$, whichever gives greater freight to the vessel.

Frustration The termination of a contract as a result of some major event which prevents fulfilment. Thus, war may frustrate a contract, or it may be frustrated by supervening illegality, some government declaring the trade illegal. If a ship chartered for a voyage sinks on the way to the port of loading the charter-party is frustrated.

GATT (General Agreement on Tariffs and Trade) An international multilateral agreement at government level designed to free trade by reducing barriers to trade, such as tariffs, quotas, etc.

General average A method of compensating those who make a sacrifice (either of goods, or of part of the ship, or of money paid out as expenses) to save the entire venture in perilous marine situations. A general average contribution is levied by the shipowner before goods are delivered at destination. Security (a *general average bond*) may be taken from a reputable institution. General average losses are usually recoverable under the terms of insurance policies.

Groupage A system of consolidation used to obtain the benefit of cheaper rates for full loads. A groupage agent (usually a freight forwarder) groups together small consignments from a number of exporters to make up a full container load or vehicle load, covering the single consignment with a bill of lading. The individual consignments are acknowledged by house bills of lading, which may be used by the importer to claim the goods from the agent's foreign de-grouper who is breaking down the grouped consignment for individual delivery of the component parts.

Groupage agent A freight forwarder, who having made up an FCL container from several LCL consignments, offers same to carrier, and undertakes payment of the freight.

GRT (Gross registered tonnage) A term used in shipping to describe a vessel's active capacity. It is calculated by measuring the wholly enclosed spaces of the ship in cubic feet, deducting certain exempt areas, e.g. staircases, and dividing the total obtained by 100, i.e. every 100 cubic feet is regarded as 1 ton.

Hague Rules The body of rules laid down by the International Convention on the Carriage of Goods by Sea originally embodied into British law by the Carriage of Goods by Sea Act 1924. The current version, the Hague–Visby Rules, were embodied in the Carriage of Goods by Sea Act 1971.

Hamburg Rules A set of UN rules for carriage of goods by sea, now ratified, but not much used because major trading nations have not yet ratified them.

Harmonised system The latest name for a Customs Co-operation System for deciding codes for commodities passing through ports.

Hazchem A set of regulations about the carriage of hazardous chemicals by road. The Hazchem scheme is an official scheme, the technical background material for which is prepared by the Chemical Industries Association, King's Buildings, Smith Square, London SW1 P34. Among the materials issued are TREM cards (transport emergency cards).

HCI (Human-computer interface) A data processing service for amending entries into H.M. Customs' CHIEF (see above).

Headway The timing between vehicles on the same track. Most frequently applied to railway operations.

HMC (Her Majesty's Customs) The Customs authority for the United Kingdom.

House air waybill, House bill of lading Documents issued by an air forwarder or freight forwarder to recognise the grouping of consignments in a groupage operation. They may be used at destination to claim the goods from the de-grouper.

IATA (International Air Transport Association) An association of air transport operators, aimed at providing safe, regular and economic air transport. Based in Geneva but drawing its legal existence from a Canadian Act of Parliament, it licenses air forwarding agents, promotes easy documentation and other procedures. It is a world-wide conference which fixes air freight rates, and is a world centre for debate on air transport developments.

ICAO (International Civil Aviation Organisation) A body which consists of national representatives and UN representatives. It aims to ensure safe and orderly growth of civil aviation, with a fair opportunity for all nations to share in air transport.

ICC (International Chamber of Commerce) An organisation based in Paris to act as an international forum for the promotion of world trade, and representing all business points of view in resolving difficulties and conflicts of law between states. Its *Incoterms* are the basis of contracts in international trade.

ICD (Inland clearance depot) Defined by H.M. Customs as a place approved by them to which goods imported in containers may be removed for entry, examination and clearance and, equally, where goods intended for exportation may be made available for export control.

IMDG Code (The International Maritime Dangerous Goods Code 1990) The IMO recommendations for carriage of dangerous goods by sea came into effect on 1 January 1991. Supplements to the code cover emergency procedures; medical first aid guide; code of safe practice for solid bulk cargoes; reporting procedures for incidents; IMO/ILO guidelines for packing cargo in containers and recommendations for the safe use of pesticides in ships. Also covers marine pollutants.

IMO (International Maritime Organisation) The new name for IMCO (International Maritime Consultative Organisation). It is a UN body based in London and mainly concerned with achieving inter-governmental co-operation on the technical aspects of shipping, especially with regard to safety at sea. In this respect it is responsible for the rules governing the carriage of hazardous cargoes by sea. It also aims to spread the introduction of improved navigation techniques by becoming the centre for an exchange of technical and legal information between member states.

Incoterms 1990 A set of thirteen internationally agreed terms of trade whose definitions of buyers' and sellers' duties are clear and may be contractually adopted to avoid ambiguities about who does what.

Inherent vice Any defect in goods which is a consequence of their nature, and cannot be blamed on a carrier, e.g. soft fruit tends to rot, powders tend to blow away, animals can be violent at times, etc. Inherent vice is one of the five common law exceptions for which a carrier is excused liability.

Interface The point in a transport system where passengers and goods are transferred between one mode of transport and another.

IRFO (The International Road Freight Office) (Westgate House, Westgate Road, Newcastle upon Tyne NE1 1TW. Tel: 0632 610031) *Inter alia*, issues permits for international journeys by goods vehicles to or through those European countries which require them.

ISO (International Standards Organisation) An international body devoted to the establishment of international standards. So far as transport is concerned, it has particular relevance in establishing internationally agreed standard sizes, e.g. for pallets and containers, and maximum permitted weights and standard design of fittings, e.g. the corner fittings of containers. These standards ensure complete compatibility with handling equipment, vehicles, etc. throughout the world.

Jettison To throw cargo overboard either because it is a hazard or as a general sacrifice in extreme circumstances.

JIT (Just in time) This is concerned with reducing stock levels to a minimum so that the factory is only geared to meeting existing orders and in turn its suppliers only deliver what is required for that day's manufacture. This may require some consolidation of loads with other suppliers to make economic loads, e.g. full lorry loads of supplies sufficient to meet factory requirements. The changeover by the power industry from coal to gas-fired boilers is an application of JIT since, whereas previously they had to stockpile coal to meet seasonal demands for power, gas can be switched on and off as required, with no waste disposal problems.

Keelage Toll levied by a port authority on vessels entering a port.

Lash (Lighters aboard ship) The first of the systems incorporating barge-carrying vessels.

Laydays The days agreed between a charterer and a shipowner when a ship will be available for the purpose of loading or discharging cargo. Laydays may be expressed in a variety of ways, some of which are beneficial to the shipowner (e.g. running days – consecutive days of twenty-four hours midnight to midnight), or to the charterer (e.g. weather working days, SHEX (Sundays and holidays excepted)). If the laydays are exceeded a payment called demurrage becomes payable, to compensate the shipowner for the fact that the vessel is idle. Where no laydays are specified the goods must be loaded or unloaded in a reasonable time.

LCL Less than container load.

Lead time The time between the receipt of an order and its satisfaction by the supply of the goods, completion of the service, etc. The aim of the physical distribution industry is to satisfy demand with the least possible lead time.

Least time track The method of 'pressure path' navigation which seeks to find optimum tracks for aircraft to take advantage of tailwinds or avoid head winds.

LEC (Local export control) A system of clearing goods through Customs at exporters' own premises.

LIC (Local import control) A similar system to *LEC* where imports are cleared for entry and duty (if any) is levied at importers' own premises.

Lighterage The charge for using a lighter or barge.

Liner terms Freight covers costs of loading and discharge. Used in charter-parties.

LNG Liquefied natural gas.

Load factor A ratio found by the formula:

$$\frac{\text{Loaded tonne-kilometres}}{\text{Capacity tonne-kilometres}} \times 100$$

If the figures were (800/1,000) × 100 the load factor would be 80 per cent. It is a measure of vehicle utilisation. It should be measured over a period and compared with a target load factor. Interpretation of the results may lead to the conclusion that the wrong type or size of vehicle is being used, or that the service is not being marketed properly, e.g. by failure to find suitable return loads. A low load factor may indicate that for most of the time the vehicle is being used in a partially loaded state, or that full-leg and empty-leg journeys are succeeding one another on most occasions.

Logistician Person overseeing the logistical processes, monitoring them and updating them where necessary or when new techniques become available. He or she aims to get goods of the right quantity and quality to the consumer as required as regards both time and price.

Logistics The management of the supply-chain from the initial movement of raw materials and in-bought components, through in-house movements to the final distribution to the customer. It embraces not only the transport element but also industrial and depot location, warehousing, stock control, waste disposal, environmental considerations, legal aspects, packing and quality control.

Lo/lo (Lift on/lift off) A container vessel using cranes for loading and discharge.

LPG Liquefied petroleum gas.

Lump sum freight A fixed sum payable for the charter of a vessel irrespective of the tonnage or nature of the cargo actually carried. Used when hiring a vessel to be used for liner purposes.

Manifest A summary of all bills of lading, sea waybills, non-negotiable receipts and parcel receipts loaded on a vessel. One copy to Customs, one copy to the port authority at loading and to each destination port, plus several copies of each destination port's cargo for that port. Nowadays manifests are transmitted to recipients by EDI.

Mate's receipt A receipted lighterage note evidencing shipment on board of goods delivered by lighter or barge to a vessel. This receipt must be exchanged in due course for a bill of lading. A similar receipt is given to a port authority for cargo loaded via their quay.

MCP (Maritime cargo processing) A network service, which interfaces with Customs' CHIEF (see above).

Metro (1) The Paris underground system. (2) The Tyneside (UK) Rapid Transit System designed to carry 20,000 passengers an hour in each direction. A new bus route network was designed to link with the Metro stations to provide an integrated transport system using through tickets.

Motorway A divided highway, with very limited access, no conflicting traffic movements, no stopping (except in emergencies), restricted to certain classes of road users, and designed and constructed for high-speed travel. Alternative names used in other countries are: *Autobahn* (Germany), *autostrada* (Italy) and *freeway* or *turnpike* (USA).

Multi-modal transport (MMT) A system whereby goods are moved by the most economical transport system from door to door. Thus, road–sea–road, road–barge–road, road–air–road systems are in use. Easy transfer from one mode to another is essential, and containerisation of cargo is very helpful in this respect.

NCR (No carbon required) A system of document copying using coated papers which avoids the use of carbon paper, to give multiple copies of a single document or aligned documentation.

NDC National distribution centre.

Non-negotiable receipt A receipt issued in place of a bill of lading for personal and household effects.

Notary public A lawyer empowered to note and protest bills of exchange and thus formally bear witness to the failure of any party to honour these documents. The notary public also 'notes protest' by the master of any vessel arriving after a deep-sea voyage to cover the carrier against 'heavy weather' damage suffered.

Not to inure A clause which effectively prevents a carrier or other bailee claiming under a cargo insurance policy, and thus destroying the insurer's subrogation rights.

NRT (Net registered tonnage) It consists of the gross registered tonnage (GRT) of a ship less allowance for the space occupied by the engine room, crew accommodation and other non-earning parts of the ship. It is usually about 55–65 per cent of the GRT and is used as the basis for the calculation of port dues, canal dues, etc. It represents the enclosed earning space of the vessel.

NVD (No value declared) Entered into 'Value for carriage' box on AWB if exporter does not wish to extend the carrier's normal liability.

NVOCC (Non-vessel-owning common carrier) Also known as NVOMMO (non-vessel owning multi-modal operator). A carrier issuing bills of lading for carriage of goods on a vessel he neither owns nor operates.

OBO Oil-bulk-ore carrier.

OOG (Out-of-gauge) A load that is too wide for a railway wagon. Some out-of-gauge working is done over short distances with the load overlapping the other track.

Operating ratio A unit of measurement used to test the viability of a service. It consists of the operating costs expressed as a percentage of receipts. The closer the figure is to 100, the less profitable is the service. If it exceeds 100, a loss will be incurred.

O/W (Over-width) A flat rack container with goods protruding over sides.

Payload That part of the total load which earns freight or fares and hence contributes to the revenue of an undertaking.

Peak The time of the day, week or year, when the demand for transport is greatest, and far exceeding the average. Satisfying this kind of demand requires an over-provision of transport facilities at other times and hence gives rise to the 'problem of the peak'.

Pence per passenger-km A costing unit found by the formula:

$$\frac{\text{Cost of operating the vehicle in pence}}{\text{Number of passenger-kilometres}}$$

to give a standard cost per passenger-kilometre.

Pence per vehicle-kilometre A costing unit found by the formula:

$$\frac{\text{cost of operating the vehicle in pence}}{\text{number of vehicle-kilometres}}$$

Percentage satisfaction The extent to which a firm can satisfy demand immediately from stock. 100 per cent satisfaction is the ideal in theory but in practice may be prohibitively expensive, tying up capital in slow-moving items.

Physical distribution A term to describe collectively a number of inter-related activities, such as freight transportation in all its forms, materials handling, storage, warehousing, packaging and unitisation.

Phyto-sanitary certificate A certificate issued by officials of the Department of Agriculture certifying that plants are free of disease.

PI Club (Protection & Indemnity Association) Shipowners' mutual liability insurer, whereby all bear some loss when a major vessel is lost at sea.

PIRA The Paper Industry Research Association.

POA Place of acceptance.

POD Place of delivery or proof of delivery.

POR Place of receipt.

Porterage Charges levied by a dock company for use of porters' services.

Port mark The main identification mark on any package, made up of four parts: (a) consignee's identifying mark; (b) order number; (c) port of destination; (d) number of the particular package.

Pratique The health certificate issued to the master of a vessel if there is no infectious disease on board.

Preferred vendor A supplier who most fulfils the requirements of your up-stream analysis covering such aspects as price, specifications; compliance with specification; reliability and frequency of deliveries, flexibility and servicing. The supplier's reputation for quality, his legal monopolistic rights as regards patents, etc.; his willingness to comply with your special requirements, e.g. bar coding of components and other supplies and his general approach to keeping his products and production methods up to date are further aspects to take into account.

Prime mover A type of engine giving motive power, which differs fundamentally from other classes of engines, e.g. a steam engine, diesel engine, etc. Sometimes used erroneously to describe the motive unit in an articulated lorry, to distinguish it from the trailer, or the combined motive unit and trailer.

Principal carrier The carrier issuing a CTD, regardless of whether or not goods are carried on his own, a third party's or consortium member's vessel.

Protest An essential act when a foreign bill of exchange is dishonoured. More formal than the ordinary noting of a bill of exchange, it involves the formal preparation of a document (the protest) which includes a copy of the wording of the bill and a declaration by the notary public that it was dishonoured. Masters of vessels also 'note protest' if they have encountered 'heavy weather' on the voyage and will need to extend this protest if the vessel is subsequently found to have incurred cargo damage due to such 'heavy weather'.

PSV Public service vehicle, e.g. a bus or coach (see Road Traffic Act 1972 for legal definitions).

QTOL (Quiet take-off and landing) Also combined with STOL (QSTOL). A number of aircraft development groups now produce QSTOL aircraft, which cause far less noise offence than existing aircraft, apart from needing runways roughly one-fifth the usual length.

Quality circles Much favoured by Japanese industrialists, they are regular meetings of staff actually engaged on a particular project, where all can air their views and suggest ways in which the work might possibly be improved. It helps to develop team spirit and management should always seriously consider such suggestions and reward them if merited.

Quasi-negotiable instrument The bill of lading is often termed a quasi-negotiable instrument ('quasi' is Latin for 'almost'). While a bill of lading can be assigned to a third party by endorsement it is not fully negotiable since it only passes on the same title as the giver of it has, nothing more. Thus, a person taking it in good faith for value is liable to lose it if the true owner proves title and the transferor's title is shown to be defective.

Rapid transit A system designed to deal with heavy surges of traffic, particularly in certain areas. The expression may be applied to either a road or rail service which has a high average speed, is capable of accepting heavy surges of traffic, and above all, operates on a completely grade-separated right of way (e.g. bus-only lanes).

RCP (Rate construction point) Part of the rubric on an air waybill which allows a rate to be constructed to take advantage of a specific commodity rate for part of a journey with possibly a cabotage rate for the remainder, which gives a lower overall rate than the normal rate. Can be constructed over any airport on the actual flight, or on another scheduled route or even over a hypothetical route which would involve transshipment.

RDC Regional distribution centre.

Real-time A computer system which controls a transport or other system by receiving data, processing them, and returning the conclusions almost simultaneously so that control can be exerted to affect the functioning of the system. Sometimes the computer is programmed to effect the necessary adjustments to the system.

Reefer Refrigerated vehicle, or container.

Release note A note signed by the consignee as a receipt for the goods.

Removal note A note which indicates goods cleared by Customs and free to proceed.

RID The regulations concerning the international distribution of dangerous goods by rail.

ROCE (Return on capital employed) The most fundamental ratio for determining the success of a business. The formula is:

$$\frac{\text{Net profit}}{\text{Capital employed}} \times 100$$

Ro/ro ship A roll-on roll-off vessel, with bow and/or stern doors through which vehicles are driven on or off, via adjustable ramps.

Ro/ro terminal A berth specially designed to facilitate the loading and unloading of roll-on roll-off ships, being equipped with ramps and extensive marshalling areas for vehicles.

SAD (Single administrative document) The customs declaration for both import and export cargo. Came into use 1 January 1988. Although not now necessary in intra-Union trade it has residual use for certain goods (e.g. goods on which duty is payable) and is still the important entry document in non-EU trade.

SCP (Simplified clearance procedure) Exporters of goods not requiring special control may submit an abbreviated pre-entry on an approved commercial document to Customs at the time of export and provide the full statistical information within fourteen days after the goods are exported.

SDR (Special drawing rights) The basket of currencies used by the International Monetary Fund as a unit of account. Used to express limitations in the Hague–Visby Rules.

Seabee The largest of the barge-carrying systems, operated by Lykes Lines with barges having a carrying capacity of just under 1,000 tons each. They are loaded/discharged two at a time by means of a large stern elevator. Barge-carriers such as the Seabee vessels mentioned above, the Lash (Lighter aboard ship) and the Baco vessels were all introduced in the late 1960s; their barges being yet another form of unit load. Their objectives were twofold. First, the speedy turnround of the mother ship, which incidentally only requires sheltered water for loading and discharge. Second, the extension of the sea voyage into navigable river and canal systems at either end using pusher tugs.

Ship's manifest A summary of the details of all bills of lading (including common short form bills of lading), sea waybills, non-negotiable receipts and parcels receipts, covering all the cargo shipped on board a vessel. It is delivered to the port authority by the master of the vessel.

Short shipment A situation where part of a consignment is shut out.

Shut outs It is not uncommon for goods sent down to a particular vessel to be shut out, i.e. not shipped. Although late arrival is possibly the most common cause, goods may be shut out for a variety of reasons, such as lack of a suitable stow or even goods which, having arrived during the early stages of the receiving period, have been overlooked in the rush to load just before the vessel closes.

SITPRO (The Simpler Trade Procedures Board) The UK representative on international panels designed to simplify international trade by the development of aligned documentation and electronic data interchange systems. Its address is given in Chapter 21 of this book.

Slot The space occupied by a container on board ship or in a container yard.

SOB (Shipped on board) An endorsement on a bill of lading confirming that crates or containers have actually been loaded.

SPARCS (Synchronous planning and real-time control system) Used at Tilbury to give an accurate technicolour computer screen representation of vessel bays, yard areas, containers and container handling equipment. It takes into account such factors as the container size and weight, the cargo characteristics, the destination and vessel stability.

SSN (Standard shipping note) A six-part document, which accompanies goods to the container base or dock and acts as a receipt for goods to the road haulier. It also records details of the container for carrier's use.

SST (Supersonic transport) Civil aircraft able to operate at a speed faster than the speed of sound. Concorde is the first example of this new generation of civil aircraft.

Standard shipping mark The new internationally agreed shipping marks in four parts: (1) initials (or abbreviated name); (2) reference number; (3) destination; (4) package number.

Standard trading conditions The terms under which a carrier contracts with a customer for the carriage of goods.

STOL (Short take-off and landing) A type of aircraft needing only short runways.

Stowage order An order from a shipowner who has been notified of valuable, fragile or hazardous cargo instructing stevedores to accept the goods and stow them in the manner specified. It equally advises the shipper when and where he is to deliver the goods.

Straight bill of lading An American term for a non-negotiable B/L, i.e. a waybill.

Stuffing/stripping Packing and unloading of a container.

Tare The unladen weight of a vehicle or container.

Tariff Terms, conditions and scale of charges by a carrier.

TEU (Twenty-foot equivalent unit) A unit for calculating the carrying capacity of container vessels.

T form procedures The EU transit document procedure which not only signals (indicates) to customs officers the status of goods in the Union, but which, provided their seals are unbroken, enables vehicles to cross frontiers without inspection. Since the Single Market they are less used than formerly but are still effective for non-EU goods and in certain other circumstances.

THC (Terminal handling charge) Charge for handling FCLs at ocean terminal.

THE (Technical help for exporters) Part of British Standards Institute, it offers technical advice on all aspects of exporting (e.g. voltages in various countries for electrical products).

TIF (Transports Internationaux par Chemin de Fer) The international railway customs procedure similar to TIR for road haulage.

Tilt A fabric cover over framework secured to the platform of a lorry to form an easily removable, covered body. When used in connection with TIR operations it must be capable of being laced and sealed with plastic-covered steel wire, and free from tears or repairs unless such repairs have been effected in accordance with the regulations. There are also tilt containers with side curtains.

TIR (Transports Internationaux par Route) The international road carnet system which enables goods in approved sealed vehicles or containers to cross frontiers without inspection by Customs, so long as the seals are unbroken and the tilts, if employed, are undamaged.

Tonne-kilometres The weight carried multiplied by the length of the haul.

Total distribution cost A concept which seeks to secure optimum efficiency in the distribution process by choosing that total system of storage, handling and transport which moves goods from the point of production to the point of consumption with the least total expense, rather than dealing with each of the operations involved on an isolated basis.

TQA (Total quality approach) An approach which advocates that a supplier only delivers a quality service or product to his customers. This is only possible if he in turn demands quality from his suppliers of both capital goods and consumer goods and services, and if he encourages professionalism in his own staff. It is therefore a policy which seeks always to raise standards in production, distribution and exchange activities.

Traffic commissioners The Licensing Authority for PSVs. The Chairman of the Traffic Commissioners is the Licensing Authority for goods vehicles.

TREM cards A series of cards issued as part of the Hazchem scheme for the transport of hazardous chemicals. Each card bears detailed information about the particular product, the safety equipment to be used, how to disperse any spillage, etc. The technical material is made available by the Chemical Industries Association, King's Buildings, Smith Square, London SW1P 3HQ. These cards are also used for European ADR movements.

Trimming a vessel This is concerned with the weight distribution over the length of the vessel, which is normally trimmed so that she is slightly down by the stern to give a more effective thrust to the propellers. The term is also used for spreading bulk cargo evenly over a hold and 'FIO and trimmed' (free in, out and trimmed) is a fairly common charter term meaning that all loading, discharging and trimming costs are for the charterer's account. Trimming is equally important in stowing aircraft and a *Trim Chart* is issued showing the weight distribution of an aircraft prior to take-off.

Trunking Movement of containers between ocean terminal and CFSs, or long-haul lorry movements between depots.

Turning radius The distance between the centre of turn point of a forklift truck and the farthest point of the truck body. It is a measure of the skill of the designer in getting capacity and stability in as small a space as possible. The degree of success achieved will affect the space which must be provided for turning and manoeuvring, e.g. in warehouses and on stacking grounds.

ULCC Ultra large crude carrier, i.e. over 300,000 tons.

ULD (Unit load device) An air traffic term.

UNCON Uncontainerable goods.

Unit load concept The concept which seeks to make one large load of many small loads by the use of pallets, containers, etc. The consolidation should take place as soon as possible in the journey from producer to consumer, the unit should be as large as can be handled by the vehicle and equipment connected with its journey, and should remain as a unit for the largest possible part of the journey before being de-consolidated.

UN number This is the number by which the United Nations has classified dangerous cargoes, so that irrespective of language they can be recognised for their dangerous qualities. It appears on the dangerous goods note (DGN).

Up-stream analysis Concerned with the manufacturer's own supply requirements.

Valuation charge An AWB rubric asks 'Value for carriage?' If completed with a value it will increase the carrier's liability to that value. In return the shipper pays a valuation charge. It is the same as an *ad valorem* surcharge by sea.

VLCC Very large crude carrier.

VTOL Vertical take-off and landing: applied to aircraft capable of vertical ascent and descent. Sometimes called jump jets. The principle has been successfully applied to military aircraft, e.g. the 'Harrier', but as yet no successful commercial aircraft has been developed.

Warsaw Convention (1929) The original international agreement covering the carriage of goods by air, which has since been modified and amended by subsequent conventions and conferences but still forms the basis of the law of international carriage of goods by air.

Wharfage Fees for use of a wharf to discharge or load cargo.

Wharfinger's receipt An acknowledgement of the receipt of goods by a wharfinger, who will warehouse them and ship them in due course.

11 Appendix: Professional institutions and other bodies

Introduction

The wide range of transport and logistical activities today requires many types of knowledge and expertise. Firms and individuals have found it advantageous to join together in voluntary associations to pool experiences and ideas. Similarly, many official bodies set up to promote or control transport are broadly-based panels of knowledgeable people chosen for their experience and understanding of the needs of society and the problems of transport and distribution. This rich pattern of expertise is available to individuals and companies who wish to join, at fairly nominal expense, associations which can assist them with their problems.

Inevitably the authors' list of institutions and organisations will be adjudged incomplete, and the references too brief. Every effort has been made to represent the activities of the institutions accurately. Readers interested in membership should apply to the addresses given.

List of institutions

American Bureau of Shipping, ABS House, 1 Frying Pan Alley, London E1 7HR. Tel: 071 247 3255; Fax: 071 377 2453
The American Bureau of Shipping is a ship classification society which certifies the soundness of merchant ships and other marine engineering structures. Its 700 surveyors include specialists in all aspects of the design, building and engineering operation of ships and offshore structures. They discuss original ideas, submit specific proposals for vessels, live with the ship throughout its construction and ensure that the Bureau's rules are carried out. The Bureau is authorised to assign Load Lines and Safety of Life at Sea Certificates.

Associated British Ports, 150 Holborn, London EC1N 2LR.
Tel: 071 486 6621; Telex: 23913; Fax: 071 430 1384
Associated British Ports is the country's largest ports business owning and operating nineteen ports in England, Scotland and Wales. Established under the Transport Act 1981 as successor to the British Transport Docks Board, ABP functions as a profitable and successful commercial enterprise and handles about a quarter of all UK seaborne trade through its ports.

Recently, the two ABP ports of Southampton and Cardiff were designated as 'freeport' areas, enabling goods to be imported and re-exported without payment of VAT or customs duty.

BAA PLC, 130 Wilton Road, London SW1V 1LQ. Tel: 071 834 9449; Fax: 071 932 6699
BAA is a private company, privatised in 1987 from the nationalised British Airports Authority. It owns and operates Heathrow Airport, Gatwick Airport and other airports at Stansted, Glasgow, Aberdeen, Edinburgh and Southampton. These airports currently handle 78 per cent of all passengers and 86 per cent of all air cargo in the United Kingdom.

The Baltic Air Charter Association (temporary address)
6 The Office Village, Romford Road, London E15 4EA.
Tel: 081 519 3909; Fax: 081 519 6967
Since 1744 the Baltic Exchange has been the shipping market of the world, where ships are found for cargoes and cargoes are arranged for ships. The new transport medium, the air freight industry, turned to the established expertise of the Baltic Exchange as the logical centre for fixing air charters. By 1949 an Airbrokers' Association had been established to foster the young but flourishing Baltic Exchange Air Market.

The Association is a non-profit-making organisation. It no longer operates on the floor of the Baltic Exchange (which is in any case at the present time being rebuilt after terrorist action). Today charters are arranged by telephone and computerised links from the members' own offices, but the Association meets regularly at the Baltic's offices to preserve that high standard of conduct which has always been a feature of the Baltic Exchange, and is even more important in the electronic era. The Association's objects are to maintain in London a world market for the charter of aircraft for the carriage of cargo and passengers; to promote uniformity in commercial transactions in the airbroking trade, especially with regard to contracts of carriage by air and air charter-parties; to represent members in all negotiations with government departments, chambers of commerce and other public, mercantile or international bodies; and to offer arbitration machinery for the settlement of disputes between members where necessary. It promotes integrity in dealings, in conformity with the principle of the Baltic Exchange, 'Our word is our bond'. A firm offer of aircraft space or cargo cannot be withdrawn once it has been made, until the time of expiry.

The Baltic and International Maritime Council (BIMCO), 161 Bagsvaerdvej, DK-2880 Bagsvaerd. Tel: +45 44 44 45 00; Telex: 19086; Fax: +45 44 44 44 50

Founded in 1905, the Baltic and International Maritime Council (BIMCO) is the world's largest private shipping organisation, grouping shipowners and managers, shipbrokers and agents, protection and indemnity clubs, defence associations, national associations of shipowners and national associations of shipbrokers, as well as other entities involved in shipping. Current membership includes nearly 1,000 shipowner members with 360 million tons deadweight, representing 55 per cent of the world merchant fleet, about 1,600 broker members, 60 club members and 30 associate members.

BIMCO provides an unparalleled shipping forum in which members from 110 countries can discuss problems of mutual interest on an equal footing.

Because BIMCO is both non-political and non-governmental, its opinions are widely respected in the international world of shipping and commerce in general, and the organisation has consultative status with international bodies such as the United Nations Conference on Trade and Development (UNCTAD) and the International Maritime Organisation (IMO).

A very large percentage of the total world transportation of goods takes place on the basis of charter-parties and other documents prepared by the Documentary Committee of BIMCO, or on charter-party terms which have been recommended by BIMCO. Throughout its existence, BIMCO has endeavoured to prepare modern, reasonable and balanced documents which are acceptable to all parties. All these documents embody apt terms and trade terminology in an effort to obviate or reduce the possibility for disputes over their interpretation.

BIMCO documents are available for transportation of general cargoes, for the carriage of ore, coal and timber, liquid gas, chemicals, vegetable oils and fertilisers, etc. All told, BIMCO has issued more than 100 charter-parties, bills of lading and other forms in current use, as well as over 140 standard clauses specifically designed to cover particular situations.

Providing detailed information for its members has been an integral part of BIMCO's activities since its foundation. Equipped with what is possibly the finest collection of data on port conditions and charges, BIMCO feeds a constant stream of facts to its members either by telephone, telex, fax, letter, or on-line from its databases, or through the regular publications.

British Association of Removers, 3 Churchill Court, 58 Station Road, North Harrow, Middlesex HA2 7SA. Tel: 081 861 3331; Fax: 081 861 3332
The British Association of Removers is the only British organisation representing the views of the removing, storage and warehousing industry. It speaks for the industry at government, local authority and European Union level.

British International Freight Association, Redfern House, Browells Lane, Feltham, Middlesex TW13 7EP. Tel: 081 844 2266; Fax: 081 844 5546
British International Freight Association (BIFA) is a trade association, representing the freight forwarding industry in discussions with official bodies about such matters as proposed legislation, documentation requirements, etc. It is also active in promoting paperless trading by computer-to-computer data links.

British Ports Federation, Victoria House, Vernon Place, London WC2B 6AH. Tel: 071 242 1200; Telex: 295741; Fax: 071 405 1069
The British Ports Federation is an association formed to promote, further and protect the general interests of port authorities and conservancy authorities. It constitutes a forum where discussion and consideration of general questions affecting the members can take place. It particularly designates in its rules that opportunities for discussion of matters affecting major ports, medium ports and small ports shall be created.

BPF is the catalyst in the discussion of port-related topics and provides a central organisation which represents the views of all ports to external bodies. There is a continuing dialogue with government and other sectors of industry which have an interest in port affairs. Views on international matters are represented through membership of, and services are performed for, the International Association of Ports and Harbours.

British Road Federation, 194–202 Old Kent Road, London SE1 5TG. Tel: 071 703 9769; Fax: 071 701 0029
The British Road Federation is an association of firms and organisations who believe in the importance of roads and road transport to the life of Great Britain. They join together to put forward constructive policies for the development of an adequate road system and to rebut uninformed opposition to road transport.

Bureau Veritas, 42 Weston Street, London SE1 3QL. Tel: 071 403 6266; Fax: 071 403 1590
Bureau Veritas is an international organisation with offices in more than 100 countries. Established originally in 1828 at Antwerp, it exists to ensure that materials and equipment used in ships, buildings, industrial activities, electrical, electronic or nuclear projects, etc. reach the required standards. It periodically issues rules for the guidance of engineers and construction firms. These rules take into account the progress made in various fields and the experience of the Bureau's Inspection Department.

Bus and Coach Council, Sardinia House, 52 Lincoln's Inn Fields, London WC2A 3LZ. Tel: 071 831 7546; Telex: 297054; Fax: 071 242 0053
The Bus and Coach Council represents operators, both public and private, who run 98 per cent of the buses and two-thirds of the coaches in the United Kingdom. BCC members are grouped into four sectors depending upon the nature of their undertakings. The four groups are: (1) the Nationalised Sector – the National Bus Company, the Scottish Bus Group and Ulsterbus; (2) the Transport Executive Sector – Passenger Transport Executives of the seven metropolitan counties and the London Transport Executive; (3) the Local Authority Sector – nearly all passenger transport operations of district councils and also the Scottish regions, and (4) the Independent Sector – more than 1,750 private bus and coach operators.

The Chamber of Shipping, 2–5 Minories, London EC3N 1BJ. Tel: 071 702 2200; Fax: 071 702 9515
The Chamber of Shipping is the trade association and employers' organisation for British shipowners and ship managers. It promotes and protects the interests of its member companies, both nationally and internationally. It represents British shipping to the government, parliament, international organisations, unions and the general public. Its activities cover all issues which have a bearing on British shipping, ranging from fiscal policy and freedom to trade, through to recruitment and training, maritime safety and the environment, navaids and pilotage.

The Chamber represents six very different commercial sectors trading at sea: deep-sea bulk, short-sea bulk, deep-sea liner, ferry, cruise and offshore support. It has 140 member companies which own or manage 686 trading ships totalling 20.8 million deadweight tonnes including some managed for foreign owners.

The Chartered Institute of Purchasing and Supply, Easton House, Easton on the Hill, Stamford, Lincs PE9 3NZ
CIPS is the professional body for all those engaged in Purchasing and Supply Chain Management. It has over 21,000 members (20% overseas) and entry to full membership is by examination or assessment. The Institute offers a wide range of open services including Education and Training, Recruitment, Booksales, and a Technical Information Centre.

Chartered Institute of Transport, 80 Portland Place, London W1 4DP. Tel: 071 636 9952; Fax: 071 637 0511
The Chartered Institute of Transport is the professional body for those engaged in transport and physical distribution. It has 20,000 members, over 40 per cent of them outside the United Kingdom and include in their membership senior transport managers in all modes. Entry is by a three-part written examination, with papers of degree standard level and there are special arrangements for candidates over the age of 30 already employed in transport 'under mature candidate rules'. Membership of the

institute is open to men and women without restriction as to nationality or place of residence. There are branches in many countries and one of its main roles is the spread of transport knowledge with special emphasis on the continuing professional education of its members.

Civil Aviation Authority, CAA House, 45–59 Kingsway, London WC2B 6TE. Tel: 071 379 7311; Fax: 071 240 1153

The Civil Aviation Authority was established by the Civil Aviation Act 1971, and came into full operation on 1 April 1972. It is an independent public body, separate from the government, with responsibilities for:

1. The economic regulation and well-being of the civil aviation industry, including the air transport licensing duties formerly carried out by the Air Transport Licensing Board.
2. Air safety, both airworthiness (formerly the responsibility of the Air Registration Board) and operational safety, including the licensing of pilots and flight engineers.
3. The National Air Traffic Services, both air traffic control and telecommunications.
4. Airport planning, as part of its general responsibility as the government's adviser on civil aviation matters; the well-being of general aviation; research; consumer interests; the collection and publication of data relating to civil aviation, and a large number of miscellaneous functions such as the ownership and operation of the Highlands and Islands aerodromes.

Confederation of British Industry, Centre Point, 103 New Oxford Street, London WC1A 1DU. Tel: 071 379 7400; Fax: 071 240 1578

The Confederation of British Industry is the premier organisation in Great Britain representing British industry and commerce. It exists to represent industry in any discussions with government, local government, international authorities or other bodies whose actions may affect its 250,000 members. Its regular meetings with the prime minister and senior cabinet members indicate its status and the high regard in which it is held.

Dun and Bradstreet International, Holmers Farm Way, High Wycombe HP12 4UL. Tel: 0494 422000

Credit management is an integral part of exporting, as it is of home business. Dun and Bradstreet offer a comprehensive range of services which include the following:

1. *A 'payment trend profile'* This is a profile of a firm or company which can be ordered over the telephone on 0800 500 900 and will be delivered by fax. It gives all the details about a company: name, address, co. registration number, number of employees, line of business, bank branch and sort-code details, graphs showing previous two-year trading history and plotting the trend of this firm against the industry.
2. *A 'D & B' rating* This rating is in two parts. It might appear on a Business Report in the form '4A 3'. The first part is a measure of the

company's financial strength, and varies from 5A, 4A, 3A, etc., down to H, and N. 5A means the company has assets with a net worth of £35 million and above. (Net worth means worth after all claims from outsiders have been fully satisfied.) 4A means a net worth of between £15 million and £34,999,999. H means the net worth is less than £8,000 while N means 'negative net worth'. This means that the company's liabilities to outsiders exceed the value of its assets.

The second part of the rating varies from 1 to 4 and refers to the level of risk. 1 indicates a low level of risk and 4 a high level of risk. This risk factor is based on well-known 'early warning' signals and is updated whenever a request for a rating is received. The risks have therefore been re-assessed every time.

3. *Monitoring services* These services offer subscribers a choice of four types of check-up. They are: (a) time critical data (such as bankruptcies, court orders, etc.); (b) legal and general data (such as mortgages, charges, change of officers, etc.); (c) D & B rating and payment data (see above), and (d) latest accounts. (The latest registered accounts are sent to the enquirer as soon as they are filed.)
4. *Business information reports* This is a full report on any required business, giving a printout of all the information available on the data base for that firm or company.

Freight Transport Association, 157 St Johns Road,
Tunbridge Wells TN4 9UP. Tel: 0892 526171; Fax: 0892 534989
This association is a UK trade association which exists solely to safeguard the interests of, and provide services for, trade and industry as operators and users of all forms of freight transport. It has two main spheres of activity. First, it provides a wide range of tangible benefits to members, assisting them with their day-to-day operations in the transport field. Such services include advice on technical, legal and practical problems, a costing service, advice on international operations, etc. Second, it seeks to influence the decisions of government, local authorities, the European Union, the providers of transport services and others.

Inland Waterways Association (Inland Shipping Group),
114 Regent's Park Road, London NW1 8UQ. Tel: 071 586 2510;
Fax: 071 722 7213
Concern for our natural environment together with the economic and energy crises has triggered new nationwide interest in inland water transport as the cheapest, the least demanding on energy, manpower and land resources, and the most environmentally beneficial form of transport. The IWA's Inland Shipping Group is energetically promoting the development of commercial waterways for modern inland shipping in the interests of industry, commerce, amenity users and the public at large.

Institute of Chartered Shipbrokers (The), 3 Gracechurch Street, London EC3V 0AT. Tel: 071 283 1361; Fax: 071 626 2319

The Institute of Chartered Shipbrokers is a professional body representing shipbrokers. It maintains standards in the shipbroking fraternity by ensuring adequate training in both theory and practice, conferring qualifications upon those entitled to them. It holds conferences and meetings for the discussion of shipbroking affairs, the reading of papers and the consideration of the law and practice of shipbroking.

Since the granting of its Royal Charter in 1920 it has been at the centre of the shipbroking fraternity, collecting, collating and publishing all relevant information of interest and service to shipbrokers.

Institute of Freight Forwarders Ltd, Redfern House, Browells Lane, Feltham, Middlesex TW13 7EP. Tel: 081 844 2266; Fax: 081 890 5546

The Institute of Freight Forwarders was formed in 1944, and seeks to promote the highest standards of professional conduct in the freight-forwarding industry. To this end it has two types of member: associates and fellows. They are qualified through its examinations and through experience in the industry to play a full professional part in the activities of their firms. Company members are now members of BIFA, the British International Freight Association. This is a trade association, representing the industry in discussions with official bodies about such matters as proposed legislation, documentation requirements, etc. It is also active in promoting paperless trading by computer-to-computer data links.

Institute of Logistics, Douglas House, Queen's Square, Corby, Northants NN17 1PL. Tel: 0536 205500; Fax: 0536 400979

The Institute was formed on 1 August 1993 following a merger of the Institute of Logistics & Distribution Management and the Institute of Materials Management.

It caters for the professional logistician whose responsibilities cover the strategic and operational issues concerned with planning and controlling the supply, movement and storage of material and goods. It has in excess of 11,000 members with a high proportion of senior managers.

Membership is open to individuals who meet the educational and professional criteria as approved by the Council.

The Institute is heavily involved in the development of education and training programmes for junior, middle and senior managers.

It provides an information service, including a lending facility for books and videos. 'Logistics Focus', the Institute's journal, is published monthly. Members also receive a Yearbook. In addition specialist publications and surveys are produced.

Conferences, seminars and workshops are held on a wide range of subjects.

The Institute has an active regional organisation throughout the United Kingdom. The thirteen regions organise visits, lectures and seminars.

Institute of Petroleum, 61 New Cavendish Street, London W1M 8AR. Tel: 071 636 1004; Telex: 264380; Fax: 071 255 1472
The Institute of Petroleum is concerned with all aspects of petroleum technology and distribution. In particular the Institute publishes *Model Codes of Safe Practice*, covering all aspects of the production of oil, its refining and the distribution of finished products.

Institute of Road Transport Engineers, 1 Cromwell Place, Kensington, London SW7 2JF. Tel: 071 589 3744; Fax: 071 225 0494
The Institute of Road Transport Engineers is an examining body which seeks to further skill, training and education in road transport engineering. Its members have reached a high standard in specialist education and training, and have acquired practical experience in the road transport industry. They seek to apply their specialist knowledge in the selection, modification, maintenance of mechanical condition and operation of wheeled, tracked and air-cushioned vehicles in the movement of goods and passengers.

Institute of Transport Administration, 32 Palmerston Road, Southampton SO1 1LL. Tel: 0703 631380; Fax: 0703 634165
The Institute of Transport Administration is a leading professional body for transport managers and staff, running a broad programme of educational courses for the basic training and full professional qualification of members. It also provides regular meetings and conferences for the presentation and discussion of papers on all aspects of transport, to assist professional transport staff to keep abreast of the latest developments.

The Institute's network of centres in Britain and overseas meet regularly, enabling staff in particular regions to meet for the mutual discussion of problems, and for social occasions.

The Institute's officers serve on a variety of official bodies to express the point of view of the transport profession generally and advance the cause of traffic administration in the service of the nation.

International Air Transport Association (IATA), Imperial House, 15–19 Kingsway, London WC1R 6UN. Tel: 071 497 1048; Fax: 071 240 9041
The International Air Transport Association is an association of air transport operators. Its members carry the bulk of the world's scheduled air traffic under the flags of over 120 nations. Its aims are to promote safe, regular and economical air transport for the benefit of the peoples of the world; to foster air commerce and to study its problems; to provide means for collaboration among the air transport fraternity and to co-operate with the International Civil Aviation Organisation and other international bodies. It has developed world air routes and traffic handling practices into a world-wide public service, despite barriers of language, currency, law

and mensuration. It represents a medium for negotiation and consultation with governments on matters of international co-operation, carriage of mails, etc. Originally founded in 1945 as the successor to the International Air Traffic Association of 1919, it draws its legal existence from a special Act of the Canadian parliament. Once two governments have drawn up a bilateral air transport agreement, and have licensed the airlines selected to perform the service, IATA's activities commence. Its functions are to simplify and standardise documentation, procedures and operational devices so that airline costs are minimised and charges to the public are reduced as much as possible commensurate with safety.

International Cargo Handling Co-ordination Association (ICHCA), Westminster Business Centre, 71 Broadway, London SW8 1SH. Tel: 071 793 1022; Fax: 071 820 1703

ICHCA is a professional co-ordinating body unique in the international transport world. It is non-political, non-commercial and non-profit-making. Its membership spans the entire spectrum of professions and occupations that have an effect on, or are affected by, technological changes in the physical distribution of goods through world transport.

International Chamber of Commerce, 38 Cours Albert 1er 75008 Paris, France and 14 Belgrave Square, London SW1. Tel: 071 823 2811; Fax: 071 235 5447

The International Chamber of Commerce operates from a headquarters in Paris, led by a Secretary-General who is chosen by, and responsible to, the ICC Council. It is one of the most important bodies in international commerce, speaking with authority for professional people of all types and seeking to promote international trade. It publishes a number of really authoritative documents, which every student should buy, such as *Incoterms 1990*, *Uniform Customs and Practice for Documentary Credits*, *Uniform Rules for Collections*, etc. These publications are available from the ICC National Committees in each particular country.

International Civil Aviation Organisation (ICAO), 1000 Sherbrooke Street, West Montreal, P.Q., Canada H3A 2R2. Tel: 95140 285 8220 1

ICAO was created in 1944 to promote the safe and orderly development of civil aviation in the world. A specialised agency of the United Nations, it sets international standards and regulations necessary for the safety, security, efficiency and regularity of air transport and serves as the medium for co-operation in all fields of civil aviation among its 164 contracting states.

The aims of the organisation are:

1. To ensure safe and orderly growth of civil aviation throughout the world.
2. To encourage the development of airports and navigation facilities for international civil aviation.

3. To reduce wasteful competition.
4. To ensure that all nations have a fair opportunity to operate international airlines.
5. To avoid discrimination between contracting nations.

Safety has always been a paramount concern of ICAO. All crews are licensed in accordance with international standards. All aircraft have certificates of airworthiness recognised by ICAO. At all times aircraft are in touch with standard air traffic control centres world-wide, and all airports, runways, equipment and facilities meet ICAO standards.

International Federation of Freight Forwarders Associations (FIATA), Baumackerstrasse 24, CH-8050 Zurich, Switzerland. Tel: + 41 1 311 65 11; Telex: 823579; Fax: + 41 1 311 90 44

The International Federation of Freight Forwarders Associations is an international body which represents the forwarding profession throughout the world. It has 74 member organisations (ordinary members) and more than 1,800 associate members (including ports and airports) from 124 countries. It has official consultative status with the Economic and Social Council of the United Nations and with many governmental and non-governmental bodies concerned with transportation on technical, legal, commercial and vocational training grounds.

FIATA has a General Council which convenes a General Council meeting every year. There are three Institutes (airfreight, Customs and facilitation and multi-modal transport) dealing with operational matters, air transport, seaborne transport, combined transport, road, rail, etc., and also with customs matters and facilitation. There are also three advisory bodies (legal matters, public relations and vocational training) dealing with relevant problems.

FIATA documents have achieved world-wide recognition, such as the forwarding agent's certificate of receipt (FCR), the forwarding agent's certificate of transport (FCT), the FIATA combined transport bill of lading (FBL) – to be replaced in a couple of months by the new FIATA multi-modal transport bill of lading – and the FIATA warehouse receipt (FWR).

International Maritime Organisation (IMO), 4 Albert Embankment, London SE1. Tel: 071 735 7611; Fax: 071 587 3210

The International Maritime Organisation is the specialised agency of the United Nations concerned solely with maritime affairs. Its interest is mainly in ships used in international services. Eighty-six states are members of IMO. Its aims are to facilitate co-operation among governments on technical matters affecting shipping, and particularly safety of life at sea. The Council consists of representatives of eighteen member states, elected by the assembly sessions. These normally take place in London every two years, the first session having been in 1959. The Assembly also chooses a Maritime Safety Committee and a Marine Environment Protection Committee.

IMO is a forum where members can exchange information on, and endeavour to solve problems connected with, maritime technical, safety and legal problems. It administers the International Convention for the Safety of Life at Sea. One of its current major problems is piracy.

International Road Transport Union (IRU), BP 44/1211 Geneva, Switzerland. Tel: 34 13 30; Telex 27017

The International Road Transport Union (IRU) has over eighty active members in almost fifty countries. It is an international federation of national road transport associations and also accepts associate members directly or indirectly involved in the sector. It has consultative status in the United Nations and in the Council of Europe and a permanent delegation to the EU. Its main objective is to contribute to the development and prosperity of national and international road transport by solving problems in the economic, social, legal and technical fields.

International Transport Intermediaries Club (ITIC), America House, 2 America Square, London EC3N 2LU. Tel: 071 338 0150; Telex: 8814516 (ITICG); Fax: 071 338 0151

The International Transport Intermediaries Club (ITIC) is a mutual, non-profit-making insurance association – the leading club in its field. Formed in 1992, ITIC was born out of the merger of two already well-established clubs: the Chartered and International Shipbrokers' P&I Club Limited (CISBACLUB), which was founded in 1925, and the Transport Intermediaries Mutual Insurance Association Limited (TIM), which started in 1985.

ITIC is run on the principles of mutuality established by shipowners' P&I Clubs. A P&I Club is a protection and indemnity club, which seeks to protect members taking very high risks on ships and other large transport facilities. It is directed exclusively by, for and in the best interests of its members.

ITIC provides insurance cover to nearly 900 members in more than 55 countries. They are primarily ship agents, ship brokers and ship managers. However, ITIC's cover may extend to many ancillary activities which are habitually undertaken by members, whether they are acting as agents or as principals. The list is as follows:

Agents: Tramp and Liner Agents, Passenger Agents, Chartering Brokers, Forwarding Agents, Sale and Purchase Brokers, Crewing Agents, Ship Managers, Lloyd's Agents, Bunker Brokers, P&I Club Representatives, Air Brokers and Travel Agents.

Principals: Ship Chandlers, Freight Forwarders (usually insured in conjunction with the Through-Transport Club), Marine Surveyors, Loss Adjusters and Crew Managers.

Ship brokers, ship agents, ship managers and other transport intermediaries provide a range of services without which the international transportation industry would be unable to operate. In performing their services they are inevitably exposed to many risks. Perhaps the most serious of these is the risk of a claim for professional negligence. Furthermore, other parties may commit errors for which the intermediary is then held liable. There is, for example, an increasing tendency for port and harbour authorities, statutory undertakings and even central government to impose responsibilities on intermediaries, simply because they offer an accessible target. A similar situation may arise when a loss results from the bankruptcy of a principal or through an act of fraud which is quite beyond the influence of the broker or agent. Not the least of the risks is that a customer should fail to settle outstanding accounts. Not only can cashflow suffer, but the legal expenses incurred in trying to recover such debts can also be substantial. ITIC can help to resolve all these problems, and many more.

International Union of Railways (IUC), 14–16 Rue Jean Rey, 75015 Paris, France. Tel: 1 273 01 20

The International Union of Railways was set up in 1922 to co-ordinate international railway transport policies on any matters where mutual interests make it desirable. With headquarters in Paris, the IUC has committees which deal with planning, commercial matters, railway operations, legal and financial problems, and study groups which review problems of management, control engineering, traffic trends, passenger services, etc. Its members include practically all the European railways, including British Rail, and railways in North America, Africa and Asia.

Lifting Equipment Engineers Association, Waggoners' Court, The Street, Manuden, Bishop's Stortford, Herts CM23 1DW. Tel: 0279 816504; Fax: 0279 816524

Formerly known as the Chain Tester's Association of Great Britain, the Lifting Equipment Engineers Association is an association representing companies or organisations in the field of lifting equipment. It is essentially a technically-oriented association providing for its members both a source of technical information and a means of authoritative representation. One of its most important objects is to promote the development of efficient methods and processes in the industry and the adoption of good standards and safety in the design, manufacture and use of all lifting equipment.

Internally the LEEA has a code of practice for members, which sets out the requirements in terms of personnel, plant, procedures and records which are essential to ensure that a member is technically competent to deal with the range of work undertaken.

Lloyd's Register of Shipping, 71 Fenchurch Street, London EC3M 4BS. Tel: 071 709 9166; Fax: 071 488 4796

Lloyd's Register of Shipping began in 1760 as a committee to produce a Register of Shipping as a guide in the assessment of maritime risks. Classification by Lloyd's Register is accepted by owners, underwriters, charterers and national authorities as a guarantee of structural and mechanical efficiency. The Register employs 2,000 full-time engineers, naval architects, metallurgists and other professionals all over the world to provide a technical inspection and advisory service, primarily for ships but increasingly for engineering projects of many kinds, marine and non-marine.

Besides designing ships to meet its classifications, and then ensuring they are built in a proper manner, Lloyd's also classifies ship machinery, surveys vessels both on the high seas and in dry dock and publishes a detailed register of shipping, with monthly supplements giving details of alterations, additions, new vessels and survey records. It also classifies and certifies the state of offshore facilities, submersibles, buoys, diving complexes, etc. It undertakes industrial surveys, giving impartial assessments of all sorts of industrial complexes and is represented on eighteen national and many international committees.

Marine Society (The), 202 Lambeth Road, London SE1 7JW. Tel: 071 261 9535; Fax: 071 401 2537

The society provides libraries on board ships and organises further education courses for seafarers. It also arranges ship adoption for schools and helps those seeking career opportunities at sea. It also runs a catering course, and is ready to assist education for seafarers, or those interested in seafaring, in any way possible.

The Maritime Information Association, c/o Marine Society (see above)

The Association was formed in 1972 to promote contact and co-operation between librarians and information officers in the marine field, and to develop a body of professional expertise in exploiting the relevant literature and information sources.

Membership is on a personal basis and no formal qualifications are required. The Association is open to all who have a primary or substantial interest in the provision of literature or information in marine subjects, including members of educational institutions, government organisations, professional bodies and industrial or commercial firms.

A conference is held annually at which members may attend lectures on marine subjects, visit organisations of common interest and meet fellow members informally. News items and information about Association activities are circulated to members throughout the year.

Road Haulage Association, 35 Monument Hill, Weybridge, Surrey KT13 8RN. Tel: 0932 841515; Fax: 0932 852516
The Road Haulage Association is a trade association of road hauliers. Its 18,000 members carry 50 per cent of all the goods transported in the United Kingdom. It has a broadly based democratic network of 140 sub-areas serving every part of the country, reaching decisions and taking action on a wide variety of matters which arise in the day-to-day operations of road haulage. These sub-areas elect representatives to the fifteen area committees and thirteen functional groups with specialist interests. These are agricultural, bulk liquid, car transporters, caravan hauliers, express carriers, heavy haulage, international, livestock, long distance, meat and allied trades, milk carriers, tipping vehicles and waste disposal.

Salvage Association (The), Bankside House, 107–12 Leadenhall Street, London EC3A 4AP. Tel: 071 623 1299; Telex: 888137; Fax: 071 626 4963
The Salvage Association (formerly known as The Association for the Protection of Commercial Interests as respects Wrecked and Damaged Property) exists to seek out the truth about any maritime casualty. It does not operate ships, salvage plant or similar services. It acts for anyone who instructs it, charging fees on a time-and-trouble basis. Its expertise and experience are also valuable in the field of loss prevention. Over 15,000 cases are handled annually, either by staff surveyors from one of the association's twenty-eight world-wide offices or by an appointed consultant.

Society of British Aerospace Companies Ltd, 29 King Street, St James's, London SW1Y 6RD. Tel: 071 839 3231; Telex: 262274 SBAC G; Fax: 071 930 3577
The Society of British Aerospace Companies Ltd is the trade association of Britain's aerospace industry. Some 300 companies are members. Its primary object is to encourage, promote and protect the best interests of the British aerospace industry towards expanding its trade and prosperity. It maintains a close liaison and working understanding with departments of government and represents the industry in deliberations with the government. The society is the exhibition authority for the industry and sponsors joint venture presentations of aerospace companies at overseas exhibitions in co-operation with the British Overseas Trade Board. At home, it organises the world-renowned Farnborough International Exhibition and Flying Display.

Society of Motor Manufacturers and Traders Ltd, Forbes House, Halkin Street, London SW1X 7DS. Tel: 071 235 7000; Fax: 071 235 7112
The Society of Motor Manufacturers and Traders Ltd is the trade association for the motor industry in Britain. It negotiates on behalf of the industry with the government on all aspects of government policy which may affect the industry. These include economic and fiscal aspects, matters to do with overseas trade and regulations about construction and safety.

SMMT organises the biennial British International Motor Show (even years) and the Garage Equipment/Auto-Equipment Exhibition (odd years).

Syntegra, Guidion House, Harvest Crescent, Ancells Park, Fleet, Hants GU13 8UZ. Tel: 0252 777000; Fax: 0252 777111; International: Tel: + 44 252 777000; Fax: + 44 252 777111

Syntegra, the systems integration business of BT, is a global organisation which provides large and complex systems integration projects for major companies. These can range from bespoke software to complete computer system solutions.

Syntegra provides systems that benefit its clients in three distinct areas:

1. Systems that facilitate and enhance the business interface between organisations, their customers and their trading partners.
2. Systems that utilise the best technology, ideas and techniques to provides improved working methods and organisational style.
3. Systems that allow organisations to improve their capability to deliver new products and services to their customers and markets.

Syntegra has a long and successful track-record of working with the transportation and freight industry. It specifically focuses on providing solutions to the logistics distribution service arena. In conjunction with the UK air cargo community, Syntegra has developed CCS-UK (Cargo Community System for the UK), which succeeds ACP 80 and ACP 90, both also developed by BT. The CCS-UK system enables airlines, freight agents, transit sheds and H.M. Customs & Excise to communicate effectively using EDI messages.

Syntegra is also undertaking systems development projects for leading airlines and transportation service providers.

Trade Indemnity PLC, 12–34 Great Eastern Street, London EC2A 3EB. Tel: 071 739 4311; Fax: 071 729 7682

Many exporters do not realise that insurance cover can be obtained for failure to pay by the buyer. One firm offering such cover is Trade Indemnity PLC. In export trade the risks are higher than in home trade, since language, customs of the trade, regulations and currency may all be different. There is usually a requirement that prudence has been displayed in checking the status of a customer with a reliable credit reference agency, and in order to spread risks as widely as possible 'whole turnover' cover is preferred. The exporter insures all shipments, not just the ones considered most risky. Protection is available from the date of dispatch, and pre-delivery protection can be provided if specialised plant has been purchased, or work-in-progress is particularly valuable. Transactions in foreign currencies may be covered, and insurance policies may be assigned to bankers or finance houses who are naturally more willing to provide finance if the eventual payment is covered against default.

Index

Other books in the *Elements of Overseas Trade* series:

Export Law
ABDUL KADAR *and* GEOFFREY WHITEHEAD

International Trade and Payments
RALPH BUGG *and* GEOFFREY WHITEHEAD

International Physical Distribution and Cargo Insurance
DENNIS BADGER, RALPH BUGG *and* GEOFFREY WHITEHEAD

Transport
and
Logistics